HIDDEN
SAN FRANCISCO
& NORTHERN
CALIFORNIA

Including Napa, Sonoma, Mendocino,
Santa Cruz, Monterey, Yosemite, and Lake Tahoe

Ray Riegert

THIRTEENTH EDITION

Ulysses Press

HIDDEN REALM

From San Francisco's glittering steel-and-glass buildings to Tahoe's windswept beaches and sparkling lakes, Northern California presents a staggering array of choices for the modern traveler. The key to finding your own perfect adventure is to experience the realm the way the locals do, visiting unique and uncommon places off the beaten tourist path. While *Hidden San Francisco and Northern California* also covers many well-loved and famous spots in the area, its true goal is to guide you on an unforgettable visit, discovering treasures most visitors never see. With highlighted listings, detailed maps, and easy-to-follow directions, you'll find secluded hiking trails, powdery white beaches, luxurious boutique hotels and quirky bed-and-breakfast inns, along with premium small-production wineries and hip gay-friendly neighborhoods. As you continue through the guide, your hidden adventure will follow the trail of the literary Bohemians of the last century, lead you to cutting-edge California cuisine and venerable dim sum palaces, point the way to quiet spots among the towering redwoods, and help you create your dream itinerary.

McClures Beach showcases Northern California at its most majestic.

LITERARY NORTHERN CALIFORNIA

John's Grill, where Sam Spade stopped in The Maltese Falcon, is steeped in San Francisco nostalgia.

From its earliest history as a part of the United States, California has been a powerful magnet for writers. Robert Louis Stevenson, Jack London, Dashiell Hammet, Mark Twain, John Steinbeck, Henry Miller, and a whole generation of Beats found adventure and inspiration here. From hip cafés to historic museums to restaurants pulled straight from the pages of well-known works, the sights here are those you can't find anywhere else. Enjoy a cocktail at the jazzy lounge where Beat giant Jack Kerouac scribbled on napkins, or spend the night in the same room where poet Allen Ginsberg used to stay. Stopping by these historic haunts will bring the area's literary legends to life.

No visit to San Francisco is complete without a visit to **City Lights Bookstore** *(p. 72)*, the epicenter of the Beat literary movement during the 1950s. At **Jack London State Historic Park** *(p. 273)* in Glen Ellen, the House of Happy Walls is a museum displaying London's first editions and original manuscripts. Along the Central Coast, stop for lunch in Salinas at the **Steinbeck House** *(p. 408)*, the Queen Anne Victorian where the author grew up. Modeled after the home in Nathaniel Hawthorne's classic *House of Seven Gables*, **Shaw House Bed & Breakfast** *(p. 355)* is a picturesque Gothic Revival–style mansion in Ferndale. In downtown San Francisco, **John's Grill** *(p. 40)* is a sure bet for fans of the private eye genre—it's the steakhouse where detective Sam Spade stopped for dinner during a tense scene in *The Maltese Falcon*.

Glimpse the beginnings of the quintessential California novelist at John Steinbeck's childhood home.

BEACHES

No natural feature defines California more than its staggering variety of beaches. Along the northern coast there are tiny coves blanketed with sands undisturbed by visitors. Some beaches are alluring for their rich tidepools and rocky trails, others for their secluded woodsy camping or spectacular sunbathing spots. At these hidden locales you can lazily hunt for sand dollars or shells while the cool ocean water laps at your feet. These are the beaches where the locals converge for crabbing or community, so you will have a chance to watch everyday life unfold while you relax—overall, a splendid coastal experience.

Manresa Uplands State Beach *(p. 414)*, popular with surfers, is a strip of white sand bookended by blufftop homes and is a favorite summertime location with good facilities. Bounded by cliffs near Point Reyes, **Kehoe Beach** *(p. 325)* is an isolated spot perfect for explorers; it's covered with wildflowers in the spring. San Francisco's sunwashed **Baker Beach** *(p. 113)* brings in the locals for its expansive corridor of powdery sand and its family-friendly picnicking areas. Tucked discreetly beneath steep cliffs, **Gray Whale Cove** *(p. 383)* is ideal for seaside sunbathing. Along the scenic Russian River, **Johnson's Beach** *(p. 291)* is a sunny, laid-back shore to launch a canoe or jump in for a swim.

Bounded by cliffs, Kehoe Beach is a glittering, secluded strip ideal for exploring.

Just south of San Francisco, Gray Whale Cove is a classic Northern California beach—a white-sand crescent nestled beside rugged cliffs and roaring ocean waves.

WINE

California winemaking began in the 18th century with Spanish *padres* who planted vineyards at the missions. Today it's a multibillion-dollar business that draws millions of oenophiles each year. Hidden small-production wineries still embody the romance of the grape, offering an intimate look at vineyards and personal tours with winemakers. Some estates feature mini-museums tracing the state's unique winemaking history, while others boast signature bistros showcasing their own varietals. Specialized shops and restaurants also cater to the wine-centric palate, offering rare bottles as ideal souvenirs and cuisines that pair perfectly.

One of the prettiest vineyards in the Northern Wine Country, **Iron Horse** *(p. 281)* is renowned for sparkling wine. Fields of pinot noir and chardonnay grapes are laid out in graceful checkerboards around the classic, barn-red winery buildings and the charming outdoor tasting area. Berkeley's Gourmet Ghetto includes the knowledgeable **Kermit Lynch Wine Merchants** *(p. 213)*, which sells high-end French and California varietals at reasonable prices. The grand estate of **Château Julien Winery** *(p. 435)*, with its signature merlot, is a stunning Old World jewel in the lush Carmel Valley. San Francisco's **1150 Hyde Café and Wine Bar** *(p. 100)* presents a fresh, creative menu that can be paired with a wide selection of quality wines.

The Sonoma Valley's cool, coastal climate is ideal for growing vividly colored pinot noir grapes for award-winning vintages.

Carmel Valley's Château Julien Winery (top) offers daily tastings in its picturesque French-Swedish mansion (bottom) on 16 verdant rolling acres.

BOUTIQUE HOTELS

This region overflows with one-of-a-kind hotels whose personalities and individual designs offer a uniquely Northern Californian lodging experience. Some offer top luxury and personal service; others are historic classics, steeped in charm and tradition. What sets them apart is their attention to decorative detail—each thematic affair is exclusively styled, from floor lamps and canopies to curtains and furnishings. You won't find these eclectic accommodations just anywhere; they originally blossomed in cities like San Francisco in the early 1980s and have remained jewels in the same metropolitan areas. For a taste of local charisma, book a room at one of these singular destinations.

At Fisherman's Wharf, the Argonaut Hotel's nautically themed rooms boast waterfront views.

At bustling Fisherman's Wharf, among the falsefront buildings and carnival-like revelry, is the **Argonaut Hotel** *(p. 86)*, a sophisticated gem in a 1907 canning warehouse. Travel back to the Beat era at **Hotel Bohème** *(p. 77)*, a European pension–style affair where Alan Ginsberg once stayed. Perched on a Sausalito hillside overlooking the Bay, **Casa Madrona Hotel & Spa** *(p. 222)* combines the styles of New England and the Mediterranean in its rooms and guest cottages. In the state capitol is the gracious 1925 **Citizen Hotel** *(p. 468)* with decidedly stately details such as brass plaques, plaster busts, and cocktail napkins printed with signatures from political greats.

Hotel Bohème gives a nod to North Beach history with its Beat-generation decor and photo retrospective.

BED & BREAKFASTS

Relax in the quiet comfort of the Gold Country at Sutter Creek Inn, an 1859 New England–style home.

As elegant as they are charming, B&Bs offer cozy accommodations along with the one exceptional detail large hotels can't provide—individualized hospitality. Whether providing fresh-cut flowers, in-house massage, hand-delivered movies, or ice-chilled champagne, the innkeepers at California B&Bs are dedicated to bringing guests all the comforts they desire. These delightful spots are full of character; some are Victorian estates boasting antiques, others are country clapboard mansions decorated with warm floral prints. Whether they're set on a hillside or nestled on a city street, these unique affairs offer sincere generosity and thoughtful amenities.

The Gold Country's **Sutter Creek Inn** *(p. 488)* offers charming guest rooms with unique swinging beds and spacious grounds. **Chateau Tivoli** *(p. 137)* is the quintessential San Francisco "painted lady," a dazzling three-story 1892 mansion with stained-glass windows, gold leaf, and elaborate woodwork. Mendocino's family- and pet-friendly **Stanford Inn by the Sea** *(p. 334)* features handsome, intimate rooms with wood-burning fireplaces, a greenhouse pool surrounded by bougainvillea, and superb vegetarian menus designed around the inn's biodynamic garden. Overlooking the harbor in the Half Moon Bay area is the **Pillar Point Inn** *(p. 380)* boasting a sleek nautical style reminiscent of Cape Cod.

The lavish boudoirs feature period furnishings and handcarved woodwork at the opulent Chateau Tivoli, a classic Victorian.

CALIFORNIA CUISINE

Alice Waters, Wolfgang Puck, and many of their highly talented chef colleagues pioneered what the world now knows as "California cuisine"—food that relies heavily on fresh local produce, seafood, poultry, and meats, then combines them in ways that allow the flavors to sing—no heavy sauces or deep-fried entrées here. The movement has produced an extraordinary array of restaurants dedicated to innovative cooking and refined tastes. When visiting the homeland of this exquisite trend, indulging in its rich and vibrant flavors is an absolute must.

Chez Panisse *(p. 209)* in Berkeley is where it all began—and where splurging on a multicourse extravaganza is worth the high price and the month-long wait for reservations. In the Mt. Shasta area, **Trinity Café** *(p. 563)* is a big-city bistro in a small-town location. The offerings include fresh seafood, steaks, salads, and a local wine list. Near Point Reyes, the casual, comfortable **Bolinas Coast Cafe** *(p. 317)* features innovative items such as tempura-style prawn tacos, as well as a sumptuous Sunday brunch—all made from local, organic ingredients. At Oakland's **Bay Wolf** *(p. 208)*, the hearty Mediterranean-inspired menu changes monthly but always includes free-range duck from Sonoma, their house specialty. For a romantic dinner in San Francisco, try the outdoor patio at **Foreign Cinema** *(p. 147)* in the Mission, where they pair fresh, local menu items—including a diverse oyster bar—with movies broadcast on a three-story-high wall.

In the East Bay, Bay Wolf offers a mouthwatering menu featuring locally grown ingredients—a feast for both the eyes and the taste buds.

ETHNIC EATERIES

At quirky, spirited Vasili's Greek Restaurant, the kitschy decor is as fun as the food.

A true melting pot, California is home to numerous ethnicities, all rich in different cultural conventions, spices, and flavors. This bountiful variety equates to an abundance of exquisite restaurants with menus offering delicious and authentic cuisines. From San Francisco's Chinese vegetable-stuffed pot stickers to Monterey's Mexican tequila-marinated *pollos borrachos*, the menus are as diverse as their chefs. To get a true taste of the local scene, make a point to reserve a table at one of the little-known gems where dishes are prepared by resident chefs who use original, time-honored recipes and traditional ingredients.

The **Moscow & Tbilisi Bakery Store** *(p. 128)* in San Francisco always has long lines for its fresh-baked desserts, pastries, and breads; the steaming piroghis filled with meat, cheese, or potatoes are delectable additions to any picnic. At the **Hong Kong Flower Lounge** *(p. 179)*, chefs prepare authentic dim sum delicacies, including shrimp or shark fin dumplings, steamed pork buns, and stuffed bell peppers. **Cha Cha Cha** *(p. 133)* dishes out a bewitching blend of Latin and Caribbean flavors like Jamaican jerk chicken or Cajun shrimp in a spicy cream sauce. In Santa Rosa, **Jhanthong Banbua** *(p. 287)* serves up a sophisticated Thai menu of curries, noodles, and creative vegetarian options. Every day is a celebration at **Vasili's Greek Restaurant** *(p. 402)* in Santa Cruz, especially when the owner comes to your table and sets your *saganaki*, a flaming cheese appetizer, ablaze.

San Francisco locals come to Cha Cha Cha for the festive atmosphere, sizzling Latin American food, and potent sangria.

REDWOODS

The colossal redwoods in Northern California are found nowhere else on earth. These towering giants must be seen up close to be truly appreciated, and there are ample places to do so without going too far afield. Silence and solitude are essential to experiencing a redwood forest, so make a point to visit these less-traversed groves where you can actually hear the twigs crack beneath your steps and where you can soak in the earthy fragrance of these magnificent wonders.

The trees in **Muir Woods National Monument** *(p. 308)* reach 260 feet and form a lofty arcade above the narrow trails. Hidden just outside Oakland's downtown is **Joaquin Miller Park** *(p. 217)*, a 500-acre area with rustic hiking trails and skyscraping redwoods. Whimsical beams of sunlight stream through cool, shady canopies at **The Forest of Nisene Marks State Park** *(p. 414)* just north of Santa Cruz. **Humboldt Redwoods State Park** *(p. 346)*, a tribute to early conservationists, is home to 17,000 acres of virgin-growth forest.

Some of the enormous, awe-inspiring trees at Humboldt Redwoods State Park are over 350 feet tall and up to 20 feet in diameter.

Wind your way through the serene grandeur of the coastal redwoods at Muir Woods National Monument.

HIKING

Sometimes putting foot to earth is the best way to get to know an area, getting off the busy roads and finding an intimate, personal connection to the land. From the San Francisco Bay's fabled hills and Monterey's sparkling coastline to Yosemite's alpine meadows and Humboldt's towering forests, California's hiking opportunities are as varied as its people. You can trek through an ancient redwood grove, breathing in the natural essence, and stroll along a secluded shore of the Pacific, reveling in the quiet crash of waves. While bright yellow buttercups bloom on the trail and great blue herons soar overhead, you'll be mesmerized by the natural beauty—and the details you'll discover miles from the tourist crowds. Few other places in the world offer the chance to explore powder-soft beaches and steep mountains in the same day.

With a sprawling 2900 acres to roam, **Samuel P. Taylor State Park** *(p. 323)* offers gentle hiking trails that meander around coastal redwoods and open grasslands bursting with native wildflowers. A high, sharp mountain range, the **Trinity Alps Wilderness Area** *(p. 557)* is made for serious hikers, with its glacial canyons, alpine lakes, pristine streams, and giant talus boulders. **San Bruno Mountain** *(p. 174)*, overlooking the entire Bay Area, features easy-to-reach hiking trails that thread through the ravines and heights; expect amazing views of the Pacific and Santa Cruz Mountains. A gorgeous natural area of rocky headlands, quiet coves, pine forests, and cypress groves, **Point Lobos State Reserve** *(p. 434)* is rich in wildlife and dotted with colorful tidepools.

Explore pine forests, cypress groves, and teeming tidepools along the rugged shore at Point Lobos State Reserve.

Trek through Trinity Alps Wilderness Area, a vast hinterland laced with trails plunging from 9000-foot cliffs to rolling canyon streams.

"OUT" AND ABOUT

California has some of the largest and strongest gay communities in the country, and is justly famous for its activism, nightlife, and ground-breaking politics. San Francisco's Castro neighborhood is lined with rainbow flags, a symbol of pride, and brims with gay-owned and -operated restaurants, theaters, boutiques, and clubs. It is one of the few places where you will see more same-sex couples holding hands than straight couples, where heterosexuals can experience life in the minority. Up north, the Russian River area has become a highly popular resort area for gay men and women. There, and throughout Northern California, bed and breakfasts, nightclubs, and bookstores catering specifically to gay clientele dot the landscape, carving out enclaves where tolerance and individuality abound.

Get in touch with the heart and soul of the city's gay community with **Cruisin' the Castro** *(p. 170)*, a two-hour walking tour that's full of entertaining history and anecdotes. Catering to a mixed clientele, particularly women, **Just For You** *(p. 162)* is a diner with counter service and tables. The **Russian River Resort** *(p. 293)* has modern, contemporary accommodations and is known for organizing festive events and holiday celebrations. In Sacramento, the three floors and three patios at gay club **Faces** *(p. 472)* provide plenty of space to dance or relax late into the night.

Cruisin' the Castro leads walks through this welcoming, vibrant neighborhood and includes a stop at the iconic 1922 Castro Theatre.

HIDDEN
SAN FRANCISCO
& NORTHERN
CALIFORNIA

Including Napa, Sonoma, Mendocino,
Santa Cruz, Monterey, Yosemite, and Lake Tahoe

Ray Riegert

THIRTEENTH EDITION

"Captures the mystique of the locale. Locals will find it refreshing;
vacationers should find it very worthwhile."
—*Los Angeles Times*

"An excellent guide. Riegert seems to have gotten everywhere
there is to get and seen everything there is to see."
—*Honolulu Advertiser*

"A great guidebook for those who will be traveling in and around the city."
—*Out & About*

Ulysses Press
BERKELEY, CALIFORNIA

Published by: ULYSSES PRESS
                P.O. Box 3440
                Berkeley, CA 94703
                www.ulyssespress.com

ISSN 1097-1572
ISBN 978-1-56975-695-9

Printed in Canada by Transcontinental Printing

40 39 38 37 36 35 34 33 32 31 30 29

UPDATE AUTHOR: Carolyn Patten
MANAGING EDITOR: Claire Chun
PROJECT DIRECTOR: Elyce Petker
COPYEDITOR: Emma Silvers
EDITORIAL ASSOCIATES: Lauren Harrison, Abigail Reser,
    Katy Loveless
PRODUCTION: Judith Metzener
CARTOGRAPHY: Pease Press
HIDDEN BOOKS DESIGN: what!design @ whatweb.com
INDEXER: Sayre Van Young
COVER PHOTOGRAPHY: front © Lee Foster;
    back © Nancy Belcher
COLOR INSERT: *page i* © Lee Foster; *page ii* © Richard Cleaver;
    page iii top © Robert Holmes; bottom © Lee Foster;
    page iv © George Grossman; *page v* © Steve Moga; *pages
    vi–vii* © Robert Holmes; *page viii* top © Jeff McCann,
    bottom © Shawn M. Winterich; *page ix* top © Sutter
    Creek Inn/Lindsay Way, bottom © Chateau Tivoli Bed
    & Breakfast/Jason Gerke; *page x* © Bay Wolf/Molly
    Decoudreaux; *page xi* top © Arlene Tsang, bottom
    © Anna L. Conti www.bigcrow.com; *page xii* © Vincent
    Zammit; *pages xiii–xiv* © Robert Holmes; *page xv* © Bryan
    Kennedy; *page xvi* © Robert Holmes

Distributed by Publishers Group West

HIDDEN is a federally registered trademark
of BookPack, Inc.

To Leslie,

for the wonderful years behind us and the many ahead

CONTENTS

MAPS

OUTDOOR ADVENTURE SYMBOLS

The following symbols accompany national, state and regional park listings, as well as beach descriptions throughout the text.

▲	Camping	🏄	Surfing
🚶	Hiking	🎿	Waterskiing
🚲	Biking	⛵	Windsurfing
🐎	Horseback Riding	🛶	Kayaking/Canoeing
⛷	Downhill Skiing	🚤	Boating
🎿	Cross-Country Skiing	🚤	Boat ramps
🏊	Swimming	🐟	Fishing
🤿	Snorkeling/Scuba Diving		

HIDDEN LISTINGS

Throughout the book, listings that reveal the hidden realm—spots that are away from tourists or reflect authentic Florida Keys and the Everglades—are marked by this icon:

There are also special maps at the start of each section that guide you to some of these hidden listings. Each place is identified with this symbol:

CALIFORNIA DREAMING

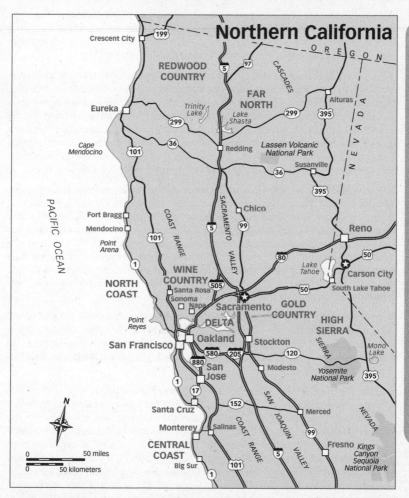

Northern California

Travelers today possess an awareness and imagination that was lacking in their predecessors. Vacations were once escapes from routine. People charted two weeks a year as an island-in-time where they changed from wool suits to bathing suits. In desperate attempts to forget office hours and car payments, they gravitated to overcrowded tourist areas where life proved as frenzied as back home.

Now travel is becoming a personal art form. A destination no longer serves simply as a place to relax: it's also a point of encounter, where experience runs feverish and reality unravels. To many, this new wave in travel customs is labeled "adventure travel" and involves trekking glaciers or dusting granite walls in a hang glider; to others, it connotes nothing more daring than a restful spell at a hidden country inn. Actually, it's a state of mind, a willingness not only to accept but to seek out the uncommon and unique.

This book is written for those taking up the challenge of this freewheeling style. It's intended not for tourists but travelers—people who are equally at ease on a mountain trail or a city boulevard. As a guide, it leads you through San Francisco, then combs the Bay Area and beyond in search of adventure.

Many traditional tourist spots are described, but I have tried to take you a step further. In San Francisco, for instance, you'll visit ever-popular Chinatown, but after walking the crowded blocks of Grant Avenue, the tour leads down an alleyway to a fortune cookie factory. I've listed well-known restaurants and also uncovered the tradition of dim sum dining. In North Beach, the walking tour carries you from Broadway's neon strip to a silent street lined with wooden sidewalks and flowering gardens. At Fisherman's Wharf, you'll skirt the tacky tourist section and wander the barnacle-caked waterfront, where fishermen still ply an ancient trade.

Then head for The Neighborhoods, far from the Gray Line crowds, to discover the soul of the city. Union Street is a strange mix of historic Victorian homes and swinging singles bars; Russian Hill contains pocket parks and hills so steep that steps replace sidewalks; the Haight, once the scene of the Summer of Love, has become thoroughly gentrified; South of Market, once called SOMA Multimedia Gulch, stood as the epicenter of SF's dot-com boom; the rapidly changing Mission District is a fascinating neighborhood with its colorful murals and authentic mariachi bands. San Francisco's gay neighborhoods, particularly Castro and Polk streets, are fully described.

You can explore Golden Gate Park, the West Coast answer to New York's Central Park. Farther afield lies the Golden Gate National Recreation Area with its joggers and hang gliders; the Presidio, a spacious forest in the midst of a major city; and Land's End, where San Francisco marks its finale in a wild tangle of fractured cliffs and untracked coastline.

For the greater Bay Area, there are descriptions of Sausalito's unique houseboat community and the secluded country towns of Port Costa and Benicia. In Berkeley, you will learn how the '60s revolution surrendered to a revolution in the kitchen. During the '70s and '80s, "California cuisine" seized the time and created some of the nation's finest restaurants. Neighboring Oakland, a city often cited for its rougher edges, boasts literary landmarks, including the haunts and homes of Jack London, where you can discover East Bay history. Locally loved jazz clubs also dot the scene and you'll be guided to some of the best. There are bayside parks galore, plus a look at the hills and dales of Silicon Valley, the nation's hub of high-tech ingenuity.

The tourism industry has a knack for transforming everyday life into a spectacle and making tourists feel like visitors to a huge, outdoor human zoo. The result is a kind of Heisenberg-uncertainty-principle-of-tourism whereby the mere presence of outsiders changes the human landscape forever. Local residents become actors, historic places are transformed into theme parks, and visitors see something that more nearly reflects themselves than the indigenous culture.

Like Heisenberg's dilemma, the phenomenon is unavoidable. But given the sensitivity and circumspection contemporary travelers are demonstrating, it is possible to gaze into America's cultural kaleidoscope without greatly disturbing the glass pieces.

In the following pages, I've provided a quiet and intimate approach to Northern California, taking you beyond the surface and into the heart of the place. Visiting the Wine Country, for instance, the book explores the burgeoning wine-growing regions of Sonoma and Napa valleys, stopping at tiny wineries where quality is a matter of family pride. Then it rolls west through the Russian River resort area, a getaway destination for gay men and lesbians. Families also vacation here because of the numerous outdoor opportunities, from canoeing to horseback riding.

Along the magnificent California coast, you'll range from Big Sur to Oregon, stopping at quaint bed-and-breakfast inns and tiny restaurants. The book describes picnics amid the redwoods, hiking trails high above the Pacific, nude beaches, and twisting country roads.

Then it heads for California's golden hills, the Sierra Nevada. Climbing through the Gold Country, where the ghosts of '49ers still wander falsefront towns, it leads to Lake Tahoe and Yosemite, destinations with unmatched beauty. Traditional tourist places are examined in detail, but the important moment is when the tour leaves the beaten track to include hideaway hotels, cozy nightspots, and remote campgrounds.

While this fresh style of travel appeals to people ranging in age from sprout to senior citizen, it has been taking shape for only a few decades. The transformation began in the '60s. The Peace Corps demonstrated we could swim freely in foreign seas; Vietnam taught us not to thrash about in the water. Then the preoccupation with self in the '70s, narcissistic though it was, opened us to unmapped experiences. We have changed from a society perceived as "ugly Americans" to a people in search of unique cultures and history. Better informed, more sensitive and adventurous, we travel for education as much as enjoyment. Rather than proclaiming answers, we ask questions. The high-tech industry, with the Bay Area as its epicenter, overlays the region with a whole new dimension of existence, and the kaleidoscope of cultures, philosophies, and dreams invites us to reach out and touch the ephemeral spirit of place.

More than anywhere in the country, Northern California is a place for creative travelers. It's a multicultural extravaganza as well as a region of exceptional natural beauty. Continents have drifted into San Francisco Bay in ways geologists will never explain. Asia overlaps the entire state, Mexico is shifting north, and tides are carrying the rest of the world closer. Chinese people are moving into Italian neighborhoods, French vintners have invaded the Wine Country, and Scandinavians are discovering the snows of the High Sierra.

Northern California is a destination best suited to a particular pattern of exploration, one requiring an open spirit and unquenchable curiosity. It's a place where experience and adventure form a pattern of overlapping layers that the new traveler, like an archaeologist, will personally uncover.

THE STORY OF NORTHERN CALIFORNIA

GEOLOGY

For billions of years, natural forces have carved the geology of California, creating a land as grand as it is beautiful. Bounded to the west by the cold waters of the Pacific and on the east by sharp mountain ranges and dense forests, Northern California has developed a diverse landscape rich in geologic history.

As a whole, the interior of Northern California can be divided into four natural regions. The first is the Sierra Nevada, the largest single mountain range in the United States. It's a solitary block of earth, tilted and uplifted, 430 miles long and 80 miles wide. A mere child in the long count of geologic history, it rose from the earth's surface a few million years back and did not reach its present form until 750,000 years ago. During the Pleistocene epoch, glaciers spread across the land, grinding and cutting at the mountains. They carved river valleys and deep canyons, and sculpted bald domes, fluted cliffs, and stone towers. In fact, San Francisco Bay is a drowned river valley. Glaciers melting 10,000 years ago created it by raising sea levels and causing the ocean to flood a canyon carved earlier by the Sacramento and San Joaquin rivers.

The glaciers left a landscape dominated by ragged peaks where lakes number in the hundreds and canyons plunge 5000 feet. There are cliffs sheer as glass that compete with the sky for dominance. It is, as an early pioneer described it, a "land of fire and ice."

Millions of years ago, the Klamath region separated from the Sierra Nevada and drifted 60 miles to the northwest. Composed of rocky uplands extending as high as 7000 feet in elevation, the Klamaths are deeply etched by the Smith, Klamath, and Trinity rivers. Heavy precipitation and fog have created dense coniferous forests that now dominate the landscape.

To the east of the Klamaths is the third natural region, which encompasses the southern extension of the volcanic Cascade Range and includes Mount Shasta and Lassen Peak. Mt. Shasta, rising over 14,000 feet, is lord of the land, a white-domed figure brooding above a forested realm. Lassen Peak, its infernal cousin, is an active volcano that last erupted in 1921. Composed of andesite volcanic rock and dated at several million years of age, the Cascade Range developed as a result of the process of subduction.

The fourth natural region consists of the Coast Ranges, which extend up the San Francisco peninsula, through Northern California to Oregon. Built of shale, sandstone, and other sedimentary rocks, the Coast Ranges are a product of pressure from the Pacific Plate beneath the western border of North America. These peaks include the Santa Cruz

Mountains, which rise to the west and south of San Francisco Bay; on the other side of the Bay are the East Bay Hills and the Diablo Range; to the north looms Mt. Tamalpais. At the mouth of the Bay is the Golden Gate, a rocky conduit through which California's major drainage system empties into the Pacific.

The California coast is lined with softly rolling hills and bounded by a pacific sea. The shoreline is actually a head-on collision between the edge of the ocean and the rim of North America. Two tectonic plates, those rafts of land that float upon the earth's core, meet in California. Here the North American Plate and the Pacific Plate push against each other in a kind of international arm wrestle. Between them, and under colossal pressure from both sides, lies the San Andreas Fault. Villain of the 1906 San Francisco earthquake, it also brought the Loma Prieta quake in 1989 that measured 7.1 on the Richter scale.

Things were not always as they are. About 150 million years ago, the California coast rested where the Sierra Nevada mountains reside today. Then the North American Plate shifted west, riding roughshod over the Pacific Plate, compressing and folding the earth upward to create the Coast Ranges, and moving the continent 100 miles westward.

Today the northern section of the San Andreas Fault runs up the San Francisco peninsula, heading briefly out to sea just south of San Francisco, then cutting north through Stinson Beach, Bodega Bay, and Point Arena, before heading seaward again near Shelter Cove. Meanwhile the Pacific Plate, carrying Los Angeles, is shifting north along the North American Plate, which holds San Francisco, at a pace that should position the rival cities next to each other in about ten million years. Anyone planning to hitch a ride north should pack extra sandwiches and prepare for a long wait at the side of the road.

HISTORY

The tiny village of Yerba Buena, pop. 400, slumbered on the edge of the bay, waiting for the whaling ships that occasionally dropped anchor there for supplies. Once the northernmost Spanish colonial capital in the Americas, it had begun to decline when the old Franciscan mission on the other side of the hill shut down. By 1846, when the region became United States territory, most Californians had moved south into Mexico. Meanwhile, a few Anglo adventurers had begun to arrive; by 1848, about 1000 of them had homesteaded in Northern California.

When local newspaper publisher Sam Brannan announced in the town plaza that gold had been discovered 150 miles inland, all hell broke loose. Within a year, the population of the village—newly renamed San Francisco after the old mission nearby (and deemed "Old Gold Mountain" by the Chinese)—grew from 400 to 24,000, and another 60,000 pioneers had taken up residence in the gold country of the Sierra. In ten more years, San Francisco's population would reach 57,000, and by 1870 it would be 150,000, while the total population of Northern California would exceed 500,000.

Many newcomers were Southerners who brought black slaves with them, but California was admitted to the Union as a free state, and in 1851 a woman named Biddy Mason won a Supreme Court decision that any slave owner who remained in the state for three years lost his property rights to his slaves, thus instantly freeing about 1000 African Americans in California. The presence of an established black community made California seem a land of opportunity for many newly freed slaves who migrated west after the Civil War.

At the same time, famine was sweeping China, and American brokers brought thousands of refugees to the United States to work in mines and build railroads. Japanese immigrants also came to California, but most dispersed in rural areas to become farmers. Prejudice ran high, and as the numbers grew, Anglo Californians prevailed on the federal government to pass laws prohibiting Asian immigration—with a few exceptions. After the Philippines became United States territory in the Spanish-American War, Filipinos could move to the U.S., and many did.

Before World War II, there were no restrictions on Mexicans entering the United States. Many Mexican citizens came to California seasonally to work in the fast-growing agricultural industry, and many stayed between seasons. During the war, fears that Mexicans would fill the jobs vacated by American soldiers prompted the federal government to tighten the border and deport many people of Mexican descent. But those who could prove they had been born in the U.S. or had been naturalized were allowed to stay and form the nucleus of a Mexican American population that has been growing ever since.

Also during World War II, Japanese Americans in California were taken from their homes and put in internment camps around the western U.S. While some returned after the war, California's Japanese population has never regained its pre-war level. Laws against Asian immigration stayed in effect until 1965. After they were lifted, the Asian population grew rapidly. Thousands of Cambodian, Vietnamese, and Laotian refugees settled in San Francisco. With the Silicon Valley high-tech boom, a new wave of highly educated immigrants from many parts of Asia arrived to meet the seemingly limitless demand for engineers and technicians.

As civil wars ravaged Central America during the 1980s, many Guatemalan, Salvadoran, and Nicaraguan people chose to live in California with its long-established Spanish-speaking community. In San Francisco, Central Americans now comprise the majority of the Latino population.

According to recent official population estimates, 66 percent of Northern Californians are of European descent; 12 percent are African American; 16 percent are Asian American; and 6 percent are "other." Latinos (who may fall into any of the above categories) account for 14 percent of Northern California's population.

In San Francisco, 43.6 percent are of European descent; 7.8 percent are African American; 30.8 percent are Asian; and 3.7 percent are "other." Within the Asian population, 63.7 percent are Chinese; 16.7 percent are Filipino; 4.7 percent are Japanese; 4.4 percent are Vietnamese; and the remaining 10.5 percent include Koreans, East Indians, Cambodians, Hmong, Laotians, and Thais. Of all San Franciscans, 14.1 percent are Latino, including 44 percent Mexican Americans, 50 percent Central Americans, 3 percent Puerto Ricans, and 1 percent Cubans.

Statistics alone, however, cannot tell the whole story of Northern California's kaleidoscope. Consider, for instance, the rich Italian heritage that infuses the Wine Country, as well as the Irish character of many communities in the Gold Country. Above all, there's San Francisco's reputation for tolerance, which has consistently attracted people whose lifestyles lie outside the American mainstream. Beatniks, gay men and lesbians, hippies, and internet pioneers have all helped shape the character of one of the most unusual and culturally vibrant cities anywhere.

FLORA

From dark redwood forests to sunny alpine meadows to a coastline colored by wildflowers, California's habitats are heaven to natural history lovers. Radical climatic differences within the state are largely responsible for creating this unique diversity.

Heavy precipitation and cold temperatures in the Sierra Nevada create the perfect environment for dense coniferous forests of Ponderosa pine, white fir, and red fir. Higher up, the sugar pines and Sierra redwoods tower over manzanita, deer brush, and Sierra gooseberry. Also included in this high-altitude habitat is California's own giant sequoia, which is the pride of Sequoia and Kings Canyon national parks. Also known as the California redwood, this is the Golden State's official tree and the tallest living thing in the world.

In the riparian woodlands of the Sierra Nevada, smaller trees and larger shrubs (including willows, cottonwoods, white alders, and dogwoods) thrive. Often bounded by lodgepole forests, Sierra meadows are home to an array of springtime wildflowers—phloxes, paintbrushes, lupines, elephants head, and the brilliant scarlet gilia.

In the Far North region of the Klamath mountains, abundant rainfall and moderate temperatures combine to create a dense forest similar to that of the Alaskan coast. Species include Alaskan cedar, Douglas fir, and silver fir. At higher elevations, wind-eroded foxtail pine, a close relative of the ancient bristlecone pine of Southern California, survive. The lower slopes along the coast are host to Pacific madrone, tan oak, and California laurel, while different species of shrubby willow trees are found from Humboldt County to Del Norte County.

East of the Klamaths, the volcanic soils of the Cascades support a unique conifer known as the Baker cypress, which flourishes despite the area's cold weather conditions. In the lowlands, rainfall and fog have created forests dotted with ponderosa and Jeffrey pine.

From the rim of the sea to the peaks of surrounding mountains, the coastline is covered with a complex variety of plant life. Several plant communities flourish along the shore, each clinging to a particular niche in the environment. Blessed with a cooler, more moderate climate near the ocean, they are continually misted by sea spray and must contend with more salt in their veins.

On the beaches and along the dunes are the herbs, vines, and low shrubs of the coastal strand community. Among their numbers are beach primrose, sand verbena, beach morning-glory, and sea figs, those tenacious succulents that run along the ground sprouting magenta flowers and literally carpeting the coast. Characterized by leathery leaves that retain large quantities of water, they are the plant world's answer to the camel.

Around the mud flats and river mouths grow rushes, pickleweed, tules, cord grass, and other members of the salt marsh community. Low, shrubby plants growing in clumps, these hearty fellows are inundated by tides and able to withstand tremendous concentrations of salt.

Coastal sage scrub inhabits a broad swath from above the waterline to about the 3000-foot elevation. White and black sage, wild buckwheat, and California sagebrush belong to this community of short, tough plants.

Along the northern coastal ranges, cold ocean waters create heavy fog, an essential nutrient for the eerily beautiful coastal redwoods. The fabled Monterey cypress inhabits a picturesque region along the Monterey coast, the only place in the world it is found. Closed-cone pines including the Monterey, Bishop, and knobcone skirt the shoreline. Shrubs in the northern coastal ranges include brown dogwood, Western rosebay, and bunchberry. Scattered along the rolling hills of the coastal interior are the dignified, gnarled oak trees while the coastal woodlands are also sown with drought-tolerant species of dry grasses and assorted wildflowers including the California poppy, the state flower.

FAUNA

From the black bears of Yosemite Valley to the black-tailed deer of the East Bay hills, Northern California is home to a variety of wildlife. This is true despite the environmental stress of humans on the state's wilderness areas, which has caused the extinction of many species. The California grizzly bear, for instance, is no longer found in the Sierra Nevada; and because of the damming of rivers and streams, salmon spawning has become a rare phenomenon. Conservation efforts have increased in the past few years, and many species are now under governmental protection. For example, attempts to preserve the habitat of the bighorn sheep have been so intense that a marked increase in their population occurred for several years. Debates continually rage over the status of mountain lions and coyotes, both of which are coming into increased contact with humans as open land has given way to residential developments.

The rich habitat of the High Sierra is home to a variety of species including ground squirrels, yellow-bellied marmots, pikas, gophers, jackrabbits, hares, snakes, lizards, golden trout, salamanders, bighorn sheep, and great gray owls. In the lower fields of the Sierra riparian woodlands, multicolored butterflies and a diverse selection of birds such as starlings, sparrows, blackbirds, American dipper, and the belter kingfisher make their homes. Lower yet, the cavities in oak trees provide shelter for gray squirrels, owls, woodpeckers, and bluebirds.

The moist forests of the Klamath region are a fertile backdrop for a wide array of wildlife. There are approximately 15 colorful species of salamanders in these northern forests, including the cave-dwelling Shasta salamander and the water-loving Olympic salamander. Colorful hummingbirds, bald eagles, pileated woodpeckers, elusive spotted owls, and the marbled murrelet dart around the forests. Other critters include chipmunks, porcupines, raccoons, weasels, river otters, and Roosevelt elk.

In the northern Coast Ranges, the insects can be as interesting as reptiles and amphibians. The monarch butterfly migrates between Canada and Central Mexico, stopping off in Pacific Grove every year. The Western pond turtle is found along the coast, while alligator lizards inhabit the coastal interior. The scrub jay helps create oak forests by storing hundreds of acorns underground. Another acorn-loving species is the acorn woodpecker, which stores its provisions in the cavities of oak trees.

Somehow the mud flats of San Francisco Bay are the last place you may think to go sightseeing, particularly at high tide, after the flood has stirred the ooze. But it is at such times that birders gather to view flocks of as many as 60,000 birds.

The California shore is one of the richest bird habitats anywhere in North America. Over 500 species are found across the state, many along the coast and its offshore islands. There are near-shore birds like loons, grebes, cormorants, and scoters, that inhabit the shallow waters of bays and beaches. Other birds are situated offshore; these include shearwaters, which feed several miles off the coast; and pelagic or open-ocean species like albatross and Arctic terns, which fly miles from land and live for up to 20 or 30 years.

Joining the shore birds along California's beaches are ducks, geese, and other waterfowl. Both waterfowl and near-shore birds flee the scene each year, flying north in spring to Canada and Alaska or south during autumn to Mexico and Central America, following the Pacific flyway, that great migratory route spanning the western United States.

The peregrine falcon nests on rock ledges and is capable of diving at 200 miles an hour to prey on ducks, coots, and terns. Among the most beautiful birds are the egrets and herons. Tall, slender, elegant birds, they live from January until July in Bolinas and other coastal towns. Together with sea gulls, sandpipers, and pelicans, they tend to turn travelers into birdwatchers and make inconvenient times, like the edge of dawn, and unusual places, like swamps, among the most intriguing possibilities Northern California has to offer.

California's marine mammals inspire great myth and magic. Foremost are the ocean-going animals like whales, dolphins, and porpoises, members of that unique Cetacean order that left the land 30 million years ago for the alien world of the sea.

While dolphins and porpoises range far offshore, the region's most common whale is a regular coastal visitor. Migrating 12,000 miles every year between the Bering Sea and Baja Peninsula, the California gray whale cruises the shoreline each winter. Measuring 50 feet and weighing 40 tons, these distinguished animals can live to 50 years of age and communicate with sophisticated signaling systems.

Six species of seals and sea lions inhabit the coast, together with sea otters, those playful creatures that delight visitors and bedevil fishermen.

WHEN TO GO

SEASONS

Northern California stretches over 400 miles from Big Sur to Oregon and almost 200 miles from east to west. Within that broad expanse lies the Pacific coastline, a broad interior valley, the lofty Sierra Nevada, and a weather pattern that varies as dramatically as the terrain.

Generally, there are three different climatic zones. San Francisco and the rest of the Pacific shore enjoy mild temperatures year-round, since the coastal fog creates a natural form of air conditioning and insulation. The mercury rarely drops below 40° or rises above 70°, with September and October being the hottest months, and December and January the coolest.

Spring and particularly autumn are the ideal times to visit. During the winter, the rainy season brings overcast days and frequent showers. Summer is San Francisco's peak tourist season, when large crowds can present problems. It's also a period of frequent fog; especially in the morning and evening, fog banks from offshore blanket the city and head inland through the Golden Gate.

The seasons vary much more in the interior valleys, creating a second climatic zone. In the Wine Country, Delta, and Gold Country, summer temperatures often top 90°. There's less humidity, winters are cooler, and the higher elevations receive occasional snowfall. Like the coast, this piedmont region experiences most of its rain during winter months.

The Sierra Nevada and Cascade Ranges experience Northern California's most dramatic weather. During summer, the days are warm, the nights cool. Spring and autumn bring crisp temperatures and colorful foliage changes (which the coastline, with its unvarying seasons, rarely undergoes). Then in winter, the thermometer plummets and snow falls so heavily as to make these mountain chains spectacular ski areas.

CALENDAR OF EVENTS

JANUARY
San Francisco   During late January or early February, the **Chinese New Year** features an extravagant parade with colorful dragons, dancers, marching bands, and fireworks.

FEBRUARY

San Francisco   The **Pacific Orchid Exposition** celebrates its floral namesake at the Fort Mason Center.

North Coast   The **World Famous Crab Races and Crab Feed** takes place in Crescent City; if you forgot to bring your own, you can rent a racing crab. Who said California lacks culture?

Central Coast   The **AT&T National Pebble Beach Pro-Am Golf Championship** swings into action early in the month.

MARCH

San Francisco   Bands, politicians, and assorted revelers parade through the city on the Sunday closest to March 17, marking **St. Patrick's Day**.

Wine Country   The blooming of wild mustard marks the start of the **Napa Valley Mustard Festival**, which runs February through March and includes cooking demonstrations, art exhibits, and (of course) chowder- and winetasting.

North Coast   Mendocino and Fort Bragg celebrate a **Whale Festival** with whale-watching cruises, art shows, and winetasting.

High Sierra   The **SnowFest** along Lake Tahoe's North Shore is a celebration with fireworks, ski races and dancing.

Far North   During the winter months, Mount Shasta Board & Ski Park sponsors a series of **Demo Days** during which you can test-drive all the latest ski and snowboarding equipment.

APRIL

San Francisco   Japantown's **Cherry Blossom Festival** features parades, tea ceremonies, theatrical performances, and martial arts displays. **Opening Day on the Bay** launches the yachting season with a blessing of the fleet and a parade of decorated boats. The **San Francisco International Film Festival** offers a wide selection of cinematic events. Cowboys do their celebrating at the **Grand National Rodeo, Horse & Stock Show**.

Wine Country   The entire town of Sebastopol turns out for the **Shenandoah Apple Blossom Festival**, staging exhibits, parades, and pageants.

North Coast   The two-day **Heron Festival and Wildflower Brunch** features boat rides to heron rookeries on Clear Lake, nature walks, slide shows, food, and fun for the kids.

MAY

San Francisco   Over 70,000 hearty souls (soles?) run the **Bay to Breakers Foot Race**, many covering the 7.5-mile course in costumes. San Francisco celebrates **Cinco de Mayo** in the Mission with arts, crafts, food, and a festive parade.

Gold Country   Up in Angels Camp, the **Calaveras County Fair and Jumping Frog Jubilee**, immortalized by Mark Twain, includes not only frog-jumping contests, but a wine show and county fair as well. A parade helps kick off a series of rodeo competitions at Sonora's **Mother Lode Round Up**.

JUNE

San Francisco   The **San Francisco Lesbian, Gay, Bisexual, Transgender Pride Parade**, with its colorful floats and imaginative costumes, marches down Market Street to the Civic Center.

Bay Area   Artists throughout the East Bay display their work two weekends every June during the **Pro Arts Open Studios**.

Central Coast   Monterey presents its **Annual Wine Festival**, with winetasting, gourmet food, and cooking demonstrations.

JULY

San Francisco   Here at Fisherman's Wharf and throughout Northern California, firework displays commemorate the **Fourth of July**.

Bay Area   The **Jewish Film Festival**, in existence for more than three decades, celebrates new independent films from around the world, focusing on Jewish history, culture, and identity.

Central Coast   Gilroy celebrates its favorite crop with a **Garlic Festival** featuring the cuisine of local gourmet chefs. The **California Rodeo** in Salinas ranges from horse races to trick riders to clown acts. Browse the wares of local artists, accompanied by live jazz, at Santa Cruz's outdoor **Art on the Wharf**.

Gold Country   Plymouth's **Amador County Fair** includes demonstrations of antique farming, mining, and lumbering equipment.

AUGUST

San Francisco   Celebrate the Bay Area's diverse Asian community at the annual **Nihonmachi Street Fair**. Local artisans display their wares, and there's live music and authentic Asian cuisine as well as an area for kids to make traditional Asian crafts. The **San Francisco Marathon** takes runners past many of the city's sights.

Bay Area   On the last Sunday of every August in Niles, over 200 vendors descend for the **Antique Faire and Flea Market**, and residents open their garages and front lawns to the bargain hunters and antique lovers that fill the streets.

Central Coast   Pebble Beach sponsors the **Concours d'Elegance Exposition of Classic Cars**, a classic auto show featuring pre- and postwar cars. Salinas celebrates its four-day **Steinbeck Festival** with walking tours, lectures, films, and plays.

Gold Country   Sample the fare of a number of local restaurants and wineries at the **Nimbus Winery Wine and Food Festival** in Rancho Cordova. Lasting until Labor Day, the capital city of Sacramento hosts the **California State Fair**, which features concerts, exhibits, and competitions galore.

SEPTEMBER

San Francisco   This month for music is marked by the opening of the **San Francisco Opera** and the **San Francisco Symphony**, as well as the annual **Opera in the Park**. The **San Francisco Jazz Festival** kicks off in late September to present two months' worth of concerts, dance, per-

The Musical Days of Summer

It's hard to beat California weather in the summertime. Add days of endless live music and good people, and you've got a recipe for fun in the sun. Here's a mini-guide to the Golden State's most golden summer music festivals.

San Francisco   The **Stern Grove Festival** (www.sterngrove.org) brings world-renowned acts every Sunday from June through August to the Stern Grove amphitheater. Performances showcase international music and dance, vocal ensembles, opera, and jazz. Come early with picnic fixings to save a good spot (don't forget a blanket!). Be a part of the activism San Francisco is famous for and dance with the free spirits in Golden Gate Park at **Power to the Peaceful** (www.powertothepeaceful.org), a pro-peace festival in September headed by reggae-rock musician Michael Franti and his group Spearhead. Love bluegrass? Don't miss the free **Hardly Strictly Bluegrass Festival** (www. strictlybluegrass.com) in October in Golden Gate Park, two non-stop days of, you guessed it, bluegrass and bluegrass-inspired music.

Bay Area   Every Labor Day weekend, downtown Oakland becomes the grounds for **Art & Soul** (www.artandsouloakland.com), a conglomerate of visual artists, musicians, food booths, and crafts vendors.

Wine Country   The Russian River flows alongside the site of the **Russian River Blues Festival** (www.omegaevents.com) held every June with artists like Al Green and Ike Turner, among others.

North Coast   **Reggae on the River** (www.reggaeontheriver.com) is one of the largest reggae festivals in the world, taking place over three days in August on the Eel River in Humboldt County. Further south on the Eel River is the September **Earthdance** (www.earthdance.org), which hosts a wide range of world music (reggae, Latin, hip-hop), as well as yoga and healing centers and children's activities.

Central Coast   The world's longest running jazz festival is the **Monterey Jazz Festival** (www.montereyjazzfestival.org), bringing in over 500 artists on several stages each September.

Gold Country & High Sierra   Held 4th of July weekend, the **High Sierra Music Festival** (www.highsierramusic.com) features bluegrass, reggae, rock, and jam bands against the backdrop of the Sierras. The **Strawberry Music Festival** (www.strawberrymusic.com) is a family-orientated event held twice a year over Memorial and Labor Day weekends. Americana, bluegrass, rock, and blues music is primarily featured.

Far North   The three-day **Trinity Tribal Stomp** (www.trinitytribalstomp. org), hosts rock, reggae, and bluegrass bands every September.

formances, and tributes to the masters. The **San Francisco Blues Festival** at Fort Mason is known not only for being the oldest of its kind in America, but also for attracting some of the best musicians in the world. The end of the month and Leather Pride Week brings a San Francisco tradition: the **Folsom Street Fair**. The event is peopled with San Francisco's kinkiest citizens (it's the biggest leather event in the world), but tolerant adults of all kinds also join in the fun.

Bay Area   The **Santa Clara Art and Wine Festival**, one of the nation's largest sidewalk art displays, features food, entertainment, and local and regional artists at Central Park. Sausalito also celebrates the arts and Memorial Day weekend with the **Sausalito Art Festival**. More than 20,000 works are displayed, accompanied by live entertainment and gourmet delights.

Central Coast   It's the magic month for the internationally renowned **Monterey Jazz Festival**.

Gold Country   The **Gold Country Fair** in Auburn features a harvest festival, livestock auction, plenty of food, and country music. Grass Valley hosts the **Nevada County Fair**, with entertainment, food, music, livestock, living-history displays, and gold panning.

OCTOBER
San Francisco   **Columbus Day** is marked by an Italian Heritage parade, bocce ball tournament, and the annual blessing of the fishing fleet. The **Castro Street Fair** features food, art, and loads of quirky San Francisco culture. **Comedy Celebration Day** is a free "comedy concert" in Golden Gate Park featuring stand-ups from around the world.

Central Coast   The **Art and Pumpkin Festival** in Half Moon Bay features food booths, crafts exhibits, and pie-eating contests.

Gold Country   The festivities at the **Calaveras Grape Stomp and Gold Rush Street Faire** include grape stomping, a team costume contest, and a waiters' race.

NOVEMBER
North Coast   Mendocino hosts a **Thanksgiving Art Fair** with over 40 crafts booths and refreshments.

DECEMBER
San Francisco   The **Great Dickens Christmas Fair**, which goes from Thanksgiving to Christmas, and the **Tree Lighting at Union Square** commemorate the holiday season. There are also **Christmas Parades** in towns throughout Northern California. The San Francisco Ballet (the country's oldest ballet company and one of the best) mounts its annual production of Tchaikovsky's classic **Nutcracker**.

Bay Area   Locals head to Oakland's Jack London Square to view the annual **Lighted Yacht Parade**.

BEFORE YOU GO

VISITORS CENTERS

Several agencies provide free information to travelers. Also consult local chambers of commerce and information centers, which are mentioned in the various area chapters.

CALIFORNIA TRAVEL AND TOURISM COMMISSION ✉ *980 9th Street, Suite 480, Sacramento, CA 95814* ☎ *916-444-4429, 800-862-2543* ✐ *www.visit*

california.com This organization will help guide you to areas throughout the state.

REDWOOD EMPIRE ASSOCIATION ✉ *1925 13th Avenue #103, Oakland, CA 94606* ✆ *800-619-2125* ✐ *www.redwoodempire.com* For information on the North Coast counties between San Francisco and Oregon, contact this association.

SAN FRANCISCO VISITORS INFORMATION CENTER ✉ *Hallidie Plaza, Lower Level; 900 Market Street, San Francisco, CA 94102* ✆ *415-391-2000* ✐ *www.onlyinsanfrancisco.com* Maps, detailed guides, and recommendations are available from this excellent resource.

PACKING

There are two important guidelines when deciding what to take on a trip. The first is as true for San Francisco and Northern California as anywhere in the world—pack light. Dress styles here are relatively informal and laundromats or dry cleaners are frequent. Most airlines allow one carry-on bag and one personal item, such as a briefcase, purse, or laptop. Other luggage will have to be checked, possibly for a fee, so try to take one suitcase and perhaps a small accessory case.

The second rule is to prepare for cool weather, even if the closest you'll come to the mountains is the top of Nob Hill. "The coldest winter I ever spent," Mark Twain remarked, "was a summer in San Francisco." While the city's climate is temperate, temperatures sometimes descend below 50°. Even that might not seem chilly until the fog rolls in and the ocean breeze picks up. A warm sweater and jacket are absolute necessities. Pack shorts for the summer or autumn. You'll encounter similar weather conditions in all coastal areas of Northern California, where the Pacific Ocean moderates the climate. If you plan to tour inland, though, it's a different story. The Wine Country, the Delta, and the Gold Country can be very hot during the summer, and you'll want the lightest, coolest clothing possible.

Yosemite and other parts of the Sierras have deep snow and subfreezing temperatures for most of the winter, so a parka, hat, gloves, and warm boots are in order. Even in early fall and late spring, campers in the Sierras will discover that the thermometer quickly plunges below freezing as the sun goes down, so pack accordingly. Whenever you're planning a trip around the interior of California, it's always a good idea to dress in layers and be prepared for anything.

LODGING

Overnight accommodations in Northern California are as varied as the region itself. They range from highrise hotels and neon motels to hostels and bed-and-breakfast inns. One guideline to follow with all is to reserve well in advance. This is an extremely popular area, particularly in summer, and facilities fill up quickly.

Throughout the book, hotel facilities are organized geographically. Check through the various regional sections of each chapter and you're bound to find something to fit your budget and personal taste.

The neon motels offer bland facilities at low prices and are excellent if you're economizing or don't plan to spend much time in the room. Larger hotels often lack intimacy, but provide such conveniences as restaurants and shops in the lobby. My personal preference is for historic hotels, those slightly faded classics that offer charm and tradition at moderate cost. Bed-and-breakfast inns present an opportunity to stay in a home-like setting. Like hostels, they are an excellent way to meet fellow travelers; unlike hostels, Northern California's country inns are quite expensive.

To help you decide on a place to stay, I've described the accommodations not only by area but also according to price (prices listed are for the high season; rates may decrease in low season). *Budget* hotels ($) are generally less than $90 per night for two people; the rooms are clean and comfortable, but lack luxury. The *moderately* priced hotels ($$) run $90 to $150, and provide larger rooms, plusher furniture, and more attractive surroundings. At *deluxe*-priced accommodations ($$$) you can expect to spend between $150 and $300 for a homey bed and breakfast or a double in a hotel or resort. You'll check into a spacious, well-appointed room with all modern facilities; downstairs the lobby will be a fashionable affair, and you'll usually see a restaurant, lounge, and a cluster of shops. If you want to spend your time (and money) in the city's very finest hotels, try an *ultra-deluxe* facility ($$$$), which will include all the amenities and a price above $300.

CALIFORNIA ASSOCIATION OF BED & BREAKFAST INNS
✉*414 29th Street, Sacramento* ☎*800-373-9251* 🖥*916-444-2738* 🖱*www.cabbi.com,*
info@cabbi.com Contact this association to give you a hand in finding a cozy place to stay.

DINING

It seems as if Northern California has more restaurants than people. Particularly in San Francisco, they line the streets; vendor stands and lunch wagons line the curbs as well. To establish a pattern for this parade of dining places, I've described not only the cuisine but also the ambience and general price structure of each establishment. Restaurants listed offer lunch and dinner unless otherwise noted.

Within a particular chapter, the restaurants are categorized geographically, with each restaurant entry describing the establishment as budget ($), moderate ($$), deluxe ($$$), or ultra-deluxe ($$$$) in price. Dinner entrées at *budget* restaurants usually cost $10 or less. The ambience is informal café-style and the crowd is often a local one. *Moderately* priced restaurants range between $10 and $20 at dinner and offer pleasant surroundings, a more varied menu, and a slower pace. *Deluxe* establishments tab their entrées above $20, featuring sophisticated cuisines, plush decor, and more personalized service. *Ultra-deluxe* dining rooms, where $30 will only get you started, are gourmet gathering places where the cooking (hopefully) is a fine art form and service is a way of life.

Breakfast and lunch menus vary less in price from restaurant to restaurant. Even deluxe-priced kitchens usually offer light breakfasts and lunch sandwiches that place them within a few dollars of their budget-minded competitors. These early meals can be a good time to test expensive restaurants.

TRAVELING WITH CHILDREN

Visiting Northern California with kids can be a real adventure, and if properly planned, a truly enjoyable one. To ensure that your trip will feature the joy, rather than the strain, of parenthood, remember a few important guidelines.

Children under age 7 or under 60 pounds must be in approved child restraints while riding in motor vehicles. The back seat is safest.

Use a travel agent to help with arrangements; they can reserve spacious bulkhead seats. Also plan to bring everything you need on board—diapers, food, toys, and extra clothes for kids and parents alike. If the trip to Northern California involves a long journey, plan to relax and do very little during the first few days.

Always allow extra time for getting places. Book reservations well in advance and make sure the hotel has the extra crib, cot, or bed you require. It's smart to ask for a room at the end of the hall to cut down on noise. Also keep in mind that many bed-and-breakfast inns do not allow children.

Most towns have stores that carry diapers, food, and other essentials; in cities and larger towns, 7-11 stores are often open all night (check the Yellow Pages for addresses).

Hotels often provide access to babysitters or you can check the Yellow Pages for state licensed and bonded babysitting agencies.

A first-aid kit is always a good idea. Also, check with your pediatrician for special medicines and dosages for colds and diarrhea. Finding activities to interest children in Northern California could not be easier. Especially helpful in deciding on the day's outing are *Fun Places to Go with Children in Northern California* (Chronicle Books) and the "Datebook" or "pink section" of the Sunday *San Francisco Chronicle*.

WOMEN TRAVELING ALONE

It is sad commentary on life in the United States, but women traveling alone must take precautions. It's entirely unwise to hitchhike and probably best to avoid inexpensive accommodations on the outskirts of town; the money saved does not outweigh the risk. Bed and breakfasts, youth hostels, college dorms, and YWCAs are generally your safest bet for lodging, and they also foster an environment ideal for bonding with fellow travelers. Lodging in a major hotel in a safe area is a fine option as well.

If you are hassled or threatened in some way, never be afraid to scream for assistance. It's a good idea to have your cell phone handy and to know the number to call in case of emergency. If your cell does not work on the U.S. network, or if you don't own a cell, you can rent a mobile device. Try **TripTel** (1525 Van Ness Avenue, San Francisco; 415-474-3330, 877-874-7835; www.triptel.com); you can pick up your rental at SFO or in San Francisco. Note that California law prohibits texting while driving and limits talking on a cell phone to hands-free devices.

Northern California boasts nearly 900 women's organizations, including rape crisis centers, health organizations, battered women's shelters, National Organization of Women (NOW) chapters, business networking clubs, artists' and writers' groups, and one-of-a-kind organizations ranging from Women as Allies in the Santa Cruz area to the Women's Mountain Bike & Tea Society (WOMBATS) in Fairfax.

Emergency services, including rape crisis and battered women's hotlines, can be found in local phone books or by calling directory assistance. A good place to start when seeking information about other resources is the local women's center, often affiliated with a university. Among them are:

University of California–Berkeley Gender Equity Resource Center
✉ *202 Cesar Chavez Student Center, Berkeley* ☎ *510-642-4786*

University of California–San Francisco Center for Gender Equity
✉ *100 Medical Center Way, San Francisco* ☎ *415-476-5222*

University of California–Santa Cruz Women's Center ✉ *Cardiff House, University of California, Santa Cruz* ☎ *831-459-2072*

Women Escaping a Violent Environment (WEAVE) ✉ *Sacramento* ☎ *916-920-2952*

Women's Center House 55 ✉ *Humboldt State University, Arcata* ☎ *707-826-4216*

University of California–Davis Women's Resources and Research Center ✉ *North Hall* ☎ *530-752-3372*

GAY & LESBIAN TRAVELERS

Without doubt, San Francisco is one of the premier gay and lesbian vacation spots in the country. In many ways, the entire city of San Francisco is a gay-friendly enclave. Gays and lesbians constitute a powerful voting block in local politics, and several serve on the Board of Supervisors. The Castro Street and Polk Street neighborhoods, as well as the South of Market district, are all major gay areas. Each offers gay-owned and gay-friendly lodging, restaurants, and nightspots. (See the "Gay Neighborhoods" and "South of Market" sections in Chapter Two, and "Gay-friendly travel" in the index.)

SAN FRANCISCO LESBIAN, GAY, BISEXUAL, AND TRANSGENDER COMMUNITY CENTER (LGBT) ✉ *1800 Market Street* ☎ *415-865-5555* 🖷 *415-865-5501* 🖳 *www.sfcenter.org, info@sfcenter.org* One of the largest of its kind, this community center offers a plethora of services from health and legal referrals to lodging and activity suggestions.

BILLY DEFRANK LGBT COMMUNITY CENTER ✉938 *The Alameda, San Jose* ☎408-293-2429 ✐*www.defrank.org* A great resource, this website has lots of information online.

CALIFORNIA AIDS HOTLINE ✉415-863-2437, 800-367-2437 *(within California)* ✐*www.sfaf.org* This is the area's best resource for counseling and referrals.

AIDS NIGHTLINE ☎415-434-2437, 800-628-9240 ✐*www.aidsnightline.org* Operators are available nightly from 5 p.m. to 5 a.m. through this hotline.

COMMUNITY UNITED AGAINST VIOLENCE SUPPORT LINE ☎415-333-4357 ✐*www.cuav.org* This support line is available 24 hours a day to assist gay, lesbian, bisexual, and transgender people who have been physically assaulted.

WOMEN'S BUILDING ✉3543 *18th Street #8, San Francisco* ☎415-431-1180 📠415-861-8969 ✐*www.womensbuilding.org* Despite its name, the Women's Building is a community center with a non-profit auditorium for rent, and bulletin boards loaded with information and job listings for gays, lesbians, and bisexuals.

LYON-MARTIN WOMEN'S HEALTH SERVICES ✉1748 *Market Street, Suite 201, San Francisco* ☎415-565-7667 📠415-252-7512 ✐*www.lyon-martin. org, info@lyon-martin.org* Medical attention for lesbian and transgender women can be found here.

THE PACIFIC CENTER FOR HUMAN GROWTH ✉2712 *Telegraph Avenue, Berkeley* ☎510-548-8283 ✐*www.pacificcenter.org, info@pacificcenter.org* Low-cost counseling, peer-support groups, job listings, and housing bulletins, as well as an information referral line for anything that is pertinent to the gay-lesbian-bisexual-transgender community is available at this center.

BAY AREA REPORTER ☎415-861-5019 For weekly updates on the gay community, pick up this paper, which focuses on local news and arts and entertainment.

SF FRONTIERS ✐*www.frontiersnewsmagazine.com* This biweekly magazine features articles of interest to the gay community.

SAN FRANCISCO BAY TIMES ☎415-626-0260 Dealing specifically with gay, lesbian, bisexual, and transgender issues, this weekly paper doubles as a resource guide as well.

The Russian River area, an hour north of the city, is another key gay and lesbian resort area. (See the "Russian River" section in Chapter Four, and "Gay-friendly travel" in the index.)

GAY/LESBIAN/BI INFORMATION REFERRAL LINE ☎707-526-0442 This is a traveler-friendly phone line that provides information and referrals about lodging, dining, and nightlife in the area, along with just about any other information you might need.

WE THE PEOPLE The local gay and lesbian newspaper is *We the People*, which comes out once a month and is available throughout the Wine Country and the Russian River region.

MOM . . . GUESS WHAT! ☎916-441-6397 ✐*www.mgwnews.com* A free bimonthly magazine, *Mom . . . Guess What!* serves Sacramento and Northern California with political scoops, travel tips, restaurant reviews, and more.

SENIOR TRAVELERS

Northern California is an ideal spot for older vacationers. The mild climate makes traveling in the off-season possible, helping to cut down on expenses. Many museums, theaters, restaurants, and hotels offer discounts to seniors (requiring a driver's license, Medicare card, or other age-identifying card). Be sure to ask your travel agent when booking reservations.

The large number of national parks and monuments in the region means that persons age 62 and older can save considerable money with an America the Beautiful–National Parks and Federal Lands Senior Pass, which allows free admission for the pass holder plus all passengers in a non-commercial vehicle (or three additional adults at per-person entrances). Apply for one in person at any national park unit that charges an entrance fee. Many private sightseeing attractions also offer significant discounts for seniors.

Be extra careful about health matters. Bring any medications you use, along with the prescriptions. Consider carrying a medical record with you—including your current medical status, and medical history, as well as your doctor's name, phone number, and address. Also be sure to confirm that your insurance covers you away from home.

AMERICAN ASSOCIATION OF RETIRED PERSONS (AARP) ✉*601 E Street NW, Washington, DC 20049* ☎*888-687-2277* ✐*www.aarp.org* Check out AARP for member discounts and escorted tours.

ELDERHOSTEL ✉*11 Avenue de Lafayette, Boston, MA 02111* ☎*800-454-5768* ✐*www.elderhostel.org* For those 55 or over, this group offers educational programs in California.

DISABLED TRAVELERS

California stands at the forefront of social reform for persons with disabilities. During the past decade, the state has responded to the needs of the blind, wheelchair-bound, and others with a series of progressive legislative measures.

Be sure to check in advance when making reservations. Many hotels and motels feature facilities for those in wheelchairs.

DEPARTMENT OF MOTOR VEHICLES ✉*1377 Fell Street, San Francisco* ☎*800-777-0133* ✐*www.dmv.ca.gov* The DMV provides special parking permits for the disabled. Many local bus lines and other public transit facilities are wheelchair accessible.

ACCESS SAN FRANCISCO ✉*1720 Market Street* ☎*415-575-4949* ✐*www.accessf.org* This free guide gives detailed information on access to the city's sights, hotels, and restaurants. It's also available from the San

There are also agencies in Northern California assisting travelers with disabilities.

CENTER FOR INDEPENDENT LIVING ✉*2539 Telegraph Avenue, Berkeley* 📞*510-841-4776* 🖨*510-841-6168* ✒*www.cilberkeley.org* For tips and information about the San Francisco Bay Area, contact this self-help group that has led the way in reforming access laws in California.

SOCIETY FOR ACCESSIBLE TRAVEL & HOSPITALITY ✉*347 5th Avenue, Suite 605, New York, NY 10016* 📞*212-447-7284* ✒*www.sath.org, sath travel@aol.com* General information and resources are available here.

MOSSREHAB RESOURCENET ✉*MossRehab Hospital, 1200 West Tabor Road, Philadelphia, PA 19141* 📞*215-456-9600* ✒*www.mossresourcenet.org* A complete resource for disabled travelers, MossRehab offers lots of helpful tips, tools, links, and facts.

FLYING WHEELS TRAVEL ✉*143 West Bridge Street, Owatonna, MN 55060* 📞*507-451-5005, 877-451-5006* ✒*www.flyingwheelstravel.com* Flying Wheels operates as a full-service travel agency for the disabled.

FOREIGN TRAVELERS

PASSPORTS AND VISAS Foreign visitors are required to obtain a passport and tourist visa to enter the United States. Furthermore, tighter U.S. Department of Homeland Security regulations now mandate that all those traveling to the U.S. by boat or air, including U.S. citizens, must show a valid passport to enter or re-enter the U.S.

CUSTOMS REQUIREMENTS Foreign travelers are allowed to carry in the following: 200 cigarettes (1 carton), 50 cigars, or 2 kilograms (4.4 pounds) of smoking tobacco; one liter of alcohol (restricted to checked luggage) for personal use only (you must be 21 years of age to bring in alcohol); and US$100 worth of duty-free gifts that may include an additional 100 cigars (except Cuban). As of August 2006, the maximum amount of liquid permitted in carry-on luggage is 3 oz. All containers with liquids must be enclosed in a 1-quart Ziploc bag. You may bring in any amount of currency, but must fill out a form if you bring in over US$10,000. Carry any prescription drugs in clearly marked containers. You may have to produce a written prescription or doctor's statement for the customs officers. Meat or meat products, seeds, plants, fruits, and narcotics are not allowed to be brought into the United States.

United States Customs and Border Protection ✉*1300 Pennsylvania Avenue NW, Washington, DC 20229* 📞*202-354-1000, 877-227-5511* ✒*www.cbp.gov* Contact the customs service for further information on allowable items and amounts.

DRIVING If you plan to rent a car, an international driver's license should be obtained prior to arrival. Some rental car companies require both a foreign license and an international driver's license, along with a major credit card and require that the lessee be at least 25 years of age. Seat belts are mandatory for the driver and all passengers. Children under the age of 7 or 60 pounds should be in the back seat in approved child-safety restraints. Cell phone users take note: You must have a hands-free system to talk (Bluetooth, speakerphone). Furthermore, all texting from cells or other mobile devices—sending, writing, or reading—is illegal for all motorists.

CURRENCY American money is based on the dollar. Bills in the United States come in six common denominations: $1, $5, $10, $20, $50, and $100. Every dollar is divided into 100 cents. Coins are the penny (1 cent), nickel (5 cents), dime (10 cents), quarter (25 cents), half-dollar (50 cents), and dollar (100 cents). You may not use foreign currency to purchase goods and services in the United States. Consider buying traveler's checks in dollar amounts. You may also use credit cards affiliated with an American company such as Interbank, Barclay Card, VISA, and American Express.

ELECTRICITY AND ELECTRONICS Electric outlets use currents of 110 volts, 60 cycles. For appliances made for other electrical systems, you need a transformer or other adapter. Travelers who use laptop computers for telecommunication should be aware that modem configurations for U.S. telephone systems may be different from their European counterparts. Similarly, the U.S. format for DVDs and videotapes is different from that in Europe; National Park Service visitors centers and other stores that sell souvenir DVDs or videos often have them available in European format on request.

WEIGHTS AND MEASUREMENTS The United States uses the English system of weights and measures. American units and their metric equivalents are as follows: 1 inch = 2.5 centimeters; 1 foot (12 inches) = 0.3 meter; 1 yard (3 feet) = 0.9 meter; 1 mile (5280 feet) = 1.6 kilometers; 1 ounce = 28 grams; 1 pound (16 ounces) = 0.45 kilogram; 1 quart (liquid) = 0.9 liter.

OUTDOOR ADVENTURES

CAMPING

CALIFORNIA DEPARTMENT OF PARKS AND RECREATION ✉P.O. Box 942896, Sacramento, CA 94296 ☎916-653-6995, 800-777-0369 The state oversees close to 300 camping facilities. Amenities at each campground vary; for more information on state-run campgrounds call or write the parks department for a free *California Escapes* guide packet. Reservations for campgrounds may be made by calling 800-444-7275.

NATIONAL PARK SERVICE ✉Golden Gate National Parks, Fort Mason, Building 201, San Francisco, CA 94123 ☎415-561-4700 ✐www.nps.gov/goga For general information on federal campgrounds, contact the national service. To reserve a National Park campsite, contact the park directly or call 800-365-2267.

U.S.D.A. FOREST SERVICE ✉ 1323 Club Drive, Vallejo, CA 94592 ✆ 707-562-8737 ✎ www.fs.fed.us/r5 This is a great resource for maps and information.

NATIONAL RECREATION RESERVATION CENTER ✆ 877-444-6777 Campsites must be booked through this reservation center. A fee is charged at these facilities and the length of stay varies from park to park. It's best to reserve in advance, though many parks keep some sites open to be filled daily on a first-come, first-serve basis.

In addition to state and national campgrounds, Northern California offers numerous municipal, county, and private facilities. See the "Beaches & Parks" sections in each chapter for the locations of these campgrounds.

PERMITS

WILDERNESS PERMITS For camping and hiking in the wilderness and primitive areas of national forests, a wilderness permit is required. Permits are largely free and are issued for a specific period of time, which varies according to the wilderness area. You can obtain permits from ranger stations and regional information centers, as described in the "Beaches & Parks" sections in each chapter. Information, but not permits, is available through the **U.S. Forest Service** (1323 Club Drive, Vallejo, CA 94592; 707-562-8737, fax 707-562-9130; www.fs.fed.us/r5).

FISHING LICENSES For information on the fishing season and state license fees, contact the **California Department of Fish and Game** (1416 9th Street, Sacramento, CA 95814; 916-445-0411; www.dfg.ca.gov).

SAN
FRANCISCO

San Francisco

It is a city poised at the end of the continent, civilization's last fling before the land plunges into the Pacific. Perhaps this is why visitors demand something memorable from San Francisco. People expect the city to resonate along a personal wavelength, speak to them, fulfill some ineffable desire at the center of the soul.

There is a terrible beauty at the edge of America: the dream begins here, or ends. The Golden Gate Bridge, that arching portal to infinite horizons, is also a suicide gangplank for hundreds of ill-starred dreamers. Throughout American history, those who crossed the country in search of destiny ultimately found it here or turned back to the continent and their own past.

Yet San Francisco is only a city, a steel-and-glass metropolis mounted on a series of hills. With a population of about 799,000, it covers 47 square miles at the tip of a peninsula bounded by the Pacific Ocean and San Francisco Bay. A gateway to Asia, San Francisco supports a multicultural population with large and growing concentrations of Chinese, Latinos, African Americans, Italians, Filipinos, Japanese, and Southeast Asians.

The myth of San Francisco originates not only from its geography, but also from its history. If, as early Christians believed, the world was created in 4004 B.C., then the history of San Francisco began on January 28, 1848. That day a hired hand named James Marshall discovered gold in California. Year One is 1849, a time etched in the psyche of an entire nation. The people swept along by the mania of that momentous time have been known forever since as "'49ers." They crossed the Rockies in covered wagons, trekked the jungles of Panama, and challenged the treacherous seas around Cape Horn, all because of a shiny yellow metal.

Gold in California was the quintessence of the American Dream. For anyone with courage and ambition, it represented a chance to blaze trails, expand a young nation, and become rich in the flash of a fortuitous find.

God granted Divine Right to Britain, creating a kingdom that ruled the oceans. To America, God gave Manifest Destiny, a hunger for territory which drove an entire nation west like a fever through the body. Gold was the currency of Manifest Destiny, a myth that lured 100,000 people across an implacable land, and created a civilization on the fringes of a continent.

San Francisco became the capital of that civilization. The peaceful hamlet was transmogrified into a hellbent city, a place to make the Wild West look tame. Its population exploded from 900 to 25,000 in two years; by 1890 it numbered 300,000.

During the Gold Rush, a Barbary Coast ghetto grew along the Bay. Over 500 businesses sold liquor; gambling, drugs, and prostitution were rampant; gangs roamed the boomtown and iron-fisted vigilance committees enforced law and order. Sailors were shanghaied and failed prospectors committed suicide at the rate of 1000 per year.

By 1850, about 500 ships, whose crews had deserted for the gold fields, lay abandoned in San Francisco Bay. Some were used as stores, hotels, even lunatic asylums; others became landfill. Speculators wildly divided the city into tiny plots.

Amid all the chaos, San Francisco grew into an international city. Ambitious Americans, displaced Mexicans, indentured Chinese, itinerant Australians, and Chilean immigrants crowded its muddy streets. The populace soon boasted over a dozen newspapers, published in a variety of languages. Because of its multicultural population, and in spite of periodic racial problems, San Francisco developed a strong liberal tradition, an openness to the unusual and unexpected, which prevails today.

Long before Americans discovered gold in the Sierra Nevada foothills, Spaniards spoke of a mythical land filled with gems and precious metal. A 16th-century Spanish novel described it as an island called California, inhabited by beautiful amazons. San Francisco lay near the northern tip of the colony that the Spanish eventually named after that fabled land.

In 1769 an expedition led by Gaspar de Portolá, intent on expanding Spanish control in California, marched up the San Francisco peninsula and discovered the Golden Gate. Then in 1776, while the American Revolution raged on the East Coast, Captain Juan Bautista de Anza established a mission and presidio near San Francisco Bay.

Of course, the Costanoan Indians had been occupying the area for thousands of years, moving among the hills, marshes, forests, and meadows. They hunted deer, elk, and grizzly bears, ground acorns to make meal, dug roots, and caught shellfish off the coast. After the conquistadors arrived, the Costanoans built churches. In ever-imperious fashion, the Spanish "civilized" the American Indians, forcibly removing them from ancestral homes, crowding the Indians into dingy quarters, and teaching them the glories of Christianity.

Using slave labor and fortifying a chain of 21 missions, the Spanish eventually colonized the coast from San Diego to San Francisco to Sonoma. When Mexico gained independence from Spain in 1821, this colonial prize became Mexican territory. At the same time, San Francisco and environs began attracting American whalers, Russian seal hunters, French adventurers, and British entrepreneurs.

Finally, in 1846, American settlers, with assistance from the United States government, fomented the Bear Flag Revolt. Seizing California from Mexico, they created an independent republic that soon became part of the United States. Just two years before gold would be found in Spain's mythic land of amazons, the stars and stripes flew over San Francisco.

The Gold Rush not only lured prospectors to the pulsing young city: many of America's finest writers were soon mining literary material. Mark Twain, fresh from the gold fields, took in the scene during the 1860s, as did local colorist Bret Harte. Ambrose Bierce excoriated everyone and everything in his column for William Randolph Hearst's *Examiner*. In 1879, Henry George published a book in San Francisco called *Progress and Poverty*, which propounded a revolutionary system of taxation. Robert Louis Stevenson explored the Bay Area a few years later, and Jack London used it as a setting for his adventure tales.

With characters like Joshua Abraham Norton roaming the streets, San Francisco was a natural place for storytellers. A riches-to-rags victim, Norton made and lost a fortune within a few years of the Gold Rush, then, unhinged by the ordeal, declared himself the emperor of the United States. Rather than committing the crackbrain, San Francisco welcomed him and made "Emperor Norton" a municipal mascot.

Even a society willing to accept eccentrics can sometimes turn upon itself, bitterly excluding part of its populace. There is a dark side of the dream that blackens the fate of some and casts a shadow upon all. During the 1860s, Chinese immigrants were brought in to build the transcontinental railroad. When they completed it in 1869, San Francisco was linked with the rest of the United States and railroad owners like the Big Four (Mark Hopkins, Leland Stanford, Collis Huntington, and Charles Crocker) were fabulously wealthy. Chinese labor helped stimulate the boom that made San Francisco a city of cable cars and stately Victorians by the end of the century. Regardless, the Chinese were victims of vitriolic racism. "Yellow Peril" hysteria was rampant in San Francisco during the 1880s, and led to beatings, murder, and a ban on Asian immigration to the United States.

Social upheaval gave way to devastating convulsions of the earth on April 18, 1906. Dream turned to nightmare at 5:12 that morning as a horrendous earthquake, 8.3 on the Richter scale, rocked and buckled the land. Actually, the infamous San Francisco earthquake owed its destructive ferocity more to the subsequent fires than the seismic disturbance. One of the few people killed by the earthquake itself was the city's fire chief. Gas mains across the city broke and water pipes lay shattered. Within hours, 50 separate fires ignited, merged, and by nightfall created firestorms that tore across the city. Three-quarters of San Francisco's houses were destroyed in the three-day disaster, 452 people died, and 250,000 were left homeless.

The city whose municipal symbol is a phoenix rising from the ashes quickly rebuilt. City Hall and the Civic Center became part of a resurrected San Francisco. The Golden Gate and Bay bridges were completed in the 1930s, and during World War II the port became a major embarkation point for men and materiel. A city of international importance, San Francisco was the site for the signing of the United Nations charter in June 1945.

It entered the post–World War II era at the vanguard of American society. San Francisco's hallmark is cultural innovation. This city at the continent's edge boasts a society at the edge of thought. During the 1950s it became the Beat capital of the world. Allen Ginsberg, Jack Kerouac, Gary Snyder, and other Beat poets began haunting places like Caffe Trieste and the Co-Existence Bagel Shop. The Beats blew cool jazz, intoned free form poems, and extolled the virtues of nothingness.

Lawrence Ferlinghetti opened City Lights Bookstore in 1953. Two years later Ginsberg publicly read a poem called "Howl" that redefined the American dream and outraged the Eisenhower society. In 1957, Jack Kerouac, ricocheting between San Francisco and the East Coast like some kind of human missile, defined the generation in *On the Road*. Later he would pen what many would call his finest book, *The Dharma Bums*, using Northern California settings and characters.

Not even Kerouac was prepared for San Francisco's next wave of cultural immigrants. This mecca for the misplaced became a mystical gathering place for myriads of hippies. The Haight-Ashbury neighborhood was the staging area for a movement intent on revolutionizing American consciousness.

Ken Kesey and his Merry Pranksters created the Trips Festival in 1966, combining dynamic light shows and massive doses of LSD in a grand effort to entertain while enlightening. The Jefferson Airplane, Big Brother and the Holding Company, and the Grateful Dead blew minds with an electric sound called acid rock. Then, in January 1967, about 20,000 people gathered in Golden Gate Park for a "Human Be-In." Ginsberg chanted, the Hells Angels blasted through on Harleys, and Tim Leary advised the assembled to "Turn on, tune in, and drop out." It was a happening of colossal proportions, leading to the fabled "Summer of Love" when hippies from around the world set out to make San Francisco the center of cosmic consciousness.

By the 1970s San Francisco was becoming home to a vital and creative minority, gay men and women. The city's gay population had increased steadily for decades; then, suddenly, San Francisco's open society and freewheeling lifestyle brought an amazing influx of gays. In 1977, Supervisor Harvey Milk became the nation's first outfront gay to be elected to a major municipal post. That same year the city passed a landmark gay rights ordinance. With an advancing population that today numbers perhaps 200,000, gays became a powerful social and political force.

Then the dark face of the dream appeared once again. More than 900 members of the People's Temple, one of the countless sects headquartered in San Francisco, committed mass suicide at their outpost in Guyana. Shortly afterwards, on November 27, 1978, in an unrelated incident, Supervisor Dan White assassinated fellow supervisor Harvey Milk and San Francisco Mayor George Moscone.

Text continued on page 30.

San Francisco
Neighborhoods

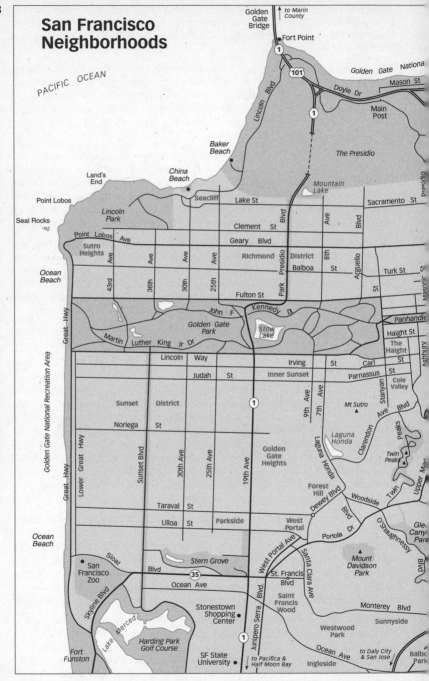

PACIFIC OCEAN

Golden Gate
Bridge

↑ to Marin
County

● Fort Point

● 1

101

to Marin County

Golden Gate Nationa

Mason St

Doyle Dr

1

Main
Post

The Presidio

Presidio

Baker
Beach

China
Beach

Land's
End

Mountain
Lake

Point Lobos

Seacliff

Lake St

Sacramento St

Seal Rocks

Lincoln
Park

Clement St

Blvd

Ave

Blvd

Point Lobos Ave

Geary Blvd

Sutro
Heights

Richmond District

8th

Turk St

Ocean
Beach

43rd

36th

30th

25th

Balboa

St

Aguello

Ave

Ave

Ave

Ave

Park

Presidio

St

Maconic

Fulton St

Kennedy Dr

Panhandle

Great Hwy

John F

Golden Gate Park

Stow
Lake

Haight St

The
Haight

Ashbury

Martin

Luther King Jr Dr

Lincoln Way

Irving St

Carl St

Golden Gate National Recreation Area

Judah St

Inner Sunset

Parnassus

St

Cole
Valley

9th Ave

7th Ave

Mt Sutro ▲

Stanyan

Ave

Blvd

Peaks

Sunset District

Laguna
Honda

Twin
Peaks ▲

Noriega St

Clarendon

Lower Great Hwy

Great Hwy

Sunset Blvd

30th Ave

25th Ave

19th Ave

Golden
Gate
Heights

Laguna Honda

Upper Mar

Twin

Forest
Hill

Dewey Blvd

Woodside

Blvd

Taraval St

Ulloa St

Parkside

West
Portal

Portola Dr

O'Shaughnessy

Gle
Cany
Par

Ocean
Beach

Sloat

Stern Grove

West Portal Ave

Blvd

Mount
Davidson
Park ▲

Skyline Blvd

● San
Francisco
Zoo

Blvd

35

Ocean Ave

St. Francis
Blvd

Santa Clara Ave

Monterey Blvd

Stonestown
Shopping
Center ●

Juniper Serra Blvd

Saint
Francis
Wood

Sunnyside

Lake Merced

Westwood
Park

Harding Park
Golf Course

1

Fort
Funston

SF State
University ●

to Pacifica &
Half Moon Bay

Ocean Ave

Ingleside

to Daly City
& San Jose

Balbo
Park

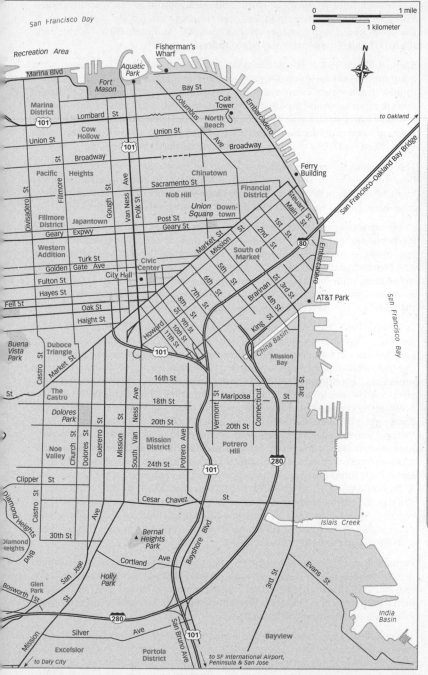

The dual murder stunned the world and outraged the gay community. When White received a relatively mild sentence the next year, a night of rioting swept the Civic Center, with damages totaling $300,000. And then, within a few years, the AIDS epidemic swept the gay community.

Throughout the 1980s, '90s, and into the 21st century, San Francisco has retained a gay supervisor whose constituency remains an integral part of the city's life. A multi-cultural society from its early days, San Francisco remains a city at the edge, open to experiment and experience. The national media still portray the region as a kind of open ward, home to flakes and weirdos. They point to events like the mayoral election in which a character named Jello Biafra, then a singer for a punk band called the Dead Kennedys, polled over three percent of the vote.

The city does sometimes seem to contain as many cults as people, but it also boasts more than its share of artists and activists. The national ecology movement, which began in this area with the pioneering work of John Muir, also flourishes here. This is headquarters for dozens of concerned organizations.

There are some problems: during the last few decades, San Francisco's skyline has been "Manhattanized," crowded with clusters of dark skyscrapers. The AIDS epidemic has taken a terrible toll, particularly among the area's gay population. And the city has allowed its port to decline. Most cargo ships travel across the Bay to Oakland, while San Francisco's once great waterfront is being converted into gourmet restaurants and chic shopping malls. It is a city in love with itself, trading the mundane business of shipping for the glamorous, profitable tourist industry.

In October 1989, television viewers across America who had tuned in for the third game of the World Series between the San Francisco Giants and neighboring Oakland Athletics in Candlestick Park witnessed a 7.1-level earthquake that rocked the stadium and rolled through Northern California, leaving 67 dead and causing more than $10 billion in damage. As with previous disasters, however, San Francisco quickly rose from the rubble to achieve a new level of prosperity. The rebuilding process provided ideal investment opportunities for the new money flooding the Bay Area thanks to booming high-tech companies in nearby Silicon Valley. Condemned warehouses were bulldozed to make way for luxury condominium and office complexes. Artsy, affordably run-down districts were transformed almost overnight into yuppie enclaves of richly renovated Victorian mansions, their former carriage houses converted to garage space for Lexuses and BMWs. Ultimately, Candlestick Park itself was abandoned by the Giants in favor of a state-of-the-art ballpark in another part of the city. But by the turn of the 20th century, the dot-com crash hit hard, knelling a death blow for much of SF's computer industry. Technology continues to be an important sector, though it has lost its explosive and vibrant nature.

Perhaps Rudyard Kipling was right. He once called the place "a mad city—inhabited for the most part by perfectly insane people." William Saroyan saw it as "a city that invites the heart to come to life . . . an experiment in living." The two thoughts do not contradict: San Francisco is madly beautiful, a marvelous and zany place. Its contribution to the world is its lifestyle.

The people who gravitate here become models—some exemplary, others tragic— for their entire generation. Every decade San Francisco moves further out along the edge, maintaining a tradition for the avant-garde and iconoclastic that dates back to the Gold Rush days. The city is a jigsaw puzzle that will never be com-

pleted. Its residents, and those who come to love the place, are parts from that **31**
puzzle, pieces that never quite fit, but rather stand out, unique edges exposed,
from all the rest.

DOWNTOWN

Visit any city in the world and the sightseeing tour will begin in a vital
but nebulous area called "Downtown." San Francisco is no different.
Here, Downtown is spelled Union Square (Geary and Stockton streets),
a tree-dotted plot in the heart of the city's hotel and shopping district.
Lofty buildings bordering the area house major department stores
while the network of surrounding streets features many of the city's
poshest shops and plushest hotels.

SIGHTS

UNION SQUARE This public square's most intriguing role is as San
Francisco's free-form entertainment center. On any day you may see a
brass band high-stepping through, a school choir singing the world's
praises, or a gathering of motley but talented musicians or mimes passing the hat for bus fare home. Union Square is a scene—where the rich
and powerful come to view the merely talented, where panhandlers
sometimes seem as plentiful as pigeons.

CABLE CARS Cable cars from the nearby turnaround station at
Powell and Market streets clang past en route to Nob Hill and Fisherman's Wharf. So pull up a patch of lawn and watch the world work
through its paces, or just browse the Square's hedgerows and flower
gardens.

SAN FRANCISCO VISITORS INFORMATION CENTER ✉*Hallidie
Plaza, Lower Level, 900 Market Street* ☎*415-391-2000* ⌨*www.onlyinsanfrancisco.com*
While you're here, you'd be wise to stop by this visitor center for some
handy brochures. Closed Sunday November through April.

FLOOD BUILDING This historic building overlooks the Powell
Street BART station and houses The Gap. This was the only downtown
building besides the U.S. Mint to survive the 1906 earthquake intact.

Riding the CultureBus

⌨*www.sfculturebus.org* Ditch the car and hop on the CultureBus—Muni line
74X—for a museum tour of San Francisco. This eco-friendly bus route (vehicles run on biodiesel) connects the SOMA Museum District, Union Square,
and the museum concourse in Golden Gate Park. Ride all day for one special
event fare, getting on and off as many times as you like. Some museums give
discounts when you show your special transfer, which can also be used on
Muni buses, the Metro, and historic streetcar service (cable cars not included)
for the rest of the day. It runs daily every 20 minutes from 8:40 a.m. to 5:50
p.m. For specific stops and times, check the website.

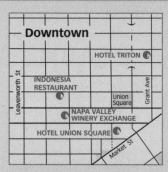

INDONESIA RESTAURANT

Authentic Indonesian curries, soups, and rice plates in a cozy, casual spot favored by those in the know

HOTEL TRITON

Hip, artistic, eco-friendly, and celebrity-inspired luxury suites, seconds from the bustle of downtown

HOTEL UNION SQUARE

Sleek, innovative, modern design—and a *Maltese Falcon* room— in one of San Francisco's original boutique hotels

NAPA VALLEY WINERY EXCHANGE

Hard-to-find, small-production California wines, gifts, and knowledgeable staff in a family-owned gem of a store

MINT PLAZA ✉ *Off 5th Street between Mission and Market streets* ☎ *415-348-4604* 🖱 *www.mintplazasf.org, info@friendsofmintplaza.org* Bounded on three sides by historic buildings, Mint Plaza offers a public open space dotted with trees and a few cafés. Stone walkways, bright orange seating, and a steel arbor amassed with vines make up the 290-foot area. As the plaza is developed throughout 2009, additional push-cart vendors will offer locally produced items, and a series of concerts and public events will be held here, including dance and theater programs.

OLD MINT BUILDING ✉ *Mission and 5th streets* Nearby, the 1874 U.S. Mint survived the 1906 earthquake due to the foresight of its architect Alfred Mullet, who knew of the region's proclivity to tremblors and designed the building to float on its foundation in a quake. The "Granite Lady" is now being restored as a cultural center and is scheduled to open to the public by 2012.

MAIDEN LANE Right off Union Square is this lane, the headiest of the city's high-heeled shopping areas. Back in Barbary Coast days, when San Francisco was a dirty word, this two-block-long alleyway was wall-to-wall with bawdy houses. But today it's been transformed from redlight district to ultrachic mall. Of particular interest among the galleries and boutiques lining this pedestrian-only thoroughfare is the building at **140 Maiden Lane**. Designed by Frank Lloyd Wright in 1948, its circular interior stairway and other unique elements foreshadow the motifs he later used for the famous Guggenheim Museum.

THE BARBARY COAST TRAIL This thoroughly urban "trail" blazed along San Francisco's sidewalks introduces you to some of the city's best-known districts on an easy four-mile trek. Because of stoplights and storefronts, city hiking takes longer than country hiking, so allow four to five hours for the whole route. The Barbary Coast Trail is marked by well-worn circular bronze plaques embedded in the sidewalks, each with one arrow pointing where you're coming from and another pointing the way you want to go.

LODGING

If you want to stay in the city's chic epicenter, book a room at a hotel near Union Square.

HOTEL UNION SQUARE

$$$ 131 ROOMS   ✉114 Powell Street   ☎415-397-3000, 800-553-1900
📠415-885-3268   🖥www.hotelunionsquare.com, reservations@personality hotels.com

Built early in the 20th century to accommodate visitors to the Panama–Pacific International Exposition, this hotel is sleekly decorated with elements from its Art Deco history and contemporary San Francisco personality. Mystery writer Dashiell Hammett, who reportedly once frequented the place, is honored with a memorial suite that features literary-themed antiques and the name of his fictional detective agency on an outfacing window. Walls upstairs have been sandblasted to expose original brick.

FOUR SEASONS HOTEL

$$$$ 277 UNITS   ✉757 Market Street   ☎415-633-3000, 800-819-5053
📠415-633-3001   🖥www.fourseasons.com

A quick detour to Market Street will bring you to this ultraposh getaway that features 231 modern rooms and 46 suites. Suites have an office area separated from the living space by French doors, and even the

---

Affordable Accommodations

The cheapest accommodations in town are found in the city's Tenderloin district. Situated between Union Square and the Civic Center, this area is an easy walk from restaurants and points of cultural interest. The Tenderloin is a sometimes dangerous, sleazy neighborhood filled with interesting if menacing characters, the kind of place you stay because of the low rent rather than the inherent charm. Still, if the spirit is willing, the purse will certainly be appreciative. Just don't flaunt the purse—or camera, for that matter.

In my opinion, the best hotel buys in San Francisco are the middle-range accommodations. These usually offer good location, comfortable surroundings, and reasonable service at a cost that does not leave your pocketbook empty. Happily, the city possesses a substantial number of these facilities.

Downtown San Francisco

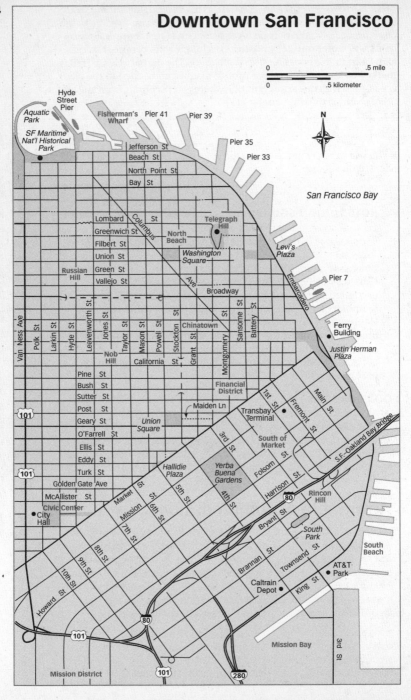

0   .5 mile

0   .5 kilometer

N

San Francisco Bay

Aquatic Park

Hyde Street Pier

SF Maritime Nat'l Historical Park

Fisherman's Wharf

Pier 41

Pier 39

Pier 35

Pier 33

Jefferson St

Beach St

North Point St

Bay St

Lombard St

Greenwich St

Filbert St

Union St

Green St

Vallejo St

Russian Hill

Columbus Ave

North Beach

Washington Square

Telegraph Hill

Levi's Plaza

Pier 7

Broadway

Chinatown

Nob Hill

California St

Financial District

Maiden Ln

Union Square

Hallidie Plaza

Yerba Buena Gardens

Transbay Terminal

South of Market

Rincon Hill

South Park

South Beach

AT&T Park

Caltrain Depot

Mission Bay

Embarcadero

Ferry Building

Justin Herman Plaza

Van Ness Ave

Polk St

Larkin St

Hyde St

Leavenworth St

Jones St

Taylor St

Mason St

Powell St

Stockton St

Grant Ave

Montgomery St

Sansome St

Battery St

Pine St

Bush St

Sutter St

Post St

Geary St

O'Farrell St

Ellis St

Eddy St

Turk St

Golden Gate Ave

McAllister St

Civic Center

City Hall

Market St

Mission St

Howard St

Folsom St

Harrison St

Bryant St

Brannan St

Townsend St

King St

3rd St

4th St

5th St

6th St

7th St

8th St

9th St

10th St

1st St

Fremont St

Main St

S.F.-Oakland Bay Bridge

Mission District

101

101

80

80

280

101

more moderate rooms have marble bathrooms complete with deep-soaking tubs. If your pampering needs exceed the comforts of your guest room, the resident spa will step in and offer massage, aromatherapy, and a tempting array of peels and wraps. There's a pool and an elegant dining room.

HOTEL METROPOLIS

$$ 105 ROOMS   ✉ 25 Mason Street   📞 415-775-4600, 800-553-1900

📠 415-775-4606   💻 www.hotelmetropolis.com

This whimsical, ten-story property takes its design sense from the elements of earth, wind, fire, and water. The rooms are small, but feel larger with compact, mid-century-style furniture in light woods; warm, cream-colored walls are set off by curtains, accessories, and artwork pillows in colors of the different elements—red for fire, brown for earth, etc. Bright white bathrooms are spiced up with colorful tiles in geometric designs. Business travelers will love the 24-hour business center, free wi-fi throughout the hotel, and well-lit writing desks. The attached Farmer Brown Restaurant serves up tasty soul food. The hotel is on the edge of an area known for panhandlers and can be noisy at night, but the value is excellent and the staff friendly and accommodating.

HOTEL NIKKO

$$$$ 533 ROOMS   ✉ 222 Mason Street   📞 415-394-1111, 800-248-3308

📠 415-394-1106   💻 www.hotelnikkosf.com, reservations@hotelnikkosf.com

Accommodations at this 25-story hotel exude *shibui*, a Japanese word that expresses elegant simplicity. Smooth-edged contemporary furnishings and natural colors. Rates include access to business services and fitness facilities, including a glass-enclosed rooftop swimming pool and whirlpool.

HOSTELLING INTERNATIONAL—DOWNTOWN

$ 272 BEDS   ✉ 312 Mason Street   📞 415-788-5604   📠 415-788-3023

💻 www.norcalhostels.org, downtown@sfhostels.org.

Within walking distance of Union Square is this comfortable, yet very affordable option. In fact, this is *the* place if you are looking for budget accommodations in the heart of the city. There are 32 private rooms as well as shared rooms with four bunks per room; a kitchen is available for guests to use. Internet access is also available. Continental breakfast included.

KING GEORGE HOTEL

$$ 154 ROOMS   ✉ 334 Mason Street   📞 415-781-5050, 800-288-6005

📠 415-391-6976   💻 www.kinggeorge.com, 1hotelreservation@kinggeorge.com

If you prefer an English theme, try this charming hotel also on Mason Street. The lobby at this tasteful establishment is done in a lovely cream with a traditional English countryside motif. A marble staircase ascends to the "Windsor Tea Room." Convenient in both price and location, featuring comfortable, spiffy rooms, the King George is a noteworthy competitor in its class.

HOTEL FRANK

$$$–$$$$ 153 ROOMS   ✉️*386 Geary Street*   📞*415-986-2000, 800-553-1900*
🖱️*www.hotelfranksf.com, info@hotelfranksf.com*

Kitty corner from the King George is this newly styled affair. Designed by award-winning Hollywood powerhouse Thomas Schoos Design, the Frank boasts a slick, hip style that stresses black and white, graphic drama, and clean lines. All rooms have two phones and writing desks. The twin penthouses have room to really stretch out and enjoy the location in the middle of the theater district. One of them also has a full kitchen and rooftop deck with fine views.

THE INN AT UNION SQUARE

$$$$ 30 ROOMS   ✉️*440 Post Street*   📞*415-397-3510, 800-288-4346*
📠*415-989-0529*   🖱️*www.unionsquare.com, inn@unionsquare.com*

When a travel writer is reduced to writing about a hotel's hallways, the establishment is either problematic or exceptional. Corridors at this inn, which is located on the north side of Union Square Park, are fashionably done along their entire length with mirrors and brass wall sconces, and most rooms leading off the halls are equipped with a brass lion-head door knocker. All that brass is a polisher's nightmare, but adds immeasurably to the charm of this pocket hotel. The entire inn numbers only 30 rooms, so intimacy is a primary consideration here. There is a small lobby with a fireplace on most floors where wine and evening hors d'oeuvres are served. Rooms are plush and cozy with quilted bedspreads, wooden headboards, and antique Georgian furnishings. In sum, a marvelous establishment, one of the city's finest small hotels.

JW MARRIOTT SAN FRANCISCO

$$$$ 327 UNITS   ✉️*500 Post Street*   📞*415-771-8600, 800-288-9290*
📠*415-398-0267*   🖱️*www.marriott.com*

Once inside this 21-story hotel, some guests simply cannot believe there are hundreds of rooms and suites here; the ambience is more like that of an intimate small hotel. Guest rooms have fine furnishings, custom cabinetry, and distinctive arched windows. Despite their size, they feel cozy, almost too much so. Oversized marble baths and attentive 24-hour butler service are extra indulgences at this ultra-deluxe-priced hotel one block west of Union Square.

PRESCOTT HOTEL

$$$$ 164 UNITS   ✉️*545 Post Street*   📞*415-563-0303, 866-271-3632*
📠*415-563-6831*   🖱️*www.prescotthotel.com, reservations@prescotthotel.com*

Home to Wolfgang Puck's Postrio eatery, the Prescott is more famous for its restaurant than its rooms. It shouldn't be, for the accommodations are equally as outstanding, from the Early California living room warmed by a big stone hearth to 164 rooms and suites beautifully arranged with Empire and neoclassical furnishings. Cherry armoires, silk wallpapers, and nightstands inlaid with black granite are embellished by rich tones of purple and gold and hunter green. There's complimentary coffee and tea in the mornings, and wine in the afternoons. And if you don't feel like going out for dinner, you can always order room service from Postrio.

ADELAIDE INN

$ 18 ROOMS   ✉5 Isadora Duncan Place   ☎415-441-2261   ✆415-359-1940

For native funk at rock bottom rates consider the Adelaide. Billed as "Old World charm less than two blocks from Union Square," it is an 18-room, family-operated establishment. There is a small lobby plus a coffee room and kitchen for the guests. The room prices, with continental breakfast included, are friendly to the pocketbook. Rooms are small, tidy, and plainly furnished; each is equipped with a sink and television; bathrooms are shared. Most important, the inn is located in a prime downtown location, not in the Tenderloin.

BERESFORD ARMS

$$$ 95 ROOMS   ✉701 Post Street   ☎415-673-2600, 800-533-6533   ✆415-929-1535
⌐www.beresford.com, info@beresford.com

The Beresford Arms is a sister hotel to the Hotel Beresford in more than name. Featuring a similar antique lobby, the Beresford Arms has gracefully decorated its public area with a crystal chandelier, leather-tooled tables, stuffed armchairs, and an old grandfather clock. Casting that same European aura, rooms often feature mahogany dressers and headboards as well as the expected amenities like wall-to-wall carpeting, tile tubs, and spacious closets and VCRs with movie rentals at the desk. The Arms has suites with whirlpools, kitchenettes, and wet bars.

VANTAGGIO SUITES

$$ 143 UNITS   ✉761 Post Street   ☎415-614-2400   ✆415-614-2500
⌐www.vantaggiosuites.com, sf@vantaggiosuites.com

This luxurious European-style hotel was built in 1929. The lobby is a fresh, bright place hung with crystal and dotted about with potted plants. Upstairs, the private rooms are brilliantly coordinated and possess an air of artistry.

HOTEL CALIFORNIA SAN FRANCISCO

$$ 83 ROOMS   ✉580 Geary Street   ☎415-441-2700, 800-227-4223   ✆415-441-0124
⌐www.thesavoyhotel.com, sanfrancisco@hotelca.com

The brilliant polished wood facade of this hotel provides only a hint of its luxurious interior. The lobby is the first word in elegance with black and white marble floors, brass fixtures, and dark woods. The rooms at this lavish but affordable hotel second the invitation of the lobby. Sporting a French-country motif, they blend floral prints with attractive wood furniture. An afternoon wine-and-cheese reception is included. Add a tile bath-shower, goosedown featherbeds, plus free wi-fi access, and you have one very noteworthy hotel.

HOTEL MONACO

$$$$ 201 ROOMS   ✉501 Geary Street   ☎415-292-0100, 866-622-5284
✆415-292-0111   ⌐www.monaco-sf.com

This small boutique hotel in the heart of the theater district offers luxury accommodations with a funky edge. Vibrant colors meet eclectic furniture in guest rooms that feature pillowtop beds, down pillows, and whirlpools (in most suites). Pop uptown for some morning shopping with their free chauffeur service, then come back for an evening wine-and-cheese reception with tarot readings and neck massages. This hotel is so pet-friendly, they even sponsor a "Guppy Love" program, matching guests up with overnight goldfish companions.

THE TOUCHSTONE HOTEL

$$ 42 ROOMS   ✉*480 Geary Street*   ☎*415-771-1600, 800-620-5889*   📠*415-931-5442*
📧*www.thetouchstone.com, reservations@thetouchstone.com*

This hotel sits smack-dab in the center of the theater district, but even more important, it is located over David's Delicatessen, one of the best delis in town. The lobby is nearly nonexistent, but the rooms are attractively done in European style, with warm woods and white duvets. This hotel is immaculately clean, and anyone would be hard-pressed to find a speck of dust anywhere. The rate includes a complimentary breakfast and discounts for the deli. This place is a true original.

HOTEL DIVA

$$$ 116 ROOMS   ✉*440 Geary Street*   ☎*415-885-0200, 800-553-1900*
📠*415-346-6613*   📧*www.hoteldiva.com, reservations@personalityhotels.com*

From its marble and glass exterior to its modern rooms with cobalt carpet and steel headboards, Hotel Diva is glossy, clean, high-tech, and hip. It's also comfortable, with luxury linens, wi-fi access, CD players, a Starbucks next door, and a consistently warm and helpful staff. There is even one sweetly chic suite for children and a collection of mini offices for guest use.

HOTEL BERESFORD

$$ 114 ROOMS   ✉*635 Sutter Street*   ☎*415-673-9900, 800-533-6533*
📠*415-474-0409*   📧*www.beresford.com, info@beresford.com*

European elegance at reasonable cost: that's what the Hotel Beresford has offered its clientele for years. You'll sense a touch of class immediately upon entering the richly decorated lobby. There's a historical flair about the place, highpointed by the adjoining White Horse Tavern and Restaurant, with its Old England ambience. Upstairs, the individually wall-papered rooms are outstanding—wooden headboards, comfortable furnishings, small refrigerators, and a marble-top vanity in the bathroom. Complimentary continental buffet. All this, just two blocks from Union Square. If you can beat it, let me know how.

HOTEL REX _____

$$$ 94 ROOMS   ✉*562 Sutter Street*   ☎*415-433-4434, 800-433-4434*
📠*415-433-3695*   📧*www.thehotelrex.com, thaney@jdvhospitality.com*

This is one of those quirky kinds of places that sets itself apart from more ordinary hostelries. The lobby looks like a library, where you long to spend the evening curled up in front of the fireplace, with a glass of sherry and an antique book chosen from the hundreds on shelves around the room. The rooms have a modern edge with a Provençal color-scheme and artwork from local artisans on the walls.

LARKSPUR HOTEL UNION SQUARE

$$$$ 114 ROOMS   ✉524 Sutter Street   ✆415-421-2865, 800-919-9779
✆415-398-6345   ✍www.larkspurhotelunionsquare.com,
sfreservations@larkspurhotels.com

A sparkling, well-run hotel in one of the best shopping blocks in town is always worth checking out—or checking into. This hotel offers eight floors of accommodations individually decorated in personally selected antiques. The attention to detail shows in touches such as plump reading pillows. There's a daily wine hour in the evenings.

CAMPTON PLACE HOTEL

$$$$ 110 UNITS   ✉340 Stockton Street   ✆415-781-5555   ✆415-955-5536
✍www.camptonplace.com, reservation.campton@tajhotels.com

It's a one-class-fits-all establishment. Of course, at this 15-story hotel, the class is definitely first: 110 luxurious rooms and suites are outfitted with sinfully comfortable beds, armoires, writing desks, limited edition art, and European baths. Innumerable services are available around the clock. Located half a block from Union Square, this is the place to stay when you can afford to pay ultra-deluxe prices.

HOTEL TRITON

$$$$ 140 ROOMS   ✉342 Grant Avenue   ✆415-394-0500, 800-800-1299
✆415-394-0555   ✍www.hoteltriton.com

From the wild and crazy lobby with its dervish chairs to the sapphire theater curtains in all its rooms, the Triton is a place with a sense of humor. If you are seeking a hotel with a fantasy mural, furniture that appears to undulate, iridescent throw pillows, starburst light fixtures, and room service from several trendy restaurants, look no further. Several of its suites were designed by celebrities (think Carlos Santana and Jerry Garcia). An added plus is its proximity to Chinatown. Pet-friendly.

HOTEL DES ARTS

$$$$ 51 ROOMS   ✉447 Bush Street   ✆415-956-3232, 800-956-4322
✆415-956-0399   ✍www.sfhoteldesarts.com, reservations@sfhoteldesarts.com

Close to Union Square and the Chinatown gates, this hotel is both installation art gallery and hotel. Hundreds of ever-changing paintings are hung throughout the space. Many of the tiny rooms have been upgraded to "Painted Rooms," which are decorated by emerging international artists such as L.A. graffiti muralist Buff Monster, whose giant pink toe graphic adds whimsy and makes up for the lack of furniture. Standard rooms have shared baths and all have refrigerators, microwaves, and wi-fi access. A complimentary continental breakfast is served. Painted rooms are only available when reserved online.

ORCHARD HOTEL

$$$$ 104 UNITS   ✉665 Bush Street   ✆415-362-8878, 888-717-2881
✆415-362- 8088   ✍www.theorchardhotel.com, mhaney@theorchardhotel.com

Opened in 2000, the Orchard exhibits the polished graces of a much-older hostelry: vaulted ceilings, marble baths, arched entryways, muted colors. But the amenities in all of the rooms and suites immediately reveal its true age: DVD and CD players, cordless phones, and internet connection in addition to minibars, safes, hairdryers, and coffeemakers. You'll also find a restaurant, a bar, and an exercise room on-site.

GRANT HOTEL

$ 76 ROOMS ✉ 753 Bush Street ✆ 415-421-7540, 800-522-0979 📠 800-686-8063
💻 www.granthotel.net, contact@granthotel.net

The Grant is basic and clean, with an air of understated elegance. The furniture is simple but comfortable. It is a well-maintained hotel, and a friendly, helpful staff makes it a pleasant place to stay. Every room has a color TV; continental breakfast is included.

WHITE SWAN INN

$$$ 26 ROOMS ✉ 845 Bush Street ✆ 415-775-1755, 800-999-9570
📠 415-775-5717 💻 www.whiteswaninnsf.com,
whiteswan@jdvhospitality.com

Elegance *and* style? That would be the White Swan. A six-story, English-style building with curved bay windows, the White Swan was originally built in 1908 as a small hotel. Today it is a fashionable bed and breakfast with a living room, library, solarium, and small courtyard. The decorative theme, reflected in the garden, wallpapers, and art prints, is English. Each room contains a fireplace, television, telephone with voicemail, wet bar, coffeemaker, and private bath. Like the public rooms, they are all beautifully appointed. Complimentary fireside wine and hors d'oeuvres are served in the evening.

DINING

JOHN'S GRILL

$$–$$$ STEAK/SEAFOOD ✉ 63 Ellis Street ✆ 415-986-3274
📠 415-989-7766 💻 www.johnsgrill.com, john@johnsgrill.com

Whether they are hungry or not, Dashiell Hammett fans always track down John's. It's the restaurant that detective Sam Spade popped into during a tense scene in *The Maltese Falcon*. Today the wood-paneled walls, adorned with memorabilia and old photos, still breathe of bygone eras. Waiters dress formally, the bartender gossips about local politicians, and the customers sink onto bar stools. The menu features broiler and seafood dishes as well as a nostalgic platter of chops, baked potato, and sliced tomato (what Spade wolfed down on that fateful day). Live jazz nightly.

BISTRO 69

$ AMERICAN/MEDITERRANEAN ✉ 69 Maiden Lane ✆ 415-398-3557
📠 415-981-3735

Maiden Lane used to be a perfect spot for slumming; today it's a fashionable shopping district. But there's one place along the high-priced strip that brings back the easy days. Bistro 69 is an unassuming restaurant/café serving an array of sandwiches, salads, homemade pastas, Mediterranean dishes, and mouthwatering pastries. Dine alfresco or pull up a chair inside this brick-walled establishment. Local newspapers routinely give this joint high marks. At lunch there will likely be a line out the door. Also open for breakfast. Closed Sunday.

SUSHI MAN

$$ JAPANESE ✉731 Bush Street ☎415-981-1313 📠415-668-3214

This is a matchbox sushi bar with matchless style. If that's not evident from the plastic sushi displays in the window, then step inside. The tiny wooden bar is decorated with serene silk screens and fresh flowers. The restaurant has earned a deserved reputation for its sushi creations. There's *sake* (smoked salmon) and *mirugai* (clam), as well as sashimi. Dinner only.

POSTRIO

$$$$ CALIFORNIA CUISINE ✉545 Post Street ☎415-776-7825
📠415-776-6702 🖱www.postrio.com, mail@postrio.com

It is the rare restaurateur who can please both Los Angeles and San Francisco, but that's exactly what Wolfgang Puck, in collaboration with chef Sies Kamimura, has done with Postrio. Puck and Sies's innovative food pairings, such as grilled quail with spinach and soft ravioli and seared ahi with Indian coconut curry, compete for attention with a stunning dining room and impressive art collection. Reserve far in advance. Breakfast is also served.

SCALA'S BISTRO

$$$–$$$$ FRENCH/ITALIAN ✉432 Powell Street ☎415-395-8555 📠415-395-8549
🖱www.scalasbistro.com, rikki.gates@scalabistro.com

The atmosphere is classy and the food fancy at Scala's. Gilt mirrors adorn the walls and deep mahogany booths evoke the charm of an upscale, modern Parisian bistro. Choose from any of their lavish regional Italian or French country dishes: seared salmon filet with buttermilk mashed potatoes or a duck confit with risotto. There's even a cheese list with scrumptious choices to peruse and sample.

TEMPURA HOUSE

$$ JAPANESE ✉529 Powell Street ☎415-393-9911

After dining at this hole-in-the-wall restaurant, you'll understand why the Financial District crowd goes out of its way to eat here. What's delivered to your table looks exactly like the plastic meals displayed in the front window, and everything's delicious. Tempura is the specialty of the house, but the grilled fish, sukiyaki, and sushi also rate highly.

FARALLON

$$$$ SEAFOOD ✉450 Post Street ☎415-956-6969 📠415-834-1234
🖱www.farallonrestaurant.com, cdurie@farallonrestaurant.com

In addition to being a dining extravaganza, this restaurant is a total immersion experience. Step into this uniquely designed restaurant and it's like plunging beneath the waves; every aspect of the decor reflects an aquatic motif. Light fixtures resembling jellyfish hang suspended two stories overhead, handrails look like tendriling kelp, and bar stools stand on octopus tentacles. The Gothic arches in the dining room (called, naturally, the "Pool Room") sport mermaid mosaics and sea urchin light fixtures. After easing into a booth, you can order from a menu laden with seafood dishes. The menu, which changes every few weeks, might feature Atlantic black bass, poached sea scallops, local petrale sole en papillote, or, for those who don't get the point—grilled filet of beef. Dinner only.

CORTEZ

$$$ MEDITERRANEAN   ✉550 Geary Street   ☎415-292-6360   ✦415-923-0906
✐www.cortezrestaurant.com, info@cortezrestaurant.com

This restaurant is like a skewed Mondrian painting brought to life. Oversized mobiles fashioned from hanging globe lamps, illuminated panels, and occasional primary color splashes provide edgy contrast to the earthy, Mediterranean-inspired menu. These small plates are best shared with friends. Favorites include the New Zealand lamb and asparagus with lemon béarnaise and crispy sunchokes. The desserts are sinful. Dinner only.

MILLENNIUM

$$$–$$$$ AMERICAN/CALIFORNIA CUISINE   ✉Hotel California San Francisco, 580 Geary Street   ☎415-345-3900   ✦415-345-3941   ✐www.millenniumrestaurant.com

Vegans and vegetarians will love this place, where all of the innovative, beautifully prepared dishes are animal-free. The menu changes daily and revolves around fresh and seasonal ingredients; past entrées have included seared emerald rice cakes with lemongrass tofu, pecan-crusted portobello mushrooms with creamy garlic polenta, and squash risotto with chanterelles. Though it's located in the Tenderloin, an area not known for upscale eateries, Millennium is a white-linen-tablecloth affair with dim lighting and rich wood paneling.

INDONESIA RESTAURANT

$ INDONESIAN   ✉678 Post Street   ☎415-474-4026   ✦415-858-8095

This beloved restaurant has developed a loyal following among the many San Franciscans who have lived or traveled in Indonesia. And for good reason. The complex and diverse flavors in this tiny, crowded hole-in-the-wall establishment tantalize the taste buds. Such favorite dishes as *gado-gado*, *soto ayam*, beef curry, *mie goreng*, *rendang*, and *sate* are included on the menu, as well as many others.

FLEUR DE LYS

$$$$ FRENCH/AMERICAN   ✉777 Sutter Street   ☎415-673-7779
✐www.fleurdelyssf.com

One of the city's most romantic dining spots, Fleur de Lys is a tented affair with fabric along the walls that rise to a gathered cluster at the center of the room. Add a chandelier and a waitstaff that glides silently between tables to create the ideal ambience for an intimate evening. Chef Hubert Keller prepares three four- and five-course dinners that are as imaginative as the surroundings—think foie gras "hamburgers," King salmon with caramelized cauliflower, and filet mignon with roasted pears. Gourmet dining at its best. Dinner only. Closed Sunday.

MASA'S

$$$$ FRENCH ✉648 Bush Street ☎415-989-7154 📠415-989-3141 🖰www.masasrestaurant.com, info@masasrestaurant.com

A small and romantic dining room, this is one of my favorite San Francisco restaurants. Elite yet understated, the decor is a mix of dark woods, softly colored upholstered chairs, and floral arrangements. Changing daily, the contemporary French menu might include filet mignon with foie gras mousse and black truffles, roasted squab with Italian butter beans, or sautéed medallions of fallow deer with caramelized apples and zinfandel sauce. Dinner only. Jackets required. Reservations highly recommended. Closed Sunday and Monday.

UNCLE VITO'S

$ ITALIAN ✉700 Bush Street ☎415-391-5008 🖰www.unclevitos.com

Craving authentic Italian pizza, but don't want to trek out to North Beach? Hit up Uncle Vito's. It's casual, homestyle Italy with what some San Franciscans claim are the best pies around. Favorites include the Tia Mia, which boasts piles of mushrooms with feta cheese and spinach sans the marinara sauce, and The Mountain, which is what it sounds like—meat aplenty.

SHOPPING

Union Square quite simply is *the* center for shopping in San Francisco. First of all, this grass-and-hedgerow park (located between Post and Geary, Stockton and Powell streets) is surrounded by department stores. Once the haven of European specialty boutiques, Union Square is becoming a hot address among sport-shoes shops, entertainment-company merchandising centers, and mass-appeal clothing stores.

MACY'S ✉170 O'Farrell Street ☎415-397-3333
Stationed along one border of Union Square, this enormous department store's bright lights add a touch of Vegas to this festive shopping area.

SAKS FIFTH AVENUE ✉384 Post Street ☎415-986-4300
This pristine department store stands guard over another corner of Union Square.

NEIMAN-MARCUS ✉150 Stockton Street ☎415-362-3900
This Texas-bred emporium has all the current fashions for savvy San Francisco shoppers.

MAIDEN LANE
This pedestrian shopping strip just off Union Square is filled with upscale boutiques and eateries.

XANADU GALLERY FOLK ART INTERNATIONAL ✉FLW building, 140 Maiden Lane ☎415-392-9999 🖰www.xanadugallery.us, info@xanadugallery.us
A notable Maiden Lane shop is this gallery, offering icons, folk sculptures, baskets, pottery, and other crafts from Africa, Oceania, Latin America,

and Asia, as well as antique jewelry from India, and gem-quality Baltic amber from Poland and Denmark. Closed Sunday and Monday.

STOCKTON STREET Along Stockton Street, one of the avenues radiating out from the square, you'll find a number of prestigious shops.

CROCKER GALLERIA ✉️*50 Post Street* ✆*415-393-1505* ✍️*www.shopat galleria.com* Then if you follow Post, another street bordering Union Square, you'll find this glass-domed promenade lined with fashionable shops. A center for well-heeled business crowds, the mall showcases designer fashions and elegant gifts. Closed Sunday.

GUMP'S ✉️*135 Post Street* ✆*415-982-1616, 800-766-7628* 📠*415-984-9361* ✍️*www.gumps.com* This eclectic home store features fine jewelry, objets d'art, and imported decorations. If you get bored looking through the antiques, china pieces, and oriental art, you can always adjourn to the Crystal Room.

H&M ✉️*150 Post Street* ✆*415-986-0156* ✍️*www.hm.com* While you're in the epicenter of high-end San Francisco shopping, an excellent stop is this hip department store with sleek, posh styles, but surprisingly affordable prices.

HATS ON POST ✉️*210 Post Street, Suite 606* ✆*415-392-3737* Nestled on the sixth floor of a building at Grant and Post, this shop features two rooms filled with elegant and expensive women's headwear. Closed Sunday.

GIORGIO ARMANI ✉️*278 Post Street* ✆*415-434-2500* 📠*415-434-2546* ✍️*www.giorgioarmani.com* For a vicarious "rich and famous" experience, take a stroll through the Armani store at Union Square. This boutique is one of only eleven American stores carrying the designer's premier Black Label line. Formalwear and sportswear are elegantly displayed under the tutelage of attentive salespeople, who discreetly disclose the cost of the apparel.

The streets all around host a further array of stores. You'll encounter jewelers, dress designers, boutiques, furniture stores, tailor shops, and more. So take a gander—there's everything out there from the unexpected to the bizarre.

BRAUNSTEIN/QUAY GALLERY ✉️*430 Clementina Street* ✆*415-278-9850* This is an outstanding place to view the work of local artists. As the catalog claims, owner Ruth Braunstein "embodies the brash, irreverent, and irrepressible energy of the San Francisco art world." This contemporary gallery also exhibits works from other parts of the world. Closed Sunday and Monday except by appointment.

LOEHMANN'S ✉️*222 Sutter Street* ✆*415-982-3215* San Francisco's answer to Boston's famous Filene's Basement discount apparel chain is this clothing store with alarmingly low-priced designer clothes.

BORDERS BOOKS & MUSIC ✉️*400 Post Street* ✆*415-399-1633* Just steps from Union Square, you'll find Borders, with four floors of books, CDs, national and international newspapers and periodicals, and chairs for serious reading.

WESTFIELD SAN FRANCISCO CENTRE ✉*865 Market Street, between 4th and 5th streets* ☎*415-512-6776* 📠*415-512-6770* 🖰*www.westfield.com/sanfran cisco* You've never seen a mall quite like the Westfield. Within this expansive complex is a nearly 400,000-square-foot, multilevel **Bloomingdale's** (415-856-5300), complete with sparkling checkered floors and chandeliers. A movie theater, a gourmet food court with international cuisine and an entire grocery store, and over 100 high-fashion boutiques have established the center as an authoritative shopping destination. In a separate wing six stacked spiral escalators ascend through an oval-shaped, marble-and-granite atrium toward the retractable skylight. Tinkling music from a grand piano welcomes patrons to the five-story **Nordstrom** (415-243-8500) that tops the west section.

NAPA VALLEY WINERY EXCHANGE

✉*415 Taylor Street* ☎*800-653-9463* 📠*415-441-9463* 🖰*wine@nvwe.com, www.nvwe.com* This tidy little wine shop, just two blocks from Union Square, has been sourcing and selling small-production California wines since the late 1980s. The knowledgable staff can recommend a wine for your picnic, hostess gift, or personal wine tasting, steering you to some of the best vintages coming out of the small vineyards in Napa.

NIGHTLIFE

Since its rowdy Gold Rush days, San Francisco has been renowned as a wide-open town, hard-drinking and easygoing. Today there are over 2000 places around the city to order a drink, including saloons, restaurants, cabarets, boats, private clubs, and even a couple of hospitals. There's a bar for every mood and each occasion.

When looking for nightlife, it is advisable to consult the *SF Bay Guardian*, the *SF Weekly*, the *Onion*, or the "Datebook" (commonly called the "pink section") in the Sunday *San Francisco Chronicle* for current shows and performers. However you decide to spend the evening, you'll find plenty of possibilities in this city by the Bay.

EDINBURGH CASTLE ✉*950 Geary Street* ☎*415-885-4074* 🖰*www.castle news.com* San Francisco's answer to a Scottish pub is this cavernous bar complete with dart board. There are chandeliers hanging from the ceiling, heavy wooden furniture, and convivial crowds—Scotland incarnate.

WARFIELD THEATRE ✉*982 Market Street* The Warfield is a well-known, old-school venue that continues to bring in top groups from around the country. Big names, such as Bob Dylan, Guns N' Roses, and the Grateful Dead have all rocked the stage.

RRAZZ ROOM ✉*Hotel Nikko, 222 Mason Street* ☎*415-781-0306, 866-468-3399* 📠*415-781-0306* 🖰*www.therrazzroom.com* This sophisticated, 190-seat cabaret club features top-quality sound and lighting in an intimate setting. An 80-seat lounge greets patrons with windows facing Mason Street.

The main performance space is a square with no pillars and no wing space. The artists, from major lounge singers such as Diane Schuur and Jane Olivor, to showbiz greats like Diahann Carroll and Chita Rivera, enter through the audience and work on a stage backed by a wall of windows. It's a place that calls for dressing up and staying up late. Cover plus a two-drink minimum.

REDWOOD ROOM ✉*Geary and Taylor streets* ☎*415-775-4700* A favored relaxing place for the hip and rich is this bar in the Clift Hotel. With contemporary lamps, candlelit tables, and burnished redwood paneling, it is nothing less than sumptuous. Dressing up is encouraged.

FILM NIGHT IN THE PARK Each year from May to September, huge outdoor screens in Union Square, Dolores Park in the Mission, and Washington Square in North Beach show everything from classics to contemporary favorites—all part of Film Night in the Park. Picnics encouraged, chairs discouraged.

BISCUITS & BLUES ✉*401 Mason Street* ☎*415-292-2583* ✐*www.biscuitsand blues.com, info@biscuitsandblues.com* Calling itself a "shrine to the blues" is no exaggeration. Located about a block from Union Square, Biscuits & Blues represents all that's right about the American South. With Southern cuisine and live music in an elegant basement nightclub, it's the perfect place to relax, appreciate the wail of a harmonica, and have a drink after taking in a play in the theater district. Closed Sunday and Monday.

RUBY SKYE ✉*420 Mason Street* ☎*415-693-0777* ✐*www.rubyskye.com* You wouldn't expect to find a vibrant nightclub in a restored Victorian ballroom, but this hot spot mixes lavish surroundings with a club atmosphere. If you're not into the bump-and-grind scene, stop in for drinks before 10 p.m. and enjoy the interior architecture. Cover.

Theater

The "On Broadway" theater scene in San Francisco is on Geary Street, near Union Square; while the "Off Broadway," or avant-garde drama, is scattered around the city.

GEARY THEATER ✉*415 Geary Street* ☎*415-749-2228* ☏*415-439-2322* ✐*www.act-sf.org* Built in 1910, this Beaux Arts–style theater reopened in 1996 after extensive repair and renovation, and now features a sky lobby. This state historic landmark is home of the **American Conservatory Theater**, or ACT, the biggest show in town. It's also one of the nation's largest resident companies. The season runs from September to July, and the repertory is traditional, ranging from Shakespeare to French comedy to 20th-century drama. Closed Monday.

CURRAN THEATRE ✉*445 Geary Street* ☎*415-551-2000* ✐*www.shnsf.com* The Curran brings Broadway musicals to town, such as *Wicked* and *Phantom of the Opera*.

GOLDEN GATE THEATRE ✉*1 Taylor Street, at the corner of 6th and Market streets* ☎*415-551-2000* This ornate theatre attracts major shows and national companies. Built in 1922, the theater is a grand affair with marble floors and rococo ceilings.

MARINES MEMORIAL THEATRE ✉609 Sutter Street ☏415-771-6900
🖘www.marinesmemorialtheatre.com Among the city's other playhouses is
the Marines Memorial, which often has comedians performing.

ORPHEUM THEATRE ✉1192 Market Street ☏415-551-2000 Close to the
Civic Center is the Orpheum, which stages top-of-the-line productions
of major plays and musicals, including *Spamalot* and *Grease*.

CIVIC CENTER

On the other side of the Downtown district, to the southwest, rises the
Civic Center, the architectural pride of the city. The prettiest pathway
through this municipal meeting ground begins in United Nations Plaza
at Fulton and Market streets.

SIGHTS

HEART OF THE CITY FARMERS' MARKET ✉Fulton and Market
streets ☏415-558-9455 Every Wednesday and Sunday the United Nations
Plaza is home to this huge farmers' market, an open-air produce fair
that draws farmers from all over Northern California.

FEDERAL BUILDING ✉7th and Missions streets A notable stop is the
eco-friendly energy-efficient Federal Building, which stands 18 stories
tall. With floor-to-ceiling windows, the spacious structure was designed to allow for natural air and light. The public can get a close-up
look at this modern edifice at the 11th floor open-air sky garden, which
is dotted with pedestrian bridges and benches. Security checks to enter
are rigorous, but worth the hassle.

SAN FRANCISCO PUBLIC LIBRARY ✉100 Larkin Street ☏415-557-4400
📠415-557-4433 🖘www.sfpl.org, webmail@sfpl.org To experience one of the
country's most modern information centers, saunter on over to the
main branch of the San Francisco Public Library. Exemplifying the fact
that libraries are not just about books anymore (in fact, critics charge
that the architectural splendor and special features have resulted in a
lack of shelf space), the main branch's facilities include 512 electronic
workstations with free connection to the internet. Among the library's 11
special-interest research centers are the San Francisco History Center,
the Gay and Lesbian Center, and the Art, Music, and Recreation Center.

CIVIC CENTER ☏415-557-4266 (tour information) 🖘www.sfcityguides.org With
its bird-whitened statues and gray-columned buildings, this is the domain of powerbrokers and political leaders; ironically, its grassy plots
and park benches also make it the haunt of the city's homeless. Guided
tours of the Civic Center begin at the San Francisco Public Library.

JOSEPH L. ALIOTO PERFORMING ART PIAZZA ✉1 Dr. Carlton B.
Goodlett Place ☏415-554-6023 🖘www.sfgov.org Named after one of San
Francisco's most beloved mayors, this area with reflecting pool and for-
mal gardens is often used for outdoor events.

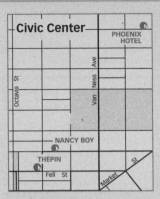

CITY HALL   City Hall's gold-leafed dome is 306 feet tall—the fifth-tallest domed building in the world, 20 feet taller than the U.S. Capitol. It also surpasses other government centers in technology, with interactive touch screens that let supervisors vote, call staff, and retrieve documents during meetings. Free guided tours of City Hall are offered Monday through Friday. Note that the two blocks of Polk Street within the Civic Center were renamed Dr. Carlton B. Goodlett Jr. Place in honor of the San Francisco civil rights leader who died in 1997.

ASIAN ART MUSEUM   ✉ *200 Larkin Street*   ✆ *415-581-3500*   ✇ *415-581-4700*   ✐ *www.asianart.org* Across from City Hall and housed in a historic 1917 Beaux Arts building, the Asian Art Museum features major pieces from China, Tibet, Japan, Korea, Iran, Syria, and throughout the continent. This institution is the largest museum in the country devoted exclusively to Asian art. Some of the 14,000-plus pieces date back 6000 years. Admission.

WAR MEMORIAL OPERA HOUSE   ✉ *301 Van Ness Avenue at Grove Street* Centerstage of the Civic Center is this opera house, home of one of the world's finest opera companies as well as the San Francisco Ballet Company. Considered by such performers as Placido Domingo to be one of the world's finest opera houses and called "the most attractive and practical building of its kind in the U.S." by *Time* magazine, the grandiose building's interior features lofty romanesque columns, a gold-leafed proscenium, and a five-story-high ceiling. Although conceived in 1918 as a tribute to the nation's World War I veterans, the opera house was not completed until 1932. Perhaps its finest moment came in 1945, when the opera house and adjacent Veterans Auditorium (now Herbst Theatre) hosted the signing of the United Nations Charter and the first official sessions of the U.N.

LOUISE M. DAVIES SYMPHONY HALL ✉*201 Van Ness Avenue;* ✆*415-552-8338 (information)* To the left, that ultramodern glass-and-granite building is the home of the San Francisco Symphony. Through the semicircle of green-tinted glass, you can peer into one of the city's most glamorous buildings. Or if you'd prefer to be on the inside gazing out, tours of the hall and its cultural cousins next door are given Monday from 10 a.m. to 2 p.m. Admission.

MUSEUM OF PERFORMANCE AND DESIGN ✉*Veterans Building, 401 Van Ness Avenue* ✆*415-255-4800* ⌁*www.mpdsf.org, info@mpdsf.org* One of the best places in town to appreciate the city's rich cultural tradition is this museum, formerly the San Francisco Performing Arts Library and Museum. Recent exhibitions include a retrospective on 75 years of design at San Francisco Ballet, an exhibition reconstructing the historic Fillmore Jazz era, and a tribute to Broadway icon Carol Channing. Library and galleries open Wednesday through Saturday. Researchers should call the librarian in advance.

LODGING

INN AT THE OPERA

$$$$ 48 UNITS   ✉*333 Fulton Street*   ✆*415-863-8400, 800-325-2708* ✆*415-861-0821*

For fans of the opera (or the symphony or the ballet), this inn is heaven on earth. Located virtually within earshot of the major performing-arts houses, it plays the ham with concierge services (especially helpful for last-minute tickets) and little touches (such as sheet-music drawer liners) in the 30 rooms and 18 suites. Rooms have tasteful furnishings with pillowtop mattresses and mini-fridges. Continental breakfast and afternoon cookies are served.

PHOENIX HOTEL

$$–$$$ 44 ROOMS   ✉*601 Eddy Street*   ✆*415-776-1380, 800-248-9466* ✆*415-885-3109*   ⌁*www.thephoenixhotel.com, pw@jdvhospitality.com*

A two-story motor court flanking a pool courtyard, spacious rooms and suites with a '50s bungalow theme, a chic southeast Asian restaurant and lounge . . . can this be the heart of San Francisco? It is, and it's the Phoenix Hotel, just a long block from Civic Center. Concierge services and a rock-and-roll clientele may make the Phoenix the hippest inn in town.

HOTEL RENOIR

$$–$$$ 133 ROOMS   ✉*45 McAllister Street*   ✆*415-626-5200, 800-576-3388* ✆*415-626-0916*   ⌁*www.renoirhotel.com, info@renoirhotel.com*

Located right on the edge of the Civic Center, this hotel is one of the more economical spots to rest. The lobby is lined with Renoir prints and decorated in gold and soft peach colors. There's a Brazilian restaurant, a lounge, and a friendly ambience about the place. The only detraction is its location on busy Market Street and proximity to the city's Tenderloin district. Rooms are basic but dignified, with floral drapes,

Civic Center

polished wood furniture, wall-to-wall carpeting, and tile bathrooms with shower-tub combinations.

DINING

HAYES STREET GRILL

$$$ SEAFOOD   ✉320 Hayes Street   ☎415-863-5545   🖷415-863-1873
🖱www.hayesstreetgrill.com

This area spotlights several outstanding dining rooms. One of the best in my opinion is this cozy grill, situated within strolling distance of the opera and symphony. Specializing in fresh fish dishes, they also serve grilled porkchops, dry-aged steak, and escarole. Excellent food. No lunch on the weekend.

CAFFE DELLE STELLE

$$ ITALIAN   ✉395 Hayes Street   ☎415-252-1110   🖷415-863-5224

Few, if any, places in the Hayes Valley gourmet ghetto are more popular than this spot. Sheer shades grace the windows, and photographs adorn the walls of this quirky, cute Tuscan trattoria. Conversation buzzes, but it's not too loud to enjoy an intimate discussion of your own. The cuisine is Italian country cooking, and meals begin with fresh bread and a bowl of *pansanela*, a dip made from olive oil, bread, tomato juice, and spices. Entrées include a selection of pastas, baked chicken, roasted salmon fillet, and daily specials like ravioli barbarossa stuffed with arugula, ricotta, and walnuts in a basil sauce.

ABSINTHE BRASSERIE AND BAR

$$$$ CONTINENTAL   ✉398 Hayes Street   ☎415-551-1590
🖷415-255-2385   🖱www.absinthe.com

This darkly romantic 1940s-style restaurant conjures up a bit of pre-war Moulin Rouge with vintage cabaret music, classic cocktails, and beautifully rendered European-style bistro food. Start out with the fresh oyster bar or a pot of French onion soup with bubbling cheese and croutons, then share an entrée of pan-roasted duck breast with fingerling potatoes, Brussels sprouts, pancetta, and roast shallots. The grilled lamb loin is succulent and crispy. At lunch, the grilled chicken sandwich is a favorite. Weekend brunch. Closed Monday.

THEPIN

$–$$ THAI   ✉298 Gough Street   ✆415-863-9335   🖅415-863-9276

A café setting that features brass fixtures, pastel walls, bentwood furniture, and Asian artwork make Thepin an inviting Thai establishment. The fare, ranging from sweet and sour duck to marinated prawns and chicken breast, is also a winner. Specialties include sautéed chicken with cashews and dried chili, marinated filet of salmon in curry sauce, and sliced green papaya salad with tomatoes and chili pepper. No lunch on Saturday or Sunday.

MAX'S OPERA CAFÉ

$$ AMERICAN   ✉601 Van Ness Avenue   ✆415-771-7300   🖅415-474-9780
✍www.maxsworld.com, maxoperasf@maxsworld.com

Max's serves a variety of fare that ranges from smoked barbecued ribs to California cuisine, but the standouts are the thick pastrami, corned beef, and turkey breast sandwiches accompanied by tangy coleslaw and potato salad. Low-carb dinner and sugar-free dessert menus available. A lively bar area features occasional impromptu entertainment by the staff, some of whom are budding tenors and sopranos.

SHOPPING

Hayes Valley lies directly west of the Civic Center and has as its focus the block bounded by Hayes, Franklin, Grove, and Gough streets.

NANCY BOY

✉347 Hayes Street   ✆415-552-3802   ✍www.nancyboy.com For all your skin-care needs, check out Nancy Boy. Their botanical-based concoctions are designed for the "styling queer dude" and created by the shop's owners. Perfumes, bath washes, soaps, and facial masks are just some of the products "tested on boyfriends, not animals."

F. DORIAN   ✉370 Hayes Street   ✆415-861-3191   ✍www.fdorian.com This diverse shop specializes in crafts from all over the world, including ethnic and contemporary items. Although their selection varies, you may be lucky enough to find antique Filipino furniture, Indian oil lamps, Indonesian diary boxes, and exotic jewelry.

OPERA PLAZA   ✉Van Ness and Golden Gate avenues   Just a few blocks away from F. Dorian lies this atrium mall with shops, restaurants, and a movie theater collected around a courtyard and fountain. It's a pretty place to sit and enjoy the day.

NIGHTLIFE

TIX BAY AREA ✉️*Union Square, Powell Street between Geary and Post streets* 📞*415-433-7827* 🖱️*www.tixbayarea.com, tba@theatrebayarea.org* San Francisco is rich culturally in its opera, symphony, and ballet, located in the Civic Center area. Since tickets to major theatrical and other cultural events are expensive, consider buying week-of-performance half-price tickets here. Open from 11 a.m. until two hours before showtime, they sell tickets at half-price on the week of the show and full price for events and tours. Closed Monday.

SAN FRANCISCO OPERA ✉️*301 Van Ness Avenue* 📞*415-864-3330* 📠*415-626-1729* 🖱️*www.sfopera.com* San Francisco takes nothing quite so seriously as its opera. The San Francisco Opera is world class in stature and invites operatic greats from around the world to perform. As a result, tickets sell out quickly. Standing-room-only tickets are always available on the day of the performance (must be purchased in-person, cash only), and at just $10 are a steal—if your legs are up to it. The international season begins in mid-September and runs through June. The box office is closed on Sunday during performance season and weekends during the off-season.

SAN FRANCISCO SYMPHONY ✉️*Davies Hall, 201 Van Ness Avenue* 📞*415-864-6000* 📠*415-554-0108* 🖱️*www.sfsymphony.org* The symphony stands nearly as tall as the San Francisco Opera on the world stage. The season extends from September through July. Michael Tilson Thomas conducts, and guest soloists have included Jessie Norman and Itzhak Perlman.

SAN FRANCISCO BALLET ✉️*301 Van Ness Avenue* 📞*415-865-2000* 📠*415-865-0740* 🖱️*www.sfballet.org, sfbmail@sfballet.info.com* Performing since 1933, this is the nation's oldest professional ballet, and one of the finest. Featuring *The Nutcracker* during December, the company's official season runs at the Opera House from January until May. In addition to original works, they perform classic ballets. The box office is only open on performance days.

GREAT AMERICAN MUSIC HALL ✉️*859 O'Farrell Street* 📞*415-885-0750* 📠*415-885-5075* 🖱️*www.gamh.com, info@gamh.com* This vintage 1907 building has been splendidly converted to a nightclub featuring a variety of entertainers. Included in the lineup are international acts such as Jimmy Cliff, Bonnie Raitt, and Shawn Colvin.

FINANCIAL DISTRICT

Beyond the Downtown district, as Maiden Lane debouches into a complex of streets, you'll come upon the "Wall Street of the West," Montgomery Street, locus of the Financial District. The center of Pacific commerce and trade, this is the roosting place for San Francisco's skyscrapers. Here you'll encounter windswept canyons of glass and steel inhabited by exotic birds dressed in three-piece suits or tailor-trim skirts.

A. P. GIANNINI PLAZA ✉*Montgomery Street, between Pine and California streets* Behind the granite and marble along Montgomery are more banks than one could imagine. A. P. Giannini Plaza, a combination mall and office building, memorializes the brilliant Italian banker who developed an upstart savings company into one of the world's largest financial institutions, the Bank of America.

WELLS FARGO HISTORY MUSEUM ✉*420 Montgomery Street* ☎*415-396-2619* ☏*415-391-8644* ✎*www.wellsfargohistory.com, historicalservices@wellsfargo.com* Another bank on Montgomery hosts this financial museum. In addition to glistening gold specimens and postal artifacts, there are photos recapturing the raffish days of the Old West. Central to the entire exhibit is an 18-passenger stagecoach reconditioned to sparkle like this year's model. (Remember, this pocket museum is open during banker's hours only.) Closed Saturday and Sunday.

PACIFIC HERITAGE MUSEUM ✉*608 Commercial Street* ☎*415-399-1124* ☏*415-989-0103* ✎*www.ibankunited.com/phm* Also consider the Bank of Canton of California (now part of United Commercial Bank), which has reconstructed a 19th-century federal mint and incorporated it into this museum. Rotating exhibitions feature the art and culture of the Pacific Basin, and the permanent collection includes artifacts from early San Francisco. Closed Sunday and Monday.

MONTGOMERY STREET The history-minded will also keep a sharp eye for the bronze markers spotted here and there along this fabled street. Montgomery has always been a center for San Francisco financial adventures. One plaque near 505 Montgomery commemorates the historic **Hudson's Bay Company headquarters**. It seems that in 1841 the British-owned company set up shop here, sending shivers through the American traders who were beginning to consider California their own preserve. On the side of the California National Bank at Montgomery and Clay streets rests a marker noting the spot where the first Pony Express rider arrived in 1860 after the dangerous relay from St. Joseph, Missouri.

TRANSAMERICA BUILDING ✎*www.thepyramidcenter.com* That bizarrely shaped edifice between Clay and Washington streets is none other than the 48-story Transamerica Building. Designed like a pyramid that's been put through a wringer, it stands 853 feet tall and is the most striking feature along San Francisco's skyline. Although not open to the public, it's still a marvel to gaze upward at. Situated on the east side of the building is a half-acre pocket park—a significant attraction in itself. It features metal sculptures, a fountain, and a child's-eye view of the stone needle rising straight above.

The land east of the Transamerica Building was San Francisco's harbor until 1855, when it was filled in. Abandoned by sailors turned gold miners, at least ten ships still lie buried beneath the streets of the Financial District.

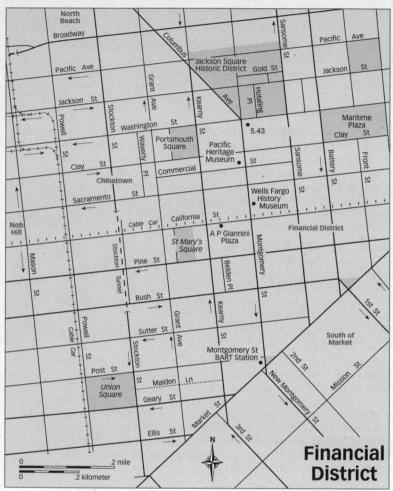

North Beach
Broadway
Columbus
Sansome St
Pacific Ave
Jackson Square Historic District
Gold St
Jackson St
Pacific Ave
Grant Ave
Kearny Ave
Hotaling Pl
Jackson St
Stockton St
Powell St
Washington St
Maritime Plaza
Clay St
5.43
Portsmouth Square
Pacific Heritage Museum
St
Sansome St
Battery St
Front St
Waverly Pl
Clay St
Chinatown
Commercial
Sacramento St
Wells Fargo History Museum
Nob Hill
Cable Car
California St
Financial District
St Mary's Square
A P Giannini Plaza
Mason St
Stockton St
Pine St
Montgomery St
Belden Pl
Tunnel
Bush St
Grant Ave
Kearny St
Powell Cable Car St
Stockton St
Sutter St
South of Market
1st St
Montgomery St BART Station
2nd St
Post St
Maiden Ln
New Montgomery St
Mission St
Union Square
Geary St
Market St
3rd St
Ellis St
N

0   .2 mile
0   .2 kilometer

Financial District

JACKSON SQUARE   The 700 block of Montgomery contains a cluster of buildings dating back to 1850. They are part of the Jackson Square area, a misnomered enclave extending from Washington to Pacific streets and from Columbus Avenue to Sansome Street. There is no "square" here, but you will find an official historic district sprinkled with brickface buildings and interior courtyards. During the 1850s, this represented the black heart of the Barbary Coast. Prospectors on the make and convicts on the lam haunted its gambling dens and flophouses. The local denizens' penchant for kidnapping drunken sailors gave rise to the word "shanghaied."

As with Downtown's Maiden Lane, a mixture of time and irony has transformed the area. Fashionable galleries and other upscale emporia have replaced the brothels and dives. Though prices here are as staggering as the neighboring skyscrapers, you might want to browse the shops, which include some of the city's finest antique stores.

SAM'S GRILL

$$ STEAK/SEAFOOD   ✉374 Bush Street   ☎415-421-0594   📠415-421-2632
🖃www.belden-place.com

Sam's, established in 1867, is a classic San Francisco businessperson's restaurant. With a new menu printed every day, it features fresh fish, shellfish from surrounding waters, charcoal-broiled steaks and chops, plus seafood casseroles. The menu is the same at lunch or dinner, and you can order a martini anytime from 11 a.m. on. There are diner car booths, waitstaff in bow ties and tuxedos, a friendly bar, and white walls adorned with hunting scenes. Closed Saturday and Sunday.

CAFE BASTILLE

$$$ FRENCH   ✉22 Belden Place   ☎415-986-5673   📠415-986-1013
🖃www.cafebastillesf.com, cafebastillesf@yahoo.com

No, you're not at a Paris metro station, even though the designer of this café would like to make you think so. This popular bistro boasts a basement dining room, with floors done in multicolored marble, walls painted with steel girders, and a giant Bastille Metro sign. You can also dine on the ground floor, by the bar, or at umbrella-covered tables in the front alleyway. The daily menu is written on a blackboard and includes crêpes, sandwiches, quiche, and such entrées as roasted chicken breast. Sunday brunch.

TADICH GRILL

$$ SEAFOOD   ✉240 California Street   ☎415-391-2373

This historic grill means business with its wood-paneled walls, tile floor, and Art Deco light fixtures. It also has a counter running the length of the grill, white linen–covered tables, and wooden booths. The history of the place is so rich it consumes the first page of the menu. It all began during that gilded year, 1849, and has continued as a businessperson's restaurant in the heart of the Financial District. A new menu is printed daily, though on any given day, lunch and dinner remain the same. The specialty is seafood (sole, salmon, snapper, swordfish, shrimp, and scallops), but charcoal-broiled steak, chops, and chicken are also available. Proud in tradition and cuisine, this San Francisco institution remains top-flight all the way. Closed Sunday.

YANK SING

hidden

$$–$$$ CHINESE   ✉101 Spear Street   ☎415-957-9300
🖃www.yanksing.com, yanksing@yanksing.com

Dim sum is the Chinese tradition of selecting dishes from trays that are continuously wheeled about the dining room at brunchtime. You'll discover designer dim sum at this restaurant that has elevated the tea house idea to a culinary art. While tea houses are usually like cafeterias, Yank Sing provides a serene setting with white linen, fresh flowers, and cane-back chairs. Simple but suave, the restaurant offers dim sum delights like stuffed snow crab claws, stuffed lotus leaf, Peking duck by the slice, and shrimp dumplings. Lunch only.

SAI'S RESTAURANT

$ VIETNAMESE   ✉505 Washington Street   ✆415-362-3689

There are only about 25 tables, but Sai's packs in the Financial District lunch crowds, who wait in line to enjoy Vietnamese food at this popular family-run establishment. The decor is simple, with a few paintings on the wall, but the food has a devoted following. Favorite dishes include lemongrass chicken, eggplant with garlic sauce, Sai's special chow mein, and coconut curries. No dinner on Saturday. Closed Sunday.

TOMMY TOY'S

$$$$ CHINESE   ✉655 Montgomery Street   ✆415-397-4888
📠415-397-0469   🖰www.tommytoys.com, info@tommytoys.com

The decor here was fashioned after the 19th-century quarters of the Empress Dowager's sitting room. The 300-year-old tapestries, silk draperies and Tommy's collection of original Chinese fans set the stage for elegant French-Chinese dishes such as a Mongolian lamb with hoisin and fresh mint or smoked black cod with camphorwood and tea leaves served with Chinese string beans and wooden mushrooms. The prix-fixe Executive Luncheon is a five-course winner for weekday lunches.

BIX

$$$$ FRENCH   ✉56 Gold Street   ✆415-433-6300   📠415-433-4574
www.bixrestaurant.com, info@bixrestaurant.com

Gatsby would feel right at home in this glamorous, '30s-style supper club with live jazz at night, white-jacketed bartenders, classic martinis, and a stunning mahogany bar. Named after jazz great Bix Biederbecke, the slick Art Deco interior belies Bix's location in a nondescript alley at the edge of the Financial District. Lunch and dinner items change daily. Fresh seasonal entrées might include grilled rack of lamb with zucchini-parmesan tart, truffled pecorino cheeseburger, or American Kobe steak. Great people watching daily. Dinner daily; lunch on Friday.

YO YO'S

$ JAPANESE   ✉318 Pacific Avenue   ✆415-296-8273

The long lines at this hole-in-the-wall spot prove there's more to a restaurant than just location. Businessfolk love to pop in and grab some sobe noodle soup, teriyaki chicken or sushi. After all, Yo Yo's is mainly take-out with little seating and a fast turn-around. So just take your fare down to the waterfront for some great views and delicious grub. Lunch only. Closed weekends.

NIGHTLIFE

CARNELIAN ROOM   ✉555 California Street   ✆415-433-7500   🖰www.carnelian room.com, contactus@carnelianroom.com   A favorite bar in this world of finance is the Carnelian atop the Bank of America. Perched on the 52nd floor, this luxurious lounge has the best views of all, sweeping from little old San Francisco Bay out across the boundless deep. Reservations strongly recommended. Dress code.

THE PUNCH LINE ✉*444 Battery Street* ✆*415-397-7573* ✐*www.punchline comedyclub.com* The comedy scene has been ripping through San Francisco since the early days of Lenny Bruce and Mort Sahl. Today the city has more stand-up comedians than cab drivers. This place books a wide variety of acts from around the country.

EMBARCADERO

Below the Financial District, where the city's skyscrapers meet the Bay, is the Embarcadero. This waterfront promenade has become increasingly appealing since the 1989 earthquake, which resulted in the dismantling of a freeway that once ran along the bayfront. Today the vistas are unobstructed and the strip is wide open for wandering.

Back in Gold Rush days, before the pernicious advent of landfill, the entire area sat beneath fathoms of water and went by the name of Yerba Buena Cove. Matter of fact, the hundreds of tall-masted ships abandoned here by crews deserting for the gold fields eventually became part of the landfill.

Nature is rarely a match for the shovel. The Bay was pressed back from around Montgomery Street to its present perimeter. As you head down from the Financial District, walk softly; the world may be four billion years old, but the earth you're treading has been around little more than a century.

SIGHTS

EMBARCADERO CENTER This skein of five skyscrapers rising sharp and slender along Sacramento Street to the foot of Market Street is the Embarcadero Center. This $645 million complex, oft tagged "Rockefeller Center West," features a three-tiered pedestrian mall that links the buildings together in a labyrinth of shops, restaurants, fountains, and gardens.

VAILLANCOURT FOUNTAIN That blocky complex of cement pipes from which water pours in every direction is not an erector set run amok. It's Vaillancourt Fountain, situated smack in the Hyatt's front yard.

JUSTIN HERMAN PLAZA This surrounding patchwork of grass and pavement is the perfect place for a promenade or picnic. Craft vendors with engraved brass belt buckles, silver jewelry, and beanbag chairs have made the plaza their storefront and skaters have made it their playground. It's also the starting point for the monthly roving bicycle protest known as Critical Mass.

FERRY BUILDING Just across the road, where Market Street encounters the Embarcadero, rises San Francisco's answer to the Statue

HERB CAEN WAY

Pedestrian walkway honoring San Francisco's late, great, Pulitzer Prize–winning columnist who first coined the term "beatnik" in 1958

KOKKARI ESTIATORIO

Gourmet Mediterranean specialties—fresh seafood and game in a comfortable restaurant complete with roaring fireplace

FOG CITY DINER

Classic diner made modern with stylish booths and exciting California cuisine

of Liberty. Or what was the city's answer at the turn of the 20th century, when the clock tower of the Ferry Building was as well-known a landmark as the Golden Gate Bridge is today. Back then there were no bridges, and 100,000 ferryboat commuters a day poured through the portals of the world's second-busiest passenger terminal. Built in 1898, the old landmark has made a comeback with a complete renovation. Now the building houses a plethora of shops and restaurants and a bustling **farmers' market** on Tuesday and Saturday. Afternoon or evening tours of the building are available through **City Guides** (415-557-4266; www.sfcityguides.org) on Tuesday, Thursday, and Saturday.

WORLD TRADE CENTER   You might want to walk the ramp that leads up to the World Trade Center, on Embarcadero at the foot of Market Street. It's lined with Covarrubias' murals that were preserved from the 1939 Golden Gate International Exposition. They look like those maps in your old sixth grade social studies book: one vividly depicts "the people of the Pacific" with aborigines sprouting up from the Australian land mass and seraped Indians guarding the South American coast. Another pictorial geography lesson features the Pacific economy with salmon swimming off the North American shore and rice bowls growing in China.

One positive result of the horrendous 1989 Loma Prieta earthquake was the demolition of the Embarcadero Freeway, a longtime eyesore that ran like a concrete scar through the waterfront area. Now that the freeway is gone, there is a lighter and brighter look to the area, with palm trees planted along the Embarcadero and more expansive views of the Bay Bridge and Treasure Island. At the same time, a new neighborhood is fast growing up around and to the south of lower Market Street with apartments, restaurants, nightspots, and parks.

HERB CAEN WAY
In 1996, the city named the pedestrian promenade that parallels the boulevard in honor of San Francisco's famous gossip columnist who died in 1997.

RINCON CENTER A popular gathering spot for locals, especially at noontime, is this cluster of eateries offering everything from Korean noodles to Indian curries. The eateries surround a central indoor courtyard dining area and spectacular, rainfall-like fountain.

RINCON ANNEX ⊠*101 Spear Street* ☏*415-777-4100* This annex is a restored 1930s post office with magnificent **WPA murals** glorifying science and technology.

SHIPPING PIERS Stretching from either side of the Ferry Building are the rows of shipping piers that once made San Francisco a fabulous harbor. Today much of the commerce has sailed across the Bay to the Port of Oakland. To recapture San Francisco's maritime era, head north on Embarcadero from the Ferry Building along the odd-numbered piers. The city looms to your left and the Bay heaves and glistens before you. This is a world of seaweed and fog horns where proverbial old salts still ply their trade. Blunt-nosed tugboats tie up next to rusting relics from Guadalcanal. There are modern jet ferries, displaying the latest aeronautical curves and appearing ready at any moment to depart from the water for open sky. The old, big-girthed ferries have been stripped of barnacles, painted nursery colors, and leased out as office space; they are floating condominiums.

Along this parade of piers you'll see cavernous concrete wharves astir with forklifts and dockhands. Locomotives shunt with a clatter, trucks jockey for an inside post, and container cranes sweep the air. Other piers have fallen into desuetude, rust-caked wharves propped on water-rotted pilings. The only common denominators in this odd arithmetic progression of piers are the seagulls and pelicans whitening the pylons.

LEVI'S PLAZA ⊠*1155 Battery Street* Across from Pier 23, this plaza features a grassy park ideal for picnicking; just beyond Pier 35 there's a waterfront park with a wonderful vantage for spying on the ships that sail the Bay.

The Embarcadero continues along the waterfront all the way to Fisherman's Wharf. Joggers, skaters, and skateboarders all favor this long smooth stretch of Herb Caen Way.

Embarcadero

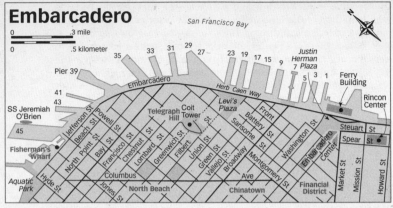

San Francisco Bay

BAY CRUISES Venturing out on the water will take you to some of San Francisco's landmark sites. Ground zero (water zero?) for the **Alcatraz Cruises** (415-981-7625, fax 415-705-5429; wwww.alcatrazcruises. com, rich_weidman@nps.gov)—which sponsors Bay cruises, Alcatraz tours, and ferry service to Angel Island, Sausalito, and Tiburon—is Pier 33 near Fisherman's Wharf, so that's where you'll want to be.

The trip to **Alcatraz** is highlighted with a National Park Service tour of the infamous prison. Originally a fort and later a military prison, Alcatraz gained renown as "The Rock" when it became a maximum security prison in 1934. Al Capone, "Machine Gun" Kelly, and Robert "Birdman of Alcatraz" Stroud were among its notorious inmates. On the tour, you'll enter the bowels of the prison, walk the dank corridors, and experience the cage-like cells in which America's most desperate criminals were kept. Be sure to tune in to the audio tour of former guards and prisoners remembering their time at The Rock.

The prison closed in 1963; then in 1969 a group of American Indians occupied the island for almost two years, claiming it as Indian territory. Today Alcatraz is part of the Golden Gate National Recreation Area.

A cruise to wind-blown **Angel Island State Park** (415-435-5390; www. angelisland.org) is a different adventure entirely. Unlike "The Rock," this star-shaped island is covered with forest and rolling hills. During previous incarnations it has served as a military installation, quarantine station, immigration center, and prisoner of war camp. Today, the largest true island in San Francisco Bay is a lacework of hiking and biking trails and flowering meadows. In 2008, wildfires drastically changed the terrain, burning 380 of the park's 740 acres. Fortunately, the island remains open to hikers and campers, despite the damage. For an overview stop by the Visitors Center at Ayala Cove. You'll find a diorama and map of the island, historical exhibits, a self-starting 20-minute video that reviews the history of the island and the light fixture from an old lighthouse. You can trek five miles around the island or climb to the top for 360° views of the Bay Area.

Deer graze throughout the area and there are picnic areas galore. It's a perfect spot for a day in the sun. If you'd like to visit the small Immigration Station Museum, which is dedicated to the history of the island's early immigration station, call ahead to reserve a spot in one of their guided tours Wednesday through Sunday. While reservations are currently accepted, tours won't begin until April 2009 when the museum is reopened after restoration. Touching photographs document the story of this "West Coast Ellis Island." Except for the visitors center, which is open year-round, the buildings on Angel Island are open weekends only April through October (and for group tours). A tram operates on weekends in the summer and with limited hours the rest of the year. (The entrance fee is included in the ferry price; however, there is a $15 day-use fee if you bring your own boat.)

LODGING

HYATT REGENCY
$$$$ 802 ROOMS ✉5 Embarcadero Center ✆415-788-1234 🖷415-398-2567
✐www.hyatt.com

The lobby of this hotel, on the corner of Market and California streets, features a towering atrium that rises 170 feet—a triangular affair lined with a succession of interior balconies that ascend to a skylighted roof. Fountains and flowering plants are all about, glass capsule elevators scale the walls, and sun flecks splash in through the roof. The 800-plus large, fashionable guest rooms, accented with tall green plants and fresh-cut flowers, come with business-oriented amenities such as two telephones, voice mail and computer hookups, as well as such luxury touches as hair dryers, plush robes, and optional turndown service. Most rooms have exterior balconies, and many have Bay views.

HOTEL GRIFFON
$$$$ 62 ROOMS ✉155 Steuart Street ✆415-495-2100, 800-321-2201
🖷415-495-3522 ✐www.hotelgriffon.com, reservations@hotelgriffon.com

Just one block from the Embarcadero and convenient to the Financial District, this lodging offers spacious attractive rooms and suites appointed with oversized mirrors, luxurious fabrics, flatscreen TVs, and, in a few cases, Bay views and terraces. A cozy lobby features a reading nook and fireplace, and there's an adjacent fitness center. An expanded continental breakfast is included.

HARBOR COURT HOTEL
$$$–$$$$ 131 ROOMS ✉165 Steuart Street ✆415-882-1300, 866-792-6283
🖷415-882-1313 ✐www.harborcourthotel.com

On the same block as the Griffon is this comfortable hotel, where some of the rooms and suites also offer marine views. Guest accommodations are small but attractively appointed with rich fabrics, modern furnishings, and canopied beds. The lobby is large and comfortable, and ideal for leisurely afternoons. Complimentary wine is served in the evening. You can also relax at the health club and indoor pool adjacent to the hotel. Pet-friendly.

HOTEL VITALE

$$$$ 185 ROOMS   ✉8 Mission Street   📞415-278-3700, 888-890-8688
📠415-278-3750   🖰www.hotelvitale.com, bookvitale@jdvhospitality.com

This eight-story hotel offers 185 guest rooms, eight suites, and six studios—each styled in natural, contemporary motifs, and many with Bay views. Amenities include 24-hour room service, twice-daily housekeeping, high-speed internet, spa-styled bathrooms, and flatscreen TVs with DVD players. The Vitale also has a waterfront restaurant, outdoor café, a spa with outdoor soaking tubs, fully equipped business center, fitness center, and free morning yoga classes. Pet-friendly.

DINING

BOULEVARD

$$$$ FRENCH/AMERICAN   ✉1 Mission Street   📞415-543-6084   📠415-495-2936
🖰www.boulevardrestaurant.com, info@boulevardrestaurant.com

Consistently ranked among the city's top restaurants, Boulevard is the brainchild of famed San Francisco chef Nancy Oakes and interior designer Pat Kuleto. Belle epoque decor unifies three distinct seating areas—a casual central section around an open kitchen where you can watch the chefs at work, a front bar, and a more formal back dining area. The food is as chic as the decor, and the menu changes regularly. Representative entrées have included glazed pork chops with roasted figs, Peking duck with champagne-grape relish, and grilled salmon in salsa verde. There's also an exceptional list of hard-to-find California wines. No lunch on weekends.

DELANCEY STREET RESTAURANT

$–$$ AMERICAN   ✉600 Embarcadero   📞415-512-5179
🖰www.delanceystreetfoundation.org

This very well-regarded restaurant serves as a training school for residents in the Delancey Street Foundation substance abuse program, and the service and menu selections are on a par with much fancier (read: more expensive) spots in the city. Daily specials feature fresh seafood and local produce. Comfort food, such as meatloaf with gravy, hefty ribs, fried chicken with red beans and rice, and matzo ball soup are usually on offer, along with a fresh oyster bar and home-style desserts like sweet potato pie. The main dining room features wood paneling and white tablecloths, though in nice weather opt for a seat on the patio, which has fantastic views of the waterfront.

KOKKARI ESTIATORIO

$$–$$$ GREEK   ✉200 Jackson Street   📞415-981-0983   📠415-982-0983
🖰www.kokkari.com

Named after a small fishing village on the island of Samos in the Aegean Sea, this restaurant is a cozy, Old World place with lots of warm wood, high shuttered windows and handmade ceramic plates. The menu is heavy on seafood and game, with traditional Greek dishes such as a lightly spicy moussaka of eggplant, lamb ragout, and creamy béchamel sauce. Lamb chops, steak, ravioli, and whole fish are staples, with seasonal specials. No lunch on Saturday. Closed Sunday.

FOG CITY DINER — **h**idden

$$–$$$ CALIFORNIA CUISINE   ✉*1300 Battery Street*   ✆*415-982-2000*
✆*415-982-3711*   🖱*www.fogcitydiner.com, gm1@fogcitydiner.com*

San Francisco's modern version of camp is Fog City, quite likely to be the most upscale diner you've ever seen. Check out the exterior with its Art Deco curves, neon lights, and checkerboard tile. Then step into a wood-and-brass paneled restaurant that has the feel of a club car on the Orient Express. Featuring California cuisine, the menu changes frequently, but might include ahi tartare with jalepeño and cilantro, or corriander-seared salmon with green lentils and artichokes. Everything is à la carte, including the Fog City T-shirts. Reservations recommended.

PIER 23 CAFE

$$ SEAFOOD   ✉*Pier 23*   ✆*415-362-5125*   🖱*www.pier23cafe.com, pier23cafe@aol.com*

Head on down to this little shack between Fisherman's Wharf and downtown, for unique waterfront dining. The place is funky but nice, with white tablecloths and linen napkins on the tables. Dine inside or on the huge back patio overlooking the bay. This restaurant specializes in seafood and offers several fish specials daily. The deep-fried calamari appetizer and the oven-roasted crab with garlic, parsley, and butter dipping sauce are two of the most popular items on the menu.

SHOPPING

EMBARCADERO CENTER   Shoppers along the Embarcadero head to this emporium located on Sacramento Street near the foot of Market Street. It's a vaulting glass-and-concrete "town" inhabited by stores and restaurants. This multifaceted mall consists of the lower three levels of five consecutive skyscrapers. You pass from one building to the next along corridors that open onto a galaxy of shops. Verily, what Disneyland is for kids, Embarcadero Center is to shoppers. The place has positively everything. There are bookstores, bakeries, jewelry stores, gift bazaars, newsstands, and camera shops. There's even a "general store," plus dozens of restaurants, cocktail lounges, and espresso bars, a luggage shop, a store devoted entirely to nature, and on and on and on in labyrinthine fashion.

NIGHTLIFE

13 VIEWS   ✉*Hyatt Regency San Francisco, 5 Embarcadero Center*   ✆*415-788-1234*
🖱*www.sanfranciscoregency.hyatt.com*   Stop into this chic lounge for a chilled

martini and a perch that overlooks the 18-story atrium on one side and the Bay skyline on the other. A wall of glass gives a clear view of "13 views" that encompass Justin Herman Plaza, the Embarcadero waterfront, the historic Ferry Building, and what looks like all of San Francisco. Quiet music, rich desserts, and a full menu for late night dining make this a top choice for romantic evenings.

THE HOLDING COMPANY ✉2 Embarcadero Center ✆415-986-0797 ✐www.theholdingco.us This is a dark-wood bar and grill crowded with young professionals on the make. With the feel of an Irish pub, it's a clean, comfortable spot to unwind with a drink and watch sports. Closed Saturday and Sunday.

PIER 23 CAFE ✉Embarcadero and Pier 23 ✆415-362-5125 ✐www.pier23cafe. com This café is a funky roadhouse that happens to sit next to the San Francisco waterfront. The sounds emanating from this saloon are live jazz, reggae, salsa, and blues. Highly recommended to those searching for the simple rhythms of life. There's music Tuesday through Sunday. Cover.

CHINATOWN

It's the largest Chinatown outside Asia, a spot that older Chinese know as *dai fao*, Big City. San Francisco's Chinatown also ranks as the city's most densely populated neighborhood. Home to more than 14,000 of the city's 153,000 Chinese, this enclave has been an Asian stronghold since the 1850s. Originally a ghetto where Chinese people were segregated from San Francisco society, the neighborhood today opens its arms to burgeoning numbers of immigrants from a host of Asian nations.

On the surface, this pulsing, noisy, chaotically colorful 70-square-block stretch projects the aura of a tourist's dream—gold and crimson pagodas, stores brimming with exquisite silks and multicolored dragons, more restaurants per square foot than could be imagined, roast ducks strung up in shop windows next door to Buddhist temples and fortune cookie factories.

But Chinatown is far more than a tourist mecca. This crowded neighborhood is peopled with families, powerful political groups, small merchants, poor working immigrants and rising entrepreneurs molding a more prosperous future. Although the "city within a city" that Chinatown once symbolized now encompasses less than a quarter of San Francisco's Chinese people, it's still a center of Chinese history, culture, arts, and traditions that have lived for thousands of years.

In appropriately dramatic fashion, you enter Chinatown through an arching gateway bedecked with dragons. Stone lions guard either side of this portal at Grant Avenue and Bush Street.

It was during the Gold Rush that "Celestials" sporting queues and exotic costumes arrived en masse in California. Often forced into indentured

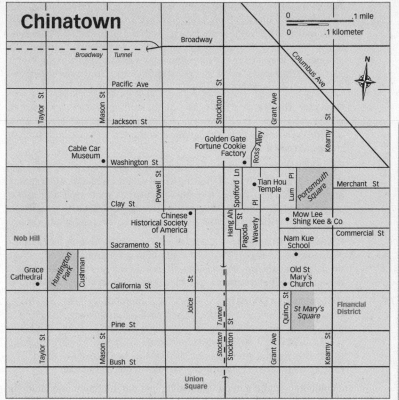

Chinatown

Broadway

Broadway Tunnel

Pacific Ave

Columbus Ave

N

Taylor St

Mason St

Stockton St

Grant Ave

Jackson St

St

Kearny

Cable Car Museum

Golden Gate Fortune Cookie Factory

Ross Alley

Washington St

Powell St

Spofford Ln

Tian Hou Temple

Lum Pl

Portsmouth Square

Merchant St

Clay St

Pl

Chinese Historical Society of America

Hang Ah St

Pagoda Pl

Waverly

Mow Lee Shing Kee & Co

Commercial St

Nob Hill

Sacramento St

Nam Kue School

Grace Cathedral

Huntington Park

Cushman

California St

St

Old St Mary's Church

Joice

Tunnel St

Financial District

Quincy St

St Mary's Square

Pine St

Stockton

Stockton St

Grant Ave

Kearny St

Taylor St

Mason St

Bush St

Union Square

servitude, they worked the gold fields and later helped build the transcontinental railroad. During the 1870s and 1880s these proud people, who had arrived in San Francisco with visions of the "Great City on the Golden Hill," became victims of the "yellow peril" mentality sweeping the nation. They were beaten and lynched, their homes torched. Racist whites, eyeing the prime real estate upon which the Chinatown ghetto had grown, tried to run the entire population out of town.

It took an earthquake to uproot them. The calamity of 1906 devastated Chinatown, leaving countless dead and homeless. When the smoke and rubble were cleared, a new Chinatown arose; gone were the opium dens and houses of prostitution for which the old ghetto was notorious; in their stead grew a neighborhood that became modern-day Chinatown.

SIGHTS

GRANT AVENUE   To stroll this eight-block length of Chinatown is to walk along San Francisco's oldest street. Today it's an ultramodern thoroughfare lined with Chinese arts-and-crafts shops, restaurants, and Asian markets. It's also one of the most crowded streets you'll ever squeeze your way through. Immortalized in a song from the musical

Flower Drum Song, Grant Avenue, San Francisco, California, U.S.A., is a commotion, a clatter, a clash of cultures. At any moment, a rickety truck may pull up beside you, heave open its doors, and reveal its contents—a cargo of chinaware, fresh produce, or perhaps flattened pig carcasses. Elderly Chinese men lean along doorways smoking fat cigars, and Chinatown's younger generation sets off down the street clad in sleek leather jackets.

OLD ST. MARY'S CHURCH   At the corner of California Street, where cable cars clang across Grant Avenue, rises this lovely brick structure. Dating to 1854, this splendid cathedral was originally built of stone quarried in China.

ST. MARY'S SQUARE   Just across the way in St. Mary's Square, there's a statue of the father of the Chinese Republic, Dr. Sun Yat Sen, crafted by San Francisco's foremost sculptor, Beniamino Bufano. You might take a hint from the crowds of businesspeople from the nearby financial center who bring their picnic lunches to this tree-shaded plaza.

NAM KUE SCHOOL   ✉*755 Sacramento Street* With an iron fence, mullioned doors, and pagoda-like facade, this is an architectural beauty ironically backdropped by a glass-and-concrete skyscraper. Since 1925, the school has been educating local children about Chinese culture.

COMMERCIAL STREET   As you walk along Grant Avenue, with its swirling roof lines and flashing signs, peek down this street. A curious brick-paved promenade, it permits a glimpse into "hidden" Chinatown. Lined with everything from a noodle company to a ginseng shop, this tightly packed street also holds the **Mow Lee Shing Kee & Co.** (774 Commercial Street), Chinatown's second-oldest establishment.

CHINESE HISTORICAL SOCIETY OF AMERICA   ✉*965 Clay Street* 📞*415-391-1188* 📠*415-391-1150* 🖱*www.chsa.org, info@chsa.org* Between Stockton and Powell streets lies this hole-in-the-wall museum that will open wide your perspective on Chinatown's history. The Chinese Historical Society of America graphically presents the history of San Francisco's Chinese population. In the museum is a magnificent collection of photos and artifacts re-creating the Chinese experience from the days of pig-tailed "coolies" to the recent advent of ethnic consciousness. Wide in scope, the museum is a treasure house with a helpful and congenial staff. Closed Sunday and Monday. Admission.

PORTSMOUTH SQUARE   ✉*Kearny and Washington streets* After you've immersed yourself in Chinese history, head down to this square for a lesson on the history of all San Francisco. Formerly the city's central plaza, it was here in 1846 that Yankees first raised the Stars and Stripes. Two years later, the California gold discovery was announced to the world from this square. Rudyard Kipling, Jack London, and Robert Louis Stevenson once wandered the grounds. At one corner of the park you'll find the bronze statue of a galleon celebrating the ocean-going Robert Louis Stevenson. Today this gracious park is a gathering place for old Chinese men playing chess and practicing tai chi.

CHINESE CULTURE CENTER ✉*750 Kearny Street* ☎*415-986-1822* ✆*415-986-2825* 🖥*www.c-c-c.org, info@c-c-c.org* From the center of Portsmouth Square, a sky bridge arches directly into this cultural center, with its displays of Chinese art. Closed Sunday and Monday.

STOCKTON STREET   Now that you've experienced the traditional tour, you might want to explore the hidden heart of Chinatown. First take a stroll along Stockton Street, which runs parallel to, and one block above, Grant Avenue. It is here, not along touristy Grant Avenue, that the Chinese shop.

The street vibrates with the crazy commotion of Chinatown. Open stalls tumbling with vegetables cover the sidewalk, and crates of fresh fish are stacked along the curb. Through this maze of merchandise, shoppers press past one another. In store windows hang Peking ducks, and on the counters are displayed pigs' heads and snapping turtles. Rare herbs, healing teas, and chrysanthemum crystals crowd the shelves.

MURAL ✉*Stockton Street* The local community's artwork is displayed in a fantastic mural that covers a half-block between Pacific and Jackson streets.

ALLEYWAYS OF CHINATOWN
To further explore the interior life of Chinatown, turn down Sacramento Street from Stockton Street, then take a quick left into Hang Ah Street. This is the first in a series of alleyways leading for three blocks from Sacramento Street to Jackson Street. When you get to the end of each block, simply jog over to the next alley.

A universe unto themselves, these alleyways of Chinatown are where the secret business of the community goes on, as it has for over a century. Each door is a barrier beyond which you can hear the rattle of mah-jongg tiles and the sounds of women bent to their tasks in laundries and sewing factories.

HANG AH STREET   Along this street, timeworn buildings are draped with fire escapes and colored with the images of fading signs. As you cross Clay Street, at the end of Hang Ah Street, be sure to press your nose against the glass at **Grand Century Enterprise** (858 Clay Street; 415-392-4060, fax 415-392-4063). Here the ginseng and other precious roots sell for hundreds of dollars a pound.

SPOFFORD LANE   The next alley, Spofford Lane, is a corridor of painted doorways and brick facades occasionally humming with the strains of Chinese melodies. It ends at Washington Street.

ROSS ALLEY   From Washington Street you can zigzag over to Ross Alley. This is the home of **Golden Gate Fortune Cookie Factory** (56 Ross Alley; 415-781-3956). At this small family establishment you can watch your fortune being made.

WAVERLY PLACE

The last segment in this intriguing tour will take you back to this two-block stretch leading from Washington Street to Sacramento Street. Readers of Dashiell Hammett's mystery story, *Dead Yellow Women*, will recall this spot. It's an enchanting thoroughfare, more alley than street. At first glance, the wrought-iron balconies draped along either side of Waverly evoke images of New Orleans. But not even the French Quarter can boast the beauty contained in those Chinese cornices and pagoda swirl roof lines.

TIAN HOU TEMPLE ✉125 Waverly Place The prize jewel in this architectural crown is this temple. Here Buddhists and Taoists worship in a tiny temple overhung with fiery red lanterns. There are statues portraying battlefields and country landscapes; incense smolders from several altars. From the pictures along the wall, Buddha smiles out upon the believers. They in turn gaze down from the balcony onto Chinatown's most magical street.

CABLE CAR MUSEUM ✉1201 Mason Street ☎415-474-1887 ☎415-929-7546 ✐www.cablecarmuseum.org Just uphill from Chinatown stands this brick goliath that houses the city's cable cars. The museum provides a great opportunity to see how these wood-and-steel masterpieces operate. The system's powerhouse, repair, and storage facilities are here, as are the 14-foot diameter sheaves which neatly wind the cable into figure-eight patterns. The museum also has on display three antique cable cars from the original cable car company. Video displays show footage of the 1906 earthquake and a ride down Market Street before the quake.

LODGING

Though you'll notice doors and stairways throughout Chinatown advertising hotel accommodations, these are usually residential buildings serving the local Chinese community. Look for the permanent "no vacancy" signs that accompany many of the hotel insignia and you'll realize that these facilities are Asian boarding houses, closed to the general public.

GRANT PLAZA HOTEL

$–$$ 72 ROOMS ✉465 Grant Avenue ☎415-434-3883, 800-472-6899 ☎415-434-3886 ✐www.grantplaza.com, info@grantplaza.com

Immediately up from the Grant Avenue gateway to Chinatown you'll encounter this hotel. Staff and management here are quite hospitable. The place features a small, mirrored lobby with chandeliers and a selection of pleasant rooms. They feature plush mauve carpeting, telephones, color televisions, and private baths. The hotel's location right on Grant Avenue has the advantage of being at the very heart of the district and the disadvantage of being noisy.

HON'S WUN TUN HOUSE

$ CHINESE   ✉648 Kearny Street   ☎415-433-3966   📠415-433-1506

Chinatown is one of the best places in the city to find exceptional food at rock-bottom prices. Look for it at the kind of plain-looking places where most of the diners appear to be from the neighborhood and children roam around as freely as if they were at home. A good example is Hon's, where spotless formica, shared tables and counter seating set the stage for noodle dishes and soups as tasty as they are affordable. Closed Sunday.

SAM WO

$ CHINESE   ✉813 Washington Street   ☎415-982-0596   📠415-982-0596

Among budget restaurants, this is a San Francisco classic. Dining in this jook house is a rare adventure. The entrance is also the kitchen, and the kitchen is just a corridor filled with pots, stovepipes, cooks, and steamy smells. Sam Wo's menu is extensive and the food is quite good for the price.

POT STICKER

$$ CHINESE   ✉150 Waverly Place   ☎415-397-9985   📠415-397-3829

Concealed along one of Chinatown's back alleyways, this eatery has the feel of a local secret, part social club, part take-out place serving neighborhood families, and so exotic that it seems a world apart from the more touristy restaurants of Grant Street. Specializing in its namesake—meat-filled dumplings that are first steamed and then fried—the Pot Sticker also offers a full menu of Mandarin-style dishes.

EMPRESS OF CHINA

$$$–$$$$ CHINESE   ✉838 Grant Avenue   ☎415-434-1345   📠415-986-1187
🖥www.empressofchinasf.com, info@empressofchinasf.com

For luxurious dining in the heart of Chinatown, no place matches the Empress. Set on the top floor of the China Trade Center, with nothing between you and heaven, it is a culinary temple. Dining rooms are adorned with carved antiques and the maitre'd dons a tuxedo. Lunch at this roof garden restaurant begins with appetizers like Shanghai dumplings and walnut prawns, then graduates to lychee chicken and Manchurian beef. Dinner is the true extravagance. The menu includes a royal variety of chicken, duck, lamb, shellfish, pork, and beef dishes. There are also unique selections like baby quail flambé, Dungeness crab in ginger and onion sauce, and almond-pressed duck.

HANG AH TEA HOUSE

$ CHINESE/DIM SUM   ✉1 Hang Ah Street   ☎415-982-5686

My favorite dim sum restaurant is tucked away in an alley above Grant Avenue. Personalized but unpretentious, more cozy than

You Dim Sum, You Win Some

The ultimate Chinatown experience is to dine dim sum style. Rather than choosing from a menu, you select dishes from trundle carts laden with steaming delicacies. A never-ending convoy of waitresses wheels past your table, offering plates piled with won tons, pork tidbits, and Chinese meatballs. It's up to you to create a meal (traditionally breakfast or lunch) from this succession of finger-size morsels.

Many dim sum establishments are cavernous restaurants, sparsely decorated like cafeterias. But each has a particular personality and generates warmth from the crowds passing through. Do not be fooled by the neon facades, for an Asian adventure waits within these dining palaces. You should be careful about prices, however: most dim sum courses cost only $2 or $3, but it's easy to lose count as you devour dish after dish.

cavernous, Hang Ah Tea House is a rare find. Enter the dining room with its Chinese wood carvings and fiberglass tables. Serving a full Mandarin cuisine as well as dim sum portions, it warrants an exploratory mission into the alleys of Chinatown.

GOLD MOUNTAIN RESTAURANT

$–$$ DIM SUM   ✉644 Broadway near Powell Street   ☎415-296-7733

The brightly lit yellow sign outside this restaurant attracts its share of tourists and passersby. Nonetheless, this clean and modern dining room serves trusty claypot specialties, traditional seafood and noodles, and dim sum at lunch. Try the three treasures in black bean sauce, a colorful dish with red bell peppers, eggplant, and stuffed tofu. No dinner.

ORIENTAL PEARL

$$–$$$ CHINESE/DIM SUM   ✉760–778 Clay Street   ☎415-433-1817
☎415-433-4541   ⬡www.orientalpearlsf.com

Overlooking Portsmouth Square on the second story of a nondescript building, this restaurant serves sophisticated, gourmet dim sum, a step above the usual Chinatown teahouse. Here dim sum is ordered from a menu, allowing diners to concentrate on conversation and cuisine, rather than being distracted by the contents of passing carts. Such treats as shrimp and scallop dumplings, pork buns, and chicken meatballs emerge hot and fresh from the kitchen. White tablecloths, mahogany chairs, and classical Chinese music make this a quiet oasis from the busy streets of Chinatown below.

LICHEE GARDEN

$$ CANTONESE   ✉1416 Powell Street   ☎415-397-2290   ⬡licheegarden.ypguides.net

Styled like a teahouse, this delicious find limits glitzy decor and concentrates on excellent, authentic Cantonese cuisine. The tables are consistently crowded with Chinese families who have come to rely on the over 60 fresh dim sum dishes that are prepared daily. Pork, beef, duck, seafood, or vegetarian dim sum options are available, along with full lunch and dinner menus, which boast all the traditional favorites.

Shopping in Chinatown brings you into immediate contact with both the common and the unique. If you can slip past the souvenir shops, many of which specialize in American-made "Chinese products," you'll eventually discover the real thing—Chinese arts and crafts as well as Asian antiques.

STOCKTON STREET Grant Avenue is the neighborhood's shopping center, but local Chinese favor this street. My advice is to browse both streets as well as the side streets between. Some of the city's best bargains are right here in Chinatown.

GRANT AVENUE After Stockton Street's soft-spoken introduction, continue on to that buzzing, clanging commercial strip called Grant Avenue. Sensory overload and crazed consumerism are facts of life along this neon thoroughfare. But don't be discouraged by the painted face: beneath that garish exterior, Grant Avenue reveals its own particular culture.

The soul of Chinatown resides somewhere between the Hong Kong souvenirs and the antique tapestries. While there is a lot of gimcrackery sold here, many specialty shops provide a sense of the richness of Chinese arts and crafts. Slip into one of the district's silk stores to admire the kimonos, or drop by a tea shop and sample one of the hundreds of varieties of teas.

CANTON BAZAAR ✉*616 Grant Avenue* ✆*415-362-5750* ✐*cantonbazaar@ aol.com* This first stop along Grant Avenue is a mandatory one: This three-story emporium is a browser's warehouse. Six-foot-high wooden statues and laughing Buddhas surround the entrance, drawing in the canny and unwary alike. From the ceramic pieces to the silver jewelry, the shelves are laden with exceptionally tasteful goods. The bottom floor is filled with furniture and decor items while the top floor is devoted to clothing and textiles. Among the antiques are Buddhist religious paintings, raw-silk wallhangings, and intricately carved statues.

CHINATOWN KITE SHOP ✉*717 Grant Avenue* ✆*415-989-5182* ✆*415-391- 8217* ✐*www.chinatownkite.com* As you continue down Grant Avenue, several specialty shops are worth noting. This kite shop is hung with a variety of kites, including dragonfly and box kites.

WOK SHOP ✉*718 Grant Avenue* ✆*415-989-3797* ✆*415-982-2299* ✐*www.wok shop.com* This shop sells every kind of wok imaginable—carbon steel, cast iron, stainless steel, electric—as well as all the accessories to cook up a tantalizing stir-fry, succulent roasted chicken, or savory *shiu mai*. There are also bamboo steamers, cleavers, claypots, and books.

FAR EAST FLEA MARKET ✉*729 Grant Avenue* ✆*415-989-8588* At this flea market you'll find everything from clothing to birdcages. Also available at this Asian emporium are fans and decorative boxes from mainland China.

CHONG IMPORTS ✉️*838 Grant Avenue* 📞*415-982-1434* At the New China Trade Center there's this store, which seems to offer every item found anywhere else on Grant Avenue. The prices at this multitiered wonderland are as alluring as the merchandise.

NIGHTLIFE

BUDDHA LOUNGE ✉️*901 Grant Avenue* 📞*415-362-1792* Head to this hole-in-the-wall haunt for a taste of the local scene. A bright-red neon sign announces this kitchy lounge, which boasts a multifarious jukebox (from standards to hip-hop to funk) and strong drinks, including Korean whiskey. The bartender will shoot dice with you for a free round—a lively spot to while away the evening.

LI PO ✉️*916 Grant Avenue* 📞*415-982-0072* This dimly lit Chinatown bar, is complete with incense, lanterns, and carved statuary, plus an incongruous jukebox featuring some Caucasian favorites mixed in with the Chinese music. The potions they mix here are powerful and exotic; the place has an air of intimacy.

NORTH BEACH

It's a region of contrasts, a neighborhood in transition. North Beach combines the sex scene of neon-lit Broadway with the brooding intellect and Beat heritage of Grant Avenue and Columbus Street. Traditionally an Italian stronghold, North Beach still retains its fabulous pasta palaces and bocce ball courts, but it's giving way to a growing influx of Chinese residents.

Introductions to places should be made gradually, so the visitor comes slowly but certainly to know and love the area. In touring North Beach, that is no longer possible, because the logical spot to begin a tour is the corner of Broadway and Montgomery streets, at night when the neon arabesque of Broadway is in full glare.

SIGHTS

BROADWAY Broadway, you see, has long been San Francisco's answer to Times Square, a tawdry avenue that traffics in sex. While the neighborhood is steadily changing, it still features strip joints, peekaramas, and X, Y, Z-rated theaters—a modern-day Barbary Coast.

CITY LIGHTS BOOKSTORE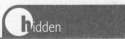

✉️*261 Columbus Avenue* 📞*415-362-8193* 📠*415-362-4921* 🖥️*www.citylights. com, staff@citylights.com* After you've dispensed with North Beach's sex scene, your love affair with the neighborhood can begin. Established in 1953 by poet Lawrence Ferlinghetti, City Lights is the old hangout of the Beat poets. Back in the heady days of the '50s, a host of "angelheaded hipsters"—Allen Ginsberg, Jack

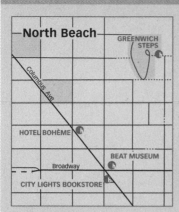

North Beach

GREENWICH STEPS

PAGE 76

Quiet walkway tucked in a historic residential part of North Beach offering views of Coit Tower

HOTEL BOHÈME

PAGE 77

European-style boutique hotel with black and white decor and iron beds—slick and classic

BEAT MUSEUM

PAGE 74

Hip gallery of '50s poetry memorabilia, including Kerouac bobble heads and first-edition books

CITY LIGHTS BOOKSTORE

PAGE 72

Lawrence Ferlinghetti's infamous literary hub where the Beat movement and its spirit of independence still flourish

Kerouac, Gary Snyder, and Neal Cassady among them—haunted its book-lined rooms and creaking staircase. Today the place remains a vital cultural scene and gathering point. It's a people's bookstore where you're invited to browse, carouse, or even plop into a chair and read awhile. You might also check out the paintings and old photos, or perhaps the window display in this official national landmark. Fifty years after the Beats, the inventory here still represents a who's who in avant-garde literature.

VESUVIO CAFÉ

✉ *255 Columbus Avenue* ✆ *415-362-3370* 🖉 *www.vesuvio.com* Just next door to City Lights, this café was another hallowed Bohemian retreat. The hip spot gained notoriety in 1955 when Neal Cassady and Dean Moriarty held a poetry reading here. From then on, it's been a literary joint popular with locals and in-the-know visitors.

CAFFE TRIESTE

✉ *601 Vallejo Street* ✆ *415-392-6739* 🖉 *415-550-1239* 🖉 *www.caffetrieste. com* Head up nearby Grant Avenue to the another café at the

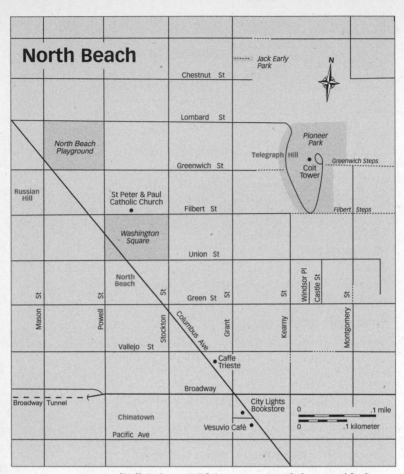

North Beach

Jack Early Park

Chestnut St

Lombard St

North Beach Playground

Pioneer Park

Greenwich St

Telegraph Hill

Greenwich Steps

Coit Tower

Russian Hill

St Peter & Paul Catholic Church

Filbert St

Filbert Steps

Washington Square

Union St

North Beach

Windsor Pl

Castle St

Mason St

Powell St

Stockton St

Green St

St

St

Columbus Ave

Grant St

Kearny St

Montgomery St

Vallejo St

Caffe Trieste

Broadway

Broadway Tunnel

City Lights Bookstore

0   .1 mile

0   .1 kilometer

Chinatown

Vesuvio Café

Pacific Ave

corner of Vallejo Street. With its water-spotted photos and funky espresso bar, the place has changed little since the days when bearded bards discussed cool jazz and Eisenhower politics.

BEAT MUSEUM _____ ⓗidden

✉540 Broadway ✆831-372-4911, 800-537-6822 ✐www.thebeatmuseum. org You're on "upper Grant," heart of the old Beat stomping grounds and still a major artery in the city's Italian enclave. You're also only a block from this hip museum, home to memorabilia from Lawrence Ferlinghetti, Allen Ginsberg, Jack Kerouac, and their buddies. The museum includes a collection of signed pictures, cards, and first edition books, as well as unusual antique items such as Kerouac-themed yo-yos and bobble heads. Rotating exhibits feature work from new and original poets and artists. Closed Monday.

Chinatown is at your back now, several blocks behind, but you'll see from the Chinese script adorning many shops that the Asian neighborhood is sprawling into the Italian. Still remaining, however, are the cafés and delicatessens that have lent this area its Mediterranean flair since the Italians moved in during the late 19th-century.

Beyond Filbert Street, as Grant Avenue continues along the side of Telegraph Hill, the shops give way to Italian residences and Victorian houses. When you arrive at Lombard Street, look to your left and you'll see the sinuous Lombard, labeled "The Crookedest Street in the World." Then turn right as Lombard carries you up to the breeze-battered vistas of Telegraph Hill.

TELEGRAPH HILL   Named for the semaphore station located on its height during the 1850s, this was a Bohemian haunt during the 1920s and 1930s. Money moved the artists out; today, this hillside real estate is among the most desirable, and most expensive, in the city.

COIT TOWER   Poking through the top of Telegraph Hill is this 180-foot-high tower (admission for elevator to observation platform). Built in 1934, this fluted structure was named for Lillie Hitchcock Coit, a bizarre character who chased fire engines and became a fire company mascot during the 1850s. Lillie's love for firemen gave rise to stories that the phallic tower was modeled after a fire hose nozzle. Architectural critics scoff at the notion. Some of the nation's most outstanding **WPA murals** decorate Coit Tower's interior. Done as frescoes by New Deal artists, they sensitively depict the lives of California laborers.

Upstaging other nearby marvelous artworks is the view from the summit. That sinewy structure to the right is the **Bay Bridge**, which stretches for eight and one quarter miles, the world's longest steel bridge. It is interrupted in its arching course by **Yerba Buena Island** and **Treasure Island**, the latter a manmade extension created for the 1939 Golden Gate International Exposition.

The Bay Bridge's gilded companion to the left is the **Golden Gate Bridge**. Between them lies San Francisco Bay. Tugs and freighters slide past in search of mooring. Fog horns groan. From this aerie the distant sloops and ketches look like children's toys blown astray in a pond puffed with wind.

The island moored directly offshore is **Alcatraz**, named for the pelicans that still inhabit it, but known for the notorious prisoners who have long since departed its rocky terrain. Looming behind America's own Devil's Island is **Angel Island**. That high point on the horizon, between the Golden Gate and Angel Island, is **Mt. Tamalpais**, crown jewel in Marin County's tiara. Across the water, where the Bay Bridge meets terra firma, are the East Bay cities of **Berkeley** and **Oakland**. Behind you, past the highrise cityscape, the hills and streets of San Francisco sweep out toward the sea.

Now that all of San Francisco has been spread before you like a tableau, it's time to descend into the hidden crannies of the city. Unlike Coit

Tower, there will be no elevator to assist on the way down, but then again there won't be any tourists either.

GREENWICH STEPS

After exiting Coit Tower, turn right, cross the street, and make your way down the brick-lined staircase. In the middle of San Francisco, with wharves and factories far below, you have just entered a countrified environment. Ferns and ivy riot on either side of these steps, while vines and conifers climb overhead.

FILBERT STEPS

At the bottom of the steps, turn right, walk a short distance along Montgomery Street, then head left down these steps. Festooned with flowers and sprinkled with baby tears, the steps carry you into a fantasy realm inhabited by stray cats and framed with clapboard houses. Among the older homes are several that date to the 1870s; if you follow the Napier Lane Boardwalk that extends from the steps, there are falsefront buildings from which sailors reportedly once were shanghaied.

WASHINGTON SQUARE   Retracing your tracks back up the steps, then descending the other side of Filbert Street, you'll arrive at Washington Square, between Filbert and Stockton streets in the heart of North Beach. Nestled between Russian and Telegraph hills, this is the gathering place for San Francisco's "Little Italy." In the square, old Italian men and women seek out wooden benches where they can watch the "young people" carrying on. From the surrounding delis and cafés you might put together a picnic lunch, plant yourself on the lawn, and catch this daily parade. But if you come early in the morning, you will see evidence of the slow transition North Beach is undergoing: 50 or more Chinese and Westerners practice tai chi in the square. Sitting amidst this garden setting, it's hard to imagine that Washington Square was a tent city back in 1906. The great earthquake and fire totally devastated North Beach, and the park became a refuge for hundreds of homeless people.

SAINTS PETER & PAUL CATHOLIC CHURCH ✉ *666 Filbert Street, between Powell and Stockton streets* ☎ *415-421-0809* ⌨ *www.stspeterpaul.san-francisco.ca.us, jitzgina@yahoo.com* This Catholic church anchors one side of the square. Its twin steeples dominate the North Beach skyline. The façade is unforgettable, an ornate affair upon which eagles rest in the company of angels. The interior is a wilderness of vaulting arches hung with lamps and decorated in gilt bas-relief. Tourists proclaim its beauty. For my taste, the place is overdone; it drips with architectural jewelry. Everything is decoration, an artistic happening; there is no tranquility, no silent spot for the eye to rest.

As a nighttime visit to North Beach will clearly indicate, this neighborhood was not made for sleeping. The "love acts" and encounter parlors along Broadway draw rude, boisterous crowds until the wee hours.

EUROPA HOTEL

$ 75 ROOMS   ✉310 Columbus Avenue   ✆415-391-5779   📠415-362-7740

If noise and neon have a soporific effect upon you, or if you have some bizarre and arcane need to know what sleeping on the old Barbary Coast was like, check out this hotel. The price is certainly right, and you get a clean, carpeted room and shared bath.

HOTEL BOHÈME

hidden

$$$ 15 ROOMS   ✉444 Columbus Avenue   ✆415-433-9111
📠415-362-6292   🖱www.hotelboheme.com, info@hotelboheme.com

Retreat a little farther from Broadway and take a step back into North Beach history here. This European pensione–style hotel has been decorated to reflect the Beat-generation era, complete with a black-and-white photo retrospective. Poet Allen Ginsberg even stayed here. Rooms feature antique wardrobes, tile bathrooms, and black iron beds. Ask for one of the rooms in the back, which are quieter than those along busy Columbus Avenue. Free wi-fi is available throughout the hotel.

DINING

TOMMASO'S NEAPOLITAN RESTAURANT

$$–$$$ ITALIAN   ✉1042 Kearny Street   ✆415-398-9696   📠415-989-9415
🖱www.tommasosnorthbeach.com

Some of the best pizza in town is served at Tommaso's, where the chefs bake in an oak-fired oven. The creations they prepare have resulted in this tiny restaurant being written up in national magazines. As soon as you walk in you'll realize it's the food, not the surroundings, that draws the attention. Entering the place is like stepping down into a grotto. The walls are lined with booths and covered by murals; it's dark, steamy, and filled with inviting smells. Filmmaker Francis Ford Coppola drops by occasionally, as should every pizza and pasta lover. Dinner only. Closed Monday.

THE STINKING ROSE

$$–$$$ ITALIAN   ✉325 Columbus Avenue   ✆415-781-7673
🖱www.thestinkingrose.com, sfcomments@thestinkingrose.com

Okay, not everybody likes garlic, but those who don't probably have no business dining in predominantly Italian North Beach anyway. On the other hand, those who *really* like garlic will love The Stinking Rose. Everything—from scrambled eggs to cocktails—is laced with garlic. Though mainly California-Italian, the menu runs the gamut from 40-

clove garlic chicken to garlic-roasted Dungeness crab. Garish inside and out, the decor is conducive to fun-loving rowdiness, and the waitpeople take their jobs anything but seriously. An added bonus is that you can get your garlic fix until 11 p.m. weeknights, midnight on weekends.

CAFFE SPORT

$$–$$$ ITALIAN   ✉574 Green Street   ☎415-981-1251   🖰www.caffe-sport.com

If there is any place in San Francisco that elevates dining to the level of high adventure, it is this restaurant. First, the place introduces itself a block before you arrive; if you're not buried beneath the waves of garlic it wafts along Green Street, you'll be visually assaulted by the garish orange facade. Once inside, you'll discover a baroque museum; the place is chockablock with bric-a-brac—faded photos, tacky candelabra and antiques circa 1972. Besides that, it's hot, steamy, unbelievably crowded, and the waiters are rude. What more can I say, except that you'll either love or hate the place. No lunch Tuesday through Thursday. Closed Monday.

NORTH BEACH RESTAURANT

$$–$$$ ITALIAN   ✉1512 Stockton Street   ☎415-392-1700   🖷415-392-0230
🖰www.northbeachrestaurant.com, northbeachrestaurant@yahoo.com

Classic Italian craftsmanship in Carrara marble, Venetian granite, Florentine floor tiles, and vaulted ceilings make a pretty frame for a busy lunch and dinner crowd enjoying the Tuscan-style food. Since 1970, this place has been a reliable spot for fresh seafood served with flair. The calamari vinaigrette appetizer is both tangy and crispy, a house specialty. For dinner there's cioppino, saltimbocca, chicken marsala, and risotto as well as the usual pasta favorites. The wine cellar boasts more than 500 bottles, with premium grappas, ports, and cognacs.

GELATO CLASSICO

$ DESSERT   ✉576 Union Street   ☎415-391-6667

Dessert in North Beach means Italian ice cream, and few places make it better than Gelato. Creamy and thick, Italian ice cream is made without air, so it's denser and more delicious than other ice cream. At Gelato Classico they also use fresh fruit and other natural ingredients to guarantee great taste. If you try it in summer, you can have fresh strawberry, blackberry, burgundy cherry, or raspberry. During the rest of the year, they serve a host of flavors ranging from coppa mista and banana to good old chocolate and vanilla (made, of course, from vanilla beans). *Viva Italia!*

CAPP'S CORNER

$$–$$$ ITALIAN   ✉1600 Powell Street   ☎415-989-2589   🖷415-989-2590
🖰www.cappscorner.com, cappscorner@netscape.net

At least once during a North Beach visit, you should dine at a family-style Italian restaurant. Dotted all around the neighborhood, these establishments have a local flavor unmatched by the area's chic new restaurants. A good choice is Capp's, a local landmark adorned with celebrity photos, more celebrity photos, and a few photos of celebrities. The prix-fixe dinner includes soup, salad, and an entrée. Among the dishes are osso buco, linguini with steamed mussels and clams, and lamb shanks.

Café Culture

The heart of North Beach beats in its cafés. Gathering places for local Italians, the neighborhood's coffee houses are also literary scenes. Step into any of the numerous cafés dotting the district and you're liable to hear an elderly Italian singing opera or see an aspiring writer with notebook in one hand and espresso cup in the other. The best North Beach breakfasts are the continental-style meals served in these cafés. But any time of day or night, you can order a croissant and cappuccino, lean back, and take in the human scenery.

Foremost among these people-watching posts is **Caffe Trieste** (601 Vallejo Street; 415-392-6739, fax 415-982-3045; www.caffetrieste.com), the old Beatnik rendezvous. Cash only.

You'll find heavenly homemade *tiramisu* and delicious espresso at **Caffe Puccini** (411 Columbus Avenue; 415-989-7033), a well-loved local spot. Decorated in classical decor, the café is named after the legendary composer of *Madame Butterfly* and *Tosca*. Cash only.

Right on Washington Square is **Mario's Bohemian Cigar Store Cafe** (566 Columbus Avenue; 415-362-0536). Known for outstanding panini sandwiches, this is the place to go for a quick bite and some local kitch. Finish your meal with a cappuccino and a slice of ricotta cheesecake.

HENRY'S HUNAN RESTAURANT

$ CHINESE ✉924 Sansome Street ✆415-956-7727
✎www.henryshunanrestaurant.com

The *New Yorker* once called Henry's "the best Chinese restaurant in the world." Those are pretty big words, hard to substantiate this side of Beijing. But it's certainly one of the best San Francisco has to offer. Understand now, we're talking cuisine, not ambience. The atmosphere is characterized by noise and crowds; there is a bar and a contemporary-style dining room adorned with color photographs. But the food will transport you to another land entirely. It's hot, spicy, and delicious. From the dining room you can watch masterful chefs working the woks, preparing pungent sauces, and serving up bean curds with meat sauce, Hunan scallops, and a host of other delectables.

SHOPPING

Shopping in North Beach is a grand escapade. As you browse the storefronts here, do like the Sicilians and keep an eye out for Italian treasures such as the hand-painted ceramics and colorful wallhangings still brightening many a home in old Italia.

CITY LIGHTS BOOKSTORE ✉261 Columbus Avenue ✆415-362-8193
✆415-362-4921 ✎www.citylights.com, staff@citylights.com This famous bookstore in North Beach stocks both the traditional and the avant-garde. Within the hallowed confines of this oddly shaped store is a treasure trove of magazines on arts and politics, plus books on everything from nirvana to the here and now.

BIORDI ART IMPORTS ✉*412 Columbus Avenue* ☎*415-392-8096* ✐*www. biordi.com, info@biordi.com* This impressive shop provides the Italian answer to gourmet living. Specializing in Italian ceramics, the place is loaded. There are hand-painted pitchers from Florence and De Simone folk art from Palermo, and hand-painted dinnerware, wall mirrors framed in ceramic fruit, hand-painted umbrella stands and other quality Italian Renaissance–style items. Walking through this singular shop is like browsing an Italian crafts fair. Closed Sunday.

DOUBLE PUNCH ✉*1821 Powell Street* ☎*415-399-9785* From the popular online toy house Ningyoushi comes this collector's dream, filled with special edition merchandise by the likes of Mark Ryden, Gary Baseman, and Jeremy Fish, as well as mainstream companies Hello Kitty and G.I. Joe. This quirky-chic boutique shop also holds art shows that feature contemporary artists.

101 MUSIC AND 101 BASEMENT These sister shops are just a few doors apart. You will find CDs and vinyl records at 101 Music (1414 Grant Avenue; 415-392-6369), while a hodgepodge of instruments, collectibles, and musical memorabilia await at 101 Basement (513 Green Street; 415-392-6368).

A. CAVALLI & COMPANY ✉*1441 Stockton Street* ☎*415-421-4219* No North Beach shopping spree would be complete without a visit to A. Cavalli. Operating since 1880, this family business caters to all sorts of local needs. They offer an assortment of Italian cookbooks as well as records and tapes ranging from Pavarotti to Italian new wave. Cavalli's also stocks Italian travel posters, Puccini opera prints, Italian movies on DVD, and magazines from Rome. Closed Sunday.

OOMA ✉*1422 Grant Avenue* ☎*415-627-6963* ✐*www.ooma.net* This store's name stands for "Objects of My Affection," and it's packed with affordable and trendy finds—flirty jersey skirts and dresses, trendy handbags, chic shoes, bright swimsuits, and a good selection of unusual jewelry. Stock changes frequently. Closed Monday.

NIGHTLIFE

North Beach, the old Beatnik quarter, is the area for slumming. It's door-to-door with local bars and nightclubs, not to mention the few topless and bottomless joints that still remain along Broadway.

VESUVIO CAFÉ

✉*255 Columbus Avenue* ☎*415-362-3370* ☎*415-362-1613* ✐*www.vesuvio. com* A diverse crowd packs the tables and barstools at this major North Beach scene, rich in soul and history. The place hasn't changed much since the Beat poets haunted it during the days of Eisenhower, Kerouac, Corso, Ginsberg, and the crew spent their nights here and their days next door at City Lights Bookstore.

SPEC'S TWELVE ADLER MUSEUM CAFÉ

✉ *12 Adler Place* ☎ *415-421-4112* Spec's is another bohemian haunt. There's nary a bald spot on the walls of this literary hangout; they're covered with all manner of mementos from bumperstickers to a "walrus' penis bone." A great place to get metaphysical.

SAN FRANCISCO BREWING COMPANY ✉ *155 Columbus Avenue*

☎ *415-434-3344* ✐ *www.sfbrewing.com, brewmaster@sfbrewing.com* To step uptown, just walk down the hill to this historic brewery. Built the year after the 1906 earthquake, it's a mahogany-paneled beauty with glass lamps and punkah wallah fans. Legend tells that Jack Dempsey once worked here as a bouncer. It's also the first pub in San Francisco to brew its own beer on the premises. Live jazz several nights a week.

MOJITOS ✉ *1337 Grant Avenue* ☎ *415-398-1120* This wide-open bar with

bright murals and a small dancefloor, offers low-priced drinks and tapas in a lively, Latin American atmosphere. A deejay spins a mix of hip-hop, '80s rock, and Cuban music all night. Locals crowd the place on Tuesdays for the $2 Tuesday menu specials.

CLUB FUGAZI ✉ *678 Green Street (Beach Blanket Babylon Boulevard)* ☎ *415-421-*

4222 ✐ *www.beachblanketbabylon.com, bbb@beachblanketbabylon.com* This club features an outlandish musical revue, *Steve Silver's Beach Blanket Babylon*, which has been running since 1973 (although the script is frequently updated with contemporary pop- and political-culture spoofs). The scores and choreography are good, but the costumes are great. The hats—elaborate, multilayered confections—make Carmen Miranda's adornments look like Easter bonnets. Cover. Closed Monday and Tuesday.

THE BOARDROOM ✉ *1609 Powell Street* ☎ *415-982-8898* If you weren't

actually on your way here, you might walk right past the unassuming front door nestled between two apartment gates. But it's well worth stopping at this neighborhood spot, especially on Tuesday night when they have a rousing game of trivia. Weekends are popular with the sports crowds; the four large-screen TVs are dedicated to college and pro matches. Known for its welcoming bartenders and cheap fish tacos, the Boardroom is a perfect lair for enjoying a beer or unwinding with friends.

BIMBO'S 365 CLUB ✉ *1025 Columbus Avenue* ☎ *415-474-0365* ✐ *www.*

bimbos365club.com This snazzy North Beach institution, jamming since 1951, showcases an eclectic mix of live music from jazz and rock to French pop. Call for a list of events. Cover.

FISHERMAN'S WHARF

Places have a way of becoming parodies of themselves—particularly if they possess a personal resonance and beauty or have some unique feature to lend the landscape. People, it seems, have an unquenchable need to change them.

Such is the fate of Fisherman's Wharf. Back in the 19th century, a proud fishing fleet berthed in these waters and the shoreline was a quiltwork of brick factories, metal canning sheds, and woodframe warehouses. Genoese fishermen with rope-muscled arms set out in triangular-sailed *feluccas* that were a joke to the west wind. They had captured the waterfront from the Chinese and would be supplanted in turn by Sicilians. They caught sand dabs, sea bass, rock cod, bay shrimp, king salmon, and Dungeness crab. Salt caked their hands, wind and sun gullied their faces.

Today the woodplanked waterfront named for their occupation is hardly a place for fishermen. It has become "Tourist's Wharf," a bizarre assemblage of shopping malls and penny arcades that make Disneyland look like the real world. The old waterfront is an amusement park with a wax gallery, a Ripley's museum, and numerous trinket shops. The architecture subscribes to that modern school which makes everything look like what it's not—there's pseudo-Mission, ready-made antique Victorian, and simulated falsefront.

But salt still stirs the air here and fog fingers through the Bay. There are sights to visit along "the Wharf." It's a matter of recapturing the past while avoiding the plastic-coated present. To do that you need to follow a basic law of the sea—hug the shoreline.

SIGHTS

PIER 39   On the corner of Embarcadero and Beach Street, this pier is an elaborately laid-out shopping mall catering primarily to tourists who spill over from neighboring Fisherman's Wharf. In addition to a plethora of waterfront shops and restaurants, Pier 39 features jugglers, yo-yo champs, and other entertainers who delight the crowd with their sleight of hand.

SEA LIONS   ☎415-289-7330 ☏415-289-7333 ✒www.tmmc.org, edu@tmmc.org
The central attraction at Pier 39 is the colony of sea lions that has taken up residence on the nearby docks. Numbering 400 at times, these thousand-pound pinnipeds are a cross between sea slugs and sumo wrestlers. They began arriving in 1989, taking over a marina, causing a ruckus, and creating the greatest stench this side of a sardine factory. But when Pier 39 attracted over 10 million people the next year, placing it behind Orlando's Walt Disney World and Anaheim's Disneyland as the most popular tourist spot in the country, the local merchants decided to welcome the smelly squatters as permanent residents. On weekends, you can join docents from the Marine Mammal Center for free educational talks about the sea lion's habitat. Meet at the K Dock at Pier 39's west marina. Reservations required.

AQUARIUM OF THE BAY   ✉Pier 39 ☎415-623-5300, 888-732-3483 ☏415-623-5324 ✒www.aquariumofthebay.com, info@aquariumofthebay.com   For an up-close look at other residents of the San Francisco Bay, including sharks and fish, go to this bright aquarium. Journey along moving walkways

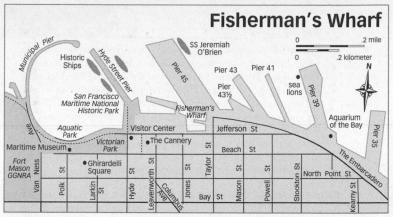

Fisherman's Wharf

through a 300-foot-long transparent tunnel into two giant two-story tanks. These tanks contain rays, salmon, crabs, jellyfish, eels, and more than 150 examples of the six shark species found in surrounding waters. Touch live seastars and other shoreline creatures in the Touch the Bay area. Admission.

FORBES ISLAND ✉Pier 39 ✆415-951-4900 ✐www.forbesisland.com Among Pier 39's attractions is this ten-foot-long fantasyland complete with live palm trees, a white-sand beach, a waterfall, and a 40-foot-tall lighthouse with an observation deck. This self-propelled 700-ton motor vessel in disguise offers dishes like roasted rack of lamb with artichokes and olives. Closed Monday and Tuesday. Admission.

PIER 45 Farther west from Pier 39 is this working wharf, bleached with bird dung and frequented by fishing boats. From here it's a short jog to the docks on Jefferson Street, located between Jones and Taylor streets. The remnants of San Francisco's fishing fleet lies gunnel to gunnel here. The *Nicky-J, Wacky Jacky, Butchy B, Phu Quy, Hai Tai Loc*, and an admiralty of others cast off every morning around 4 a.m. to return in late afternoon. With their brightly painted hulls, Christmas tree rigging, and roughhewn crews, they carry the odor and clamor of the sea.

MUSÉE MÉCANIQUE ✉Pier 45 ✆415-346-2000 ✐www.museemechanique. org At the intersection of Taylor Street and the Embarcadero is this museum that houses a collection of vintage mechanical amusements dating to a simpler time. You can still put in your change and see them do their thing.

S.S. JEREMIAH O'BRIEN ✆415-544-0100 📠415-544-9890 ✐www.ss jeremiahobrien.org, liberty@ssjeremiahobrien.org Docked at Pier 45 at the Embarcadero is one of two 2751 World War II Liberty Ships still remaining in original condition (the other is docked in Baltimore). A beamy hulk, the *Jeremiah O'Brien* numbers among its combat ribbons the D-Day invasion of Normandy. Visitors may walk the decks of the old vessel, explore the sailors' quarters, descend into the depths of the engine room, and chat with a volunteer crew member. Call ahead for tour information. Admission.

84

FISH ALLEY _____

This nostalgic nook is tucked into the narrow corridor next to Castagnola's Restaurant on Jefferson Street toward Scoma's Restaurant. Those corrugated metal sheds lining the docks are fish-packing operations. The fleet deposits its daily catch here to be processed for delivery to restaurants and markets. This is an area of piers and pilings, hooks and hawsers, flotsam and fish scales, where you pay a price to recapture the past: as you work farther into this network of docks, approaching nearer and nearer the old salty truths, you'll also be overwhelmed by the putrefying stench of the surrounding businesses.

SAN FRANCISCO MARITIME NATIONAL HISTORICAL PARK
☎415-447-5000 📠415-556-1624 ✎www.nps.gov/safr For a breather, it's not far to the Hyde Street Pier, where history is less offensive to the nose. Here you'll find this historical park with historic ships docked along the pier. You can board the _Eureka_, an 1890 paddlewheeler that ferried commuters between San Francisco and Sausalito for almost 30 years. Recently the largest floating wooden structure on earth, it served as police headquarters for the crime-fighting crew on TV's now-defunct "Nash Bridges." To walk this pier is to stride back to San Francisco's waterfront at the turn of the 20th century. The _Eppleton Hall_ is an old paddlewheeler and the _Alma_ a "scow schooner" with a flat bottom and square beam. A three-masted merchant ship built in Scotland in 1886, the _Balclutha_ measures 301 feet. This steel-hulled craft sailed around Cape Horn 17 times in her youth. She loaded rice in Rangoon, guano in Callao, and wool in New Zealand. Today the old ship's cargo boasts exhibits and a hold full of memories. Stop by the Small Boat Shop and watch volunteers work on restoration projects or try your hand at knot-tying and block-and-tackle work. A visitors center is located across from the Hyde Street Pier. Admission to board the ships.

SAN FRANCISCO MARITIME MUSEUM ✉Beach and Polk streets
☎415-447-5000 📠415-556-1624 ✎www.nps.gov/safr This nearby maritime museum, which looks like a ferryboat run aground, is actually an Art-Deco building designed to resemble the bridge of a passenger liner complete with wildly colorful murals along the first floor. Onboard there's a weird collection of body parts from old ships plus models, scrimshaw displays, and a magnificent photo collection. But perhaps the neatest exhibit is "Sparks, Waves and Wizards." Using a live feed from the U.S. Coast Guard, visitors can use a telescope to spot a vessel entering the Golden Gate, find the ship on a computer screen, and with a click of a button pull up all sorts of information, from vessel speed to cargo contents. The museum is closed until 2009 for extensive renovations.

AQUATIC PARK All these nautical showpieces are anchored in this lovely lawn that rolls down to one of the Bay's few sandy beaches. A mélange of sounds and spectacles, the park has a bocce ball court where you'll encounter old Italian men exchanging stories and curiously eyeing the tourists. There are street vendors galore. If that's not enough,

84

you can watch the Powell and Hyde Street cable cars being turned around for their steep climb back up Nob Hill. Or catch an eye-boggling glimpse of San Francisco Bay. Alcatraz lies anchored offshore, back-dropped by one of the prettiest panoramas in this part of the world.

THE CANNERY ✉Jefferson and Leavenworth streets ☎415-771-3112 Of course, no tour of Fisherman's Wharf is complete without a stop at this 1907 brick warehouse converted into a shopping center with 30 specialty shops.

GHIRARDELLI SQUARE ✉900 North Point Street ☎800-877-9338 ✐www. ghiradellisq.com Be sure to stop at this former site of the chocolate factory, which has been converted into an open-air shopping courtyard. For more information, see "Shopping" below.

LODGING

Fisherman's Wharf contains more hotels than fishermen. Most facilities here are overpriced and undernourished. I'm only going to mention a few, since I think you'll do much better financially and experience San Francisco more fully in a downtown or neighborhood hotel.

THE WHARF INN
$$$ 51 ROOMS   ✉2601 Mason Street   ☎415-673-7411, 877-275-7889 ☎415-776-2181 ✐www.wharfinn.com, info@wharfinn.com
This four-story affair has moderate-size rooms at decent prices. Unlike its nearby competitors, free onsite parking is included. The place is clean and bright, offering the same type of facility you could have downtown at a lesser cost. In an area of pricey hotels, The Wharf Inn has some of the best rates around.

SHERATON FISHERMAN'S WHARF
$$$$ 531 ROOMS   ✉2500 Mason Street   ☎415-362-5500, 800-325-3535 ☎415-956-5275 ✐www.sheratonatthewharf.com
This sprawling facility features spacious rooms tastefully furnished in contemporary, sophisticated fashions, plus room service and nightly turndown service. The hotel has other alluring features like a bright, colorful entranceway, liveried doormen, swimming pool, and an attractive gift shop.

HYATT AT FISHERMAN'S WHARF
$$$$ 313 ROOMS   ✉555 North Point Street   ☎415-563-1234, 800-233-1234 ☎415-749-6122 ✐www.fishermanswharfhyatt.com
The Hyatt is a luxury retreat that is faced in antique brick and illuminated through skylights. It comes complete with a pool, a spa, and a fitness center.

TUSCAN INN BEST WESTERN
$$$–$$$$ 221 ROOMS   ✉425 North Point Street   ☎415-561-1100, 800-648-4626 ☎415-561-1199 ✐www.tuscaninn.com
This Italian-style boutique hotel features a garden court and an Italianate lobby complete with fireplace. The rooms here are richly decorated and intimate. Pet-friendly.

ARGONAUT HOTEL

$$$–$$$$ 265 ROOMS   ✉495 Jefferson Street   ☎415-563-0800, 866-415-0704   📠415-563-2800   🖅www.argonauthotel.com

If you're looking for a place with a little more history, try the Argonaut. Housed in the old Haslet warehouse and built in 1907 to store canned goods, this four-story building takes its nautical theme to the limit: a steamer-like front desk, wooden plank floors, and yellow and deep blue hues dominate the decor. It can be a bit much, but certainly adds to the experience. Some rooms feature great views of Alcatraz Island or the Golden Gate Bridge; the Maritime National Historical Park Visitors Center and Interactive Museum is located adjacent to the lobby. Evening wine reception included.

DINING

Dining at Fisherman's Wharf usually means spending money at Fisherman's Wharf. The neighborhood's restaurants are overpriced and overtouristed. If you look hard enough, however, it's possible to find a good meal at a fair price in a fashionable restaurant.

SEAFOOD COCKTAIL STANDS

$ SEAFOOD   ✉Jefferson Street

The easiest way to dine is right on the street. An old wharf tradition, these curbside vendors began years ago feeding bay fishermen. Today they provide visitors an opportunity to sample local catches like crab, shrimp, and calamari.

BOUDIN BAKERY

$$ BAKERY   ✉156 Jefferson Street   ☎415-928-1849   📠415-351-5577

A San Francisco favorite, sourdough bread, can be tasted at this Bay Area bakery chain. A pungent French bread particularly popular in seafood restaurants, sourdough is the staff of life in these parts. Boudin Bakery, founded in 1849, has had plenty of time to fit its recipe perfectly to the local palate.

EAGLE CAFÉ

$–$$ AMERICAN/SEAFOOD   ✉Pier 39   ☎415-433-3689   📠415-434-9253   🖅www.eaglecafe.com

This old-time restaurant is so much a part of San Francisco that plans to tear the place down years ago occasioned a public outcry. Instead of flattening the old woodframe building, they lifted it—lock, stock, and memories—and moved it to the second floor of the Pier 39 shopping mall. Today it looks like an ostrich at a beauty pageant, a plain all-American café surrounded by glittering tourist shops. The walls are covered with faded black-and-white photos, Eagle baseball caps, and other memorabilia. Actually, the bar is more popular than the restaurant. Who wants to eat when they can drink to old San Francisco? The bar is open all day and into the night.

BUTTERFLY

$$$–$$$$ CALIFORNIA CUISINE/ASIAN ✉Pier 33 ☎415-864-8999
🖰www.butterflysf.com, info@butterflysf.com

The excellent food here is California-Asian fusion (think *kalua* pig with butter lettuce cups and hoisin barbecue sauce) while the decor is cool and modern, studded with glass and views of the bay. Live jazz or dee-jay music accompanies your meal.

CAFE FRANCISCO

$ AMERICAN/CONTINENTAL ✉2161 Powell Street ☎415-397-2602
🖰www.cafefrancisco.com, ziadcf@cafefrancisco.com

Situated between the Wharf and North Beach, this café enjoys the best of both worlds—it's strolling distance from the water and possesses a bohemian flair. A great place for light and inexpensive meals, this trendy café serves salads and sandwiches for lunch. Breakfast at the espresso bar ranges from a continental repast to bacon and eggs. Decorated with changing exhibits by local artists, it attracts a neighborhood crowd.

ALIOTO'S

$$–$$$ SEAFOOD ✉#8 Fisherman's Wharf (Taylor and Jefferson streets)
☎415-673-0183 🖰www.aliotos.com

This San Francisco staple started as a fresh fish stall in 1925, added a seafood bar in 1932, and is still one of the best places to pick up fresh crab and shrimp cocktails. Upstairs, diners choose a just-caught fish special served with veggies and hot sourdough. The tiramisu and the view of the bay are delicious.

SCOMA'S

$$$–$$$$ SEAFOOD ✉Pier 47 on Al Scoma Way; Near the foot of Jones Street ☎415-771-4383, 800-644-5852 📠415-775-2601
🖰www.scomas.com, seafood@scomas.com

Would you believe a hidden restaurant in tourist-mobbed Fisherman's Wharf? Scoma's is the place. Seafood is the password to this chummy restaurant. There's *cioppino alla pescatore*, a Sicilian-style broth; *calamone alla anna*, squid prepared "in a totally different manner," or just plain old sole, snapper, shrimp, or scallops. There's lobster tail, too, and Dungeness crab.

RESTAURANT GARY DANKO

$$$$ SEAFOOD ✉800 North Point Street ☎415-749-2060 📠415-775-1805
🖰www.garydanko.com, info@garydanko.com

Dinner at this top-rated restaurant in the current Zagat guide, is an extravaganza. The eponymous owner, who once built stage sets, envisions each evening as a "performance" featuring a "multi-act meal." The restaurant setting is certainly dramatic enough—with contemporary paintings on taupe walls and a decor that combines oak panels, plantation-style shutters, and pin-spot lights to create an intimate but active atmosphere. The seasonal cuisine focuses on freshness and includes signature dishes like lamb loin and roast lobster. They also boast an exceptional wine cellar, special tea service, and a granite cheese cart for which they are renowned. It's a special place for special occasions. Highly recommended. Dinner only.

MCCORMICK & KULETO'S

$$–$$$ SEAFOOD   ✉ *Ghirardelli Square, 900 North Point Street*   ☎ *415-929-1730,*
888-344-6861   ✎ *www.mccormickandkuletos.com*

Crisp, clean, and classy is the way to describe this popular seafood restaurant in Ghirardelli Square. Natural woods predominate, white tablecloths adorn the tables, and faux tortoiseshell lamps hang from the high ceilings, but the focus of attention is the incredible view of the bay from the floor-to-ceiling windows. The extensive menu changes daily depending on what fish is available and may include such specialties as crab cakes, seafood pastas, cashew-crusted tilapia, and Atlantic salmon stuffed with crab, shrimp, and Brie. There's also a very lengthy wine list.

ALBONA RISTORANTE ISTRIANO

$$$ ITALIAN   ✉ *545 Francisco Street*   ☎ *415-441-1040*   📠 *415-441-5107*

This high-heeled hole-in-the-wall is a small but fashionable restaurant that features Venetian and Central European dishes. The interior is a mélange of beveled mirrors, white linen tablecloths, burgundy banquettes, and fresh flowers. The menu, not to be upstaged, includes sauerkraut braised with prosciutto, pan-fried gnocchi, and exotic entrées like braised rabbit with juniper berries and *brodetto de pesse a la istriana* (fish stew). Valet parking is available. Dinner only. Closed Sunday and Monday.

SHOPPING

Fisherman's Wharf is a shopper's paradise . . . if you know what you're doing. If not, it's a fool's paradise. This heavily touristed district houses a mazelike collection of shops, malls, arcades, and galleries. Most of them specialize in high-priced junk. How someone can arrive in the world's most splendid city and carry away some trashy trinket to commemorate their visit is beyond me. But they do. Since you're certainly not the type searching out an "I Got Crabs at Fisherman's Wharf" T-shirt, the best course is to go where the natives shop.

STREET VENDOR STALLS   For locally crafted goods, be sure to watch for the street vendor stalls. Located along Beach Street between Hyde and Larkin, and on side streets throughout the area, they offer hand-fashioned wares with homemade price tags. You'll find jewelry, leather belts, statuary, framed photos of the bay city, tie-dye shirts, kites, and anything else the local imagination can conjure.

PIER 39   ✉ *Embarcadero and Beach Street*   ☎ *415-981-7437*   ✎ *www.pier39.com*
Though its wooden boardwalks and clapboard buildings look promising, this isn't the place for bargains or antiques. It's a haven for tourists and features gift stores that range from cutesy card shops to places selling ceramic unicorns. There are restaurants and stores galore, plus an amusement arcade. Kids often enjoy the carnival atmosphere here.

My main objection is to the ticky-tacky shops. Every year, however, millions of tourists disagree with me. They flock to this two-tiered mall, popping in and out of the more than 110 shops and enjoying the ersatz early-20th-century atmosphere.

THE GOLDEN GATE NATIONAL PARK STORE ✉*Pier 39* ☎*415-433-7221* One noteworthy exception to Pier 39's tourist-oriented selection of shops is this national park store, the only bookshop I know that comes with a view of sea lions basking in the sun. It offers a complete selection of travel, hiking, and wildlife books and also sells educational toys, and other gifts.

COST PLUS WORLD MARKET ✉*2552 Taylor Street* ☎*415-928-6200* ✍*www.costplusworldmarket.com* Before people buy anything in the City, they come to this internationally themed store and see if they can find it here. If so, it's cheaper; if not, maybe they don't really need it. You'll find ceramics, wallhangings, and a host of other items.

THE CANNERY ✉*Jefferson and Leavenworth streets* ☎*415-771-3112* ✍*www. thecannery.com, info@thecannery. com* Another popular spot among San Franciscans is this old brick canning factory. Thanks to innovative architects, The Cannery has been transformed into a tri-level marketplace dotted with interesting shops. The central plaza, with its olive trees and potted flowers, contains picnic tables, several cafés, and snack kiosks, and features free daily entertainment. Among the dozens of shops are many selling handcrafted originals.

GHIRARDELLI SQUARE ✉*900 North Point Street* ☎*800-877-9338* ✍*www. ghirardellisq.com, info@ghirardellisq.com* Chocoholics will be delighted to discover the home of Ghirardelli chocolate. This early 20th–century factory is another example of old industrial architecture being turned to contemporary uses. Around the factory's antique chocolate-making machines are myriad shops varying from designer outlets to sundry stores. There are also import stores, boutiques, and a creamery where you can order your favorite ice cream creation with gobs of Ghirardelli chocolate on top.

So there you have the secret of shopping Fisherman's Wharf: simply ignore everything else and beeline between the street vendors, Cost Plus, The Cannery, and that brick-red chocolate factory.

NIGHTLIFE

EAGLE CAFÉ ✉*Pier 39* ☎*415-433-3689* This café appears like some strange bird that has landed in the wrong roost. All around lies touristville, polished and preening, while the Eagle remains old and crusty, filled with waterfront characters. Old photos and baseball caps adorn the walls, and in the air hang age-old memories.

LOU'S PIER 47 RESTAURANT AND BLUES CLUB ✉*300 Jefferson Street* ☎*415-771-5687* ✍*www.louspier47.com, louspier47@yahoo.com* Don't know any local people, but still like to party? Head to Lou's, have a meal, and dance the afternoon and night away. For eats, there are sandwiches, burgers, pastas, and fried, grilled, or sautéed fish and seafood. The bands that play each week in the glass-enclosed nightclub upstairs play mostly rhythm-and-blues but you can also hear Motown and light rock occasionally. The music begins around 4 p.m. daily. Cover.

BUENA VISTA CAFÉ ✉ *2765 Hyde Street* 📞 *415-474-5044* Situated near Fisherman's Wharf, this pub is popular with local folks and tourists alike. There's a fine old bar and friendly atmosphere, and the place claims to have introduced America to the Irish coffee.

RUSSIAN HILL

Among the city's better-kept secrets is a tumbling residential area called Russian Hill. According to legend, the neighborhood's vaulting slopes were once the site of a cemetery for Russian seal hunters. The Russians have long since departed, leaving the district to local folks and a few canny travelers.

SIGHTS

GEORGE STERLING PARK

This park, honoring the poet who named San Francisco the "cool grey city of love," stands at the southwest corner of Lombard and Hyde streets. Its wooded stone walkways and sunny tennis courts are a cool counterpoint to the surrounding cityscape. They're also a prelude to the trip down Lombard Street.

LOMBARD STREET There's a single block amid Russian Hill's checkerboard streets that stands out in the public imagination. Located between Hyde and Leavenworth, it has earned for Lombard the sobriquet of "The Crookedest Street in the World." (The nearby block where Filbert Street plummets from Hyde to Leavenworth is the steepest street in the city.) Whether this block represents the planet's most serpentine road remains to be measured; it is certainly the street most congested with shutter-snapping visitors.

Visitors come from around the world to stand astride Lombard's crest and take in the postcard views that stretch in several directions. The western window opens onto the Presidio's wooded expanse; to the north are moored the old ships of Hyde Street Pier and just offshore, Alcatraz Island; eastward rises Telegraph Hill, crowned by Coit Tower and backdropped by Yerba Buena Island.

This dizzying descent happens to be along a beautifully landscaped street. The brick-paved road winds around hedgerows and banks of hydrangea bushes; at the corners, where zig gives way to zag, trees have been planted. You'll have to see for yourself: It's one of those places so cluttered with tourists you never want to admit visiting, but so beautiful you don't want to miss it.

MACONDRAY LANE

Heaven always seems to evoke images of pearl-encrusted gates and shimmering white boulevards. One hopes the saintly place possesses a few country paths as well. If so, they'll undoubtedly be modeled on Macondray Lane. To those who wish a preview of eternal life, Macondray waits off Jones between Green and Union streets. For a solitary block, its cobblestone path leads through a garden, then opens onto a wooden staircase overlooking the Bay. You enter a tunnel of greenery, walled on one side with shingle houses and on the other with an ivy-embowered hillside. It's a realm of flower pots and fluttering birds, one of San Francisco's secret and magical walks.

VALLEJO STREET   Lombard Street represents only one of Russian Hill's two crests. Tourists jam the first, while literary historians know the second. To join the cognoscenti, travel up Vallejo Street to the 1000 block. Together with Russian Hill Place and Florence Street, nearby cul-de-sacs, this enclave was a gathering place for 19th-century writers. Ambrose Bierce, Frank Norris, and a sheaf of other California authors were part of the area's famous salon. The beauty they sought can be found among the Mediterranean-style haciendas lining **Russian Hill Place**, and the Pueblo Revival houses that have taken over **Florence Street**.

In 1893, Willis Polk, the master architect for whom Polk Street is named, designed and occupied the gingerbread brown-shingle house at **1013–1019 Vallejo Street**. A few things have been added to the Bay view that Polk enjoyed. Today it sweeps from Fisherman's Wharf to Coit Tower to San Francisco's skyscrapers. Nor did Polk have the steps that lead down Vallejo Street's eastern flank one block to **Ina Coolbrith Park** at Vallejo and Taylor streets. This steep swath of green was named for the Oakland librarian who helped a young fellow named Jack London find his way around the literary world.

UNION STREET

People go to Union Street for two reasons—shopping and singles bars. Sightseeing is an afterthought. The fact of the matter, however, is that many of the district's trendy shops are housed in magnificent Victorians. So sightseeing can become a case of shopping in architectural wonders.

SIGHTS

OCTAGON HOUSE ⊠ *2645 Gough Street* ☎ *415-441-7512* Built in 1861, this eight-sided heirloom is capped with a turret. The National Society of Colonial Dames of America, which runs the old place, opens it to the public on the second and fourth Thursdays and second Sunday of each month (except January) from noon until 3 p.m.

The park next door, with its easy slope and tall timber, is a lone remnant from the days when Union Street was "Cow Hollow." Thirty dairies once operated from this grassy dale. What is today the sidewalk of Union Street was then the shoreline of "Washerwoman's Lagoon," a small lake where housewives gathered on laundry day.

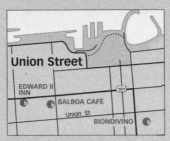

EDWARD II INN

PAGE 93

English-style B&B luxury with well-appointed rooms and complimentary sherry

BALBOA CAFÉ

PAGE 95

California cuisine since 1914: calamari *fritti*, pork chops, and New York steak with warm brass and oak decor

BIONDIVINO

PAGE 96

Chic, sophisticated stop for over 490 bottles and hard-to-find vintages from Italy, Austria, and Slovenia

TWIN WEDDING HOUSES The structure at 1980 Union Street gained a mark on the map when an eccentric father built this Siamese twin of a house for his two daughters. It seems they were newlyweds needing dowries, who soon found themselves cozily ensconced in these Twin Wedding Houses.

1923–1929 UNION STREET Actually, a grander example of the Victorian-in-a-mirror can be seen in the imposing pair of houses across the street from the Twin Wedding Houses.

VENDANTA TEMPLE ✉*2963 Webster Street* This temple is another structural curiosity. No, it wasn't levitated here from Moscow. It was built on the spot to celebrate the Hindu religion. At the risk of trying to portray the indescribable, it's a sprawling three-story house, maroon and gray, capped with several towers. One tower sports battlements, another a bulbous dome, and yet another a cluster of cupolas.

EPISCOPAL CHURCH OF ST. MARY THE VIRGIN ✉*2325 Union Street* ☎*415-921-3665* 🖷*415-921-6194* 🖱*www.smvsf.org* Don't neglect the brick courtyard of this church, where there's a fresco by a student of Diego Rivera. Graced with a garden and wood-shingled church, St. Mary's also has a fountain. A very special fountain. It's actually a spring where early dairy farmers watered their herds back in Cow Hollow days.

CASEBOLT HOUSE ✉*2727 Pierce Street* This historic house is the last link in this chain of architectural jewels. With two magnificent palm trees guarding the entranceway and a flanking retinue of willows, it presents an imposing sight. Dating from 1865, it was built in an Italian-ate style; today the ornate white edifice, set on a rise above the street, is as grand as it was back in California's younger days.

Amid elegant shops and Victorian homes are some of San Francisco's stateliest bed-and-breakfast inns.

HOTEL DEL SOL

$$$ 68 UNITS ✉3100 Webster Street ✆415-921-5520, 877-433-5765
✆415-931-4137 ✎www.thehoteldelsol.com

An affordable and hip hotel in the Marina just three blocks from Union Street? Yes, Virginia, it does exist. Formerly a '50s-style motor lodge, this hotel uses vibrant colors to re-create the feel of a California beach house. Lounge around the courtyard pool, browse the pillow-lending library (yes, pillow-lending), or borrow the hotel's stash of sports equipment and beach balls to entertain the kids. Fifty-seven guest rooms, ten one-bedroom suites (three with kitchenettes, two with fireplaces), and one family suite complete with trundle beds, toys, and board games are available. Continental breakfast included.

UNION STREET INN

$$$$ 6 ROOMS ✉2229 Union Street ✆415-346-0424 ✆415-922-8046
✎www.unionstreetinn.com, innkeeper@unionstreetinn.com

The emphasis at this hostelry is on personalized service. Guests are often served full breakfast in the garden, an urban oasis of fruit trees and flowering plants. The rooms are quite cozy, grandly decorated, and imaginatively furnished. The Golden Gate Room features burgundy decor. Cherrywood armchairs cluster around an oriental rug and the bed is covered with a quilted spread and topped by a canopy. The "carriage house," a cottage snugly set in the garden, and two other rooms feature private jacuzzis.

EDWARD II INN _____ hidden

$$$ 30 ROOMS ✉3155 Scott Street ✆415-922-3000, 800-473-2846
✆415-931-5784 ✎www.edwardii.com, innkeeper@edwardii.com

"Ours is an attempt to return to the original B&B concept popularized in Britain: a modest room at a practical price." The proprietors here have fully realized their motto. Taking the old Hotel Edward, which provided accommodations for the nearby Panama–Pacific International Exposition of 1915, they transformed it into the 30-room (four of which are suites) Edward II. In the process they provided an opportunity for guests to enjoy bed-and-breakfast luxury at a lower cost. The room I saw was English in decor and included such features as quilted bedspread and a dresser with beveled mirror; the bathroom was tiled and trimmed in wood. Guests enjoy a complimentary continental breakfast and evening sherry. While I highly recommend this facility, I also advise that you ask for a room in back, away from noisy Lombard Street.

MARINA MOTEL

$$ 39 UNITS   ✉ *2576 Lombard Street*   📞 *415-921-9406, 800-346-6118*
📠 *415-921-0364*   🖥 *www.marinamotel.com, marinamotel@value.net*

Among the many motels lining busy Lombard Street, only this one seems to possess character; others are part of the mondo condo world. The Marina is located near a noisy thoroughfare, but most guest rooms are set back off the street. This 39-unit motel resembles a white adobe structure with the clean and tidy rooms surrounding a flower-filled courtyard. About half have kitchens, while all have fridges, private garages, and wi-fi. Dogs are welcome in certain rooms.

DINING

PANE E VINO

$$ ITALIAN   ✉ *1715 Union Street*   📞 *415-441-2111*   📠 *415-346-2111*
🖥 *www.paneevinotrattoria.com*

This unassuming little spot consistently turns out tasty thin-crust pizzas and pasta dishes that satisfy the need for a simple, inexpensive dinner. Fresh grilled fish and meats are also on the menu, along with a delightful dessert, *mela caramellata* (a huge baked apple with caramelized brown sugar, served with chilled sour cream and almond sauce). Service is relaxed but spot-on. High ceilings, a big brick pizza oven and open dining room with white linens on the tables give it a rustic, yet elegant atmosphere. In nice weather, the walled garden patio is a big favorite. Dinner only.

LUISA'S

$$–$$$ ITALIAN   ✉ *1851 Union Street*   📞 *415-563-4043*

Romantic candlelight and hanging Chianti bottles create an inviting ambience at Luisa's. The cuisine is Italian with the accent on dishes such as linguine with calamari and osso buco. There are numerous pasta dishes along with homemade gnocchi and bread. Dinner only.

PERRY'S UNION STREET

$$$ AMERICAN   ✉ *1944 Union Street*   📞 *415-922-9022*   📠 *415-922-0843*
🖥 *www.perryssf.com, unionstreet@perryssf.com*

Hankering for good food and the feel of an Upper East Side bar? Try Perry's. Their menu runs the gamut from grilled ahi tuna sandwiches to meatloaf and chicken enchiladas, with more traditional American fare dominating the selection. Wednesday and Saturday nights mean "Lobster Madness" (one and a quarter pounds of fresh Maine catch for a reasonable price) and crowds, so make reservations. You might also enjoy their weekend brunch, especially if you secure a coveted spot outside.

LEFT AT ALBUQUERQUE

$$ SOUTHWESTERN   ✉ *2140 Union Street*   📞 *415-749-6700*   🖥 *www.leftatalb.com*

A casual, airy place with floor-to-ceiling windows, this spot draws a big crowd every night. The chef fire-roasts chiles and vegetables each day for the sauces and salsas, and makes dessert fresh each morning. Servings are huge and meant to be shared with a zingy margarita, made from one of the more than 75 different tequilas and mescal potions behind the bar. The Hatch chile *relleno* is a fluffy masterpiece and the

Navajo chicken stack blends white-meat chicken, beans, cheese, salsa, and fry bread into a memorable treat.

BALBOA CAFÉ

$$$ CALIFORNIA CUISINE   ✉3199 Fillmore Street   ☎415-921-3944
📠415-921-3957   🖳www.balboacafe.com, balboa@plumpjack.com

The history of this café is almost as rich as its brass, oak, and stained-glass interior. In operation since 1914, it specializes in California cuisine. The menu varies from lunch to dinner, and includes fresh fish, pork chops, and New York steak. There are appetizers like warm spinach salad and calamari *fritti*. A splendid restaurant.

BRAZEN HEAD

$$–$$$ CONTINENTAL   ✉3166 Buchanan Street   ☎415-921-7600   📠415-921-0164
🖳www.brazenheadsf.com

Check out this cozy spot for an intimate pub setting. Its low ceiling, deep woodwork, and burgundy carpeting make it a warm getaway from any lingering SF fog. Meat is the standard fare here, and those who like solid Continental dishes will get their fill. There's an extensive wine list and full bar. Dinner only.

JUDY'S CAFÉ

$–$$ AMERICAN/DINER   ✉2268 Chestnut Street   ☎415-922-4588   📠415-922-0149
🖳www.chestnutshop.com

Over on Chestnut Street, a few blocks from the chic Union Street corridor, you'll find Judy's. As the local crowds flowing in here every day attest, it's an excellent choice. Judy's is small, intimate, and decorated with signed artwork. There's sidewalk dining where you can enjoy a lunch menu that features sandwiches and omelette specials. Judy's also offers breakfast and Sunday brunch. No dinner.

YUKOL PLACE THAI CUISINE

$$ THAI   ✉2380 Lombard Street   ☎415-922-1599

For inexpensive Asian food, try this yummy place. The dinner menu includes fried mussels with chile, ginger chicken, and sautéed pork. It's a comfortable restaurant. Dinner only.

RISTORANTE PARMA

$$ ITALIAN   ✉3314 Steiner Street   ☎415-567-0500   📠415-567-0457

This tiny place is decorated with mirrored walls and leatherette banquettes, and serves popular southern European dishes nightly. Offerings range from eggplant scallopine, stuffed veal, and saltimbocca to prawns in garlic and lemon-butter sauce or baked petrale. Closed Sunday.

MEL'S DRIVE IN

$–$$ DINER   ✉2165 Lombard Street   ☎415-921-3039   📠415-921-3521
🖳www.melsdrive-in.com

For all-American eats, check out this classic '50s-style joint with push-button jukeboxes and posters of vintage cars. I don't have to tell you we're talking burgers, hot dogs, and chili here. For something more substantial, try the meat loaf or a "ground round plate." And don't forget a side of "lumpy mashed potatoes" or "wet fries" (with gravy). Open 24 hours Friday and Saturday.

LA FOLIE

$$$$ FRENCH ✉2316 Polk Street ✆415-776-5577 📠415-776-3431 🖰www.lafolie.com, lafoliep@aol.com

Fashionable, French, intimate, and imaginative—this place combines all the ingredients required of a small San Francisco restaurant. Those heavy French sauces of yore have been replaced with natural sauces and vegetable purées. The menu includes specialties like roti of quail and squab stuffed with mushrooms and wrapped in crispy potato strings, and poached lobster with butternut squash ravioli. Dinner only. Closed Sunday, except in December.

SHOPPING

No doubt about it, Union Street is a budget-busting boulevard. Rich in designer fashions and rare imports, this Victorian street sports some of the finest merchandise and heftiest price tags in town. But as the saying goes, it doesn't cost to look.

BIONDIVINO

✉1415 Green Street ✆415-673-2320 🖰www.biondivino.com Sophisticated wine buyers head to this stylish boutique to peruse the selection of 490 varietals from Italy and its regional outskirts, such as Austria and Slovenia. Specializing in small producers, Biondivino is loved by locals for its hard-to-find vintages as well as its accommodating hours—they're open until 11 p.m. except Sunday. This chic shop is also known for having a knowledgable, friendly staff.

CHAN'S TRAINS & HOBBIES ✉2450 Van Ness Avenue ✆415-885-2899

Model railroad engineers will find enough new and old model trains, including Marklin, Lionel, and LGB brands, to engineer for the rest of their lives at Chan's. A mecca for Bay Area hobbyists, model trains chug on tracks overhead and in the front display window. You'll have to drag your kids out of this place—and maybe yourself, as well.

KOZO ARTS ✉1969-A Union Street ✆415-351-2114 🖰www.kozoarts.com, info@kozoarts.com This art supply store sells sheets of exquisite Japanese handmade paper, beautiful fountain pens, blank books, and handmade photo albums, all excellent examples of one of Japan's many art forms.

ENCHANTED CRYSTAL ✉1895 Union Street ✆415-885-1335 🖰www.enchantedcrystal.com Aglitter with art glass pieces by about 70 artists, this glass palace is also known for its world-class collection of quartz pieces. The window displays—extravagant, wildly imaginative affairs in rock and glass—are magical. As a matter of fact, in addition to its ordinary clientele, this shop caters to metaphysical covens and others knowledgeable in the mesmerizing powers of crystal.

IMAGES OF THE NORTH ✉2036 *Union Street* ✆415-673-1273 🖱*www. imagesnorth.com, gallery@imagesnorth.com* Collectors come from all over the country to purchase the Alaskan and Canadian Inuit art sold here. This gallery represents artists from across the Artic and sells museum-quality stone sculptures of people, wildlife, and mythological beings carved from soapstone, serpentine, and musk-ox horn, as well as walrus ivory jewelry. The gallery also features prints, masks, jewelry, and photography. Even if you can't afford to buy, it's a great place to look. Closed Sunday and Monday.

NIGHTLIFE

THE ROYAL OAK ✉2201 *Polk Street* ✆415-928-2303 For an archetypal San Francisco fern bar, head here. With its plush Victorian parlor couches, it's a cozy spot for a nightcap. Be sure to open the drawers of any end table; you'll find them full of napkins scrawled with poetry.

PERRY'S ✉1944 *Union Street* ✆415-922-9022 To take a rest from the crowds, drop into Perry's, where you can actually get a seat at the bar on the weekends. It's a friendly spot and reminiscent of San Francisco in decades past.

BALBOA CAFÉ ✉3199 *Fillmore Street* ✆415-921-3944 If you're in the mood for another kind of action, check out the scene at this hot spot. It's a meat market for the young and upwardly mobile.

NOB HILL

Perhaps the most famous of all the knolls casting their loving shadows on San Francisco is a prominent prominence called Nob Hill. It is a monument to San Francisco's crusty rich—those old powerbrokers who trace their heritage back to the Big Four. It seems that in the 19th century, Misters Crocker, Huntington, Hopkins, and Stanford—the tycoons who built the transcontinental railroad—chose Nob Hill as the place to honor themselves. They all built estates on top of the 338-foot rise, each more ostentatious than the other. It became, as Robert Louis Stevenson described it, "the Hill of palaces." Until 1906, that is: the fire that followed the great earthquake burned Nob Hill's mansions to the ground.

SIGHTS

PACIFIC UNION CLUB ✉1000 *California Street* All that remains from the robber baron age is this blocky brownstone built in 1855 for a silver king named James Flood.

FAIRMONT HOTEL ✉950 *Mason Street* Built just prior to 1906, the shell of this grand building endured; the interior was refurbished in time for the hotel to open on the first anniversary of the earthquake. Today the hotel lobby, with its marble columns and gilt bas-relief, evokes memories of the Big Four.

LUXURY HOTELS   Once the domain of San Francisco's wealthiest families, Nob Hill now is home to the city's finest hotels. Strung like pearls along California Street, a doorman's whistle from the Fairmont, are three luxurious hotels. Fittingly, the **Stanford Court Hotel**, **Mark Hopkins Inter-Continental Hotel**, and the **Huntington Hotel** were built upon the ruins of Big Four mansions. That tree-dotted resting place across the street, *naturalement*, is **Huntington Park**.

GRACE CATHEDRAL   ✉*1051 Taylor Street* This massive church marks San Francisco's attempt at Gothic architecture. Consecrated in 1964 and constructed of concrete, it's not exactly Notre Dame. But this mammoth, vaulting church does have its charm. Foremost are the doors atop the cathedral steps; they represent Lorenzo Ghiberti's "Doors of Paradise," cast in bronze from the artist's original work in Florence. The church interior is graced with a series of wall murals and tiers of stained-glass windows picture such latter-day luminaries as labor leader John L. Lewis, social worker Jane Addams, and astronaut John Glenn. In addition to these architectural adornments, the cathedral is filled with objects as dear as they are sacred—a 15th-century carved oak altar piece, a 13th-century Spanish crucifix, a 16th-century Belgian tapestry, and an organ boasting 7000 pipes.

Cathedral, hotels, the park—all are perched in a gilded nest known sarcastically among local folks as "Snob Hill." When you're ready to come down from these heady heights, you might want to decompress slowly by touring some of the area's small townhouses.

SACRAMENTO STREET   You needn't be a millionaire to live along Sacramento Street; you just need lots of money. Take the sprightly **townhouse** at 1172 Sacramento, for instance. With its mansard roof and cast-iron filigree, it could probably be had for a relative pittance. The **1200 block of Sacramento** boasts a string of lovely townhouses, including two structures adorned with wrought-iron tracery. At 1298 Sacramento Street, **Chambord Apartments** is a singular Beaux Arts–style building featuring curved balconies and elaborate exterior ornamentation.

It's only the three square blocks at the very top of Nob Hill that possess the pretension of wealth. The neighborhood below, where the hill slopes westward, is rather folksy. One enclave is downright rural. That, of course, is Priest Street.

PRIEST STREET ————————————————— **h**idden

✉*From Washington Street between Jones and Leavenworth* Priest is not really a street but a staircase, an ivy-banked country lane in the heart of San Francisco. It requires a bit of imagination to fully experience the place. For one thing you have to always gaze to the right, where slender townhouses are bordered with hedges. On the left side someone has built an astonishingly hideous apartment house. To add irony to insult, they've barricaded the beast behind a chain-link fence topped with a menacing roll of barbed wire.

REED STREET   Follow the trail at the end of Priest Street and emerge on an overgrown hill that looks out upon the city. If you continue on this semicircular course, you'll come out on Reed Street. Like its counterpart, this "street" is a narrow walkway planted with gardens and tucked between clapboard houses.

Perhaps we should call Priest and Reed streets "the Tiny Two," the common folk's answer to Nob Hill's "Big Four." You can take any of the city's three cable car lines to Nob Hill's **Powell–California Street stop**, the only spot in San Francisco where they all intersect.

LODGING

THE STANFORD COURT

$$$$ 392 ROOMS   ✉ *905 California Street*   ☎ *415-989-3500*   📠 *415-391-0513*
🖱 *www.marriott.com*

There's an emphasis on style and service at this stately hotel. Its hallmark is the *porte cochère*, illuminated through a leaded-glass dome. The guest rooms combine antiques and modern pieces to create a singular effect. Indulge in a personal morning wake-up call, where tea or coffee is brought to your room. There is a restaurant, a fitness room, and a piano lounge, plus an excellent staff. Of the several well-known hotels that adorn Nob Hill, this is my favorite.

THE HUNTINGTON

$$$$ 140 ROOMS   ✉ *1075 California Street*   ☎ *415-474-5400, 800-227-4683*
📠 *415-474-6227*   🖱 *www.huntingtonhotel.com, reservations@huntingtonhotel.com*

Of major Nob Hill hotels, this hotel is no doubt the least well-known, and it seems to like it that way. Constructed in the 1920s as an apartment house, the building was the first steel-and-brick highrise west of the Mississippi. An aura of understated elegance pervades the hotel and its 140 guest rooms and suites, most of which are individually decorated. A standout is the Mulholland suite, which features fine leather furnishings and warm gold, cream, and bronze decor. The Big 4 restaurant, named after the four great railroad magnates—Stanford, Hopkins, Crocker, and Huntington—is a mini-museum of San Francisco and Western memorabilia and also serves exceptional meals in a comfortable, clublike atmosphere.

NOB HILL HOTEL

$$$ 84 ROOMS   ✉ *835 Hyde Street*   ☎ *415-885-2987, 877-662-4455*   📠 *415-921-1648*
🖱 *www.nobhillhotel.com, nobhill@nobhillhotel.com*

From the Huntington, head northwest toward Japantown where you'll find this upscale hotel. It boasts rooms and suites decorated in Victorian style, appointed with antiques and marble bathrooms. In addition, suites are equipped with wet bars and jacuzzi tubs. There's a complimentary wine tasting every evening. Continental breakfast included.

CARLTON HOTEL

$$ 161 ROOMS   ✉ *1075 Sutter Street*   ☎ *415-673-0242, 800-922-7586*
📠 *415-673-4904*   🖱 *www.hotelcarltonsf.com, carltonres@jdvhospitality.com*

In Lower Nob Hill, northwest of the Nob Hill Hotel, is this quality establishment. The Carlton features a rich lobby with marble floors, brass wall sconces, and a fireplace. The earth tone-themed rooms have been decorated with pieces from around the world and are reasonably priced. A morning town car takes guests to downtown shopping. Located about five blocks from Union Square, the Carlton is highly recommended and is a certfied green business. Pet-friendly.

DINING

1550 HYDE CAFÉ
AND WINE BAR

$$$ CALIFORNIA CUISINE   ✉ *1550 Hyde Street* ☎ *415-775-1550*
🖳 *www.1550hyde.com, 1550hyde@earthlink.net*

Hop off the cable car and stroll into this chic restaurant and bar for sumptuous California cuisine paired with top-shelf wines. With a prix-fixe menu that changes daily, the emphasis here is always on the fresh and seasonal. Creative entrées such as wild stinging nettle and chanterelle risotto and ruby grapefruit and fennel sardines set the standard. The wine list is equally impressive, with a selection of affordably priced rare varietals. Dessert is just as delicious, boasting delights such as huckleberry apple crostada. Closed Monday.

THE TERRACE

$$$$ AMERICAN   ✉ *Ritz-Carlton, 600 Stockton Street* ☎ *415-773-6198,*
800-241-3333 🖷 *415-291-0288* 🖳 *www.ritzcarlton.com*

Reserve a Sunday for this brunch, possibly the best in Northern California. A jazz quartet sets the mood for this feast, and dining in the outside courtyard is an option when the sun's out. The gourmet spread includes traditional brunch fare such as eggs Benedict and crêpes, plus a stomach-expanding banquet featuring several varieties of charcuterie, an assortment of sushi, exotic salads, fresh-from-the-sea crab legs, and oysters on the half shell. And if that isn't enough, you'll definitely want to save room for the to-die-for desserts, such as the strawberry arugula tart and peach galette with crème fraîche ice cream. Top it off with a glass of champagne, mimosa, or fresh-squeezed orange juice and you won't have to eat for a week. It's worth the splurge for the ultra-deluxe price. Reservations advised.

NIGHTLIFE

TOP OF THE MARK ✉ *999 California Street* ☎ *415-392-3434, 415-616-6916*
🖳 *www.topofthemark.com* If San Francisco tourists were given an association test and asked the first thing that came to mind when a "bar with a view" was mentioned, about 101 out of every 100 would list this place. With good reason: from its roosting place in Nob Hill, this venerable lounge provides extraordinary 360° vistas of the bay and beyond. Famed for its 100 Martinis menu, there's also live music Tuesday through Saturday. Dress code. Usually a cover.

BIG 4 ✉ *1075 California Street* ☎ *415-771-1140* 🖳 *www.big4restaurant.com*
There's nothing shabby about the view at the Huntington Hotel's elegant lounge. The intimate, softly lit, wood-paneled bar has comfort-

able chairs encircling round tables, and live piano music is performed nightly.

JAPANTOWN

Center of culture for San Francisco's burgeoning Japanese population is Japantown, a self-contained area bounded by Geary, Post, Laguna, and Fillmore streets. This town-within-a-city consists of two sections: the old part, where residential housing is located, and a newer commercial area. During the April Cherry Blossom Festival, August Street Fair, Autumn Bon Dances, and the Aki Matsuri festival in September, Japantown turns out in splendid costumes for musical celebrations.

SIGHTS

JAPAN CENTER ✉*Between Post Street and Geary Boulevard* ✑*www.sfjapan town.org* Designed by architect Minoru Yamasaki, this shopping center is a five-acre monstrosity. Built in 1968, it exemplifies the freeway architecture of the era. There are, nonetheless, fascinating shops and outstanding restaurants located in this Asian mall.

PEACE PAGODA ✉*Japantown Peace Plaza; Between Post Street and Geary Boulevard* This five-tiered structure near Japan Center was designed by world-renowned architect Yoshiro Taniguchi as an expression of friendship and goodwill between the people of Japan and America.

NIHONMACHI MALL ✉*Buchanan Street* Year-round you can enjoy this mall with its cobblestone pathway and lovely Ruth Asawa origami fountains. There are also park benches featuring bas-reliefs done by local children and a *torii* gate, which designates holy ground.

KABUKI SPRINGS & SPA ✉*1750 Geary Boulevard* ✆*415-922-6000* ✇*415-922-6005* ✑*www.kabukisprings.com* For the ultimate in relaxation after a full day of sightseeing, visit this spa, where the main attraction is a series of hot and cold traditional Japanese communal baths. The baths are open to women only on Sunday, Wednesday, and Friday, and men only on Monday, Thursday, and Saturday, bathing suits optional. Tuesday is coed, suits required. In addition, a wide range of spa services are available, including shiatsu and Swedish massage, seaweed wraps, acupuncture, and Javanese *lulur* body treatments. None of this is inexpensive, of course, but you'll leave feeling like a million bucks.

LODGING

Japantown has two excellent hotels that provide a "chance to experience the tranquilities of the East and the amenities of the West."

BEST WESTERN HOTEL TOMO

$$–$$$ 125 ROOMS ✉*1800 Sutter Street* ✆*415-921-4000* ✇*415-923-1064* ✑*www.jdvhotels.com/tomo*
One of the most reasonable accommodations in the area, this hotel has been newly-renovated and redecorated with a Japanese pop-culture

Nob Hill, Pacific Heights, and Japantown

Broadway

Stockton St

Powell St

Chinatown

St

Mason St

Cable Car

Broadway

Tunnel

Jackson St

Washington St

Cable Car

Clay St

St

Nob Hill

Priest St

Reed St

Hyde St

Cable Car

Broadway

Broadway

Sacramento St

California St

Stockton Tunnel

Union Square

Powell St

Fairmont Hotel

Pine St

Pacific Union Club

Huntington Park

Grace Cathedral

Cable Car

Bush St

Sutter St

Post St

Geary St

O'Farrell St

Mason St

Taylor St

Jones St

Leavenworth St

Hyde St

Larkin St

Tenderloin

Vallejo St

Polk St

Pacific Ave

Jackson St

Washington St

Clay St

Sacramento St

Van Ness Ave

Pine St

Bush St

Sutter St

Post St

Polk St

Geary St

101

Broadway

Haas-Lilienthal House

Glenlee Terrace

Golden Gate Church

Franklin St

California St

Gough St

Royal Swedish Consulate

Whittier Mansion

Spreckels Mansion

Lafayette Park

Octavia St

Kokoro (old Soto Zen Mission)

Laguna St

0.5 mile

N

0.5 kilometer

0

0

Hamlin School

Bourn Mansion

Pacific Heights Ave

Whittier Mansion

Spreckels Mansion

Sacramento St

Buchanan St

Buchanan Mall

Japantown

Peace Plaza

Broadway

Pacific St

Jackson St

Upper Fillmore

Fillmore St

Webster St

Pine St

Bush St

Sutter St

Post St

Japan Center

Geary Blvd

theme. The lobby is simple but comfortable, featuring plump armchairs. There is also a restaurant on the premises.

HOTEL KABUKI

$$$–$$$$ 218 ROOMS ✉ *1625 Post Street* ☎ *415-922-3200* 🖅 *415-614-5498*
🖱 *www.jdvhotels.com/kabuki*

Foremost among the city's Asian-style hotels is the Kabuki, exuding a harmonious East-meets-West elegance. Pass through the sliding glass doors and you'll enter an oriental milieu. The private rooms are adorned with Japanese prints; a welcome tea service, based on the traditional Japanese tea ceremony, is served to guests after checking in. Be sure to ask for a traditional Japanese soaking tub. There is one traditional Japanese suite available, complete with sunken living space, shoji screens, and bamboo and sand garden. The Kabuki represents one of the city's most exotic hotels.

DINING

KOJI OSAKAYA

$$ JAPANESE ✉ *Kintetsu Mall, 1737 Post Street* ☎ *415-922-2728*

The Japan Center building houses several Japanese dining establishments, including this *shokuji dokoro*, or traditional bistro. Here the atmosphere is mannered and reserved. Japanese tradition at its finest.

ISOBUNE

$$–$$$ JAPANESE ✉ *Kintetsu Mall, 1737 Post Street* ☎ *415-563-1030*

Tired of humdrum sushi bars? Bored with sea urchin platters? Then this is the place for you. Here those raw fish finger foods scud past you on wooden boats along a miniature canal. No joke—we're talking sushi on a stream. You simply sit at the counter and pluck off your favorite cargo as the boat goes by. There are numerous sushi selections, as well as soup and sashimi.

SANPPO RESTAURANT

$$ JAPANESE ✉ *1702 Post Street* ☎ *415-346-3486*

Recommended by local residents and gourmets alike, this restaurant serves excellent food at fair prices. In addition to outstanding sushi, they offer lemon steak, garlic chicken, *chanko nabe* (a fish, chicken, and vegetable dish), tempura, and *donburi* dishes. The interior is unsophisticated café-style, but the cuisine is worthy of a plush establishment.

SHOPPING

In this Asian neighborhood, most shopping is done in Japan Center, a modern mall. As you'll discover, most of the listings below are located in this commercial complex.

SHIGE NISHIGUCHI KIMONO & ANTIQUES ✉ *1730 Geary Boulevard #204* ☎ *415-346-5567* Open since 1968, this small, unassuming shop specializes in antique kimonos, those gorgeous heavy silk garments

but have new kimonos as well. They also have dolls dressed in kimono miniatures.

ASAKICHI ✉*1730 Geary Boulevard #150* 📞*415-921-2147* 📠*415-928-1987* 🖥*www.asakichi.com* Here you'll find antique furniture as well as Asian arts and crafts. Take special note of those heavy wood antique chests called *tansu*. Cluttered but fascinating, this shop also carries porcelain dinnerware, sake cups, tea ceremony utensils, and antique fabrics.

KINOKUNIYA STATIONERY AND GIFT ✉*1581 Webster Street* 📞*415-567-7625* 📠*415-567-4109* 🖥*sf@kinokuniya.com* Also worthy of notice is this stationary store, which stocks Japanese books, postcards, calendars, and writing supplies.

MASHIKO FOLKCRAFT ✉*1581 Webster Street* 📞*415-346-0748* One of Japan Center's most captivating stores is this museum-cum-shop displaying Japanese folk art and antiques. Among the exhibits, you might find an 18th-century tobacco set or a hand-painted papier-mâché pillow. The prices often match the age of these precious objects, but there are affordable items—like ceramic dishes and porcelain chopstick rests. Closed Thursday.

PACIFIC HEIGHTS

San Francisco's most prestigious neighborhood resides on a hill looking down upon the Bay. In addition to Rolls-Royces and Mercedes Benzes, Pacific Heights contains some of the city's most outstanding architecture. Stroll the wide streets and you will encounter straitlaced Tudor homes, Baroque confections, and elaborate Victorians.

SIGHTS

VICTORIANS The best place to begin touring this palatial ridgetop is the corner of Franklin and California streets. That twin-turreted structure on the corner is a **Queen Anne–style Victorian**, built for a 19th-century figure who made his fortune in gold and lumber. Its poorer neighbors up the hill are **Italianate-style Victorians**, characterized by slanting edge bay windows; both date to the 1870s.

Head north on Franklin Street to 1735 Franklin, a brick **Georgian-style house** built at the turn of the 20th century for a family of coffee barons.

GOLDEN GATE SPIRITUALIST CHURCH ✉*1901 Franklin Street* 📞*415-885-9976* 🖥*http://ggsc.org* This church is a Baroque Revival structure built in 1900 for the Crockers, one of California's most powerful families.

HAAS-LILIENTHAL HOUSE ✉*2007 Franklin Street* 📞*415-441-3004* 🖥*www.sfheritage.org, info@sfheritage.org* The grandest of all San Francisco's Victorians is this Queen Anne gingerbread fantasy adorned with gables and bas-relief figures. Despite the bold tower, ornate design, and sheer size of the place, it cost less than $20,000 to build. Of course, that was back in 1886. Today it's a house museum, operated by San Francisco

Architectural Heritage, open to the public Wednesday, Saturday and Sunday on docent-led tours only. Admission.

GLENLEE TERRACE ✉ *1925 Jackson Street* Turn left on Jackson and continue uphill to this next site. With its white stucco facade and red tile roof, this sophisticated apartment house follows a Mission Revival motif and dates from 1912. Across the street from Glenlee Terrace, you can admire a stately brick building.

WHITTIER MANSION ✉ *2090 Jackson Street* This red sandstone structure was built in 1896 by local shipping magnate William Frank Whittier. Interestingly, this home was sold to the Third Reich in 1938 and remained a German consulate until the U.S. entered World War II in 1941. Today it is once again a private residence.

HAMLIN SCHOOL ✉ *2120 Broadway* Turn right on Laguna, go downhill, then left on Broadway. Here you'll find a stern three-story edifice with lions on either side of the entranceway. Designed as a Baroque Revival mansion, the Hamlin School was constructed in 1901.

RENAISSANCE-STYLE PALAZZO ✉ *2222 Broadway* ✇ *www.floodmansion. org* James Flood, the man who commissioned several Pacific Heights buildings, also built this white marble Renaissance-style palazzo.

BOURN MANSION ✉ *2550 Webster Street* Go back a half-block and turn uphill on Webster Street. This Georgian townhouse was built in 1896 by William Bourn, one of California's wealthiest businessmen.

SPRECKELS MANSION ✉ *2080 Washington Street* Take a left on Washington Street and continue to **Lafayette Park** between Washington and Laguna streets, a beautiful tree-dotted park with a rolling lawn. Across the street rises this ornate edifice with a white limestone surface that is beginning to fall to the forces of San Francisco's wind and weather. This mansion is home to author Danielle Steele. There are literally hundreds more houses to visit in this neighborhood. If this thumbnail tour has merely whetted your architectural appetite, you can continue alone, strolling these heights, searching out vestiges of San Francisco's baronial history.

FILLMORE DISTRICT From its time as an economic hub after the 1906 earthquake to its transformation into a community for Japanese residents during World War II to its eventual emergence as the stomping ground for early greats of the jazz era, this San Francisco district has a long, rich history. Today, the area bounded by McAllister, Post, Steiner, and Webster streets has been dubbed The Historic Fillmore Preservation District, but for residents of this vibrant area its boundaries remain largely undefined. The neighborhood is dotted with notable jazz clubs, historic buildings, and memorial sites.

JAZZ HERITAGE CENTER ✉ *1320 Fillmore Street* ☏ *415-255-7745* ✇ *www. jazzheritagecenter.org, info@jazzheritagecenter.org* This complex is entirely devoted to San Francisco's jazz history. Part gallery and part museum, the center details local jazz culture as it was in the 1940s and follows it through to contemporary musicians performing today, including those featured at the renowned on-site club, Yoshi's.

LODGING

HOTEL MAJESTIC

$$$$ 58 ROOMS ✉ *1500 Sutter Street* ☎ *415-441-1100, 800-869-8966*
📠 *415-673-7331* 🖎 *www.thehotelmajestic.com, info@thehotelmajestic.com*

In lower Pacific Heights, a mile or two from the Downtown district and bordering Japantown, stands this five-story structure. The building dates from 1902 and opened as one of the city's first grand hotels. It underwent several incarnations before finally being reincarnated as The Majestic. The current 58-room establishment features a restaurant, bar, and attractive lobby. All rooms are strikingly appointed with elegant features; some include canopied beds, European antiques, and marble bathrooms.

HOTEL DRISCO

$$$$ 48 ROOMS ✉ *2901 Pacific Avenue* ☎ *415-346-2880, 800-634-7277*
📠 *415-567-5537* 🖎 *www.jdvhotels.com/drisco*

This hotel survived the 1906 earthquake and fire and went on to serve four generations of guests. Located in the city's poshest area, the Drisco is one of the best places to mingle with upper-class San Franciscans. Both the small standard rooms and the roomier suites combine modern and antique furnishings and offer oversized baths. And the place still retains some of its old charms—like the downstairs dining room, the dark wood lobby, the nightly wine reception, and the complimentary buffet breakfast.

LAUREL INN

$$$ 49 ROOMS ✉ *444 Presidio Avenue* ☎ *415-567-8467, 800-552-8735*
📠 *415-928-1866* 🖎 *www.thelaurelinn.com, khegre@jdvhospitality.com*

Chain establishments sometimes get a bad rap, but this boutique hotel is truly lovely. The Art Deco interior hides super-modern comforts. Eighteen of the forty-nine colorful guest rooms have kitchenettes; many have pretty views of the neighborhood. A continental breakfast is included, as is a lending library of CDs and videos.

DINING

HELMAND PALACE

$$ AFGHAN ✉ *2424 Van Ness Avenue* ☎ *415-345-0072*
🖎 *www.helmandpalace.com, service@helmandpalace.com*

Dining here is like visiting the home of an upper-class Afghani family. Lush handmade Afghan carpets, beautiful chandeliers, and paintings add a touch of elegance, and the food is first-rate. You can feast on grilled rack of lamb, roasted chicken, and many vegetarian dishes. Aushak, Afghan ravioli stuffed with leeks and topped with ground beef marinated in yogurt, can be habit-forming. Dinner only. Closed Monday.

While Pacific Heights is primarily residential there are a few options. You'll also find dining rooms in the "upper Fillmore" area and along Sacramento Street. Both of these gentrified districts feature a host of gourmet restaurants. The best way to uncover them is by exploring the area. Upper Fillmore reaches from Bush Street to Jackson Street, wedged between a proletarian neighborhood and posh Pacific Heights. The accent is on the latter locale, however, and the street is lined with good dining places. Most are restaurants characterized by canvas awnings, hand-lettered signs, brass rails, and ever-changing menus.

SWAN OYSTER DEPOT

$$ SEAFOOD   ✉1517 Polk Street   ☎415-673-1101

Dollar for dollar, this is the best dining spot along Polk Street. It's a short-order place serving fresh prawns, crabs, lobster, shrimp, and oysters, all displayed in trays out front. The place consists simply of a counter lined with stools and is almost always packed. The depot opens at 8 a.m. and closes at 5:30 p.m. Closed Sunday.

THE GRUBSTAKE

$$ AMERICAN/PORTUGUESE   ✉1525 Pine Street   ☎415-673-8268
✐www.sfgrubstake.com, fcsantos@comcast.net

Running a close second to Swan Oyster Depot is this brightly painted café adorned with a skylight and exotic murals. The menu consists of hamburgers, sandwiches, salads, omelettes, and a number of Portuguese dishes. At night they serve pork chops, steaks, and a daily fish special. Better yet, it stays open until 4 a.m. Lunch is only served on the weekend.

CORDON BLEU
VIETNAMESE RESTAURANT

 hidden

$ VIETNAMESE   ✉1574 California Street   ☎415-673-5637

There are about a thousand restaurants in San Francisco named Hunan, and the second most popular name seems to be Cordon Bleu. The place claiming to be the original Cordon Bleu is this simple café-style establishment serving a few good Southeast Asian dishes. There are imperial rolls, shish kabobs, and five-spice roast chicken. No lunch on Sunday. Closed Monday.

LITTLE JOE'S

$$ ITALIAN   ✉2550 Van Ness Avenue   ☎415-433-4343   ✐www.little-joes.com

The food here is outstanding and is prepared before your eyes by some of the city's great showmen. Working a row of oversized frying pans, these jugglers rarely touch a spatula. Rather, with a snap of the wrist, they flip sizzling veal, steak, or calamari skyward, then nonchalantly catch it on the way down. This restaurant also serves delicious fish, roast chicken, and sausage dishes, each accompanied by pasta and sautéed vegetables. Very crowded, especially on weekends.

ÉLITE CAFÉ

$$$–$$$$ CREOLE   ✉2049 Fillmore Street   ☎415-673-5483
✐www.theelitecafe.com

My personal favorite is this spiffy Art Deco establishment with overhead fans and private oak-paneled booths. Open for dinner and weekend brunch, the Élite specializes in the flavors of New Orleans. Appetizers include gumbo and Gulf oysters; the main courses vary daily and may feature blackened fish, filet mignon with Cajun butter, housemade sausage and jambalaya, or broiled sea bass with pecan rice.

LA MÉDITERRANÉE

$$ MEDITERRANEAN ✉2210 Fillmore Street ☎415-921-2956
🖉www.cafelamed.com

La Med, as regulars like to call it, is an excellent Mediterranean restaurant squeezed into small digs. The lighting is low and seating cozy, but the hummus and tabbouleh are to die for. Customers rave about the Mezze, which lets couples sample almost everything on the menu. Try the Middle Eastern plate or opt for a phyllo dough creation.

OSTERIA

$$ ITALIAN ✉3277 Sacramento Street ☎415-771-5030 🖉www.osteriasf.com
Away from the hustle and bustle of Fillmore Street lies this charming neighborhood eatery. With a soft cream-colored interior and murals of vineyards on the walls, rural Tuscany comes to life. Fresh pastas (wonderful capellini and homemade gnocchi) and tasty salads keep a consistent clientele coming back for more. Friendly service and great food make this little place a true find. Dinner only. Closed Monday.

SHOPPING

Upper Fillmore and Sacramento Street are convenient shopping districts close to Pacific Heights. "Upper" Fillmore is a double entendre referring to class as well as altitude. Stretching from Sutter Street to Jackson Street in Pacific Heights, it's a gently sloping boulevard lined with designer shops. Along this seven-block row are galleries, gourmet food outlets, boutiques, and bath accessory stores. Très chic.

BETSEY JOHNSON ✉2031 Fillmore Street ☎415-567-2726 🖉www.betsey johnson.com The clothing here may look used, but the pricetags will tell you otherwise. The ultimate in retro designer fashion, Betsey's will make you wish you hadn't thrown out those old clothes in the back of your closet. You could sell them and make a fortune.

SECONDS TO GO ✉2252 Fillmore Street ☎415-563-7806 For great second-hand items, consider this fantastic find, which has vintage couture clothing for guys and gals.

NEST ✉2300 Fillmore Street ☎415-292-6199 🖉www.nestsf.com Francophiles will adore this international shop, with its funky collection of handbags, jewelry, and French-inspired houseware.

SACRAMENTO STREET 🖉www.sacramentostreetshop.com One of the streets crossing this upper Fillmore promenade is Sacramento. Follow it several blocks west and you'll discover another fast-growing shoppers' strip. The stores here are not as concentrated, but scattered between Broderick and Lyon streets are a number of boutiques and trendy shops.

A real neighborhood shopping area, this street combines galleries, boutiques, and antique stores with shops serving the immediate needs of local folks. You can combine your shopping with a tour of this vintage area, which contains a number of impressive Victorian homes.

NIGHTLIFE

FILLMORE ✉1805 Geary Boulevard ☎415-346-6000 ⌨www.thefillmore.com
Located just below Pacific Heights in the Fillmore District, national rock, folk, blues, and country acts rock this Victorian-style venue that continues the legacy started by promoter Bill Graham in 1966, when bands such as the Jefferson Airplane and the Grateful Dead rang in a new era. Stained-glass chandeliers highlight the huge dancefloor and balcony seats.

YOSHI'S ✉1330 Fillmore Street ☎415-655-5600 ⌨sf.yoshis.com/sf/jazzclub
The owners of this renowned jazz club have been featuring premier musicians—as in legends Dizzy Gillespie, Harry Connick Jr., and Branford Marsalis—in their Oakland establishment since 1973. In 2007, Yoshi's opened this sleek Fillmore District venue, which offers top-of-the-line jazz performances as well as rock, soul, and world music.

GOLDEN GATE NATIONAL RECREATION AREA

One of San Francisco's most spectacular regions belongs to us all. The Golden Gate National Recreation Area, a 74,000-acre metropolitan park, draws about 20 million visitors annually. A place of natural beauty and historic importance, this magnificent park stretches north from San Francisco throughout much of the Bay Area. In the city itself, the Golden Gate National Recreation Area forms a narrow band around the waterfront. It follows the shoreline of the Bay from Aquatic Park to Fort Mason to the Golden Gate Bridge. On the ocean side it encompasses Land's End, an exotic and untouched preserve, as well as the city's finest beaches.

SIGHTS

GOLDEN GATE PROMENADE The most serene way to begin exploring the Golden Gate National Recreation Area is via this promenade. This three-and-a-half-mile walk will carry you across a swath of heaven that extends from Aquatic Park to the shadows of the Golden Gate Bridge.

MUNICIPAL PIER Just start in the park and make the short jaunt to this hook-shaped cement walkway that curls several hundred yards into the Bay. As you follow its curving length, a 360-degree view unfolds—from the Golden Gate to the Bay Bridge, from Mt. Tamalpais to Alcatraz to downtown San Francisco. The pier harbors fisherfolk and seagulls, crabnetters and joggers; few tourists seem to make it out here.

Golden Gate National Recreation Area & the Presidio

LAND'S END · EL POLIN SPRING · TASTE OF THE HIMALAYAS · KHAN TOKE THAI HOUSE

LAND'S END

PAGE 114

Cliffs poised over the tumultuous sea where waves and winds control the earth—San Francisco's grand finale

TASTE OF THE HIMALAYAS

PAGE 118

The place for authentic Tibetan, Nepalese, and Indian cuisine like *momos* and *alu bhanta* to tantalize your taste buds

KHAN TOKE THAI HOUSE

PAGE 118

Thai delicacies served in a welcoming, exotic locale with a sunken-floor, intricate wood carvings, and gold inlay

EL POLIN SPRING

PAGE 119

Enchanting glade where hiking trails lead outward into surrounding hills dotted with eucalyptus and conifers

FORT MASON CENTER ✉ *Marina Boulevard and Buchanan Street* ☎ *415-441-3400* 🖷 *415-441-3405* 🖳 *www.fortmason.org, contact@fortmason.org* From Municipal Pier it's uphill and downstairs to this complex of old wharves and tile-roof warehouses that was once a major military embarkation point. Fort Mason today is the cultural heart of avant-garde San Francisco. This National Historic Landmark houses theaters, museums, and a gourmet vegetarian restaurant, and hosts thousands of programs and events.

Nearly all the arts and crafts are represented—several theater groups are home here; there is an on-going series of workshops in dance, creative writing, painting, weaving, printing, sculpture, music, and so on. A number of environmental organizations also have offices in the center. As one brochure describes, "You can see a play, stroll through a museum or gallery, learn how to make poetry films, study yoga, attend a computer seminar, or find out about the rich maritime lore of San Francisco."

MUSEO ITALOAMERICANO ✉*Fort Mason Center, Building C* ☎*415-673-2200* 📠*415-673-2292* 💻*www.museoitaloamericano.org, sfmuseo@sbcglobal.net* This museum is dedicated to displaying the works of Italian and Italian-American artists and culture. The permanent collection features the work of several artists, some of whom have made San Francisco their home for years. Rotating exhibits include readings, lectures, and concerts. Docent-led group tours available by appointment. Closed Monday except by appointment. Admission.

MARINA Now that you're fully versed in the arts, continue on the shoreline to the Marina, along Marina Boulevard. (The remainder of the tour can be completed by car, though walking is definitely the aesthete's and athlete's way.) Some of this sailor-city's spiffiest yachts are docked along the esplanade.

MARINA GREEN This stretch of park paralleling the Bay is a landlubber's haven. Bicyclers, joggers, jugglers, sunbathers, and a world of others inhabit it. The park's most interesting denizens are the kitefliers who fill the blue with a rainbow of soaring colors.

Continue on past a line-up of luxury toys—boats with names like *Haiku*, *Sea Lover*, *Valhalla*, and *Windfall*. When you arrive at the far end of that small green rectangle of park, you'll have to pay special attention to your navigator; you're on Marina Boulevard at the corner of Yacht Road; if going by car, proceed directly ahead through the U.S. Army gate and follow Mason Street, Crissy Field Avenue, and Lincoln Boulevard, paralleling the water, to Fort Point; if on foot, turn right onto Yacht Road, then left at the waterfront, and follow the shoreline toward the Golden Gate Bridge.

PALACE OF FINE ARTS Turn left at Yacht Road, cross Marina Boulevard, and proceed to that magnificent Beaux-Arts monument looming before you. This domed edifice is built of arches and shadows. Adorned with molded urns and bas-relief figures, it represents the only surviving structure from the 1915 Panama–Pacific International Exposition. Happily, it borders on a sun-shivered pond. The pond in its turn is peopled by mallards and swans, as well as pintails and canvasbacks from out of town. Together, the pool, the pillars, and surrounding park make this one of the city's loveliest spots for sitting and sunning.

EXPLORATORIUM ✉*Marina Boulevard and Lyon Street* ☎*415-397-5673* 📠*415-561-0370* 💻*www.exploratorium.edu* If education is on your mind, note that the Palace of Fine Arts, which boasts this great museum, is a great place to bring children. This "hands-on" museum, with imaginative exhibits demonstrating the principles of optics, sound, animal behavior, etc., was once deemed "the best science museum in the world" by *Scientific American*. It's an intriguing place with constantly changing temporary exhibits and permanent displays that include a "distorted room" lacking right angles and an illusionary mirror into which you seemingly pass. Also check out the Tactile Dome (reservations required; separate admission), a pitch-black crawlspace of textural adventures. Closed Monday and selected holidays. Admission.

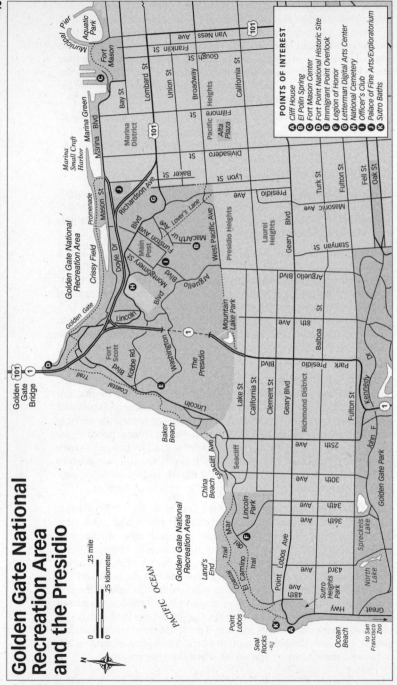

Golden Gate National Recreation Area and the Presidio

112

N

PACIFIC OCEAN

0 .25 mile
0 .25 kilometer

POINTS OF INTEREST

- **Ⓐ** Cliff House
- **Ⓑ** El Polin Spring
- **Ⓒ** Fort Mason Center
- **Ⓓ** Fort Point National Historic Site
- **Ⓔ** Immigrant Point Overlook
- **Ⓕ** Legion of Honor
- **Ⓖ** Letterman Digital Arts Center
- **Ⓗ** National Cemetery
- **Ⓘ** Officer's Club
- **Ⓙ** Palace of Fine Arts/Exploratorium
- **Ⓚ** Sutro Baths

But enough for detours; we were embarked on a long march to the bridge. If you cheated and drove, you're already at Fort Point, and we'll catch up with you later; otherwise you're on foot, with the Bay at your side and the Golden Gate dead ahead. This is a land where freighters talk to foghorns, and sloops scud along soundlessly. The waterfront is a sandy beach, a rockpile in seeming upheaval, then beach again, sand dunes, and occasional shade trees. That wooded grove rising to your left is the Presidio; those bald-domed hills across the Bay to the right are the Marin Headlands, and the sharp-rising buildings poking at your back are part of the San Francisco skyline. You'll pass a Coast Guard Station and a fishing pier before arriving at the red brick fort that snuggles in the arch of the Golden Gate Bridge.

FORT POINT NATIONAL HISTORIC SITE ✉️*End of Marine Drive* 📞*415-556-1693* 📠*415-561-4390* 🖥️*www.nps.gov/fopo* Modeled on Fort Sumter and completed around the time Confederate forces opened fire on that hapless garrison, this site represents the only brick fort west of the Mississippi. With its collection of cannons and Civil War–era re-enactments and exhibits, it's of interest to history buffs. Also, if you follow the spiral granite staircase to the roof, you'll stand directly beneath the Golden Gate Bridge and command a sentinel's view out into the Pacific. Open Friday through Sunday. Call for hours and information on guided tours and special programs.

GOLDEN GATE BRIDGE From Fort Point, a footpath leads up to the observation area astride the Golden Gate Bridge; if driving, take Lincoln Boulevard to the vista point. By whichever route, you'll arrive at "The Bridge at the End of the Continent." Aesthetically, it is considered one of the world's most beautiful spans, a medley of splayed cable and steel struts. Statistically, it represents one of the longest suspension bridges anywhere—6450 feet of suspended concrete and steel, with twin towers the height of 65-story buildings and cables that support 200 million pounds. It is San Francisco's emblem, an engineering wonder that has come to symbolize an entire metropolis.

If you're game, you can walk across, venturing along a dizzying sidewalk out to one of the most magnificent views you'll ever experience. The Bay from this height is a toy model built to scale; beyond the bridge, San Francisco and Marin, slender arms of land, open onto the boundless Pacific.

The Golden Gate Promenade ends at the bridge, but Lincoln Boulevard continues along the cliffs that mark the ocean side of San Francisco. There are **vista points** overlooking the Pacific and affording startling views back toward the bridge.

BAKER BEACH

✉️*Off Lincoln Boulevard on Gibson Road* After about a mile you'll reach this wide corridor of white sand. Ideal for picnicking and sunbathing, this lovely beach is a favorite among San Franciscans. Adventurers can follow this strand, and the other smaller beaches with which it connects, on a fascinating walk back almost all the way to the Golden Gate Bridge. With the sea unfolding on one side and rocky crags rising along the other, it's definitely worth a little sand in the shoes. As a final reward, there's a **nude beach** on the northern end, just outside the bridge.

CHINA BEACH ✉*Turn right on 25th Avenue, left on Sea Cliff Avenue, then follow until it dead ends.* Lincoln Boulevard transforms into El Camino del Mar, which winds through Sea Cliff, one of San Francisco's most affluent residential neighborhoods. This exclusive area has something to offer the visitor in addition to its scenic residences—namely China Beach (formerly known as James Phelan Beach). More secluded than Baker, this pocket beach is backdropped by a rocky bluff atop which stand the luxurious plate-window homes of Sea Cliff. Named for the Chinese fishermen who camped here in the 19th century, the beach has a dilapidated beach house and restroom facilities.

LEGION OF HONOR ✉*Lincoln Park, 34th Avenue and Clement Street* ☎*415-750-3600* 📠*415-750-3656* ⬗*www.legionofhonor.org, guestbook@famsf.org* Continuing on El Camino del Mar as it sweeps above the ocean, you'll come upon San Francisco's prettiest museum. With its colonnaded courtyard and arching entranceway, the Legion of Honor is modeled after a gallery in Paris. In fact, a mini pyramid mirroring the one at the Louvre sits in the courtyard, letting light into the gallery below. Appropriately, it specializes in European art and culture. The exhibits trace European aesthetic achievements from ancient Greek and Roman art to the religious art of the Middle Ages to Renaissance painting, the Baroque and Rococo periods, and the Impressionists of the 19th and 20th centuries. Closed Monday. Admission.

After you've drunk in the splendid view of city and Bay from the museum grounds, head downhill on 34th Avenue past the golf course, turn right on Geary Boulevard, which becomes Point Lobos Avenue, then turn right on to El Camino del Mar and follow it to the end. (Yes, this is the same street you were on earlier; no, I'm not leading you in circles. It seems that, years ago, landslides collapsed the midriff of this highway, leaving among the survivors two dead-end streets known forever by the same name.)

LAND'S END

This thumb-like appendage of real estate seems to have been stolen from the sea by San Francisco. It is the nearest you will ever approach to experiencing this area as the Costanoan Indians knew it. Hike the trails that honeycomb the hillsides hereabout and you'll enter a wild, tumbling region where winds twist cypress trees into the contours of the earth. The rocks offshore are inhabited by slithering sea creatures. The air is loud with the unceasing lash of wave against shoreline. Land's End is San Francisco's grand finale—a line of cliffs poised at the sea's edge and threatening imminently to slide into eternity. From the parking lot located at the end of El Camino del Mar, walk down the steps that begin at the U.S.S. *San Francisco* Memorial Flagpole, and head east on the trail to the water. That dirty blonde swath of sand is a popular **nude beach**, perfectly situated here in San Francisco's most natural region. (Note: While hiking the footpaths in the region, *beware!* Land's End is plagued by landslides and foolish hikers. Remain on the trails. Exercise caution and this exotic area will reward you with eye-boggling views of Marin's wind-chiseled coast.)

SUTRO BATHS ✎*www.sutrobaths.com* Continuing down Point Lobos Avenue, at the corner where the road turns to parallel the Pacific Ocean, rest these ruins. From the configuration of the stones, it's a simple trick to envision the foundation of Adolf Sutro's folly; more difficult for the mind's eye is to picture the multitiered confection that the San Francisco philanthropist built upon it in 1896. Sprawling across three oceanfront acres, Sutro's baths could have washed the entire city. There were actually six baths total, Olympian in size, as well as three restaurants and 500 dressing rooms—all contained beneath a stained-glass dome.

CLIFF HOUSE ✉*1090 Point Lobos Avenue* ✆*415-386-3330* ✎*415-387-7837* ✎*www.cliffhouse.com, info@cliffhouse.com* Towering above Sutro Baths was this Gothic castle that survived the earthquake only to be consumed by fire the next year. Following several reincarnations, the Cliff House houses two restaurants, two bars, a cocktail lounge, and a gift shop. Three observation decks jut over the rocky edge of the continent; from this crow's nest you can gaze out over a sweeping expanse of ocean.

CAMERA OBSCURA ✆*415-750-0415* ✎*www.giantcamera.com* A controversy once surrounded this camera-shaped kiosk near the Cliff House. The National Park Service, which leases the land on which this venerable old-time tourist attraction stands, wanted to tear the building down and move the camera's inner workings to a visitors center. Public outcry resulted in the addition of the Camera Obscura to the National Register of Historic Places, which protects it permanently. So rest assured that you'll be able to stand inside this dark chamber and watch as a rotating lens and mirror, based on a 16th-century design by Leonardo da Vinci, projects a panoramic view that takes in the Cliff House, the Sutro Baths and the Golden Gate Bridge, and **Seal Rocks**, which lie just offshore. (The seals for which the rocks were named have all moved to Pier 39 at Fisherman's Wharf, but other sea lions take up residence on the rocks during the spring months.) Admission. Closed in inclement weather.

OCEAN BEACH Below the Cliff House, extending to the very end of vision, is the Great Highway. The slender ribbon of salt-and-pepper sand that runs beside it is this beach, which decorates three miles of San Francisco's western perimeter. Remember, this is San Francisco—land of fog, mist, and west winds—and beachwear here more often consists of sweaters than swimsuits. The water, sweeping down from the Arctic, is too cold for mere mortals; only surfers and polar bear swimmers brave it. Nevertheless, to walk this strand is to trek the border of eternity. American Indians called San Francisco's ocean the "sundown sea." If you'll take the time some late afternoon, you'll see that the fiery orb still settles nightly just offshore.

FORT FUNSTON   Located on Skyline Boulevard at the far end of Ocean Beach, this is the prettiest stretch to stroll. The fort itself is little more than a sequence of rusting gun emplacements, but there is a half-mile nature trail here that winds along cliffs overlooking the sea. It's a windblown region of dune grass and leathery succulent plants, with views that span San Francisco and alight on the shore of Marin. Hang gliders dust the cliffs of Fort Funston, adding another dramatic element to this spectacle of sun and wind.

LAKE MERCED   This U-shaped reservoir has the unusual distinction of once having been salt water. Bounded by the Harding Park golf links and hiking trails, it provides a pretty spot to picnic. If you decide to pass up the hang gliding at Fort Funston, you might rent a rowboat or canoe at the clubhouse here and try a less nerve-jangling sport. The lake is stocked with catfish and trout.

SAN FRANCISCO ZOO   ✉*47th Avenue and Sloat Boulevard*   ☎*415-753-7080*   🖥*www.sfzoo.org, guestservices@sfzoo.org* Heading back along the Great Highway, you'll encounter the local zoo. Guests can stroll from the Entry Village on the Great Highway up Zoo Street and visit the African Savanna, a three-acre habitat housing giraffes, antelope, and birds. Guests can continue on to the Lemur Forest, while Puente al Sur ("bridge to the south") brings together such South American species as the giant anteater, tapir, and capybara. There's a children's zoo, home to the Meerkat and Prairie Dog exhibits, as well as an extensive facility for classes and educational programs. Be sure to stop at Grizzly Gulch, a one-acre grizzly bear habitat with a meadow and a 20,000-gallon pool. Other unique exhibits include the Gorilla Preserve, one of the world's largest gorilla habitats; Koala Crossing, one of the few zoo habitats of this teddy bear–like marsupial; and the Primate Discovery Center, a home for rare and endangered apes, monkeys, and lemurs. The daily (except Monday) big-cat feeding at the Lion House is especially popular. More than most zoos, this one goes out of its way to prove it's not just for kids. Besides a full calendar of events for children and families, the zoo sponsors adults-only mating season parties, including a popular Valentine's Day Woo at the Zoo sex tour. Admission.

LODGING

HOSTELLING INTERNATIONAL– SAN FRANCISCO–FISHERMAN'S WHARF

$ 142 BEDS   ✉*Fort Mason, Building 240, Bay and Franklin streets*   ☎*415-771-7277*   📠*415-771-1468*   🖥*www.norcalhostels.org, fishermanswharf@sfhostels.com*

Say the word "hostel" and the first pictures to come to mind are spartan accommodations and shabby surroundings. At this hostel that is simply not the case. Set in Fort Mason, an old military base that is now part of a magnificent national park, the hostel overlooks San Francisco Bay. In addition to eye-boggling views, the facility is within walking distance of the Marina district and Fisherman's Wharf. The hostel itself is contained in a Civil War–era infirmary and features a living room, kitchen, and laundry, as well as a café that offers stunning views of the bay. The rooms, carpeted and quite clean, are dorm-style with 4 to 24 bunk beds in each. Rates also include a continental breakfast and wi-fi. No smoking or alcohol-imbibing; strict noise curfew at 11:00 p.m. Free walking tours, music, and movies are offered. Reservations recommended.

SEAL ROCK INN

$$–$$$ 27 ROOMS   ✉*545 Point Lobos Avenue*   ☎*415-752-8000, 888-732-5762*
📠*415-752-6034*   🖱*www.sealrockinn.com, reservations@sealrockinn.com*

If you're seeking a hotel near the ocean, removed from the hubbub of downtown San Francisco, consider this inn. Perched on a bluff overlooking the Pacific, it's located just outside the Golden Gate National Recreation Area, a stone-skip away from Ocean Beach and Golden Gate Park. The 27 guest rooms are spacious, easily sleeping four people. Furnishings and decor are unimaginative but quite comfortable; the rooms are carpeted wall-to-wall and equipped with televisions and phones. Also, a godsend in this region of frequent fog, some rooms have fireplaces. These are a little extra, as are rooms featuring mini-kitchenettes and panoramic ocean views. Make reservations far in advance.

OCEAN PARK MOTEL

$$ 24 ROOMS   ✉*2690 46th Avenue*   ☎*415-566-7020*   📠*415-665-8959*
🖱*www.oceanparkmotel.com, ocnprk36@aol.com*

San Francisco's first motel is this Art Deco beauty. Built in 1936, the same year as the Golden Gate Bridge, it has modern furnishings and cedar paneling. In addition to attractive rooms with microwaves and refrigerators (some with kitchens) and large family suites, it offers guests an outdoor hot tub, garden courtyard, and small playground. Dogs are welcome (extra fee).

DINING

GREENS AT FORT MASON

$$–$$$ VEGETARIAN   ✉*Fort Mason Center, Building A*   ☎*415-771-6222*
📠*415-771-3472*   🖱*www.greensrestaurant.com*

One of San Francisco's most popular vegetarian restaurants is incongruously situated in an old waterfront warehouse. With pipes exposed and a metal superstructure supporting the roof, this restaurant at Fort Mason possesses the aura of an upscale airplane hangar. But this eatery, run by the Zen Center, has been deftly furnished with burlwood tables, and there's a view of the Golden Gate out of the warehouse windows. The lunch menu includes vegetable brochettes fired over mesquite charcoal, pita bread stuffed with hummus, grilled tofu, soups, and daily specials. Dinner menu is à la carte Monday through Friday, pre-set on Saturday. The menu changes daily: A typical multicourse repast would be soft polenta with grilled portobello mushrooms; spinach linguine with artichokes, shiitake mushrooms, pine nuts, rosemary, and parmesan; Tunisian salad; eggplant soup; Gruyère tart; lettuce salad; tea; and dessert. Reservations recommended for lunch and dinner. No lunch on Monday, brunch on Sunday.

TASTE OF THE HIMALAYAS

$$ TIBETAN ✉*2420 Lombard Street* ☎*415-674-9898*
✐*www.tasteofnepalsf.com*

In a city famed for its amazing array of ethnic restaurants, this is the only place where you can try Tibetan cuisine. This place serves it right, as well as Nepalese and Indian dishes. The minute you wrap your taste buds around any item served here, you'll know you're not in Kansas any more. Go for the *momos* (dumplings with veggies or meat) or the *alu bhanta* (Himalayan-style eggplant with potatoes). The warm, friendly staff, mainly Tibetan refugees, and the authentic decorative touches make a meal here a memorable experience.

BISTRO AT THE CLIFF HOUSE

$$–$$$ AMERICAN ✉*1090 Point Lobos Avenue* ☎*415-386-3330* 📠*415-387-7837*
✐*www.cliffhouse.com, info@cliffhouse.com*

Try as you might to escape the trodden paths, some places in the world are simply inevitable. This historic structure at the edge of the sea is positively inundated with tourists. Still, the Bistro at the Cliff House offers great views of the Sutro Baths, the Marin coastline, and the Golden Gate Bridge. The breakfast and lunch menu boasts omelettes as well as soups and sandwiches. At dinner there are pasta dishes, several seafood selections, and a few chicken, steak, or lamb entrées. **Sutro's**, a more formal two-story dining room, offers an upscale seafood menu for lunch and dinner.

LOUIS'

$$ DINER ✉*902 Point Lobos Avenue* ☎*415-387-6330*

For a tad less expensive meal than at the nearby Cliff House, head uphill a few steps to this cliffside café that's been family-owned since 1937. The dinners, served with soup or salad, include New York steak, prawns, scallops, and hamburger steak. Breakfast and lunch are similar all-American affairs. Add a postcard view of the Sutro Baths and Seal Rocks and you have one hell of a bargain. Limited dinner hours during winter.

PACIFIC CAFÉ

$$ SEAFOOD ✉*7000 Geary Boulevard* ☎*415-387-7091*

Seafood lovers start lining up early at this popular this café in the outer Richmond District where the wait for a table is soothed by a complimentary glass of wine and convivial talk. Then it's time to sink into a high-backed wooden booth and ponder the daily specials, which always include a wide assortment of grilled fresh fish and frequently ahi tuna garnished with wasabe butter, crab cakes, and garlic-infused steamed mussels. Dinner only.

KHAN TOKE THAI HOUSE

$$ THAI ✉*5937 Geary Boulevard* ☎*415-668-6654*

Leave your shoes at the door and step into Southeast Asian elegance. This restaurant offers all the culinary and aesthetic delights of fine dining without the hefty price. Sunken-floor seating, intricate wood carvings, and gold inlay transform the interior into an exotic locale. Try the fried tofu appetizer with peanut sauce, green curry chicken, or any of their other Thai delights. Ask for a spot in the back and get your own secluded table. Reservations suggested. Dinner only.

NIGHTLIFE

MAGIC THEATRE ✉*Fort Mason Center, Building D* ✆*415-441-8822* 📠*415-771-5505* 🖱*www.magictheatre.org, info@magictheatre.org* This theatre has premiered several plays by Pulitzer Prize–winning dramatist Sam Shepard, who was playwright-in-residence here for several years. Plays by new playwrights are performed nearly year-round.

THE PRESIDIO

What was previously the oldest active military base in the country is now part of the country's largest urban national park. The Presidio is also a National Historic Landmark. It was established by the Spanish in 1776 and taken over by the United States in 1846. Civil War troops trained here, and the Sixth Army established the base as its headquarters. Even when it was a military base, the Presidio had the feel of a country retreat. Hiking trails snake through the 1400 acres of undulating hills sprinkled with acacia, madrone, pine, and redwood trees, and there are expansive bay views. Although still under development, there are plans for new hiking trails, museums, education centers, and conference facilities.

SIGHTS

VISITOR CENTER ✉*Building 50, Moraga Avenue* ✆*415-561-4323* 📠*415-561-4310* 🖱*www.nps.gov/prsf* The best way to explore the Presidio is by stopping first at this visitor center. The folks here are very knowledgeable, they'll provide you with a map and information about free public programs. The center is temporarily located at the **Officers' Club**, a tile-roof, Spanish-style structure. It includes part of the original 1776 Presidio, one of the first buildings ever constructed in San Francisco.

NATIONAL CEMETERY ✉*Lincoln Boulevard* This cemetery, with rows of tombstones on a grassy knoll overlooking the Golden Gate Bridge, is San Francisco's salute to the nation's war dead.

EL POLIN SPRING idden
✉*Located at the end of MacArthur Avenue* The remainder of our Presidio tour is of a more natural bent. This is the spot where, as the brass plaque proclaims, "the early Spanish garrison attained its water supply." History has rarely been made in a more beauti-

ful spot. The spring is set in a lovely park surrounded by hills upon which eucalyptus trees battle with conifers for strategic ground. Hiking trails lead down and outward from this enchanted glade.

LOVER'S LANE ⊠*In the southeast corner of the Presidio* The battle lines of the forest are drawn here. March, or even stroll, along this narrow pathway, and review these armies of nature. On one side, standing sentinel straight, out-thrust arms shading the lane, are the eucalyptus. Mustered along the other front, clad in darker uniforms, seeming to retreat before the wind, are the conifer trees. Forgetting for a moment these silly games soldiers play, look around. You are standing in an awesome and spectacular spot, one of the last forests in San Francisco.

IMMIGRANT POINT OVERLOOK ⊠*Washington Boulevard between Central Magazine and Compton roads* This overlook features stone benches and terraces, and affords outstanding views of the Pacific Ocean and the Golden Gate Bridge.

MOUNTAIN LAKE PARK ⊠*Lake Street between 8th and Funston avenues* Stationed along the Presidio's southern flank, this is another idyllic locale. With grassy meadows and wooded walkways, it's a great place to picnic or stroll. The lake itself, a favorite watering hole among ducks visiting from out of town, is skirted with tule reeds and overhung with willows. There's also a playground here.

LETTERMAN DIGITAL ARTS CENTER ⊠*Corner of Lyon Street and Lombard Street* The Presidio's newest addition centers around this 865,000-square-foot office complex (one of the largest developments in San Francisco history). It is now home to employees of Lucasfilm, Ltd. George Lucas, of *Star Wars* fame, has extended his Marin-based digital media firm southward across the Golden Gate. This sprawling campus also includes open acreage and beautiful views of the bay.

PRESIDIO WALL The base's prettiest walk is actually in civilian territory along this wall bordering Lyon Street. Starting at the Lombard Street Gate, where two cannons guard the fort's eastern entrance, walk uphill along Lyon Street. That wall of urbanity to the left is the city's chic Union Street district, breeding place for fern bars and antique stores. To the right, beyond the Presidio's stone enclosure, are the tumbling hills and towering trees of the old garrison.

After several blocks, Lyon ceases to be a street and becomes a staircase. The most arduous and rewarding part of the trek begins; you can follow this stairway to heaven, which happens to be Broadway, two heart-pounding blocks above you. Ascend and the city falls away—the Palace of Fine Arts, Alcatraz, the Marina, all become landing points for your vision. Closer to hand are the houses of San Francisco's posh Pacific Heights district, stately structures looming several stories and sprawling across the landscape. When you reach the stone steps at the top of Broadway, they will still rise above, potent and pretentious, hard contrast to the Presidio's leafy acres.

PRESIDIO CAFÉ

$$ CALIFORNIA CUISINE/AMERICAN ✉ *300 Finley Road (at the Arguello gate)* ☎ *415-561-4661 ext. 203* ✎ *www.presidiogolf.com*

Creative California cuisine may be everywhere you look in San Francisco, but rarely will you find it served in such a restfully sylvan setting as at this café, located in the clubhouse of the Presidio Golf Course. The indoor 'dining area features an exposed-beam cathedral ceiling, a massive stone fireplace, and picture windows looking out on the golf course, while the outdoor area is sandwiched between the links and the forest. The menu features specialty sandwiches, like the Presidio club or the pulled pork simmered in Zinfandel barbecue sauce. Prices are reasonable, and there's ample free parking. Hours are late morning to afternoon, with appetizers and cocktails served until evening. (Hours vary slightly on weekends.)

PRESIDIO SOCIAL CLUB

$$ AMERICAN ✉ *Building 523, 563 Ruger Street* ☎ *415-885-1888* ✎ *www.presidiosocialclub.com*

Good, familiar food—grilled steaks and chops, fresh oysters, beef stroganoff, sloppy joes, and burgers—is served throughout the day here. The restaurant is set in century-old Building 563, one of only four remaining structures in the Army's East Cantonment, and once home barracks for the famed Buffalo Soldiers. Both building and location are rooted in the history of its beautiful surroundings, providing a welcome meeting place to a revitalized Presidio. Dinner only Monday through Saturday. Weekend brunch.

GOLDEN GATE PARK

It is the Central Park of the West. Or perhaps we should say that Central Park is New York's answer to Golden Gate Park. It extends from the Haight-Ashbury neighborhood, across nearly half the width of the city, all the way to the ocean. With its folded hills and sloping meadows, its lakes and museums, Golden Gate is everyone's favorite park.

Once an undeveloped region of sand dunes, the park today encompasses over 1000 acres of gardens, lawns, and forests. The transformation from wasteland to wonderland came about during the late-19th and early-20th centuries through the efforts of a mastermind named John McLaren. A gardener by trade, this Scotsman could rightly be called an architect of the earth. Within his lifetime he oversaw the creation of the world's largest human-made park.

What he wrought was a place that has something to suit everyone: there are tennis courts; lawn bowling greens; hiking trails; byways for bicyclists, rollerskaters, skateboarders, even unicyclists; a nine-hole golf course; an archery field; flycasting pools; playgrounds; fields for soccer and football; riding stables; even checker pavilions. Facilities for renting bikes and skates are located just outside the park along Haight and Stanyan streets.

Or, if you'd prefer not to lift a finger, you can always pull up a shade tree and watch the parade. The best day to visit Golden Gate Park is Sunday when many of the roads in the eastern end of the park are closed to cars but open to skaters, jugglers, cyclists, troubadours, mimes, skateboarders, impromptu theater groups, sun worshippers, and anyone else who feels inspired.

Touring the park should be done on another day, when you can drive freely through the grounds. There are two roads spanning the length of the park. Each begins near Stanyan Street on the east side of Golden Gate Park and runs about four miles westward to the Pacific. The best way to see this area is to travel out along John F. Kennedy Drive and back by Martin Luther King, Jr. Drive, detouring down the side roads that lead into the heart of the park.

SIGHTS

MCLAREN LODGE ⬚*Stanyan and Fell streets* ☎*415-831-2700* ✎*415-221-8034* ✐*www.parks.sfgov.org* The first stop along John F. Kennedy Drive lies immediately after the entrance. The red-tile building is park headquarters and home base for maps, brochures, pamphlets, and information. Closed Saturday and Sunday.

CONSERVATORY OF FLOWERS ⬚*John F. Kennedy Drive* ☎*415-666-7001* ✐*www.conservatoryofflowers.org, info@conservatoryofflowers.org* This Victorian glass palace was built in 1878. It houses a plant kingdom ruled by stately palm trees and peopled with tropical flowers, pendent ferns, and courtly orchids. The Conservatory makes for a stunning photo op. Closed Monday. Admission.

RHODODENDRON DELL   Just down the street from the conservatory is a lacework of trails threading through this 20-acre garden; if you're visiting in early spring, when the rose-hued bushes are blooming, the dell is a concert of colors.

DE YOUNG MEMORIAL MUSEUM ☎*415-750-3600* ✎*415-750-7386* ✐*www.thinker.org, guestbook@famsf.org* Just beyond this garden beats the cultural heart of Golden Gate Park. Located around a tree-studded concourse, this museum first opened in 1895; an earthquake in 1989 closed its doors until 2005, when it re-opened in a contemporary copper structure with a 144-foot-high twisting tower. A sculpture garden and thoughtful landscaping create a feast for the eyes. Skylit courts, floor-to-ceiling windows, and avant-garde free-standing furniture bring a modern touch to the interior. Exhibits trace the course of American art from colonial times to the mid-20th century, including an important collection of colonial-era art donated by the Rockefellers; the Art of the Americas gallery features ancient art from Central and South

America as well as North American art of the past 400 years. There's also an intriguing display of works from Africa and Oceania, as well as a supreme collection of rare objects from New Guinea. The de Young has one of the largest collections in the nation. Closed Monday. Admission.

CALIFORNIA ACADEMY OF SCIENCES ✉ *55 Music Concourse Drive* 📞*415-379-8000* 🖱*www.calacademy.org* Several years of planning and construction have given this venerable scientific museum a completely new identity. In fact, the place might consider changing its name to somehow tip off visitors to the stunning combination of artistry and nature here. Designed by world-famous architect Renzo Piano, the building is encased by glass walls that allow natural light to stream into 90 percent of the public areas. The result is a place that, from almost every vantage point, lets visitors enjoy views of the Golden Gate on one side and extraordinary exhibits on the other. A highlight is the two-and-a-half-acre Living Roof, showcasing native California plants and covering the major exhibits with seven hills that echo the city's topography. At Rainforests of the World, you can take a glass elevator into an Amazonian flood forest, with anacondas, piranhas, and electric eels, or walk through a clear tunnel beneath a river of Amazonian fish swimming overhead. The world's largest all-digital planetarium, a coral reef ecosystem, and virtual African safari are more of the standout exhibits, guaranteeing that you'll be back for multiple visits. Admission.

JAPANESE TEA GARDEN If you're like me, you won't be in Golden Gate Park more than an hour or two before museum fatigue sets in and all the art starts looking like kindergarten crafts. It's time for a break at this peaceful garden. Here you can rest your heavy eyes on carp-filled ponds and handwrought gateways. There are arch footbridges, cherry trees, bonsai gardens, and, of course, a tea house where Japanese women serve jasmine tea and cookies. Admission.

MUSIC CONCOURSE All these cultural gathering places cluster around this concourse, a grand civic amphitheater designed for cultural events. It was originally constructed as a center for an international fair in 1900.

STOW LAKE You can get back on John F. Kennedy Drive and resume your self-guided tour by continuing to this donut-shaped body of water with an island as the hole in the middle. From the island's crest you can gaze across San Francisco from Bay to ocean. Or, if an uphill is not in your day's itinerary, there's a footpath around the island perimeter that passes an ornate Chinese pagoda. There are also rowboats, pedalboats, and electric motorboats for rent, and a small snack bar.

RAINBOW FALLS Next along John F. Kennedy Drive you'll pass Rainbow Falls. That monument at the top, from which this cascade appears to spill, is **Prayerbook Cross**, modeled after an old Celtic cross.

MEADOWS This is followed close on by a chain of meadows, a kind of rolling green counterpoint to the chain of lakes that lie ahead. **Speedway Meadow** and **Lindley Meadow** offer barbecue pits and picnic tables; both are fabulous areas for sunbathing.

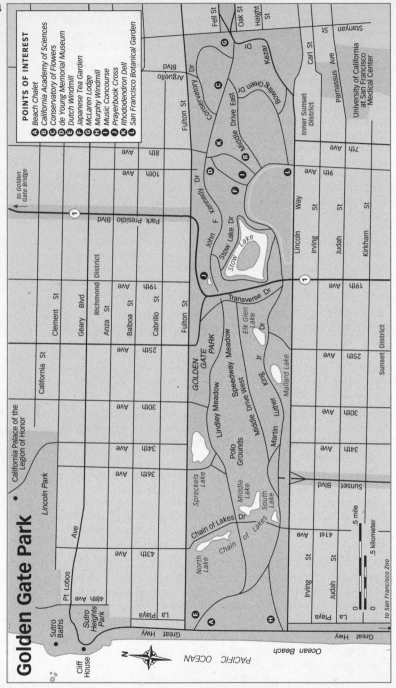

Golden Gate Park

SPRECKELS LAKE   This lake is home to ducks, seagulls, and model sailboats. Nearby is the **Buffalo Paddock**, where American bison still roam, though within the confines of a barbed wire fence.

CHAIN OF LAKES   Immediately beyond Stowe Lake is this string of three reservoirs stretching the width of the park, perpendicular to John F. Kennedy Drive. Framed by eucalyptus trees, they offer hiking paths around each shoreline. As you circumnavigate these baby lakes, you will notice they are freckled with miniature islands. Each lake possesses a singular personality: North Lake is remarkable for its hip-deep swamp cypress; Middle Lake features an island tufted with willows; and South Lake, tiniest of the triplets, sprouts bamboo along its shore.

WINDMILLS   If the Chain of Lakes ponds be babies, the great mother of them all rests nearby—the Pacific Ocean. Where the road meets the Pacific you'll come upon the **Dutch Windmill**, a regal structure built in 1903. With its wooden struts and scale-like shingles, it stares into the face of the sea's inevitable west winds. The Dutchman's cousin, **Murphy Windmill**, lives several hundred yards down the coast.

SAN FRANCISCO BOTANICAL GARDEN   ✉*9th Avenue at Lincoln Way* ☎*415-661-1316* 📠*415-661-3539* 🖱*www.sfbotanicalgarden.org* From the lake at continent's edge, it's a four-mile trip back through the park along Martin Luther King, Jr. Drive. After picking it up at Murphy Windmill, you'll find that this softly curving road passes lakes and forests, meadows and playgrounds. More importantly, it borders this place specially made for garden lovers. The garden is a world within itself, a 55-acre flower quilt stitched together by pathways. Over 7000 species peacefully coexist here—dwarf conifers and sprawling magnolias, as well as plants from Asia, the Andes, Australia, and America. There is a "redwood trail" devoted to native California plants, a "garden of fragrance" redolent of flowers, and a Japanese moon-viewing garden. It's a kind of park within a park, a glorious finale for your visit to this park within a city.

DINING

DE YOUNG MUSEUM CAFÉ
$–$$ AMERICAN   ✉*Golden Gate Park, 50 Hagiwara Tea Garden Drive* ☎*415-750-2614* 🖱*www.deyoungmuseum.org*
This first-class café serves a seasonal menu and prepares dishes from the freshest locally grown and sustainably produced ingredients from small family farmers and artisans. Patrons are lit from above through original, hand-blown glass light fixtures and the dining room features views of the museum's sculpture garden. Museum admission is not required to eat at the café, and in fact visitors with a park picnic in mind now have the option of ready-to-go salads and sandwiches. Closed Monday.

ACADEMY CAFÉ
$–$$ INTERNATIONAL   ✉*California Academy of Science, 55 Music Concourse Drive* ☎*415-379-8000*
The chef-designer duo who earned a distinguished reputation for the

Slanted Door restaurant teamed up again to establish this upscale café, which is part of the California Academy of Sciences. While admission to the academy is required for café entry, the assortment of pastas, soups and sandwiches are decidedly affordable. The cafeteria-style dining room features entrees such as Lebanese lentils and pumpkin stew and Vietnamese halibut with rice noodles. A light and airy atmosphere that includes an extensive aquarium complements the rich cuisine.

For any city in the country, there's a rule of thumb to good eating: to dine where the locals dine, go where the locals live. In San Francisco that means Clement Street. Paralleling Golden Gate Park and the Presidio and set midway between the two, this friendly street is the center of a multicultural neighborhood. Irish, Russians, Chinese, Japanese, Jews, and others have called the district home for varying periods of time. The result is a marvelous mix of ethnic restaurants. Stroll Clement Street, from 1st to 12th Avenue or 19th to 26th Avenue, and encounter Italian, Danish, Thai, and Indonesian restaurants. There are Irish bars, French patisseries, bistros, health food stores, open-air vegetable stands, and numerous Asian dining places. The only difficulty you'll encounter is deciding on a particular place (and maybe finding parking). I have a few suggestions, but if they don't fit your fancy, you'll doubtless find a dozen places that do.

MAI'S   hidden

$ VIETNAMESE   ✉*316 Clement Street*   ☎*415-221-3046*

I heartily recommend this restaurant. The dining room is small and informal with a simple decor. Serene and personable, Mai's prepares a host of tempting entrées, among them coconut chicken, lemongrass barbecued beef, Vietnamese pork shish kebab, as well as several vegetarian dishes.

TOY BOAT DESSERT CAFE

$ DINER   ✉*401 Clement Street*   ☎*415-751-7505*   🖷*415-751-7505*

End your meal on a sweet note with a shake, malt, or sundae from this cafe. Though mainly an ice cream parlor, you'll also find espresso drinks, breakfast items, sandwiches, pies, cakes, and cookies. If you're young at heart, you probably won't be able to resist the mind-boggling display of old and new collectible toys. Their price tags, however, are another matter.

KING OF THAI NOODLE HOUSE

$ THAI   ✉*639 Clement Street*   ☎*415-752-5198*

This is a genuine hole in the wall: a narrow, fluorescent-lit eatery with a few tables in the back where young locals hang out late into the night. The food, like the atmosphere, more closely approximates what you'd actually find in Thailand than what you'd expect of a Thai restaurant in the U.S.—an assortment of spicy soups and noodle bowls ranging from vegetarian to meat and seafood.

HAIG'S DELICACIES

$–$$ MEDITERRANEAN   ✉642 Clement Street   ☎415-752-6283
🖅www.haigsdelicacies.com, info@haigsdelicacies.com

Haig's, a long-established specialty food shop, is where many chefs from San Francisco's finest restaurants go for unusual and hard-to-find ingredients from around the world, such as Indian chutneys, Turkish olive oil, Israeli soup mixes, and Lebanese hot red-pepper sauce. There are a few tables where diners can eat on the premises (but why not pick up the makings for a classy picnic and head up to Golden Gate Park?). The hummus and tabbouleh come highly recommended. Closed Sunday.

YET WAH

$$ CHINESE   ✉2140 Clement Street   ☎415-387-8040   ☎415-387-8333
🖅www.yetwah.com

With over 300 dishes from all over China to choose from, this place has something for everyone. The main dining room is rather large and franchise-esque, sporting the same look as other popular Chinese restaurants. But that doesn't detract from the food, which remains tasty and well-prepared. Lunchtime dim sum is especially popular, with carts whizzing by and chatter filling the room.

BILL'S PLACE

$$ DINER   ✉2315 Clement Street   ☎415-221-5262   ☎707-824-0295
🖅www.billsplace.qpg.com

Chandeliers in a hamburger joint? Bill's ain't just any hamburger joint! Many San Franciscans insist it's a hamburger palace, the best in the city. There's the '49er burger with bacon and avocado; the Giants burger; the Letterman burger; the Red Skelton burger (garnished like a clown); and so on. If you want to be gauche, you can order a sandwich or hot dog instead. And if you'd rather forego the counter or table service out front, there's an open-air patio in back. Bill's is *the* place for fast food with a flair.

INDIA CLAY OVEN

$–$$ INDIAN   ✉2436 Clement Street   ☎415-751-0544   ☎415-751-3610
🖅www.indiaclayoven.com

For north Indian cooking, it's hard to beat the house specialties here including chicken *tikka* and other tandoori oven–cooked entrées. Bright decor suggestive of an Indian village sets the tone in this low-key family restaurant.

One block south of and parallel to Clement Street, Geary Boulevard is a broad street with storefronts that harken back to an earlier decade. It, too, boasts an array of ethnic eateries, old-fashioned ice cream parlors, and friendly watering holes.

MOSCOW & TBILISI
BAKERY STORE

$ BAKERY ✉5540 Geary Boulevard ✆415-668-6959 📠415-752-5721

If you're a fan of baked goods, prepare to spend some time in this bakery. Sure, you'll have to get in line to purchase the freshly baked black, rye, and white breads, but that's not why you'll take so long—it's the process of deciding which desserts and pastries *not* to buy! To make things more difficult, the pierogis, filled with meat, cheese, or potatoes, are delectable. Closed Sunday.

NIGHTLIFE

TRAD'R SAM ✉6150 Geary Boulevard ✆415-221-0773 Here, you sit in booths named Guam, Samoa, and various Hawaiian islands and slowly sip such tropical concoctions as Tahitian deep purples, mai tais, and banana cows. Soak in the 1940s Polynesian atmosphere. This bar is a classic.

THE PLOUGH AND THE STARS ✉116 Clement Street ✆415-751-1122 🖱www.theploughandstars.com Perhaps the closest thing to an authentic Dublin pub in San Francisco is this spot with its burnished wood paneling and framed political cartoons hanging on the walls. A stage in the back presents rousing Irish folk bands on most nights. Cover on Friday and Saturday.

THE HAIGHT

Places that are part of the cultural mythology have usually gained their prominence centuries before. For the Haight that is simply not the case. This neighborhood of quiet streets and Victorian houses blazed across the public consciousness within the past decades, leaving a vapor trail that may never vanish.

For an entire generation, 1967 was the "Summer of Love," a heady season when psychedelic drugs were food for thought and acid rock was king. On January 14, 1967, about 20,000 enlightened folks streamed through the Haight on the way to a "Human Be-In—A Gathering of the Tribes," where they tuned in to a succession of speakers, singers, and seers. By that summer, San Francisco had become a mecca for young people seeking religious truth and righteous dope. A new breed thronged to the Haight—clad in motley and carrying bells, feathers, beads, and cymbals. For one brief period it was a kind of dreamland, a creation of the collective imagination. Like all dreams, it was ephemeral, momentarily transmogrified into reality by Vietnam and an increasingly repressive society.

SIGHTS

While many of us will carry the memory of those days to the grave, the Haight has lost many of its countercultural trappings. As it was before

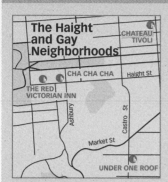

The Haight and Gay Neighborhoods

CHATEAU TIVOLI

CHA CHA CHA — Haight St

THE RED VICTORIAN INN

Ashbury

Castro St

Market St

UNDER ONE ROOF

THE RED VICTORIAN INN

PAGE 132

Inviting B&B, where each room boasts a different theme from the Summer of Love and friendly conversation waits below in The Peace Cafe

CHA CHA CHA

PAGE 133

Local treasure offering Latin and Caribbean flavors from Cajun shrimp and jerk chicken to lightly battered calamari with lemon aïoli

CHATEAU TIVOLI

PAGE 137

San Francisco's greatest "painted lady"—a lavishly decorated inn with a long list of infamous guests including Mark Twain

UNDER ONE ROOF

PAGE 139

One-of-a-kind retail store with soaps, jewelry, books, and more donating all profits to HIV/AIDS organizations

the first hippie floated along its streets, the Haight is an upper-middle-class neighborhood resplendent with tree-lined avenues and backyard gardens. With its multihued Victorian houses, it is continually undergoing a process of gentrification. Old buildings are remodeled and chic shops move. As a result, shoppers will find that Haight Street is a hip, bustling boulevard.

ASHBURY HEIGHTS   Tucked between two of San Francisco's prettiest parks—Golden Gate and Buena Vista—the Haight sports some of the city's loveliest Victorians. There are Queen Anne styles marked by solitary turrets and boldly painted facades. On Ashbury Heights, the hillside overlooking Haight Street, are houses drawn from a gingerbread cakeboard. In the entire neighborhood there are over a thousand Victorians.

HAIGHT STREET   Today the Haight is still an area in transition. The district has been partially gentrified but still retains vestiges of its bohemian past. On Haight Street, between Masonic and Stanyan streets, the sidewalks are door-to-door with mod shops, trendy bars, used clothing stores, art galleries, and funky restaurants.

BUENA VISTA PARK ✉*Haight and Lyon streets* Before strolling Haight Street, be sure to explore this park. Dense with conifers and eucalyptus trees, the park's angling hills offer splendid views of San Francisco from

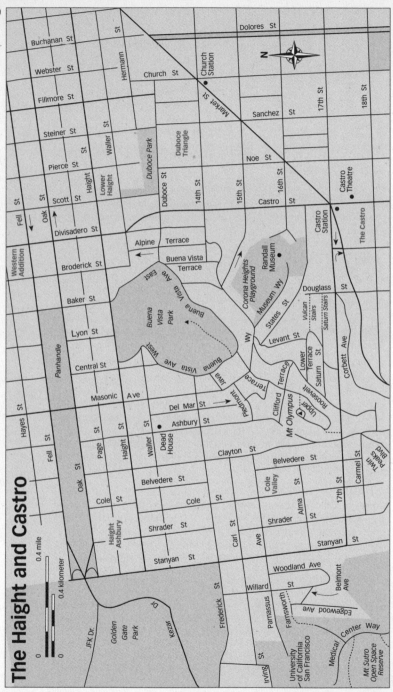

The Haight and Castro

ocean to bay. Buena Vista possesses the beauty of Golden Gate Park but lacks the crowds.

MURAL   Just off Haight Street are several spots vital to the history of the '60s counterculture. For a vibrant retrospective on psychedelic art, wander past the mural that decorates an entire outside wall at 1807 Page Street. Painted in striking colors, it pictures a visionary eye radiating down upon a multiracial band of musicians. Along one side, green hills roll to infinity, while from the other extends the open sea. In the busy but vital style of the era, it is packed with an endless series of images.

636 COLE STREET   To add a ghoulish element to your otherwise pleasant tour, check out the nondescript house at 636 Cole Street. It served during the "Summer of Love" as home to a man named Charles Manson.

DEAD HOUSE   Or, if you like visiting these places-that-are-still-spoken-of-around-town-even-though-they-are-no-longer-what-they-are-known-for, you'll be interested in the pretty Victorian at 710 Ashbury Street. Back in the halcyon days of live music and electric drugs it was the Dead House, home to San Francisco's foremost acid rock ensemble, the Grateful Dead.

CORONA HEIGHTS

A rewarding way to discover the Haight is by wandering on your own through the neighborhood, seeking out old Victorians and soaking up local ambience. You might also head to Corona Heights for a city view known only to San Franciscans. This six-block uphill walk from Haight Street carries one past some pretty Victorians (take Masonic Street to the end, then continue one-half block after it turns into Roosevelt Avenue). At the top is a rocky, wind-haunted outcropping that commands a sweep of the city from Russian Hill to the Financial District to the southern stretches of the Bay. Backdropped by Twin Peaks, Corona Heights is a lesser promontory, but one that you'll often have to yourself.

RANDALL MUSEUM ✉ *199 Museum Way* ☎ *415-554-9600* 📠 *415-554-9609* 🌐 *www.randallmuseum.org, info@randallmuseum.org* Near the southern edge of Corona Heights Park is this kid-friendly spot. Interactive exhibits focus on the culture of San Francisco, from science to art. Free audience-participation animal sessions are held every Saturday at noon. A model railroad exhibit is also open Saturday. There's a playground adjacent to the museum. Closed Sunday and Monday.

EDGEWOOD AVENUE

Beauty appears not only in open spaces, but in narrow corridors as well. After descending Corona Heights, you might consider a stroll on this avenue. The climb begins on Farnsworth Lane (off Parnassus Avenue, above the University of California Medical Center). Farnsworth is a country lane banked with ivy and trim hedges that someone accidentally placed in the city. It opens on to Edgewood Avenue, a brick-paved street that local resident Else Reisner considers one of San Francisco's prettiest walks. If you ever plan to live in San Francisco, you might as well settle here; you'll never find a more congenial place. The houses on either side are faced with brown shingle or brick; they end at the edge of a forest amid trees heavy with vines. If you're game, a hiking path leads into this primeval wood.

LODGING

THE RED VICTORIAN INN

$$–$$$$ 18 ROOMS   ✉1665 Haight Street   ☎415-864-1978
📠415-863-3293   🖱www.redvic.com, reservations@redvic.com

One of San Francisco's most reasonable B&B hotels can be found right along Haight Street, center of the fabled Summer of Love. This inn evokes a sense of that era. Owner Sami Sunchild promotes an individualistic atmosphere in her hotel. Each chamber is decorated according to a different theme. The Peacock Suite and the Rainbow Room reflect the style of the 1960s. All rooms are nicely appointed with handsome wood tables and chairs and lacy curtains. Some have shared baths. The public areas display the owner's artwork as well as historic photos of Golden Gate Park and San Francisco. A light breakfast is served.

INN 1890

$$–$$$ 16 ROOMS   ✉1890 Page Street   ☎415-386-0486, 888-466-1890
📠415-386-3626   🖱www.inn1890.com, inn1890@pacbell.net

If the wackiness of Haight Street proves too much, retreat to this stately Victorian built in, you guessed it, 1890. It boasts rooms with brass or iron queen-sized beds, down comforters, 12-foot ceilings, and kitchenettes. A full kitchen and dining room is available around the clock and guests enjoy nearby health club facilities (slight fee). Continental breakfast included.

DINING

KAN ZAMAN

$$ MIDDLE EASTERN   ✉1793 Haight Street   ☎415-751-9656

Stepping into this dining room is like entering into a dream of Arabian Nights. The lighting is dim, and the walls are covered with desert murals done in relaxing earth tones. Lounge on the big, comfortable cushions set on the floor around low tables and choose from couscous, falafel, grape leaves, and so on. After dinner you may want to indulge in one of the large hookah pipes filled with your choice of apricot, honey, strawberry or apple tobacco. No lunch on weekdays.

CHA CHA CHA

$$ CARIBBEAN ✉1801 Haight Street ✆415-386-7670 ✎415-386-0417
✐www.cha3.com

Amid Santería altars and glittering shrines hanging on the black brick walls, this restaurant conjures up a bewitching mix of Latin and Caribbean flavors that can range from Jamaican jerk chicken over white rice to Cajun shrimp in a spicy cream sauce or fried plantains with black beans and sour cream. Fortunately, most menu choices are tapas plates allowing diners to sample a variety of tastes.

MEMPHIS MINNIE'S BARBECUE

$–$$ BARBECUE ✉586 Haight Street ✆415-864-pork ✎415-864-8081
✐www.memphisminnies.com, info@memphisminnies.com

Never mind the squat red-painted brick building and bare bones furnishings. This is the home of mouth-watering meats, slow-smoked over white oak and served steaming hot. Order yours topped with tangy slaw as a sandwich on a crusty roll or straight up with down-home sides. Pork ribs, chicken, turkey, and beef ribs share the menu with big sides of chilli cheese fries, fried cheese grits sticks, greens, mac and cheese, and sweet potatoes. You won't find beer or wine, but there's a great selection of premium *sake* (go figure) and soft drinks. Closed Monday.

SHOPPING

PIPE DREAMS ✉1376 Haight Street ✆415-431-3553 Though the hippies of the Haight may have gone off to graze in greener pastures, their spirit infuses this anachronistic '60s survivor that still has a good selection of pipes, rolling papers, nostalgic posters, roach clips, and water pipes, as well as a small selection of shirts, books, and incense burners.

PIEDMONT BOUTIQUE ✉1452 Haight Street ✆415-864-8075 ✐www.piedmontsf.com Dress to fit your fantasy at this boutique. Join the drag queens and strippers who frequent the store for fancy custom-made gowns, boas, baubles, and bangles. You can buy a great outfit for a costume party or something to help you blend into the Haight Street fashion scene. There aren't too many stores like this one.

ASHBURY MARKET ✉205 Frederick Street near Ashbury Street ✆415-566-3134 Located a couple blocks south of Haight is this great neighborhood market for picnic stuff to bring to Golden Gate Park. You'll find fresh-baked breads, California wines, a wide array of deli items and tempting gourmet specialties.

DISTRACTIONS ✉1552 Haight Street ✆415-252-8751 This shop offers underground electronic CDs, smoking paraphernalia, and popular items of the hippie era such as bells, incense, jewelry, and reggae and urban clothing. In the back, a special section specializes in waterpipes and used records and CDs.

OFF THE WALL ✉*1669 Haight Street* ☎*415-863-8170* In addition to an imaginative name, this gallery has an appealing collection of contemporary poster art and a large line of new rock art. There are assorted eclectic artworks, particularly by ethnic artists.

AMOEBA MUSIC ✉*1855 Haight Street* ☎*415-831-1200* ✐*www.amoeba music.com* Music lovers will have a field day at Amoeba, a former bowling alley jammed with new and used CDs, records, and even cassettes.

Unique Bookstores

San Francisco has a long tradition of supporting unusual, often quirky bookstores, large and small. Yes, these days you'll find bookselling behemoths Borders, Barnes & Noble, and B. Dalton downtown, but serious readers still head for personality-packed independent shops.

MCDONALD'S BOOKSHOP ✉*48 Turk Street* ☎*415-673-2235* ✐*mc donaldsbookshop@prodigy.net* This musty warren of crowded aisles could keep you browsing for hours. It boasts more than a million books and a vast array of magazines that date back to the 1920s, including a complete selection of *Life*, which began publication in 1936. There are also hundreds of old photos and a collection of James Dean pictures and books. Closed Sunday and Monday.

GREEN APPLE BOOKS ✉*506 Clement Street* ☎*415-387-2272* ✐*www. greenapplebooks.com* A destination for discriminating book lovers for more than 40 years, this bookstore sells, buys, and trades new and used books, CDs, and DVDs in virtually every genre.

CITY LIGHTS BOOKSTORE ✉*261 Columbus Avenue* ☎*415-362-8193* ☎*415-362-4921* ✐*www.citylights.com*, *staff@citylights.com* Once a roosting place for Beat writers like Allen Ginsberg, Jack Kerouac, and Neal Cassady, San Francisco's most famous independent bookshop still remains a vital gathering point for local artists. The book selection is unique, featuring many contemporary poetry and prose volumes that are unavailable elsewhere.

KINOKUNIYA BOOKSTORE ✉*Japan Center, 1581 Webster Street* ☎*415-567-7625* ✐*www.kinokuniya.com* This Japantown bookstore is a warehouse of a store, chockablock with volumes on Japanese language and culture. Among the works in both English and Japanese are books on history, travel, and cooking.

BROWSER BOOKS ✉*2195 Fillmore Street* ☎*415-567-8027* In Pacific Heights, this shop is noteworthy. Its stock focuses on literature, psychology, religion, and philosophy.

A DIFFERENT LIGHT ✉*489 Castro Street* ☎*415-431-0891* ✐*www.adl books. com* This bookstore in the heart of the Castro carries the most popular titles for and about the lesbian, gay, bisexual, and transgender community.

GET LOST TRAVEL BOOKS ✉*1825 Market Street* ☎*415-437-0529* ✐*www.getlostbooks.com* This travel bookstore carries an extensive selection of guidebooks, travel literature, language instruction manuals and CDs, maps, luggage, and a host of other travel accessories.

Located a block north of Haight Street, this store has stained-glass supplies and creates custom windows. Closed Sunday.

NIGHTLIFE

The Lower Haight is home to many bars and clubs, and on weekends they seem to have a revolving door as people cruise from one to the other and back again.

MAD DOG IN THE FOG ⊠*530 Haight Street* ☏*415-626-7279* ⏴*www.maddoginthefog.com* Mad Dog resembles a British pub and attracts quite a crowd with its dart boards and extensive beer selection (20 on tap plus about 35 bottled). There are deejay-spun tunes on Friday night, live music on Saturday night, and a pub quiz on Tuesday and Thursday. On weekend mornings, they show live English soccer via satellite, if you're so inclined.

NOC NOC ⊠*557 Haight Street* ☏*415-861-5811* A bit quirkier than Mad Dog is this bar, with decor that is somehow reminiscent of both the Jetsons and the Flintstones.

NICKIE'S BBQ ⊠*460 Haight Street* ☏*415-621-6508* ⏴*www.nickies.com* For a game of pool or serious dancing go to Nickie's. There's a different deejay or band Monday through Saturday, playing everything from hip-hop to Latin and jazz. Closed Sunday. Cover.

GAY NEIGHBORHOODS

San Francisco's gay neighborhoods center around Castro Street, Polk Street, and in the South of Market area. The city's lesbian community has its roots along Valencia Street in the Mission District. With a population that today numbers perhaps 200,000, the community has become a powerful social and political force. In 1977, Supervisor Harvey Milk became the nation's first openly gay man elected to a major municipal post. Since then, despite the AIDS epidemic, San Francisco has retained gay supervisors and the gay community has remained an integral part of the city's life.

SIGHTS

SAN FRANCISCO LESBIAN GAY BISEXUAL TRANSGENDER COMMUNITY CENTER ⊠*1800 Market Street* ☏*415-865-5555* ☏*415-865-5501* ⏴*www.sfcenter.org, info@sfcenter.org* The community center ("the Center" for short) houses 11 nonprofit organizations and is a major meeting point for the LGBT community, as well as their friends and families. Each week more than 2000 people use their services and the hundreds of meetings and events encompass education, arts and social events, programs for children and youth, health screening and referrals.

SAN FRANCISCO OFFICIAL GAY & LESBIAN MAP & GUIDE
For a detailed map of the city's premier gay spots, drop by the **San Fran-**

cisco **Visitors Information Bureau** (900 Market Street; 415-391-2000, fax 415-362-7323; www.onlyinsanfrancisco.com, vic1@sfcvb.org) for this free guide. Within its 18 pages you'll find information on superb places to eat, shop, play, and stay, including notes on clientele and whether a locale is transgender-friendly.

CASTRO THEATRE ✉429 Castro Street ✆415-621-5288 ext.15 ✆415-864-0119 ✐www.castrotheatre.org, castrotheatre@yahoo.com This 1920s theater is the iconic heart of the Castro; its huge, neon pink and blue sign is one of the most recognizable neighborhood sights. In 1977, the city acknowledged the theater as its 100th registered historic landmark. Today you can view classic, independent, and foreign films here.

LODGING

Throughout the Castro and Polk districts are numerous hotels catering primarily to gay travelers. Others in these areas serve a wide-ranging clientele, including many gay guests.

INN ON CASTRO

$$–$$$ 8 ROOMS ✉321 Castro Street ✆415-861-0321 ✆415-861-0321 ✐www.innoncastro.com, innkeeper@innoncastro.com

This eight-room bed and breakfast is housed in an old Victorian. A class establishment all the way, the inn adds subtle touches like fresh flowers and complimentary brandy in the evening. Each room is decorated in a different fashion, and the house atmosphere is comfortable and personal. Most rooms have private baths. Because of its popularity, the hotel recommends reservations.

24 HENRY

$–$$ 10 ROOMS ✉24 Henry Street ✆415-864-5686, 800-900-5686 ✆415-864-0406 ✐www.24henry.com, reservations@24henry.com

This charming 1870s Victorian B&B is right in the middle of the Castro on a quiet little side street. The ten guest rooms have high ceilings, period furniture, and comfortable beds. Just three have private baths and all have TVs and wi-fi. Breakfast is served in the parlor.

THE WILLOWS BED AND BREAKFAST INN

$$–$$$ 12 ROOMS ✉710 14th Street ✆415-431-4770, 800-431-0277 ✆415-431-5295 ✐www.willowssf.com, innkeeper@willowssf.com

Several blocks from Castro Street is this beautiful facility that attracts both gay and straight guests. Each room has been furnished with antique wooden pieces and adorned with French art prints (while all have a contemporary mini-fridge). The trademark of this cozy hostelry, however, is the willow-branch furniture designed expressly for the Inn. It's personal touches like this that make it a special place. Shared bath.

CASTRO SUITES

$$$$ 2 UNITS ✉927 14th Street ☎415-437-1783 🖷415-437-1784
✍www.castrosuites.com, castrosuites@comcast.net

Here you'll find a beautiful pair of comfortable and colorfully decorated apartments a couple of blocks from the heart of the Castro. The kitchens include a dishwasher, laundry facilities, and a microwave. (The upstairs kitchen is painted an appropriate bright purple.) If you give them some warning, they'll have the kitchen fully stocked for you.

PARKER GUEST HOUSE

$$$–$$$$ 21 UNITS ✉520 Church Street; 888-520-7275 🖷415-621-4139
✍www.parkerguesthouse.com, info@parkerguesthouse.com

Catering primarily to a gay clientele, this guest house sits between the Castro, Haight, and Noe Valley districts, making it a great location for exploring the area. The inn itself is a 1909 Edwardian mini-mansion and is meticulously appointed with rich woods and mellow cream hues. The rooms are outfitted with down comforters. Enjoy a continental breakfast and afternoon wine service. The inn's gardens provide a restful haven from the hustle and bustle of the city.

METRO HOTEL

$$ 24 ROOMS ✉319 Divisadero Street ☎415-861-5364 🖷415-863-1970
✍www.metrohotelsf.com, info@metrohotelsf.com

Midway between Castro Street and the Haight-Ashbury neighborhood is this hotel. Appealing to a mixed clientele, there is a small lobby, an adjoining café downstairs, and an English garden. The guests rooms are carpeted wall-to-wall, furnished with oak pieces, and decorated with wallhangings. Each has a private bath (shower only) and color television with cable. Set in a white Victorian building, it is clean and comfortable. Free wireless internet.

CHATEAU TIVOLI

$$–$$$$ 9 UNITS ✉1057 Steiner Street ☎415-776-5462, 800-228-1647
🖷415-776-0505 ✍www.chateautivoli.com, mail@chateautivoli.com

Those in search of the quintessential "Painted Lady" Victorian will not want to miss this dazzling three-story 1892 mansion resplendent with gold leaf, stained-glass windows, and elaborate woodwork. Many of the rooms and suites are named for famous painted ladies of San Francisco, including actress Lola Montez and flapper Aimee Crocker. Accommodations consist of nine rooms and suites, seven of which have private baths. The clientele is both straight and gay. There's a complimentary breakfast, as well as afternoon wine and cheese. Nonsmoking.

DINING

LUNA

$$ CALIFORNIA CUISINE ✉558 Castro Street ☎415-487-1511

Over in the Castro Street neighborhood, this is a good choice for a tasty meal. You can dine indoors or outside on a tree-studded patio. They feature a breakfast menu that includes poached eggs, omelettes, and eggs Benedict. Lunch consists of hamburgers, sandwiches, salads, and pasta. The restaurant serves dinner as well.

ANCHOR OYSTER BAR

$$–$$$ SEAFOOD   ✉*579 Castro Street*   ☎*415-431-3990*
✑*www.anchoroysterbar.com*

This hole-in-the-wall café happens to serve delicious shellfish. There are oysters on the half shell, steamed clams and mussels, seafood cocktails, and various daily specials. Recommended for lunch or dinner. No lunch on Sunday.

SWEET INSPIRATION

$–$$ DESSERT   ✉*2239 Market Street*   ☎*415-621-8664*
✑*www.sweetinspirationbakery.com*

To appease your sugar cravings, stop in at this café. Along with rotating exhibitions of local artists' works, it has the most delectable cakes and pastries around. The slices are so huge, you'll have to share. Try the cheesecake, tiramisu, or fresh fruit tart.

CAFE FLORE

$–$$ AMERICAN   ✉*2298 Market Street*   ☎*415-621-8579*   ✑*www.cafeflore.com*

Exceptionally popular with the locals, this café has a partially enclosed outside patio and sidewalk, where diners can watch life in the Castro go by. Inside, the floor is tiled, the atmosphere casual and relaxed. You order at the window from a blackboard menu listing breakfast frittatas, salads, sandwiches, and the daily special. There's also a full bar and an espresso bar.

SPARKY'S DINER

$ AMERICAN   ✉*242 Church Street*   ☎*415-626-8666*

After a long night of clubbing or an attack of the midnight munchies, hit up Sparky's. Open 24 hours, they serve traditional American fare— burgers, fries, and omelettes—to a less-than-typical clientele. The restaurant gets packed in the wee hours of the morning, offering a loud and vibrant environment while the rest of the city sleeps.

PEASANT PIES

$ FRENCH/BAKERY   ✉*4108 24th Street*   ☎*415-642-1316*   ✑*www.peasantpies.com*

For a bite between bar hopping or a quick snack, try a pie here. This shop has a few stools and a counter, but the business is mostly carry-out. There's a good selection of sweet and savory pies that include clam and tomato, spicy eggplant, Moroccan lentil, mushroom and zucchini, cherry, banana and chocolate, and blueberry pear.

ORPHAN ANDY'S

$–$$ DINER   ✉*3991 17th Street*   ☎*415-864-9795*

A good place after a late movie at the Castro Theatre is this spot, one of the few San Francisco restaurants open 24 hours. Decorated with a colorful 1950s diner theme with a counter and leatherette booths, Orphan Andy's serves good burgers, sandwiches, omelettes, and other classic coffee-shop fare.

The Castro Street shopping district stretches along Castro from 19th Street to Market Street, then continues for several blocks on "Upper Market"; there are also several interesting stores along 18th Street. The entire area is surprisingly compact, but features a variety of shops. Together with Polk Street, it represents the major gay shopping area in San Francisco.

HUMAN RIGHTS CAMPAIGN ACTION CENTER & STORE

✉*600 Castro Street* ✆*415-431-2200* 🖷*415-431-2203* 🖳*www.hrc.org* This unusual store offers a unique fusing of education and grassroots advocacy with HRC's signature merchandise. The Castro store has the company's most complete line of Equality Wear—from caps to pullovers to watches, as well as many gift items not found on the website.

WORN OUT WEST ✉*582 Castro Street* ✆*415-431-6020* A cut above the
neighborhood's other resale shops, this one has a great selection of high-quality used leather jackets and boots, along with new T-shirts, underwear, and accessories.

BRAND X ANTIQUES ✉*570 Castro Street* ✆*415-626-8908* Speaking of
generic names, how about Brand X? They feature an assortment of antiques and decorative artworks that are perfect as gifts and souvenirs. Estate jewelry is another very popular part of their line. Silver cigarette cases, glass figurines, Chinese Buddhas, rare porcelain, and objets d'art are often among the extraordinary pieces in this fascinating shop.

UNDER ONE ROOF

✉*549 Castro Street* ✆*415-503-2300* 🖷*415-503-2301* 🖳*www.underone roof.org* Shopping here is like giving to a good cause. This store is underwritten by individuals and corporations, so 100 percent of the profits are donated to dozens of AIDS service organizations. It sells a wide selection of items, including candles, soaps, lotions, candy, T-shirts, jewelry, and gay and lesbian books. Most of the personnel are volunteers.

THE BEAD STORE ✉*417 Castro Street* ✆*415-861-7332* For African trade
beads, turquoise and silver jewelry, as well as other bodily adornments, try this tiny one-room shop positively crammed with attractive items.

Polk Street is wall to wall with designer fashion shops, boutiques, and all manner of clothing outlets. The central gay area stretches from Post Street to Washington Street, but savvy shoppers will continue on to Union Street, since several intriguing stores lie on the outskirts of the neighborhood.

TIBET SHOP ✉*4100 19th Street* ✆*415-982-0326* At this diverse shop are
sili bangles, painted lanterns, Buddha figurines, prayer beads, and monastic incense. This wonderful little shop also has vests, skirts, dresses, shirts, and jackets made in Nepal, Tibet, and Bhutan.

NAOMI'S ANTIQUES TO GO ✉*1817 Polk Street* ✆*415-775-1207* There are enough plates, saucers, pitchers, bowls, and cups at Naomi's to furnish an entire neighborhood of dining rooms, whether in the homes of hip young professionals or traditional grandparents. Closed Sunday and Monday.

GOOD VIBRATIONS ✉*603 Valencia Street* ✆*415-522-5460* ✍*www.good vibes.com, customerservice@goodvibes.com* This sex toy, book, and video emporium designed in the late 1970s especially for women, has become a Bay Area institution. The store sells erotic literature, self-help sex books, feminist erotica, videos and sex education films, and an unbeatable array of vibrators and electric massagers. A highlight of the store is an antique vibrator museum with some rather unusual items like a cranked version that looks like a rolling pin.

X21 ✉*890 Valencia Street* ✆*415-647-4211* ✇*415-695-0797* ✍*www.x21modern. com* The stuff for sale here is strewn throughout a 8500-square-foot, two-story space. There's a huge assortment of mid-20th-century design fixtures, vintage office furniture, paintings, sculpture, industrial design, glass, and ceramics.

NIGHTLIFE

One example of San Francisco's wide-open tradition is the presence of almost 200 gay bars in the city. There's everything here from rock clubs to piano bars to stylish cabarets. Some are strictly gay, others mix their customers, and some have become so popular that straights have begun to take them over from gays.

CASTRO THEATRE ✉*429 Castro Street* ✆*415-621-5288 ext.15* ✇*415-864-0119* ✍*www.castrotheatre.org, castrotheatre@yahoo.com* Since 1922, this ornate theater has been showing an array of first- and second-run movies as well as occasional live productions in its Spanish-style, 1600-seat auditorium, complete with mezzanine. Cash only.

TWIN PEAKS TAVERN ✉*401 Castro Street* ✆*415-864-9470* ✍*www.twin peakstavern.com* There are a dozen or so bars in the Castro Street area, many open from early morning until the wee hours. Among the nicest is this tavern with its overhead fans and large windows overlooking the street.

THE CAFÉ ✉*2369 Market Street* ✆*415-861-3846* ✍*www.cafesf.com* San Francisco's lesbian bars are located not only around Valencia Street, but in other parts of the city as well. Catering to a mixed gay and lesbian crowd, this is a mirrored club with pool tables, pinball machines, three full bars and outdoor patios. Occasional cover. There's deejay music nightly in the lounge.

CAFE DU NORD ✉*2170 Market Street* ✆*415-861-5016* ✍*www.cafedunord. com* This café is *the* hip hangout for gays and straights alike. Built in 1907, the historic building's past life as a speakeasy is still visible in its bordello-red interior and dim lighting. Sidle up to the 40-foot mahogany bar or hunker down in a separate room where there's live entertainment every night.

KIMO'S ✉️*1351 Polk Street* 📞*415-885-4535* This is the nicest of all the Polk Street neighborhood bars. New ownership granted this local haunt with a slick face lift. Red walls, dim lighting, and plenty of open space now dominate the hip venue. Cover for live music.

N'TOUCH ✉️*1548 Polk Street* 📞*415-441-8413* 🖱️*www.ntouchsf.com* This club has a disco dancefloor plus video monitors. There's always a lively Asian crowd here. With flashing lights and ample sound, it's a good spot for dancing and carousing and watching the go-go boys. Most nights have shows or other entertainment. Occasional cover.

THEATRE RHINOCEROS _____ ⓗidden

✉️*2926 16th Street* 📞*415-861-5079* 🖱️*www.therhino.org* Plays with gay, bisexual, transgender, and lesbian themes are the focus of this acclaimed company that presents performances at two theaters, Rhino's Mainstage and Rhino's Studio.

MISSION DISTRICT

Depending on your personal taste or maybe just your mood, you'll come away from the Mission District thinking it either a poem or a ghetto. In truth, it's both. "The Mission," San Francisco's own Spanish barrio, is the vibrant home of the city's Mexican, Colombian, Guatemalan, Nicaraguan, and Salvadoran population. It's a neighborhood where brilliant murals vie with graffiti-scrawled walls, and where children compete with old folks for a seat on the bus or park bench.

The Mission District is a scene not just of transition but of social turmoil. In the early 1990s, zoning regulations opened the neighborhood to "live/work lofts," which originally meant artists' studios, and "bohos" (short for bohemians) moved in. Then city planners created NE-MIZ—the Northeast Mission Industrial Zone—to encourage development of biotechnology industries. But while an influx of capital from pre-Communist Hong Kong poured in to finance new construction, the biotech boom passed San Francisco by. As a result, all that development money went into luxurious, very expensive live/work loft projects to accommodate the overflow of dot-com firms from the South of Market district, creating population densities that are now approaching ten times what city planners anticipated—with no increase in parking spaces. Skyrocketing rents and property taxes are rapidly forcing long-time Latino residents, bohemian artists, and the vibrant lesbian subculture out of the Mission.

Today, the Mission is a controversy-ridden patchwork quilt of a neighborhood, where young multimillionaires pedal down the bike lanes of Valencia Street, one of the fastest-gentrifying streets in the city, passing within a block or two of makeshift car repair shops and hole-in-the-wall *taquerías* that could as easily be in Guatemala City, and equally close to chic boutiques, restaurants, and galleries; where hilly, quiet, beautiful

NOE'S NEST

PAGE 146

Unique and eclectic B&B featuring elaborate decorations and an even more elaborate hostess that knows all the local hotspots

FOREIGN CINEMA

PAGE 147

A daily California/Mediterranean–inspired menu in a chic industrial building where food and film unite

THE ABANDONED PLANET BOOKSTORE

PAGE 149

Quintessential used-book lover's heaven with leather bound classics, cushy easy chairs, and resident cats to curl up with

TRUCK

PAGE 149

The "best gay bar" in the city—tasty food, interesting company, and fun events like go-go dancer Thursdays

Dolores Street rolls down past the park of the same name, shared by picnicking families and one of the city's largest concentrations of drug dealers; where the same magical murals that brighten the exteriors of dozens of buildings are also displayed with pride on dozens of websites. Here you'll find the oldest building in San Francisco and some of the newest. In fact, wandering the streets of the Mission, you'll probably find whatever you want, along with a few things you never imagined.

SIGHTS

The *corazón* of the Mission is 24th Street with its outdoor markets and indoor murals. Start your tour at 24th and York streets, about six blocks east of Mission Street.

ST. FRANCIS FOUNTAIN AND CANDY ✉*2801 24th Street* ☎*415-826-4200* This soda fountain, right on the corner, is a classic. With its cozy booths, old-fashioned fountain, and pink ceiling, the place seems to have been suspended in time since 1955. Actually this after-school ice cream parlor dates from 1918.

GALERÍA DE LA RAZA ✉*2857 24th Street* ☎*415-826-8009* 📠*415-826-6235* 🖱*www.galeriadelaraza.org, info@galeriadelaraza.org* Those **murals** in the park across the street are a striking example of *la raza* (the Latino people). The artists who worked those walls might be part of the everchanging exhibits at this gallery. Innovative and provocative, the gallery is as liable to feature a show on the revolutionary movement in El Salvador as a photographic display or artistic exhibit. Hours vary—call for details. There's also a gift shop. Closed Sunday through Tuesday.

CHINESE-STYLE MURAL ✉*2884 24th Street* Another mural on the side of 2884 24th Street depicts scenes that also correspond with this theme, and is modeled after the style of Chinese peasant paintings.

CHILDREN'S MURAL ✉*On the corner of 24th Street and Balmy Avenue* Even the alleyways hereabouts are home to art—check out the colorful children's mural decorating the Mission Neighborhood Family Center.

OTHER MURALS There's more street art just past South Van Ness Avenue—a **wall mural** depicting multihued parrots and thrashing fish. Then, space-age counterpoint to this folk art, is the **mural** at 24th and Mission streets, illustrating San Francisco's BART subways.

MISSION STREET If 24th Street is the heart of the barrio, this street is its nerve center, a neon ganglia delivering electric charges throughout the community. By day it's a collection of shoe stores, hair salons, and pawn shops. At night, particularly on weekends, the area is transformed into a cruising strip. Although the gaudy, outrageous low-riders have been pushed out of the Mission in recent years, there are still plenty of macho cars competing with spit-shine sleek vans with multicolored designs.

VALENCIA STREET Not so long ago, this street was a funky mix of Latino-owned car-repair shops, seedy dives, and women-owned stores and bars. Though a number of these businesses still thrive, this area has become quickly gentrified. Bistros and coffee shops abound, among them spots featuring cuisine from Ethiopia, Colombia, South India, China, Thailand, and, of course, Mexico. Art galleries and hip clothing boutiques have crowded out the auto repair shops and given this area a much-needed shot of vitality.

LEXINGTON CLUB ✉*3464 19th Street* ☎*415-863-2052* ⌨*www.lexingtonclub.com* San Francisco's best-known lesbian bar, this club is a holdout from the days when Valencia was the epicenter of the lesbian community.

WOMEN'S BUILDING ✉*3543 18th Street, between Valencia and Guerrero streets* ☎*415-431-1180* ⌨*www.womensbuilding.org* This is an important community gathering place. Don't miss the incredible **mural** on its walls.

QUANE STREET

Unless you've sidetracked down Mission or Valencia, you're still on the corner of 24th and Mission, staring at that futuristic mural. Cross Mission and continue along 24th Street uphill several blocks to Quane Street. Walk the three-block length of this alleyway and you'll be convinced the city fathers and mothers meant to name it Quaint Street. It's not much—just picket fences, shade trees, and clapboard houses—but rarely has so little spoken so eloquently.

The Mission

Jackson Playground

Carolina St

Mariposa St

18th St

19th St

20th St

Potrero Hill

Southern Heights Ave

De Haro St

Rhode Island St

16th St

17th St

Kansas St

22nd St

23rd St

Vermont St

Vermont St

San Bruno Ave

McKinley Square

San Bruno Ave

San Francisco General Hospital

Utah St

101

Potrero Ave

Potrero Ave

Hampshire St

Franklin Square

22nd St

York St

St Francis Candies

Theater Artaud

Mariposa St

18th St

19th St

21st St

Bryant St

Galeria de la Raza

Florida St

Alabama St

China Books

Harrison St

Harrison St

Treat Ave

Treat Ave

Folsom St

16th St

17th St

18th St

19th St

20th St

Shotwell St

24th St

South Van Ness Ave

Book Building

Capp St

Mission St

16th Street Mission BART Station

23rd St

24th Street Mission BART Station

Valencia St

Valencia St

16th St

17th St

Lapidge St

Women's Building

Guerrero St

Murphy House

Dolores St

Mission Dolores

Chula Ln

Dolores Park

Liberty St

Church St

.5 mile

.5 kilometer

18th St

19th St

20th St

21st St

22nd St

Noe Valley

0

0

N

MURPHY HOUSE ✉*159 Liberty Street* When this woodframe corridor debouches into 21st Street, turn left, then take a quick right onto Dolores Street. Head down for one block and take a right onto Liberty Street for a view of some magnificent old Victorians. Built in 1878, this Italianate-style home gained notoriety in 1896 when the famous suffragette Susan B. Anthony visited. Five other majestic Victorians, including a turreted Queen Anne–style structure, sit just beyond this fine old home.

DOLORES PARK ✉*Between Dolores and 20th streets* Back on Dolores Street, you can continue downhill along one of San Francisco's prettiest boulevards. Bordered on either side by bay window homes, Dolores Street's proudest feature is the grassy median planted with stately palm trees. Better still, this marvelous promenade opens onto Dolores Park, a rectangle of rolling hills dotted with magnolia and pepper trees. You can follow the sinuous walkways down to the tennis courts or head for the high ground and a luxurious view of the city. Remember, this is the Mission District, the city's sunniest sector, and there's no better place than Dolores Park for hanging out, people watching, and sunbathing.

MISSION SAN FRANCISCO DE ASÍS (MISSION DOLORES)

📞*415-621-8203* 📠*415-621-2294* 🖰*www.missiondolores.org, parish@missiondolores. org* Farther downhill, at Dolores and 16th streets, stands the historic building that gave the neighborhood its name. The crown jewel of the city (also known as Mission Dolores), completed in 1791, this was one of the 21 Spanish missions established along the California coast by Franciscans. Its thick adobe walls—and perhaps a few prayers—helped the church survive the 1906 earthquake and fire; today it is the city's oldest building. Here you can wander back to the last great days of the Spanish empire: the tabernacle came from the Philippines, the main altar along with two side altars were imported from Mexico, the designs on the ceiling are from the Ohlone Indians—all unfortunate subjects of 18th-century Spain. There's a mini-museum behind the chapel and a massive 20th-century basilica next door, but the most intriguing feature on the mission grounds is the cemetery. Studded with yew trees and tombstones, it is the last resting place of several famous (and infamous) San Francisco figures. Captain Louis Antonio Arguello, California's first Mexican governor, is interred here. So are Charles Cora and James Casey, a notorious pair who died at the hands of San Francisco's Vigilance Committee. All in all, 11,000 individuals were buried here between 1777 and 1898, 6000 of them local Indians. Admission.

LODGING

ELEMENTS HOTEL

$–$$ 30 ROOMS ✉*2524 Mission Street* 📞*415-647-4100, 866-327-8407* 🖰*www.elementssf.com*

The hip new resting spot for the urbane and on-the-move 20s-to-30s crowd is this hotel. This Mission District lodging offers both private rooms and hostel-style shared dormitory options (the latter going for as little as $25 per night), and has an on-site

ATM, 24-hour check-in, and laundry facilities. Stays include access to a high-speed internet lounge, nightly rooftop parties, and movie nights—all for free. Linens and towels also provided.

INN SAN FRANCISCO

$$–$$$ 11 UNITS ✉*943 South Van Ness Avenue* 📞*415-641-0188,*
800-359-0913 (reservation) 📠*415-641-1701* 🖱*www.innsf.com,*
innkeeper@innsf.com

This inn resides in a 19th-century world. Set in a grand four-story Victorian, this splendid mansion has been furnished entirely with period pieces. There are gilded mirrors and beveled glass in the parlors, wall sconces and marble sinks in many rooms, as well as other antique flourishes. The rooftop sundeck provides a great view of the city, and an English garden in the back has a gazebo and hot tub. Room prices in this elegant establishment all include a full buffet breakfast; the moderate prices are for shared bath; some deluxe rooms have private facilities; ultra-deluxe rooms come with jacuzzis. The clientele is both gay and straight.

NOE'S NEST

$$$–$$$$ 5 ROOMS ✉*1257 Guerrero Street* 📞*415-821-0751*
📠*415-821-0723* 🖱*www.noesnest.com, noesnest@aol.com*

A short six blocks away from the Mission District, Noe's could be your home away from home. This lavish domicile features a hot tub, steam room, fireplace, and gorgeous views of the city. The cozy rooms at this bed and breakfast have private baths. Children are welcome. Reservations recommended.

DINING

BANGKOK 16

$–$$ THAI ✉*3214 16th Street* 📞*415-431-5838* 🖱*www.bangkok16sf.com*

The traditional Thai paintings and statuary add to the charm of this restaurant. Thai specialties served at your table include duck in a spicy lemon sauce, calamari salad, yellow curry, pad Thai noodles, lamb on a skewer served with a peanut sauce, and filet of snapper in a spicy tamarind sauce. Try the fried bananas for dessert. Dinner only. Closed Monday and Tuesday.

TI COUZ

$$ FRENCH ✉*3108 16th Street* 📞*415-252-7373*

In Brittany, *ti couz* means "The Old House," and worn hardwood floors, blue-and-white-painted walls, and wooden china cabinets give this restaurant that homey feeling. The seafood bar (available at dinner only) features oysters, shrimp, and fresh whole crab. But it's the savory crêpes that draw the crowds. Made from buckwheat flour in the style of Brittany, the crêpes are cooked to order one at a time, filled with cheese, sausage, or smoked salmon, and garnished with crème fraîche. Flavored butters, ice cream, white chocolate, and fruit are folded into the sweet crêpes. Delicious.

TAQUERIA LA CUMBRE

$ MEXICAN ✉*515 Valencia Street* ☎*415-863-8205*

It looks and smells like south of the border here. By the size of the crowd, those rumors about the best burritos must be true. For a price comfortable to any budget, you can order pork, tongue, chicken, or steak burritos, as well as tacos and other Mexican finger foods. They also feature vegetarian dishes at this simple but special *taquería*.

MARIACHI'S

$ MEXICAN ✉*508 Valencia Street* ☎*415-621-4358*

If you're craving something less traditional, head across the street to this place, where you'll find tacos and burritos with a decidedly Californian twist. Bright and festive decorations match the equally zesty menu. Try the snapper soft tacos with tangy mango salsa. Vegan dishes available.

DOSA

$$–$$$ INDIAN ✉*995 Valencia Street* ☎*415-642-3672*
✍*www.dosasf.com, comments@dosasf.com*

Warm woods matched with burnt orange decor set the ambiance at this delectable South Indian restaurant in the Mission. Soft, crispy rice– and lentil-based *dosas* (similar to crêpes) are served with a variety of rich flavors, including red and green chiles, cinnamon, and coconut mixed with vegetables, chicken, or fish. An array of *soju* cocktails are available, along with wine and beer (some from India). A sumptuous experience.

ESPERPENTO

$$ SPANISH ✉*3295 22nd Street* ☎*415-282-8867*

This place shines among the city's many tapas places, distinguished by its colorful atmosphere. Fans, ceramic plates, shawls, and pictures of bullfights adorn the walls, and the tables are painted with flowers and giant suns. You can linger over plates of paella and tapas of fried fish, garlic shrimp, pork kebab, and salads, while enjoying lively conversation and good Spanish wine. Closed Sunday.

FOREIGN CINEMA

$$$–$$$$ CALIFORNIA CUISINE/MEDITERRANEAN ✉*2534 Mission Street* ☎*415-648-7600* ✍*www.foreigncinema.com*

Food and films go hand in hand at this favorite evening destination for locals. The menu, which changes daily, might include lavender-scented pork chop and King salmon with green olive tapenade. There's also a full oyster bar. But it's the atmosphere here that's most distinctive. The high, stark, concrete walls create a warehouse-like feel that's at odds with the elegant dining and conciliatory service. In the large courtyard outside, films (mainly foreign and art flicks) are projected onto a 25-foot wall. If you plan to focus on the movie, eat outdoors: There are heat lamps. Weekend brunch available.

SHOPPING

This Latin American neighborhood once favored shoe stores and groceries over boutiques and galleries. Today, however, those old-timey stores are being joined by some screamingly modern places.

ARIK'S ✉2650 Mission Street ✆415-285-4770 This shop stocks American Army surplus clothing. They also have outdoor wear, boots, camping equipment, and rain gear.

PAXTON GATE ✉824 Valencia Street ✆415-824-1872 ⬧www.paxtongate.com Sometimes a person needs to find that perfect mounted beetle, exotic plant, or rare Japanese gardening tool. If this should occur on your San Francisco travels, stop here, where all your butterfly needs will be met.

COMMUNITY THRIFT STORE ✉623 Valencia Street ✆415-861-4910 ⬧415-861-7483 The Mission is known for its secondhand shops, but few beat this one. When people donate items to this massive emporium of previously owned furniture, books, posters, records, dishes, and clothes, they designate their favorite charity, which receives the proceeds. Because of the store's policy, it receives better-than-average donations.

NEEDLES & PENS ✉483 14th Street ✆415-255-1534 ⬧www.needles-pens. com This tiny, brick hole-in-the-wall houses an assortment of DIY goods created by local artists. You'll find funky T-shirts, bags, and accessories, as well as zines ranging from glossy numbers to xeroxed-and-stapled productions. There's also an art gallery. Closed Monday through Wednesday.

RAINBOW GROCERY COOPERATIVE ✉1745 Folsom Street ✆415-863-0620 ⬧415-863-8955 ⬧www.rainbow.coop This co-op has always been a perfect expression of the spirit of the Bay Area for me. It's a one-of-a-kind food emporium offering a wide array of organic, vegetarian, and health food items, as well as specialty cookbooks, aromatherapy candles, massage, and other household necessities. More importantly, the grocery has been worker-owned and -operated since 1976.

BOOK BUILDING ✉2141 Mission Street The Mission offers perhaps the richest and most eclectic mix of used and special-interest bookstores in the city. This building offers worthwhile shops to browse. Go to **Bolerium Books** (415-863-6353, fax 415-255-6499; www.bolerium. com, info@bolerium.com) for writing on American labor and radical history, gay and lesbian history, African-American history, Spanish Civil War, and other ethnic social movements. They also specialize in psychoceramics (the study of crackpots, of course). Closed Sunday. At

Meyer Boswell Books (415-255-6400, fax 415-255-6499; www.meyer bos.com, rarclaw@mcycrbos.com) you'll find books on the history of law. Closed weekends.

THE ABANDONED PLANET BOOKSTORE

✉518 Valencia Street ✆415-861-4695 Of all the used bookstores in the Mission, none is more pleasant to browse than this one. Neatly arranged books, dark woods, and a red carpet create a used-book lovers' heaven. There are easy chairs for serious readers, and resident cats to pet. In the back room is a poetry mural painted by the late Beat poet Jack Micheline.

MODERN TIMES BOOKS ✉888 Valencia Street ✆415-282-9246 ✐www.moderntimesbookstore.com Specializing in books on contemporary culture, feminism, sexuality, and politics, Modern Times also has a multicultural, international selection of children's books and books in Spanish. They frequently host author readings.

NOE VALLEY This district near the Mission features an opportunity to shop far from the tourist areas. All along 24th Street between Church and Castro streets, small stores line either side of the road. There are bookstores, galleries, handicrafts shops, open-air fruit stalls, and numerous other locally owned establishments. There's a distinctive neighborhood feeling here, which makes shoppers seem more like friends than consumers.

NIGHTLIFE

ROCCAPULCO SUPPER CLUB ✉3140 Mission Street ✆415-648-6611 ✐www.roccapulco.com At the edge of the Outer Mission, this club features live music on Friday and Saturday. For beginners, there are salsa lessons on Wednesday. The ballroom is as big as a warehouse, with enough tables and dance space to fit a Latin American army. It's hot. Closed Sunday through Tuesday and Thursday. Cover and dress code.

TRUCK

✉1900 Folsom Street ✆415-252-0306 ✐www.trucksf.com, truck@trucksf.com A rowdy—sometimes shirtless—crowd takes over this very hip gay bar for dancing and drinking on a nightly basis. Revolving events, such as theme parties and contests, up the flirtatious ante and make for a colorful evening. While it's clearly a male-centric venue, you'll find women on both sides of the bar also taking place in the festivities. *S.F. Weekly* voted this spot "the best gay bar" in the city—which means it probably is.

Valencia street between 15th and 20th streets teem with trendy watering holes:

ELBO ROOM ✉*647 Valencia Street* ✆*415-552-7788* *www.elbo.com* This bar is lively and the people are having a blast. There are a few pool tables, and live music upstairs ranges from jazz to rockabilly. Upstairs cover.

2202 OXYGEN BAR SUSHI & SAKE LOUNGE ✉*795 Valencia Street* ✆*415-255-2102* *www.oxygensf.com* Are loud, smoky nightspots passé? Find out for yourself at this trendy alternative lounge. The oxygen is combined with various scents such as lavender ("for the severely uptight") or a geranium blend ("the euphoria mix"). Paying for what you can get free may seem frivolous, but it's a surprisingly pleasant feeling to sit and breathe herb-infused air for a while. When you get the bill, remember to take a deep breath. Closed Monday.

LEXINGTON CLUB

✉*3464 19th Street* ✆*415-863-2052* *www.lexingtonclub.com, contact@ lexingtonclub.com* Self-proclaimed as the "friendly neighborhood dyke bar," this is a mellow nightspot especially popular with lesbians. There's a pool table, a jukebox, and, perhaps most significantly, two women's restrooms. Closed Sunday.

THE MARSH THEATER ✉*1062 Valencia Street* ✆*415-826-5750* *www.the marsh.org* San Francisco's answer to off-off-Broadway is this small, informal theater billed as a "breeding ground for new performances," which offers plays and spoken-word entertainment. Monday nights are reserved for performers trying out new work.

MARGARET JENKINS DANCE COMPANY ✉*3973-A 25th Street* ✆*415-826-8399* *www.mjdc.org* This area is also home to many outstanding dance companies. Featuring modern and experimental dance, they include this dance company.

ODC/SAN FRANCISCO ✉*3153 17th Street* ✆*415-863-9834* *www.odc dance.org* This modern dance center produces world-class performances.

SOUTH OF MARKET

In the 1970s, South of Market, popularly known as SOMA, had the reputation as one of the most unattractive and unsafe neighborhoods in the city. Filled with residential hotels, vacant warehouses, and seedy bars, it was long ignored by many of the city's residents. This neglect presented an opportunity for those who wanted to be isolated, and SOMA became a hub for the gay bathhouse crowd and the gay leather crowd.

During the '80s SOMA metamorphosed again. Gay bathhouses were closed in a sweeping move by government officials and replaced by trendy nightclubs; gay leather bars with names like "The Arena" converted into popular dance clubs with names like the "DNA Lounge."

The underutilized warehouses then brought in a different countercultural crowd—artists. Modeling themselves after the residents of New York City's SOHO (South of Houston) district, Bay Area artists converted SOMA warehouses into combination live/work spaces featuring art galleries, music studios, and performance spaces. Many of San Francisco's most creative people still live and display (or perform) in small galleries and theaters throughout SOMA.

Ephemeral as ever, SOMA next burst into another transitional phase, flaunting its formerly low-profile cyber-art industry with the promotional flair of a P. T. Barnum. Centering on Yerba Buena Gardens as the town square of the area, developers quickly packed the blocks between Market Street and Moscone Convention Center with family-oriented entertainment attractions, many of them showcasing interactive media.

Meanwhile, decrepit old hotels and office buildings in the surrounding neighborhood were replaced by upscale live/work complexes as builders petitioned City Hall for exemptions from San Francisco's strict anti-growth regulations, claiming that more condominiums and office suites in SOMA were needed to keep high-tech companies from moving elsewhere. Today, the artist and gay communities are being squeezed out of SOMA block by block. And oddly enough, all this urban redevelopment is meeting with less public protest than the traffic and noise associated with the big, glitzy nightclubs that are replacing the local leather bars of old.

Still, there are many restaurants and cafés that offer a true SOMA twist to their atmosphere and menu. Don't be surprised if your café table has a computer hooked up to the internet, or the restaurant you're dining at has decor created during the slow hours before lunch.

SIGHTS

MOSCONE CONVENTION CENTER ✉ *Howard Street between 3rd and 4th streets* Named for George Moscone, the San Francisco mayor who was assassinated in 1978, this mammoth convention center extends across 11 acres. With restaurants, hotels, apartments, and stores encircling it like satellites, the center is the dominant feature in San Francisco's fastest-changing district. Smack on top of the building sits a 60,000-square-foot solar installation—the largest city-owned solar array in the U.S.—which over the next 30 years will reduce carbon dioxide emissions by 35,000 tons.

YERBA BUENA GARDENS An important addition to the area is this garden, a project that was 30 years in the making but has proven to be worth the wait by providing a forum for the visual and performing arts as well as some much-needed green space.

YERBA BUENA CENTER FOR THE ARTS One component of the ten-acre complex located on top of the underground Moscone Convention Center are these two buildings, one designed by the acclaimed Japanese architect Fumihiko Maki. It includes three galleries devoted to visual arts and high-tech installations, as well as a screening room for video and film. A large multipurpose room called "The Forum" hosts special events. In addition, a 755-seat theater offers a diverse lineup of music, dance, and performance art. Closed Monday. Admission.

MARTIN LUTHER KING JR. MEMORIAL ✉ *415-820-3550* 📠 *415-820-3554* 🖱 *www.yerbabuenagardens.com, info@yerbabuenagardens.com* Softening the

South of Market

Market St

CARTOON ART MUSEUM

THE STUD

SOUTH PARK CAFÉ

CARTOON ART MUSEUM

PAGE 155

One-of-a-kind showplace for comic books, animation, and political cartoons with screening room and bookstore

SOUTH PARK CAFÉ

PAGE 157

Cheery café near South Park with imaginative, French-inspired California cuisine menu

THE STUD

PAGE 158

Eclectic gay bar with theme nights throughout the week and live deejay performances on the weekends

contemporary hard edges of Yerba Buena is a five-and-a-half-acre esplanade of gardens and outdoor public art. A focal point of Yerba Buena Gardens is this graceful waterfall spilling over Sierra granite. Behind the waterfall are a series of 12 thick glass panels etched with quotations drawn from speeches Dr. King made in San Francisco. Each quote is paired with a translation into a different language, including Chinese, Spanish, Hebrew, and Swahili, and representing the origins of the city's major ethnic groups.

SAN FRANCISCO MUSEUM OF MODERN ART ✉151 3rd Street ✆415-357-4000 🖷415-357-4158 ⌕www.sfmoma.org This modern art museum is one of the top-ten most-visited museums in the United States. The building, designed by Swiss architect Mario Botta, is a Modernist work of art in itself, distinguished by a tower finished in alternating bands of black and white stone. Inside are three large galleries and more than 20 smaller ones, totaling 50,000 square feet. The second floor displays selections from the museum's permanent collection. The third-floor gallery features photographs and works on paper. The top two gallery floors accommodate special exhibitions and large-scale art from the museum's collection. Closed Wednesday. Admission.

METREON ✉101 4th Street ✆415-369-6000 ⌕www.westfield.com/metreon, metreon@westfield.com This peculiar blend of theme park and shopping mall combines San Francisco's largest motion picture complex (15 screens plus an IMAX theater), six restaurants, play areas based on children's books, a futuristic video arcade, and seven retail stores, plus plenty of high-tech advertising. The self-styled "entertainment center" looks like a giant concrete cube from the outside and stands four stories tall to accommodate the 50-by-100-foot IMAX screen. Almost everything here is associated with Sony's entertainment and technology empire and supported by sponsorships from other huge corporations, and many of the management team members are veterans of Disney, so don't be surprised if you feel like you've stepped into the world's largest advertisement for corporate America. If you're traveling with kids, the Metreon is a must-see—sort of. Among the multimedia "tie-ins" is the 175-seat Action Theatre featuring anime movies and live performances Friday through Sunday. You might have to be a teen to fully appreciate the **Playsation Store**, where you can try the latest expensive video games played against opposing teams instead of against the computer. Meanwhile, mom and dad can play with the latest high-tech toys at **Sony Style**.

ROOFTOP AT YERBA BUENA GARDENS ✉*221 4th Street* ✆*415-820-3320* ✐*www.zeum.org, info@zeum.org* Just over a second-floor walkway from the Metreon, on top of the Moscone Convention Center, sits another collection of family-oriented attractions, this time created not by megacorporations but by the San Francisco Redevelopment Agency. The high-tech draw here is **Zeum**, an art-and-technology center that offers hands-on, behind-the-scenes experiences in animation, video production, digital photography, web page design, 3-D modeling, and stage set design and production. Closed Monday and Tuesday during the school year; closed Monday in summer. Admission.

CHARLES LOOFF CAROUSEL ✉*4th and Howard streets* In striking contrast to the futuristic-style kids' museum Zeum is this antique carousel. Originally built in 1906 by Charles Looff, it was the centerpiece of San Francisco's former Playland-at-the-Beach amusement park. The large, beautifully restored carousel has all-white horses that gleam like new. Admission.

YERBA BUENA ICE SKATING CENTER & YERBA BUENA BOWLING CENTER ✉*750 Folsom Street* ✆*415-820-3532* ✆*415-820-3520* ✐*www.skatebowl.com* The rooftop complex at Yerba Buena includes this this Olympic-size ice rink (admission) with huge windows overlooking the San Francisco skyline to create the feel of skating outdoors, and an adjoining 12-lane bowling alley.

YERBA BUENA LANE This spiffy pedestrian mall connects Mission and Market between 3rd and 4th streets. In addition to functioning as a convenient walkway from BART to Yerba Buena Gardens and Moscone Convention Center, the streetscape acts as a retail corridor and includes a dozen cafés, restaurants, and retailers.

MUSEUM OF CRAFT & FOLK ART ✉*51 Yerba Buena Lane* ✆*415-227-4888* ✆*415-227-4351* ✐*www.mocfa.org, store@.mocfa.org* A magnet for artistic ventures of all sorts, the area plays host to numerous museums, including this craft museum. Exhibitions range from Cook Island quilts to San Simeon architect Julia Morgan's craftware. You'll also want to visit the gift shop, where they sell native and tribal goods, as well as a wide variety of jewelry and contemporary craft. Closed Wednesday. Admission.

CONTEMPORARY JEWISH MUSEUM ✉*736 Mission Street* ✆*415-655-7800* ✆*415-655-7815* ✐*www.thecjm.org, info@thecjm.org* Founded in 1984, this museum opened in a 63,000-square-foot facility in 2008. The $43 million space showcases scholarly and artistic work relating to the Jew-

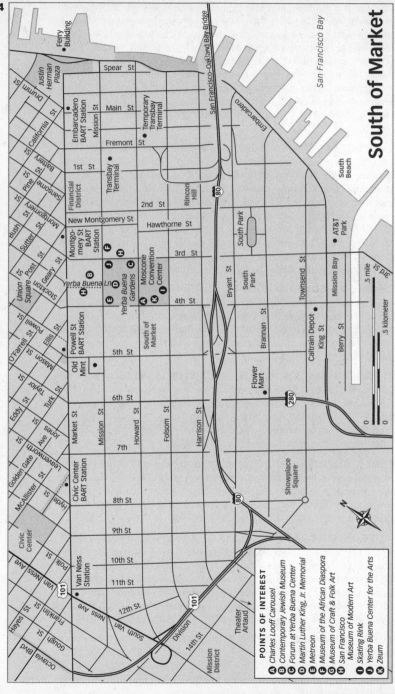

South of Market

San Francisco Bay

San Francisco-Oakland Bay Bridge

Ferry Building

Justin Herman Plaza

Embarcadero BART Station

Financial District

Transbay Terminal

Temporary Transbay Terminal

Rincon Hill

South Beach

AT&T Park

New Montgomery St

Montgomery St BART Station

Moscone Convention Center

South Park

Yerba Buena Gardens

Yerba Buena Ln

Union Square

Powell St BART Station

South of Market

Old Mint

Flower Mart

Caltrain Depot

Mission Bay

Civic Center BART Station

Showplace Square

Van Ness Station

Civic Center

Mission District

Theater Artaud

N

POINTS OF INTEREST

- **A** Charles Looff Carousel
- **B** Contemporary Jewish Museum
- **C** Forum at Yerba Buena Center
- **D** Martin Luther King, Jr. Memorial
- **E** Metreon
- **F** Museum of the African Diaspora
- **G** Museum of Craft & Folk Art
- **H** San Francisco Museum of Modern Art
- **I** Skating Rink
- **J** Yerba Buena Center for the Arts
- **K** Zeum

.5 mile

.5 kilometer

0

0

ish experience. A non-collecting museum, CJM partners with national and international cultural institutions to present a wide-ranging exhibition program that includes contemporary art and historical objects, film and music, conversations, lectures, literary readings, and other live performances. The museum store has a good selection of jewelry, gifts, toys, books and contemporary Judaica. There's also an on-site café. Guided tours are available. Closed Wednesday. Admission (under 18 free).

MUSEUM OF THE AFRICAN DIASPORA ✉*St. Regis Hotel and Residences, 685 Mission Street* ✆*415-358-7200* ✐*www.moadsf.org* Near the Yerba Buena center is this 20,000-square-foot museum, which offers film screenings, traveling and media-based exhibits, live music, and colloquiums and panels on a wide variety of topics central to the African diaspora. Closed Monday and Tuesday.

CARTOON ART MUSEUM

✉*655 Mission Street* ✆*415-227-8666* ✆*415-243-8666* ✐*www.cartoonart. org, office@cartoonart.org* Also located in the Yerba Buena neighborhood, this museum features rotating exhibits of cartoon art in all its various incarnations: newspaper strips, political cartoons, comic books, and animation are amply represented. Highlights include an animation screening area and a bookstore. One of the only museums of its kind in the United States, this rare treat should not be missed. Closed Monday. Admission.

SOUTH PARK Tucked into an area bordered by Bryant, Brannan, 2nd, and 3rd streets is this oval-shaped park ringed by cafés and artists' studios. The surrounding neighborhood is an industrial district that includes multimedia companies operating out of lofts in converted warehouses.

479 AND 483 TEHAMA STREET To see a startling example of the force with which the 1906 earthquake warped and buckled San Francisco buildings, drive down the alleyway between 5th and 6th streets just south of Mission Street to 479 and 483 Tehama Street. These old warehouses look like the earth collapsed beneath them at the same time a giant hand shoved them backwards.

AT&T PARK ✉*24 Willie Mays Plaza* ✆*415-972-1800* ✆*415-947-2925* ✐*www. sanfrancisco.giants.mlb.com* This baseball park is situated on the south side of the South of Market warehouse district, along the China Basin waterfront and readily accessible from the Embarcadero or Route 280. Baseball's San Francisco Giants left 3Com Park (known as Candlestick Park until a Silicon Valley conglomerate bought the naming rights) in favor of this more cost-efficient facility, which has just over one-half the seating capacity. The $319 million ballpark features classic architecture inspired by Wrigley Field and Fenway Park, together with state-of-the-art lighting and electronics and an innovative seating alignment that provides the best possible views of the field from most seats. Speaking of views, fans also find themselves surrounded by a panorama of the San Francisco skyline, the Bay, and the distant East Bay Hills. Just outside the stadium, **AT&T Park Tours** (King Street between 2nd and 3rd streets; 415-972-2400; toursinfo@attpark.com) a wharfside promenade near center field operated by the park, lets passersby view ball games knothole-style. They also offer daily tours (fee) at 10:30 a.m. and 12:30 p.m. except game days, which include looks at the press box and the dugout.

LODGING

W HOTEL

$$$$ 410 ROOMS   ✉*181 3rd Street*   ✆*415-777-5300*   📠*415-817-7823*
🖱*www.whotels.com*

This popular hotel provides trendy types upscale accommodations done in sleek Euro-Asian style. In addition to the usual high-end conveniences, special touches include goose-down duvets, complimentary boutique toiletry packs, in-room "munchie boxes," and "whatever, whenever" service. Rooms are spacious enough to launch a start-up inside.

ST. REGIS HOTEL

$$$$ 306 ROOMS   ✉*125 3rd Street*   ✆*415-284-4000*   📠*415-284-4100*
🖱*www.stregis.com/sanfrancisco*

The elegant St. Regis is a bit more than just a hotel. These unusually spacious rooms (up to 3200 square feet) include first-rate amenities such as deep soaking tubs, original art, 42-inch plasma TVs, wi-fi, and great views. The premises include underground parking, two restaurants, spa, café, and two lounges.

DINING

RESTAURANT LULU

$$–$$$ AMERICAN   ✉*816 Folsom Street*   ✆*415-495-5775*   📠*415-495-7810*
🖱*www.restaurantlulu.com*

A hot spot not far from the Yerba Buena Gardens complex is this noisy warehouse-sized restaurant that draws in crowds at lunch and dinner for superb meats and chicken prepared on a brick rotisserie. Also noteworthy are the shellfish selections such as iron skillet–roasted mussels and Dungeness crab with garlic. Reservations recommended.

OOLA RESTAURANT & BAR

idden

$$$ CALIFORNIA CUISINE   ✉*860 Folsom Street*   ✆*415-995-2061*
📠*415-995-2065* 🖱*www.oola-sf.com*

Brick walls, gossamer fabric, intimate lighting, and sleek black tables create the backdrop for this restaurant's rustic fare. This split-level eatery uses organic meats and produce in classically prepared dishes such as lamb daube with root vegetables, seafood stew, and soy-glazed baby back ribs. The scene really picks up later in the night, when patrons come to eat (food is served until 1 a.m. most evenings) and sip watermelon cosmos and ginger snaps (whiskey with fresh ginger syrup). Dinner only.

CAFFE MUSEO

$$ CALIFORNIA CUISINE ✉151 3rd Street ☎415-357-4500
🖱www.caffemuseo.com

After taking in the SFMOMA, pause at this café for a delicious afternoon meal. Specializing in "edible art," Caffe Museo serves up fresh soups, salads, and sandwiches along with steamed mussels and braised artichokes. Its large picture windows and outdoor seating make it the perfect place for people watching. Dessert dishes are worth more than just a bite. Closed Wednesday.

SUPPERCLUB SAN FRANCISCO

$$$ CONTINENTAL ✉657 Harrison Street ☎415-348-0900
🖱www.supperclub.com

Spend three hours eating in bed at the first U.S. outpost of the original Amsterdam Supperclub. There is only one seating per night, beginning at 7:30 p.m. Dinner is served in four courses—all delivered to your bed. In between courses stroll around, meet other diners, hit the dancefloor, or get a massage. The meal is at the whim of the chef, so there's no printed menu. Entertainment varies but has included aerial performers, exotic dancers, and rollerskaters.

SOUTH PARK CAFÉ

$$–$$$ FRENCH-CALIFORNIA CUISINE ✉108 South Park
☎415-495-7275 🖱www.southparkcafesf.com

This café is a sunny and cheery dining spot facing, as its name suggests, South Park. With only a long zinc bar and a few tables, it is a popular gourmet dining spot known for its imaginative salads and daily meat and fish specials. Closed Sunday. No lunch Saturday; no dinner Monday.

COCO500

$$–$$$ CALIFORNIA CUISINE ✉500 Brannan Street ☎415-543-2222
🖱www.coco500.com

Transformations abound in the City. Ever-popular Bizou has morphed into this find at the hands of chef and owner Loretta Keller. Her culinary skills (perfected in New Orleans and Paris) now center around a rotating small-plates menu with a Mediterranean focus. Dishes feature organic and local produce, and most entrées are baked in a wood oven. The restaurant's sleek lines, teak tables, and loud customer chatter give it a modern, hip vibe. Great SOMA spot for a stylish and tasty lunch or dinner. Closed Sunday.

BRAIN WASH

$–$$ DINER ✉1122 Folsom Street ☎415-861-3663 🖱www.brainwash.com,
contact@brainwash.com

If you're looking to nosh on a bagel, burgers, sandwich, or salad while your duds spin around in the suds, drop by here. This innovative address combines a café with a laundromat. Check out their cheap ($4.99) breakfasts Monday through Friday.

ASIASF

$$$ ASIAN   ✉*201 9th Street*   📞*415-255-2742*   🖥*www.asiasf.com*

There's another side to San Francisco beyond the bridge-dotted skyline and bustling capitalism; past the elaborate Victorians and winding streets; behind the inline skaters and Sunday strollers. It's a world of camp and fashion, where the drinks are mixed, the music is intoxicating, the clothing is sleek, and the men are women. Welcome to AsiaSF. Make no mistake, the food is good: grilled seafood, chicken satay, "baby got back" ribs, and other Asian-influenced entrées. But no one comes for the food. They come for the "gender illusionists"—men you'd swear on your partner were women—performing cabaret numbers on a red runway when they're not filling water glasses. After dinner, work off the calories in the state-of-the-art danceclub downstairs.

AZ RUSTICO CAFÉ

$ INTERNATIONAL   ✉*California College of the Arts, 1111 8th Street*   📞*415-252-0180*
📟*415-252-1533*

This café offers excellent pizza, panini, calzone, sandwiches, and salads. Homemade soups, quiche, vegetarian lasagna, and tasty tarts are also served in the dining area or at sidewalk tables. Convenient to the South of Market discount outlets, this is the place to refuel on the bargain trail.

SHOPPING

BONHAMS & BUTTERFIELDS   ✉*220 San Bruno Avenue*   📞*415-861-7500*
🖥*www.butterfields.com* This highly regarded auction house has regular sales that are open to the public. You must register for viewing before you can bid.

FLOWER MART   ✉*6th and Brannan streets*   📞*415-781-8410* Also located South of Market is this flower market where dozens of florists offer excellent prices. Closed Sunday.

Walking or driving around will net additional possibilities, from furniture stores to gallery shops and artist studios.

NIGHTLIFE

SOMA is the epicenter of San Francisco's nightclub scene, and "something for everybody" seems to be the motto.

THE STUD _____

✉*399 9th Street*   📞*415-863-6623*   🖥*www.studsf.com* Near the Flower Mart, you'll find everybody's favorite gay bar. Everybody in this case includes aging hippies, multihued punks, curious straights, and even a gay or two, all packed elbow to armpit into this pulsing club. Cover on most nights. Occasionally closed on Monday.

WISH BAR AND LOUNGE   ✉*1539 Folsom Street*   📞*415-278-9474* For upscale drinks in a fashionably low-brow setting, head to this spot where deejays spin hits nightly.

THE EAGLE TAVERN ✉398 *12th Street* ☎*415-626-0880* ✐*www.sfeagle. com* The scene is different down the street at this Levis and leather bar when there is live music. Cover on Thursday.

TWO ROCKING NIGHTCLUBS ✉*715 Harrison Street* ☎*415-339-8686* ✐*www.sfclubs.com* There is only one thing in the world better than a rocking nightclub: two rocking nightclubs. That's what you get over at 3rd and Harrison streets. On Friday **the X** (18-plus) jumps to the sound of Top 40, hip-hop, R&B, and house; and on Saturday, it's 18-plus hip-hop night at **City Nights**. Cover.

BRAIN WASH ✉*1122 Folsom Street* ☎*415-861-3663* ✐*www.brainwash.com* For some live acoustic sounds from local bands or deejay-spun jazz, check this place out. There's always something happening at this hip café that also doubles as a . . . laundromat! Tuesday is acoustic open mic night, Wednesday is spoken word night (female performers only), Thursday is comedy night, and Friday and Saturday feature live bands.

1015 ✉*1015 Folsom Street* ☎*415-431-1200* ✐*www.1015.com* Not sure what you're in the mood for tonight? Then head to this SOMA club with three floors and five separate dance environments, each featuring a different sound from house to trance to techno. The club is open after-hours, often going on until 7 a.m. Open Friday and Saturday. Cover.

CAT CLUB ✉*1190 Folsom Street* ☎*415-703-8965* ✐*www.catclubsf.com* Hip, black-clad twenty-somethings with funky haircuts and dancing feet converge on the two dancefloors here. Deejays spin '80s hits, Brit pop, indie rock, and hip-hop most nights; on Tuesday, bands crank out rock and metal. Cover.

DNA LOUNGE ✉*375 11th Street* ☎*415-626-1409* ✐*www.dnalounge.com* This lounge has lasted much longer than most trendy clubs. The scene is high-decibel with a mixed crowd clearly born to dance. And dance they do, all over this two-story club. There's also occasional live music. Cover.

BUTTER ✉*354 11th Street* ☎*415-863-5964* ✐*www.smoothasbutter.com, contact@ smoothasbutter.com* A self-proclaimed "trailer-trash bistro," Butter serves up a host of snacks and drinks — all to the sound of a funky house beat provided by deejays. Just follow the 30-something model-chic hipsters in always-fashionable black. Closed Sunday.

SLIM'S ✉*333 11th Street* ☎*415-255-0333* ✐*www.slims-sf.com* Some of the classic Bay Area rock and blues performers play here, possibly because entertainer Boz Scaggs is an owner. But there is also a hefty line-up of alternative rock bands, so the crowd could be gray- or green-haired at this all-ages club. Tickets required for entry; box office on-site.

ASIAN AMERICAN THEATER COMPANY ✐*www.asianamerican theater.org, aatcspace@gmail.com* An important member of the city's group of small theaters is this company, which represents the city's burgeoning Asian community. They perform at venues throughout the Bay Area.

3 BABES AND A BUS ✉*415-552-2582, 800-414-0158* ✐*www.threebabes.com, info@threebabes.com* If you find SF's nightlife options overwhelming, this company allows you a taste of different scenes, from '70s disco and Top-40 to salsa and R&B. For a flat fee, this nightclub-touring company takes care of the driving and cover charges while ensuring priority entry to a number of clubs on this four-hour tour. Reservations recommended.

SAN FRANCISCO'S "BACKYARD"

There is an area of San Francisco, stretching across the southern sector of the metropolis that I call the city's "Backyard." Dotted throughout this sprawling residential region are a number of inviting places. Most are unknown to tourists; some remain hidden even to native San Franciscans. To find them you'll require a feel for adventure, a touch of patience, and a good road map, plus a special desire to uncover secret locales.

SIGHTS

VERMONT STREET Everyone knows about the 1906 quake, just as everyone has heard of Lombard, San Francisco's "crookedest street." Few are aware of Vermont Street, even though it might just be crookeder than the crookedest. That's because it's located out on **Potrero Hill**, a clapboard neighborhood that has been gentrified by artists, craftspeople, and imaginative others. From a public park at Vermont and 20th streets, there's a back-door view of San Francisco's skyline; in the opposite direction loom Twin Peaks, Mt. Davidson, and a ridgeline of lesser hills. From this coign of vantage, Vermont snakes down to 22nd Street in a mesmerizing series of zigs and zags.

BERNAL HEIGHTS For another splendid view, head to this working-class neighborhood, similar to Potrero Hill, though economically more upscale and geographically a bit upslope. Bernal Heights Boulevard encircles a shale-strewn hill from the top of which the entire Bay Area spreads before you. Just park on the street and climb a short distance uphill. To the north stands the Golden Gate and beyond it the fog-curled mountains of Marin. Then as the eye moves clockwise, the San Francisco skyline appears in the foreground. The Bay, long and narrow here, draws a line along the eastern perimeter as it ebbs and flows from San Jose. Complete this 360° sweep and your eye will hike the ridgeline that protects San Francisco from the rolling fogs of the Pacific Ocean.

TWIN PEAKS Of course, the view of views is from these peaks on Twin Peaks Boulevard. Atop these bald knobs the eye traces a circle around the entire Bay. The Golden Gate Bridge becomes a mere corridor that opens onto a mountain range called Marin. The Bay is a pond inhabited by sailboats. The cityscape lies before you, and buildings appear as out of the wrong end of a telescope. Jostled and teeming, civilization stretches to the west, only to pile up at the Pacific's edge. It is a view for travelers who can wander back in the mind to the days before humankind when wind and water were all the land could see.

GLEN CANYON PARK   After leaving the metropolis in the dust, spur your mount toward this park. With its meandering stream, dense underbrush, and twisted geologic formations, there's something about this steep canyon that evokes the Old West. Granted, the sunglinted windows of civilization surround the hillsides, but deep in the heart of this draw are hiking trails that are escapes from urbanity. Like all treasures, Glen Canyon is hard to find and requires a map. Most visitors to the park come along Portola Drive to O'Shaughnessy Boulevard, then down to Elk Street. Turning left onto Elk, there's a ballfield and tennis courts, followed immediately by a road. Turn onto the road as it parallels the courts; it becomes a dirt road that forks into several hiking trails.

MT. DAVIDSON   Another wooded retreat rests nearby atop this mountain. A trail from the corner of Myra Way and Sherwood Court climbs sharply to the 938-foot summit of San Francisco's highest peak. The concrete cross at the top measures another 103 feet; for more than 60 years there have been Easter sunrise services here. If today doesn't happen to be Easter, you can still peer through the eucalyptus forest out over the Pacific.

STERN GROVE   ✉ *Corner of 19th Avenue and Sloat Boulevard* ☎ *415-252-6252* 🖷 *415-252-6250* 🖰 *www.sterngrove.org, info@sterngrove.org* This park is known for its free summer concerts. Aficionados of jazz, world, classical music, and more flock every Sunday to this natural amphitheater. The San Francisco Symphony and Ballet perform each summer here. Regardless of the day or season, the grove offers visitors grassy meadows, shady spots, and a tiny lake encircled by eucalyptus trees. It's a beautiful stroll from the Trocadero House (once an infamous gambling den) to the lake, even when there's nary a symphonic sound to be heard.

DINING

CARÊME 350

$$$ FRENCH/AMERICAN   ✉ *350 Rhode Island Street* ☎ *415-216-4329* 🖷 *415-771-2194* 🖰 *www.baychef.com*

The California Culinary Academy's restaurant, this place offers everything from a half pint of delicious potato salad to a global buffet. Students under faculty supervision hone their talents here. Located in a skylit neoclassic hall, this Potrero Hill restaurant serves three-course lunches and dinners as well as buffets. Closed Saturday through Monday.

MOKI'S SUSHI & PACIFIC GRILL

$$ PACIFIC RIM/SUSHI   ✉ *615 Cortland Avenue* ☎ *415-970-9336* 🖰 *www.mokisushi.com*

Moki's, one of Bernal Heights' hottest sushi joints, serves up Hawaiian-Japanese fusion fare. Expect to see coconut, mango, and macadamia nuts paired with salmon, tuna, and a range of other fresh raw seafood. While you're there, try the spicy corn fritters, Hawaiian chicken, or coconut-fried tofu. Expect long waits on Friday and Saturday nights at this upscale tropical eatery.

JUST FOR YOU

$$ AMERICAN ✉732 22nd Street ☎415-647-3033
✑www.justforyoucafe.com

Open for breakfast and lunch and catering to a mixed clientele, though particularly popular with women, is this diner, just outside the Potrero Hill district. It has counter service and tables and is decorated with artwork by local artists. The menu has a lot to offer, with cornmeal pancakes and grits for breakfast, hamburgers and crabcake sandwiches at lunch.

SHOPPING

PETCO ✉1685 Bryant Street ☎415-863-1840 Near Potrero Hill, this is much more than a pet shop. It's more like a zoo. Petco has all kinds of exotic birds, reptiles, and snakes, as well as more run-of-the-mill pets such as hamsters and goldfish. Bring Fluffy home a new jeweled collar or buy yourself some animal motif jewelry.

NIGHTLIFE

THE WILD SIDE WEST ✉424 Cortland Avenue ☎415-647-3099 This Bernal Heights bar operates out of a purple Victorian house. The bar is open to all, but is mainly frequented by women. The red walls and ceiling are adorned with photos and paintings, as well as masks and shoes. Guests can play video games and pool, and enjoy music from the jukebox.

PROJECT ARTAUD COMPLEX ✉450 Florida Street ☎415-626-4370 **Theater of Yugen Noh Space** (415-621-7978; www.theaterofyugen. com) and **A Traveling Jewish Theatre** (415-522-0786; www.atjt.com) are among the companies in permanent residence in the Project Artaud complex.

OUTDOOR ADVENTURES

SPORTFISHING

WACKY JACKY ✉Fisherman's Wharf, Berth 1 ☎415-586-9800 If you hanker to spend a day deep-sea fishing for rock cod, bass, salmon, and other gamefish, check out Wacky Jacky, which takes you out on her 50-foot *Delta*, often heading out to the Farallon Islands in search of salmon. Bring a lunch and dress warmly.

SAILING & NATURE CRUISES

SIGNATURE HOSPITALITY GROUP ✉Pier 39 ☎415-788-9100, 800-292-2487 ✑www.signaturesf.com, sales@signaturesf.com Some of the world's most challenging sailing can be found on San Francisco Bay. Spend a

Sunday morning cruising the Bay on a motorized yacht with this company, which has a luxury 150-foot yacht. The two-hour Sunday brunch excursion is available from April to October.

OCEANIC SOCIETY ✉*Fort Mason Center, Building E* ✆*415-474-3385, 800-326-7491* 📠*415-474-3395* 🖥*www.oceanicsociety.org* From the deck of this non-profit's 56-foot vessel you'll observe elephant seals and sea lions, dolphins, puffins, porpoises, and humpback, blue, and gray whales also frequent the waters. Day-cruises to the Farallon Islands are offered mid-May through November; whale-watching tours go from December until mid-May. Reservations required.

HANG GLIDING

MERLIN FLIGHT SCHOOL ✆*415-456-3670* 🖥*www.merlinflightschool.com, wally@merlinflightschool.com* If you like to soar the skies, try hang gliding. There is a site at Fort Funston (Skyline Boulevard at the far end of Ocean Beach). For lessons in paragliding, contact this flight school that offers views of the coastline. If you're not ready to test those wings, you'll find it's fun just to watch.

SKATING

When weekends roll around, several hundred folks are apt to don inline skates and rollerskates and careen along the sidewalks and streets of Golden Gate Park. John F. Kennedy Drive, on the east side of the park, is closed to cars on Sundays and holidays. It's great exercise, and a lot of fun to boot.

PURPLE SKUNK ✉*5820 Geary Boulevard between 22nd and 23rd avenues* ✆*415-668-7905* 🖥*www.purpleskunk.com* Rentals are available near the park at this cute shop. Closed Monday. Try their 1219 Polk Street location, too.

GOLDEN GATE PARK SKATES AND BIKES ✉*3038 Fulton Street at 6th Avenue* ✆*415-668-1117* You can also rent skates on the park's north side from this neighborhood shop.

JOGGING

In a city of steep hills, where walking provides more than enough exercise, jogging is nevertheless a favorite pastime. There are actually places to run where the terrain is fairly level and the scenery spectacular. Most popular are the Golden Gate Bridge, the Presidio Highlands, Glen Canyon Park Trail, Ocean Beach, Golden Gate Park, and Angel Island.

Parcourses, combining aerobic exercises with short jogs, are located at Justin Herman Park (the foot of Market Street near the Ferry Building; half course only), Marina Green (along Marina Boulevard near the foot of Fillmore Street), Mountain Lake Park (Lake Street between 8th and Funston avenues), and the Polo Field in Golden Gate Park.

SWIMMING

AQUATIC PARK ✉*502 Jefferson Street (Dolphin Club)* ☎*415-441-9329* ✉*500 Jefferson Street (South End Rowing Club)* ☎*415-776-7372* Although the air temperature remains moderate all year, the ocean and bay around San Francisco stay cold. If you're ready to brave the Arctic current, join the hearty swimmers who make the plunge regularly at this park. Many of these brave souls belong to either the **Dolphin Club** or the **South End Rowing Club**. Both clubs are open to the public (on alternating weekdays, call for open dates) and provide saunas and showers for a small fee (bring your own towel and swimgear). Closed Sunday and Monday.

SURFING

OCEAN BEACH West of Golden Gate Park there are several spots along this wide, sandy beach; however, the conditions vary seasonally and, because of strong rip currents, this is not a place for beginners.

FORT POINT Located on the bay side of the Golden Gate Bridge's south tower, this is another surf break in the city. Fast-flowing currents moving out the Gate make this another spot for experts only.

GOLF

For the earthbound, golf can be a heavenly sport in San Francisco. Several courses are worth checking out.

GLEN EAGLES GOLF COURSE AT MCLAREN PARK ✉*2100 Sunnydale Avenue* ☎*415-587-2425* With two separate tee boxes, this course at McLaren Park features a nine-hole course that's hilly and narrow. This public course rents power carts.

GOLDEN GATE PARK GOLF COURSE ✉*47th Avenue and Fulton Street* ☎*415-751-8987* The golf course in Golden Gate Park is a short but tricky nine-hole course close to the ocean. They rent pull carts and clubs at this public course.

HARDING PARK GOLF COURSE ✉*99 Harding Park Road* ☎*415-661-1865* Harding Park is considered to be one of the finest public courses in the country. There is an 18-hole course and a 9-hole course. Power carts are available for rent, as well as golf clubs.

PRESIDIO GOLF COURSE ☎*415-561-4664* ⌕*www.presidiogolf.com* This 18-hole golf course, the only golf course in a U.S. national park, was originally built in 1895 for Army officers to use and doubled as a drill field for troop reviews. Opened to civilians in 1995, it has quickly gained a reputation as one of the finest public courses in Northern California. Cart and club rentals are available.

TENNIS

With more than 150 free public courts, San Francisco could easily be called The City of Nets. For more information on all city courts call the San Francisco Parks and Recreation Department.

GOLDEN GATE PARK ✉John F. Kennedy and Middle drives 21 courts. Fee.

GEORGE MOSCONE PLAYGROUND ✉Chestnut and Buchanan streets Four lighted courts.

DOLORES PARK ✉18th and Dolores streets Six lighted courts.

ALICE MARBLE MEMORIAL PLAYGROUND ✉Greenwich and Hyde streets Three courts.

CHINESE PLAYGROUND ✉Sacramento Street and Waverly Plaza One lighted court.

NORTH BEACH PLAYGROUND ✉Lombard and Mason streets ☎415-831-6302 Three lighted courts.

BIKING

San Francisco is not a city designed for cyclers. Some of the hills are almost too steep to walk and downtown traffic can be gruelling. There are places, however, that are easy to ride and beautiful as well. **Golden Gate Park**, the **Golden Gate Promenade**, and **Lake Merced** all have excellent bike routes.

Among the city's most dramatic rides is the bicyclists' sidewalk on the **Golden Gate Bridge**. Or, if you're less adventurous, the **Sunset Bikeway** begins at Lake Merced Boulevard, then carries through a residential area and past views of the ocean to the Polo Field in Golden Gate Park.

CRITICAL MASS If you find yourself on a bike on the last Friday of the month, head over to Justin Herman Plaza at 5:30 p.m. and join this huge group ride. This slow-paced, moderate bike expedition lasts about two hours; the route varies each time, but expect to bring traffic to a halt as you maneuver through thoroughfares and up inclines with hundreds of other two-wheelers.

Bike Rentals

BLAZING SADDLES BIKE RENTALS ✉1095 Columbus Avenue ☎415-202-8888 ∅www.blazingsaddles.com Near Fisherman's Wharf is this bike rental shop, with mountain bikes, hybrids, and tandems.

BIKE AND ROLL ✉734 Lombard Street ☎415-771-8735, 888-544-2453 ∅www.bicyclerental.com Here you'll find comfort and touring hybrids.

WHEEL FUN RENTALS Two locations: ✉Golden Gate Park, 50 Stow Lake Drive ☎415-668-6699 ✉Fisherman's Wharf, 2739 Taylor Street ☎415-673-6700 ∅sfbicyclerentals.com This company offers many bicycle and bike-like options—from the standard two-wheel variety, tandems, and cruisers, to three- and four-wheeled buggies, choppers, and Mad Max–inspired all-terrain contraptions.

AVENUE CYCLERY ✉756 Stanyan Street ☎415-387-3155 Near the southeast corner of Golden Gate Park is this shop, which rents mountain bikes, hybrids, and kids' bicycles.

ANGEL ISLAND COMPANY ✉Angel Island ☎415-897-0715 ∅www.angelisland.com This company rents 21-speed mountain bikes and junior bikes to explore that state park's paved paths.

TRANSPORTATION

CAR

The major highways leading into San Francisco are **Route 1**, the picturesque coastal road, **Route 101**, California's coastal north–south thoroughfare, and **Route 80**, the transcontinental highway that originates on the East Coast.

AIR

SAN FRANCISCO INTERNATIONAL AIRPORT ✉ www.flysf.com

Better known as SFO, this airport sits 15 miles south of downtown San Francisco off Routes 101 and 280. A major destination from all points of the globe, the airport is always bustling.

Most domestic airlines fly into SFO, including Alaska Airlines, American Airlines, Continental Airlines, Delta Air Lines, Hawaiian Airlines, jetBlue, Northwest, Southwest, United Airlines, and Virgin America.

International carriers are also prominent here: Air Canada, British Airways, China Airlines, Japan Airlines, KLM, Lufthansa, Mexicana, Philippine Airlines, Singapore Airlines, TACA International Airlines, and Virgin Atlantic have regular flights into San Francisco's airport.

SFO GROUND TRANSPORTATION INFORMATION SERVICE

This free service will help you plan your way to and from the airport via buses, shuttles, taxis, limousines, and more. There's an information booth in the baggage claim area of each SFO terminal.

BART ☎ 650-992-2278 ✎ www.bart.gov This rapid transit service runs from the airport to all its destinations.

SUPERSHUTTLE ☎ 415-558-8500 ✎ www.supershuttle.com To travel from the airport to downtown San Francisco, call this shuttle company, which provides door-to-door service.

SAN MATEO COUNTY TRANSIT ☎ 800-660-4287 ☎ 650-817-1717 ✎ www.samtrans.org You can catch the SamTrans bus to the Transbay Terminal (425 Mission Street).

Taxi and limo service are also available, or try **Lorrie's Airport Service** (415-334-9000; www.lorries-shuttles.com).

BUS

GREYHOUSE BUS LINES ✉ Transbay Terminal, 425 Mission Street ☎ 415-495-1569, 800-231-2222 ✎ www.greyhound.com Greyhound services San Francisco from around the country.

GREEN TORTOISE ✉ 494 Broadway ☎ 415-956-7500 ✎ www.greentortoise.com, tortoise@greentortoise.com An alternative to Greyhound is this New Age company with a fleet of funky buses. Each is equipped with sleep-

ing platforms that allow travelers to rest as they cross the country. The buses stop at interesting sightseeing points en route. The Green Tortoise, an endangered species from the '60s, travels to and from the East Coast, Grand Canyon, Alaska, Baja Mexico, and elsewhere. It provides a mode of transportation as well as an experience in group living.

TRAIN

AMTRAK ✉5885 Horton Street, Emeryville ✆800-872-7245 ✐www.amtrak.com
For those who prefer to travel by rail, Amtrak has train service via the "Coast Starlight," "California Zephyr," and "San Joaquin." These trains arrive at and depart from the Emeryville train station, with connecting bus service to San Francisco's Ferry Building, where Market Street meets the Embarcadero.

CAR RENTALS

The easiest way to explore San Francisco is by foot or public transit. Driving in San Francisco can be a nightmare. Parking spaces are rare, parking lots expensive. Then there are the hills, which require you to navigate along dizzying inclines while dodging cable cars, trollies, pedestrians, and double-parked vehicles. The streets of San Francisco make Mr. Toad's wild ride look tame.

If you do decide to rent a car, most major rental agencies have franchises right at the airport. These include **Alamo** (800-462-5266), **Avis Rent A Car** (800-331-1212), **Budget Rent A Car** (800-527-0700), **Dollar Rent A Car** (800-800-4000), **Enterprise Rent A Car** (800-261-7331), **Hertz Rent A Car** (800-654-3131), **National** (800-227-7368) and **Thrifty Car Rental** (800-847-4389).

PUBLIC TRANSIT

SAN FRANCISCO MUNI ✆415-673-6864 or 311 ✐www.sfmta.com San Francisco is a city where public transit works. To get anywhere in the City, call San Francisco Muni and an operator will direct you to the appropriate mode of public transportation.

Over 90 bus lines travel around, about, and through the city. Trolley buses, street cars, light-rail subways, and cable cars also crisscross San Francisco. Most lines operate daily (with a modified schedule on weekends and holidays). Free transfers allow a 90-minute stopover or connection to two more lines. Exact fares are required. For complete information on the Muni system, purchase a copy of the "Muni Street and Transit Map" from the Visitor Information Center (900 Market Street; 415-391-2000), the Information Desk at City Hall, or local bookstores and corner groceries.

For an earth-conscious tour of the city's major museums, catch a ride on Muni's biodiesel-fueled **CultureBus** (www.sfculturebus.org), which stops in Union Square, at the SOMA musuems, and at Golden Gate Park's Music Concourse. The flat-rate all-day ticket can also be used on other Muni vehicles (cable cars excluded).

BAY AREA RAPID TRANSIT SYSTEM (BART) ☎ 650-992-2278
🖱 www.bart.gov Unlike San Francisco's classic cable cars, BART operates
streamlined cars that zip beneath the city's streets. This system travels
from Downtown to the Mission District, Glen Park, and SFO. It also
runs under the San Francisco Bay to the cities of Oakland, Berkeley, and
other parts of the East Bay. Trains run every 8 to 20 minutes depending
on the time of day. BART opens at 4 a.m. (6 a.m. on Saturday and 8 a.m.
on Sunday) and closes at midnight every night at most stations—be
sure to check the website for current schedules.

GOLDEN GATE TRANSIT ☎ 415-923-2000 🖱 www.goldengatetransit.org
Many surrounding communities feature transportation services to and
from San Francisco. To the north, this transit company provides both
bus and ferryboat service.

SAN MATEO COUNTY TRANSIT ☎ 800-660-4287 🖱 www.samtrans.
com South of San Francisco, SamTrans offers bus service as far south as
Palo Alto.

CALTRAIN ✉ Fourth and Townsend streets ☎ 800-660-4287 🖱 www.caltrain.com
Caltrain provides daily commuter service from San Jose to San
Francisco with stops along the way.

ALAMEDA–CONTRA COSTA TRANSIT ☎ 510-839-2882 🖱 www.ac
transit.org Across the Bay, AC Transit carries passengers from Oakland,
Berkeley, and other East Bay cities to the Transbay Terminal in San
Francisco.

For more information on ferry services, see the "Transportation" section in Chapter Three.

CABLE CARS

Those clanging symbols of San Francisco, are *the* way to see this city of
perpendicular hills. This venerable system covers a ten-mile section of
downtown San Francisco.

The cable car was invented in 1873 by Andrew Hallidie and works via an
underground cable that travels continuously at a speed of nine and a half
miles per hour. Three of the system's original twelve lines still operate
year-round. The Powell–Mason and Powell–Hyde cars travel from the
Downtown district to Fisherman's Wharf; the California Street line runs
east to west and passes through Chinatown and Nob Hill.

Built partially of wood and furnished with old-style running boards, these
open-air vehicles are slow and stylish. Edging up the city's steep heights,
then descending toboggan-run hills to the Bay, these open-air vehicles
provide many of San Francisco's finest views. Half the joy of riding, however, comes from watching the operators of these antique machines. Each
has developed a personal style of gripping, braking, and bell-ringing. In
addition to the breathtaking ride, they will often treat you to a clanging
street symphony.

Cabs are plentiful, but flagging them down is a trick—it's best to call by phone. The main companies are **DeSoto Cab Company** (415-970-1300), **Luxor Cabs** (415-282-4141), **Veteran's Taxi Cab Company** (415-552-1300), and **Yellow Cab** (415-626-2345).

WALKING TOURS

San Francisco is a city made for walkers. Appropriately, it offers a number of walking tours that explore various neighborhoods and historical spots.

CHINESE HERITAGE WALKS ✆ *415-986-1822* ✐ *www.c-c-c.org, info@c-c-c.org* Conducted by the Chinese Culture Center, these walks reveal the true Chinatown. They also offer a **Culinary Walk** that visits markets and herb shops, then stops for lunch in a dim sum restaurant. Call ahead for tour times. Reservations required. Fee.

WOK WIZ WALKING TOURS ✉ *750 Kearny Street* ✆ *650-355-9657, 415-981-8989* ✐ *www.wokwiz.com, shirley@wokwiz.com* This tour company, led by cookbook author Shirley Fong-Torres and her team, features local markets, herbal pharmacies, temples, and other attractions. A dim sum lunch is optional. This daily two-and-a-half-hour walk is a tasty way to get acquainted with Chinatown's historical and culinary world. Tours gather at the Hilton Hotel. Reservations required. Fee.

DASHIELL HAMMETT WALKING TOUR

✉ *P.O. Box 8755, Emeryville, CA 94662* ✐ *www.donherron.com/tour.html, dashdude@donherron.com* This walking tour is a three-mile search for the old haunts of the mystery writer and his fictional sleuth, Sam Spade. Hammett lived in the bay city from 1921 to 1929, and used it as the setting for numerous short stories and novels, including *The Maltese Falcon*. Following the tracks of Sam Spade, the tour combs the city from the Tenderloin to Nob Hill. The tour is given every Sunday in May and September and begins at noon at the northwest corner of the San Francisco Public Library at 100 Larkin and Fulton streets. Fee.

SAN FRANCISCO CITY CLUB ✉ *155 Sansome Street* ✆ *415-285-0495* ✇ *415-441-7683* Folks at the Mexican Museum lead a tour of this early-20th-century building that once housed the San Francisco Stock Exchange and features a fresco by Diego Rivera. First Wednesday of every month at 3 p.m. Fee.

PRECITA EYES MURAL ARTS CENTER ✉ *2981 24th Street* ✆ *415-285-2287* Tours are available through this arts center. Fee.

CITY GUIDES ✆ *415-557-4266* ✐ *www.sfcityguides.org, tours@sfcityguides.org* This volunteer non-profit organization sponsored by the San Francisco

Public Library, offers free tours of various locations throughout the city. They include separate tours of the Ferry Building, Pacific Heights Victorians, North Beach, Nob Hill, Coit Tower, and other points of interest.

VICTORIAN HOME WALK ☎*415-252-9485* ✐*www.victorianwalk.com,* *victorianwalk@yahoo.com* For a look at some of San Francisco's tourist-free zones and their array of Victorian homes, consider this two-and-a-half-hour home tour. Hosted by Jay Gifford, the tour's pace and tone are set by the group of two or more. Tours depart daily from Union Square. Fee.

CRUISIN' THE CASTRO

☎*415-255-1821* ✐*www.cruisinthecastro.com, cruisinthecastro@yahoo.com* Experience the heart and soul of San Francisco's gay community with host Kathy Amendola. Approximately two hours long, this entertaining walking tour includes a visit to the 1922 vintage Castro Theatre, Pink Triangle Memorial Park (the first of its kind to commemorate gays who died in WWII's concentration camps), and a stop at civil rights activist Harvey Milk's former residence and camera shop. Reservations required. No tours Sunday. Fee.

J WALKS ☎*415-806-0049* ✐*www.jwalks.com, tours@jwalks.com* Discover the sights and tastes of the Mission and Noe Valley with these guides. Tours last three hours and include a substantial amount of snacking at shops and cafés. Join native San Franciscan Jean Feilmoser and discover the pretty Victorians, funky shops, and vibrant murals that dominate the neighborhood. Reservations required. No tours December through April. Fee.

URBAN SAFARI ✉*30 Harry Street* ☎*415-282-5500, 866-6971317* ✐*www.theurbansafari.com, daniel@theurbansafari.com* Urban Safari's Daniel Oppenheim offers truly personalized, off-the-beaten-path tours of San Francisco. These spontaniety-driven excursions, which take place in a zebra-striped Land Rover, last anywhere from four to seven hours. Politely skirting tourist traps like Lombard Street and Fisherman's Wharf, Oppenheim prefers to take visitors into the heart of residential neighborhoods, or to the city's out-of-the-way curios. Fee.

HAIGHT-ASHBURY FLOWER POWER WALKING TOUR ✉*P.O. Box 170106, San Francisco, CA 94117* ☎*415-863-1621* ✐*www.hippygourmet.com, hasfs525@sbc.net* If your teenagers ever start dressing in bell bottoms and beads, take them on this tour, which explores the neighborhood made famous during the hippie era of the 1960s. Along with sites from the Summer of Love, the tour takes a longer look back at the area's Victorian architecture, which dates to the days when the once-rural Haight was a weekend resort. Tours are conducted on Tuesday and Saturday mornings. Fee.

BAY AREA

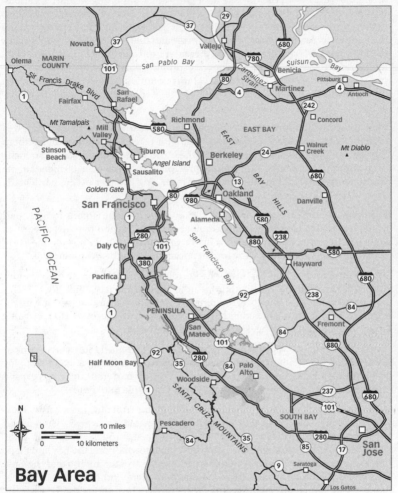

Bay Area

Geologists demythologize even the most romantic places. San Francisco Bay, they state, is a drowned river valley. Glaciers melting 10,000 years ago created it by raising sea levels and causing the ocean to flood a canyon that earlier had been carved by the Sacramento and San Joaquin rivers.

Mountains surround the entire area. The Santa Cruz Mountains rise to the west and south; on the other side are the East Bay Hills and Diablo Range; to the north looms Mt. Tamalpais. At the mouth of the Bay is the Golden Gate, a rocky conduit through which California's major drainage system empties into the Pacific.

Then the geographers take over, explaining that San Francisco Bay covers 900 square miles. It extends 50 miles south from the Golden Gate to San Jose, and ranges east for 30 miles through San Pablo and Suisun bays to the Delta.

Along the west side of the Bay sits the Peninsula. Containing wealthy suburban towns, it reaches to Palo Alto, home of Stanford University. Santa Clara Valley, better known as Silicon Valley, capital of the computer industry, sprawls along the South Bay. San Jose, with a population greater than San Francisco, dominates the area. The East Bay, directly across the water from San Francisco, features Oakland, one of the world's largest container shipping ports, and the dynamic campus town of Berkeley. To the north lies Marin County, a posh enclave highlighted by the town of Sausalito, with its aura of the Mediterranean. (Western Marin, along the Pacific, is covered in Chapter Five.)

That last word is important to meteorologists, who use it to describe the Bay Area climate. With an average temperature of 57°, it resembles sections of southern Europe. Summers are warm and dry and the warm winters bring plentiful rainfall. Though snow is extremely rare, annual precipitation varies from 20 inches in the warm South Bay to 33 inches in cooler Marin. Fog is a fact of life, particularly around the Golden Gate.

Historians perceive the area differently. They begin with the Ohlone Indians, part of the Costanoan language group, who occupied the region perhaps as early as 7000 B.C. In Marin, the Coast Miwok held sway. By the 18th century, on the eve of the white man's appearance, the Indian population numbered about 9000.

The Spanish arrived in 1769. Gaspar de Portolá explored the length of the Peninsula, and was probably the first European to see San Francisco Bay. By 1777, his countrymen founded San Jose, building Mission Santa Clara de Asís and establishing a pueblo with 66 residents. They pressed on to Marin in 1817, creating Mission San Rafael Archangel in the town of San Rafael.

By then the Spanish were already in decline, and San Rafael represents the next-to-last of their 21 California missions. The Bay was becoming a major shipping point for merchants from several countries. Traders bartered sugar, spices, and other goods for cattle hides, better known as "California banknotes."

After the Americans took over California in 1846, the fruit farming industry blossomed in the South Bay and lumbering dominated elsewhere. Timber was stripped from surrounding mountains and shipped through the Golden Gate. Then the Gold Rush brought further prosperity to towns along the Bay and made the Delta a vital corridor for goods shipped upriver to Sacramento and the Gold Country. After Chinese and other workers built a labyrinthine system of levees later in the century, the Delta became the nation's richest agricultural area.

Communities in the East Bay and Marin bloomed after the 1906 earthquake as thousands of refugees sought new homes. When the Golden Gate and Bay bridges opened during the 1930s, another trans-Bay migration occurred.

By the 1950s, the South Bay was moving to center stage. The electronics boom sounded and computer manufacturing replaced fruit farming. Between 1940 and 1998, the population of Santa Clara County increased exponentially, from about 300,000 to almost 1,700,000. Today, a staggering percentage of the nation's high-tech components originate from this Silicon Valley region. A victim of its own success, Santa Clara County began losing population in 1999 as high rents and real estate prices forced many Silicon Valley workers to live in other counties and commute an average of 150 miles a day. By the beginning of the 21st century, however, the high-tech industry and the astronomical housing prices were in retreat. But mini-booms abound, and the region has its ups and downs—albeit remaining arguably more prosperous and dynamic than the majority of the country. History in the 1960s was written in red and black. Berkeley became a rallying point, first for the Free Speech Movement in 1964, and later for the anti–Vietnam War mobilization. Its provocative populace set the pace for a nationwide movement that helped force the United States out of Southeast Asia. In 1967, Huey Newton and Bobby Seale founded the Black Panther Party in Oakland. The East Bay was a staging ground for revolution with demonstrations and riots continuing into the early 1970s.

Later in that decade, as the "Me Generation" matured, sybaritic Marin became known for its hot tubs and peacock feather massages. Berkeley politics mellowed and moved from the radical fringes to the liberal center. Oakland expanded its port at the expense of San Francisco's shrinking waterfront, and San Jose overtook San Francisco as the state's third largest city. Meanwhile, the entire Bay Area (including San Francisco) grew to a population of more than six million.

Over time, the growing population has spread to the suburbs, with housing developments spiraling out from the city centers and into the surrounding valleys and hillsides. Parts of the Bay Area have become hotbeds for technology (you'll find Silicon Valley and the Apple, Inc. headquarters in the South Bay, while Google makes its home on the Peninsula), making this one of the wealthiest places in the nation. In the East Bay, Berkeley has become an increasingly expensive place to live, drawing fewer radicals and more white collar–workers, but the undercurrent of protest has never left. Although this vibrant area originally made a name for itself in the 1960s and '70s, in the 21st century it is ever-changing, ever-growing, and never, ever boring.

Rather than visualizing the Bay Area as geologists and historians, it's time to look at the region through the eyes of the traveler. To ease the visitor's entry, this chapter is divided into five sections. Proceeding counterclockwise from San Francisco, they are the Peninsula, South Bay, East Bay, and Marin, followed by a northeastern tangent out into the Delta.

Within this lazy loop reside two of the nation's finest universities—Stanford, with its 8100-acre campus, and Berkeley. There is also the Santa Clara Valley, where the box-shaped architecture of the high-tech industry gives way to fruit orchards and rolling hills. Marin, one of the nation's richest counties, features picturesque towns and opulent estates. The Delta is a dreamy maze of waterways linked by drawbridges. Together these diverse sections form a circle and salient, along which lies some of the prettiest land west of the Atlantic.

THE PENINSULA

The Peninsula of which San Francisco is the tip extends south and encompasses some of the Bay Area's wealthiest bedroom communities. Here you will find Hillsborough, Atherton, and Palo Alto, a series of high-toned towns adorned with wooded realms and prestigious homes.

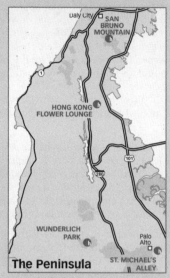

The Peninsula

SAN BRUNO MOUNTAIN STATE & COUNTY PARK

PAGE 182

Meandering, forested, peak-top trails with sweeping views of the entire Bay Area

HONG KONG FLOWER LOUNGE

PAGE 179

Authentic dim sum delicacies such as shrimp dumplings and stuffed bell peppers served in a bright eatery

ST. MICHAEL'S ALLEY

PAGE 180

Intimate sidewalk bistro with fresh California cuisine— seared apple-cider sea scallops and sweet potato gnocchi

WUNDERLICH PARK

PAGE 183

Dense forest with canopies of towering redwoods and numerous running springs

SIGHTS

SAN BRUNO MOUNTAIN

✉*Summit Road, Brisbane* The best way to explore an area is to scout it out first. So the initial stop in a Peninsula tour should be San Bruno Mountain, a bald-domed rise from which to survey the entire region. With its steep flanks and wooded ravines, this park overlooks all the Bay Area. To get there, take Bayshore Boulevard to Guadalupe Canyon Parkway, which goes through the park to the summit. You'll have to share the heights with radio antennas, but there are nearby hiking trails to escape civilization. Peer south and the world spreads before you, with the Pacific to the west, San Francisco Bay to the east, and the Santa Cruz Mountains running down the Peninsula like a spine. (The ocean side of the Peninsula is covered in Chapter Six.)

To explore the Bay side of the Peninsula, you can choose between three highways. Route 101, closest to the Bay, is a major freeway that streams past San Francisco International Airport, then beelines south. It is quick, painless (except during commute hours), and downright ugly. Route 82, or El Camino Real, named for the old royal road, is a commercial highway lined with shopping areas. Passing through the heart of most peninsula towns, it involves a lot of stop-and-go traffic and is largely uninteresting. The third option is Route 280, farther inland. To call a parkway pretty takes gall and imagination, but this high-speed freeway does possess beautiful stretches. It has been nicely landscaped and skirts the eastern fringe of the Santa Cruz Mountains.

All these highways will pass some of the Bay Area's most exclusive towns. Like Marin County to the north, the Peninsula is a suburban enclave filled with wealthy bedroom communities. In the towns of Hillsborough, Belmont, and Atherton, along winding roads above the Bay, are outlandish mansions and secluded estates.

WOODSIDE   This town is a rural version of the elite communities of Hillsborough, Belmont, and Atherton. Situated near Route 280 along the Santa Cruz Mountains, its fabulous homes are tucked away in forested heights.

FILOLI ✉*Canada Road, Woodside* ✆*650-364-8300* 📠*650-366-7836* ✐*www.filoli. org, friends@filoli.org* The most splendid of all of the unbelievable homes in the area is this sumptuous 43-room mansion designed in 1915 by Willis Polk. Built for William Bourn II, whose wealth derived partially from the Empire Mine in Grass Valley, the house features an elegant ballroom. Murals decorate the ballroom, and the marble work is impeccable. The gardens surrounding the house, equally beautiful, require the maintenance of 14 horticulturists and garden volunteers. Visitors may take a self-guided tour with a brochure; docent-led tours available by reservation. A café on the grounds serves light lunches. Last admission at 2:30 p.m. Closed Sunday and Monday, and late October to mid-February. Admission.

WOODSIDE STORE ✉*3300 Tripp Road (at King's Mountain Road), Woodside* ✆*650-851-7615* This bare wood structure dates back to 1854. A general store in the days when this region was a lumbering center, the establishment is now a three-room museum containing old tools and other artifacts. Closed Monday, Wednesday, and Friday.

SCENIC DRIVE   If you decide to follow Route 280 and visit Woodside, consider getting off the freeway in Hillsborough and taking the small side roads that parallel the main road. Skyline Boulevard (Route 35), Ralston Avenue, and Canada Road link together to form an alternate north–south route between Hillsborough and Woodside. Passing through the **San Francisco State Fish and Game Refuge**, they provide splendid views of Crystal Springs Reservoir and the Santa Cruz Mountains. Regardless of the highway you take, you will ultimately arrive in Palo Alto, home to one of America's prettiest college campuses. Named for a "tall tree" that served as an early landmark, this wealthy community is still noted for its beautiful arbors.

STANFORD UNIVERSITY ✉*Palo Alto* ✆*650-723-2560* 📠*650-725-6232* ✐*www.stanford.edu, visitorinfo@stanford.edu* The centerpiece of Palo Alto is its university, an immense campus created by railroad baron Leland Stan-

The Peninsula

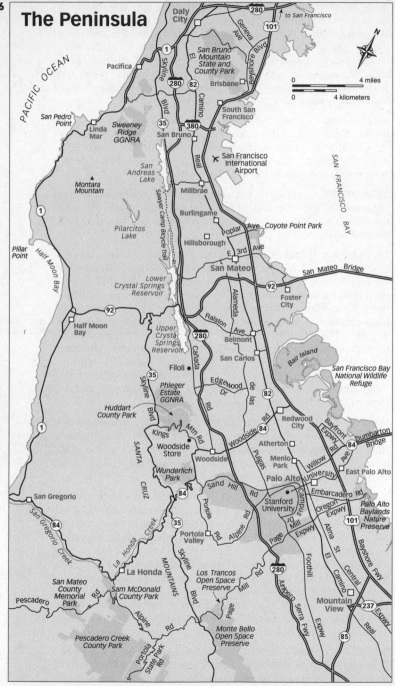

PACIFIC OCEAN

SAN FRANCISCO BAY

to San Francisco

Daly City

San Bruno Mountain State and County Park

Brisbane

South San Francisco

Pacifica

Skyline Blvd

El Camino Real

Geneva Ave

Bayshore Blvd

San Pedro Point

Linda Mar

Sweeney Ridge GGNRA

San Bruno

San Francisco International Airport

Montara Mountain

San Andreas Lake

Sawyer Camp Bicycle Trail

Pilarcitos Lake

Millbrae

Burlingame

Pillar Point

Half Moon Bay

Hillsborough

Poplar Ave

Coyote Point Park

Lower Crystal Springs Reservoir

E 3rd Ave

San Mateo

San Mateo Bridge

Half Moon Bay

Upper Crystal Springs Reservoir

Alameda

Ralston Ave

Foster City

Filoli

Cañada

Belmont

San Carlos

Phleger Estate GGNRA

Edgewood Dr

de las Pulgas

Bair Island

San Francisco Bay National Wildlife Refuge

Huddart County Park

Skyline Blvd

Woodside Rd

Redwood City

Bayfront Expwy

Dumbarton Bridge

Kings Mtn Rd

Woodside Store

Atherton

Menlo Park

Willow Rd

East Palo Alto

SANTA CRUZ

Wunderlich Park

Woodside

Sand Hill Rd

Palo Alto

University

Embarcadero Rd

San Gregorio

Portola Rd

Alpine Rd

Stanford University

Campus Dr

Oregon Expwy

Palo Alto Baylands Nature Preserve

San Gregorio Creek

La Honda Creek

Portola Valley

Junipero Serra Fwy

Page Mill Rd

Alma St

El Camino Real

Bayshore Fwy

San Mateo County Memorial Park

La Honda

Sam McDonald County Park

MOUNTAINS

Skyline Blvd

Los Trancos Open Space Preserve

Page Mill Rd

Foothill Expwy

Central Expwy

Pescadero

Alpine Rd

Portola State Park Rd

Monte Bello Open Space Preserve

Mountain View

El Camino Real

Pescadero Creek County Park

MONTARA MOUNTAINS

0 — 4 miles
0 — 4 kilometers

ford during the 1880s. For information on walking tours, call Stanford Visitor Information.

CANTOR ARTS CENTER AT STANFORD ⊠*Stanford University, Museum Way and Lomita Drive, Palo Alto* ✆*650-723-4177* ✆*650-725-0464* ✎*www.stanford.edu/dept/ccva* The arcade of trees lining the entrance along Palm Drive will provide an idea of Palo Alto's arboreal heritage and of Stanford's magnificent landscaping. You'll also pass the arts center here. Among the pieces in this diverse collection are an Egyptian mummy, California landscape oil paintings, a 19th-century Yurok canoe carved from a redwood log, and the golden spike that marked completion of the transcontinental railroad. Ongoing exhibits highlight art and artifacts from around the world. One of the main attractions is the outdoor Rodin sculpture garden, accessible 24 hours a day. Closed Monday and Tuesday.

QUADRANGLE ⊠*Stanford University, end of Palm Drive* The center of campus, this elegant Spanish-style courtyard is built of sandstone and capped with red tile. The architecture throughout the university is Romanesque, and the Quad's colonnaded walkways evoke the image of a cloister.

MEMORIAL CHURCH ⊠*Stanford University* This sacred building anchors the far edge of the plaza. That tile mosaic facade portraying the Sermon on the Mount was fashioned in Venice, Italy. Inside, the cathedral is a vaulting structure illuminated through stained glass and adorned with stone filigree. Behind the altar, past the candelabra and solitary cross, hangs "The Last Supper," re-created from the Sistine Chapel original with special permission from the Pope.

HOOVER TOWER ⊠*Stanford University* ✆*650-723-2053* ✆*650-725-6232* ✎*www.hoover.org* Just east of the Quad rises this 285-foot landmark from the top of which you can survey the campus and beyond. Home to the Hoover Institution, a conservative think tank, the tower also houses the memorabilia of one of Stanford's most famous graduates, President Herbert Hoover. Closed during finals and other relevant academic occasions. Admission.

MUSEUM OF AMERICAN HERITAGE ⊠*351 Homer Avenue, Palo Alto* ✆*650-321-1004* ✆*650-473-6950* ✎*www.moah.org, mail@moah.org* Ingenuity is the password to this museum. Housed in a 1907 Earnest Coxhad home, this little showplace traces the history of mechanical, electrical, and technological inventions with a variety of permanent and rotating displays. Fixed exhibits include both an early 20th-century print shop, kitchen, and radio repair shop. Changing displays may feature historic instruments along with myriad domestic and industrial technology. A handful of workshops are available for middle school–aged students. Closed Monday through Thursday.

PALO ALTO BAYLANDS NATURE PRESERVE

⊠*Located on the east end of Embarcadero Road, Palo Alto* ✆*650-329-2506*
In addition to the historic and academic heights, Palo Alto pos-

sesses mucky lowlands along the shores of San Francisco Bay. Though the contrast between the two is startling, both are well worth exploring. The nature preserve is a land of pickleweed and cord grass, home to the endangered clapper rail and salt marsh harvest mouse. It takes a special person to appreciate the beauty of a salt marsh. For those who don't mind black mud and pungent smells, this preserve offers unique opportunities. There's a small interpretive center here, as well as a boardwalk that leads through the marsh to the edge of the Bay. More important, the preserve is a birdwatcher's paradise. A major stop along the Pacific Flyway, the marshlands are visited by over one million birds each year. Closed Monday.

BYXBEE ART PARK ✉*Embarcadero Road* Near Baylands is this 40-acre park, created on an old landfill site. This waterfront spot features environmental art displays and plenty of room for peacefully contemplating the universe. Mysteriously arranged poles scattered across the moguled landscape make this an intriguing place (as do the wind waves, oyster shell pathways, and industrial flair).

ARBOREAL ROUTE To get in tune for a visit to these mudflats, you can follow a route from Stanford that leads along one of Palo Alto's tree-shaded streets. Most people take University Avenue, the main drag. Instead take Hamilton Avenue, one block to the south, then turn right on Greer Road, and pick up Embarcadero Road to the Bay. Along this arboreal route are trees exotic in name and appearance—Irish yews, sugarplums, bottle-brushes, bunya-bunyas, Australian brush cherries, and monkey puzzle trees.

LODGING

BEST WESTERN GROSVENOR HOTEL

$$ 206 ROOMS ✉*380 South Airport Boulevard, South San Francisco*
📞*650-873-3200, 800-722-7141* 📠*650-589-3495* ⌨*www.grosvenorsfo.com*

You're just ten minutes from the San Francisco Airport (which is really the only reason to check in to the hotel in the first place) at this nine-story facility. There are rooms and suites; the suites feature queen-sized beds and comfortable sofas. If you like watching planes take off, this is the place for you. Fortunately, the rooms are all soundproofed. There's a pool and airport shuttle, and an extensive business center on the ground floor.

STANFORD PARK HOTEL

$$$$ 171 UNITS ✉*100 El Camino Real, Menlo Park* 📞*650-322-1234, 800-241-2431*
📠*650-322-0975* ⌨*www.stanfordparkhotel.com*

Just half a mile from the Stanford campus, the European-style Stanford Park Hotel offers 163 rooms and 8 suites. English yew wood furniture adds to the charm of rooms decorated with landscape paintings. Many offer courtyard views. You can work out in the exercise room and relax by the spa or pool. This is a place that manages to retain Old World hospitality.

TOWNHOUSE INN

$$ 77 ROOMS ✉4164 El Camino Real, Palo Alto ☎650-493-4492, 800-458-8696
📠650-493-3418 ✐www.townhouseinn.com, hosts@townhouseinn.com

Located on the main drag, the Townhouse is a convenient place to stay in Palo Alto. The digs are comfortable and spacious, done up in typical motel decor. Some rooms have kitchenettes; laundry facilities are on site. Free high-speed internet access. A continental breakfast is included in the rates.

COWPER INN

$$$ 13 ROOMS ✉705 Cowper Street, Palo Alto ☎650-327-4475 📠650-329-1703
✐www.cowperinn.com

This cozy inn sits just a few blocks from University Avenue, and minutes away from Palo Alto's chic shops and many eateries. Thirteen comfortable and well-maintained rooms (two with a shared bath) fill a restored Craftsman-style home. A large parlor with bay windows is perfect for afternoon lounging, and a tasty homemade breakfast awaits guests every morning.

DINING

HONG KONG FLOWER LOUNGE

$$–$$$ CHINESE ✉51 Millbrae Avenue, Millbrae ☎650-692-6666
✐www.flowerlounge.net

There's no need to fly across the Pacific for authentic dim sum. Just head here, where servers wheel around carts laden with savory delicacies such as shrimp dumplings, steamed pork buns, stuffed bell peppers, and shark-fin dumplings. In addition to this lunchtime favorite, diners can order traditional Cantonese dishes from the menu.

ALICE'S RESTAURANT

$$ AMERICAN ✉Skyline Boulevard and La Honda Road, Woodside ☎650-851-0303
✐www.alicesrestaurant.com

This eatery is located at the only busy intersection for miles around. It sports little more than a counter, a few tables and chairs, and a spacious outdoor eating area facing Route 35. Alice's is open for breakfast, lunch, and dinner, primarily serving speciality burgers, egg dishes, sandwiches, and a variety of vegetarian entrées.

MACARTHUR PARK

$$–$$$$ NEW AMERICAN ✉27 University Avenue, Palo Alto ☎650-321-9990
📠650-321-1403 ✐www.macarthurparkpaloalto.com

To dine in style while visiting Stanford, I recommend eating here. Located between campus and downtown, it rests in a 1918 building designed by noted Bay Area architect Julia Morgan. Originally serving as a World War I hospitality house, the structure now contains a lovely restaurant specializing in food prepared in an oakwood smoker or mesquite grill. There's roasted chicken breast, barbecued baby back ribs, lobster ravioli, and fresh fish. Vegetarian dishes are also available. The menu is similar at lunch and dinner. No lunch on Saturday and Sunday.

TRESIDDER MEMORIAL UNION

$ MEXICAN/AMERICAN   ✉*Stanford University, 518–520 Lagunita Drive, Palo Alto*

This facility on the Stanford University campus houses **The Treehouse**, serving Mexican food. At **Bon Appetit** in the Arbuckle Lounge, you can order breakfast pastries, or sandwiches and salads at lunch. Each place will be crowded with students. Since the eateries are located near the central Quadrangle, they're convenient when touring the campus.

STRAITS CAFE

$$–$$$ ASIAN FUSION   ✉*3295 El Camino Real, Palo Alto*   ✆*650-494-7168*
✍*www.straitscafepaloalto.com*

Singaporean cuisine meets dot-com trendiness here. Entrées reflect a pan-Asian romance—Indian-flavored noodles listed next to tuna sashimi, for instance. The setting is equally exotic with teak, orchids, and a lavish patio. Appetizers are plentiful and highly recommended, especially the grilled scallops, Poh Pia (a spring roll creation), and Dungeness crab cakes with mango salsa. No lunch on weekends.

PALO ALTO CREAMERY FOUNTAIN & GRILL

$ AMERICAN   ✉*566 Emerson Street, Palo Alto*   ✆*650-323-3131*
✍*www.paloaltocreamery.com*

When the yuppified streets of Palo Alto prove too much, find solace in old-fashioned fare at this unpretentious diner. Known as the Peninsula Creamery to regulars, this joint has been turning out burgers and fries since the 1920s. Breakfast is served all day, the jukebox spits out oldies nonstop, and there's a tantalizing display case full of deliciously sinful desserts. Forgoing a milkshake is criminal.

ST. MICHAEL'S ALLEY

$$–$$$ CALIFORNIA CUISINE   ✉*806 Emerson Street, Palo Alto*
✆*650-326-2530*   📠*650-326-1436*   ✍*www.stmikes.com*

St. Michael's is an intimate bistro—a good place to go for quiet conversation and a taste of hearty California cuisine. Seasonal entrées may include artichoke and cheese ravioli, pork medallions, Idaho trout, or potato gnocchi. Closed Sunday night and Monday. Weekend brunch available.

ALPINE INN

$ AMERICAN   ✉*3950 Alpine Road, Portola Valley*   ✆*650-854-4004*

Way up in the hills above Palo Alto, there's a roadhouse called the Alpine Inn that dates back to the 1850s. It's a simple, homey place serving locally famous hamburgers, sandwiches, and other basic fare. The spot is very popular with local folks. You can dine indoors beneath trophy heads or outside at a picnic table.

UNITED STATES GEOLOGICAL SURVEY EARTH SCIENCE INFORMATION CENTER ✉*345 Middlefield Road, Menlo Park* ✆*650-329-4390* 🖷*650-329-5130* For detailed maps and cartographic information, it's hard to top this center. In addition to excellent USGS topographic maps, this facility sells thematic maps and various literary works. Closed weekends.

KEPLER'S BOOKS ✉*1010 El Camino Real, Menlo Park* ✆*650-324-4321* 🖅*www.keplers.com, books@keplers.com* One of the Peninsula's best bookstores, Kepler's is a "literary living room" where residents of the Stanford University area come to meet friends, argue politics, and share gossip. The huge, eclectic stock of books is hand-picked to appeal to an extremely well-educated, affluent clientele, and the staff stays knowledgeable by meeting daily to compare notes on the latest books they have read. Kepler's hosts a number of monthly discussions as well as author appearances. If you've got kids in tow, the Sunday-morning children's storytime is a great alternative to TV cartoons.

If you can't find it at Kepler's Books, that elusive volume will doubtless be in one of downtown Palo Alto's many bookstores. This campus town has practically as many booksellers as restaurants. To browse shops in downtown Palo Alto, plan to stroll University Avenue from Alma Street to Webster Street, then return along Hamilton Avenue. Like the side streets between, these thoroughfares are door-to-door with boutiques, galleries, and knickknack shops.

GALLERY HOUSE ✉*320 California Avenue, Palo Alto* ✆*650-326-1668* An exceptional example of this area's fabulous art shops is this gallery, which contains striking works of contemporary art and pottery by local artists. Closed Sunday and Monday.

University Avenue boasts countless galleries, shops, and restaurants, making it a neat place to do some browsing.

MEADOWLARK GALLERY ✉*516 University Avenue, Palo Alto* ✆*650-330-1490* 🖷*650-330-1493* Meadowlark, which represents over 400 American artists, sells a multitude of hand-crafted objects like ceramics, jewelry, furniture, and woodwork.

GLEIM JEWELERS ✉*322 University Avenue, Palo Alto* ✆*650-323-1331* If you're ready to plunk down some serious moolah, visit this high-end shop and drool over their dazzling collections of "old-time" jewelry. Closed Sunday.

NIGHTLIFE

MOLLOY'S TAVERN ✉*1655 Old Mission Road, Colma* ✆*650-755-9545* Night owls flying south from San Francisco will find plenty of diversions along the Peninsula. Molloy's Tavern, a few miles from the City, is a century-old bar crowded with memories and memorabilia. Plus there's karaoke on Thursday and occasional live banjo, Latin jazz, or reggae on the weekend.

CARIBBEAN GARDENS

✉1306 Bayshore Avenue, Burlingame ✆650-344-1797 In an unlikely spot near the San Francisco International Airport, this funky spot bills itself as an international dance club and is undoubtedly one of the peninsula's hottest places to dance to salsa, merengue, reggae, African, house, and soca music. Closed Monday and Tuesday. Cover.

EMPIRE GRILL & TAP ROOM ✉651 Emerson Street, Palo Alto ✆650-321-3030 With a warm atmosphere and 16 microbrewed beers on tap, the Empire is a choice spot for a candlelit evening drink. Out back, the spacious patio is complemented by lush greenery and a fountain.

BLUE CHALK CAFÉ ✉630 Ramona Street, Palo Alto ✆650-325-1020 This café dishes up Southern-inspired dishes, and it's a great nightspot for drinks at the bar along with a game of pool or darts in the billiards room.

FANNY & ALEXANDER ✉412 Emerson Street, Palo Alto ✆650-326-7183 Known as F&A's, this place has a beer garden, and gets busy at night with dancing, deejays, and occasional live music. Cover.

Check the "Intermission and Nightlife" sections of the *Stanford Daily* and other university publications for information about programs on the Stanford campus (www.standforddaily.com).

BEACHES & PARKS

SAN BRUNO MOUNTAIN STATE & COUNTY PARK

✉In Brisbane a few miles south of San Francisco. From 101 South, take the Sierra Point exit to Lagoon Road. Follow through to Bayshore Boulevard and go right. Follow to Guadalupe Canyon Parkway and go left. ✆650-992-6770 ✆650-992-1682

🚶🚲 This 2000-acre facility seems to be perennially under construction. After bitter debates between conservationists and developers, the park was finally established in the late 1970s. Today, it is one of San Francisco's last wild places, harboring 14 endangered plant species and three endangered butterflies. A spectacular time to visit is during the wildflower season from February through May. Scenically, it provides one of the Bay Area's most amazing views, a 360° panorama from atop 1314-foot San Bruno Mountain. This hillside park is also a fine place to picnic. There are 12 miles of hiking trails, picnic areas, and toilets. Day-use fee, $5.

COYOTE POINT PARK

✉ *Located in San Mateo; from Route 101 south take the Poplar Avenue exit to Coyote Point Drive.* 📞 *650-573-2592* 📠 *650-573-3727* 🖊 *www.coyotepointmuseum.org*

A multi-use facility, this bayshore park contains everything from a museum to a firing range, with stops in between for a marina and two playgrounds. There's a pebble beach for sunbathers, a nearby golf course, a salt marsh ideal for wildlife viewing, and the Coyote Point Museum (admission), which houses rotating exhibits of local wildlife. Because of the proximity to San Francisco Airport, jets pass overhead continually, but there are excellent views of the Bay, and the park is extremely popular with local residents. Facilities include restrooms, picnic areas, a large playground, showers, and a museum (admission). Day-use fee, $5.

HUDDART COUNTY PARK

✉ *Located in Woodside; take Woodside Road off Route 280, then go three and a half miles west to 1100 Kings Mountain Road.* 📞 *650-851-0326, 650-851-1210* 📠 *650-851-9558*

Situated on the Bay side of the Santa Cruz Mountains, this densely forested park provides a touch of the wild within whistling distance of San Francisco. Rising to 2000 feet, it features redwood and mixed evergreen forests. More than 25 miles of hiking trails crisscross the landscape, and the park is a habitat for blacktail deer, raccoons, coyotes, and an occasional bobcat or gray fox. There are picnic areas (some with shelters and electricity), restrooms, a playground, and an archery range. Day-use fee, $5.

WUNDERLICH PARK

✉ *Route 84 in Woodside, two miles west of the town center* 📞 *650-851-1210* 📠 *650-851-9558*

Set along the eastern slopes of the Santa Cruz Mountains, this facility is dominated by redwoods. Though largely undeveloped, it does have a private stable and is very popular with equestrians. Hikers also favor the 25 miles of trails that wind along mountain streams, across rolling meadows, and through redwood groves. The only facilities here are portable toilets.

MIDPENINSULA REGIONAL OPEN SPACE DISTRICT

✉ *From Route 280 in Palo Alto, take Page Mill Road seven miles southwest. The entrances to both preserves are along the roadside.* 📞 *650-691-1200* 📠 *650-691-0485* 🖊 *www.openspace.org, info@openspace.org*

The contiguous preserves of Los Trancos and Monte Bello cover more than 3000 acres of rolling countryside. They're located in the hills above Palo Alto and provide sweeping views from San Francisco to Mount Diablo. The terrain varies from grassland to mixed evergreen forest to canyons shaded with oak trees. Most visitors are drawn here by the San Andreas Fault, which bisects Los Trancos and can be explored along one of the area's many hiking trails. From these heights, it's possible to visually follow the fault past San Francisco. The only facilities are toilets at Monte Bello. Day-use fee, $5.

▲ Campers can spend the night at the very primitive Black Mountain Backpack Camp, which is a one-and-a-half-mile hike from Page Mill Road. A permit is required for overnight camping.

THE SOUTH BAY

Located about 50 miles south of San Francisco, the San Jose area is a sprawling collection of cities and towns laid out like Los Angeles. It's one of California's wealthiest sections, home to the state's vaunted high-tech industry. Scattered around this Santa Clara Valley region are several points of interest.

SIGHTS

SAN JOSE   Today, this city is best known as the super-rich "capital" of Silicon Valley, epicenter of the microelectronics industry in America. Among the city's custom home developments, shopping malls, and congested thoroughfares, though, visitors can discover some unique and eccentric reminders of an earlier, simpler time.

SAN JOSE CONVENTION & VISITORS BUREAU ✉ *150 West San Carlos Street, San Jose* ✆ *408-295-9600, 800-726-5673* ✐ *www.sanjose.org, concierge@ sanjose.org* For sightseeing information, your best resource is this visitors bureau. Located in San Jose Convention Center, it can provide details and directions for the entire area. The bureau's unique, free concierge service will make hotel and restaurant reservations for you and arrange theater, sports, and special events tickets, all at discounted prices.

SAN JOSE SILICON VALLEY CHAMBER OF COMMERCE ✉ *310 South 1st Street, San Jose* ✆ *408-291-5250* ✆ *408-286-5019* ✐ *www.sjchamber. com, info@sjchamber.com* For information on San Jose and the Santa Clara Valley in general, contact the chamber of commerce. Closed Saturday and Sunday.

SAN JOSE MCENERY CONVENTION CENTER ✉ *West San Carlos Street between Almaden Boulevard and Market Street, San Jose* ✆ *408-277-3900* ✆ *408-277-3535* ✐ *www.sjcc.com* Downtown, a billion-dollar renovation brought a metamorphosis to this formerly rundown area. Center stage stands this 425,000-square-foot convention center. Critical raves met this unique soft peach–colored structure—with its enormous vaulted entranceway highlighted by a porcelain-tile mural, its multilevel glass-enclosed arcade and concourse, and its black-and-white marble terrazzo promenade—upon its completion in 1989.

PLAZA PARK   High-class hotels, restaurants, shops, and financial centers dot the area, where people zip along via a modern light-rail system. Landscaping has not been forgotten amid all this glass and concrete. The city planted 600 sycamore trees to shade the downtown transit mall, and there's this green oasis with palms and acres of grass along Market Street across from the convention center.

SAN JOSE MUSEUM OF QUILTS AND TEXTILES ✉*520 South 1st Street, San Jose* ☎*408-971-0323* ✆*408-971-7226* ⌨*www.sjquiltmuseum.org, info@sjquiltmuseum.org* This is a recommended stop. Quilts and other textiles from around the world are featured in changing exhibits. Closed Monday. Admission.

CHILDREN'S DISCOVERY MUSEUM ✉*180 Woz Way, San Jose* ☎*408-298-5437* ✆*408-298-6826* ⌨*www.cdm.org* An amazing collection of interactive exhibits is on display here. Kids can climb on real fire trucks and ambulances, operate traffic lights along simulated roadways, make their own cornhusk doll, or build a bridge. Your kids can also explore a hands-on art studio and an interactive bubble exhibit. Closed Monday except in July and August. Admission.

TECH MUSEUM OF INNOVATION ✉*201 South Market Street, San Jose* ☎*408-294-8324* ✆*408-279-7167* ⌨*www.thetech.org* For older kids and adults there's the Tech Museum. Here you'll discover a collection of interactive exhibits in which you can drive a space rover through a Martian landscape, compare genetic profiles with other visitors, or take a virtual bobsled ride, complete with auditing and visual feedback. The museum's 87-foot Hackworth IMAX Dome Theater, which wraps the audience in images ten times larger than the largest conventional movie screens. Admission.

SAN JOSE MUSEUM OF ART ✉*110 South Market Street, San Jose* ☎*408-294-2787* ✆*408-294-2977* ⌨*www.sanjosemuseumofart.org, info@sjmusart.org* Housed in a century-old Romanesque-style building, this museum is complemented by a wing featuring a barrel-vaulted ceiling and two outdoor sculpture courts. Focusing on 20th- and 21st-century art, the collection includes such contemporary artists as Robert Arneson, Richard Diebenkorn, Rupert Garcia, Raymond Saunders, and Deborah Oeopallo. The museum features changing exhibitions of contemporary art, as well as a number of special programs. Closed Monday.

CITY HALL ✉*200 East Santa Clara Street, San Jose* ☎*408-535-3500, 408-292-673* ⌨*www.sanjoseca.gov* Just over on Santa Clara Street stands San Jose's pride and joy—the recently completed 18-story City Hall. Agencies and offices that were once scattered throughout the nation's tenth largest city are now housed in one location. A large glass rotunda standing 100 feet tall serves as the gateway to the building and connects directly to the public plaza.

RESTORED HOUSES ✉*175 West St. John Street, San Jose* ☎*408-993-8300* ✆*408-993-8088* ⌨*www.historysanjose.org, education@historysanjose.org* Two restored historic houses in San Pedro Square, the Fallon House and Peralta Adobe, form a living-history museum designed to honor the city's roots. The **Peralta Adobe**, San Jose's only surviving adobe structure, illustrates California pueblo life in both the 1790s and 1840s. The **Fallon House**, an Italianate Victorian mansion built by an early mayor, shows how a prosperous family lived in the 1850s. Both can be toured by appointment (408-993-8300). Admission.

HABANA CUBA

PAGE 192

Tomato- and pepper-sautéed seafood, spicy citrus pork, and tangy baked lamb from an airy Havana-style restaurant

HOTEL LOS GATOS & SPA

PAGE 191

Old World boutique inn with sumptuous Tuscan design—iron chandeliers, dark woods, and rich fabrics

SANBORN-SKYLINE COUNTY PARK

PAGE 194

Mountain landscape lushly forested with second-growth redwoods towering above Santa Clara Valley

HOTEL MONTGOMERY

PAGE 190

Slickly exquisite rooms and suites featuring custom leather furnishings and a bounty of gold decor

JAPANESE AMERICAN MUSEUM OF SAN JOSE

✉ *535 North 5th Street* ☎ *408-294-3138* 📠 *408-294-1657* 🖥 *www.jamsj.org,* *mail@jamsj.org* Closed through early 2009 for a major expansion, JAM is currently conducting walking tours of San Jose's Japan-town, the only one in the country still in its original location. A docent will take you around to all the historic sites, including Dobashi's market, one of the first Japanese businesses here and the Buddhist Church, which served as temporary shelter for Japanese Americans after they were released from the World War II internment camps. The new 6,400-square foot museum will resemble a Japanese farmhouse, with extensive exhibits and col-lections that tell the story of Japanese Americans in California. To schedule a tour, contact Mimi Suga (408-265-8693, mimi@ jamsj.org).

KELLEY PARK ✉*Story and Senter roads, San Jose* ☎*408-277-5254* ☏*408-297-0779* South of the downtown core, this park contains more than 150 wooded acres with picnic areas and recreation facilities. There's a petting zoo (admission) for children that also contains rides and puppet shows. Next to this playland sits the Japanese Friendship Garden, a serene six-acre setting with *koi* pond, footbridges, and a teahouse.

HISTORY SAN JOSE ✉*Kelley Park, 1650 Senter Road, San Jose* ☎*408-287-2290* ☏*408-287-2291* ⌖*www.historysanjose.org* Of Kelley Park's several attractions, the highlight is this outdoor museum featuring several antique buildings in a plaza setting. Inside the old Pacific Hotel, you'll find displays tracing San Jose's history from the Indians through the trappers, miners, and farmers. The nearby soda fountain, still operating, is definitely the high point of any visit. Not far from here rise the old firehouse, a clapboard livery stable complete with rickety wagons, a printing office, a Gothic-style house from the 1870s, a Chinese temple, and a 1927 gas station with gravity-feed pumps. Closed Monday. Admission.

ROSICRUCIAN EGYPTIAN MUSEUM ✉*1342 Naglee Avenue, San Jose* ☎*408-947-3636* ☏*408-947-3638* ⌖*www.egyptianmuseum.org* Certainly San Jose's most unique and exotic site is this museum. The landscaping and buildings throughout the elaborate complex effectively re-create ancient Egypt. There are sphinxes, and temples decorated with hieroglyphs. The museum entranceway is lined on either side by stone statues of rams, reproducing an ancient avenue in Thebes. Inside are mummies dating back 3000 years, alabaster urns, bronze pieces portraying lion-headed goddesses, incense burners in the shape of falcon heads, statues of the Nile gods, and mummy shrouds painted with holy insignia. Also featuring Babylonian, Persian, and Assyrian artifacts, it's a place to make you ponder the texture of life and the structure of infinity. Admission.

WINCHESTER MYSTERY HOUSE ✉*525 South Winchester Boulevard, San Jose* ☎*408-247-2101* ☏*408-247-2090* ⌖*www.winchestermysteryhouse.com* If the Rosicrucian Museum represents humankind's search for universal meaning, the Winchester Mystery House is a study in the meaningless lives of the idle rich. Numbering 160 rooms and covering four acres, this Victorian monstrosity is still unfinished. It was built by Sarah Winchester, heiress to the Winchester rifle fortune, who kept adding on rooms for 38 years. She believed that the ghosts of everyone killed by Winchester rifles were out to get her and hoped to lose them within the maze of the house. Unfortunately for her, the floor plans weren't revenge-proof—she died in 1922. Her legacy is an architectural riddle complete with stairways leading nowhere and closets that open onto walls. The interior design is very beautiful, however, and there are ghost stories galore surrounding the house and its unbalanced owner. Admission.

SANTANA ROW ✉*355 Santana Row, San Jose* ☎*408-551-4611* ⌖*www.santanarow.com* Nearly destroyed by fire on the eve of its completion in 2002, Santana Row rose from the ashes to become a thriving San Jose addition. Its wide treelined sidewalks, homey storefronts, and old-town streetlamps hide the chic and upscale shops that dominate the setting.

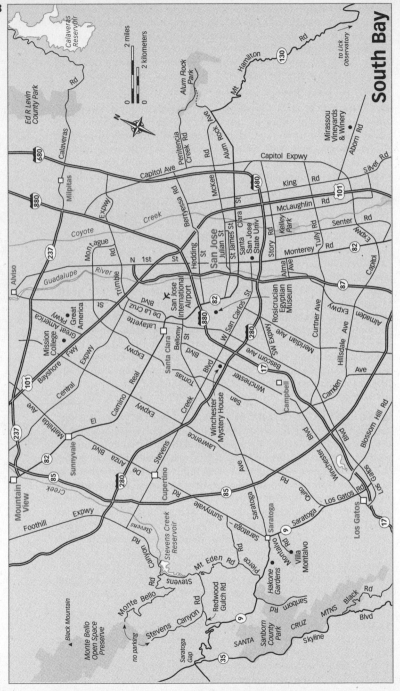

South Bay

People come here to spend, spend, spend, whether it be on dinner, deluxe accommodations, or a new Gucci tote.

PARAMOUNT'S GREAT AMERICA ✉*Great America Parkway, Santa Clara* ☎*408-988-1776* 📠*408-986-5855* 🖱*www.pgathrills.com* For hair-raising excitement, visit this amusement center. The 100-acre theme park features movies, theatrical revues, concerts, video galleries, a flight simulator, and white-knuckle rides with menacing names such as Invertigo, Demon, Vortex, Xtreme Skyflyer, and Drop Zone, an 822-foot freefall ride. For the wee ones, there's Nickelodeon Central, which features kid-themed rides like SpongeBob's Boatmobile or the Rugrats Runaway Reptar Rollercoaster. Closed in winter. Admission.

INTEL MUSEUM ✉*2200 Mission College Boulevard, Santa Clara* ☎*408-765-0503* 📠*408-765-1217* 🖱*www.intel.com/museum* This is one of the few places visitors can learn firsthand about the technology industry that drives Silicon Valley. Exhibits trace the history of microchip development and the pioneers who made the tech revolution happen. Visitors can experience work in a contamination-free microchip factory and even try on a clean-room bunny suit. There's a plethora of interactive exhibits. Closed Sunday.

LOS GATOS The South Bay's other features are farther afield, and far more placid. Los Gatos, a wealthy and luxurious town in the foothills of the Santa Cruz Mountains, provides peaceful country lanes and Carpenter Gothic–style homes.

SARATOGA This wealthy city contains sumptuous hillside homes throughout its various neighborhoods. Once an industrial town, today Saratoga is a quiet community dotted with orchards.

MONTALVO ARTS CENTER ✉*15400 Montalvo Road, Saratoga* ☎*408-961-5800* 📠*408-961-5850* 🖱*www.montalvoarts.org, info@montalvoarts.org* This Mediterranean-style mansion and surrounding estate was home to James Phelan, a three-term mayor of San Francisco and former U.S. Senator. Today his 19-room house serves as a cultural center featuring artistic exhibits and events; the luxurious grounds have been converted to an arboretum laced with nature trails. There are gardens, rare plants, creeks, and forests of maple and oak. Call or check the website for hours and events.

HAKONE GARDENS ✉*21000 Big Basin Way, Saratoga* ☎*408-741-4994* 📠*408-741-4993* 🖱*www.hakone.us, hakone@hakone.com* A lovely Japanese-style retreat, these garden are abloom with wisteria. Irises and rushes border the *koi* pond and a waterfall spills across the landscape. A perfect place to meditate, or simply soak up the sun, this enchanting garden also contains a house built without nails that serves as a cultural exchange center. Tea ceremonies and docent-led tours of the grounds are available by reservation. On the third Sunday afternoon of each month, a public tea ceremony is performed. Admission.

LICK OBSERVATORY ✉*Mount Hamilton Road, San Jose* ☎*408-274-5061* 🖱*www.ucolick.org* The 45-minute drive to this observatory, atop 4209-foot Mount Hamilton, will carry you even farther from the smoggy center of San Jose. One of the world's largest telescopes, a giant eye

120 inches in diameter, it stares heavenward from this lofty perch. In operation since 1888, the observatory sponsors guided tours and a visitors center.

MOUNT HAMILTON ROAD ⊠*Route 130* This scenic road winds over 20 miles past rolling ranch lands, oak groves, and flowering fields en route to the summit. With the white-domed observatory above you and the entire South Bay spread below, there are views no telescope can hope to match.

LODGING

HOTEL DE ANZA

$$$$ 100 ROOMS ⊠*233 West Santa Clara Street, San Jose*
☎*408-286-1000, 800-843-3700* 🖷*408-286-0500* 🖑*www.hoteldeanza.com*

An Art Deco gem restored to its 1931 grandeur is the Hotel De Anza, a 100-room boutique hotel that is a fine component of the impressive urban facelift that took place in downtown San Jose. Rooms and suites are light and airy, decorated with the blond woods and geometric prints reflective of the 1930s.

HOTEL MONTGOMERY

$$$$ 86 ROOMS ⊠*211 South 1st Street, San Jose* ☎*408-282-8800,*
866-823-0530 🖷*408-282-8850* 🖑*www.jdvhotels.com/montgomery*

Listed in the National Register of Historic Places, this renovated jewel has a prime location in downtown San Jose and an obsession with detail and service. Rooms have Burberry chairs, leather wall covers, pocket doors, and high-speed internet and iPod docking stations. The mini-bars are stocked with local gourmet chocolates and California merlot as well as the usual chips and soda. Bocce ball courts, a 24-hour business center, overnight shoeshine, and French brasserie–style cuisine in the Paragon Restaurant & Bar add to the appeal.

DOLCE HAYES MANSION

$$-$$$ 214 ROOMS ⊠*200 Edenvale Avenue, San Jose* ☎*408-226-3200*
🖷*408-362-2388* 🖑 *www.dolce-hayes-mansion-hotel.com*

The Dolce Hayes is an exquisite fusion of turn-of-the-20th-century luxury and high-tech convenience. This meticulously renovated Spanish Colonial Revival–style manor is as opulent as it must have been when it was a private home more than 100 years ago. Just a dozen miles south of the San Jose Airport, the mansion seems to exist in its own world of perfectly groomed lawns, lush gardens, and impeccable service. Rooms have a classic, traditional decor, refrigerators, coffee makers, writing desks, and free wi-fi. Amenities include a day spa, heated outdoor pool, tennis courts, two restaurants, and two lounges.

HOTEL LOS GATOS & SPA

$$$$ 72 ROOMS   ✉210 East Main Street, Los Gatos   ☎408-335-1700,
866-335-1700 📠408-335-1750 🖥www.hotellosgatos.com

In the heart of charming downtown Los Gatos, away from the hustle and bustle of San Jose, this boutique hotel exudes luxury and sophistication inside and out. Tuscan landscaping surrounds fountains and a courtyard, which leads into the lobby done in Old World burgundy, gold, and mahogany. The guest rooms and suites don't miss a beat and are perfectly in keeping with the sumptuous, indulgent decor of vibrant colors and dark woods; many feature in-room jacuzzis. An on-site spa, award-winning restaurant, swimming pool, and free wi-fi round out the amenities at this "mini-resort."

THE CYPRESS HOTEL

$$$$ 254 ROOMS   ✉10050 South De Anza Boulevard, Cupertino   ☎408-253-8900,
800-499-1408 📠408-253-3800 🖥www.thecypresshotel.com

Where do the rich and famous stay and play when not in Hollywood? The Cypress Hotel. Built at the height of the dot-com boom, this nine-story extravaganza caters to the lavish lifestyles of the region's nouveau riche. Don't let the hotel's suburban surroundings fool you: inside are plush comforters, richly decorated rooms, and all the trappings of a Mediterranean villa with splashes of animal print and deep velvet fabrics.

DINING

EULIPIA RESTAURANT AND BAR

$$$–$$$$ ITALIAN/SEAFOOD   ✉374 South 1st Street, San Jose   ☎408-280-6161
🖥www.eulipia.com, eulipia@eulipia.com

In downtown San Jose, home of business professionals and urban developers, there's this invitingly informal place. With its local crowd and light, airy, bistro-like atmosphere, the place is a prime choice when you're in the mood for casual dining. They offer an array of fresh fish, chicken, and pasta dishes. Dinner only. Closed Monday.

BELLA MIA

$$–$$$ ITALIAN   ✉58 South 1st Street, San Jose   ☎408-280-1993 📠408-280-5624
🖥www.bellamia.com, bellamia@bellamia.com

Part of a whole new infusion of sophisticated bistro-style restaurants in downtown San Jose is Bella Mia, which packs in the upwardly mobile at lunch and dinner for pizzas, pastas such as gnocchi with truffle oil, and succulent entrées such as parmesan-crusted halibut. No lunch on weekends.

EMILE'S

$$$$ CONTINENTAL   ✉545 South 2nd Street, San Jose   ☎408-289-1960
📠408-998-1245 🖥www.emilesrestaurant.com

Tucked away in a neighborhood near downtown San Jose, Emile's offers gourmet dining in intimate surroundings. The dining room—adorned with murals and mirrors—contains only a dozen tables. The cuisine is an unusual combination of French and Swiss cuisine, including dishes like lamb chops Parisienne and medallions of beef with sautéed prawns in a Bordelaise sauce. The wine list is international, creatively selected and comfortably priced. In fact, *Wine Spectator* has given this restaurant their Award of Excellence since 1994—high praise for a consistently fine wine cellar. Given the friendly staff and excellent service, there's no question why the corridor is lined with all those restaurant awards. Dinner only. Closed Sunday and Monday.

HABANA CUBA

$$-$$$ CUBAN   ✉238 Race Street, San Jose   ☎408-998-2822
  ⌨www.998cuba.com, info@998cuba.com

This airy, simply decorated eatery has been serving up a taste of old Havana for decades. Their signature dish is Zarzuela de Mariscos—seafood sautéed in light tomato sauce with peppers and onions. The slow-roasted pork marinated in citrus juices, fresh seafood, juicy steaks, and spicy salads are all favorites, and they have a wide selection of Spanish and South American wines. It's a festive, loud place, with live music on Saturday and a dog-friendly outdoor patio. Closed Monday.

AMBER INDIA

$$-$$$ INDIAN   ✉377 Santana Row, San Jose   ☎408-248-5400
  ⌨www.amber-india.com

This charming restaurant offers standards like *baingan bharta* and *palak paneer*, but their best dishes are seasonal ones that combine classic regional spices with Western favorites. Try the shiitake mushroom *kofta* and the mint salmon *tikka*. Yummy lunch buffets available.

BELLA SARATOGA

$$-$$$ CONTINENTAL   ✉14503 Big Basin Way, Saratoga   ☎408-741-5115
  ☎408-868-9774 ⌨www.bellasaratoga.com

In the heart of Saratoga village, this spot serves a menu of pastas and entrées such as eggplant parmigiana, cioppino, grilled salmon, rack of lamb, and veal marsala. This yellow Victorian house with sunny patio offers diners a laid-back atmosphere. Sunday brunch available.

STEAMER'S GRILLHOUSE

$$$$ SEAFOOD   ✉31 University Avenue, Los Gatos   ☎408-395-2722
  ☎408-354-4203 ⌨www.steamers-restaurant.com

You'll have to travel many leagues to find a restaurant as good as Steamer's. Specializing in seafood, they also offer steak and chicken. Dine on spice-crusted ahi with *mirin*-braised shiitake mushrooms while enjoying views of the Santa Cruz mountains. This gourmet spot is usually very crowded.

LINCOLN AVENUE   Much of San Jose's downtown district is continuing to be refurbished. Already upgraded, amid the stately palms and 1920s houses of the Willow Glen neighborhood is Lincoln Avenue, a street lined with craft and antiques shops, cafés, and gourmet delis.

NICHI BEI BUSSAN   ✉*140 East Jackson Street, San Jose*   ✆*408-294-8048*   ⊘*www.nbstore.com, nichibei@nbstore.com*   For gifts at reasonable prices, step over from the Japan Center to this store, brimming with Japanese items. Here is a huge collection of Asian wares ranging from standard kimonos and martial arts supplies to Japanese cultural books and rice paper wallets; they specialize in Japanese textiles. There are also a few special treasures, such as Noren wallhangings and Japanese shoes. Closed Sunday.

WESTFIELD SHOPPINGTOWN—VALLEY FAIR   ✉*2855 Stevens Creek Boulevard, San Jose*   ✆*408-248-4450*   This remains the mall to end all malls, with department store stalwarts Macy's and Nordstrom, and a dizzying array of some 200 shops, including the flagship Banana Republic.

SANTANA ROW   ✉*355 Santana Row, San Jose*   ✆*408-551-4600*   ⊘*www.santanarow.com*   Across the street from Valley Fair is this posh shopping center and its high-end stores like Burberry, Ann Taylor, and Escada.

SAN JOSE FLEA MARKET   ✉*1590 Berryessa Road, San Jose*   ✆*408-453-1110*   📠*408-437-9011*   ⊘*www.sjfm.com*   For hours of interesting shopping and some of the best bargains in the South Bay, head for the flea market. It has over 2000 vendors selling everything from bicycles to books and more than 30 food stalls for a quick order of chow mein or a plate of nachos. You could get lost here. Closed Monday and Tuesday.

Some of the area's better shops have moved to the suburbs, where they cater to Silicon Valley's affluent young executives. Saratoga and Los Gatos are particularly noteworthy.

SARATOGA AVENUE   ✉*Saratoga*   Saratoga features an upscale shopping strip in the center of town along this broad avenue. There are antique stores and galleries galore, as well as malls with an assortment of shops.

SANTA CRUZ AVENUE   ✉*From Saratoga–Los Gatos Road to Main Street, Los Gatos*   Los Gatos is quite simply a window shopper's dream. Along Santa Cruz Avenue are block on block of posh establishments. There are stores specializing in antique interiors, teddy bears, magic tricks, and travel accessories. You'll find high-fashion boutiques, gourmet food outlets, novelty shops, custom clothiers, and antique garment stores.

OLD TOWN   ✉*50 University Avenue, Los Gatos*   ⊘*www.shopsatoldtowncenter.com*   A misnomered mall, this is another prime shopping enclave. Attractively landscaped with flowering gardens, it features a string of stores in a hacienda-style building.

NIGHTLIFE

CENTER FOR THE PERFORMING ARTS ✉*255 Almaden Avenue, San Jose* ☎*408-453-7100, 888-455-7469* ✦*www.amtsj.org* The focus for San Jose high culture is this center, located in the downtown district. The **American Musical Theatre of San Jose**, which puts on wonderful productions of Broadway musicals, performs here.

SAN JOSE REPERTORY COMPANY ✉*San Jose Repertory Theatre, 101 Paseo de San Antonio, San Jose* ☎*408-367-7255* ✦*www.sjrep.com* This repertory company features full-scale productions of new and classic plays. They also have ongoing "Out and About" nights, which cater to the LGBT community.

AGENDA ✉*399 South 1st Street, San Jose* ☎*408-287-3991* ✦*www.agenda lounge.com* Head on over to Agenda in SOFA, South of First Street Area, San Jose's SOHO/SOMA/hip and trendy district. This three-level establishment is a dinner club serving California regional cuisine on the ground floor, a lounge with deejay music nightly upstairs, and a speakeasy in the basement. On the patio there's live jazz on the weekend. Restaurant closed Monday and Tuesday; speakeasy only open Friday and Saturday.

V BAR ✉*355 Santana Row, San Jose* ☎*408-551-0010* Scores of bars and restaurants make Santana Row great for late-night drinks. With its mesh metal curtains, red lights, and swank crowds, the Hotel Valencia's V bar is one of the poshest.

ROOSTER T. FEATHERS COMEDY CLUB ✉*157 El Camino Real, Sunnyvale* ☎*408-732-7781* ✦*www.roostertfeathers.com* For some laughs, hit up Rooster T., where top-bill comedians make their South Bay debuts Thursday through Sunday and there's open mic on Wednesday. Reservations recommended. Cover.

MOUNTAIN CHARLEY'S SALOON ✉*15 North Santa Cruz Avenue, Los Gatos* ☎*408-395-8880* Mountain Charley's is a down-home drinking hole with a magnificent old wooden bar that must weigh four tons. Closed Sunday. Occasional cover.

BEACHES & PARKS

SANBORN-SKYLINE COUNTY PARK

✉*Off Route 9 about three miles west of Saratoga, the park is at 16055 Sanorn Road.* ☎*408-867-9959* 📠*408-867-1859* ✦*www.parkhere.org*
🚶🐕🐎⛵ Rising from the foothills of the Santa Cruz Mountains to 3000 feet, this outstanding area is covered with Douglas fir and second-growth redwoods. It covers about 3600 acres, spreading across several ecological zones. Along the 20 miles of hiking trails, there are extraordinary views of the Santa Clara Valley; the trails also connect with a network leading all the way to the Pacific. Facilities include restrooms, picnic areas, a science mu-

seum, and a hostel. Dogs and bikes are not allowed on the trails. Day-use fee, $5.

⚠ There are 33 walk-in sites (closed in winter) at $12 per night; 15 RV sites with full hookups at $25 per night; reservations required. Reservations, 408-355-2201.

THE EAST BAY

Point your compass east from San Francisco, cross the Bay Bridge, and lo and behold, you have arrived in the East Bay. Framed by wooded hills and looking out on the Golden Gate, Oakland and Berkeley are the two key towns in this suburban enclave.

SIGHTS

OAKLAND In past decades, this city had a reputation as the Bay Area's bad neighborhood, notwithstanding the gracious hillside homes that line the city's higher elevations. Since the mid-1990s, however, urban renewal and an influx of high-tech money have done much to transform Oakland into a multi-ethnic enclave as welcoming as it is diverse.

OAKLAND CONVENTION AND VISITORS BUREAU ✉*463 11th Street, Oakland* ☎*510-839-9000* 📠*510-839-5924* ⌂*www.oaklandcvb.com, info@oaklandcvb.com* To tour Oakland, a city of 400,000 people, pick up the maps and brochures available from the visitors bureau.

CHABOT SPACE AND SCIENCE CENTER ✉*10000 Skyline Boulevard, Oakland* ☎*510-336-7300* ⌂*www.chabotspace.org, info@chabotspace.org* Secluded among the trees of the Oakland hills is this science center. The space theme is reflected in the modern-looking concrete and steel architecture of the facility. In addition to interactive science exhibits there is a dome theater where wide-format science films are shown, and a planetarium that offers a variety of shows. The three powerful telescopes are open for public viewing on weekend evenings. Closed Monday and Tuesday. Admission.

OAKLAND ZOO ✉*9777 Golf Links Road, Oakland* ☎*510-632-9525* 📠*510-635-5719* ⌂*www.oaklandzoo.org* In the hills is the Oakland Zoo, which displays a wide array of native and exotic animals, and is known for its efforts in elephant breeding. Admission.

1899 DUNSMUIR HELLMAN HISTORIC ESTATE ✉*2960 Peralta Oaks Court, Oakland* ☎*510-562-0328* 📠*510-562-8294* ⌂*www.dunsmuir.org, info@dunsmuir.org* One of the grandest mansions in the Bay Area, this 1899 estate sits in a hidden valley in the Oakland hills. The 37-room mansion, carriage house, and formal 50-acre grounds make this baronial spot a favorite retreat of mine and practically everyone who has visited. Mansion tours are offered (fee) Wednesdays from April through September. Admission. Closed Monday.

LAKE MERRITT ✉*Sailboat House: 568 Bellevue Avenue, Oakland* ☎*510-238-2196* 📠*510-238-7199* ⌂*www.oaklandnet.com/parks* The prettiest place in all of Oakland is this unassuming body of water that happens to be the

East Bay

BLACK OAK BOOKS
PAGE 212

Scholarly selection of new and used titles—and monthly author readings—in a venerable Berkeley landmark

REDWOOD REGIONAL PARK
PAGE 216

Lush green enclave of colossal redwoods and twisting trails hidden outside downtown Oakland

BAY WOLF
PAGE 208

Gourmet California cuisine such as duck a l'orange, fresh arugula salad, and sautéed halibut served in a restored Victorian

ROSE GARDEN INN
PAGE 205

Cozy 1903 Tudor-style bed and breakfast with floral prints, antique furnishings, and country flair

world's biggest saltwater tidal lake located within a city. Now that you've digested another meaningless statistic, you can work it off by joining the legions of joggers and bicyclists who continually circle the lake's three-mile perimeter. Or you can practice lawn bowling, stroll the park's botanical gardens, or rent a sailboat, rowboat, paddle boat, kayak, or canoe. Romantics can hire a gondola (510-663-6603, 866-737-7199, www.gondolaservizio.com). For complete information about Lake Merritt, stop by the **Office of Parks and Recreation** (250 Frank A. Ogawa Plaza, Suite 3330, Oakland; 510-238-7275, fax 510-238-2224; www.oaklandnet.com).

CHILDREN'S FAIRYLAND ✉699 Bellevue Avenue, Oakland ☎510-238-6876 ☎510-452-2261 ⌲www.fairyland.org Complete with rides, playsets, and the oldest operating puppet theater in the U.S. is Fairyland. The fairytale-themed park is said to have been Walt Disney's inspiration for Disneyland. Closed Monday and Tuesday in the spring and fall; closed Monday through Thursday in winter. Admission.

CAMRON-STANFORD HOUSE ✉1418 Lakeside Drive, Oakland ☎510-444-1876 ☎510-874-7803 ⌲www.cshouse.org, pelican@cshouse.org This 1876 Victorian home is decorated with art and furniture from that historic era. Open the third Wednesday of each month. Admission.

CATHEDRAL OF CHRIST THE LIGHT ✉2121 Harrison Street, Oakland ☎510-271-1932 ⌲www.christthelightcathedral.org, info@christthelightcathedral.org Across from Lake Merritt looms this modern replacement of the 1893

Cathedral of Saint Francis de Sales, which was damaged beyond repair in the 1989 Loma Prieta earthquake. The new cathedral's contemporary design features two gentle curves of glass swooping toward each other in the shape of a bishop's miter, or of two hands coming together in prayer. The structure was built to last for centuries and to have the lightest eco-footprint possible—during the day the worship space is lit only by the natural, luminous light filtered in from overhead. You can take a self-guided tour during the day, or meet at the entrance at 12:45 p.m. for a guided one Monday through Friday.

OAKLAND MUSEUM OF CALIFORNIA ✉ *1000 Oak Street, Oakland* ☎ *510-238-2200, 888-625-6873* 📠 *510-238-4901* ✎ *www.museumca.org, webmaster@museumca.org* Located just a few blocks from Lake Merritt, this is California's only museum exclusively dedicated to documenting the state's art, history, and environment. The facility first opened in 1960; it's currently undergoing a massive, $53 million renovation that began in 2008 and will continue for four years. The entire facility will be closed from late August 2009 through early 2010. When it reopens, the Art Gallery, History Gallery, and Oak Street entrance will be upgraded and the Art Gallery will have over 4000 square feet of new, high-ceiling gallery space. Check the website for details. Meanwhile, the Special Gallery in the back of the building features "The Art and History of Early California" with highlights from the museum's collections. The museum has one of the largest collections of California artifacts in the state, and is famous for its early oil paintings of Yosemite and San Francisco. Admission.

CHINATOWN _____ **h**idden

Chinatown in Oakland is a miniature neighborhood compared to San Francisco's crowded enclave, but it's still an intriguing area to stroll. Most of the markets and restaurants lie along 8th and 9th streets between Harrison and Franklin streets. Early morning is the time to visit. That's when you'll see live catfish being delivered to local restaurants and shopkeepers shelving daikon roots, Napa cabbage, and other Chinese-style vegetables.

PRESERVATION PARK ✉ *1233 Preservation Park Way, Oakland* ☎ *510-874-7580* On 9th Street between Broadway and Washington is this cul-de-sac of historic homes. The buildings are preserved as they were in another era. Most of the structures are used by nonprofit organizations today, but the scene provides an ideal picnic spot. Stop by the park office for information and self-guided history tour materials.

All around this cluster of old Victorian houses, downtown blocks are being refurbished and developed. Hotels, restaurants, shops, and offices are moving to this formerly rundown section of town and promise to turn it into one of Oakland's premier commercial districts.

JACK LONDON SQUARE ✉ *At the foot of Broadway, Oakland* This is a favorite Oakland sightseeing spot. Today it harbors retail shops, overpriced restaurants, and heavily touristed bars, but the place packs a lot of history. Located on the Alameda estuary and overlooking one of the world's busiest ports, it marks the city's early days. Richard Henry Dana

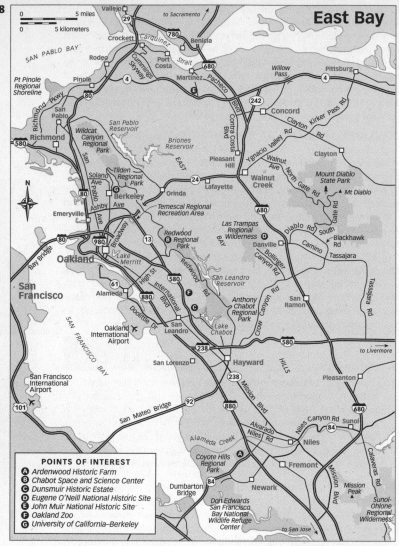

East Bay

San Pablo Bay

Vallejo

to Sacramento

Crockett

Carquinez

Benicia

Rodeo

Port Costa

Strait

Pt Pinole
Regional
Shoreline

Pinole

Martinez

Pacheco

Willow
Pass

Pittsburg

Richmond

San
Pablo

Wildcat
Canyon
Regional
Park

San Pablo
Reservoir

Briones
Reservoir

Contra Costa Blvd

Concord

Clayton

Kirker Pass Rd

Clayton

Richmond

EAST

Pleasant
Hill

Ygnacio Valley Rd

Walnut
Ave

North Gate Rd

Mount Diablo
State Park

Mt Diablo

Berkeley

Solano
Ave

Tilden
Regional
Park

Orinda

Lafayette

Walnut
Creek

Gate Rd

South

Emeryville

Ashby

Broadway

Temescal Regional
Recreation Area

Las Trampas
Regional
Wilderness

Diablo Rd

Blackhawk

Camino

Tassajara

Oakland

Lake
Merritt

Redwood
Regional
Park

BAY

Danville

Bollinger
Canyon Rd

Crow Canyon Rd

Tassajara Rd

San
Francisco

Alameda

High St

International Blvd

Redwood Rd

San Leandro
Reservoir

Anthony
Chabot
Regional
Park

San
Ramon

to Livermore

Bay Bridge

Doolittle Dr

Oakland
International
Airport

San
Leandro

Lake
Chabot

HILLS

San Francisco
International
Airport

SAN FRANCISCO BAY

San Lorenzo

Hayward

Pleasanton

San Mateo Bridge

Mission Blvd

Alvarado

Niles Canyon Rd

Sunol

Dumbarton
Bridge

Alameda Creek

Niles Rd

Niles

Calaveras Rd

Mission Peak

Coyote Hills
Regional
Park

Fremont

Newark

Mission
Peak

Sunol-
Ohlone
Regional
Wilderness

Don Edwards
San Francisco
Bay National
Wildlife Refuge
Center

to San Jose

POINTS OF INTEREST

- **A** Ardenwood Historic Farm
- **B** Chabot Space and Science Center
- **C** Dunsmuir Historic Estate
- **D** Eugene O'Neill National Historic Site
- **E** John Muir National Historic Site
- **F** Oakland Zoo
- **G** University of California–Berkeley

visited the area in 1835 while gathering material for *Two Years Before
the Mast*; by 1852 the waterfront boasted a couple of rickety wharves
from which the hamlet's oak timber was shipped to San Francisco.

JACK LONDON CABIN

✉*Jack London Square, Oakland* Jack London, who grew up in Oakland, was in turn a sailor and oyster pirate along this hard-bitten
waterfront. You can stroll the boardwalks, conjuring visions of
the fabled adventure writer, then visit this cabin. It's a classic log

cabin, little more than a dozen feet across, where London lived in 1897 during the Klondike gold rush. Back then it rested along the north fork of Henderson Creek up in the Yukon.

HEINOLD'S FIRST AND LAST CHANCE SALOON

✉56 Jack London Square, Oakland ✆510-839-6761 This is a funky woodframe saloon that Jack London haunted as a young man. They still serve spirits, so you can engage in a little historical research while toasting the writer who made Oakland infamous.

USS POTOMAC ✉540 Water Street, Oakland ✆510-627-1502 (reservations), 510-627-1215 ✈510-839-4729 ✐www.usspotomac.org, usspotomac@aol.com At the edge of Jack London Square, in the shadows of the port's loading cranes, is Franklin D. Roosevelt's 165-foot yacht, the USS *Potomac*. A step back to another era, the beautifully refurbished vessel allows you to see where FDR liked to escape to and relax during the Depression years. Open for dockside tours on Wednesday, Friday, and Sunday. From May to November, historic bay cruises are held alternating weeks on Saturday and Thursday. Admission.

ROSENBLUM CELLARS

✉2900 Main Street, Alameda ✆510-865-7007 ✈510-865-9225 ✐www.rosenblumcellars.com, rcwinerytour@rosenblumcellars.com Rosenblum uses 120 small lots of grapes, 30 different types of yeast and barrels from 55 different coopers around the world, all to create small-batch zinfandels and rhone varietals that are consistent award-winners. The Alameda tasting room is inside an old railroad building, a rustic place with a warm staff and relaxed atmosphere. The tasting menu changes frequently and includes zinfandels, syrahs, petite syrahs, white rhones, and desserts. A flight is complimentary, with a fee for an additional reserve flight. Winery tours are by appointment.

USS HORNET MUSEUM ✉Pier 3, Alameda Point, Alameda ✆510-521-8448 ✈510-521-8327 ✐www.uss-hornet.org, info@uss-hornet.org The recovery ship for the *Apollo 11* and *12* astronauts, and a significant player in World War II, the USS *Hornet* has a long history of American service. Cavernous hangar bays, claustrophobic hallways, and a wide-open flight deck create an unusual contrast of environments well worth experiencing. Closed Tuesday. Admission.

BERKELEY It's been a long time since the Free Speech Movement put "Berzerkeley" on the map, but the city remains a melting pot of people, cultures, philosophies, and food. While it's still a breeding ground for liberal views, the energy of the university keeps the city young at heart. Next to the hippies with flowers you'll meet hipsters on road bikes, and beside decades-old co-op houses you'll find the all-American family with two kids and a dog. Just remember that no matter what you might think, you'll never look out of place in the other city by the bay.

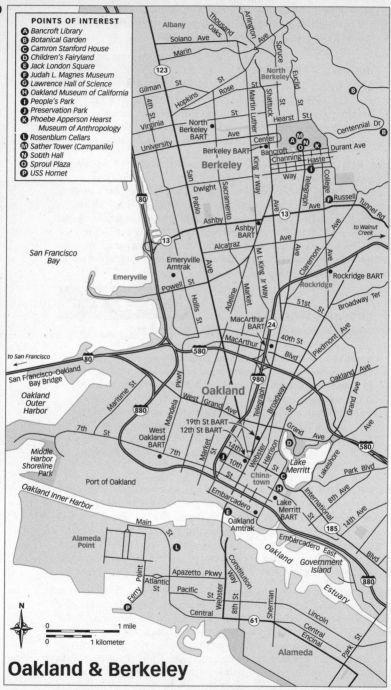

POINTS OF INTEREST
- **A** Bancroft Library
- **B** Botanical Garden
- **C** Camron Stanford House
- **D** Children's Fairyland
- **E** Jack London Square
- **F** Judah L. Magnes Museum
- **G** Lawrence Hall of Science
- **H** Oakland Museum of California
- **I** People's Park
- **J** Preservation Park
- **K** Phoebe Apperson Hearst Museum of Anthropology
- **L** Rosenblum Cellars
- **M** Sather Tower (Campanile)
- **N** South Hall
- **O** Sproul Plaza
- **P** USS Hornet

Oakland & Berkeley

TELEGRAPH AVENUE   During the tumultuous '60s and early '70s, Telegraph was the battleground for a wave of riots. Demonstrators protesting the Vietnam War spilled out from the campus to confront phalanxes of police and National Guardsmen. Protesters trashed the Bank of America's plate-glass windows so many times the bank finally replaced them with brick. Police brutality ran rampant.

The area around the UC campus, particularly on Telegraph and Durant avenues, is crowded with an array of cheap eats: pizza, salads, ramen, falafel, sushi, curry. On weekends vendor stands line Telegraph Avenue, peddling an eclectic selection of handicrafts.

The **mural** at the corner of Telegraph Avenue and Haste Street brilliantly depicts this chaotic era. Tracing the history of Berkeley in overlapping images, it portrays the Free Speech Movement, anti-war protests, flower children, and the battle for People's Park.

PEOPLE'S PARK ⊠*Bowditch Street between Haste Street and Dwight Way, Berkeley* In May 1969, a patch of Berkeley ground became a symbol for an entire generation. A vacant lot owned by the University, this park was expropriated early in 1969 by radicals and converted to a public facility. The University responded by fencing the area, demonstrators promptly tore down the enclosure, and several days of vicious rioting followed. National Guardsmen and police occupied the town, killing one bystander and blinding another. Today the park remains a public area planted with flowers and occupied by street people as well as neighborhood folks looking for a game of frisbee or basketball.

UNIVERSITY OF CALIFORNIA–BERKELEY ⊠*101 University Hall, 2200 University Avenue, Berkeley* ☎*510-642-5215* ⊘*www.berkeley.edu, visitor_info@ pa.urel.berkeley.edu* One of the nation's finest schools, Cal Berkeley is home to over 30,000 students. Founded in 1868, it covers over 1200 acres and is easy to tour with a map available at University Hall. Guided tours are given Monday through Saturday at 10 a.m. and Sunday at 1 p.m.

SPROUL PLAZA   From University Hall you can stroll across this plaza, site of countless rallies and demonstrations during the Vietnam era. Sproul Hall, the administration building, was the scene of a massive sit-in during the 1964 Free Speech Movement. Led by Mario Savio, over 700 people were dragged from the building, the largest mass arrest in California history.

SATHER TOWER   The centerpiece of the campus is this 307-foot spire modeled after St. Mark's campanile in Venice. A 61-bell carillon tolls from this lofty perch, and an elevator (admission) carries visitors to an observation perch offering extraordinary views. Just west of the campanile sits **South Hall**, the oldest and prettiest building on campus. **Bancroft Library** houses the world's finest Western Americana collection.

PHOEBE A. HEARST MUSEUM OF ANTHROPOLOGY ⊠*UC Berkeley, Kroeber Hall* ☎*510-643-7648, 510-642-3682* ☎*510-642-6271* ⊘*www.hearst museum.berkeley.edu, pahma@berkeley.edu* Among its many features, the University also offers several important museums. This one promotes the history and diversity of human cultures through research, exhibitions, and programs, with collections of American Indian artifacts and archaeological and ethnographic materials from Europe, Asia, Egypt, South America, and the Pacific Islands. Call to find out what is currently on display, as all exhibits are temporary. Closed Monday and Tuesday.

BERKELEY ART MUSEUM ✉*2626 Bancroft Way, Berkeley* ☎*510-642-0808* 🖨*510-642-4889* 🖱*www.bampfa.berkeley.edu* This museum, with its skylights and spiraling ramps, features a permanent collection of Western and Asian artworks. There are oils by old masters and contemporary artists alike, as well as a sculpture garden on the grounds. Closed Monday and Tuesday. Admission.

JUDAH L. MAGNES MUSEUM

✉*2911 Russell Street, Berkeley* ☎*510-549-6950* 🖨*510-849-3673* 🖱*www.magnes.org, info@magnes.org* Not far from the university, this museum is an important center for Jewish history and art. Occupying a stately 1908 three-story house, its collections include ceremonial pieces from around the world, works by contemporary and traditional artists, and a wealth of rare books, oral histories, and original documents. Closed Friday and Saturday.

UC BOTANICAL GARDEN ✉*200 Centennial Drive, Berkeley* ☎*510-642-3343* 🖱*www.botanicalgarden.berkeley.edu, garden@uclink4.berkeley.edu* One of the finest in the state, this garden contains over 12,000 species arranged geographically over 34 acres. There are environments planted with African, South American, Mexican–Central American, Asian, Mediterranean, New World Desert, Australian, and Californian species, as well as Western and Chinese medicinal herb gardens, a Japanese pool, and a palm garden. Closed first Tuesday of the month. Admission.

LAWRENCE HALL OF SCIENCE ✉*Centennial Drive, Berkeley* ☎*510-642-5132* 🖱*www.lawrencehallofscience.org, lhsweb@berkeley.edu* Uphill from the UC Garden is this oddly shaped structure that looks more like a Southwestern rock formation than a building. Intended for the 8-to-80 set, this marvelous place is a hands-on museum with labs where you perform experiments and play computer games. Kids can handle animals in the biology lab, and the planetarium features a series of stellar shows on weekends (daily shows during summer). Admission.

BERKELEY HILLS For a tour of the Berkeley hills, follow Centennial Drive up to Grizzly Peak Boulevard and continue north; Euclid Avenue will lead you back down to central Berkeley. All through these magnificent hills are splendid houses of brick and brown shingle; others re-create Spanish styles with red tile roofs and whitewashed facades. The views spread across the Bay to San Francisco and out beyond the Golden Gate.

TILDEN REGIONAL PARK Off Grizzly Peak Boulevard and stretching across the hills of Berkeley and Oakland, this 2000-acre park is a popular recreation spot, especially on sunny weekends. A wonderland for kids, the park offers a refurbished antique carousel with beautiful carved horses, a miniature steam train, golf course, and a small farm. See "Beaches & Parks" below for more information.

ARDENWOOD HISTORIC FARM ⊠ *34600 Ardenwood Boulevard, Fremont* ☏ *510-796-0663* 🖷 *510-796-0231* ✉ *ardenwood@ebparks.org* To experience some of the East Bay's lesser-known locales, head about 30 miles south on Route 880 to this 205-acre historic farm. It's a charming farmstead preserving the region's agrarian tradition. Tour the Queen Anne home, watch a blacksmith at work, enjoy craft and cooking displays, visit the cornfield, and see living history demonstrations. Closed Monday. Admission.

**DON EDWARDS
SAN FRANCISCO BAY
NATIONAL WILDLIFE REFUGE**

⊠ *Marshland Road, near the junction of Route 84 and Thornton Avenue, Fremont* ☏ *510-792-0222* 🖷 *510-792-5828* ✉ *desfbay.fws.gov* Located down the freeway from the Ardenwood Historic Farm is this wildlife refuge. Within this broad, flat expanse of marsh and pickleweed you'll find 30 miles of trails and 250 bird species. A visitors center includes exhibits on the region and affords a wonderful vista of the bay. The center also offers various nature programs. Center closed Monday.

NILES Heading east on Route 84 will bring you to the town of Niles. Actually part of Fremont, this falsefront community played an important role in the history of Hollywood (it has its own "Hollywood" sign constructed on a neighboring hillside—only this one proclaims "Niles"). More than 450 one-reel films were shot here after Essanay Studios made it their West Coast headquarters around 1910. Charlie Chaplin's classic *The Tramp* was filmed in town. You can still see a few of the silent stars' cottages on 2nd Street between F and G streets.

**ESSANAY STUDIOS
SILENT FILM MUSEUM**

⊠ *37395 Niles Boulevard, Fremont* ☏ *510-494-1411* ✉ *www.nilesfilmmuseum. org* The old Essanay Studio has been transformed into this museum, which chronicles the region's long-gone ties to the industry. Check out hand-crank movie cameras, film projectors, original movie posters, and artifacts from the studio's heyday. Every Saturday night a silent film classic is screened at the museum's theater and accompanied by live piano music—just like in the days before "talkies." Open Saturday and Sunday afternoons.

NILES MAIN STREET ASSOCIATION ☏ *510-742-9868* ✉ *www.niles. org* Niles remains a great neighborhood with a renovated Main Street filled with countless antique stores and craft shops, restored storefront facades, and wide sidewalks. Many of the buildings retain their original Old West flavor, recalling the area's agricultural roots. The Main Street Association offers a self-guided walking tour of the area and highlights historic buildings along the main drag and quaint side streets.

NILES RAILWAY DEPOT MUSEUM ✉36997 *Mission Boulevard, Fremont* 📞*510-797-4449* Railway aficionados will love this railway museum. Set along the railroad tracks that bisect the town, this restored depot sports a cheery coat of yellow paint and houses model railway sets, historic photos of Niles, and a library with more than 500 books on railway history. They also provide tours of an old caboose situated along the town's Main Street. The museum is currently undergoing major renovations and will be closed through 2009.

If you head east into Niles Canyon on Route 84, you'll pass the rolling hills where Bronco Billy filmed his fabled Westerns.

NILES CANYON RAILWAY ✉*Along Route 84, Sunol* 📞*925-862-9063* 🖰*www.ncry.org, pla_ncry@ncry.com* While you're in the canyon, you can board a vintage train here. The trip, which runs on the first and third Sunday of the month October through March (night trains in November and December), and every Sunday April to October, lasts about an hour. Admission.

EUGENE O'NEILL NATIONAL HISTORIC SITE

📞*925-838-0249* 📠*925-838-9471* 🖰*www.nps.gov/euon* Over the East Bay hills in Danville rests this historic site. In 1937, America's only Nobel Prize–winning playwright Eugene O'Neill built and resided in a beautiful home overlooking Mt. Diablo while writing some of his greatest dramas—*The Iceman Cometh*, *A Moon for the Misbegotten*, and *Long Day's Journey into Night*. Decorated in the fashion of the era, Tao House and its grounds are open to the public. Access is by reservation only; arrangements can be made through the National Park Service. Tours are run twice a day, Wednesday through Sunday, at no charge. Closed Monday and Tuesday.

BLACKHAWK MUSEUM ✉*3700 Blackhawk Plaza Circle, Danville* 📞*925-736-2277* 📠*925-736-4818* 🖰*www.blackhawkmuseum.org, museum@blackhawkmuseum. org* Pay homage to Henry Ford's invention at this museum, which has a collection of classic cars dating back to the 1890s—among them Clark Gable's 1935 Duesenberg convertible. The museum also houses traveling exhibits from the Smithsonian. Closed Monday and Tuesday. Admission.

LODGING

OAKLAND MARRIOTT CITY CENTER

$$$–$$$$ 484 ROOMS   ✉*1001 Broadway, Oakland* 📞*510-451-4000* 📠*510-835-3466* 🖰*www.marriott.com*

Just a short jaunt from BART, the Oakland Marriott sits at the heart of downtown. It's standard large-chain fare with 484 rooms stacked into 21 stories, but you can expect the top-quality services and amenities that come with a big hotel. The location is across the street from Chinatown and perfect for easy access to the Bay Area's countless treasures.

THE WASHINGTON INN

$$$, 47 ROOMS ✉495 10th Street, Oakland ☎510-452-1776
📠510-452-4436 ✐www.thewashingtoninn.com

For a smaller, more personable hotel, try The Washington. This 1915 brick-facade building boasts warm hues, sleek lines, and luxury rooms and suites. It's across the street from the Oakland Convention Center and minutes away from Jack London Square and Chinatown.

ROSE GARDEN INN

$$$–$$$$ 40 ROOMS ✉2740 Telegraph Avenue, Berkeley
☎510-549-2145, 800-992-9005 📠510-549-1085
✐www.rosegardeninn.com, info@rosegardeninn.com

One of the coziest spots in the Bay Area is this 1903 Tudor-style house converted to an inn. The public areas in this homey establishment include several ornately designed sitting rooms as well as a spacious yard and deck. There are 11 guest rooms in the main house plus 29 more in four adjacent buildings. Many are creatively appointed with hand-carved headboards, antique wardrobes, quilts, and plump armchairs, but the primary antiques at the inn are the houses themselves. The price includes a full buffet breakfast. The Rose Garden Inn provides the best of both worlds: a country inn in the city.

HOTEL DURANT

$$$–$$$$ 143 ROOMS ✉2600 Durant Avenue, Berkeley ☎510-845-8981,
800-238-7268 📠510-486-8336 ✐www.hoteldurant.com,
reservations@hoteldurant.com

When looking for a convenient location, it's hard to top the Durant. This facility sits just one block from the Berkeley campus and includes a restaurant and pub. The rooms are cozy, with dark hardwood furniture and plush linens, and feature all the creature comforts, including flat-screen TVs and complimentary wi-fi. Plus, the hotel is green certified and pet-friendly.

BERKELEY CITY CLUB

$$$$ 30 ROOMS ✉2315 Durant Avenue, Berkeley ☎510-848-7800
📠510-848-5900 ✐www.berkeleycityclub.com

Set amidst a treelined section of Durant Avenue is this Gothic-style building. Built in 1929, this historic landmark functions as both a private social club and a bed and breakfast. The rooms in this Julia Morgan–designed building feature private baths and are small and spartan (no TVs), recalling women's residences of the 1920s. Among the amenities here are a grand indoor swimming pool, a fitness center, a hair salon, and continental breakfast. It's located just a block from the UC Berkeley campus. Tours of the club are held the fourth Sunday of every month except December.

BANCROFT HOTEL

$$$ 22 ROOMS ✉2680 Bancroft Way, Berkeley 📞510-549-1000, 800-549-1002 📠510-549-1070 🖱www.bancrofthotel.com, reservations@bancrofthotel.com

Right across the street from the Berkeley campus is this 22-room boutique hotel listed on the National Register of Historic Places. A prime example of the Arts and Crafts architecture that once flourished in Berkeley, the 1928 building was designed by Walter T. Steilberg, one of Julia Morgan's associates, as a private club-house for the College Women's Club. Many rooms feature balconies and the rooftop has panoramic views of San Francisco Bay. Continental breakfast included.

DINING

Oakland's Chinatown has no shortage of eateries to fit all budgets. Most, of course, are Chinese, but you'll also find Vietnamese gems. Here, there's a restaurant that can compete dish for dish with many of San Francisco's popular Chinese restaurants.

HUNAN RESTAURANT

$$ CHINESE ✉396 11th Street, Oakland 📞510-444-1155 📠510-444-0219

Hunan serves Mandarin-style cuisine with special flair. Among the dozens of dishes are smoked tea duck, Szechuan prawns, Peking spare-ribs, squid, braised fish, and ginger crab. This family restaurant is highly recommended.

SILVER DRAGON

$$ CHINESE ✉835 Webster Street, Oakland 📞510-893-3748 📠510-893-4918 🖱www.silverdragonrestaurant.com

Located in the heart of Chinatown, this Cantonese restaurant started out as a small café in 1956. Today it's a cavernous, three-story establishment that has become the "occasion" place of choice for Chinese weddings, special dinners, birthdays, and banquets. Customer favorites include Peking duck and roasted chicken stuffed with sweet rice, shark fin soup, glazed honey walnut prawns, fried stuffed crab claws, and abalone braised with sea cucumber.

IL PESCATORE

$$–$$$ ITALIAN/SEAFOOD ✉31 Webster Street, Oakland 📞510-465-2188 📠510-465-0238 🖱www.ilpescatoreristorante.com

Jack London Square, a high-rent area situated along the Oakland waterfront, specializes in expensive restaurants. Il Pescatore, however, is a reasonably priced place with a view of the marina and estuary. The decorative motif is nautical and the menu follows the theme, specializing in seafood entrées like scampi, calamari, and salmon. There are also numerous Italian-style dishes, including veal scallopine, chicken cacciatore, and eggplant parmigiana. Saturday and Sunday champagne brunch.

YOSHI'S AT JACK LONDON SQUARE

$$–$$$ JAPANESE/SUSHI   ✉510 Embarcadero West, Oakland   ☎510-238-9200
✆510-238-4551   🖱www.yoshis.com

Exquisite Japanese meals, ranging from teriyaki and tempura to yakitori and sushi, are served at Yoshi's. There's smoked Kobe *tataki*, *maki* sushi, and carpaccio. Yoshi's also presents hot jazz sounds in the adjoining club. No lunch Saturday through Monday.

LE CHEVAL

$–$$ VIETNAMESE   ✉1007 Clay Street, Oakland   ☎510-763-8495
🖱www.lecheval.com

Off the main drag lies this large bright dining room with a delicious Vietnamese menu. There isn't a lot for decoration, aside from the giant bronze horse in the foyer (hence its name), but it's a convivial place with well-prepared dishes. Some good choices: the claypot rice combination with seafood, beef, and vegetables and the lemongrass calamari topped with peanuts. It's a popular place, so reservations are recommended. No lunch on Sunday.

PACIFIC COAST BREWING COMPANY

$–$$ AMERICAN   ✉906 Washington Street, Oakland   ☎510-836-2739
✆510-836-1987   🖱www.pacificcoastbrewing.com, info@pacificcoastbrewing.com

Old-town Oakland with its red-brick facades has catered to the new trend in social life, the microbrewery. Down on Washington Street, a block away from the Convention Center, this brewing company boasts award-winning microbrew and an elbow-polished hardwood bar where executives battle for the bartender's attention after 5. At lunch, expect hearty blue-collar fare like bangers and mash or meat pies. The service is notoriously slow, but beer gourmets don't mind.

QUINN'S LIGHTHOUSE

hidden

$$ SEAFOOD   ✉1951 Embarcadero, Oakland   ☎510-536-2050
✆510-532-4156   🖱www.quinnslighthouse.com, quinnslighthouse@aol.com

Quinn's claims to be Oakland's best-kept secret, and it may very well be. Hidden away across from Coast Guard Island along the Oakland/Alameda estuary, the building where Quinn's is located dates to 1903, once served as the Oakland harbor entrance lighthouse, and was moved to its present site in 1965. The main dining room is decorated in a nautical motif and has views of the marina below and downtown Oakland in the distance. An upstairs deck proves a wonderful place to dine on a sunny day. Specialties of the house include salmon Wellington, blackened prawns, and seafood pastas.

The Birthplace of California Cuisine

During the past several decades, Berkeley has shed its image as a center of revolt and assumed the role of gourmet capital. The shift in sensibility first occurred during those dolorous days in the '70s when Berkeley's affluent graduates traded barriers for *boulliabaisse*. Since then, culinary consciousness has become a cause célèbre here. It means repudiating the fast food–frozen dinner mentality and taking up the banner of fresh fruits and vegetables. Berkeley champions the Slow Food Movement (started in Italy in 1986 when a McDonald's set up shop in Rome), emphasizing a strong connection between the plate and the planet. The Bay Area's passion for this movement culminated in 2008, when San Francisco hosted the first U.S.-based Slow Food Nation festival. Vendors and representatives from across the country and around the world gathered to celebrate California cuisine and the value of knowing where your food comes from, and eating locally and sustainably.

Several exemplary restaurants were born of these movements. Developing a cooking style termed "California cuisine," they serve select dishes to small groups. All ingredients, from spice to shellfish, are fresh; the focus is on locally produced foods in season. Menus change daily and sometimes include dishes invented that afternoon to be tested on an adventurous clientele.

Alice Waters, owner of the world-renowned Chez Panisse in Berkeley and international vice president of Slow Food, is credited with "inventing" this now-popular cooking style that's been widely adapted in other regions of the country. She has long been the guiding light in Berkeley kitchens, and her reputation is so imposing that the Dalai Lama stopped in for dinner during a Bay Area visit, as did former president Bill Clinton. You can experience California cuisine first-hand at Chez Panisse or any number of other eateries across the Bay Area.

BAY WOLF RESTAURANT

$$$ CALIFORNIA CUISINE ✉*3853 Piedmont Avenue, Oakland*
✆*510-655-6004* ✎*510-652-0429* ◁*www.baywolf.com*

At Bay Wolf, three partners founded a gourmet restaurant in a woodframe house. Its two dining rooms are decorated with modern art pieces, and the heated outdoor terrace is as cozy as the indoors. Run by a friendly staff, the place has the feel of home. Lunch menus change by the week and dinner menus vary by the month. If they're not serving sautéed duck breast or swordfish with braised leeks, the chefs may be preparing roast leg of lamb, fresh pasta with scallops and mushrooms, or pork loin with artichoke purée. In any case, the food is outstanding, the service impeccable, and the ambience soft as candlelight. No lunch on weekends.

ZACHARY'S CHICAGO PIZZA

$$ PIZZA ✉*Two locations: 5801 College Avenue, Oakland* ✆*510-655-6385*
✉*1853 Solano Avenue, Berkeley* ✆*510-525-5950* ◁*www.zacharys.com*

College Avenue, running directly from Broadway in Oakland to the Berkeley campus, boasts a bevy of cafés, bistros, trattorias, diners, and restaurants in all price ranges. One is Zachary's, blessing the East Bay with Chicago-style stuffed pies. Think: dough, then cheese and toppings, then more dough, then sauce; spinach and mushroom is a favorite. The result is so good that both locations of the restaurant are constantly packed, however, as locals know, the wait is well worth it.

PIZZAIOLO

$$ ITALIAN   ✉5008 Telegraph Avenue, Oakland   ✆510-652-4888   📠510-428-2122
🖳www.pizzaiolooakland.com

A proponent of the Slow Food movement, this elegant little place in Oakland's Temescal district features locally grown, organic, and seasonal meats and produce cooked by a Chez Panisse–trained chef. It's know for the delectable pizza. Toppings range from traditional Margherita with fresh mozzarella, tomatoes, and basil, to pizza with wild nettles and ricotta salata or butternut squash and gorgonzola. Freshly made pasta and a few meat selections make a more substantial meal, and the soups are outstanding. Come early and have a cocktail while you wait on one of their sidewalk benches or call after 3 p.m. to make a dinner reservation.

SHEN HUA

$$ CHINESE   ✉2914 College Avenue, Berkeley   ✆510-883-1777

In the Elmwood district of College Avenue lies this local gem. A favorite among East Bay folk, this is, simply put, a fantastic Chinese restaurant. The dining room is light and airy with full-length sliding glass windows, high ceilings and an open kitchen, while the food is exquisite. Along with a host of delightful meat, poultry, and seafood dishes, you'll also find veggie selections like braised green beans and Szechuan eggplant. Reservations recommended.

The area around the UC campus, particularly on **Telegraph and Durant avenues**, is crowded with an array of cheap eats: pizza, salads, ramen, falafel, sushi, curry, all at budget prices.

CHEZ PANISSE

$$$$ CALIFORNIA CUISINE   ✉1517 Shattuck Avenue, Berkeley
✆510-548-5525 (dinner reservations), 510-548-5049 (café information)
📠510-548-0140 🖳www.chezpanisse.com

The vanguard of California cuisine is Chez Panisse. Set in a modest woodframe building, it hardly looks the part of a world-famous restaurant. Dinner is served downstairs in this two-tiered establishment and features a prix-fixe menu nightly. It's a multi-course extravaganza from appetizer to sorbet. A typical evening might include warm cabbage and spinach salad with goose confit and roasted apples, local fish and shellfish soup with garlic mayonnaise, grilled rack of lamb with green olive sauce, fried artichokes and celery root purée and passionfruit and kiwi sherbet Pavlova—all for an ultra-deluxe price. Reservations are *de rigueur* and may be made one month to the day in advance. Upstairs, however, the café offers more moderately priced meals in a lively setting, and reservations are also accepted up to a month in advance, but need only be made a week or two ahead of time. Open for lunch and dinner, it may serve calzone with goat cheese, oysters on the half shell, and sorrel soup, plus daily specials such as fettuccine with sweetbreads and grilled steak with rosemary butter. If time and budget permit, indulge yourself: This is where it all began. Closed Sunday.

CÉSAR

$$–$$$ TAPAS/SPANISH ✉ *1515 Shattuck Avenue, Berkeley* ☎ *510-883-0222*
🖱 *www.barcesar.com*

Located in Berkeley's gourmet ghetto is this tapas bar next door to Chez Panisse. Opening at noon, the lively atmosphere invites you to have a drink and light fare, or sample the wide variety of tapas and stay until the midnight closing time. A communal table is available in the center of the room, with private tables along the wall. The eclectic menu includes items such as Spanish cheeses, salt cod, and potato *cazuela*, and organic strawberries with rose for dessert. A fine selection of wines, cocktails, and beers complements the Spanish-inspired fare.

CAFÉ FANNY

$ CALIFORNIA CUISINE ✉ *1603 San Pablo Avenue, Berkeley*
☎ *510-524-5447* 🖱 *www.cafefanny.com*

Alice Waters of Chez Panisse fame created this spinoff restaurant to accommodate those who wished to eat well without the hassle and expense of a "serious" restaurant. The bright little café is illuminated by a huge skylight and windows, and floored in handmade tiles. Most of the produce is purchased from local ranches that promote ecologically sound farming practices. The menu is simple and delicious: light sandwiches and gourmet salads. Breakfast favorites include buckwheat crêpes with fruit and organic yogurt. No dinner.

LALIME'S

$$$$ MEDITERRANEAN ✉ *1329 Gilman Street, Berkeley* ☎ *510-527-9838*
📠 *510-559-7025* 🖱 *www.lalimes.com, ouresya@yahoo.com*

When I first dined here, I felt as though I had stumbled into a secret retreat. Set in the midst of a pretty residential neighborhood, the restaurant looks like an ordinary home from the outside. But I've never been in a private residence that serves roast California yellowtail with a succotash of sweet corn and cranberry beans. The service is excellent, as is the Mediterranean-inspired food, and the intimate setting is ideal for a quiet evening out. Dinner only.

CAFÉ ROUGE

$$$$ CONTINENTAL ✉ *1782 4th Street, Berkeley* ☎ *510-525-1440* 📠 *510-525-2776*
🖱 *www.caferouge.net*

The gentrification of 4th Street in West Berkeley has produced a host of trendy restaurants. A popular eatery is this split-level café, which serves a mix of southern French and northern Italian cuisine in a warm, modern setting. A cherrywood zinc bar rounding the west wall adds a European flair. The menu changes weekly but may include a charcuterie plate and raw oysters for starters, and entrées such as spit-roasted chicken, steak *frite*, and seafood risotto. Sunday brunch. No dinner on Monday.

RIVOLI RESTAURANT

$$$ CALIFORNIA CUISINE   ✉1539 Solano Avenue, Berkeley
☎510-526-2542   📠510-525-8412   🖰www.rivolirestaurant.com,
roscoe@rivolirestaurant.com

Rivoli's owners set out to establish a neighborhood eatery featuring California cuisine. They've maintained the mom-and-pop feel despite the popularity of the place. Service is flawless and unobtrusive, and the restaurant is elegantly lit. Tables, set close together, line a large dining room that looks out plate-glass windows onto a beautifully landscaped garden. The ever-changing menu consists of dishes made from local organic produce. One delicacy that is a constant on the menu, luckily, is the portobello mushroom fritters with lemon aïoli, parmesan, arugula, and caper vinaigrette. Dinner only.

CAFFE VENEZIA

$$–$$$ ITALIAN   ✉1799 University Avenue, Berkeley   ☎510-849-4681
📠510-849-3104   🖰www.caffevenezia.com, caffevenezia@sbcglobal.net

Berkeley may be known for California cuisine, but one of the great finds here is an Italian restaurant called Caffe Venezia. The walls in this eatery are decorated with murals portraying an Italian street scene. Adding three-dimensional reality is a clothesline hung with laundry stretched from one wall to another and a fountain. There are pasta dishes like cannelloni *al forno*, spaghetti puttanesca, and ravioli, plus fresh fish, chicken, and milk-braised pork. Rate this restaurant with a night sky worth of stars! No lunch on weekends and Monday.

MEAL TICKET

$ AMERICAN   ✉1235 San Pablo Avenue, Berkeley   ☎510-526-6325

Definitely off the beaten path is this small restaurant hidden in the flatlands. Its red facade and yellow overlay provide a bright contrast to the dingy grays of the surrounding warehouses and garage shops. Inside are mouth-watering breakfast and lunch plates. Locals swear by the cornmeal blueberry pancakes and grilled salmon with eggs your way. No dinner. Closed Monday and Tuesday.

THE NILE COFFEE SHOP

$ AMERICAN   ✉121 I Street, Fremont   ☎510-791-6049

This coffee shop offers yummy breakfasts and salad and sandwich lunches, along with occasional theme dinners. It's a tiny place with folding chairs and Egyptian-inspired wall murals. You'll find locals sitting around and discussing town gossip every morning.

JACK LONDON SQUARE ✉*Oakland* Situated on the Oakland waterfront, Jack London Square offers many opportunities for shopping. In addition to several national chains, there are interesting boutiques, specialty shops, and gift emporiums. Every Sunday, locals flock to the **farmers' market** for fresh fruit, produce, bread, and flowers. If you favor a literary respite, **Barnes & Noble** (510-272-0120), one of the largest bookstores in northern California, will occupy you for hours.

COLLEGE AVENUE This street is one of the East Bay's major shopping sections. From its starting point at Broadway in north Oakland all the way to Russell Street in Berkeley, this thoroughfare hosts every type of store imaginable, from antique shops to clothing boutiques to children's secondhand stores. Some of the most notable are in Berkeley's Elmwood District.

GLOBAL EXCHANGE ✉*2840 College Avenue, Berkeley* ☎*510-548-0370* ✐*www.globalexchange.com* For earth-friendly items, stop at this shop, which proffers handmade Fair Trade gifts from around the world.

JEREMY'S ✉*2967 College Avenue, Berkeley* ☎*510-849-0701* This boutique carries salvaged designer-label clothing and shoes for men and women.

ROOMPAM SAREES ✉*1044 University Avenue, Berkeley* ☎*510-848-2642* ✐*www.roompam.com* An outpost of a famous Indian fashion house, Roompam has rooms and rooms of traditional men's and women's clothing. Women will love the *salwar kameez* (tunic and pants) in rich cottons for everyday and silks for dressier events. Prices are reasonable and the staff are very friendly and accommodating.

SHATTUCK AVENUE Shattuck, a broad boulevard complete with landscaped median, is Berkeley's central district. The street divides into two entirely different sections, with University Avenue as a line of demarcation. To the south, from Durant Avenue to University, lies the city's old downtown section.

The section along Shattuck Avenue north of University Avenue is far more interesting than the downtown area. This area, nicknamed "the gourmet ghetto" for its specialty food shops, is home to many upscale retailers and restaurants.

THE CHEESE BOARD ✉*1504 Shattuck Avenue, Berkeley* ☎*510-549-3183, 510-549-3055 (pizzeria)* ☎*510-549-9514* ✐*www.cheeseboardcollective.com* Run by an eclectic collective, this North Berkeley shop stocks a dizzying inventory of cheeses. With its baguettes, pizzas, and other breads, it's a perfect place to stock up for a picnic or pop down a few storefronts to their pizzeria that offers pizza Tuesday through Saturday. Closed Sunday.

BLACK OAK BOOKS

✉*1491 Shattuck Avenue, Berkeley* ☎*510-486-0698* ✐*www.blackoakbooks. com, blackoak@infoconex.com* Don't miss this exceptionally fine bookstore and important literary gathering place that hosts numerous author readings every month. It has been a haven for local scholars and casual bookworms alike since the '80s.

TELEGRAPH AVENUE   A shopping district of another sort lies along Berkeley's Telegraph Avenue between Dwight Way and Bancroft Way. While this campus area is being steadily remodeled and made to conform to the chic standards of the new century, it still retains the native funk of Berkeley circa 1968. Street vendors line either side of the thoroughfare, selling clothes, metalwork, leather goods, and jewelry. Most of these artisans produce their own handiworks: There are painters, potters, weavers, and woodworkers here, dividing their days between studios at home and this open-air marketplace.

MOE'S BOOKS   ✉*2476 Telegraph Avenue, Berkeley* ✆*510-849-2087* ✎*www. moesbooks.com, moe@moesbooks.com* Moe's, founded by a cigar-chomping bibliophile named Moe Moskowitz, contains four floors of new and used titles. It's a prime place to pick up secondhand books at reduced prices.

KERMIT LYNCH
WINE MERCHANTS
✉*1605 San Pablo Avenue, Berkeley* ✆*510-524-1524* ✐*510-528-7026* ✎*www.kermitlynch.com, info@kermitlynch.com* In a tiny off-shoot of Berkeley's Gourmet Ghetto, beside Café Fanny, Kermit Lynch's store specializes in French imports—a departure from the usual California wines you'll find in this area. Although the bare-bones decor (narrow aisles of wine cases, no wall hangings, no music) might be intimidating to newcomers, the staff here is knowledgeable and ready to help you whether you know anything about wine or not. Closed Sunday and Monday.

SMITH AND HAWKEN   ✉*1330 10th Street* ✆*510-527-1076* ✎*www.smith andhawken.com* West Berkeley has become a center for design stores, art galleries, and discount outlets. Among the renovated warehouses and stores is this trendy gardening supply store that also sells sportswear, books, and vases.

EARTHWORKS CERAMICS CO-OP   ✉*2547 8th Street #33* ✆*510-841-9810* At Earthworks you'll find several potters creating functional dinnerware and decorative work. Fluctuating hours, call ahead.

GARY HOLT   ✉*1449 5th Street* ✆*510-527-4183, 888-567-5367* ✎*www.garyholt. com* Many potters in the area offer open studios. One of the best is Gary Holt, whose award-winning work has an Asian influence. Call ahead.

FOURTH STREET   A refurbished warehouse district in West Berkeley, this has become ground zero for savvy shoppers. Outlet stores and stylish gift shops abound along this tree-lined street.

CASTLE IN THE AIR   ✉*1805 4th Street, Berkeley* ✆*510-204-9801* This is an upscale shop full of whimsical art pieces and quality craft supplies. Whether or not you're in the market for fantasy-themed gifts, this unique store is worth a walkthrough for its imaginative displays.

THE GARDENER ✉*1836 4th Street, Berkeley* ☎*510-548-4545* ⌕*www.the gardener.com* Stop here for rustic home furnishings and upscale gardening supplies.

NILES Niles is practically synonymous with antiques. The downtown is chock-full of great shops proffering turquoise jewelry, wooden furniture, and a mind-spinning array of bric-a-brac. Plenty of these shops also double as craft houses featuring work from local artisans. Good bets include **Empty Nest** (37541 Niles Boulevard, Fremont; 510-792-6292), **Remember When** (37557 Niles Boulevard, Fremont; 510-795-1919), and **My Friends & I** (37521 Niles Boulevard, Fremont; 510-792-0118).

NIGHTLIFE

Across the Bay from San Francisco, the evening activities revolve around places of high culture and those specializing in high spirits.

OAKLAND BALLET ✉*The Ron Guidi Foundation, 2626 Harrison Street, Oakland* From September to December, the Oakland Ballet, a nationally acclaimed company, presents dazzling premieres and performs classic ballets at theaters throughout the Bay Area.

PARAMOUNT THEATRE ✉*2025 Broadway, Oakland* ☎*510-893-2300* ⌕*www. paramounttheatre.com, tours@paramounttheatre.com* If you have the chance, don't miss the Oakland Ballet's annual *Nutcracker* performance here. This fully restored Art Deco building is a showcase of flourishes and decorative details. The sumptuous theater alone is worth the price of admission. In addition to performing arts events and concerts, the Paramount hosts semimonthly tours.

HEINOLD'S FIRST AND LAST CHANCE SALOON ✉*56 Jack London Square, Oakland* ☎*510-839-6761* As for spirits, there's Heinold's, a roisterous little bar once frequented by Jack London. It's been around since the late 1800s and upon entering—watch for the very slanted floor—you feel like you've gone through a time warp.

YOSHI'S AT JACK LONDON SQUARE ✉*510 Embarcadero West, Oakland* ☎*510-238-9200* ⌕*www.yoshis.com* Yoshi's, one of the nation's premier jazz clubs, brings in locally and nationally known acts, such as Branford Marsalis, Harry Connick Jr., and Pete Escovedo. Cover.

CLUB ANTON ✉*428 3rd Street, Oakland* ☎*510-463-0165* ⌕*www.clubanton. com* Oakland's hot Latin club is the place to dress up and bust out the salsa moves. Live entertainment and top deejays keep the temperature turned up on the weekends, with every genre of Latin music, as well as hip-hop and reggae. Mid-week is a bit milder, but you can still expect a real workout on the dancefloor. Cover.

ELI'S MILE HIGH CLUB ✉*3629 Martin Luther King Jr. Way, Oakland* A long-time blues bar, Eli's changed ownership in 2008 and reopened as a venue for twentysomething rock 'n' rollers. It managed to maintain its vintage Oakland vibe and is a perfect spot for late-night drinks, burgers, and live music with an edge. Closed Sunday through Tuesday. Cover.

BENCH & BAR

 hidden

✉2111 Franklin Street, Oakland ☎510-444-2266 ✑www.bench-and-bar.com Near the Oakland Museum, this place is popular with gay men and women (particularly men). Billing itself as a "Latin nightclub," get your groove on to Latin dance music almost every night of the week. "Kinky karaoke" is Tuesday.

PARKWAY THEATER ✉1834 Park Boulevard, Oakland ☎510-814-2400

☎510-848-1940 ✑www.speakeasytheaters.com, will@speakeasytheaters.com In its latest incarnation, the historic Parkway, which first opened in 1926, is a combination movie theater, pub, and pizzeria screening not-so-recent releases and experimental and foreign films at about half the price of a movie ticket anywhere else. Settle into a couch, cocktail lounge chair, or theater seat, put your pizza and beer on the table beside you, wait for the lights to dim, and enjoy the show.

CALIFORNIA SHAKESPEARE THEATER ✉Gateway Boulevard, Orinda

☎510-548-3422, 510-548-9666 (box office) ✑www.calshakes.org This theater is another highly visible example of the East Bay's rich dramatic tradition. Once devoted exclusively to Shakespeare, the Festival's recent change in management led to the inclusion of at least one non-Shakespeare production a season. Cal Shakes is perfect for a picnic dinner under the Orinda skies, accompanied by a bottle of wine and the Bard. Season runs May through October.

BERKELEY REPERTORY THEATRE ✉2025 Addison Street, Berkeley

☎510-647-2900, 510-647-2949 (box office) ✑www.berkeleyrep.org The brick-fa-caded Berkeley Rep offers an intimate alternative to the more commercial theaters in San Francisco, despite the 600-seat proscenium theater added to the original 400-seat theater. This Tony award–winning group has a growing reputation in the performing-arts community, and is known for undertaking ambitious projects.

CAL PERFORMANCES ✉UC Berkeley, 101 Zellerbach Hall ☎510-642-9988

✑www.calperfs.berkeley.edu Check this venue for a current listing of cultural events. They regularly present jazz concerts, chamber music, ballet and modern dance companies, ethnic performances, and countless other programs.

PACIFIC FILM ARCHIVE ✉Bancroft at Bowditch, Hearst Annex Field Building,

Berkeley ☎510-642-1412 ✑www.bampfa.berkeley.edu Connected with the University, this is an extraordinary showcase for early and artistic movies. Closed Monday.

SKATES ON THE BAY ✉100 Seawall Drive, Berkeley ☎510-549-1900

✑www.skatesonthebay.com On the Berkeley waterfront, this spot provides otherworldly views of the Bay and San Francisco skyline. Just pull up to a plate-glass window, order a cocktail, and watch nature perform.

BECKETT'S ✉*2271 Shattuck Avenue, Berkeley* ✆*510-647-1790* ✐*www.becketts irishpub.com* Being a college town, you'd expect Berkeley to have a healthy stash of bars. But here, espresso appears to be the addiction of choice, with cafés far outnumbering pubs. Still, there are a few good watering holes if you look for them. Beckett's, an authentic Irish pub, has a cozy and intimate atmosphere with stone walls, lots of woodwork, and a roaring fire. Occasional live entertainment.

JUPITER ✉*2181 Shattuck Avenue, Berkeley* ✆*510-843-7625* ✐*www.jupiter beer.com* You can sample over 30 of the best local brews here. The setting is an early-20th-century building that originally housed a lumber merchant, with decor that the owner calls "beer gothic." This popular hangout also serves pizzas, focaccia sandwiches, and salads, and there's summer jazz several evenings a week in the beer garden out back. Other musical acts also make their appearance during warmer months.

TRIPLE ROCK BREWERY AND ALE HOUSE ✉*1920 Shattuck Avenue, Berkeley* ✆*510-843-2739* ✐*www.triplerock.com* Another often-crowded brewery is Triple Rock Brewery. Choose from a pale ale, an amber, or a porter and relax inside at one of the large wooden tables or outside on the rooftop sundeck.

FREIGHT AND SALVAGE COFFEE HOUSE ✉*2020 Addison Street, Berkeley* ✆*510-548-1761* ✐*www.freightandsalvage.org* The Freight and Salvage is a folk and acoustic music venue with national renown. Performers have included bluegrass legend Doc Watson, folksinger Tom Paxton, and country blues star Taj Mahal. Local musicians perform here as well, and on occasional Tuesday nights, the famous (or infamous) open mic is, at $5.50 at the door, a great entertainment deal for the good-humored. Cover. No alcohol served.

ASHKENAZ ✉*1317 San Pablo Avenue, Berkeley* ✆*510-525-5054* ✐*www.ash kenaz.com* A legend among Berkeleyites, this popular music and dance community center is a mecca for those who love world music. Artists play world beat, salsa, folk, Cajun, or reggae most nights of the week. Cover.

BEACHES & PARKS

For online information on the East Bay's regional parks, go to www. ebparks.org.

ANTHONY CHABOT REGIONAL PARK AND REDWOOD REGIONAL PARK

✉*The parks are located off Route 580 and can be entered from Skyline Boulevard or Redwood Road in Oakland or San Leandro.* ✆*510-635-0135* ✐*510-569-4319* These contiguous facilities spread across nearly 7000 acres in the hills above Oakland. Foremost among their features are Lake Chabot, a haven for anglers and boaters, and the second-growth redwoods in Redwood Park.

Chabot Park alternates between grass-covered hills and dense stands of eucalyptus, live oak, and madrone; the forests of Redwood Park are home to deer, raccoons, squirrels, and bobcats. Both parks have restrooms, picnic areas, and hiking trails. Chabot offers a golf course, an equestrian center, and a shooting range. Redwood has an archery range. There's a $5 parking fee at both parks.

▲ There are 75 sites (12 with RV hookups) near the lake in Chabot; $18 to $25 per night.

TEMESCAL REGIONAL RECREATIONAL AREA

✉️*Located at the intersection of Routes 24 and 13 in Oakland. There are entrances from both highways; take the Broadway exit from Route 24, or the Broadway Terrace exit off Route 13.* ☎️*510-652-1155* ✒️*510-652-0241*

🚶🚴🏊🍴 The highlight of this 48-acre park is Lake Temescal, created in 1868 when the Temescal Creek was dammed to supply water to Oakland. But soon larger reservoirs replaced Temescal and in 1936 it opened as one of the first recreational areas in the East Bay. Today this park, enhanced by lush growth of live oak, willow, and laurel, is a favorite spot among locals for swimming, sunbathing, fishing, picnicking, and hiking. In addition to a rose garden, fishing piers, and both paved and unpaved trails, facilities include picnic areas, restrooms, and showers. Swimming fee, $2 for kids and $3 for adults; fishing permit, $4; parking fee on weekends and holidays only (April through October), $5.

JOAQUIN MILLER PARK

✉️*3590 Sanborn Drive, Oakland* ☎️*510-283-2725, 510-238-3187 (reservations)* 🖥️*www.oaklandnet.com/joaquinmillerpark*

🚶🚴🐎 When Joaquin Miller, a poet, pony-express rider, judge, teacher, and gold prospector, settled in the hills above the "City of the Oaks" in 1886, he planted 75,000 trees including Monterey cypress, Monterey pines, eucalyptus, and olive. After his death, the city purchased the land and in 1929, the Save the Redwoods League donated the Redwood Grove to the park. Just nine miles from downtown Oakland, at this peaceful retreat you'll forget you were ever in the bustling, noisy city. In addition to one of the only urban second-growth redwood groves in existence, you'll also find forests of oak trees, lush creekside slopes, and sprawling meadows. The heavily used park is popular with hikers, joggers, equestrians, birdwatchers, and bicyclists, and is perfect for a picnic.

TILDEN REGIONAL PARK AND
WILDCAT CANYON REGIONAL PARK

✉️*Tilden Park is off Wildcat Canyon Road in the Berkeley hills; Wildcat Canyon Park is reached from McBryde Avenue in Richmond.* ☎️*510-635-0135* ✒️*510-569-4319*

🚶🚴🐎🏊🍴 These two gems lie side by side in the hills above Berkeley. Tilden, by far the more diverse and popular, is a magnificent park. Stretching over 2000 acres, it features swimming in Lake Anza, a botanical garden that condenses California's 160,000 square miles of

218

plant life into a six-acre preserve, a small environmental education center, and a rolling landscape that varies from volcanic rock to grassy meadows. Wildcat Canyon Park, with its meandering creek and forested arroyos, is a rustic counterpoint to Tilden's crowded acres. Both parks have restrooms, picnic areas, and hiking trails. Tilden also has a snack bar and a golf course. Day-use fee, $5.

POINT PINOLE REGIONAL SHORELINE

✉*Off Route 80; it can be reached by taking Hilltop Drive to San Pablo Avenue to Atlas Road in Richmond.* ✆510-635-0135 ✉510-569-4319

🚶🚴🛶 Located along San Pablo Bay, this 2400-acre park offers diverse possibilities. There are salt marshes to explore, as well as eucalyptus groves, open grasslands, and sea cliffs with sweeping vistas and pebble beaches. Anglers gravitate to the fishing pier, which extends several hundred yards into the Bay. Steelhead, salmon, sturgeon, striped bass, and leopard shark are a few of the game fish swimming these waters. Facilities include restrooms and picnic areas. Parking fee, $3 on weekends and public holidays (April through October).

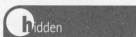

MOUNT DIABLO STATE PARK

✉*Located five miles east of Danville off Route 680, the park is reached via Mount Diablo Scenic Boulevard or North Gate Road out of Walnut Creek.* ✆925-837-2525 ✉925-673-0160

🚶🚴🐎 Rising 3849 feet above sea level, Mount Diablo is the Bay Area's second loftiest peak (Mount Hamilton is the highest). From this surveyor's vantage point you can gaze east to the Sierra Nevada and west to the Pacific. Americans Indians considered it a place of power, the only point not submerged by the primordial flood. The mountain landscape ranges from shady cottonwood canyons to open woodlands to hillsides carpeted with wildflowers. Golden eagles, red-tailed hawks, and horned larks number among the many birds here. Rabbits, raccoons, coyotes, foxes, blacktail deer, bobcats, and an occasional mountain lion are also seen. In all, the park covers almost 20,000 acres. There are restrooms, picnic areas, and over 160 miles of hiking trails. There's a visitors center at the summit. Day-use fee, $6.

⛺ There are 55 tent sites; $15 to $20 per night. Campers must arrive and check in before sunset.

LAS TRAMPAS REGIONAL WILDERNESS

✉*Off Route 680 about seven miles northwest of San Ramon, the preserve lies along Bollinger Canyon Road.* ✆510-635-0135 ✉510-569-4319

🚶🚴🐎 Within this 5000-acre expanse are sheer sandstone cliffs, chaparral-coated hillsides, and grassy meadows. It's a rugged region crossed by two ridges and containing a box canyon. Geologic forces have twisted and uplifted large sections of rock, which the wind has sculpted into exotic shapes. Golden eagles are often spotted here and wildlife is plentiful. The only facilities are picnic areas, restrooms, and stables. Day-use fee, $5.

COYOTE HILLS REGIONAL PARK

Paseo Padre Parkway and Route 84 off Route 880, north of the Dumbarton Bridge, Fremont &510-795-9385 &510-795-8012 *chvisit@ebparks.org*

Adjacent to the Don Edwards San Francisco Bay National Wildlife Refuge, this 966-acre wildlife sanctuary provides both environmental education and recreation. Two shellmounds spanning more than 2000 years harken back to the days when American Indians settled this region of freshwater marshes, willow runs, fallow fields, and grassy hills. Trails traverse these habitats and a boardwalk extends through the marsh, allowing glimpses of native plants and wildlife, including thousands of migratory birds. The visitors center features exhibits and nature programs; closed Monday. There are picnic areas and restrooms. Parking fee, $5.

QUARRY LAKES REGIONAL PARK

2100 Isherwood Way, Fremont &510-795-4883

Quarry Lakes borders the north side of Fremont's Niles district. Of its 450 acres of usable space, 350 are taken up by manmade lakes. However, there is ample picnicking and trail space. The lakes are routinely stocked with catfish and rainbow trout, and fishing permits can be picked up on-site. Swimming (fee) is also allowed in designated areas. One of the park's best features is its access to the Alameda Creek Regional Trail. This leisurely trail, which affords views of Alameda Creek, is popular with dog-walkers, bikers, joggers, and hikers. Boats with gas engines are not allowed into the park. Day-use fee, $5.

SUNOL/OHLONE REGIONAL WILDERNESS

Located about eight miles due east of Fremont, the park is at the end of Geary Road. &925-862-2244 &925-862-0810

An area of oak-covered hills, grasslands, and tumbling streams, this preserve stretches across more than 15,000 acres. Much of the land is cattle-grazing country, but more remote sections are covered with willows and inhabited by coyotes, mountain lions, and eagles. The foothills rise to almost 4000 feet, forming one of the wildest sections of the Diablo Range. An excellent trail system crosses the park. Facilities include a visitors center, restrooms, and picnic areas. Day-use fee, $5 (seasonal); trailer fee, $4.

There are four tent sites; $12 per night; there is also a backpack camp available for $5 per person ($2 backpacker permit required). Reservations: 510-636-1684.

MARIN COUNTY

While the Pacific side of Marin County, described in Chapter Five, is known for its wave-lashed shoreline, the San Francisco Bay side of this wealthy region is renowned for posh homes and sleek shopping areas. Towns like Sausalito, Tiburon, and Mill Valley sit on dramatic hillsides and gaze out over the Bay toward the San Francisco skyline.

Once across the Golden Gate Bridge in Sausalito, sightseeing begins on Bridgeway, a sinuous road paralleling the waterfront. I won't even begin to describe the views of Belvedere, Angel Island, and Alcatraz along this esplanade. Suffice it to say that the Sausalito waterfront offers the single element missing from every vista in San Francisco—a full-frame view of the city itself. It is also a perfect introduction to Marin County, a collection of luxurious bedroom communities that comprise one of the wealthiest counties in the nation.

SIGHTS

SAUSALITO   This is a shopper's town: galleries, boutiques, and antique stores line Bridgeway, and in several cases have begun creeping uphill along side streets. **Plaza Vina del Mar** (Bridgeway and El Portal), with its elephant statues and dramatic fountain, is a grassy oasis in the midst of the commerce. Several strides seaward of this tree-thatched spot lies **Gabrielson Park**, where you can settle on a bench or plot of grass at water's edge.

BAY MODEL VISITOR CENTER ⊠*2100 Bridgeway, Sausalito* ☎*415-332-3871* 🖷*415-289-3004* 🖅*www.spn.usace.army.mil/bmvc* Continue along the piers past chic yachts, delicate sloops, and rows of millionaires' motorboats. To get an idea of the inland pond where the rich sail these toys, check out the U.S. Army Corps of Engineers' visitor center. Built to scale and housed in a two-acre warehouse, this hydraulic model of San Francisco Bay is used to simulate currents and tidal flows. A self-guided map and audio tour leads you around the mini-Bay. When the model actually runs, you can watch the tide surge through the Golden Gate, swirl around Alcatraz, and rise steadily along the Berkeley shore. The tidal cycle of an entire day takes 15 minutes as you witness the natural process from a simulated height of 12,000 feet. Also part of the permanent exhibit is a display portraying Sausalito during World War II, when it was converted into a mammoth shipyard that produced almost 100 vessels in three years. Call ahead to make sure the model will be operating. Closed Sunday and Monday in winter and Mondays the rest of the year.

BAY AREA DISCOVERY MUSEUM ⊠*557 McReynolds Road, East Fort Baker, Sausalito* ☎*415-339-3900* 🖷*415-339-3905* 🖅*www.baykidsmuseum.org, contact@badm.org* Imagine a cluster of eight historic buildings and more than 100 hands-on activities all devoted to children ages 6 months to 8 years. Throw in a performing-arts theater, a 2.5-acre sea cave, and an indoor/outdoor "Tot Spot" for infants and toddlers and what you have is a place called the Bay Area Discovery Museum. Closed Monday and last two weeks of September. Admission.

RICHARDSON BAY AUDUBON CENTER AND SANCTUARY ⊠*376 Greenwood Beach Road, Tiburon* ☎*415-388-2524* 🖅*www.tiburonaudubon.org, richardsonbaycenter@audubon.org* I heartily recommend the quarter-mile self-guided tour through this center. The 900-acre preserve will provide an inkling of what Marin was like before the invention of cars and condominiums. During the winter months harbor seals can be seen in sanctuary waters. You can wander through dells and woodlands, past salt marshes and tidepools. Also contained on the property is **Lyford House**, a magnificent Victorian that commands a strategic spot on the shore of Richardson Bay. Closed Sunday.

MARIN COUNTY CIVIC CENTER ✉*3501 Civic Center Drive, San Rafael*
📞*415-499-7009* ✐*sardaiz@co.marin.ca.us* This building is constructed of
concrete and steel, which nevertheless evokes the rolling golden hills
and blue-domed sky of Northern California. Perhaps that is because
the Marin County Civic Center was designed by Frank Lloyd Wright, an
architect with a passion for blending a building to the surrounding
landscape. Take Route 101 north to the North San Pedro Road exit in
San Rafael; before even leaving the highway you'll see this long, low,
graceful building that seems almost a land bridge between the three
hills it spans. A self-guided tour will reveal interior corridors brilliantly
illuminated by skylights and landscaped with trees and shrubs; there
are docent-led tours Wednesday at 10:30 a.m. (fee). A singular structure, it represents the last commission of Frank Lloyd Wright, who died
in 1959, several years before the Civic Center's dedication. There's also
a café on-site. Closed Saturday and Sunday.

LODGING

CAVALLO POINT–THE LODGE AT THE GOLDEN GATE

$$$–$$$$ 142 ROOMS ✉*Fort Baker, 601 Murray Circle, Sausalito* 📞*415-339-4700,*
888-651-2003 📠*415-339-1792* ✐*www.cavallopoint.com,*
reservations@cavallopoint.com

Just over the Golden Gate Bridge, this hotel is much more than the
"lodge" it claims to be. Located in historic Fort Baker in Golden Gate
National Park, the rooms and suites all have views of the San Francisco
skyline, the Golden Gate Bridge, or the Marin headlands. Clustered
around a lush green lawn, the 68 "historic" rooms are found in pictur-
esque turn-of-the-20th-century Colonial Revival buildings originally
used by the Fort Baker officers; they are filled with beautifully restored
original floors and moldings. All the accommodations are done in
bright, inviting colors and most have fireplaces, so you'll stay warm
when that fog rolls in off the bay.

THE GABLES INN

$$$–$$$$ 15 ROOMS ✉*62 Princess Street, Sausalito* 📞*415-298-1100,*
800-966-1554 📠*415-339-0536* ✐*www.gablesinnsausalito.com,*
innkeeper@gablesinnsausalito

Tucked away in Sausalito, this little bed and breakfast has just
the right mix of charm and elegance. Originally built in 1869 as a
hotel for shipyard workers and travelers, the Gables was com-
pletely updated in 2008 with warm spaces that welcome you
into what feels like a family home. The 15 spacious rooms all
have ultracomfortable beds and are sparsely decorated in a
modern style with clean, crisp linens and dark furniture. Many
rooms have jacuzzis and views. For a real indulgence, stay in the
Bay Room, which looks out on a spectacular panorama that in-
cludes San Francisco, Alcatraz, Treasure Island, Angel Island,
and the Bay Bridge. There's complimentary wine and cheese in
the evening.

PANAMA HOTEL

PAGE 223

Bright, gay-friendly, Key West–inspired bed and breakfast boasting tropical kitch and tons of character

EAST BROTHER LIGHT STATION

PAGE 223

Enchanting 1873 lighthouse-cum-upscale-inn nestled in San Pablo Bay—only accessible by boat

CASA MADRONA HOTEL & SPA

PAGE 222

Opulent boutique hotel offering both clean, contemporary rooms and Victorian-style suites

THE GABLES INN

PAGE 221

Modern honeymoon-style bed and breakfast with polished decor and panoramic bay views

CASA MADRONA HOTEL & SPA

$$$$ 63 ROOMS   ✉*801 Bridgeway, Sausalito* ✆*415-332-0502,* *800-288-0502* 📠*415-332-2537* ✐*www.casamadrona.com,* *casa@casamadrona.com*

Casa Madrona features a New England–style complex of rooms attached to a 19th-century landmark house and an expansive new Mediterranean wing. You'll find this tiered structure on a Sausalito hillside overlooking San Francisco Bay. The guest rooms in the B&B-style house have a personal feel and individual names. The "Artist's Loft" is decorated with antique artists' supplies and enjoys a bay view from its large deck, while the "La Posada" is styled after a grand Victorian. The contemporary wing features lavish accommodations with deep soaking tubs and fireplaces. There are also five private cottages available at this resort.

THE WATERS EDGE

$$$$ 23 ROOMS   ✉*25 Main Street, Tiburon* ✆*415-789-5999, 877-789-5999* 📠*415-789-5888* ✐*www.marinhotels.com, watersedgehotel@jdvhospitality.com*

Staying here is like a sleepover at Martha Stewart's house. The elegant guest rooms, including two suites, all have fireplaces and are meticulously decorated in simple, modern design complete with vaulted wood ceilings. But you don't stay here for clever shelving or decorating tips. Wrap yourself in a hand-knitted blanket, curl up on the chaise lounge, and spend the day gazing at the view and pretending to turn a page every few hours. A continental breakfast is served in your room and there's complimentary wine and cheese every evening.

PANAMA HOTEL

$$$ 15 UNITS   ✉4 Bayview Street; San Rafael   ✆415-457-3993, 800-899-3993   ☏415-457-6240   ✐www.panamahotel.com, innkeeper@panamahotel.com

If you're longing to get away to a quiet hideaway in a tropical setting reminiscent of Key West (but actually located in a residential Victorian neighborhood), book a room at the Panama. The 13 rooms and two garden cottages are decorated with a hodgepodge of antiques, some with clawfoot tubs. Most have ceiling fans and either a balcony or garden patio. Continental breakfast included. Gay-friendly.

EAST BROTHER LIGHT STATION

$$$$ 5 ROOMS   ✉117 Park Place, Point Richmond, CA 94801 (mailing address)   ✆510-233-2385   ✐www.ebls.org, info@ebls.org

Calling the accommodations here unusual is a slight understatement. Where else can you find a bed-and-breakfast inn located within a lighthouse on an offshore island? The old beacon was built back in 1873 and has been operational for over a century. Today the two-story house and light station feature five bedrooms furnished with period pieces. Guests travel out to this one-acre hideaway by motorboat and enjoy wine and hors d'oeuvres followed by a multicourse dinner as well as breakfast the next morning. Of course, there's a premium on such seclusion: rates run in the ultra-deluxe range and reservations should be made. Shared and private bathrooms are available. Open Thursday through Sunday, this San Pablo Bay retreat is a unique opportunity to trade the trappings of civilization for your own private island.

DINING

HAMBURGERS

$ AMERICAN   ✉737 Bridgeway, Sausalito   ✆415-332-9471

You'll know the bill of fare by the name—Hamburgers; and you can tell the quality of the food by the line outside. Local folks and out-of-towners alike jam this postage stamp–sized eatery. They come not only for charcoal-broiled burgers, but for grilled chicken and steak sandwiches as well. It's tough securing a table, but you can always pull up a bench in the park across the street.

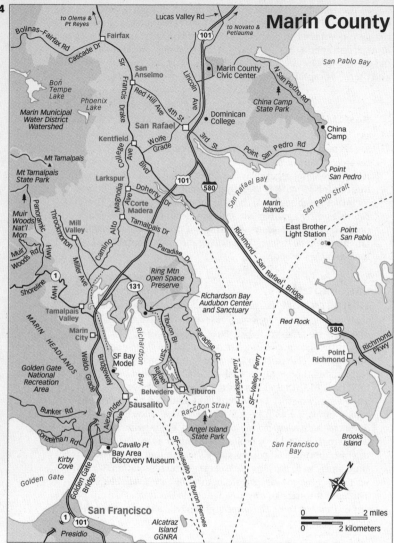

Marin County

SEVEN SEAS

$$–$$$ SEAFOOD ✉ *682 Bridgeway, Sausalito* 📞 *415-332-1304* 📠 *415-331-8015*

Sausalito sports many seafood restaurants, most of which are over-priced and few of which are good. So it's best to steer a course for this divine eatery. It lacks the view of the splashy establishments, but does feature an open-air patio in back. The menu includes scallops, bouilla-baisse, and salmon. Landlubbers can choose from several meat plat-ters; at lunch sandwiches are served. Closed January to mid-February.

HORIZONS

$$–$$$ SEAFOOD   ✉558 Bridgeway, Sausalito   ☎415-331-3232   🖷415-332-0400
🖱www.horizonssausalito.com, horizons@horizonssausalito.com

If you long for a sea vista and an eyeful of San Francisco skyline, try Horizons. Housed in the early-20th-century San Francisco Yacht Club, this spiffy seafood restaurant has a wall of windows for those inside looking out, and a porch for those who want to be outside looking farther. Then, of course, there's the food: shellfish and other aquatic fare, with chicken, pasta, and steak dishes added for good measure. Some beautiful carpentry went into the design of this place. There's also a popular bar here, making it a choice spot to drink as well as eat. Open for brunch, lunch, and dinner.

GUAYMAS

$$–$$$ MEXICAN   ✉5 Main Street, Tiburon   ☎415-435-6300   🖷415-435-6802
🖱www.guaymas.com

If the tide doesn't carry you, current trends may very well deliver you here. This upscale Mexican restaurant makes fresh tortillas and tamales daily. Pork, steak, and shrimp dishes are prepared on a mesquite grill; or try the duck with pumpkin seed sauce or the daily fresh fish catch. Located next door to the ferry dock, Guaymas rounds out the bill of fare with a bay view.

BUNGALOW 44

$$$ NEW AMERICAN   ✉44 East Blithedale Avenue, Mill Valley   ☎415-381-2500
🖱www.bungalow44.com

Sit down to a creative seasonal menu at this inviting dining room decorated in brown leather and hardwood. An open kitchen and a packed bar add a lot of energy to this popular eatery. The menu offers rib-eye steak with bacon and bleu cheese baked potatoes, New Zealand mussels and *frites* with chorizo, and Kobe beef hamburgers. Leave room for desserts such as the warm chocolate-hazelnut brioche. Dinner only.

JOE'S TACO LOUNGE

$$ MEXICAN   ✉382 Miller Avenue, Mill Valley   ☎415-383-8164

Fish tacos get raves—big moist chunks of fish on fresh tortillas.The many varieties of bottled hot sauce range from moderately hot to tongue-searing and the salsas are made fresh daily. Roasted corn on the cob, black bean soup, and pizza with a cornmeal crust are excellent. The decor is velvet-Elvis-meets-Virgin-of-Guadalupe—lots of color and verve that makes the perfect backdrop for the food. This place is a local favorite, and draws fans from across the Bay, so the wait can be long and reservations are not taken.

THE MARIN BREWING COMPANY

$–$$ AMERICAN   ✉1809 Larkspur Landing Drive, Larkspur   ☎415-461-4677
🖷415-461-4688   🖱www.marinbrewing.com

A bayside spot that's accessible by ferry is this brewing company. Famous for the beer (the Blueberry Ale has won a gold medal and Mt. Tam Pale Ale is a regional favorite), this spot also serves delicious pub grub. Clams, burgers, buffalo wings, and pizzas from the wood-fired oven are all tasty accompaniments to your brew of choice. The 50-foot-long wooden bar is claimed to be one of the longest in California.

LARK CREEK INN

$$$ NEW AMERICAN ✉ *234 Magnolia Avenue, Larkspur* 📞 *415-924-7766* 📠*415-924-7117* 🖱 *www.larkcreek.com*

Sometimes I'll find a restaurant where the food is perfectly complemented by the surroundings. Lark Creek is one such locale: a late-19th-century yellow house surrounded by redwoods, gardens, and a meandering creek, the Inn has garnered acclaim for its menu, farm-fresh ingredients, and country elegance. Dinner might feature duck confit with a morel mushroom risotto. Sunday brunch may find diners enjoying poached eggs in a green garlic béarnaise sauce with Yukon gold potatoes, sweet corn, and heirloom squash cakes. Dinner only except for Sunday brunch.

SHOPPING

The best shopping spot in all Marin is the town of Sausalito. Here you can stroll the waterfront along Bridgeway and its side streets, visiting gourmet shops, boutiques, and antique stores. One of the Bay Area's wealthiest towns, Sausalito sports few bargains, but it does host an assortment of elegant shops.

JEWELRY BY THE BAY ✉*660 Bridgeway, Sausalito* 📞*415-332-0660*

Several shops in the mini-mall at 660 Bridgeway are worth a browse. This shop is the largest jewelry store in Sausalito, and features contemporary jewelry.

LOUIS ARONOW GALLERY ✉*686 Bridgeway, Sausalito* 📞*415-331-4000* A

standout among the art galleries lining Sausalito's streets is Louis Aronow. Two floors exhibit an extensive collection of original paintings and limited-edition prints, as well as glass and bronze sculptures.

HEATH CERAMICS ✉*400 Gate 5 Road, Sausalito* 📞*415-332-3732 ext.13* 📠*415-332-3204* 🖱*www.heathceramics.com* Stop by the factory store of this

company that has been producing high-quality ceramic dinnerware for over 50 years. In addition to new ceramics, they also sell seconds and imperfect pieces at reduced prices, as well as linens, tiles, and flatware.

BOOK PASSAGE ✉*51 Tamal Vista Boulevard, Corte Madera* 📞*415-927-0960,*

800-999-7909 🖱*www.bookpassage.com* Your next trip begins the minute you step in to this spot. Travel guides, maps, and accessories make this store a favorite among Bay Area travelers. After you've selected the books you need, sit down with an Italian soda in the café and begin plotting your itinerary.

NORTHGATE MALL ✉*5800 Northgate Mall, San Rafael* 📞*415-479-5955* 🖱*www.themallatnorthgate.com* This is an enclosed shopping center with

about 100 stores, including the Gap, Macy's, Bath & Body Works, and other chains. There are several forgettable restaurants and a 15-screen movie theater. By summer 2009, major mall renovations are scheduled for completion, including a new indoor/outdoor food court, new parking lot, and new boutique area.

OVEDA MAURER ANTIQUES ✉ *34 Greenfield Avenue, San Anselmo*
☎ *415-454-6439* Stretching for a half-mile and numbering two dozen stores is the antique-shop district of San Anselmo. Look for pewter and Early American furniture here. Open by appointment only.

NIGHTLIFE

NO NAME ✉ *757 Bridgeway, Sausalito* ☎ *415-332-1392* The window simply reads "Bar"; the address is 757 Bridgeway in Sausalito; and the place is famous. Famous for its name, the no name, and because it's a favored hangout among young swingers and old salts alike. With an antique bar, piano, and open-air patio, it's a congenial spot to bend an elbow. You'll hear live jazz on Friday and Saturday, a variety of musical styles during the week including blues, folk, and Dixieland, and open mic every Tuesday.

MARIN THEATRE COMPANY ✉ *397 Miller Avenue, Mill Valley* ☎ *415-388-5208* ⌘ *www.marintheatre.org, info@marintheatre.org* This is one of the top repertory theater groups in the Bay Area. Classic and contemporary dramatic works are performed in a state-of-the-art playhouse that many larger troupes would envy.

SWEETWATER STATION ✉ *32 Miller Avenue, Mill Valley* ☎ *415-388-2820* ⌘ *www.sweetwatersaloon.com* This place jams every night. Featuring blues and rock sounds, the club often headlines big-name groups. Cover.

MAMA'S ROYAL CAFÉ ✉ *387 Miller Avenue, Mill Valley* ☎ *415-388-3261* If you're in the mood for a mellow evening, several coffeehouses offer live acoustic music. Mama's has live piano music, ranging from jazz to cat house blues, during the day on weekends.

MARIN SHAKESPEARE COMPANY ✉ *Forest Meadows Amphitheater, Dominican University of California, Grand Avenue off Mission, San Rafael* ☎ *415-499-4488* ⌘ *www.marinshakespeare.org* For a dose of outdoor drama, head to this group's amphitheater, where serious stage-strutting and fretting occur throughout the summer season, courtesy of the company's skilled, professional players.

BEACHES & PARKS

CHINA CAMP STATE PARK
✉ *Located along North San Pedro Road about five miles east of San Rafael*
☎ *415-456-0766* 🖷 *415-456-1743*

🚶 🚵 🏇 ⛵ ⚓ 🛶 ⚓ This 1540-acre park, located shoreside along San Pablo Bay, is a perfect picnic spot. Heavily wooded and adorned with several smaller islands just offshore, it has a particular lure. Part of the attraction is the old Chinese fishing village, dating to the 1860s. This ghost community of tumbledown houses was home to thousands of Chinese who were uprooted by the 1906 San Francisco earthquake and fire. Now it's a peaceful park inhabited by shore birds, anglers, and daytrippers. The park has picnic areas, restrooms, and 20 miles of hiking trails.

▲ There are 30 developed walk-in sites; $25 per night. Reservations: 800-444-7275.

THE DELTA REGION

California's two major rivers, the Sacramento and San Joaquin, flow together around Sacramento, creating the state's fertile delta region. The heart of this bayou country lies about 70 miles northeast of San Francisco. From the city, the fastest way to go is by following Route 80 east to Fairfield, turning right on Route 12 and taking it to Route 160 in Rio Vista. Route 160 leads north through the heart of the Delta.

An alternative course is to take Route 4 instead of Route 12. This will allow you to see a greater stretch of the Delta along Route 160. It will also carry you near two waterfront towns—Port Costa and Benicia—that should not be missed.

SIGHTS

PORT COSTA   Port Costa enjoyed its heyday early in the century when the town served as a major grain-shipping port. Today it's a lazy community at the end of a country lane. A few sagging stores have been converted to artists' quarters and antique shops, and one of the warehouses has become a cavernous restaurant. Otherwise, the wrinkled hills all around seem like time warps in which this church-steeple village rests suspended. Farmland and forest enclose Port Costa, so finding your way becomes half the enjoyment of exploring the town: Well-marked side roads lead to it from Route 4.

JOHN MUIR NATIONAL HISTORIC SITE ____ ✉ *4202 Alhambra Avenue, Martinez* ☎ *925-228-8860* ✐ *www.nps.gov/jomu, jomu_interpretation@nps.gov* A few miles farther along this highway, past rounded hills tufted with grass, sits this historic site. This grand 17-room Victorian on a nine-acre estate was home to the renowned naturalist for almost a quarter-century until his death in 1914. It was here that Muir wrote voluminously on conservation and became a founder of the Sierra Club. Muir also helped create Yosemite National Park; he personally led Theodore Roosevelt through the Sierra, admonishing him for hunting big game and urging the president to preserve other wilderness areas. Admission. Closed Monday and Tuesday.

The countryside that once surrounded the Scottish conservationist's house has given way to suburban plots. But nine acres of the orchards Muir once managed remain. Within the house, many rooms have been restored to their original appearance. Muir's "scribble den," or study, remains littered with manuscripts and research materials, the family quarters are opulently furnished, and the parlor is filled with Victorian effects. While John Muir's primary love was the wild, a tour of his estate provides a singular glimpse into the life of the man. Closed Monday and Tuesday. Admission.

MARTINEZ From Port Costa, it's a short drive southeast on Route 4 to this bayside town. Established as a trading post in the late 1840s, Martinez began to grow, enhancing its position by becoming a shipping port, county seat, and railroad center, not to mention the terminus for the longest-running ferry service west of the Mississippi. Today the town is low-key, off the beaten track, relaxed, and friendly—more like a small town than a metropolitan suburb. Early-20th-century homes can be found scattered about town, and a historic downtown district boasts 23 antique stores.

BENICIA ✉ *From Route 4 in Martinez continue east a few miles, then take Route 680 north to Route 780.* Across the Carquinez Strait from Port Costa looms Benicia, a community whose early dreams proved to be delusions of grandeur. The folks who founded the town foresaw it as the state capital. In 1853 it was actually named the seat of government, but by 1854 dissatisfied legislators had moved their operation to Sacramento. The founding mothers and fathers also pictured Benicia as a magnificent port.

BENICIA CAPITOL ✉ *West 1st and G streets, Benicia* 📞 *707-745-3385* 📠 *707-745-8912* 🖱 *www.parks.ca.gov, benicia@napanet.net* This capitol is an imposing brick building marked by twin pillars. True to antiquity, every desk in the Senate chamber is set up to be illuminated by candle and has a spittoon by its side. Closed Monday and Tuesday. Admission.

BENICIA HISTORICAL MUSEUM AT THE CAMEL BARNS idden

✉*2060 Camel Road, Benicia* 📞 *707-745-5435* 📠 *707-745-2135* 🖱*www.beneciahistoricalmuseum.org, info@beneciahistoricalmuseum.org* A relic of the past that didn't quite work out, the yellow sandstone Benicia Museum recalls the days in the 1850s when the U.S. Army imported a herd of dromedary camels from the Middle East in the belief that they might help open the desert. The museum houses various other displays, including ones on carpentry and shipbuilding. Open Wednesday through Sunday. Admission.

BENICIA CHAMBER OF COMMERCE ✉*601 1st Street, Benicia* 📞*707-745-2120, 800-559-7377* 🖱*www.beniciachamber.com, beniciachamber@aol.com* There are walking tour booklets at the Capitol to lead you past the other historic sites that make Benicia the little town that couldn't. The local chamber of commerce also has pamphlets and maps.

SIX FLAGS DISCOVERY KINGDOM ✉*2001 Marine World Parkway, off Route 80, Vallejo* 📞*707-643-6722* 📠*707-644-0241* 🖱*www.sixflags.com* Visitors following Route 80 can stop at this 160-acre theme park that fuses education with an adrenaline rush. A 300,000-gallon shark tank, an aquarium of killer whales, and a 55-acre lake host a variety of stunt shows (both animal and human). On the thrill side, more than a dozen head-spinning rides with names like Zonga, Hammerhead Shark, and Boomerang defy gravity. Among other land-based attractions are the Elephant Encounter (where you'll have a chance to ride Asian and African species), Butterfly World, an animal nursery, and Looney Tunes Seaport (geared towards the under-48-inch set). Closed November through February (open some weekends during winter). Steep admission.

The Delta Region

BLACK DIAMOND MINES REGIONAL PRESERVE

PAGE 231

Seven-thousand-acre park with centuries-old Welsh cemetery, historic mines, and a museum in an underground chamber

AL'S PLACE

PAGE 235

Steak, steak, and steak served in an off-the-wall eatery with a dollar-bill-plastered ceiling

DELTA DAZE INN BED & BREAKFAST

PAGE 234

Quirky yet charming inn with individually themed rooms, some with casino decor, some with an Asian motif

ISLETON JOE'S

PAGE 235

Fresh-catch diner specializing in all things crawdad—platters, omeletes, and sandwiches

THE DELTA   On Route 160, you can travel north along the Sacramento River all the way to the current state capital. En route is a dreamy land of drawbridges, meandering waterways, and murky mists. This bayou country is as dateless as the Deep South. Sam Goldwyn once claimed that the California Delta "looks more like the Mississippi than the real thing," and chose it as the movie location for *Huckleberry Finn*.

Back in the 1850s, steamboats sidewheeled upriver from San Francisco to the Gold Country outside Sacramento. Residents still tell of the pirates who stretched chains across the river to snag steamboats laden with gold. The area is renowned among anglers for its striped bass, blue gill, sturgeon, and black bass. Waterskiers and other aquatic enthusiasts favor it as well.

The Delta is an endless expanse of flatlands and orchards, levees and dikes. A thousand miles of waterways meander through this mazework. There are channels bearing names like Hog, Whiskey, Disappointment, and Montezuma Slough.

BETHEL ISLAND   The gateway to the Delta is this island, one of the 55 that comprise the Delta. Featuring marinas, motels, restaurants, and boat rentals, it sits a few miles east of the intersection of Routes 4 and 160. Like the rest of the Delta, it is busiest during summer and on weekends. In the winter, many local businesses close for the season, so it's best to check in advance.

BLACK DIAMOND MINES REGIONAL PRESERVE

✉Somersville Road, three miles south of Route 4, Antioch ☎925-757-2620 📠925-757-0335 ☞www.bdvisit@ebparks.org Listed on the National Register of Historic Places, this preserve, a 6286-acre park at the foot of Mt. Diablo, features a 19th-century cemetery complete with cracked tombstones engraved in Welsh. Approximately 65 miles of hiking and biking trails traverse the park, which has picnic areas and campsites. In the lowest level, of one of the mines is a visitors center that displays old photographs and mining artifacts. Two first-come, first-served underground tours of the mines begin at 12 p.m. and 3 p.m. on the weekend (arrive early to buy tickets) from April to November. Advance-reservation tours begin at 11 a.m., 1 p.m., and 2 p.m. on weekends (April through November). Check for seasonal hours. Parking fee weekends and holidays.

WESTERN RAILWAY MUSEUM ✉5848 Route 12, between Suisun City and Rio Vista ☎707-374-2978 📠707-374-6742 ☞www.wrm.org This museum features dozens of vintage railroad cars, many of them in working order. Wander this 25-acre, open-air museum and you'll come across an Australian tram and a Gay Nineties streetcar. A nine-mile ride on one of the many historic cars is offered. Open on the weekends only September through May; open Wednesday through Sunday June through August. Admission.

JELLY BELLY CANDYLAND TOUR ✉One Jelly Belly Lane, Fairfield ☎707-428-2838, 800-522-3267 ☞www.jellybelly.com Chances are, you've marveled at the realistic, gritty texture of the pear Jelly Belly, or the frothiness of the cappuccino-flavored bean. The Herman Goelitz company's tour will show you how it's done. During this 40-minute tour, you will receive samples and a color-coded Jelly Belly identification menu. In addition to the trademark beans, you will see the creation of Wiggle Worms, Tummy Bears, and Gummi Pet rats and tarantulas. Factory machinery does not operate on the weekends, though tours are still offered.

LOCKE

✉Route 160 ☞www.locketown.com The high point of any Delta trip is a visit to Locke (population 85; elevation 13 feet), a creaky community of clapboard houses and falsefront stores. This intriguing town, located on Route 160, is the only rural community in the entire country built and occupied by Chinese. Many contemporary residents trace their ancestry back to the pig-tailed Asian immigrants who mined California gold fields and helped build the transcontinental railroad, then moved on to construct the Delta's intricate levee system.

During its heyday in the early 1900s, Locke was a wide-open river town. Chinese people and non-Asians alike frequented its gam-

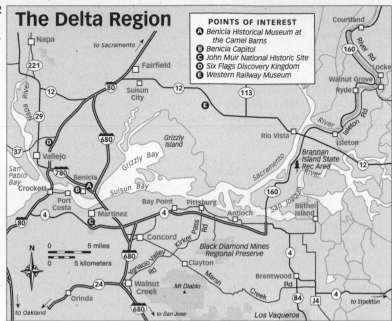

The Delta Region

POINTS OF INTEREST
- **A** Benicia Historical Museum at the Camel Barns
- **B** Benicia Capitol
- **C** John Muir National Historic Site
- **D** Six Flags Discovery Kingdom
- **E** Western Railway Museum

bling parlors, speakeasies, and opium dens. These raffish denizens have long since disappeared, but little else has changed.

Today Locke is like an outdoor museum, an example of what America's small towns would be like if time were measured not in terms of human progress, but in the eternal effects of the elements. You can still stroll along wooden sidewalks, which now slope like the pathways in an amusement park funhouse. Elderly people sit in the doorways reading Chinese newspapers.

On either side of the town's block-long Main Street, there are tumble-down, two-story buildings with balconies that lean toward the road. Rust streaks the tin roofs, and some structures have sagged so heavily that the doors are rectangular forms collapsing into parallelogram shapes. Some of the outer walls are covered with rose vines, others are buried in an avalanche of honeysuckle. Along the edge of town are the trim orchards and communal gardens that Chinese residents have tended for generations.

Every building has a story to relate. As you wander through town, glance up near the ridgetops of the falsefront buildings. On many, you can still discern the outlines of hand-lettered signs proclaiming that once this place was a Chinese "Bakery and Lunch Parlor," the "Star Theatre," or "Waih & Co. Groceries & Dry Goods." A guided walking tour (fee) of the town is available. Call 916-776-1661 for reservations and information.

ISENBERG CRANE RESERVE ⊠*In Woodbridge, ten miles southeast of Locke* ☏*209-948-7708* In the 1980s, the Department of Fish and Game purchased the land of a duck hunting club to create this reserve. Every Sunday and certain Saturdays and Thursdays from October through February, thousands of nature lovers embark on a two-hour tour to witness the gregarious nature and hear the trumpet-like gargling call of the sandhill crane. Marked by gray plumage and a bald red forehead, this threatened species stands at five feet tall with a seven-foot wingspan. Reservations required and mail-in registration needed, call for information.

THE MEADOWS

A Delta adventure lies along the filigree of waterways just behind Locke in a place known as The Meadows. The best way to explore this preserve is in a boat. By car, go south from Locke about 200 yards and turn left on the first paved road (just before the concrete bridge). Proceed about 100 feet and turn left on the gravel road; a mile in length, it leads into The Meadows. Generally considered the Delta's most picturesque region, The Meadows is like an everglades. Its narrow canals are shaded by oak and walnut trees that droop Spanish moss to the water's edge. Frogs croak in the lily pads. Pheasant, great horned owls, Canada geese, and a variety of ducks inhabit the place, and along the riverbanks you can pick blackberries and grapes.

LODGING

INN AT BENICIA BAY

$$$–$$$$ 9 ROOMS ⊠*145 East D Street, Benicia* ☏*707-746-1055* 📠*707-745-8361* ⌨*www.theinnatbeniciabay.com, theinnatbb@sbcglobal.net*
In a little yellow house circa 1854, surrounded by eucalyptus trees, and dotted with antiques and original art (most of which are for sale), this inn is the epitome of quaint. All nine rooms are individually decorated and some feature pretty decks overlooking the garden. An expanded breakfast with homemade bread is included.

B & W RESORT MARINA

$$ 23 ROOMS ⊠*964 Brannan Island Road, Isleton* ☏*916-777-6161* 📠*916-777-5199* ⌨*www.bandwresort.com, bandwresort@citlink.net*
Good lodging places are rare around the Delta, but there's one that I recommend. Set on the Mokelumne River, this place features a covey of wood-frame cottages scattered across spacious grounds. There's a marina as well as a picnic area and small beach. The units include one-bedroom cottages and two-bedroom duplexes. These are tidy efficiency units with knotty-pine walls, linoleum floors, and no decoration; they include kitchenettes but no utensils. During July and August, peak season, the minimum stay is one week.

DELTA DAZE INN
BED & BREAKFAST

$$ 10 ROOMS ✉ *20 Main Street, Isleton* 📞 *916-777-7777*
✍*www.deltadazeinn.com, info@deltadazeinn.com*

From the country antiques and fluffy bed linens, you'd never know this two-story charmer had another life as a bordello before it was rebuilt in 1926. In the middle of an 800-person village on the Sacramento River, it's a quiet, comfy headquarters for exploring. Rooms all have private baths, cable TV, and phones, amenities not all that common in this area. The breakfast room serves as a dining room, conference center, and bridge parlor—depending on the need. Each room has a different theme, from Asian to patriotic American, with thoughtful touches such as lots of books and rocking chairs.

RYDE HOTEL

$$$ 42 ROOMS ✉ *14340 Route 160 at Route 220, Walnut Grove* 📞 *916-776-1318,*
888-717-7933 📠 *916-776-1195* ✍*www.rydehotel.com, rydehotel@hotmail.com*

A former speakeasy once owned by a family member of Lon Chaney, Jr., a star of early Hollywood horror flicks, the Ryde retains its Art Deco charm with 32 period-decorated guest rooms and a restaurant reminiscent of a 1930s supper club complete with arched windows, palms, and a grand piano. The restaurant is open for Sunday brunch year-round.

The most adventurous lodging on the Delta is aboard a houseboat. These vessels are quite simple to operate with 45 minutes of instruction and require no captain's license. There's no finer way to experience California's bayou than by spending a few lazy days on the river.

HERMAN & HELEN'S MARINA

$$$$ RENTALS ✉ *At the end of Eight Mile Road, Stockton* 📞 *209-951-4634,*
877-468-7326 📠 *209-951-6505* ✍*www.houseboats.com, hth@inreach.com*

Among the many companies renting houseboats is Herman & Helen's, which also has a restaurant.

DINING

FIRST STREET CAFÉ

$$–$$$ ITALIAN ✉ *440 1st Street, Benicia* 📞 *707-745-1400* ✍*www.firststcafe.com*

In Benicia, en route to the Delta, First Street Café serves standard breakfast fare, soups, salads, and sandwiches for lunch, and Cajun- and Italian-influenced seafood, meat, and pasta dishes for dinner. A contemporary café, this popular spot has an espresso machine and offers an assortment of fresh baked desserts. Head upstairs Thursday through Sunday and munch on appetizers while gazing at the Carquinez Strait. Take out meals are also available. Weekend brunch.

THE POINT

$$–$$$ AMERICAN ✉ *120 Marina Drive, Rio Vista* 📞 *707-374-5400*
📠 *707-374-2542* ✍*www.pointrestaurant.com, pointman@pointrestaurant.com*

For riverside dining, head for this spot, tucked into the Delta Marina Yacht Harbor in Rio Vista. A variety of seafood, pasta, steak, and chicken dishes are offered. You can dine in a cozy booth by the window and watch the Sacramento River scene in the River Room or on an enclosed patio known as the Garden Room. There's entertainment in the lounge on some Saturday nights during the summer, and brunch on Sunday. Closed Monday.

ISLETON JOE'S

$-$$ SEAFOOD   ✉212 2nd Street, Isleton   ☎916-777-6510
⌨www.isletonjoes.com

Look for the two-story brick building in the middle of town with a giant crawdad painted on the side. No surprise—crawdads are the reason people come back again and again, though fans of big, sloppy burgers and crisp fried chicken will have their cravings satisfied here. The menu offers crawdad platters, crawdad cocktails, crawdad omelets, crawdad sandwiches, and more crawdad platters. Breakfasts are huge and hearty—chicken fried steak, biscuits and gravy, and fluffy Texas French toast. It's a plain, diner-style joint with a long bar that is usually crowded with fishermen and locals. Lunch and breakfast daily, dinner Thursday through Monday.

GIUSTI'S

$$ SEAFOOD   ✉14743 Old Walnut Grove Road, Walnut Grove   ☎916-776-1808
⌨www.giustis.com

For local color, nothing compares to Giusti's, a reasonably priced seafood and prime rib restaurant. Dating to 1896, it's housed in a wooden building with a timeworn exterior. It's the kind of place where the walls are decorated with autographed photos inscribed to the owner and the ceiling is covered with 1250 baseball caps. At lunch they serve steaks, burgers, pasta, and daily specials; then for dinner, Giusti's features prawns, grilled halibut, veal cutlets, and fresh fish. Seasonal brunch. Closed Monday.

LOCKE GARDEN CHINESE RESTAURANT

$ CHINESE   ✉13967 Eva Road, Locke   ☎916-776-2100

It seems almost too obvious to eat at a Chinese restaurant in Locke (founded and occupied by Chinese). But where better to find authentic Chinese cuisine? Locke Garden occupies the town's first building, a 1912 structure that looks like a transplant from the Midwest. Formerly a beer parlor, the spacious dining room features basic but tasty Cantonese staples such as cashew chicken, Szechuan beef, and chow mein. Closed Monday.

AL'S PLACE

$$ AMERICAN   ✉Main Street, Locke   ☎916-776-1800

The Delta's most bizarre restaurant is Al's, better known as "Al the Wop's." It may be the strangest joint you've ever entered. The bar out front is a saloon with hunting trophies protruding from the walls and a fading mural of a cowboy challenging a bucking bronco. The high ceiling is plastered with dollar bills (it'll cost you a buck to find out how they got there). Dinner consists primarily of steak and steak. A stack of sliced bread accompanies your slab of meat. At lunch, every table is set with big jars of peanut butter and jelly. The idea is to swab the peanut butter on the bread, add a dollop of jelly, and enjoy it with your steak. Sorry you asked?

SHOPPING

ASILEE'S VICTORIAN ANTIQUES ✉*608 Ferry Street, Martinez* ☎*925-229-0653* Martinez is popular with antique collectors. Its plentiful stores offer a wild variety of items, with prices a bit lower than the city stores. Most are closed on Sunday, however, and some on other days, so call ahead. At Asilee's, you'll discover a collection of colorful, elegant lamps, and other antiques. Closed Sunday.

HAGEN'S HOUSE OF CLOCKS ✉*513 1st Street, Benicia* ☎*707-745-2643* Historic downtown Benicia is antique store heaven. Hagen's features a vast array of timepieces. Closed Sunday and Monday.

BENICIA ANTIQUE SHOP ✉*305 1st Street, Benicia* ☎*707-745-0978* To discover hidden treasures, head to this shop, where you'll find silver, glassware, furniture, and jewelry. Closed Monday.

RIVER ROAD GALLERY ✉*13944 Main Street, Locke* ☎*916-776-1132* ✎*www.locketown.com* In the Delta, try the antique community of Locke, where you can combine shopping with a search for the town's historic roots. River Road is housed in a building that has experienced several incarnations as a grocery, pool hall, and old-fashioned ice cream parlor. Today it contains oil and pastel paintings, ceramics, and silver jewelry, all created by local artists. Closed Monday through Thursday, and January through February.

NIGHTLIFE

RYDE HOTEL ✉*Route 160, Ryde* ☎*916-776-1318* ✎*www.rydehotel.com, rydehotel@hotmail.com* By car or boat you can cruise to several spots around the Delta, including the Ryde Hotel. This rambling, multistoried affair features a plush bar and an intimate dining room; the bar is open on weekends. Back in Prohibition days, the hotel was a notorious speakeasy. Today it is one of the hottest nightspots in the Delta.

BEACHES & PARKS

BRANNAN ISLAND STATE RECREATION AREA
✉*Route 160 about four miles south of Rio Vista* ☎*916-777-6671* ☎*916-777-7703* Located along the Sacramento River, this park sits in the midst of the Delta Country. With sloughs and levees all around, it's a region of willows and cottonwoods. There's a beach for swimmers, picnic tables for daytrippers, and a maze of waterways for anglers. Black bass, sturgeon, catfish, and perch number among the

Delta's many gamefish. There are picnic areas, restrooms, showers, and a visitors center that is open weekends.

▲ There are over 140 sites; fees vary with season (they also have wi-fi at the campground).

LOS VAQUEROS

✉9990 Los Vaqueros Road, Byron   ✆925-371-2628, 925-688-8225   ✉925-513-2084
🖥www.ccwater.com/losvaqueros

🚶🚴🐎⛵🚣🎣 This 18,500-acre watershed between Brentwood and Livermore is an ideal destination for a daytrip and picnic. The hiking is excellent, with a particularly pleasant eight-mile stroll along the side of the reservoir itself. The water and countryside are spectacular, but don't get so distracted that you forget to watch out for snakes. Because the reservoir stores drinking water, swimming and gas-powered boats are not allowed. Only electric-motor boats rented from the marina are allowed on the lake. Fishing's good here; the reservoir has been stocked with more than 200,000 gamefish such as rainbow trout and largemouth bass. In addition to picnic facilities, the recreation area has restrooms, a marina that rents electric boats, an interpretive center open Friday through Sunday, and 55 miles of hiking trails, including over 12 miles for biking and horseback riding.

OUTDOOR ADVENTURES

FISHING

Deep-sea and Bay expeditions for salmon, rock cod, halibut, and bass draw countless anglers to the Bay Area.

East Bay

BERKELEY MARINA SPORT CENTER ✉225 University Avenue, Berkeley ✆510-237-3747 🖥www.berkeleysportfishing.com For charters, contact this center. Depending on the season, they fish the bay or the ocean. Bait is provided and tackle is for sale.

Marin County

SALTY LADY SPORTFISHING ✉At the foot of Harbor Drive, Sausalito ✆415-760-9362, 415-674-3474 (reservations) 🖥www.saltylady.com Salty Lady fishes the ocean for salmon (and sometimes tuna) aboard a 56-foot cabin cruiser. Bait is included in the price; tackle can be rented.

LOCH LOMOND LIVE BAIT HOUSE ✉Loch Lomond Marina, San Rafael ✆415-456-0321 This bait house handles charter reservations.

Delta Region

THE FISH HOOKERS SPORTFISHING ✉1759 Circle Drive, Isleton ✆916-777-6498 🖥www.fishhookers.com Go out on one of this company's six-pack fishing boats and try your luck at catching striper, sturgeon, or halibut.

SAILING

Nothing is more visually stunning than the sight of the sailboats on a clear, breezy San Francisco morning. Don't miss the experience of capturing the wind and drinking in endless vistas.

East Bay

CAL ADVENTURES ✉*U.C. Aquatic Center, foot of University Avenue, Berkeley* ☎*510-642-4000* ⌘*www.oski.org* From March through November, this group offers lessons and rentals on 15-foot Coronados.

OLYMPIC CIRCLE SAILING ✉*1 Spinnaker Way, Berkeley* ☎*510-843-4200, 800-223-2984* ⌘*www.ocscsailing.com* For lessons and rentals on larger boats (24 to 43 feet), try this outfitter, also at the Berkeley Marina.

Marin County

CASS' RENTAL MARINA ✉*1702 Bridgeway, Sausalito* ☎*415-332-6789, 800-472-4595* ⌘*www.cassmarina.com* In the North Bay, try Cass. In addition to running a sailing school, they rent keel sloops.

OCEAN VOYAGES ✉*1709 Bridgeway, Sausalito* ☎*415-332-4681, 800-299-4444* ⌘*www.oceanvoyages.com* For charters on San Francisco Bay call Ocean Voyages, which has luxury vessels.

KAYAKING

Your trip will take on a new dimension as you paddle among seals and seagulls, along the cityfronts and through the harbors of the world's largest landlocked bay. The popularity of kayaking has soared in the past few years, and the Bay Area certainly hasn't missed the boat; there are several small companies that cater to kayakers and would-be kayakers of all physical and financial abilities. While the most convenient place to paddle is on the Bay itself, there are also wonderful locations to the north in Marin County.

East Bay

CALIFORNIA CANOE & KAYAK ✉*409 Water Street, Oakland* ☎*510-893-7833, 800-366-9804* ⌘*www.calkayak.com* At Jack London Square, California Canoe offers classes, sea and whitewater kayaking trips, retail sales, and rentals.

Marin County

SEA TREK OCEAN KAYAKING CENTER ✉*Schoonmaker Point Marina, Sausalito* ☎*415-488-1000* ⌘*www.seatrekkayak.com* To paddle across Richardson Bay under the bright silvery moon, contact this kayaking center. They also do trips to Angel Island and guided tours all over Northern California, teach classes, and rent all the equipment you'll need.

WINDSURFING

The surf may not be up on San Francisco Bay, but the wind almost always is! The choice spot to windsurf in the East Bay is the Berkeley

Marina. In Marin, everyone goes to Larkspur Landing. Candlestick Point in South San Francisco is also a very popular spot.

East Bay

CAL ADVENTURES ✉*U.C. Aquatic Center, foot of University Avenue, Berkeley* ✆*510-642-4000* ⌨*www.oski.org* For sailboard rentals and lessons go to these experts.

GOLF

It may not be the Monterey Peninsula, but the Bay Area offers many golfing opportunities at challenging, picturesque courses. Most places rent golf clubs and carts.

Peninsula

CRYSTAL SPRINGS GOLF COURSE ✉*6650 Golf Course Drive, Burlingame* ✆*650-342-4188* Duffers and professionals alike tee off at Crystal Springs. This 18-hole course runs along the foothills with views of Crystal Springs Lake.

South Bay

SAN JOSE MUNICIPAL GOLF COURSE ✉*1560 Oakland Road, San Jose* ✆*408-441-4653* This treelined course has 18 holes and is more than 6700 yards long. It was designed by Robert Muir Graves and boasts a primarily flat terrain.

East Bay

LAKE CHABOT GOLF COURSE ✉*11450 Golf Links Road, Oakland* ✆*510-351-5812* With steep rolling hills, Lake Chabot Golf Course is quite challenging. Designed in the 1920s, the 18th hole is par 6.

TILDEN PARK GOLF COURSE ✉*Grizzly Peak Boulevard and Shasta Road, Berkeley* ✆*510-848-7373* Traversed by a creek and dotted with redwood and pine trees, this 18-hole course is a choice spot. There's a driving range and putting green.

SUNOL VALLEY GOLF CLUB ✉*6900 Mission Road, Sunol* ✆*925-862-2404* ⌨*www.sunolvalley.com* Located in a valley surrounded by rolling hills, this club encompasses two full golf courses.

Marin County

PEACOCK GAP GOLF AND COUNTRY CLUB ✉*333 Biscayne Drive, San Rafael* ✆*415-453-4940* Situated in a valley surrounded by the China Camp Recreation Area, Peacock Gap is a relatively flat 18-hole course.

TENNIS

The Bay Area is the third most active region in the nation for tennis. Cities all around the Bay have public courts, many lighted for night play.

Peninsula

PEERS PARK ✉*1899 Park Boulevard, Palo Alto* Two courts.

MITCHELL PARK ✉*600 East Meadow Park, Palo Alto* ✆*650-463-4900* Seven lighted courts.

South Bay
WALLENBERG PARK ✉*Corner of Curtner and Cottle avenues, San Jose* Eight lighted courts.

PAUL MOORE PARK ✉*Corner of Hillsdale and Cherry avenues, San Jose* Four lighted courts.

East Bay
ROSE GARDEN ✉*1201 Euclid Avenue, Berkeley* Four courts.

LIVE OAK PARK ✉*Walnut and Berryman streets, Berkeley* Two lighted courts. The city of Berkeley has courts in six other locations. Call 510-981-5150 for information.

CHABOT ✉*Patton Avenue and Broadway* Three lighted courts.

LANEY ✉*900 Fallon Street* Ten lighted courts.

DAVIE TENNIS STADIUM ✉*198 Oak Road* ✆*510-238-3494* Five lighted courts.

Marin County
SOUTHVIEW PARK ✉*North Street* One court.

MARINSHIP PARK ✉*North end of the San Francisco Bay Model* Three lighted courts.

M.L.K. PARK ✉*Coloma and Olima streets* ✆*415-289-4152* Five courts.

BIKING

With its Mediterranean climate and gentle terrain, the Bay Area is a perfect place to travel by bicycle. Thousands of local folks commute to work on two-wheelers. Bike paths are appearing everywhere and some public transportation systems accommodate passengers with bikes.

Peninsula
Cycling is a great way to explore the sights of the Peninsula. There's a beautiful 15-mile loop through Portola Valley with an interesting side trip to the quaint town of Woodside. For a journey through a eucalyptus grove, try the four-mile loop in Coyote Point Park. To ride through academia, check out the numerous paths at Stanford University in Palo Alto.

South Bay
If you take your bicycle on a sightseeing tour of the South Bay, Kelley Park in San Jose is a great place to begin. There are 150 acres of rolling hills with numerous sights along the way. Another jaunt travels between two stunning garden parks—Villa Montalvo and Hakone Gardens. More challenging is the steep 24-mile climb up Mount Hamilton Road to the Lick Observatory.

East Bay

CESAR CHAVEZ PARK ✉*Located at the west end of University Avenue, Berkeley* There are diverse routes for two-wheeling sightseers in the East Bay. This Berkeley Marina park offers a gently rolling paved loop with sweeping views of the Bay Bridge, San Francisco, and the Golden Gate Bridge. You'll also find inline skaters, joggers, kite enthusiasts (the park is almost always windy) and dog owners (there's a dog park here) all sharing the same pavement.

OAKLAND In Oakland, there's a bike path around **Lake Merritt**, the city's saltwater lake. **Tunnel Road** and **Skyline Boulevard** climb the East Bay hills to several regional parks. The 3.5-mile paved Bayview Trail in **Coyote Hills Regional Park** treats bikers to views of marshes, hills, and the Bay. Out at **Point Pinole Regional Shoreline**, a path takes cyclists through grassy meadows to the shores of San Pablo Bay.

Marin County

In Marin, the Sausalito Bikeway carries along the shoreline past marshes and houseboats. Another bikeway in Tiburon offers spectacular views of Sausalito and San Francisco.

Delta Region

For a truly enjoyable bike ride past mud flats, ponds, sloughs, rickety towns, country lanes, and levees, take your bike to the Delta. The roads are flat, lightly traveled, and offer cyclists a chance to experience Huck Finn's Mississippi right here in Northern California.

Bike Rentals

THE BIKE CONNECTION ✉*2011 El Camino Real, Palo Alto* ☎*650-853-3000* ⌨*www.bikeconnection.net* On the peninsula, try this shop for all your rental needs.

SUMMIT BICYCLES ✉*1031 California Drive, Burlingame* ☎*650-343-8483* ⌨*www.summitbicycles.com* For mountain bikes and trail information, check out this store where the people are friendly and eager to help.

BICYCLE OUTFITTER ✉*963 Fremont Avenue, Los Altos* ☎*650-948-8092* ⌨*www.bicycleoutfitter.com* This store sells road, mountain, hybrid, and tandem bikes. On Sunday mornings a 20-plus-mile tour through Portola Valley leaves from the shop. Several other local tours also leave from here.

ACTION SPORTS ✉*27365 Industrial Boulevard #F, Hayward* ☎*510-786-1025* ⌨*www.sportsbay.com* In the East Bay, this spot rents mountain, racing, and children's bikes.

KARIM CYCLE ✉*2800 Telegraph Avenue, Berkeley* ☎*510-841-2181* ⌨*www.teamkarim.com* Karim rents and sells mountain and touring bikes, as well as inline skates. Closed Sunday.

HIKING

Though much of the landscape has been built up to serve growing urban needs, some of the surrounding wilderness regions have been preserved. So the Bay Area still offers diverse terrains for hikers—grassy hillsides, open meadows, stark mountainsides, and meandering creek beds. Where the pavement ends and the pathways begin, you can often find solitude and serenity. All distances listed for hiking trails are one way unless otherwise noted.

Peninsula

SAN BRUNO MOUNTAIN STATE AND COUNTY PARK   Several trails wind through this park, offering spectacular views of the Bay Area. The **Summit Loop Trail** (3.1 miles) takes you past mountain springs to views of the bay and the ocean. An easy walk, the **Old Guadalupe Trail** (.8 mile) passes through a "fog forest" of fern-bedecked Monterey cypress and eucalyptus. The easy-looking but strenuous **Ridge Trail** (2.5 miles) to East Peak Vista offers a hawk's eye perspective on the Bay.

SAN FRANCISCO STATE FISH AND GAME REFUGE   The **Sawyer Camp Historic Trail** (6 miles) provides access to the beautiful preserve in the Santa Cruz Mountains. The road is paved, but open only to hikers, skaters, equestrians, and bicycle riders. The trail climbs past San Andreas and Crystal Springs lakes, providing excellent opportunities for birdwatchers and wildflower-gazers.

LOS TRANCOS OPEN SPACE PRESERVE   A fascinating journey through earthquake country is the high point of a trek through this preserve. The **San Andreas Fault Trail** (.6 mile) is a self-guided path along a portion of California's infamous earthquake fault. A brochure points out sag ponds, benches, and scarps near the fault. The **Franciscan–Lost Creek Loop Trail** (4.3 miles roundtrip) crosses a high meadow, cuts through stands of bay and oak, and crosses Los Trancos Creek. Its final destination is open countryside dotted with wildflowers.

East Bay

ANTHONY CHABOT REGIONAL PARK   This regional park teems with wildlife and offers several good hikes. Near Anthony Chabot Campground, the **Hidden Canyon Trail** (1.1 miles) leads through stands of oak to an amphitheater set in a eucalyptus grove. The **East Shore** and **West Shore Trails** (3.5 miles), bicycle paths with gentle slopes, also make for an enjoyable hike along Lake Chabot. If waterfalls, grass valleys, weeping willows, and wooded hillsides sound inviting, try the **Cascade** and **Columbine Trails** (4 miles). For a trek that covers the length of the park, there's the **MacDonald–Brandon Trail** (10 miles). It's part of the 31-mile-long Skyline National Recreation Trail that connects Chabot with other regional parks. After the first uphill mile, the hike is fairly easy as it passes ridges and ravines, offering wonderful views to the south.

TILDEN REGIONAL PARK   This is the most popular park in the East Bay and is a playground for naturalists. Its trails lead through nature areas, around lakes, and along mountain ridges. Be sure to visit the nature center. The **Jewel Lake Trail** (.9 mile) is an easy walk through woods and fields to a marsh pond. Frogs, ducks, and bog vegetation are part of the setting. The **Laurel Canyon** and **Wildcat Peak Trails** (2.2 miles) begin at the Little Farm and present striking views of the park as they carry you through groves of eucalyptus and Monterey pine. The **Sylvan Trail** (.6 mile) is another gentle hike, which lies along this stretch. The **Nimitz Way Trail** (5.5 miles) is also part of the 31-mile-long Skyline National Recreation Trail connecting six Bay Area parks. This section, a paved road, traverses San Pablo ridge.

MOUNT DIABLO'S STATE PARK   The granddaddy of East Bay mountains, Mount Diablo's State Park is appealing both for its challenges and rewards. If you enjoy a challenge, try the six-mile uphill **Summit Trail** climb across stark, rocky terrain. The views are outstanding; bring water. The three-mile **Devil's Slide** and **Oyster Point Trail** traverses rolling grasslands and oak forests en route to another stunning vista. The **North Peak Trail** (2.3 miles) goes up steep slopes and down through shady woods. In the end it arrives atop Mount Diablo's second peak and offers marvelous views of the Bay Area.

LAS TRAMPAS REGIONAL WILDERNESS   Hiking through the wild and rugged chaparral country of Las Trampas Regional Wilderness evokes dreams of the early West. The **Chamis Trail to Las Trampas Ridge Trail** (4.8 miles roundtrip) begins in a valley and climbs 1000 feet to an impressive view point. The **Creek Trail** (.6 mile) is an easy, shady trail through hardwood forests and grasslands past Bollinger Creek. The **Devil's Hole Trail** (1.5 miles) requires a strenuous 2000-foot climb, both out and back. The rewards include a small creek, fern gorge, and magnificent views. Bring food and water.

SUNOL REGIONAL WILDERNESS   This wilderness area offers several pathways through hills and along tumbling creeks. To get to the end of the **Flag Hill Trail** (1.3 miles) you'll have to trek a 1000-foot climb to a grand view of the park. The **McCorkle Trail via Cerro Este** (3.2 miles) follows Alameda Creek, then climbs a hill en route to a backpacking camp. To get away from other hikers, try the **Maguire Peaks Loop Trail** (4.3 miles). It carries past streams, oaks, and sage-scented grasslands to a pair of wind-sculpted peaks.

ALAMEDA CREEK REGIONAL TRAIL ✆ *510-562-7275* ✐ *www.eb parks.org/parks/alameda.htm* Starting up in Niles Canyon, this 12-mile trail follows Alameda Creek out to the San Francisco Bay. Hikers will find a gravel and sometimes paved path. It's popular with dog-walkers, bikers, and joggers. Access from Fremont, Union City, and Newark.

See Chapter Five for descriptions of hiking in Marin.

TRANSPORTATION

CAR

The Bay Area is a sprawling region threaded with major highways. Along the Peninsula, **Routes 101, 280**, and **82** travel north and south. All three lead to the South Bay; from here, **Routes 880** and **80** travel up along the East Bay.

From San Francisco, **Route 101** streams north to Marin, and **Route 80** cuts through the East Bay and connects with other roads leading into the Delta.

AIR

Three major airports service the Bay Area: **San Francisco International Airport** (see Chapter Two), **Norman Y. Mineta San Jose International Airport**, and **Oakland International Airport.** To avoid the crowds and parking problems at San Francisco's mammoth airport, consider landing in Oakland, located just across the Bay. If you're interested in touring the South Bay or Central Coast, San Jose is very convenient.

NORMAN Y. MINETA SAN JOSE INTERNATIONAL AIRPORT

Airlines flying here include Alaska Airlines, American Airlines, Continental Airlines, Delta Air Lines, Frontier Airlines, Hawaiian Airlines, Horizon Air, jetBlue Airways, Southwest Airlines, and United Airlines.

Several bus companies provide ground transportation from the San Jose airport. Check with the **Airport Connection** (408-730-5555) for schedules and destinations. **Santa Clara Valley Transit Authority** (408-321-2300) provides frequent service to downtown San Jose. Taxi cabs are also available: **United Cab** (408-971-1111) or **Yellow Cab** (408-293-1234).

OAKLAND INTERNATIONAL AIRPORT

Oakland's airport is serviced by Alaska Airlines, American Airlines, Continental Airlines, Delta Air Lines, Hawaiian Airlines, jetBlue, Mexicana, North American Airlines, Southwest Airlines, Taca, United Airlines, and US Airways.

Excellent ground transportation to and from the Oakland airport makes it one of the most convenient terminals in the area. **Bayporter Express** (415-467-1800) serves both the Oakland and San Francisco airports. **Alameda–Contra Costa Transit**, or **AC Transit** (510-817-1717; www.actransit.org), stops regularly at the terminal and transports passengers to downtown Oakland. For a quick trip to various East Bay points, climb aboard the **Oakland Air-Bart,** which connects the airport with the **Bay Area Rapid Transit**, or BART (510-465-2278; www.bart.gov), system.

Several cab and shuttle companies service the airport as well: try **Friendly Cab** (510-536-3000) or **Yellow Cab** (510-848-1234).

BUS

GREYHOUND BUS LINES ✆800-231-2222 🖉www.greyhound.com Greyhound offers extensive bus service to the Bay Area from around the country. There are stations in Oakland at 2103 San Pablo Avenue and in San Jose at 70 South Almaden Avenue.

TRAIN

AMTRAK ✆800-872-7245 🖉www.amtrak.com Amtrak has several trains coming into the Bay Area daily. Two cover extensive California routes: the "Coast Starlight" runs from San Diego to Seattle with stops in San Jose, Oakland, Emeryville, and Martinez. The "San Joaquin" covers the San Joaquin Valley, stopping in Oakland, Emeryville, Richmond, and Martinez. From Chicago, the "San Francisco Zephyr" traverses the western United States to Emeryville.

Most towns in the Bay Area have car rental agencies; check the Yellow Pages to find the best bargains. A shuttle will take you from the airport to the rental service you choose. Your options include **Avis Rent A Car** (800-331-1212), **Budget Rent A Car** (800-527-0700), **Dollar Rent A Car** (800-800-4000), **Hertz Rent A Car** (800-654-3131), or **National Car Rental** (800-227-7368).

At the Oakland airport, check with **Avis Rent A Car** (800-331-1212), **Budget Rent A Car** (800-527-0700), **Dollar Rent A Car** (800-800-4000), **Hertz Rent A Car** (800-654-3131), or **National Car Rental** (800-227-7368). Several other companies, listed in the Yellow Pages, offer free pickup and delivery to both airports.

PUBLIC TRANSIT

Most sections of the Bay Area are accessible by some form of public transportation. It may be a bus, subway, or ferry boat, but it will get you to your destination.

SAN MATEO COUNTY TRANSIT (SAM TRANS) ☎ 800-660-4287
✐ www.samtrans.com On the Peninsula, this transit agency carries passengers from San Francisco as far south as Palo Alto.

SANTA CLARA COUNTY TRANSIT ☎ 408-321-2300 ✐ www.vta.org
The South Bay is traversed by county transit buses and the **Light-Rail System**, with service extending from Mountain View through San Jose.

ALAMEDA–CONTRA COSTA COUNTY TRANSIT ☎ 510-839-2882
✐ www.actransit.org A network of bus routes crisscrosses the East Bay. Call AC Transit for schedules.

GOLDEN GATE TRANSIT ☎ 415-923-2000 ✐ www.goldengatetransit.org
These transit buses can take you from points in San Francisco to locations throughout Marin County (Sausalito, San Rafael, and beyond).

CALTRAIN ✉ 4th and Townsend streets ☎ 800-660-4287 ✐ www.caltrain.com
Daily commuter trains run the length of the Peninsula from San Francisco to San Jose.

BAY AREA RAPID TRANSIT (BART) ☎ 510-465-2278 ✐ www.bart.gov
BART runs from Fremont north to Richmond, stopping in Oakland and Berkeley; from the SF airport through San Francisco and Oakland to Pittsburg/Bay Point; and from Millbrae through San Francisco and Oakland to Dublin/Pleasanton.

GOLDEN GATE TRANSIT ☎ 415-923-2000 ✐ www.goldengateferry.org
Public transportation from San Francisco to Marin can become a sight-seeing adventure when you book passage on a Golden Gate Transit ferry boat. Cruises to Sausalito and Larkspur from the Ferry Building in San Francisco are crowded with commuters and vacationers alike.

ALAMEDA/OAKLAND FERRY ☎ 510-522-3300 ✐ www.eastbayferry.com
This ferry provides service from the East Bay to the Ferry Building, Pier 41, and AT&T Park in San Francisco.

WINE COUNTRY

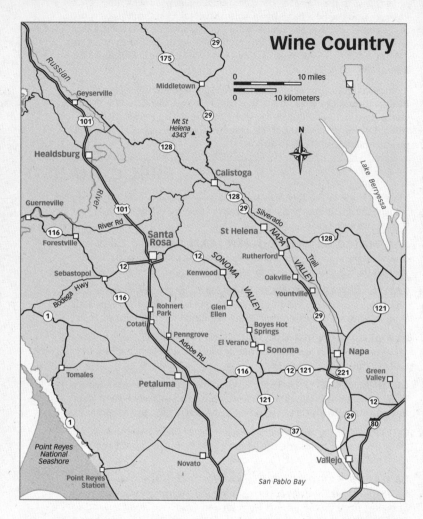

Wine Country

Just one hour from the streets of San Francisco lies an agricultural area that can match farmlands anywhere in the country for beauty. It's a region of tree-tufted mountains and luxurious valleys. Tilled fields create quiltlike patterns across the landscape and country roads wind into its hills.

Despite the grandeur of the place, its visual appeal is only a secondary feature. The lure of the land is its temptation to all the senses, particularly taste and smell. The plants stippling those picturesque fields are grapes and the product is wine, fine vintages that rival even those of France.

Winemaking in California dates back to the 18th century, when Spanish padres planted vineyards at the missions. The Franciscans grew black grapes for sacramental wines, crushing them by foot in hide troughs, then fermenting the harvest in leather sacks.

Spanish vineyards spread north to Sonoma, where in 1823 church fathers established their last mission. In Napa Valley, across the mountains east of Sonoma, George Yount, the area's original settler, cultivated grapes in 1843. During the next decade, numerous Europeans, drawn initially by the Gold Rush, forsook prospecting for planting. A Prussian immigrant named Charles Krug became a pioneer in commercializing Napa wines. He also taught other early vintners like Jacob Beringer and Carl Wente, whose names even today adorn wine bottles.

In 1857, Agoston Haraszthy, a Hungarian count, founded the Buena Vista Winery in Sonoma. Commissioned by the California governor, he traveled through France, Italy, and Germany a few years later, collecting cuttings from 300 grape varieties. Soon thereafter, the University of California perfected fermentation techniques and established a national center for viticulture and enology at its Davis campus.

California's wine business boomed. Four million gallons were produced in 1869, 28 million in 1900, and by 1911 the total rose to 58 million gallons. Then came Prohibition. From 1920 until 1933, an entire industry withered on the vine. Many wineries shut down; others converted their fields to orchards.

It took nearly 30 years for the industry to recover. Not until the 1960s, when wine became an increasingly popular national drink, did California's vineyards burgeon once more. This long-awaited renaissance proved extraordinary. Within a five-year period, vineyard acreage doubled. Wineries mushroomed in the Napa and Sonoma valleys, along the Russian River, and elsewhere throughout the state. Family-run wineries blossomed, national companies like Coca-Cola and Nestlé moved into the vineyards, and formerly aloof French winemakers, impressed with the quality of the wines, formed partnerships with local growers. Winemaking is now a multibillion dollar business, with millions of people touring California's vineyards each year.

The natural elements for this success story have always been present, though only recently did the social factors begin to coalesce. Geography and climate play vital roles in winemaking and combine north of San Francisco to create ideal growing conditions. Here several valleys—Napa, Sonoma, and the Russian River—are protected by mountains from the cold winds and rain along the Pacific coast. They enjoy hot (very hot!) summers and cool, moist winters, ensuring good harvests. In fact, zinfandel wines are only made in California, not in Europe. The origin of this grape was a mystery until modern DNA testing traced it to an obscure vineyard in northern Italy.

In Napa Valley, sun, low hills, and fog drifting up from San Francisco Bay produce one of the world's finest winegrowing regions. Today, the area is so well-known and fashionable that it is drawing more than fog from San Francisco. Celebrities and millionaires are moving here faster than new wineries. Gourmet restaurants and country inns have multiplied, and tourists are causing weekend traffic jams in this once-rustic realm. Even the health spa at Calistoga has gained such importance that France's Perrier took over the mineral water bottling. It's a far cry from a century ago when a penniless writer named Robert Louis Stevenson explored the isolated farming community.

Sonoma Valley's history traces back further than that of Napa, but lately the "valley of the moon" has been hard-pressed to keep pace with its starstruck neighbor. Resting between the volcanic Sonoma Mountains and the Mayacamas Mountains to the east, it was once inhabited by Coastal Miwok, Pomo, Wappo, and Patwin Indians. They gathered berries and acorns, fished the waters of nearby San Pablo Bay, and stalked the mountains for bear and deer. The advent of the Spanish mission changed their lifestyle unalterably and ushered in an era of international intrigue. During the early 1840s, Mexico's General Mariano Guadalupe Vallejo controlled Sonoma. Then in 1846 a band of roughhewn Americans arrested Vallejo and declared California the Bear Flag Republic. Within weeks the United States took control, eventually converting Sonoma to a military base.

Novelist Jack London settled in the nearby town of Glen Ellen in 1904, living there until his death in 1916. Interested in ranching as well as writing, London chose a region that today is an important dairy farming and sheep ranching area. The Sonoma Valley is also noted for its apple orchards, not to mention many excellent wineries.

Like the Russian River region to the north, this area is planted with an extraordinary variety of grapes. Moving in a southerly course from Mendocino County, the Russian River passes Alexander Valley, Dry Creek Valley, and other regions that have greatly contributed to California's wine renaissance. Then, as it turns west toward the sea, it has given birth to a different sort of rebirth, a gay renaissance. Since the 1970s, the area around Guerneville, long popular for its excellent canoeing and fishing, has become Northern California's top gay destination.

Country inns, restaurants, and nightclubs catering to gays from San Francisco and around the country have mushroomed along the riverbanks and in the region's deep redwood forests.

Any of these areas—providing opportunities to taste fine wines, tour vineyards, visit historic sites, and explore the Russian River—can be visited in the course of a day trip from San Francisco. But you might want to take longer—a week, or a lifetime perhaps, to wander California's luscious Wine Country. Then you can decide for yourself whether it's the beauty of the landscape or the flavor of the wine that creates the magical lure of the place.

A tour of the Wine Country will give you an opportunity to sample choice vintages, explore vineyards, and experience the art of winemaking. You'll find that most wineries, large or small, welcome visitors and provide tours and tasting.

To visit the area, pack a picnic lunch, wander through the growing region, and plan to stop at only three or four wineries during the day. Small wineries, where the operation is family run and tours are personalized, create the most memorable experiences. Usually the winemaker or a member of the family will show you around, providing a glimpse into their lives as well as their livelihoods. Since the winemakers will be leaving their normal duties to help you, small wineries usually require advance reservations. It's also a good idea to ask directions to these secluded vineyards.

Large wineries schedule tours and tasting all day and permit you to drop by unannounced. Though impersonal, they're convenient to visit and provide a wider variety of wines. Many are housed in beautiful buildings of historic interest.

Both family-run and multinational wineries are described here, though the vineyards listed are a small fraction of those you can visit. They also represent my favorites and are liable to the follies and foibles of my personal taste. So test for yourself; somewhere out there lies a hidden vineyard or unheralded vintage, waiting to be discovered.

NAPA VALLEY

California's premier winegrowing region is a long, narrow valley, laid out like a checkerboard and stretching 35 miles. Here grape arbors alternate with wild grasses and rich bottom land gives way to forested slopes. If natural beauty were a question for the palate, Napa Valley would be the rarest of vintages. It is a landscape of windmills and wooden barns, clapboard cottages and stone wineries.

The region is also a millionaire's preserve, a freshly fashionable place which draws the most affected people imaginable. There are pinch-faced connoisseurs who purse their lips as they taste, then comment on the wine in mangled French. It draws hordes of visitors and is fast becoming one of the state's most popular tourist attractions.

Try to visit during the week, and plan to explore not only the main highway, but also the Silverado Trail. An ideal itinerary will carry you up the valley on Route 29, then back down along the parallel roadway.

SIGHTS

NAPA VALLEY CONFERENCE AND VISITORS BUREAU
✉*1310 Napa Town Center, Napa* ☎*707-226-7459* ✆*707-255-2066* ⌨*www.napa valley.com, info@napavalley.org* The visitors bureau is a good place to get started. They will supply you with maps and brochures for the area.

NAPA VALLEY WINE TRAIN ✉*1275 McKinstry Street, Napa* ☎*707-253-2111, 800-427-4124* ✆*707-253-5264* ⌨*www.winetrain.com, reservations@winetrain. com* An unusual option for touring the Wine Country is to climb aboard this train, which runs daily between the city of Napa and the vineyards slightly north of St. Helena. Travelers may choose the luncheon, brunch, or dinner trip, each of which takes three hours and smoothly chugs past some of the most scenic parts of the valley. The 1915–47 Pullman cars have been beautifully restored; the dining car is straight out of a romance novel.

NAPA FIREFIGHTERS MUSEUM ✉*1201 Main Street, Napa* ☎*707-259-0609* ⌨*www.napafirefightersmuseum.org, info@napafirefighters.org* If someone in your traveling party wants to be a fireperson when she grows up, the whole family might like a brief stop at this museum, just a couple of blocks away from the visitors bureau. Engines, ladder trucks, hose carts, and other equipment, as well as uniforms and old photos are on display. Closed Sunday through Tuesday.

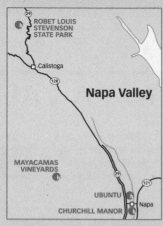

ROBERT LOUIS STEVENSON STATE PARK

PAGE 269

Rugged evergreen-strewn plaza that inspired scenes in *Treasure Island*

MAYACAMAS VINEYARDS

PAGE 251

Unexpected, yet extraordinary winery set in the mountains astride an extinct volcano

UBUNTU

PAGE 263

Innovative California cuisine in a Zen-inspired atmosphere

CHURCHILL MANOR

PAGE 259

Grand Napa Valley bed and breakfast full of hospitality—afternoon cookies, evening wine, and tandem bicycles

SILVERADO TRAIL   This old stagecoach road parallels Route 29 on the east and links with it via a succession of cross-valley roads as it runs 29 miles from Napa to Calistoga. Fully paved, the route is a favorite among cyclists as well as leisurely drivers. In addition to glimpses of Napa Valley as it was in the 1960s, it's an excellent place to search out small wineries. All along this rural stretch are family-owned vineyards, set on the valley floor or tucked into nearby hills. To reach it, you can follow Trancas Street east from Route 29 through Napa and turn left onto the Silverado Trail.

MONTICELLO CELLARS ✉4242 Big Ranch Road, Napa ☎707-253-2802 ✆707-253-1019 ⬧www.corleyfamilynapavalley.com, wine@corleyfamilynapavalley. com Head north from Napa on Route 29 to Oak Knoll Avenue and turn right. You will arrive at this winery, which is a replica of Thomas Jefferson's mansion. The classic estate offers tastings daily in their picnic grove, courtyard, or tasting cellar. Wine seminars are available by appointment. Tasting fee.

SHAFER VINEYARDS ✉6154 Silverado Trail, Napa ☎707-944-2877 ✆707-944-9454 ⬧www.shafervineyards.com, info@shafervineyards.com About two miles north of the Oak Knoll intersection on the Silverado Trail, this vineyard lies at the base of a rocky outcropping surrounded by fields of chardonnay, merlot, and cabernet sauvignon grapes. Removed from the road, it's a placid spot with views of the fields and the valley. Tours of the winery and wine cave are by appointment only, as are tastings. Closed weekends.

HESS COLLECTION

✉ *4411 Redwood Road, Napa* ☎ *707-255-1144, 877-707-4377* 📠 *707-253-1682* ⌨ *www.hesscollection.com, info@hesscollection.com* If you do choose to tour the Wine Country on your own, you'll find one of the area's most interesting wineries right in Napa. Located on the site of the former Christian Brothers' Mont LaSalle winery, the Hess Collection is where fine wine meets fine art. The self-guided tour is unique: It is the only winery in the valley that includes two floors displaying some 130 museum-quality artworks by contemporary international artists. The Hess Collection also refers to the cabernets and chardonnays that are just being released and are available for sampling in the ground-floor tasting room. Tasting fee.

MAYACAMAS VINEYARDS

✉ *1155 Lokoya Road, Napa* ☎ *707-224-4030* 📠 *707-224-3979* ⌨ *www. mayacamas.com, mayacama@napanet.net* This vineyard provides an entirely different setting from the wineries on the valley floor. Located deep in the mountains west of Napa Valley, it sits astride an extinct volcano. The blocks of vineyard appear hewn from surrounding rock walls. Indeed, the fields of chardonnay and cabernet sauvignon rest on terraces along the mountainside. Like the encircling hills, the winery is made of stone, built in 1889. Tours of this special place are by appointment; it lies about ten miles off Route 29 along winding mountain roads. Closed weekends.

YOUNTVILLE As you proceed north, the next group of major wineries lies clustered around this rural town. Residents claim that their town is "where it all began." George Yount, the municipal namesake, was the first American to settle in Napa Valley. Arriving in 1836, he took control of an 11,000-acre land grant and built a Kentucky-style log house.

NAPA VALLEY MUSEUM ✉ *55 Presidents Circle, Yountville* ☎ *707-944-0500* 📠 *707-945-0500* ⌨ *www.napavalleymuseum.org, info@napavalleymuseum. org* This museum, which is practically next door to Domaine Chandon, is not your mother's museum. Far from stuffy, it's a vibrant center for the arts. But its most stunning attribute is the high-tech permanent exhibit, "California Wine: The Science of an Art." The space celebrates the history, culture, and lifeblood of the area with changing exhibits of arts and crafts. Closed Tuesday. Admission.

DOMAINE CHANDON ✉ *1 California Drive, Yountville* ☎ *707-944-2280* 📠 *707-944-1123* ⌨ *www.chandon.com, info@chandon.com* Owned by France's

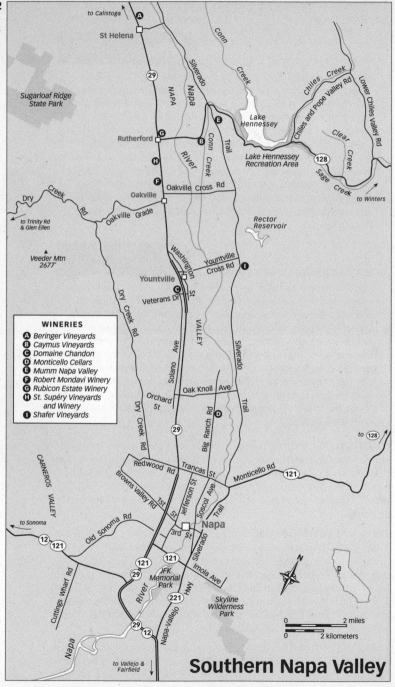

to Calistoga

Ⓐ St Helena

29

Silverado

NAPA

Napa

Conn Creek

Chiles Creek

Chiles and Pope Valley Rd

Lower Chiles Valley Rd

Lake Hennessey

Ⓔ

Sugarloaf Ridge State Park

River

Conn Creek

Trail

Lake Hennessey Recreation Area

Clear Creek

Sage Creek

Ⓖ Rutherford

Ⓑ

128

to Winters

Ⓗ

Ⓕ

Oakville Cross Rd

Dry Creek Rd

to Trinity Rd & Glen Ellen

Ⓕ Oakville

Oakville Grade

Rector Reservoir

Veeder Mtn 2677'

Washington

Yountville Cross Rd

Ⓘ

Dry Creek Rd

Ⓒ Yountville

Veterans Dr

St

VALLEY

Silverado

WINERIES

Ⓐ Beringer Vineyards
Ⓑ Caymus Vineyards
Ⓒ Domaine Chandon
Ⓓ Monticello Cellars
Ⓔ Mumm Napa Valley
Ⓕ Robert Mondavi Winery
Ⓖ Rubicon Estate Winery
Ⓗ St. Supéry Vineyards and Winery
Ⓘ Shafer Vineyards

Solano Ave

Oak Knoll Ave

Trail

Orchard St

Big Ranch Rd

Ⓓ

Dry Creek Rd

29

to **128**

CARNEROS VALLEY

Redwood Rd

Trancas St

Monticello Rd

121

Browns Valley Rd

1st St

Jefferson St

Soscol Ave

Trail

to Sonoma

Old Sonoma Rd

12 **121**

121

3rd St

Napa

Cuttings Wharf Rd

121 **121**

29

JFK Memorial Park

Imola Ave

Silverado HWY

Skyline Wilderness Park

N

River

221

Napa-Vallejo HWY

29 **12**

Napa

to Vallejo & Fairfield

0   2 miles
0   2 kilometers

Southern Napa Valley

fabled champagne producer Moët & Chandon, this estate sits on a knoll west of town. Producing some of California's foremost sparkling wines, this winery provides a close look into the production and bottling of the bubbly. It's housed in a modernistic building with barrel-vaulted ceilings and contains exhibits by local artists as well as a gourmet restaurant. There's a tasting salon and terrace. The regularly scheduled tours are free. Tasting fee.

ROBERT MONDAVI WINERY ✉ 7801 St. Helena Highway, Oakville ☎ 707-968-2022, 888-766-6328 🖥 www.robertmondaviwinery.com, robertmondavi.reservations@robertmondaviwinery.com Among the most well-known in the Napa Valley, this winery is a Spanish mission–style building offering a variety of seasonal informative tours by reservation. They range from a basic production tour with tasting to a 75-minute look at the entire process from vineyard to laboratory to winery. The chardonnay and fumé blanc are excellent, and you can sample reserve wines by the glass. Tour reservations are strongly recommended. Tasting fee.

ST. SUPÉRY VINEYARDS AND WINERY ✉ 8440 St. Helena Highway, Rutherford ☎ 707-963-4507, 800-942-0809 📠 707-963-4526 🖥 www.stsupery.com, divinecab@stsupery.com Continuing along Route 29 you'll drive through the tiny town of Rutherford, passing a patchwork of planted fields. St. Supéry features a first-rate gallery with numerous exhibits on Napa Valley winemaking. Three-dimensional displays include a replica of an actual grapevine growing out of deep soil, smell-a-vision (a contraption that enables you to smell eight of the aromatic components of wine), and topographical maps that show why the valley is good for grapes. Guided tours available; call ahead. An outdoor tasting area and a restored Victorian add spice to the winery tour. Tasting fee.

RUBICON ESTATE WINERY ✉ 1991 St. Helena Highway, Rutherford ☎ 707-968-1100, 800-782-4266 📠 707-963-9084 🖥 www.rubiconestate.com, info@rubiconestate.com One of the prettiest wineries in Rutherford is this winery, where movie great Francis Ford Coppola and his wife Eleanor have been making wine since 1975. In 1995 they purchased the adjacent Inglenook Château and vineyard, unifying the original 1879 estate of winemaker Gustave Niebaum. The ivy-draped château houses the Centennial Museum, where the history of winemaking at the estate is chronicled. Specialties here include rubicon, cabernet franc, merlot, and zinfandel. Steep admission includes wine tasting.

CAYMUS VINEYARDS ✉ 8700 Conn Creek Road, Rutherford ☎ 707-963-4204 (general information), 707-967-3010 (reservations) 📠 707-963-5958 🖥 www.caymus.com This unpretentious winery run by Chuck Wagner was established by his parents, who were Napa winemakers in the early 1900s. Caymus focuses exclusively on its delicious cabernet sauvignon. Open by appointment only.

MUMM NAPA VALLEY ✉ 8445 Silverado Trail, Rutherford ☎ 707-967-7700, 800-686-6272 📠 707-967-7796 🖥 www.mummnapa.com, mumm_info@mummnapa.com A winery with an old French name, the Mumm estate is a good place to see *methode champenoise* production via daily tours. Located on an oak-shaded hillside, the pitched-roof winery looks like a redwood barn.

In the tasting room you can sample flutes of sparkling wine. Don't miss the permanent exhibit of Ansel Adams photographs. Tasting fee.

ST. HELENA This falsefront town is the capital of the Wine Country. Surrounded by vineyards, the old farm town still retains much of its early charm.

IOOF BUILDING ✉*1352 Main Street, St. Helena* In Victorian-style downtown St. Helena, this brick-and-stone building looms several stories above the pavement, as it has for a century.

RITCHIE BLOCK ✉*1331 Main Street, St. Helena* The cynosure of St. Helena is this block, a stone structure with brick-and-wood facade built in 1892. Featuring more frills and swirls than a wedding cake, it is a study in ornate architecture.

ROBERT LOUIS STEVENSON SILVERADO MUSEUM

✉*1490 Library Lane, St. Helena* ☎*707-963-3757* 📠*707-963-0917* 🖱*www. silveradomuseum.org* This museum houses a collection of artifacts from Robert Louis Stevenson's life and his sojourn in the Napa Valley. Having visited Monterey and San Francisco, the Scottish author arrived in Calistoga in 1880 while en route to Hawaii and seeking a salubrious environment in which to escape his lifelong illnesses. Among the memorabilia at the museum are manuscripts, art, letters, photographs, and first editions, as well as personal effects left behind by the globe-girdling Victorian. Closed Monday and Tuesday.

BERINGER VINEYARDS ✉*2000 Main Street, St. Helena* ☎*707-967-4412* 📠*707-963-8129* 🖱*www.beringer.com* Beringer, which was established in 1876, occupies a huge, landscaped parcel of land on the north side of St. Helena. While there is much to be said for visiting boutique producers, only a winery as large and historic as Beringer can offer visitors so many different experiences. Its crowning glory is the 1884 Rhine House, a Queen Anne–style mansion embellished with spires, turrets, gables,

---

Cruisin' through the Country

WEST CRUISE ✉*2301 5th Avenue, Suite 401, Seattle, WA 98121* ☎*888-851-8133* 📠*206-441-4757* 🖱*www.cruisewest.com, experience@cruisewest.com* If you're in San Francisco and are planning to tour the Wine Country, the most unusual—and likely the most luxurious—way to do so is by boat. Catch the West Cruise at San Francisco's China Basin for three- or four-night excursions up the Sacramento River to Sonoma, Napa Valley, and Old Town Sacramento. In addition to soaking up views of the Bay and riverfront towns from the decks of these 100-passenger ships, you'll get to enjoy gourmet meals served in the dining room; and an on-board wine expert will impart knowledge about winemaking. So rest up in your comfortable stateroom before heading out to visit those wineries and historic sites.

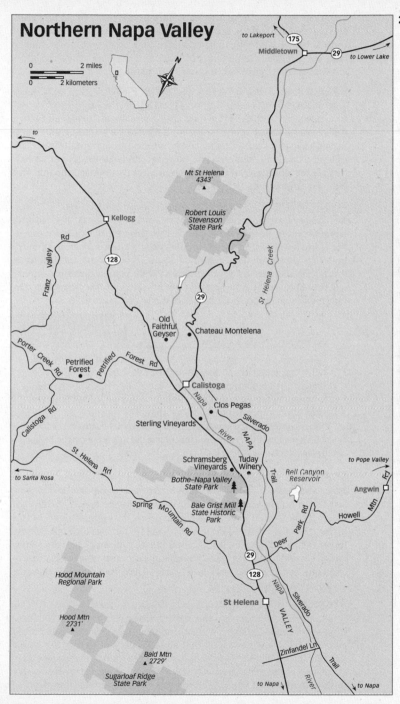

Northern Napa Valley

0   2 miles

0   2 kilometers

to Lakeport

Middletown

175

29

to Lower Lake

to

Mt St Helena
4343'

Robert Louis
Stevenson
State Park

Kellogg

Franz Valley Rd

128

29

St Helena Creek

Old
Faithful
Geyser

Chateau Montelena

Porter Creek Rd

Petrified
Forest

Petrified Forest Rd

Calistoga

Napa

Clos Pegas

Silverado

NAPA

Calistoga Rd

Sterling Vineyards

River

to Santa Rosa

St Helena Rd

Schramsberg
Vineyards

Tuday
Winery

Bell Canyon
Reservoir

to Pope Valley

Bothe–Napa Valley
State Park

Trail

Angwin

Spring Mountain Rd

Bale Grist Mill
State Historic
Park

Deer Park Rd

Howell Mtn

Hood Mountain
Regional Park

29

128

St Helena

Silverado

Hood Mtn
2731'

NAPA VALLEY

Bald Mtn
2729'

Zinfandel Ln

Trail

Sugarloaf Ridge
State Park

to Napa

River

to Napa

and a mansard roof. The interior is illuminated through stained glass and paneled in hand-carved hardwoods. Also of interest are 1000 feet of tunnels handcut into the neighboring hillside by 19th-century Chinese laborers. The adjacent historic bottling room has been converted into a gift shop/tasting room. Fee for tours and tastings.

BALE GRIST MILL STATE HISTORIC PARK ⊠Route 29, St. Helena ✆707-942-4575 ✇707-942-9560 North of St. Helena, this state park is a picturesque stop. Sitting beside a tumbling stream, an 1846 waterwheel mill creates a classic scene. It was built for a Mexican land grantee and served as an early gathering place for farmers throughout the area. The mill is now partially restored and there are guided tours. There's a visitors center plus a pair of raw wood buildings that housed the mill and granary. Admission.

TUDAL WINERY ⊠1015 Big Tree Road, St. Helena ✆707-963-3947 ✇707-968-9691 ⌕www.tudalwinery.com, info@tudalwinery.com Not far past the old mill stream, a side road leads from Route 29 to this winery. Touted as one of the world's smallest wineries, it consists of a cluster of contemporary buildings surrounded by luxurious grape arbors. Tours and tasting at this family affair are by appointment. A walk around the entire winery will probably take a grand total of ten minutes, after which the owner may regale you for hours with tales of the Wine Country.

LITTO HUBCAP RANCH

⊠6654 Pope Valley Road, Pope Valley It's easy to find this unusual sight. Just take Howell Mountain Road east from the Silverado Trail in St. Helena to the hamlet of Pope Valley. Head north three miles until you see at least a thousand points of light. Those are Litto Damonte's hubcaps, more than 5000 strong, adorning houses, barns, fences, and pastures. Just to make sure you know who's responsible, Damonte has plastered his name on the barn in—what else—hubcaps.

SCHRAMSBERG VINEYARDS ⊠Schramsberg Road, Calistoga ✆707-942-4558, 800-877-3623 ✇707-942-5943 ⌕www.schramsberg.com, info1@schramsberg.com When Robert Louis Stevenson visited here, he tasted 18 different wines. Today, you'll have to settle for a tour (by appointment) of this historic facility. The road up to Schramsberg burrows through a dense forest before arriving at the original owner's home. The winery has added several buildings since Stevenson's day and now specializes in sparkling wine, but the old tunnels and cellars remain. Tasting available only on the tour.

STERLING VINEYARDS ⊠1111 Dunaweal Lane, Calistoga ✆800-726-6136 ✇707-942-3467 ⌕www.sterlingvineyards.com, svinfo@svclub.com In the 19th century, roads were unpaved and no modern conveyances transported guests to hillside wineries. All that has changed at Sterling. Set atop a knoll near the head of Napa Valley, this Greek monastery–style winery is reached via an aerial tramway (fee). The gondolas carry visitors to a multitiered brilliant white building that commands sentinel views of the surrounding valley. Once atop this lofty retreat, a self-guided tour leads through various winemaking facilities to an elegant tasting room where guests are served five different varietals. It also has 18th-century church bells that add an exotic element to this unusual winery. Tour and tasting fee.

CALISTOGA Back on terra firma, you'll arrive in this quaint town. Founded in 1859, this well-known health spa village owes its origin and name to Sam Brannan. Brannan, of course, is the shrewd Mormon journalist and entrepreneur who first alerted San Francisco to the gold discovery. A decade later he saw liquid gold in Napa Valley's mineral springs and geysers. Determined to create a California version of New York's famous Saratoga spa, he named the region Calistoga. Indeed, its hot springs and underwater reservoirs were perfectly suited to a health resort. Today, Brannan's idea is carried on by numerous spas and health resorts. After imbibing at vineyards throughout the valley, visitors arrive in Calistoga to luxuriate in the region's mineral waters. I highly recommend that you sign up for "the works" at one of the local spas. You'll be submerged in a mud bath, led into a whirlpool bath, then a steam room, wrapped head to toe in a blanket, and finally given a massage. By the end of the treatment, your mind will reside somewhere in the ozone and your body will be completely loose.

DR. WILKINSON'S SPA AND RESORT ✉ *1507 Lincoln Avenue, Calistoga* ☎ *707-942-4102* ✆ *707-942-4412* ☞ *www.drwilkinson.com* If you are in search of an Old-World style mud bath with real peat and volcanic ash, head over to this family-owned spa. One of the oldest hot springs resorts in Calistoga, Dr. Wilkinson's provide a variety of massage styles without the pretense you might get at more expensive resorts. Guests enjoy two outdoor mineral pools and an indoor hot whirlpool. Here's a tip: If you're going to stay here and you'd like more luxurious accommodations, ask to stay in their Victorian house, located on-site, or their hideaway cottages off the Calistoga strip.

OLD FAITHFUL GEYSER ✉ *1299 Tubbs Lane, Calistoga* ☎ *707-942-6463* ✆ *707-942-6898* ☞ *www.oldfaithfulgeyser.com, geyser@oldfaithfulgeyser.com* More evidence of Calistoga's infernal geology issues forth from this geyser, a subterranean stream heated to 350° that blows skyward approximately every 30 minutes, reaching 60 to 100 feet high. This geothermal gusher, a hokey but interesting tourist attraction, is caused when hot magma heats water deep within the earth and intense pressures force it violently to the surface. Admission.

PETRIFIED FOREST ✉ *4100 Petrified Forest Road, Calistoga* ☎ *707-942-6667* ✆ *707-942-0815* ☞ *www.petrifiedforest.org, manager@petrifiedforest.org* About 3.5 million years ago, a volcano near Mount St. Helena exploded. Evidently, eruptions from this firepit leveled an entire redwood grove, which transformed over the ages into a petrified forest. Located six miles from Calistoga, this eerie spot contains a succession of fallen giants. Redwoods measuring over 100 feet long and eight feet in diameter lie along the forest floors, perfectly preserved in stone. Unfortunately, the place has the makings of a tourist trap. Admission.

SHARPSTEEN MUSEUM ✉*1311 Washington Street, Calistoga* ✆*707-942-5911* ☎*707-942-6325* ⌗*www.sharpsteen-museum.org, museum@napanet.net* A worthwhile stop is this museum and the adjacent **Sam Brannan Cottage**. Dedicated to the town's original settlers, the museum displays tools from a blacksmith's shop and an early California kitchen. Sam Brannan's cottage is furnished in period fashion with Victorian furniture and a glorious old piano. The highlight of the entire display, however, is an elaborate diorama portraying Brannan's health resort in miniature. Representing Calistoga circa 1865, it contains everything from railway station to racetrack, hotel to distillery.

CLOS PEGASE ✉*1060 Dunaweal Lane, Calistoga* ✆*707-942-4981, 800-366-8583* ☎*707-942-4993* ⌗*www.clospegase.com, cp@clospegase.com* The tasting room here is a post-modern affair designed by architect Michael Graves that features Honduran mahogany flourishes and antique glass decorations. There's a sculpture garden and fine works of art shown throughout the premises. A glass wall exposes the upright tank room where vintners make cabernet sauvignon, merlot, and chardonnay. Tasting fee.

CHATEAU MONTELENA ✉*1429 Tubbs Lane, Calistoga* ✆*707-942-5105* ☎*707-942-4221* ⌗*www.montelena.com, reservations@montelena* It's worth going a little off course to find this charming winery, where the attractions include a lake surrounded by classic Chinese landscaping. Established in the 1880s, the castle-like winery became the seventh-largest in the Napa Valley by 1896. Its main claim to fame, however, came at the legendary Paris Tasting of 1976, when its 1973 chardonnay was one of the top whites in the contest that pitted California's best against France's finest. Current releases of chardonnay, cabernet sauvignon and zinfandel are available in the tasting room. Tasting fee.

MOUNT ST. HELENA If you go north on the Silverado Trail after arriving in Calistoga, the road trades the warm, level terrain of the valley for the cool, rugged landscape of the mountains. It climbs and winds through thick coniferous forests and past bald rockfaces. In touring Napa, you've undoubtedly noticed the stately mountain that stands sentinel at the north end of the valley. Mount St. Helena, named by 19th-century Russian explorers for their empress, rises 4343 feet, dominating the skyline.

LODGING

LA BELLE EPOQUE _____

$$$$ 7 UNITS ✉*1386 Calistoga Avenue, Napa* ✆*707-257-2161, 800-238-8070* ⌗*www.labelleepoque.com, roxann@labelleepoque.com* This colorful Queen Anne–style number, built in 1893 by noted architect Luther M. Turton, houses five spacious rooms and two suites named for wine varietals. Antiques such as an Eastlake queen bed, silk oriental carpets, and a Belgian armoire distinguish the accommodations, several of which have canopied beds and/or stained-glass windows. Many rooms boast whirlpool

tubs and fireplaces, and all feature free wi-fi. The breakfasts are so elaborate that a menu for tomorrow's meal is displayed each afternoon. Tastings are held in the wine cellar each evening. The inn, which is near downtown shops and restaurants, also has two luxury suites in a Victorian across the street.

OLD WORLD INN

$$$$ 9 ROOMS   ✉1301 Jefferson Street, Napa   ✆707-257-0112, 800-966-6624 📠707-257-0118 ⌨www.oldworldinn.com, innkeeper@oldworldinn.com

This inn is at its most glorious in spring and summer, when wisteria and jasmine and then roses and other shrubs are at their peak of flowering. Rooms are decorated in cool colors such as mint green or blue and yellow; the ninth room is in a detached cottage on the far side with an indoor hot tub. A full breakfast is included, as is early evening wine and cheese, and chocolate desserts at night. Two-night minimum with a Friday or Saturday stay.

CHURCHILL MANOR

$$–$$$ 10 ROOMS   ✉485 Brown Street, Napa   ✆707-253-7733, 800-799-7733 📠707-253-8836 ⌨www.churchillmanor.com, be@churchillmanor.com

Reasonably priced bed and breakfasts are nearly nonexistent in the Wine Country, with one exception—Churchill Manor. Located on an acre of landscaped, flower-filled grounds just south of downtown Napa, the manor, built in 1889, is now a ten-room inn. The rooms are furnished with European antiques, and exquisite 100-year-old redwood columns front the main staircase. The innkeepers serve a full breakfast in the mosaic mable-floored sunroom, and on nice mornings you can take it out on the veranda, which surrounds three sides of the home. In the afternoon, cookies and lemonade are served, and in the evenings, there is wine and cheese. Tandem bikes are available to ride and a sitting room with games and puzzles offers space to relax.

WHITE HOUSE INN & SPA

$$$ 17 ROOMS   ✉443 Brown Street, Napa   ✆707-254-9301 ⌨www.napawhitehouseinn.com

Located in old town Napa, this former mansion has been refurbished with sleek moderne design and contemporary furniture, a nice contrast to the high ceilings and architectural details of the past. Rooms are spacious, with sitting areas and large windows that provide lots of light. Some have fireplaces and all have luxury linens, private baths, flat screen TVs, and free wi-fi. The in-house chef prepares an ample breakfast buffet and tasty snacks for the nightly wine reception.

MAISON FLEURIE

$$$ 13 ROOMS ✉6529 Yount Street, Yountville ☎707-944-2056, 800-788-0369
📠707-944-9342 🖉www.maisonfleurienapa.com 🖉fleurie@foursisters.com

A lodging place since 1873, this stone building is still a fashionable country inn. There are seven rooms in the old ivy-covered structure and six others in two adjacent buildings, each room crowded with antiques. Quilts and teddy bears adorn the beds, while chandeliers and brass lamps illuminate the historic setting; all have private baths and many have fireplaces and spa tubs. As a contemporary touch, there are a swimming pool, a hot tub, and bikes available for guest use. Breakfast is buffet style, and afternoon wine and tea are served daily.

VINTAGE INN NAPA VALLEY

$$$$ 80 ROOMS ✉6541 Washington Street, Yountville ☎707-944-1112,
800-351-1133 📠707-944-1617 🖉www.vintageinn.com

This inn in Yountville features rose gardens and trickling fountains surrounding smart-looking, two-story villas with brick facades and wood shingles on the roof. The rooms are like mini-suites, adorned with fireplaces and shuttered windows, marble wet bars and whirlpool baths—all in all, some of the most desirable rooms in the valley. The champagne breakfast buffet is quite extensive, and complimentary bottles of wine (upon arrival), afternoon tea, coffee, and cookies are served. A hot tub, a large pool, and tennis courts are also found here, and Yountville's exclusive shops and eateries are but a short stroll.

AUBERGE DU SOLEIL

$$$$ 13 UNITS ✉180 Rutherford Hill Road, Rutherford ☎707-963-1211,
800-348-5406 📠707-963-8764 🖉www.aubergedusoleil.com,
info@aubergedusoleil.com

Perched on a hillside studded with olive trees, this property includes French Mediterranean–style cottages named after French winegrowing regions that are decorated in a breezy California/Southwest style. Bare Mexican tile floors, louvered doors, fireplaces, and private terraces are a refreshing change from the cluttered feel of older hotels in the valley. Thirteen cottages stagger down the hill, all but two of them containing four rooms. There's also a deluxe spa that includes a heated private pool.

RANCHO CAYMUS INN

$$$$ 26 ROOMS ✉1140 Rutherford Road, Rutherford ☎707-963-1777,
800-845-1777 📠707-963-5387 🖉www.ranchocaymus.com, info@ranchocaymus.com

Crafted from white oak, this Spanish Colonial inn is a romantic retreat with stained-glass windows, a colonnade, a courtyard, and gardens. There is a total of 26 rooms; in the split-level rooms you'll find queen-sized carved walnut beds and private balconies; some feature charming adobe beehive fireplaces. Five master suites have king-sized beds and jacuzzi tubs.

HOTEL ST. HELENA

$$–$$$$ 18 ROOMS ✉1309 Main Street, St. Helena ☎707-963-4388, 888-478-4355
📠707-963-5402 🖉www.hotelsthelena.net

In the center of town, this hotel is a traditional falsefront building dating to 1881. It features 18 guest rooms, all but four of which have private baths (the four share two European-style bathrooms down the hall).

Many rooms include such decorative flourishes as caneback chairs, brass beds, antique armoires, marbletop vanities, and bent-willow headboards. Each is painted in warm pastel colors and plushly carpeted. Guests share an indoor reading room and sitting room with fireplace, plus other facilities like the hotel's wine bar. Continental breakfast is included.

THE INK HOUSE BED & BREAKFAST _____

$$–$$$ 7 ROOMS   ✉1575 St. Helena Highway, St. Helena
📞707-963-3890, 866-963-3890 📠707-968-0739 ✐www.inkhouse.com,
inkhousebb@aol.com

This gracious Victorian, topped with a fanciful cupola affording 360-degree views of the Napa Valley, is a pleasant and serene place to stay. The 1884 house is encircled by a wide veranda with white wicker chairs and offers seven antique-filled guest rooms, five with private bath. In addition to a full gourmet breakfast, wine and appetizers are served in the afternoon and early evening. There's a game room with an antique pool table; mountain bikes are available for guests.

MEADOWOOD

$$$$ 85 ROOMS   ✉900 Meadowood Lane, St. Helena 📞707-963-3646,
800-458-8080 📠707-963-3532 ✐www.meadowood.com, info@meadowood.com

Secluded at the end of a tree-shaded country road, this lavish hotel is comprised of 85 accommodations, a top-tier restaurant, a nine-hole golf course, two croquet lawns, two pools, tennis courts, a fitness center, a spa, and hiking trails. Guests may choose to stay in cozy cottages or in the Croquet Lodge; either way, they'll have comfortable furnishings and serene views of the grounds.

CALISTOGA INN & BREWERY

$–$$ 18 ROOMS   ✉1250 Lincoln Avenue, Calistoga 📞707-942-4101
📠707-942-4914 ✐www.calistogainn.com, info@calistogainn.com

This 18-room hostelry sits atop a restaurant and pub that serve their own Napa Valley Brewing Company beer. The European-style accommodations are small but tidy, carpeted wall-to-wall, and plainly decorated. The furniture is simple and baths are shared, but each room does have its own sink. These reasonably priced rooms include a continental breakfast.

MOUNT VIEW HOTEL

$$$–$$$$ 32 UNITS   ✉1457 Lincoln Avenue, Calistoga 📞707-942-6877,
800-816-6877 📠707-942-6904 ✐www.mountviewhotel.com,
info@mountviewhotel.com

Built in 1914, this hotel has the aura and feel of a classic small-town hotel. It's a comfortable affair with dining room and lounge downstairs and Victorian flourishes throughout. The spacious lobby features a fireplace and contemporary artwork. Guest rooms are nicely decorated with a mix of Victorian and modern touches. In addition, there are three cottages, each with a private hot tub. Guests are free to use the hotel's pool and spa. Continental breakfast is delivered to your room.

INDIAN SPRINGS RESORT

$$$$ 24 ROOMS ✉ *1712 Lincoln Avenue, Calistoga* ☎ *707-942-4913*
📠 *707-942-4919* 🖥 *www.indianspringscalistoga.com*

Located on the same grounds as the town's original resort, this lodging offers bungalow-style cottages (actually duplexes) that feature warm California colors, plankwood floors, plush beds, and kitchenettes. There is also a renovated lodge featuring 24 rooms, some with private patios. Overnight guests are welcome to use the spa's Olympic-sized mineral pool (heated between 90° and 102°), tennis courts, shuffleboard, croquet, hammocks, and bocce ball court. Indian Springs also features volcano ash mud baths, steam baths, massages, and facials, making it an excellent resting place for the health-minded.

SOLAGE CALISTOGA

$$$$ 89 UNITS ✉ *755 Silverado Trail, Calistoga* ☎ *707-226-0800, 866-942-*
📠 *707-226-0809* 🖥 *www.solagecalistoga.com, reservations@solagecalistoga.com*

Solage offers romantic, contemporary luxury amid Wine Country scenery. It's resort-chic with sleek furnishings like solid print Italian linens, dark hardwoods, and glass double doors leading to semiprivate patios. With a nod to the environment, the on-site spa and outdoor pool are geothermal, and solar panels generate indoor heat. Complimentary bikes are available for guests. If you have a four-legged friend with you, Solage will provide a plush dog bed and all-natural treats.

MEADOWLARK COUNTRY HOUSE

$$$$ 7 ROOMS ✉ *601 Petrified Forest Road, Calistoga* ☎ *707-942-5651,*
800-942-5651 📠 *707-942-5023* 🖥 *www.meadowlarkinn.com,*
info@meadowlarkinn.com

This beautiful 19th-century home with 20 acres of wooded grounds features an enclosed mineral pool (clothing optional), hot tub, and sauna. Each of the seven rooms has contemporary or English country antique furniture, comforters, and a view of forest or meadow. There is also a luxurious poolside guesthouse with a whirlpool tub, kitchen, and private deck. A generous breakfast is served each morning and you will find the serene veranda a great place to catch up on your reading. Gay-friendly. Not recommended for families with young children.

FOOTHILL HOUSE BED & BREAKFAST

$$$-$$$$ 4 ROOMS ✉ *3037 Foothill Boulevard, Calistoga* ☎ *707-942-6933,*
800-942-6933 📠 *707-942-5692* 🖥 *www.foothillhouse.com, info@foothillhouse.com*

If you like your lodgings intimate, check into this aptly named bed and breakfast in the foothills on the north side of town. Accommodations include four rooms that have been carved out of an early-20th-century farmhouse and feature garden views from private patios. All have private entrances, small refrigerators, and woodburning stoves or fireplaces. Most rooms have whirlpool tubs. A full breakfast is included and can be enjoyed in the sunroom, the terrace, or in the comfort of your room.

HARBIN HOT SPRINGS

$$-$$$ 13 UNITS ✉ *18424 Harbin Springs Road, Middletown* ☎ *707-987-2477,*
800-622-2477 📠 *707-987-0616* 🖥 *www.harbin.org, reception@harbin.org*

These hot springs are the perfect place to hike in the hills, eat vegetarian, and bask naked (optional, of course) in a steaming pool full of New

Agers. Although it may not be for everyone, it's a popular place, as witnessed by the weekend crowds. Natural springs feed the warm, hot, and cold mineral-water pools of this New Age retreat center. There is also a sauna and separate steam room. You may stay in a dormitory, a retreat room, an ultra-deluxe-priced cabin, or camp out, and enjoy quiet conversation with the other guests. There's a restaurant serving breakfast and dinner, or you can bring your own vegetarian food to cook in a communal kitchen. Also on the vast property are a health food store, bookstore, temple, and garden. Massage and Watsu available.

DINING

CELADON

$$–$$$$ THAI/INDONESIAN   ✉️*500 Main Street, Suite G, Napa*   📞*707-254-9690*
📠*707-254-9692*   🖱️*www.celadonnapa.com*

Downtown Napa isn't the easiest place in the valley to reach, but this restaurant, located in the historic Hatt Market, makes the trip well worth the effort. Seafood is tops on Greg Cole's menu of "global comfort food," as are many Thai- and Indonesian-influenced dishes, a number available in small servings ideal for mixing and matching. A great selection of wines by the glass rounds out the attractions in this high-ceilinged spot, painted a lovely shade of celadon-green and decorated with old French advertising posters. Reservations are recommended.

DOWNTOWN JOE'S AMERICAN GRILL AND BREWHOUSE

$–$$ AMERICAN   ✉️*902 Main Street, Napa*   📞*707-258-2337*
🖱️*www.downtownjoes.com*

Joe's continues a city tradition that goes back to his grandmother, Grace, who opened Ruffino's Restaurant in 1944. Unpretentious and friendly (even to dogs), it's a local favorite, where the dozen TVs are tuned to sports, live music is offered five nights a week, and the food is reliably satisfying. Highlights include Zio Mario's cioppino—a seafood stew that's been a family recipe for more than 90 years, an eight-inch tall cheeseburger with fries and a salad, fish and chips, seared ahi sandwich, and low-carb selections, along with several hand-crafted ales.

THE GENERAL CAFÉ

$–$$ ASIAN/AMERICAN   ✉️*540 Main Street, Napa*   📞*707-259-0762*
📠*707-258-8793*   🖱️*www.napageneralstore.com, jim@napageneralstore.com*

Tucked into the Napa General Store, this café is an ultracasual spot for small plates of pan-Asian food and traditional American fare. Black and blue ahi sashimi, mahimahi spring rolls, and spicy tiger prawns are featured alongside bacon cheeseburgers, deli sandwiches, and pizza. Lunch only.

UBUNTU

$$$ CALIFORNIA CUISINE/VEGETARIAN   ✉️*1140 Main Street, Napa*
📞*707-251-5656*   🖱️*www.ubuntunapa.com*

This stylish restaurant and yoga studio is the latest darling of the California cuisine movement. Chef Jeremy Fox, formerly of Manresa in San Francisco, coaxes the most sensuous flavors and textures from Ubuntu's locally grown organic produce. While some might cringe at the thought of a meal without meat, the dishes here are completely delicious and filling—even to the most committed carnivore. Try the creamy cauliflower purée served with crostini or roasted Brussels sprouts with house-made apple barbecue sauce. For dessert, the popular cheesecake in a jar will blow your mind. If you feel a little too full after your meal, check out the schedule for the Ubuntu yoga studio, located upstairs.

BISTRO DON GIOVANNI

$$$–$$$$ MEDITERRANEAN   ✉4110 Howard Lane, Napa   ☎707-224-3300
🖷707-224-3395   🖉www.bistrodongiovanni.com, pasta@bistrodongiovanni.com

Blessed with one of the loveliest settings in the Wine Country, this bistro evokes Tuscany for some. The fare is decidedly Mediterranean—delectables like focaccia, grilled meats, housemade pastas, seared fish fillets, and pizza. In warm weather, linger on the shaded porch; when it turns cool, warm yourself in front of the large, open fireplace.

E'TOILE AT DOMAINE CHANDON

$$$$ SEAFOOD/STEAK   ✉1 California Drive, Yountville   ☎707-204-7529,
800-736-2892   🖷707-944-1123   🖉www.chandon.com, customerservice@chandon.com

E'toile has maintained itself as a dependable choice for outstanding Wine Country cooking. This is a grown-up restaurant, where seasonal entrées arrive as complete dinners such as pan-roasted Alaskan halibut with artichokes and white corn, olive oil–poached cardinal snapper with cranberry beans, beef tenderloin with English pea coulis, and seared duck breast with white peaches. Prices are steep, but in keeping with modern surroundings, sophisticated food, and ultra-smooth service. There's an outdoor patio for more casual lunch dining. Closed Tuesday and Wednesday.

BOUCHON

$$–$$$ FRENCH   ✉6534 Washington Street, Yountville   ☎707-944-8037
🖷707-944-2769   🖉www.bouchonbistro.com

This glamorous and glorified bistro has lots of sparkle in the decor and on the menu. Entrées lean to marinated leg of lamb, sole meuniere, onion soup, roast chicken, sautéed seasonal vegetables, fruit tarts, and soufflés. Yet its most unusual feature may be its late-night dining—as late as 12:30 a.m. as a courtesy to night owls such as workers from area restaurants.

FRENCH LAUNDRY

$$$$ AMERICAN/FRENCH   ✉6640 Washington Street, Yountville   ☎707-944-2380
🖉www.frenchlaundry.com

Set in a two-story 1890s building, this legendary restaurant features contemporary American cuisine with a classic French influence. Fare may include sirloin of young rabbit, veal sweetbreads with lobster ravioli, pan-seared duck breast, and monkfish fricassée. The award-winning food is excellent, the wine list extensive, and the prix-fixe menu changes nightly. Owner Thomas Keller is considered one of the top chefs in the world due to his innovative and ever-changing creations. It's very popular; reservations must be made two months in advance. No lunch Monday through Thursday.

MUSTARDS GRILL

$$–$$$ AMERICAN   ✉7399 St. Helena Highway, Yountville   ☎707-944-2424
📠707-944-0828   🖱www.mustardsgrill.com

An ultramodern brass-rail restaurant, Mustards is complete with track lighting and contemporary wallhangings. There's an attractive wooden bar and paneled dining room, but the important features are the wood-burning grill and oven. Here the award-winning chefs prepare rabbit, grilled pork chops, smoked duck, and hangar steak. This eatery specializes in fresh grilled fish like sea bass, ahi tuna, and salmon.

AUBERGE DU SOLEIL

$$$$ CALIFORNIA CUISINE   ✉180 Rutherford Hill Road, Rutherford   ☎707-963-1211,
800-348-5406   📠707-963-8764   🖱www.aubergedusoleil.com

This hillside dining room overlooking the vineyards has been revered as a destination restaurant for more than two decades. Modern in design, this gourmet hideaway is a curving stucco structure with a wood-shingle roof. The circular lounge is capped by a skylight-cum-cupola and the dining area is an exposed-beam affair with an open fireplace. Al fresco dining is available on a deck that has views of the surrounding vineyards and gardens. Even architecture such as this pales in comparison with the menu, which changes seasonally. Lunch might begin with the foie gras terrine and *torchon* with a cherry compote and candied pistachios, then might move on to wild King salmon with corn pudding, zucchini, and toasted almond broth. Dinner entrées include quail with smoked ham, lobster risotto, or herb-basted lamb loin. There's an extensive wine list.

TRA VIGNE

$$$–$$$$ ITALIAN   ✉1050 Charter Oak Avenue, St. Helena
☎707-963-4444   🖱www.travignerestaurant.com, travigne@napanet.net

This restaurant can claim the most dramatic interior in the Wine Country. Soaring ceilings, unusual lighting, and festive displays of peppers and garlic make the setting as exciting as the menu. The theme here is regional Italian: chewy breads, bold pizzas, hearty salads, rabbit, chicken, and grilled seafood dishes, and a first-rate wine list that rotates weekly and features more than 200 choices, including local and Italian varietals. There's also unusual antipasti such as melon with shaved prosciutto and parmesan gelato.

PIZZERIA TRA VIGNE

$–$$ ITALIAN   ✉1016 Main Street, St. Helena   ☎707-967-9999
🖱www.travignerestaurant.com/pizzeria

This pizzeria is a terrific place to bring the family. It's kid-friendly as well as budget-friendly, with thin-crust Neopolitan-style pizzas, pasta, salads, and other easy-to-eat fare in an upbeat setting. Inexpensive wines are sold by the glass.

TERRA

$$$–$$$$ PAN-ASIAN/FRENCH   ✉ *1345 Railroad Avenue, St. Helena*
📞 *707-963-8931*   🖊 *www.terrarestaurant.com*

St. Helena's leading restaurant for the past decade, this eatery serves an exotic blend of French, California, and Asian cuisine. You might be treated to appetizers such as fried rock shrimp, foie gras tortellini, and *tataki* of tuna on the seasonally changing menu. Entrées feature unique preparations of seafood, beef, and squab. By way of ambience there are stone walls, terra-cotta features, and a wooden trim that lends an Asian overtone to this comfortable, Tuscan farmhouse–style dining room. Dinner only. Closed Tuesday.

THE WINE SPECTATOR
GREYSTONE RESTAURANT

$$$–$$$$ CALIFORNIA CUISINE   ✉ *2555 Route 29, St. Helena*
📞 *707-967-1010*   📠 *707-967-2375*   🖊 *www.ciachef.edu, wsgr@culinary.edu*

This cavernous restaurant—just call it Greystone—is located in an 1889 National Historic Landmark in north St. Helena. The complex includes a top-notch cooking school, but not to worry—the chefs are for real. The inspired, seasonal menu ranges from crabmeat mariposa to a carmelized red snapper paella. It's great fun to match dishes with different wines. Flanked by century-old stone walls, the restaurant is large enough to have cooking, baking, and grilling stations in full view, which provide a terrific distraction for fidgety kids. Closed two weeks in January.

BOSKOS

$$ ITALIAN   ✉ *1364 Lincoln Avenue, Calistoga*   📞 *707-942-9088*   📠 *707-942-9661*
🖊 *www.boskos.com*

The setting here is informal and the menu Italian. Day or night, you'll find fresh pasta dishes like bay scallops, mushrooms, and pesto cream over fettuccine, linguine with bay shrimp and asiago cream sauce, and spaghetti with meatballs. Or you can have a meatball, sausage, or Italian ham sandwich on their homemade focaccia. The wine list is extensive and the meals they offer are good and filling.

BRANNAN'S GRILL

$$$ AMERICAN   ✉ *1374 Lincoln Avenue, Calistoga*   📞 *707-942-2233*
🖊 *www.brannansgrill.com, info@brannansgrill.com*

With an award-winning wine list featuring small-production vintages by the glass and a menu of naturally farmed and humanely harvested seafood, poultry, and meats, this is a good choice for creative cuisine without the attitude. Choose the outside patio in warm weather or slip into a cozy wood-wrapped booth by the fieldstone fireplace on cool evenings. Appetizers include filet mignon tartare with aged balsamic, roasted peppers, egg yolk, and Black Sea salt, fresh oysters, and potato-herb gnocci. A signature dish is the Mediterranean shellfish stew, with crab, shrimp, scallops, and mussels in a red pepper aïoli broth.

$$–$$$ INTERNATIONAL   ✉1226 South Washington Street, Calistoga
📞707-942-4712 📠707-942-4741 ✍www.wappobar.com, wappo@napanet.net

Wappo dishes up dazzling food that spans the globe with Asian noodles with shiitake mushrooms, Thai shrimp curry, Ecuadorian braised pork, osso bucco, *chiles rellenos* with walnut pomegranate sauce, and Turkish mezze (that hard-to-find treasure that in this case includes an herb-and-cheese-stuffed eggplant sandwich, white bean salad, carrots, golden beets, shaved fennel, cracked green olives, hummus, yogurt sauce, and, believe it or not, more). Everything tastes better on the sun-dappled patio. Closed Tuesday.

SHOPPING

V MARKETPLACE ✉6525 Washington Street, Yountville 📞707-944-2451 📠707-944-2453 ✍www.vmarketplace.com, laurel@vmarketplace.com Almost by definition, shopping malls are unattractive. This marketplace is a rare exception to a modern rule. Housed in the historic Groezinger Winery, a massive brick building smothered in ivy, it contains several dozen fashionable shops. Wooden corridors, designed with an eye to antiquity, lead along two shopping levels. There are clothing stores galore, and several restaurants, as well as specialty shops offering collectibles and fine art.

GROEZINGER
WINE COMPANY

✉6484 Washington Street, Suite E, Yountville 📞707-944-2331, 800-356-3970 Across the street from V Marketplace, this shop features hard-to-find premium wines from California, Oregon, and Washington. The owners are vaults of knowledge and they will just as soon talk wine with you as pick up a banjo and jam. Closed Sunday, except by appointment.

OAKVILLE GROCERY ✉7856 St. Helena Highway, Oakville 📞707-944-8802, 800-973-6324 📠707-944-1844 ✍www.oakvillegrocery.com, napavalley@oakville grocery.com This grocery is a prime place to stock up for a picnic. This falsefront country store, which is on the National Register of Historic Places, sells wines and cheeses, fresh fruits, specialty sandwiches, and baked goods, as well as a host of gourmet and artisanal items. In addition, there's a coffee and espresso bar for a pick-me-up.

For people living in northern Napa Valley, going on a shopping spree means heading for either St. Helena or Calistoga. Both towns combine local businesses with general merchandise stores. Main Street, St. Helena, is a falsefront boulevard lined with a hardware store, stationery shop, newspaper office, and grocery. Of interest to visitors are the boutiques, bookstore, jewelers, and wine shop.

ART ON MAIN ✉1359 Main Street, St. Helena 📞707-963-3350 Stop here to find original works by primarily Northern California artists as well as sculptures, bronze work, and limited-edition etchings and serigraphs.

NAPA VALLEY OLIVE OIL MANUFACTURING CO. ✉*835 Charter Oak Avenue, St. Helena* ☏*707-963-4173* ✆*707-963-4173* This store is more than a gourmet shopping spot: It's a sightseeing adventure as well. Housed in a former oil manufacturing plant, it contains the original press and crusher. Wagon tracks run along the cement floor, and posters of old Italia cover the walls. Today, this tiny factory sells its own olive oil, along with delicious cheeses, salami, pasta, and condiments.

ST. HELENA MARKETPLACE ✉*3111 North St. Helena Highway, St. Helena* ☏*707-963-7282* ✍*www.sthelenamarketplace.com* Up the road in St. Helena you will find a shopping mall with premium outlet clothing stores and an assortment of other shops.

Up in Calistoga, shops of general interest are mixed with those catering to local concerns. Along Lincoln Avenue, near the barber shop and town cobbler, are antique stores, clothing shops, and a bookstore.

CALISTOGA DEPOT ✉*1458 Lincoln Avenue, Calistoga* ✍*calistogawinestop. net* This historic depot has been converted to a mall. Within this former railway station are assorted stores, including the **Calistoga Wine Stop** (707-942-5556, 800-648-4521), housed in an antique railroad car.

HURD BEESWAX CANDLES ✉*1255 Lincoln Avenue, Calistoga* ☏*707-942-7410, 800-977-7211* ✆*707-942-7415* ✍*www.hurdbeeswaxcandles.com* Since 1954, Hurd has elevated candlemaking to the level of art. The waxworks resemble statues rather than tapers; fashioned by hand, they are formed into myriad intricate shapes (some are also handpainted). There's also a demonstration beehive and winetasting on the premises.

NIGHTLIFE

The Napa Valley has yet to learn the fine art of evening entertainment. Perhaps by nightfall visitors are already tipsy from tasting wine all day. In any case, there's not a lot to do; what scene there is centers around the wineries and the hotel and restaurant bars.

RING'S LOUNGE ✉*1075 California Boulevard, Napa* ☏*707-253-9540* This upscale lounge at the Embassy Suites Napa Valley is a pleasant spot for quiet conversation.

DOWNTOWN JOE'S AMERICAN GRILL AND BREWHOUSE ✉*902 Main Street, Napa* ☏*707-258-2337* ✍*www.downtownjoes.com* Joe's features live music four nights a week, Tuesday through Saturday. Sports fans will appreciate the large satellite TVs, and all guests can enjoy their local brews and American menu.

PARKS

BOTHE–NAPA VALLEY STATE PARK
✉*On Route 29 about five miles north of St. Helena* ☏*707-924-4575* ✆*707-942-9560* ✍*www.napanet.net/~bothe, bothe@silverado.cal-parks.ca.gov*
🏃 🏊 Rising from the valley floor to about 2000 feet elevation, this outstanding park is fully developed along one side, wild and rugged on the other. Until 1960, the park was a private resort called Paradise Park,

owned by Reinhold Bothe. For those seeking to escape the Wine Country crowds, there are ten miles of hiking trails leading along sloping hillsides through redwood groves. More than 100 bird species inhabit the area, including hawks, quail, and six types of woodpecker. There are also coyotes, bobcats, deer, and fox here. The park's developed area features spacious picnic groves, campgrounds, a swimming pool open in the summer, restrooms, and showers (fee). Day-use fee, $4 per vehicle.

▲ There are 40 tent/RV sites and ten walk-in sites; $16 per night per site. Reservations: 800-444-7275.

ROBERT LOUIS STEVENSON STATE PARK

✉ Route 29, about eight miles north of Calistoga ☎ 707-942-4575
🖥 707-942-9560

🏃 Perched on the side of Mount St. Helena is this scenic state park. The Scottish writer and his wife honeymooned in these parts, camping in the hills and enjoying the recuperative air. Here he wrote sections of *The Silverado Squatter* and studied settings later used in *Treasure Island*. Today the Memorial Trail leads through this undeveloped park one mile to an old mine and a monument commemorating the spot where Stevenson spent his honeymoon. Then a fire road continues four more miles to the top of Mount St. Helena. From this impressive aerie the entire Napa Valley lies before you, with views stretching from the Sierra Nevada to San Francisco.

SONOMA VALLEY

Touring the wineries of Sonoma provides a perfect excuse not only for tasting California's fine varietals, but also for exploring the state's beautiful interior. Cutting a long, luxurious swath between the ocean and the distant Sierra, this piedmont country divides its terrain among vineyards, ranches, and dense forest.

SIGHTS

PETALUMA   On the way to the Sonoma Valley via Route 101, you may want to make a slight detour to this community. Once the state's largest egg producer, Petaluma has such a quintessential small-town flavor that it was chosen as the location for filming the coming-of-age classic *American Graffiti* and several other movies about middle America. The city's downtown district is listed on the National Register of Historic Places.

SONOMA   The logical place to begin a tour of the valley is in this Spanish-style town of 9200 people. And the spot to begin this tour-within-a-tour is the **Plaza**, bounded by 1st Street East, 1st Street West, Spain, and Napa streets. The center of Sonoma for more than 150 years, this shady park is an excellent picnic place. The largest plaza in the state, it contains a playground, an open-air theater, a duck pond, and a rose garden.

JACK LONDON STATE HISTORIC PARK

PAGE 273

Former stomping grounds of renowned outdoor writer—now a scenic area and spectacular museum

YETI

PAGE 278

Tiny, bright Indian eatery with colorful paper lanterns serving amazing naan and delicious *pakoras*

SANTÉ RESTAURANT

PAGE 277

Butter-poached lobster, black truffle pasta, and white asparagus salad—elegant and delectable California cuisine in a sleek hotel

GOLTERMANN GARDENS & COUNTRY INN

PAGE 275

Genuinely warm innkeepers at a Craftsman-style farmhouse set in a meadow of country perennials and wisteria

SONOMA VALLEY VISITORS BUREAU ✉*453 1st Street East, Sonoma* ☎*707-996-1090, 866-966-1090* 📠*707-996-9212* 🖥*www.sonomavalley.com, info@sonomavalley.com* There are maps and brochures of the area here. They also provide recommendations for local restaurants and lodgings.

SONOMA COUNTY TOURISM BUREAU ✉*420 Aviation Boulevard, Suite 106, Santa Rosa* ☎*707-522-5800, 800-576-6662* 📠*707-539-7252* 🖥*www.sonomacounty.com, info@sonomacounty.com* For information on Sonoma County, contact this bureau. Closed weekends.

SONOMA MISSION ✉*1st Street East and East Spain Street, Sonoma* ☎*707-938-9560* Spanish adobes, stone buildings, and falsefront stores surround the historic square. Mission San Francisco Solano, or Sonoma Mission, stands at the southeast corner. Founded in 1823, this was the last and most northerly of the 21 California missions. With its stark white facade, the low-slung adobe houses a small museum. There are dozens of paintings portraying other California missions; the chapel has also been painted brilliant colors and adorned with carved wood statues.

SONOMA BARRACKS ✉*1st Street East and East Spain Street, Sonoma* ☎*707-939-9420* Across the street from Sonoma Mission are these historic barracks, which were built with Indian labor during the 1830s to house the troops of Mexico's General Mariano Guadalupe Vallejo. A two-story adobe with sweeping balconies, it's now a museum devoted to early California history.

TOSCANO HOTEL ✉*20 East Spain Street, Sonoma* ☎*707-938-1519* Next door to the Sonoma Barracks, this hotel is furnished in 19th-century fashion with wood-burning stoves, brocade armchairs, and two gambling tables. Dating to 1851, this wood-frame structure was built as a general store but later was used to house Italian workers. Free tours are available Saturday through Monday.

LA CASA GRANDE ✉*West Spain Street between 1st Street East and 1st Street West, Sonoma* The only remains of General Vallejo's 1840 home is this servant's house with its sagging adobe facade.

SONOMA STATE HISTORIC PARK ✉*Sonoma* ☎*707-938-1519* ✆*707-938-1406* ✍*www.napanet.net/~sshpa* La Casa Grande, the Sonoma Mission, and other historic buildings encircling the plaza, are all part of this historic park. They can be toured for a single admission price.

DEPOT PARK MUSEUM ✉*270 1st Street West, Sonoma* ☎*707-938-1762* ✆*707-938-1762* ✍*www.vom.com/depot, depot@vom.com* Just north of the plaza stands this museum, where the displays commemorate railway history and the Bear Flag uprising when Americans revolted against General Vallejo in 1846. You can also see Sonoma as it was at the turn of the 20th century. Closed Monday and Tuesday.

LACHRYMA MONTIS ✉*At the north end of 3rd Street West, Sonoma* ☎*707-938-9559* ✆*707-938-9559* About one-half mile northeast of the town square, you'll find another antique structure. This was the home General Vallejo completed in 1852, after the United States had assumed control of California. Vallejo successfully made the change to American rule, becoming a state senator, a mayor, a vintner and an author of a five-volume history of early California. Something was lost in the transition, however, and this yellow Gothic Revival house with pretty green shutters fails to evoke images of a Mexican general.

Nevertheless, it's well worth touring. Every room is appointed in 19th-century style, as though Vallejo were expected to arrive any moment. The old pendulum clock still swings and the dinner table is set. Out back, the cookhouse contains personal effects of the Chinese cook. Part of Sonoma State Historic Park, it also features a mini-museum and picnic area. Admission.

BUENA VISTA CARNEROS WINERY ✉*18000 Old Winery Road, Sonoma* ☎*707-938-1266, 800-926-1266* ✆*707-939-0916* ✍*www.buenavistacarneros.com, tastingroom@buenavistacarneros.com* While Vallejo was settling into his American-style home, Count Agoston Haraszthy, a Hungarian aristocrat, moved to Sonoma and founded this winery in 1857. Popularly known as the "father of the California wine industry," he eventually imported 100,000 vines from Europe. Today, the actual winemaking occurs at the vineyard estate in the Carneros area, but you can taste sample vintages in the old stone winery and take a self-guided tour around the grounds. Now a historical monument, the winery also has picnic tables for the crowds that visit. Tasting fee.

SONOMA TRAINTOWN ✉*20264 Broadway, Sonoma* ☎*707-938-3912* ✍*www.traintown.com* If you're traveling with children, here's a trick that might make your trip a little easier: Kids who tire of all the dusty history

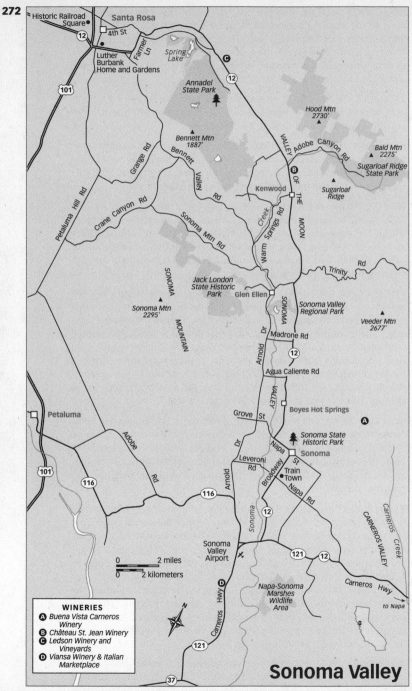

Historic Railroad Square

Santa Rosa

4th St

Luther Burbank Home and Gardens

Spring Lake

Annadel State Park

Hood Mtn 2730'

Bennett Mtn 1887'

Adobe Canyon Rd

Bald Mtn 2275'

Sugarloaf Ridge State Park

Grange Rd

Bennett Valley Rd

Crane Canyon Rd

Petaluma Hill Rd

Kenwood

VALLEY OF THE MOON

Sugarloaf Ridge

Sonoma Mtn Rd

Warm Springs Rd

Creek

Trinity Rd

SONOMA

Jack London State Historic Park

Glen Ellen

Sonoma Mtn 2295'

MOUNTAIN

SONOMA

Sonoma Valley Regional Park

Veeder Mtn 2677'

Madrone Rd

Arnold Dr

Agua Caliente Rd

VALLEY

Grove St

Boyes Hot Springs

Petaluma

Adobe Rd

Sonoma State Historic Park

Napa St

Sonoma

Train Town

Leveroni Rd

Broadway

Arnold Dr

Napa Rd

Sonoma

Sonoma Valley Airport

Carneros Hwy

CARNEROS VALLEY

Carneros Creek

Napa-Sonoma Marshes Wildlife Area

Carneros Hwy

to Napa

0   2 miles
0   2 kilometers

N

WINERIES
Ⓐ *Buena Vista Carneros Winery*
Ⓑ *Château St. Jean Winery*
Ⓒ *Ledson Winery and Vineyards*
Ⓓ *Viansa Winery & Italian Marketplace*

Sonoma Valley

can be bribed with a visit to TrainTown. Miniature steam engines chug around a ten-acre park, passing over trestles and bridges, through two tunnels, and arriving at a scale-model Western town. Also visit the petting zoo, antique carousel, vintage Ferris Wheel, and cabooses. Closed Monday through Thursday during winter. Admission.

GLORIA FERRER CHAMPAGNE CAVES ⊠*23555 Carneros Highway (Route 121), Sonoma* ✆*707-996-7256* ✎*707-601-0307* ✐*www.gloriaferrer.com, mission models@yahoo.com* One of Spain's premier winemaking families began winning awards with their very first vintages from here. The Ferrers carved caves (typical in their native country) out of the hillside for storing premium sparkling wines. The wines are available for purchase or for tasting (at a nominal fee) either indoors or on a wide patio with lovely views of the surrounding countryside. Guided tours are offered three times daily (fee) and include wine tastings. Tasting fee.

VIANSA WINERY & ITALIAN MARKETPLACE ⊠*25200 Arnold Drive (Route 121), Sonoma* ✆*707-935-4700, 800-995-4740* ✎*707-996-4632* ✐*www. viansa.com, tuscan@viansa.com* This Tuscan-style sanctuary sits atop a small hill with a commanding view north to much of the valley. Viansa produces a variety of wines made from well-known Italian grapes such as sangiovese and pinot grigio, lesser known varieties such as arneis, aleatico and primitivo, as well as several California varietals, including cabernet sauvignon, cabernet franc, chardonnay, and merlot. The marketplace is the size of a dining hall and is stocked with all kinds of California-Italian comestibles and condiments (many set out for sampling) as well as wines available for tasting. Touring and tasting fee.

GLEN ELLEN   If the Napa Valley is Stevenson country, Sonoma Valley belongs to Jack London. A world adventurer and self-described "sailor on horseback," London was not the type to settle down. Illegitimate son of an astrologer, he was in turn an oyster pirate, socialist, gold prospector, and internationally renowned author. But settle he did, a few miles northwest of Sonoma in the town of Glen Ellen.

Calling this area "the valley of the moon," London and his wife Charmian acquired a 1400-acre ranch and began construction of the Wolf House, an extraordinary mansion with 26 rooms and nine fireplaces. In 1913, when nearly completed, London's dream house mysteriously burned, probably the result of a spontaneous combustion caused by oil-soaked rags left inside the house. Three years later, after producing 51 books and becoming America's first millionaire author, he died of kidney failure at age 40.

JACK LONDON STATE HISTORIC PARK ⊠*2400 London Ranch Road, Glen Ellen* ✆*707-938-5216* ✎*707-938-4827* ✐*www.jacklondonpark.com* At this state park, you can tour what London called his Beauty Ranch. Docents can guide you throughout the grounds, detailing London's life or you can wander on your own. At the east end of the park, the House of Happy Walls, occupied by his wife Charmian after her husband's death, is a museum containing first editions and original manuscripts.

Now London's study is adorned with the original artwork for his stories, and many keepsakes from his world adventures are here. A half-mile path leads past the author's grave, simply marked by a stone, to the west side of the park and the tragic ruins of the Wolf House, a monument to a lost dream. Nearby, the cottage where London lived and wrote from 1911 until his death in 1916 still stands (only open on weekends). Admission.

California Winetasting

The Greeks, who believed that the gods drank nectar, had it all wrong. Anyone who has explored the vineyards of California knows that wine, not sweet ambrosia, is the drink of the gods. It's also obvious that deciding on the finest wine is as simple as determining the "true" religion. This is not to say that a tour of the Wine Country is a pilgrimage, though it can have a lifelong effect on the drinking habits of mere mortals.

In order to find that ultimate wine, keep in mind a few principles. The best season to visit the vineyards is during the harvest in late September and early October. The scent of freshly fermenting wine fills the air and the vineyards are colored brilliant red and gold. Winter is the rainy season and a fallow period. It's also less crowded than the rest of the year and allows opportunities for more relaxed and personalized tours, particularly at small wineries. The growing season begins in March, when buds appear on previously bare, gnarled vines. By early summer, the buds are miniature grape clusters that ripen during the torrid months of midsummer.

Once the grapes are picked in autumn, the activity shifts from the vineyard to the winery. The berries are crushed; white wines are then filtered or clarified and fermented in temperature-controlled tanks. Red wines are fermented, together with their skins and seeds, at higher temperatures (70° to 90°). Later the wines are racked, or stored, in wooden barrels to add flavor, and then bottled. Requiring two or three years to reach their potential, reds mature more slowly than whites.

There are two basic types of California wine: *varietals*, made primarily from a particular type of grape such as cabernet sauvignon or zinfandel, and lower-quality *generics*, wines generally blended from several different grapes and often named for a European wine region like Burgundy.

The true test, of course, is in the tasting. Unfortunately, winetasting also becomes a test of the taster's wine knowledge. Folks unversed in the liturgy and lexicon of wine sampling can feel mighty uncomfortable. Adding to their consternation are the region's self-styled wine connoisseurs.

Not to worry. It really only requires a sensitive nose, tongue, and eye to master the art of tasting. Just remember a few simple criteria. The look or appearance is important: wine should be clear and brilliant, not cloudy, in the glass. Consider the smell or *nose* of the vintage: this includes *aroma*, or scent of the grapes themselves, and *bouquet*, the smell from fermentation and aging. Of final importance is the taste. Let the wine wash around your mouth a moment and you'll be able to tell if it's sweet or dry, light-bodied (watery) or full-bodied, rough or mellow.

LEDSON WINERY & VINEYARDS ✉7335 Route 12, Kenwood 📞707-537-3810 📠707-538-3003 💻www.ledson.com, info@ledson.com Gray and almost brooding in the shadow of the Mayacamas Mountains, this winery was originally intended as a residence. Plans changed midway, however, and the sprawling Normandy-style château now houses Ledson Winery. Steve Ledson claims he used more than two million bricks in constructing what locals refer to as "the castle." The winery is best known for its estate-grown merlot and zinfandel and its Russian River chardonnay. The well-stocked marketplace sells glassware, collectibles, fresh sandwiches, and some 100 cheeses, which may be enjoyed at oak-shaded picnic tables. Tasting fee.

CHÂTEAU ST. JEAN WINERY ✉8555 Sonoma Highway, Kenwood 📞707-833-4134 📠707-833-4200 💻www.chateaustjean.com This strikingly beautiful winery sits beside a colonnaded mansion built during the 1920s. The winery has added several similar buildings. Wine, not extraordinary vistas, is the business here, and the winery has won several awards for its chardonnays and cabernet sauvignons. You can taste these and other varietals, explore the gardens, and set out a picnic at one of the redwood-shaded tables.

LODGING

GOLTERMANN GARDENS & COUNTRY INN

$$ 6 UNITS ✉1000 Skillman Lane, Petaluma 📞707-762-1761 💻www.goltermangardens.com/banb, agolt@comcast.net

Immerse yourself in a bit of Petaluma history and stay at this inn, a 1913 Craftsman-style farmhouse on six acres of country gardens. All rooms have king- or queen-sized beds with fine linens and private baths. A fully furnished cottage is also available. The buildings sit three miles outside of town in Leghorn Valley, where 100 farms once raised more than one million leghorns. Today only one chicken farm remains.

FAIRMONT SONOMA MISSION INN & SPA

$$$$ 228 ROOMS ✉100 Boyes Boulevard, Boyes Hot Springs 📞707-938-9000, 866-540-4499 📠707-938-4250 💻www.fairmont.com/sonoma, smi.reservations@fairmont.com

This inn lives up to its excellent reputation. The pale pink stucco facade on this gracious Mission Revival–style hotel harks back to the days when American Indians enjoyed the natural mineral waters of this area. The accommodations are appointed in earthy tones, with wooden shutters and ceiling fans adding a hint of the plantation to the place; some rooms have fireplaces. A full-service spa, two restaurants, two swimming pools, and an 18-hole golf course nearby add up to one of the best retreats in the Wine Country.

SWISS HOTEL

$$–$$$ 5 ROOMS ✉18 West Spain Street, Sonoma 📞707-938-2884 📠707-938-3298 💻www.swisshotelsonoma.com

This hotel, in an adobe building circa 1840, is a State Historical Landmark and hostelry that features rooms with private baths and refrigerators. One has a four-poster bed and pine furniture; others have a variety of antique and modern pieces. The hotel rests on the town's central plaza and contains a bar and restaurant downstairs.

SONOMA HOTEL

$$–$$$ 16 ROOMS   ✉110 West Spain Street, Sonoma   ☎707-996-2996,
800-468-6016   ☎707-996-7014   ✐www.sonomahotel.com, sonomahotel@aol.com

Sonoma's plaza features this historic hostelry, which dates to around 1879 and is decorated entirely with French Country furnishings. The lobby has a stone fireplace and the adjoining restaurant features a handcarved bar. Combining history with comfort, this vintage hotel is worth a visit. Continental breakfast is included, as is complimentary wine service.

EL DORADO HOTEL

$$$ 27 ROOMS   ✉405 1st Street West, Sonoma   ☎707-996-3220,
800-289-3031   ☎707-996-3148   ✐www.eldoradosonoma.com/el_dorado_hotel,
info@eldoradosonoma.com

Located on the square, this small hotel is a gem. Originally an adobe built in 1843, this refurbished stucco establishment offers small- to moderate-size rooms, as well as a full-service bar and restaurant. Appointed with four poster beds, down comforters, Mexican tile floors, and California/Spanish style–furniture, each has a private balcony. There's a heated swimming pool and complimentary morning coffee.

DINING

MCNEARS SALOON & DINING HOUSE

$–$$ AMERICAN   ✉23 Petaluma Boulevard, Petaluma   ☎707-765-2121
✐www.mcnears.com

Join the local crowd for a burger or some barbecued ribs and a brew at McNears. Old pictures, mirrors, signs, and even tennis rackets decorate the brick walls of this popular hangout in a historic building that dates to 1886. Along with traditional favorites, McNears offers entrées such as giant stuffed potatoes, tequila lime chicken, and pan-fried apricot salmon filet. Brunch available on weekends.

CAFÉ LA HAYE

$$–$$$ AMERICAN   ✉140 East Napa Street, Sonoma   ☎707-935-5994
✐www.cafelahaye.com, saul@cafelahaye.com

Don't let the simplicity of the menu fool you. The half-dozen or so main courses here are the result of a sophisticated chef who manages to create delectable dishes in a postage stamp–size kitchen. Chicken, beef, pasta, and daily fish and risotto selections get the deluxe treatment in this split-level storefront restaurant just off the Sonoma Plaza. Dinner only. Closed Sunday and Monday.

DELLA SANTINA

$$–$$$ ITALIAN   ✉133 East Napa Street, Sonoma   ☎707-935-0576   ☎707-935-7046
✐www.dellasantinas.com, ndellasantina@mindspring.com

If you dine here on a mild day, head to a table on the brick-lined back patio. This Italian favorite is the only place in town to order petrale sole (occasionally available). There are other daily fish and veal specials as well as classic northern Italian dishes: lasagna, tortellini, cannelloni, and so on; rabbit, duck, turkey, pork, and chicken rotate on the rotisserie. Della Santina's is especially known for its gnocchi; here a bowl of the little dumplings runs less than $14. The wine list, of course, incorporates Italian as well as California vintages.

THE RED GRAPE

$–$$ ITALIAN   ✉529 1st Street West, Sonoma   ☎707-996-4103
✐www.theredgrape.com, theredgrape@vom.com

This restaurant is best known for thin-crusted, New Haven–style pizzas, but it's also a favorite for its outstanding fresh pastas, served with either marinara, pesto cream, white wine and butter sauce, or olive oil. The high-ceilinged room features glass walls on three sides and an open kitchen; there's also patio seating.

LA CASA

$–$$ MEXICAN   ✉121 East Spain Street, Sonoma   ☎707-996-3406, 800-766-2832
📠707-938-0285   ✐www.lacasarestaurant.com, lacasafood@aol.com

Located just off the plaza, this colorful restaurant offers a full menu from south of the border. There are margaritas and other tequila drinks at the bar, plus a bill of fare ranging from fish tacos to *chile verde* to chimichangas. Enjoy your meal on their outdoor patio.

SONOMA CHEESE FACTORY

$ DELI   ✉2 West Spain Street, Sonoma   ☎707-996-1931, 800-535-2855
✐www.sonomajack.com, retailstore@sonomajack.com

This is the spot to stop on the way to the picnic grounds. In addition to a grand assortment of cheeses, it sells wines, sandwiches, and gourmet specialty foods. There's also a small, outdoor patio for diners.

THE GIRL & THE FIG

$$–$$$ FRENCH   ✉110 West Spain Street, Sonoma   ☎707-938-3634
📠707-938-2064   ✐www.thegirlandthefig.com, info@thegirlandthefig.com

This intimate eatery occupies most of the ground floor of the historic Sonoma Hotel, which has seen half a dozen restaurants come and go in as many years. The muted color scheme of ivory and moss green takes a back seat to the seasonal "country food with a French passion" such as steak and *frites*, roasted dijon chicken, regional seafood with local produce, and the bistro's signature fig salad with arugula, toasted pecans, and local goat cheese. The large brick patio out back is the best place to sample the brasserie menu between lunch and dinner.

idden

SANTÉ RESTAURANT

$$$$ CALIFORNIA CUISINE   ✉Fairmont Sonoma Mission Inn & Spa,
100 Boyes Boulevard, Boyes Hot Springs   ☎707-938-9000   📠707-938-4250

This restaurant presents innovative but unpretentious fare in an elegant dining room of dark, highly polished woods. Prepared with local produce, entrées may include celery root agnolotti with chestnut and black truffle cream, butter-poached Maine lobster with glazed winter vegetables, and roasted rib-eye steak with grilled hen of the woods mushrooms. Resortwear for men and women is required. Dinner and Sunday brunch are served.

BIG 3 DINER

$$–$$$ AMERICAN ✉️*Fairmont Sonoma Mission Inn & Spa, 100 Boyes Boulevard, Boyes Hot Springs* 📞*707-938-9000* 🖨️*707-938-4250*

This bistro-style eatery serves tasty, healthful American fare with a northern Italian influence. You'll find pastas, pizzas, and salads on the lunch and dinner menu, while breakfast features freshly baked goods, pancakes, and egg dishes.

YETI _____ **h**idden

$$–$$$ INDIAN ✉️*14301 Arnold Drive, Glen Ellen* 📞*707-996-9930*

Bright paper lanterns, starched white tablecloths, and an exposed kitchen provide a cozy and exotic ambiance at this deliciously fragrant Indian restaurant in Jack London Village. Watch chef-owner Narayan Somname prepare mixed vegetable *pakoras* with potato, cauliflower, spinach, and eggplant; lamb kabobs with onion and green peppers; chicken tandoori; or a variety of curries. Don't miss their naan—with garlic, butter, or honey—which has earned a reputation as some of the best around.

CAFE CITTI

$–$$ ITALIAN ✉️*9049 Sonoma Highway, Kenwood* 📞*707-833-2690* 🖨️*707-539-6255*

The strong aroma of garlic envelopes this family-owned and -operated Italian trattoria set amongst the vineyards of Kenwood. The place is extremely popular with Sonoma Valley locals, who love its casualness and friendly atmosphere. Flowers and candles on the tables add a bit of romance, while summertime allows patio dining. The Italian chef serves up a variety of pastas; rotisserie chicken stuffed with fresh herbs, garlic, and rosemary; and weekend specials. He also makes his own mozzarella cheese and biscotti.

SHOPPING

Petaluma is a great place to shop, with some 25 antique stores and a factory outlet mall.

SUMMER COTTAGE ✉️*153 Kentucky Street, Petaluma* 📞*707-776-2873* 🌐*www.summercottageantiques.com* More than 25 dealers display their antiques, vintage clothing, furniture, and country collectibles at this charming shop.

PETALUMA VILLAGE PREMIUM OUTLETS ✉️*2200 Petaluma Boulevard North, Petaluma* 📞*707-778-9300* 🌐*www.premiumoutlets.com* Bargain seekers will discover lots of good deals at this outlet mall. Coach, Brooks Brothers, Jones New York, and Saks Fifth Avenue all have outlets here, as do Gap, Puma, Vans, and Tommy Hilfiger.

The old Spanish town of Sonoma contains a central plaza around which you'll find its best shops. Stroll the square (bounded by 1st Street East, 1st Street West, Spain, and Napa streets) and encounter gourmet stores, boutiques, a designer lingerie company, antique stores, poster galleries, and a brass shop. Many of these establishments are housed in historic Spanish adobes.

ARTS GUILD OF SONOMA ✉*140 East Napa Street, Sonoma* ☎*707-996-3115* This art guild contains works by local artisans. Here are paintings, ceramics, sculptures, and mixed-media art. Closed Tuesday through Thursday.

EL PASEO DE SONOMA ✉*414 1st Street East, Sonoma* This mall contains more off-street shops.

THE SIGN OF THE BEAR ✉*435 1st Street West, Sonoma* ☎*707-996-3722* This shop celebrates the pleasures of life in the Wine Country. There's a huge selection of gadgets, cookware, cookbooks, bakeware, ceramics, linens, and tools for the wine enthusiast.

ROBIN'S NEST ✉*116 East Napa Street, Sonoma* ☎*707-996-4169* Robin's specializes in discount kitchen accessories and gifts such as Italian bowls and platters. Closed Tuesday.

BACCHUS GLASS ✉*21707 8th Street East, Sonoma* ☎*707-939-9416* ✐*www.bacchusglass.com, sales@bacchusglass.com* The chandeliers, lamps, shades, and wall sconces created at this shop are available for sale in the adjacent gallery. Closed weekends.

THE OLIVE PRESS *24724 Arnold Drive, Glen Ellen* ☎*707-939-8900, 800-965-4839* 🖷*707-939-8999* ✐*www.theolivepress.com, oliveoil@theolivespress.com* This store is a unique source of local olive oils, each of them pressed on the premises. In addition to the oils, some of which are always available for sampling, you'll find tabletop merchandise such as plates, platters, and bowls.

NIGHTLIFE

MCNEARS MYSTIC THEATRE ✉*21 Petaluma Boulevard, Petaluma* ☎*707-765-2121* ✐*www.mystictheatre.com, info@mystictheatre.com* Locally and nationally known bands, playing a variety of music to satisfy nearly every taste, pack in the crowds at Mystic Theatre Thursday through Saturday nights. Cover.

LITTLE SWITZERLAND ✉*19080 Riverside Drive, El Verano* ☎*707-938-9990* ✐*www.lilswiss.com, info@lilswiss.com* Northeast of Sonoma's city center, this century-old dance hall is where you can dance the polka and waltz and pretend you're in another time and place. There's live music on certain nights. Join your partner on the main dancefloor inside or in the beer garden outside. Dinners of steak, pasta, and chicken are also served. Reservations recommended; call ahead for details. Cover.

As in the Napa area, Sonoma Valley nightlife revolves around summer events at the wineries. Check local calendars for concerts, theatrical performances, and other special programs. If that seems uninteresting, or it's not summertime, you'll have to rely on hotel and restaurant bars for entertainment.

SWISS HOTEL ✉18 West Spain Street, Sonoma ✆707-938-2884 ✉707-938-3298 With old photos adorning its walls, this historic bar is a favorite meeting place of locals and travelers alike. You can also get a pretty filling meal here.

JACK LONDON SALOON ✉Jack London Lodge, 13740 Arnold Drive, Glen Ellen ✆707-996-3100 ✉707-939-9642 ⏷www.jacklondonlodge.com Out in Jack London country, this saloon is a pretty, brick-faced bar that draws a mixture of locals and visitors. Fashionably decorated with Tiffany-style lamps and old movie posters, it's a good drinking place.

PARKS

SUGARLOAF RIDGE STATE PARK
✉Located east off Route 12 between Sonoma and Santa Rosa, the park is at 2605 Adobe Canyon Road in Kenwood ✆707-833-5712 ✉707-833-5712

🚶🚴🏇🚣 Within this 2700-acre facility lie two different ecological systems, as well as 25 miles of hiking trails from which to explore. There are chaparral-coated ridges (you can see San Francisco and the Sierra Nevada from the top of Bald Mountain), plus forests of maple, laurel, madrone, and alder. Sonoma Creek tumbles through the park; you can try for trout here. Spring brings a profusion of wildflowers, and autumn is another popular season in the park. Facilities include picnic areas and restrooms. Day-use fee, $6.

▲ There are 50 sites; $20 per site. Camping here is a reasonably priced lodging option for a visit to the Wine Country and is popular with Bay Area families. Reservations: 800-444-7275.

NORTHERN WINE COUNTRY

Sonoma's vine-rich county continues north of Santa Rosa along Route 101 to Cloverdale, but the secret to touring this region resides along country lanes paralleling the highway. At the center of this area is Healdsburg, a country town centered on a plaza and dating back to 1852.

SIGHTS

SANTA ROSA The largest city in Sonoma County, this place is perhaps best known as the home of Luther Burbank, the great horticulturist who worked miracles on plant life, creating the Santa Rosa plum, Shasta daisy, spineless cactus, and hundreds of other hybrids.

LUTHER BURBANK HOME & GARDENS ✉Santa Rosa and Sonoma avenues, Santa Rosa ✆707-524-5445 ✉707-524-5827 ⏷www.lutherburbank.org, burbank home@lutherburbank.org Luther Burbank's legacy remains in full bloom here, where visitors can stroll through gardens filled with the descendants of his plant "inventions" and tour the Victorian house where he lived for 20 years. The house is open Tuesday through Sunday from April through October. Admission to tour the house.

REDWOOD EMPIRE ICE ARENA ✉*1667 West Steele Lane, Santa Rosa* ☏*707-546-7147* ✍*www.snoopyshomeice.com, info@snoopyshomeice.com* This ice rink may be the only sports facility ever created by a cartoonist. It was built by Charles Schulz of "Peanuts" fame for his children. Snoopy's Gallery and Gift Shop, also part of the facility, sells Snoopy memorabilia, books, clothing, and life-size comic strip characters. Call ahead to confirm the arena is open to the public on the day you wish to visit. There are limited public skating hours.

HISTORIC RAILROAD SQUARE ✉*4th and Wilson streets, located west of Route 101 and east of the railroad tracks, Santa Rosa* On the western edge of downtown, this square once was a busy commercial and transport center. Today its buildings, some of which survived the great 1906 earthquake that destroyed much of the city center, contain antique and specialty shops and restaurants.

CALIFORNIA WELCOME CENTER ✉*9 4th Street, Santa Rosa* ☏*707-577-8674, 800-404-7673* ☏*707-571-5949* ✍*www.visitsantarosa.com* The old Santa Rosa Depot has been restored and turned into this visitors center, including a **Rail Room Gallery**. The gallery in the former ticket office has a small display of memorabilia from the depot's past, including photographs and a model train the kids can operate. The center also provides basic visitor information about the region's wineries and attractions, and offers free wine-tasting coupons.

SONOMA COUNTY MUSEUM ✉*425 7th Street, Santa Rosa* ☏*707-579-1500* ☏*707-579-4849* ✍*www.sonomacountymuseum.org, info@sonomacountymuseum.org* Housed in a former 1909 post office, this museum provides a historical and cultural perspective on the region with changing exhibits, some of them designed especially for kids. Closed Monday. Admission.

FISHER VINEYARDS ✉*6200 St. Helena Road, Santa Rosa* ☏*707-539-7511* ☏*707-539-3601* ✍*www.fishervineyards.com, info@fishervineyards.com* In the mountains outside Santa Rosa, hidden along country lanes, lies this vineyard. Tucked into a fold in the hills and surrounded by redwood forest, this picturesque winery is a family-style operation. The main building, a lofty board-and-batten structure, was built with wood cut and milled on the site. It follows a contemporary California design and overlooks the surrounding vineyards. Planted primarily with cabernet sauvignon, chardonnay, and merlot vines, the winery produces a small but delicious quantity of wine each season. Visiting by appointment only; steep fee. Closed weekends.

Just north of Santa Rosa, around the tiny towns of **Forestville** and **Windsor**, are numerous family wineries.

IRON HORSE VINEYARDS

✉*9786 Ross Station Road, Sebastopol* ☏*707-887-1507* ☏*707-887-1337* ✍*www.ironhorsevineyards.com, info@ironhorsevineyards.com* Without doubt, one of the prettiest vineyard settings in all California belongs to this one, which is most famous for several types of sparkling wine. Despite a Sebastopol address, it's actually lo-

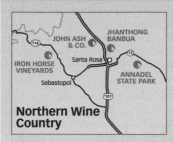

Northern Wine Country

JOHN ASH & CO.

PAGE 287

Fresh California cuisine paired with regional wines in an exquisite inn set on a lush vineyard estate

JHANTHONG BANBUA

PAGE 287

Spicy ginger lime salad, crispy stuffed prawns, and chicken curry with coconut milk—excellently prepared Thai dishes

IRON HORSE VINEYARDS

PAGE 281

Checkerboard fields of pinot noir and chardonnay grapes at a graceful, classic farm-style family winery

ANNADEL STATE PARK

PAGE 289

Wildflower-lined trails winding for 40 miles around a volcanic mountain, a lake, and a misty marsh

cated off Route 116 in Green Valley. The driveway snaking into this hidden spot is bordered with flowers, olive trees, and palm trees. Hills roll away in every direction, revealing a line of distant mountains. The winery buildings, painted barn-red, follow the classic architecture of American farms. Laid out around them in graceful checkerboard patterns are fields of pinot noir and chardonnay grapes. At harvest time these will be handpicked and then barrel-aged, for the emphasis at this elegant little winery is on personal attention. The outdoor tasting area is open seven days a week until 3:30 p.m. Tours are offered Monday through Friday at 10 a.m. only; reservations required.

SEBASTOPOL In addition to wineries, there are countless orchards around Sebastopol, another town that has become gentrified in recent years. Known as the Gold Ridge region, it is California's premier apple-producing area.

SEBASTOPOL CHAMBER OF COMMERCE ✉*265 South Main Street, Sebastopol* ☎*707-823-3032, 877-828-4748* 📠*707-823-8439* ⌨*www.sebastopol.org, info@sebastopol.org* For details on Sebastopol's local farms, contact the chamber of commerce and ask for a Sonoma County Farm Trails map. It will lead you to farms producing apples, pears, berries, cherries, peaches, and vegetables—some of which you can pick yourself. Closed weekends.

FLORENCE AVENUE

✉*Sebastopol* Sebastopol is also known for being a slightly funkier Wine Country town. While its Main Street houses standard antique shops and art galleries, visitors can also find hemp gear, goddess statuary, loose herbs, and homemade body oils. But the town's quirkiness really shines through a few streets over on Florence Avenue. This residential side street serves as an outdoor gallery. Huge sculptures fashioned out of trash, like old car parts, dot the front yards of a dozen or so homes. You might stumble across a motorcycle-riding skeleton, an Elvis statue mid hip-swing, or a giant Tarzan lifting weights. It all makes for an interesting and amusing detour.

OSMOSIS: THE ENZYME BATH SPA
✉*209 Bohemian Highway, Freestone* ☎*707-823-8231* 📠*707-874-3788* 🖱*www.osmosis.com, reservations@osmosis.com* West of Sebastopol on Route 12 in the historic town of Freestone is this five-acre spa. While hot springs soaks and mud baths are possible at countless locations, Osmosis claims to be the only place in North America offering cedar enzyme baths, composed of cedar fiber, rice bran, and more than 600 active enzymes. Tea is served in a lovely Japanese meditation garden as part of most treatments.

HEALDSBURG CHAMBER OF COMMERCE & VISITORS BUREAU
✉*217 Healdsburg Avenue, Healdsburg* ☎*707-433-6935, 800-648-9922* 📠*707-433-7562* 🖱*www.healdsburg.org, info@healdsburg.org* You can pick up maps, brochures, and other information on the region here.

DRY CREEK VALLEY
This valley encompasses a luxurious landscape of vineyards and forest. It stretches to the west of Healdsburg and is known for its plethora of family-owned wineries.

DRY CREEK VINEYARD
✉*3770 Lambert Bridge Road, Healdsburg* ☎*707-433-1000, 800-864-9463* 📠*707-433-5329* 🖱*www.drycreekvineyard.com, dcv@drycreekvineyard.com* This vineyard sits in an ivy-covered building surrounded by shade trees. There's tasting every day and the winery provides picnic tables for guests. Among the excellent wines produced are chenin blancs, fumés, cabernets, chardonnays, merlots, and zinfandels. Tasting fee.

A. RAFANELLI WINERY
✉*4685 West Dry Creek Road, Healdsburg* ☎*707-433-1385* 📠*707-433-3836* 🖱*www.arafanelliwinery.com* Along the far rim of Dry Creek Valley rises this classic family-style enterprise, now in its fourth generation. Known for producing excellent wines in limited quantities, the winery itself consists of a 100-year-old barn that connects to underground caves behind the original family home. Backdropped by forested hills, it overlooks the valley and surrounding countryside. Tasting is by appointment.

ALEXANDER VALLEY
East of Healdsburg lies Alexander Valley, which is highly regarded for its distinct viticultural characteristics. Because of its warm climate, the valley is sometimes compared with the Bordeaux area of France.

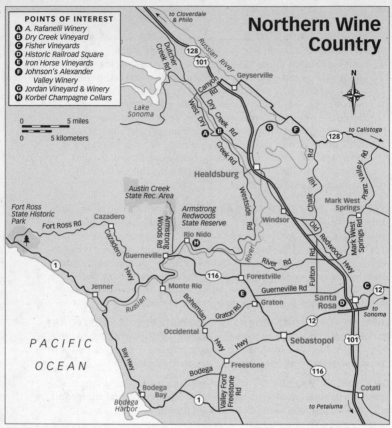

POINTS OF INTEREST
- Ⓐ *A. Rafanelli Winery*
- Ⓑ *Dry Creek Vineyard*
- Ⓒ *Fisher Vineyards*
- Ⓓ *Historic Railroad Square*
- Ⓔ *Iron Horse Vineyards*
- Ⓕ *Johnson's Alexander Valley Winery*
- Ⓖ *Jordan Vineyard & Winery*
- Ⓗ *Korbel Champagne Cellars*

Northern Wine Country

JORDAN VINEYARD & WINERY
✉1474 Alexander Valley Road, Healdsburg ☎707-431-5250, 800-654-1213 📠707-431-5259 🌐www.jordanwinery.com, info@jordanwinery.com This hilltop facility, built along the lines of a Bordeaux château, is housed in a grand building that overlooks the Alexander Valley. Tours are a real treat, providing a glimpse into a winery whose elegance matches its excellence. Tours and tastings by appointment. Closed Sunday and for one week at Christmas.

JOHNSON'S ALEXANDER VALLEY WINERY
✉8333 Route 128, Healdsburg ☎707-433-2319, 800-888-5532 📠707-433-5302 🌐www.johnsonavwines.com, sales@johnsonavwines.com A long road leads to an unpainted redwood barn housing this family-owned winery. There is a wealth of modern equipment around the place, which produces fine pinot noirs, zinfandels, and cabernets as well as buttery chardonnays and light rieslings. Tastings are offered anytime.

J. RICKARDS WINERY
✉24505 Chianti Road, Cloverdale ☎707-758-3441 📠707-857-4808 🌐www.jrwinery.com, info@winery.com This family-owned and -operated winery is nestled on the east side of Chianti Mountain. Sur-

rounded by a picturesque mountain countryside, including several ponds, the winery is a study in charm and beauty. To fully appreciate the grounds, opt for a tour of the vineyards, which boast sustainable farming practices. Complementary wine tastings are offered daily; try their blended petite sirah for an intense fruitiness characteristic of their vineyards. Closed Sunday and Monday.

ROUTE 128 Route 101 streams north past Ukiah and several more wineries. A more interesting course lies along Route 128, which leads northwest from Cloverdale through piedmont country. En route, the two-lane road meanders like an old river, bending back upon itself to reveal sloping meadows and tree-tufted glades. It's a beautiful country drive through rolling ranch land. Sheep graze the hills and an occasional farmhouse stands along the roadside, its windows blinking sunlight at solitary cars.

BOONVILLE As Route 128 rolls down into Anderson Valley, it passes Boonville, a farming community of about 2000 folks. Back in the 1880s, this town invented a kind of local pig Latin, "boontling," known only to residents. With a vocabulary of over 1000 words, it neatly reflected Anderson Valley life. A photo became a "Charlie Walker" after the Mendocino fellow who took portraits. Because of his handlebar whiskers, "Tom Bacon" lent his name to the moustache. Rail fences were "relfs," heavy storms became "trashmovers," and pastors (those heavenly sky-pilots) were "skipes." Vestiges of the old lingo remain—restaurants, for instance, still boast of their "bahl gorms," or good food. They also produce good wine in these parts, and several award-winning wineries dot the Anderson Valley.

LODGING

HOTEL LA ROSE
$$$ 28 ROOMS ✉308 Wilson Street, Santa Rosa ☎707-579-3200, 800-527-6738
707-579-3247 www.hotellarose.com, reservations@hotellarose.com

You can stay in the heart of Santa Rosa's fascinating Historic Railroad Square at this hotel, built in 1907 by the same Italian stonemasons who were responsible for the Santa Rosa depot. It has been listed on the National Register of Historic Places and is a member of Historic Hotels of America. English country style describes the decor, with floral patterns and dark wood furniture. Some guest rooms sport four-poster beds. The fourth-floor attic rooms have sloping ceilings, and some are brightened by skylights. A sundeck is available to guests, and a complimentary continental breakfast is served.

VINTNERS INN
$$$ 44 UNITS ✉4350 Barnes Road, Santa Rosa ☎707-575-7350, 800-421-2584
707-575-1426 www.vintnersinn.com, info@vintnersinn.com

Surrounded by 92 acres of vineyards, this inn has the ambience of a European estate, despite the proximity of a major highway. Its spacious and luxurious rooms and suites are housed in a cluster of two-story townhouses interspersed with courtyards, fountains, and landscaping.

HAYDON STREET INN

$$$–$$$$ 11 ROOMS ✉ *321 Haydon Street, Healdsburg*
📞*707-433-5228, 800-528-3703* 📠*707-433-6637* 🖝*www.haydon.com,*
innkeeper@haydon.com

Healdsburg, located farther north along Route 101, is a perfect
jumping-off point for visiting the many wineries in the area.
Numerous country inns dot the area, including this lovely bed
and breakfast set in a vintage 1912 Queen Anne house and
Victorian-style cottage situated near the town plaza. Each room
is beautifully appointed with antique furniture and artistic wall-
hangings. Both the private rooms and the common areas are
quite spacious. The tree-shaded lawn, comfortable living room,
and wraparound front porch are a perfect expression of Main
Street, America. Serving a full breakfast and afternoon refresh-
ments, the inn has eight rooms in the main building and three
rooms in the carriage house, all with private baths and air condi-
tioning. (Several rooms feature jacuzzi tubs and/or fireplaces.)

HOTEL HEALDSBURG

$$$$ 55 UNITS ✉*25 Matheson Street, Healdsburg* 📞*707-431-2800, 800-889-7188*
📠*707-431-0414* 🖝*www.hotelhealdsburg.com, frontoffice@hotelhealdsburg.com*

In an area dotted with B&Bs and charming little hostelries, this hotel is a
good option if you're looking for something a bit more modern. Its rooms
and suites come in a palette of lime greens and butter yellows, with wood
floors, Tibetan rugs, and sleek furnishings. Shuttered French doors lead
to balconies with views of the plaza or the countryside. All accommoda-
tions have extra-large baths, high-speed internet connections, two-line
portable phones, a mini-fridge, and luxuries like Frette bathrobes. On
site are a restaurant, a spa, a garden pool, and a café/newsstand.

MADRONA MANOR WINE COUNTRY INN

$$$–$$$$ 31 UNITS ✉*1001 Westside Road, Healdsburg* 📞*707-433-4231, 800-258-*
4003 📠*707-433-0703* 🖝*www.madronamanor.com, info@madronamanor.com*

Built in 1881 as a private summer retreat, this inn is a charming exam-
ple of Gothic Victorian architecture, complete with a balconied porch,
turrets, and gables. The best rooms are in the main house with fire-
places; they are spacious (two upstairs sport a shared veranda) and fur-
nished in serious antiques, including chaises longues and armoires.
There are an additional 12 accommodations in several outbuildings on
an eight-acre site as well as a carriage house. Guests enjoy the pool and
a breakfast buffet. The on-site restaurant whips up eclectic California
cuisine. Children under 12 are not allowed.

ISIS OASIS

$$ 16 ROOMS ✉*20889 Geyserville Avenue, Geyserville* 📞*707-857-4747,*
800-679-7387 📠*707-857-3544* 🖝*www.isisoasis.org, isis@isisoasis.org*

If you're yearning to retreat back into the '60s, check out this ten-
acre hideaway that combines bed-and-breakfast facilities with
massage, tarot readings, and past-life experiences. Set in the tiny

DINING

JOHN ASH & CO.

$$$$ CALIFORNIA CUISINE   ✉ *4330 Barnes Road, Santa Rosa*
📞 *707-527-7687, 800-421-2584* 📠 *707-527-1202* 🖥 *www.vintnersinn.com,*
johnash@vintnersinn.com

One of the first Wine Country restaurants to champion the region's natural resources, this place continues that mission long after its namesake departed the kitchen. Produce from nearby fields, fish from the sea and locally made cheeses and breads still star on the menu, along with Sausalito Springs watercress, roasted pears, Sonoma greens, fresh-picked herbs, and locally raised beef, pork, and chicken. Three large rooms, with high ceilings and plenty of windows, overlook a glass-enclosed patio that is heated in the winter and opens up when weather permits. Small plates are available in the Front Room. No lunch on Saturday.

PAMPOSH

$$–$$$ INDIAN   ✉ *52 Mission Circle, Santa Rosa* 📞 *707-538-3367*

There's no way you'd find this restaurant without good directions; it's in a modest shopping strip that gives no hint of the exotic decor and cuisine inside. To get your taste buds hopping, start your meal with samosas—thin pastry stuffed with spiced potatoes and peas—alongside refreshing housemade chutneys. Chef's specials such as chicken with mushrooms and creamy tomatoes offer a departure from otherwise traditional Indian fare.

JHANTHONG BANBUA

$$ THAI   ✉ *2400 Mendocino Avenue, Santa Rosa* 📞 *707-528-8048*

You cannot find fresher or tastier Thai food than what comes out of the kitchen here. Located in front of a motel near the Santa Rosa Junior College campus, this pretty place decorated in gold and pastels knocks itself out with service and a menu with something for everyone. Particularly fine are the pad thai and anything with shrimp. No lunch on Saturday. Closed Sunday.

ZAZU

$$$$ AMERICAN/ITALIAN   ✉ *3535 Guerneville Road, Santa Rosa* 📞 *707-523-4814*
🖥 *www.zazurestaurant.com*

The chefs here are full of clever innovations, such as pairing seared tuna with bing cherries and making the combination work. In a ramshackle building west of Santa Rosa, Zazu's weekly changing menu peddles a seasonal mix of playful American food and northern Italian fare—with a twist—split between small and big plates. Typical of the former are jingle bell peppers with housemade sausage and poppyseed–crusted soft-shell crab; of the latter, star anise–rubbed duck and grilled rack of lamb with quinoa tabbouleh. Many housemade desserts feature fresh local fruit such as strawberry rhubarb crisp with rose geranium ice cream. Closed Monday and Tuesday.

SASSAFRAS

$$–$$$ AMERICAN   ✉1229 North Dutton Avenue, Santa Rosa   ☎707-578-7600
⌨www.sassafrasrestaurant.com, info@sassafrasrestaurant.com

This restaurant specializes in all-American fare with an upscale twist. The marinated tilapia is prepared with pineapple salsa and achiote and served with cilantro rice with plantain chips. Entrées range from classic pizzas to pastas, seafood, and rib-eye steak. No lunch on weekends.

EAST-WEST CAFÉ

$–$$ MEDITERRANEAN/INTERNATIONAL   ✉128 North Main Street, Sebastopol
☎707-829-2822   📠707-539-4193   ⌨www.eastwestcafesebastopol.com,
hisamshaboon@hotmail.com

Find a taste of the Middle East along Sebastopol's Main Street at East-West Café. This cute little place serves up both Mediterranean staples like *baba ghanoush* and tabbouleh alongside fajitas, turkey pastrami melts, and Thai stir fry. It's a real mix of dishes that will please carnivores, vegetarians, and vegans alike.

HOPMONK

$$ AMERICAN   ✉230 Petaluma Avenue, Sebastopol   ☎707-829-7300
📠707-829-7300   ⌨www.hopmonk.com, hopmonk@glodownead.com

If you're craving a beer after all the winetasting, grab a table at this local brewery, which serves independent, handcrafted ales. Hearty traditional fare such as burgers, fish and chips, and bleu cheese steak pair perfectly with sides of mac and cheese or corn on the cob. They also boast original salads with fresh local produce and a late-night menu with pork adobo bites and curried samosas. An adjacent beer garden and music venue offer a festive atmosphere.

SCREAMIN' MIMI'S

$ DESSERT   ✉6902 Sebastopol Avenue, Sebastopol   ☎707-823-5903
⌨www.screamingmimisicecream.com, info@screaminmimisicecream.com

For mouth-watering, homemade ice creams and sorbets, pop into Mimi's. The shop's signature flavor, Mimi's Mud, is a sinful mixture of coffee ice cream with fudge and cookies. Many of the concoctions are seasonal and include real fruit chunks.

BOONVILLE HOTEL

$$–$$$ CALIFORNIA CUISINE   ✉Route 128, Boonville   ☎707-895-2210
📠707-895-2243   ⌨www.boonvillehotel.com

In the prime Mendocino County winegrowing region of Anderson Valley, there are a few cafés and family-style restaurants in the small towns along rural Route 128. When hunger strikes, Boonville presents the best possibilities. Particularly recommended for dinner is this outstanding restaurant with a gourmet menu. Entreés run along the lines of mussels steamed with red Thai curry, crusted Alaskan halibut, and grilled rib-eye steak. Dinner only.

SHOPPING

Winetasting is a much more popular sport in these parts than window-browsing. If intent on shopping, you'll have to skip from town to town searching out a few interesting stores. An exception to this is Santa Rosa, which has a busy downtown district and the Historic Railroad Square, with its many excellent shops.

DISGUISE THE LIMIT ✉100 4th Street, Santa Rosa 📞707-575-1477 📠707-579-4542 It's Halloween all year here, where you can find the paraphernalia to be a clown, a queen, or an alien creature. Also here are toys and a few magic tricks to put up your sleeve.

ANTIQUE ROW ✉Gravenstein Highway (Route 116) between Route 101 and Route 12, Sebastopol Antique addicts beware: Sebastopol's Antique Row may be your undoing. Two hundred dealers in a dozen locations within eight miles? Lead on.

SUMBODY ✉118 North Main Street, Sebastopol 📞707-823-2053 🖱www.sumbody.com If you're tired of the standard antique and art gallery get-ups, try this shop with its handmade skin care and bath products.

MILK & HONEY ✉123 North Main Street, Sebastopol 📞707-824-1155 You'll find female-empowering jewelry, books, and goddess statuary here.

REAL GOODS SOLAR LIVING CENTER ✉13771 South Route 101, Hopland 📞707-744-2100 📠707-744-1342 🖱www.realgoods.com Fifteen miles north of Cloverdale, this store showcases products utilizing renewable energy sources as well as items manufactured from natural fibers and alternative materials. Merchandise includes natural bed and bath products, cotton clothing, and gourmet kitchenware. More than just a retail store, the center also presents water-conservation and solar-panel demonstrations and offers guided tours of the facilities.

NIGHTLIFE

Some of the area wineries feature programs during the summer. Otherwise, there are bars and hotel lounges scattered throughout the area in towns such as Healdsburg, Geyserville, Cloverdale, and Boonville.

PARKS

ANNADEL STATE PARK ✉Off Route 12, about five miles east of Santa Rosa 📞707-539-3911 📠707-538-0769
🚶🛶 Possessing a wealth of possibilities, this 5500-acre facility has 40 miles of trails through meadow and forest. A volcanic

mountain flanks one end of the park and a lake provides fishing for black bass and bluegill. There's also a marsh where many of the area's 160 bird species flock. Blacktailed deer and coyotes roam the region. The park has picnic areas and pit toilets. Day-use fee, $4.

RUSSIAN RIVER

With its headwaters in Mendocino County, the Russian River rambles south through north central California to Healdsburg. Here it turns west toward the sea, as the surrounding landscape changes from rolling ranch land to dense redwood forest. The area around Guerneville, where the river begins its headlong rush to the Pacific, has enjoyed a rebirth as a gay resort area. Earlier a family vacation spot, the Guerneville–Forestville–Monte Rio area became a raffish home to bikers and hippies during the '50s and '60s. Then in the '70s, gay vacationers from San Francisco began frequenting the region.

Today, the Russian River is San Francisco's answer to Fire Island. There are many gay resorts in and around Guerneville, and almost without exception every establishment in town welcomes gay visitors. The area is also a popular family resort area. This stretch of the river offers prime fishing and canoeing opportunities. As the river rumbles downslope, it provides miles of scenic runs past overhanging forests. Black bass, steelhead, bluegill, and silver salmon swim these waters, and there are numerous beaches for swimming and sunbathing. From Santa Rosa, the winding, two-lane River Road follows the northern edge of the Russian River taking you to the ocean, where it stops at Jenner.

SIGHTS

VISITORS INFORMATION CENTER ✉ *16209 1st Street, Guerneville* 📞 *707-869-9000, 877-644-9001* 📠 *707-869-9009* 🖃 *www.russianriver.com, info@russianriver.com* This visitors center provides maps and brochures on facilities and water sports.

VISITORS BUREAU AT KORBEL STATION ✉ *13250 River Road, Guerneville* 📞 *707-869-4096* There is more information for visitors at this stop at Korbel Station.

KORBEL CHAMPAGNE CELLARS ✉ *13250 River Road, Guerneville* 📞 *707-824-7000* 📠 *707-869-2981* 🖃 *www.korbel.com, info@korbel.com* Founded in 1882 by three brothers, Korbel produces today's most popular sparkling wines. On any day of the week you may taste these award-winning. The tasting room and attached gift shop sell nine different champagnes, some of which are available nowhere else; also on the premises is a gourmet delicatessen. While guided tours are offered throughout the year, I recommend visiting during spring and summer when the winery's century-old garden, which you can tour separately, is alive with roses, tulips, and daffodils. No garden tours on Monday.

ARMSTRONG REDWOODS
STATE RESERVE

✉17000 Armstrong Woods Road, Guerneville ✆707-869-2015 📠707-869-5629 As you first arrive in downtown Guerneville you will come to a traffic signal at the intersection of Armstrong Woods Road. Turning north will take you to this state reserve (2.5 miles down the road), where you will undoubtedly marvel at the grove of ancient redwoods dating back 2000 years and reaching heights of 350 feet. Admission.

JOHNSON'S BEACH

✉South end of Church Street, Guerneville ✆707-869-2022 Of course, Guerneville would never have developed into a resort destination had it not been for the waters of the Russian River. The most popular spot around Guerneville to plunge in for a swim or launch a canoe is Johnson's Beach. Located just two blocks from the heart of downtown, this sunny waterfront strip is also home to many summer events, including the renowned Russian River Jazz Festival.

Dozens of wineries distinguish the Russian River region. Russian River wines are distinctive because a 70-foot-deep stratum of gravel lies beneath the valley, forcing vine roots to reach deeper for water and adding trace minerals that give the grapes a complex flavor. Several outstanding ones can be found along Westside Road and smaller roads that are sometimes little more than a lane, while others are located south on heavily traveled routes such as Route 116 (Gravenstein Highway).

RUSSIAN RIVER VINEYARDS ✉5700 Gravenstein Highway (Route 116), Forestville ✆707-887-3344 🖥www.russianrivervineyards.com, info@russianrivervineyards.com Along Route 116 you will find this rambling complex. The winery is known for its cutting-edge techniques such as biodynamic farming, which is believed to produce more vital crops by capitalizing on natural forces that tend to have minimal negative impact on the land. But the real fun is in the tasting room, where a wide array of wines, including some unusual varietals are available for sampling. Tasting fee.

LODGING

APPLEWOOD INN

$$$–$$$$ 19 UNITS ✉13555 Route 116, Guerneville ✆707-869-9093, 800-555-8509 📠707-869-9170 🖥www.applewoodinn.com, relax@applewoodinn.com

I love sleeping in the *casas* here, where I'm surrounded by giant redwoods that give the illusion of camping out in a treehouse. They're the prettiest accommodations in this neck of the red-

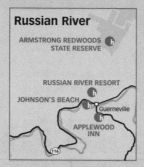

Russian River

ARMSTRONG REDWOODS STATE RESERVE

PAGE 297

Paths meandering through a deep, cool forest of 2000-year-old redwoods over 350 magnificent feet tall

RUSSIAN RIVER RESORT

PAGE 293

Cheerful, modern rooms catering to gay men, and an action-packed activities schedule that never stops

JOHNSON'S BEACH

PAGE 291

Sunny riverside strip just blocks from downtown—the perfect place to plunge in

APPLEWOOD INN

PAGE 291

Treehouse-like *casas* nestled amid towering redwoods, secluded in a tiny pocket canyon

woods, hidden on a hillside in tiny Pocket Canyon. Belden House, the original family home built in 1922, has the older, more staid rooms, while two two-story *casas* across the courtyard offer more space that in some cases includes a small balcony. An additional three suites are nestled in the new Gate House, which overlooks the courtyard. With a pool, hot tub, and excellent restaurant (which uses produce from its own gardens), this estate, secluded among the redwoods, is the kind of place to which you can retreat and never leave the grounds until your visit is over.

DAWN RANCH LODGE

$$–$$$$ 54 UNITS   ✉16467 River Road, Guerneville   ☎707-869-0656
🖱www.dawnranch.com, info@dawnranch.com

Resting on 15 waterfront acres on the edge of downtown Guerneville is Dawn Ranch. In addition to a restaurant and a bar, Dawn Ranch offers such facilities as a beach, a pool, and volleyball courts. There are 51 refurbished individual cottages and cabins that were built in the early 1900s. Each is simply but comfortably furnished with a queen-sized bed and without TV or phone. The historic Olive's cottage boasts two rooms, a patio, and a fireplace.

RUSSIAN RIVER RESORT

$$$ 23 ROOMS ✉16440 4th Street, Guerneville ☎707-869-0691,
800-417-3767 📠707-869-0698 🖋www.russianriverresort.com,
info@russianriverresort.com

Fondly called "triple R," this resort offers cheerfully decorated guest rooms situated around a hot tub area. Whereas most other resorts in the area can be described as rustic, this resort provides more modern, contemporary accommodations; each room is carpeted and has a private bath and cable TV (several have pellet stoves as well). Throughout the year, the Russian River Resort organizes 15 to 20 events celebrating major holidays and festivities such as Women's Weekend. The guests are almost exclusively gay male but lesbians and gay-friendly straights are welcome. A restaurant and several bars are located on the premises, and there's a pool.

THE WOODS

$–$$ 20 UNITS ✉16484 4th Street, Guerneville ☎877-887-9218
🖋www.rrwoods.com, info@rrwoods.com

Accommodations range from small "bunkhouse" rooms with private showers to cabins and cottages with full kitchens, fireplaces, and decks overlooking the large outdoor pool. Surrounded by redwoods and nestled in a quiet bend of Fifes Creek—but also a short walk away from downtown—The Woods caters to gays and lesbians. The large outdoor stone fireplace, fountains, and softly lighted landscaping give it an air of serenity and romance.

HIGHLANDS RESORT

$$–$$$ 16 UNITS ✉14000 Woodland Drive, Guerneville ☎707-869-0333
📠707-869-0370 🖋www.highlandsresort.com, muffins@highlandsresort.com

Catering primarily to gays and lesbians, Highlands sits on three acres. Accommodations here come in many forms. Some are individual cabins with fireplaces, private baths, and kitchenettes; others are more standard motel-style rooms. The pool suite has both a queen- and king-sized bed, a TV, a refrigerator, and a view of the pool, where sunbathing is *au naturel*. A hot tub, a continental breakfast, and a guest lounge with a piano, TV, VCR, and books complete the amenities. There is also space for 20 tents.

FERN GROVE COTTAGES

$$–$$$ 21 UNITS ✉16650 River Road, Guerneville ☎707-869-8105, 888-243-2674
📠707-869-1615 🖋www.ferngrove.com, innkeepers@ferngrove.com

These cottages sit at the foot of a mountain and are a five-minute walk from town. The 21 mustard-colored Craftsman cottages were built in 1926 and are furnished with antiques. Some have jacuzzi tubs, fireplaces, wood-burning stoves, or kitchens. Guests enjoy a buffet-style breakfast. There's a two-night minimum on peak-season weekends.

Russian River Area

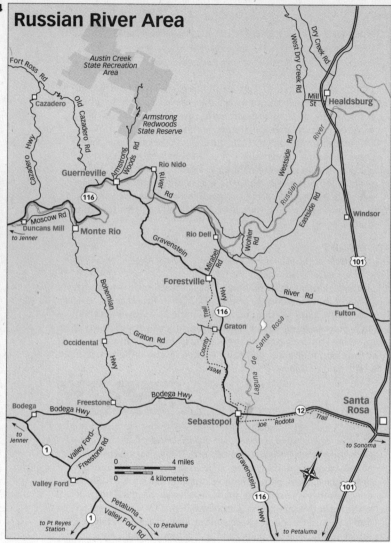

VILLAGE INN

$$$ 10 ROOMS   ✉20822 River Boulevard, Monte Rio   ☎707-865-2304, 800-303-2303

🖰www.villageinn-ca.com, info@villageinn-ca.com

This refurbished woodframe complex on the river draws a mixed clientele. This cozy country inn, set amid redwood trees, has a homey, old-time feel. All rooms come with private bath. They're trim little units: clean, carpeted, and decorated with an occasional piece of art. You'll also find a good restaurant and bar with river views.

FARMHOUSE INN

$$$$ 10 ROOMS   ✉ 7871 River Road, Forestville   📞 707 887 3300, 800 464 6642
📠 707-887-3311   ✎ www.farmhouseinn.com, innkeep@farmhouseinn.com

This inn is a vision in yellow, with rose gardens and grapevines growing right out the front door. A stone's throw from the old farmhouse, the attached cottages are decorated with distinction; one is done in peach-and-sage velvet, another in paisley prints, another in cream and green. All have fireplaces, jet tubs, and CDs and TV/VCRs. On-site amenities include a pool, restaurant, and day spa.

DINING

COFFEE BAZAAR

$ COFFEEHOUSE/DELI   ✉ 14045 Armstrong Woods Road, Guerneville
📞 707-869-9706

While even remote Guerneville now offers more than a couple of places to get an espresso, none are better than this stop. Located on Armstrong Woods Road a block off the main strip, this café's food and beverages are tasty and affordable. There is a wide range of coffee creations and a generous selection of pastries each morning. Lunch choices include soups, salads, sandwiches, quiches, and calzones; many vegetarian options are available. There is plenty of seating inside, but take a sidewalk table to peoplewatch.

ROADHOUSE RESTAURANT
AT DAWN RANCH LODGE

 hidden

$$–$$$ CALIFORNIA CUISINE   ✉ 16467 River Road, Guerneville
📞 707-869-0656   ✎ www.dawnranch.com

This restaurant is sophisticated and relaxing in California Modern fashion. You'll also find a sundeck for warm-weather dining. The menu changes seasonally. Sunday through Thursday, a limited pub-style menu is available, with burgers and fried fish. On Friday and Saturday, a more sophisticated dinner menu is available. This menu may include sweet orange chili–glazed calamari, grilled Harris Ranch top sirloin with smoked paprika and cauliflower gratin, and butternut squash risotto with Gala apple chutney. Reservations required on Friday and Saturday. Dinner only.

CAPE FEAR CAFÉ

$$ SOUTHERN/CALIFORNIA CUISINE   ✉ 25191 Main Street, Duncans Mill
📞 707-865-9246

The founder of this café hails from North Carolina, and the Southern influence cuts through the eclectic influences of Asian and Californian cuisine. Most notably, the place serves the unusual but tasty shrimp grits: a side of grits in a pool of broth and shrimp. Other entrées such as salmon crab cakes, and Carolina chicken are also delicious. The place is casual (as most restaurants around here are) and decorated with works by local artists.

FARMHOUSE INN

$$$–$$$$ CALIFORNIA CUISINE ✉7871 River Road, Forestville
📞707-887-3300 📠707-887-3311 ✐www.farmhouseinn.com

The walls in the dining room at the Farmhouse Inn are the same yellow as the exterior, making a pretty backdrop for dining. (There's also patio seating.) The seasonal menu changes nightly but usually includes the chef's special rabbit dish and features what's growing in the garden. Other local sources and the availability of fresh wild fish also dictate the inspired offerings. Desserts are housemade. Dinner only. Closed Monday through Wednesday.

MOSAIC RESTAURANT & WINE LOUNGE

$$$–$$$$ CALIFORNIA CUISINE ✉6675 Front Street, Forestville 📞707-887-7503
📠707-887-7513 ✐www.mosaiceats.com, tai@mosaiceats.com

Eight miles southeast of Guerneville, downtown Forestville is not exactly a gourmet ghetto. So it's nice that after Chez Marie closed, this restaurant moved into the building, streamlined the decor, remodeled the back room into a wine lounge, and installed a garden for alfresco dining. Chef Tai Olesky lets his creativity shine through dishes like a vanilla-bean-and-anise-rubbed pork shoulder, a coffee-encrusted filet mignon that incorporates cabernet, chocolate and bleu cheese, and chili-lime-glazed prawns with macadamia nuts.

SHOPPING

RIVER READER, INC. ✉16355 Main Street, Guerneville 📞707-869-2240
✐riverreader@gmail.com This excellent bookstore and true community resource has a small but strong selection of books, magazines, cards, games, music, and gifts. Visitors will find plenty of choices for poolside reading in all categories including fiction, spirituality, and regional topics. There is also a good selection of gay reading material including books and magazines.

KOZLOWSKI FARMS ✉5566 Gravenstein Highway (Route 116), Forestville
📞707-887-1587, 800-473-2767 ✐www.kozlowskifarms.com, koz@kozlowskifarms.com
On the main road to Forestville from Guerneville, you'll do your sweet tooth a favor by stopping at this farm. They make and sell more than 100 different items like all-fruit preserves, chutney, spreads, dessert sauces, apple cider blends, and a variety of baked goods. Other condiments include mustards, salad dressings, salsas, and chipotle sauces, among others. The farm also has a picnic area, a bakery, and an espresso bar.

NIGHTLIFE

DAWN RANCH ✉16467 River Road, Guerneville 📞707-869-0656 ✐www.dawn
ranch.com One of the area's first gay resorts, this beautiful bar extends through several pine-paneled rooms and out to a poolside deck.

RUSSIAN RIVER RESORT ✉16390 4th Street, Guerneville ✆707-869-0691 🖰www.russianriverresort.com Like Dawn Ranch, this resort is a gay-friendly establishment that invites nonguests to enjoy the facilities and mingle with guests at the bar and around the pool. The bar isn't large but the crowd is friendly and if nothing is jumping in town, there will surely be some people hanging out at the "Triple R."

RAINBOW CATTLE COMPANY ✉16220 Main Street, Guerneville ✆707-869-0206 🖰www.queersteer.com Also in the middle of downtown is this definitively hip gay bar. Offering nothing more than a couple of pool tables, three pinball machines, bar stools, and long benches, this nightspot doesn't provide much in the way of entertainment, but it's a congenial place for socializing and drinking.

CLUB YAMAGATA

✉16225 Main Street, Guerneville ✆707-869-9875 🖰www.clubyamagata. com Every Friday through Monday night at this self-proclaimed "pansexual club" is a dance party featuring deejays and a small crowd. Wednesday is devoted to locals performing open mic, from rock-and-roll to jazz. The clientele tends to be gay males, but dance nights attract a mix. On any regular evening, this is a comfortable place to enjoy a sandwich or some sushi along with a strong cocktail.

STUMPTOWN BREWERY ✉15045 River Road, Guerneville ✆707-869-0705 📠707-869-8169 🖰www.stumptown.com/brews Home of the Rat Bastard Pale Ale, Stumptown is a small seven-barrel brew pub. They have a deck overlooking the river that also offers access to their two-acre beach.

PARKS

ARMSTRONG REDWOODS STATE RESERVE AND AUSTIN CREEK STATE RECREATION AREA

✉17000 Armstrong Woods Road, Guerneville ✆707-869-2015 📠707-869-5629

🚶🚴🐎🌲⛵ These two parks, one above the other, are a study in contrasts. Armstrong features a deep, cool forest of redwood trees measuring over 350 feet high and dating back 2000 years. Rare redwood orchids blossom here in spring and there is a 1200-seat amphitheater that was once used for summer concerts. Austin Creek offers sunny meadows and oak forests. Fox, bobcats, deer, wild pigs, and raccoons inhabit the region, and a nearby shallow bullfrog pond has sunfish and bass. A four-mile hike takes you to a backcountry creek that offers relief from the sun. There are 22 miles of trails threading the park. Facilities include picnic areas, restrooms, and a visitors center. Day-use fee, $6.

⛺ Permitted in Austin Creek at Bullfrog Pond Campground,

which has 24 sites and 3 hike-in backcountry sites ($15 per night). For restrictions and permit information call 707-869-2015.

OUTDOOR ADVENTURES

WATER SPORTS

There are many opportunities for boating in the Wine Country, primarily along the Russian River. In addition, the lakes, rivers, and hot springs–fed swimming pools provide great places to swim during the sweltering Wine Country summers.

Napa Valley

LAKE BERRYESSA ✉*Off Route 21, 25 miles northeast of Napa* This lake on the eastern edge of Napa County attracts weekend crowds, who come to swim, boat, water-ski, and fish.

GETAWAY ADVENTURES ✉*2228 Northpoint Parkway, Santa Rosa* ☎*707-568-3040, 800-499-2453* ✐*www.getawayadventures.com* Contact this company for day-long kayak trips and four-day-long biking and kayaking trips.

Sonoma Valley

MORTON'S WARM SPRINGS ✉*1651 Warm Springs Road, Glen Ellen* ☎*707-833-5511* ✐*www.mortonswarmsprings.com* The three swimming pools at Morton's stay at 85°F and are open mid-May through mid-September. There's a snack bar on the grounds.

INDIAN SPRINGS RESORT AND SPA ✉*1712 Lincoln Avenue, Calistoga* ☎*707-942-4913* ☎*707-942-4919* The historic Olympic-sized pool at Indian Springs is fed by the mineral water from three natural geysers. Nuisance suits forced the resort to close the pool to the general public in 1997, but guests can still swim in what I consider one of the best swimming pools in Northern California, if not anywhere.

Russian River

This river is *the* place to explore in a canoe or kayak. Most folks rent for the day, canoe one way, and are picked up by the outfitter and shuttled back. The scenery, ranging from rolling ranch land to dense redwood groves, is stunning. The experience of floating timelessly along this magnificent river will long be remembered.

The Russian River is a Class I from April to October, and during that time canoe and kayak rentals are plentiful. Several outfits offer everything from one-day excursions to five-day expeditions.

BURKE'S CANOE TRIPS ✉*At the north end of Mirabel Road at River Road, Forestville* ☎*707-887-1222* ✐*www.burkescanoetrips.com* If you're ready for the adventure, contact Burke's Canoe Trips. They offer a ten-mile day trip to Guerneville (they bus you back) and outfit you with a canoe, life jacket, and paddles before sending you on a self-guided ride through the redwoods. Reservations required.

RIVER'S EDGE KAYAK & CANOE TRIPS ✉18340 Old Redwood Highway, Healdsburg ☎707-433-7247 🖰www.riversedgekayakandcanoe.com This outfitter offers half- or full-day kayaking trips, which include paddles and life vests. Many packages also provide lunch.

The Russian River is also good for a swim. A popular spot is **Memorial Beach** in the town of Healdsburg. Other favorites are **Monte Rio Beach** in Monte Rio and **Johnson's Beach** in the town of Guerneville.

BALLOON RIDES

All puns aside, no sport in the Wine Country has taken off like hot-air ballooning. Every morning, colorful balloons dot the sky, providing riders with a billowing crow's nest from which to view the sweeping countryside.

Napa Valley

ALOFT NAPA VALLEY ✉6525 Washington Street, Yountville ☎707-944-4408, 800-627-2759 🖰www.napavalleyaloft.com For a ride straight from the pages of *Around the World in 80 Days*, call this company. The one-hour ride drifts over vineyards and wineries, and includes a champagne breakfast after the ride.

Sonoma Valley

A BALLOON OVER SONOMA ✉109 Wikiup Meadows Drive, Santa Rosa ☎707-546-3360 📠707-579-4301 🖰www.aballoonoversonoma.com This company launches from a variety of locations in the Sonoma Valley. They can accommodate up to 16 people, and following the hour-long flight (all in all, the excursion is close to three hours), you'll be treated to a champagne breakfast (Belgian waffles? eggs benedict? steak-and-eggs?—your choice) at Kal's Kaffe Mocha Grill.

GOLF

The Wine Country's excellent weather makes golf a popular pastime. This is one of the few places in the world where you can play golf amidst beautiful grape vines.

Napa Valley
NAPA GOLF COURSE

✉2295 Streblow Drive, Napa ☎707-255-4333 This 18-hole course at Kennedy Park is on the bank of the Napa River and has been used as a championship course. The clubhouse rents clubs and carts, and there is an on-site restaurant.

MOUNT ST. HELENA GOLF COURSE ✉Napa County Fairgrounds, Calistoga ☎707-942-9966 In Calistoga, the public nine-hole course here has views of Mt. St. Helena. This mom-and-pop-style establishment has seven par 4s and two par 3s, and rents clubs and carts. Closed for five days over the Fourth of July weekend.

Sonoma Valley

WINDSOR GOLF COURSE ✉1340 19th Hole Drive, Windsor ✆707-838-7888
🖰www.windsorgolf.com Play a challenging game at this public 18-hole
course. The 6650-yard greens include lakes and oak trees.

OAKMONT GOLF CLUB ✉7025 Oakmont Drive, Santa Rosa ✆707-539-0415
🖰www.oakmontgc.com Oakmont hass a par-72 championship course and
a par-63 executive course. This treelined, semiprivate club rents clubs
and carts.

Russian River

NORTHWOOD GOLF CLUB ✉19400 Route 116, Monte Rio ✆707-865-1116
🖰707-865-1290 🖰www.northwoodgolf.com This Alister MacKenzie–designed
golf club has nine holes. Clubs and carts are available for rent.

SEBASTOPOL GOLF COURSE ✉2881 Scott's Right of Way, Sebastopol
✆707-823-9852 Tee off here for peaceful, countryside golfing. This public
nine-hole course rents clubs.

BIKING

BACKROADS ✉801 Cedar Street, Berkeley ✆510-527-1555, 800-462-2848
🖰www.backroads.com, goactive@backroads.com One of the nicest ways to explore the region is to bike the backroads, pedaling between wineries,
historic sites, and health spas. To see the area by an organized bike tour,
contact Backroads. They offer week-long trips throughout Northern
California (and the rest of the world), giving you challenge options. The
Wine Country excursion pedals through the towns of Healdsburg,
Calistoga, Yountville, Sonoma, and Bodega Bay. Bikes, helmets, most
meals, and lodging are included.

Napa Valley

SILVERADO TRAIL This trail through Napa Valley is the best road
to travel. It's less crowded than Route 29, the main thoroughfare, and is
fairly level. Several steep mountain roads lead from Napa Valley across
to Sonoma Valley through vineyards.

Sonoma Valley

A bike path on the western edge of Sonoma passes numerous sightseeing spots.

BALD MOUNTAIN TRAIL At Sugarloaf Ridge, try this trail (9
miles) to Gray Pine and then through the meadow loop. You'll pass
open meadows sprinkled with oak trees.

Russian River

River Road, between Windsor and Guerneville, meanders past rolling
hills and rural scenery, but carries a moderate amount of traffic.

Bike Rentals

SPOKE FOLK CYCLERY ✉201 Center Street, Healdsburg ✆707-433-7171
This shop includes helmets, locks, and backpacks with their rental
bikes (hybrid, tandem, road). You can buy a bike and accessories, as
well as have repairs done. Closed Tuesday in winter.

ST. HELENA CYCLERY ✉1156 Main Street, St. Helena ✆707-963-7736 For rentals (hybrids and tandems) and repairs, check out this spot. Along with a sidebag, lock, and helmet, they'll throw in some suggested routes. Closed Monday in winter.

NAPA VALLEY BIKE TOURS ✉6488 Washington Street, Yountville ✆800-707-2453 ⌲www.napavalleybiketours.com This tour company does rentals and outings throughout the Wine Country.

GETAWAY ADVENTURES ✉2228 Northpoint Parkway, Santa Rosa ✆707-568-3040, 800-499-2453 ⌲www.getawayadventures.com Bike rentals and day-long, weekend, and six-day cycling tours of the wineries are available from this outfitter.

NORCAL BIKE SPORT ✉425 College Avenue, Santa Rosa ✆707-573-0112 ⌲www.norcalcycling.com In the Sonoma area, head to this shop. If you're in the mood to buy a bike, you can find a large selection of them here. They also do repairs.

HIKING

BACKROADS ✉801 Cedar Street, Berkeley ✆510-527-1555, 800-462-2848 ⌲www.backroads.com, goactive@backroads.com For backpackers and day-trippers, state parks in the Wine Country offer a chance to escape the crowds while exploring forests, meadows, and mountain ridges. Back-roads organizes five- to six-day hiking jaunts; most meals and lodging are included.

GETAWAY ADVENTURES ✉1718 Michael Way, Calistoga ✆707-942-0332, 800-499-2453 ⌲www.getawayadventures.com This group operates weekend and six-day trips.

All distances listed for hiking trails are one way unless otherwise noted.

Napa Valley
BOTHE–NAPA VALLEY STATE PARK For those interested in communing with nature amid splendid redwood groves, Bothe–Napa Valley State Park has ten miles of hiking trails.

A fairly strenuous hike, the **History Trail** (1.2 miles) begins at the picnic area and leads near an old pioneer cemetery, the site where an 1853 church once stood, and past Mill Creek en route to Old Bale Grist Mill.

The **Coyote Peak Trail** (1.5 miles) is moderately difficult and heads away from Ritchey Creek, then climbs up to 1170 feet elevation for scenic views of the Napa Valley.

A scenic trek, the **Ritchey Canyon Trail** (3.9 miles) starts off easy on an 1860 roadbed that wanders beside a stream and is shadowed by red-woods and firs. Farther along, the trail becomes moderate and leads past a small cascade that flows into a small canyon.

A tranquil hike along Ritchey Creek can also be found on the **Redwood Trail** (1 mile). In spring, redwood orchids and trilliums add to the beauty of this tree-shaded pathway.

The **South Fork Trail** (.9 mile) is a moderately strenuous hike that circles across the rim of Ritchey Creek and arrives at a vista point overlooking the canyon.

Sonoma Valley

SUGARLOAF RIDGE STATE PARK ☏707-833-5712 The trails here provide opportunities to explore ridges and open fields. Every spring, wildflowers riot throughout the meadows.

Sugarloaf's most popular walk is along the **Creekside Nature Trail** (.8 mile roundtrip). A self-guided stroll, it begins at the day-use picnic area and carries past stands of oak, alder, ash, maple, and Douglas fir. Watch for several species of lichen *and* poison oak!

If you are up for a steep climb, try the hike up Bald Mountain on the **Bald Mountain Trail** (2.7 miles) that leads to the top of the mountain. At an elevation of 2729 feet, the summit offers spectacular views of the Sonoma and Napa valleys. In fact, on a clear day, you'll see as far as San Francisco, the Golden Gate Bridge and the Sierra Nevada. The climb begins at the day-use parking lot near the campground, which is already 1000 feet in elevation.

ANNADEL STATE PARK ☏707-539-3911 Once inhabited by Pomo and Wappo Indians, this state park is a mix of forest and meadow laced with 35 miles of hiking paths. Because this is a wildlife corridor, there are plenty of wild animal sightings, including the occasional mountain lion, so no dogs are allowed.

The **Warren B. Richardson Trail** (2.7 miles) wanders through a forest of Douglas fir en route to Lake Ilsanjo. Spring brings redwood orchid blossoms, adding a rare experience to an already splendid hike.

A scenic trek, the **Marsh Trail** (4 miles) climbs the side of Bennett Mountain and offers grand views of Lake Ilsanjo as well as nearby mountain ranges. For a trip to an old quarry site where cobblestones were once excavated, head down the aptly named **Cobblestone Trail** (2 miles).

TRANSPORTATION

CAR

The quick, painless, and impersonal way to the Napa Valley is along **Route 80**. From San Francisco, the freeway buzzes northeast to Vallejo, where it connects with **Route 37** and then **Route 29**, the main road through Napa Valley.

An alternative course leads north from San Francisco along **Route 101**. From this freeway you can pick up Route 37, which skirts San Pablo Bay en route to its junction with Route 29.

For the most scenic drive, turn off Route 37 onto **Route 121**. This rural road, which also connects with Route 29, provides a preview of the Wine Country. The curving hills along the way are covered with vineyards, ranches, and sheep farms. Route 121 also connects with **Route 12**, which leads into the Sonoma Valley.

Route 101 runs like a spine through the Russian River region. Vineyards lie in clusters on either side of the highway. Another road, **Route 116**, leaves this freeway and heads to the gay resort area around Guerneville and on to the Pacific Ocean.

BUS

GREYHOUND BUS LINES ℡800-231-2222 ✐www.greyhound.com Greyhound has frequent service to the Sonoma area. It also stops in Healdsburg, Geyserville, and points farther north.

PUBLIC TRANSIT

NAPA COUNTY TRANSPORTATION AND PLANNING AGENCY ℡707-259-8631 ✐www.nctpa.net This agency provides full information about public transportation in Napa Valley and how to connect with the San Francisco ferry in Vallejo.

SONOMA COUNTY TRANSIT ⊠355 West Robles Avenue, Santa Rosa ℡707-576-7433 ✐www.sctransit.com In Sonoma, this transit system covers the area from Sonoma to Santa Rosa, stopping in Glen Ellen and Kenwood; it continues from Santa Rosa to Windsor, Healdsburg, and Geyserville. Sonoma County Transit also serves the area between Healdsburg and Guerneville.

GOLDEN GATE TRANSIT ℡510-455-2000, 415-455-2000, 707-455-2000 ✐www.goldengate.org Bus service from San Francisco to some Sonoma County towns is available from this agency. Allow around two hours to reach Santa Rosa and another half-hour to reach Healdsburg. These buses serve commuters; on weekends, you must disembark in Santa Rosa and transfer onto Sonoma County Transit buses to reach other towns.

NORTH COAST

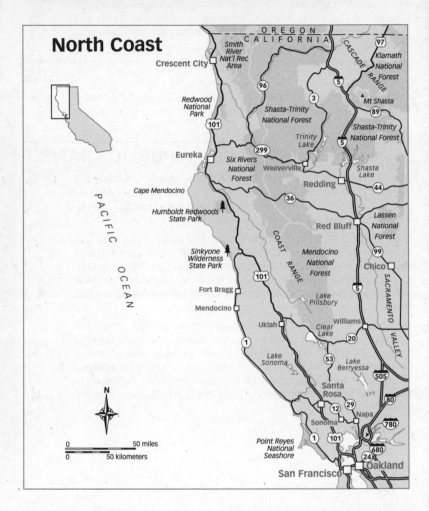

North Coast

OREGON
CALIFORNIA

Crescent City · Smith River Nat'l Rec Area · 97 · Klamath National Forest · CASCADE RANGE

96

Redwood National Park · 101 · Shasta-Trinity National Forest · 3 · 5 · Mt Shasta · 89

299 · Trinity Lake · Shasta-Trinity National Forest · 5

Eureka · Six Rivers National Forest · Weaverville · Redding · Shasta Lake · 44

Cape Mendocino

Humboldt Redwoods State Park · 36 · Red Bluff · Lassen National Forest

COAST RANGE

Sinkyone Wilderness State Park · 101 · Mendocino National Forest · 99 · Chico · SACRAMENTO VALLEY

Fort Bragg · Lake Pillsbury · 5

Mendocino · Ukiah · Clear Lake · Williams · 20

1 · Lake Sonoma · 53 · Lake Berryessa · 505

Santa Rosa · 12 · 29 · Napa · 80

Sonoma · 780

1 · 101 · Point Reyes National Seashore · 24 · 680 · Oakland

San Francisco

PACIFIC OCEAN

N

0 — 50 miles
0 — 50 kilometers

When visitors to San Francisco seek a rural retreat, paradise is never far away. It sits just across the Golden Gate Bridge, along a coastline stretching almost 400 miles to the Oregon border. Scenically, the North Coast compares in beauty with any spot on earth.

There are the folded hills and curving beaches of Point Reyes, Sonoma's craggy coast and old Russian fort, plus Mendocino with its vintage towns and spuming shoreline. To the far north lies Redwood Country, silent domain of the world's tallest living things.

Along the entire seaboard, civilization appears in the form of fishing villages and logging towns. Matter of fact, a lot of the prime real estate is saved forever from developers' heavy hands. California's Coastal Commission serves as a watchdog agency protecting the environment.

Much of the coast is also preserved in public playgrounds. Strung like pearls along the Pacific are a series of federal parks—Golden Gate National Recreation Area, Point Reyes National Seashore, and Redwood National Park.

The main highway through this idyllic domain is Route 1. A sinuous road, it snakes along the waterfront, providing the slowest, most scenic route. Paralleling this road and following an inland course is Route 101. This superhighway streaks from San Francisco to Oregon. It is fast, efficient, and at times boring. In the town of Leggett, Route 1 merges into Route 101, which continues north through Redwood Country.

Route 1 runs through San Francisco into Marin County, passing Sausalito before it branches from Route 101. While the eastern sector of Marin, along San Francisco Bay, is a suburban sprawl, the western region consists of rolling ranch land. Muir Woods is here, featuring 1000-year-old redwoods growing within commuting distance of the city. There is Mt. Tamalpais, a 2571-foot "sleeping maiden" whose recumbent figure has been the subject of numerous poems.

According to some historians, Sir Francis Drake, the Renaissance explorer, landed along the Marin shore in 1579, building a fort and claiming the wild region for dear old England. The Portuguese had first sighted the North Coast in 1543 when they espied Cape Mendocino. Back then Coastal Miwok Indians inhabited Marin, enjoying undisputed possession of the place until the Spanish settled the interior valleys during the early 1800s.

To the north, in Sonoma County, the Miwok shared their domain with the Pomo Indians. After 1812 they were also dividing it with the Russians. The Czar's forces arrived in California from their hunting grounds in Alaska and began taking large numbers of otters from local waters. The Russians built Fort Ross and soon proclaimed the region open only to their shipping. Of course, these imperial designs made the Spanish very nervous. The American response was to proclaim the Monroe Doctrine, warning foreign powers off the continent.

By the 1830s the Russians had decimated the otter population, reducing it from 150,000 to less than 100. They soon lost interest in the area and sold their fort and other holdings to John Sutter, whose name two decades hence would become synonymous with the Gold Rush.

Many of the early towns along the coast were born during the days of the '49ers. Established to serve as pack stations for the mines, the villages soon turned to lumbering and fishing. Today these are still important industries. About seven percent of California's land consists of commercial forest, much of it along the coastal redwood belt. Environmentalists continue to battle with the timber interests as they have since 1918 when the Save-the-Redwoods League was formed.

The natural heritage they protect includes trees that have been growing in California's forests since before the birth of Christ. Elk herds roam these groves, while trout and steelhead swim the nearby rivers. At one time the forest stretched in a 30-mile-wide swath for 450 miles along the coast. But in little more than a century the lumber industry has cut down over 90 percent of the original redwoods. Presently, 87,000 acres of ancient trees remain, over 90 percent of which are protected in parks. The fate of one unprotected grove, the Headwaters Forest in Humboldt County, which contains the world's largest privately owned stand of old-growth redwoods, has been an emotional issue, resulting in the arrest of scores of protesters during the past several years. The federal government has recently purchased 7500 acres of old-growth and second-growth redwoods in the forest from the Pacific Lumber Company.

Another, much younger, cash crop is marijuana. During the '60s and early '70s, Mendocino and Humboldt counties became meccas for counterculturalists intent on getting "back to the land." They established communes, built original-design houses, and plunged into local politics. Some also became green-thumb outlaws, perfecting potent and exotic strains of sinsemilla for personal use and black-market sale. They made Northern California marijuana famous and helped boom the local economy. In 1996, California voters passed Proposition 215, an initiative legalizing the use of marijuana for medical purposes. Although 38 other states already had similar laws, and the herb had actually been available to cancer patients prior to the Reagan administration, marijuana was not currently available to patients anywhere because it was (and still is) prohibited by federal law. When bars where the recreational herb was actually dispensed for medical purposes began to open in San Francisco, the U.S. Drug Enforcement Administration was quick to close them down. The California statute reached the U.S. Supreme Court for a final determination of its legality and that of similar laws in other states across the country, in 2001, but the ruling, which deemed that state and federal laws need not conform with each other, only served to continue the dissonance. Despite occasional Federal raids, pot clubs flourish throughout California.

The North Coast has become home to the country inn as well. All along the Pacific shoreline, bed and breakfasts serve travelers seeking informal and relaxing accommodations. Local artisans have also proliferated while small shops have opened to sell their crafts.

The great lure for travelers is still the environment. This coastal shelf, tucked between the Coast Ranges and the Pacific, has mountains and rivers, forests and ocean. Once the habitat of Yuki, Athabascan, Wiyot, Yurok, and Tolowa Indians, it remains an adventureland for imaginative travelers. Winters are damp, mornings and evenings sometimes foggy, but the weather overall is temperate. It's a place where you can fish for chinook and salmon, go crabbing, and scan the sea for migrating whales. Or simply ease back and enjoy scenery that never stops.

MARIN COAST

As frequently photographed as the Golden Gate Bridge, the coast of Marin County consists of rolling ranch lands and spectacular ocean bluffs. It extends from San Francisco Bay to Tomales Bay, offering groves of redwoods, meadows filled with wildflowers, and miles of winding country roads.

GOLDEN GATE BRIDGE   An exploration of this vaunted region begins immediately upon crossing the Golden Gate Bridge on Route 101. There's a vista point at the far north end of the bridge affording marvelous views back toward San Francisco and out upon the Bay. (If some of your party want to start off with an exhilarating walk across the bridge, drop them at the vista point on the city side and pick them up here a little later.)

Once across the bridge, take the first exit, Alexander Avenue; then take an immediate left, following the sign back toward San Francisco. Next, bear right at the sign for Marin Headlands.

For what is literally a **bird's-eye view** of the Golden Gate Bridge, go three-tenths of a mile uphill and stop at the first turnout on the left. From here it's a short stroll out and up, past deserted battery fortifications, to a 360° view point sweeping the Pacific and Bay alike. You'll practically be standing on the bridge, with cars careening below and the tops of the twin towers vaulting above you.

POINT BONITA   Continue along Conzelman Road and you will pass a series of increasingly spectacular views of San Francisco. Ahead the road will fall away to reveal a tumbling peninsula, furrowed with hills and marked at its distant tip by a lighthouse. That is Point Bonita, a salient far outside the Golden Gate. After proceeding to the point, you can peer back through the interstices of the bridge to the city or turn away from civilization and gaze out on a wind-tousled sea.

MARIN HEADLANDS   Nature writes in big letters around these parts. You're in the Marin Headlands section of **Golden Gate National Recreation Area**, an otherworldly realm of spuming surf, knife-edge cliffs, and chaparral-coated hillsides. From Point Bonita, follow Field Road, taking a left at the sign for the **Marin Headlands Visitors Center** (415-331-1540, fax 415-331-6963; www.nps.gov/goga), where you can pick up maps and information about the area, or make a camping reservation.

RODEO BEACH   This sandy corridor separating the Pacific from a tule-fringed lagoon is alive with waterfowl. Miles of hiking trails lace up into the hills (see the "Hiking" section at the end of this chapter). At the far end of the beach you can trek along the cliffs and watch the sea batter the continent.

MARINE MAMMAL CENTER ✉ *1065 Fort Cronkhite; From Alexander Avenue take Conzelman Road and follow the signs.* ✆ *415-289-7325* ✆ *415-289-7333* ✍ *www.marinemammalcenter.org, sales@tmmc.org* At this center are seals, sea lions, and other marine mammals who have been found injured or orphaned in the ocean and brought here to recuperate. Workers here conduct rescue operations along 600 miles of coastline, returning the animals to the wild after they have gained sufficient strength.

Bunker Road leads through a long tunnel and out of the park. You've completed a lazy loop and will emerge near an entrance to Route 101.

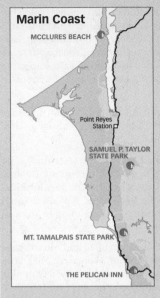

Marin Coast

MCCLURES BEACH

Point Reyes
Station

SAMUEL P. TAYLOR
STATE PARK

MT. TAMALPAIS STATE PARK

THE PELICAN INN

MCCLURES BEACH

PAGE 325

Secluded strip of white sand bookended with granite cliffs beside the Pacific Ocean's thundering waves

SAMUEL P. TAYLOR PARK

PAGE 323

Cool, dense redwood forest where black-tailed deer leap among rolling hills dotted with wildflowers

MT. TAMALPAIS STATE PARK

PAGE 321

Over 50 miles of trails through pockets of cypress, Douglas fir, California laurel, and teeming wildlife

THE PELICAN INN

PAGE 315

Period-print chambers, canopied beds, and a downstairs pub serving meat pies—16th-century England at its most delightful

Follow this north a few miles, then pick up Route 1. You'll be on the northern leg of one of the most beautiful roads in America. With its wooded sanctuaries and ocean vistas, Route 1 is for many people synonymous with California.

MUIR WOODS
NATIONAL MONUMENT

📞 *415-388-2596* 📠 *415-389-6957* 🖮 *www.nps.gov/muwo* When Route 1 forks after several miles, turn right on Panoramic Highway toward Muir Woods and Mt. Tamalpais; the left fork leads to Stinson Beach, but that comes later. It's uphill and then down to this 560-acre park inhabited by *Sequoia sempervirens*, the coast redwood. Though these forest giants have been known to live over two millennia, most enjoy a mere four-to-eight-century existence. In Muir Woods they reach 260 feet, while farther up the coast they top 360 feet (with roots that go no deeper than 10 feet!).

Facts can't convey the feelings inspired by these trees. You have to move among them, walk through Muir's Cathedral Grove where redwoods form a lofty arcade above the narrow trail. It's a forest primeval, casting the deepest, most restful shade imaginable. Muir Woods has the double-edged quality of being the redwood forest nearest to San Francisco. It can be horribly crowded. Since silence and solitude are vital to experiencing a redwood forest, plan to visit early or late in the day, and allow time to hike the more remote of the park's six miles of trails. Admission.

MT. TAMALPAIS   Back up on Panoramic Highway, the road continues through Mt. Tamalpais State Park en route to Mt. Tamalpais' 2571-foot peak. Mt. Tam, as it is affectionately known, represents one of the Bay Area's most prominent landmarks. Rising dramatically between the Pacific and the Bay, the site was sacred to Indians. Even today some people see in the sloping silhouette of the mountain the sleeping figure of an Indian maiden. So tread lightly up the short trail that leads to the summit. You'll be rewarded with a full-circle view that sweeps across the Bay, along San Francisco's miniature skyline, and out across the Pacific. Contrary to rumor, on a clear day you cannot see forever, but you can see north toward Redwood Country and east to the Sierras.

Continue on Panoramic Highway as it corkscrews down to Stinson Beach. Better yet, take the longer but more spectacular route to Stinson: Backtrack along Panoramic to where the fork originally separated from Route 1 (Shoreline Highway). Turn right and head north on Route 1.

GREEN GULCH FARM ✉1601 Shoreline Highway, near Muir Beach ☎415-383-3134 ℱ415-383-3128 ⌕www.sfzc.org, ggfoffice@sf2c.org Green Gulch is a 115-acre Zen retreat tucked serenely in a coastal valley. Residents here follow a rigorous program of work and meditation. There is a temple on the grounds and guests are welcome to tour the organic farm. Sunday is the best day to visit since a special meditation program and speaker is offered then. Closed January.

MUIR BEACH   It's not far from Green Gulch Farm to this crescent-shaped cove with sandy beach. Though swimming is not advised, this is a good spot for picnicking. About a mile farther up the road, follow the "vista point" sign to **Muir Beach Overlook**. Here you can walk out along a narrow ridge for a view extending from Bolinas to the coastline south of San Francisco. It's an outstanding place for whale watching in winter. Matter of fact, this lookout is so well placed it became a site for World War II gun batteries, whose rusty skeletons remain.

You have entered a realm that might well be called the Land of a Thousand Views. Until the road descends to the flat expanse of Stinson Beach, it follows a tortuous route poised on the edge of oblivion. Below, precipitous cliffs dive to the sea, while above the road, rock walls edge upward toward Mt. Tamalpais. Around every curve another scene opens to view. Before you, Bolinas is a sweep of land, an arm extended seaward. Behind, the San Francisco skyline falls away into the past. If God built highways, they'd look like this.

STINSON BEACH   This broad sandy hook at the bottom of the mountain is one of Northern California's finest strands. Anglers haunt the rocks along one end in pursuit of blenny and lingcod, while bird-

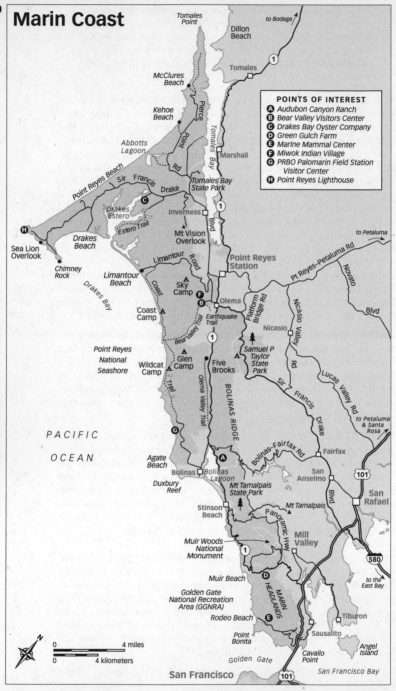

Marin Coast

to Bodega

Tomales
Point

Dillon
Beach

Tomales

1

McClures
Beach

Kehoe
Beach

POINTS OF INTEREST
Ⓐ Audubon Canyon Ranch
Ⓑ Bear Valley Visitors Center
Ⓒ Drakes Bay Oyster Company
Ⓓ Green Gulch Farm
Ⓔ Marine Mammal Center
Ⓕ Miwok Indian Village
Ⓖ PRBO Palomarin Field Station
   Visitor Center
Ⓗ Point Reyes Lighthouse

Abbotts
Lagoon

Marshall

Pierce
Point
Rd

Tomales Bay

Point Reyes Beach

Sir
Francis
Drake

Tomales Bay
State Park

1

Drakes
Estero

Ⓒ

to Petaluma

Inverness

H

Sea Lion
Overlook

Drakes
Beach

Estero Trail

Mt Vision
Overlook

Chimney
Rock

Drakes Bay

Limantour
Beach

Limantour

Road

Point Reyes
Station

Blvd

Pt Reyes–Petaluma Rd

Novato

Sky
Camp

Coast

Coast
Camp

Bear Valley Trail

Ⓕ
Ⓑ
Earthquake
Trail

Olema

Platform Bridge Rd

Nicasio

Blvd

Nicasio Valley

Lucas Valley Rd

Point Reyes
National
Seashore

Wildcat
Camp

Glen
Camp

Five
Brooks

1

Olema Valley Trail

Samuel P
Taylor
State
Park

Sir
Francis
Drake

to Petaluma
& Santa
Rosa

Rd

PACIFIC

OCEAN

Ⓖ

Agate
Beach

BOLINAS RIDGE

Bolinas–Fairfax Rd

Fairfax

101

Bolinas
Duxbury
Reef

Bolinas
Lagoon

Ⓐ

San
Anselmo

San
Rafael

Mt Tamalpais
State Park

Stinson
Beach

Mt Mt Tamalpais

Blvd

101

Muir Woods
National
Monument

1

Panoramic Hwy

Mill
Valley

580

Muir Beach

Ⓓ

to the
East Bay

Golden Gate
National Recreation
Area (GGNRA)

Rodeo Beach

Ⓔ

MARIN
HEADLANDS

Tiburon

Sausalito

Angel
Island

Point
Bonita

Cavallo
Point

0   4 miles
0   4 kilometers

Golden Gate

San Francisco Bay

San Francisco

101

watchers are on the lookout for sandpipers, shearwaters, and swallows. Everyone else comes for sand, surf, and sun.

AUDUBON CANYON RANCH ✉*Route 1* 📞*415-868-9244* 📠*415-868-1699* 🖰*www.egret.org, acr@egret.org* Birdwatchers flock to this ranch, located astride Route 1 on Bolinas Lagoon. Open on weekends and holidays from mid-March to mid-July (or by appointment), the ranch includes four canyons, one of which is famed as a rookery for egrets and herons. From the hiking trails here you can see up to 90 bird species as well as gray fox, deer, and bobcats. Closed Monday.

BOLINAS LAGOON This lagoon is also a bird sanctuary. Great egrets, ducks, and great blue herons make this one of their migratory stops. A colony of harbor seals lives here permanently and is joined in summer by migrating seals from San Francisco.

BOLINAS To reach the next point of interest you'll have to pay close attention. That's because you're approaching Bolinas. To get here from Route 1, watch for the crossroad at the foot of the lagoon; go left, then quickly left again and follow the road along the other side of the lagoon; take another left at the end of the road.

There should be signs to direct you, but there probably won't be—not because the state neglected them or highway workers forgot to put them up. It seems that local residents subscribe to the self-serving philosophy that since Bolinas is beautiful and they got here first, they should keep everyone else out. They tear down road signs and discourage visitors. The rest of Northern California is fair game, they seem to say, as long as Bolinas is left as some sort of human preserve.

The place they are attempting to hide is a delightful little town that rises from an S-shaped beach to form a lofty mesa. There are country roads along the bluff that overhangs the beach.

Whether you stroll the beach or hike the highlands, you'll discover in the houses here a wild architectural array. There are domes, glass boxes, curved-roof creations, huts, ranch houses, and stately brown-shingle designs. Bolinas, abutting on the Point Reyes National Seashore, is also a gateway to the natural world.

PRBO PALOMARIN FIELD STATION VISITOR CENTER 🖰*www.prbo.org* Follow Mesa Road for several miles outside town and you'll encounter this visitor center, where scientists at a research station study a bird population of over 200 species.

BOLINAS MUSEUM ✉*48 Wharf Road, Bolinas* 📞*415-868-2006* 📠*415-868-0607* 🖰*www.bolinasmuseum.org, info@bolinasmuseum.org* The award-winning Bolinas Museum features exhibits on the history of the Marin coast, including displays of Miwok Indian artifacts and Coastal Marin Artist's Gallery shows, which present the work of Marin County artists. Open Friday through Sunday and by appointment.

DUXBURY REEF
On the way back to town take a right on Overlook Drive, then a right on Elm Road; follow it to the parking lot at road's end.

Hiking trails lead down a sharp 160-foot cliff to this mile-long shale reef. Tidepool-watching is great sport here at low tide: starfish, periwinkles, abalone, limpets, and a host of other clinging creatures inhabit the marine preserve. In 1971 and again in 2007 huge oil spills endangered this spectacular area, but volunteers and trained personnel from all around the state worked day and night to save the reef and its tenacious inhabitants. The long-term effects of the most recent spill are being monitored and the Duxbury Reef Restoration program is working to maintain the habitat.

AGATE BEACH   Just north of rocky Duxbury Reef is this beach, an ideal spot to find agates, driftwood, and glass balls (however, no collecting is permitted).

SAN ANDREAS FAULT   Back on Route 1, continue north through Olema Valley, a peaceful region of horse ranches fringed by forest. Peaceful, that is, until you realize that the global suture that shook San Francisco back in 1906 cuts through the valley. As a matter of fact, the highway you are traveling parallels the fault line. During the great quake, houses collapsed, trees were uprooted, and fences decided to mark new boundaries.

NORTH AMERICAN PLATE   As you turn off Route 1 onto Sir Francis Drake Boulevard headed for the Point Reyes Peninsula, you'll be passing from the North American Plate, one of the six tectonic plates on which the entire earth's surface rides, to the Pacific Plate, which extends across the ocean. It is the pressure formed by the collision of these two great land masses that causes earthquakes. No sign will notify you as you cross this troubled geologic border, no guide will direct you along the rift zone. If you're like the people who live hereabouts, within 15 minutes of crossing over you'll have forgotten the fault exists. Especially when you see what is served on the Pacific Plate.

POINT REYES NATIONAL SEASHORE   With 88 miles of shoreline, this seashore is without doubt one of the finest seaside parks on any of the world's six plates. It is a realm of sand dunes and endless beaches, Scottish-type moors and grassy hillsides, salt marshes and pine forests. Bobcats, mountain lions, fox, and elk inhabit its wrinkled terrain, while harbor seals and gray whales cruise its ragged shoreline. More than 45 percent of North American bird species have been spotted here. The seashore also supports dairies and cattle ranches. In 1995, fire ripped through Point Reyes, burning 12,000 acres. However, all areas have been steadily returning to their natural habitat and await your exploration. All trails listed here and in the "Hiking" section are open and additional trails lead through the charred area, giving you a close-up look at the awesome healing power of nature.

BEAR VALLEY VISITORS CENTER ⊠ *Bear Valley Road* ✆ *415-464-5100* 🖷 *415-464-5149* ✐ *www.nps.gov/pore* The first stage in exploring Point Reyes National Seashore involves a stop at this visitors center. Here you can obtain maps, information, and camping permits.

MIWOK INDIAN VILLAGE A short hike from the visitors center will lead you to a Miwok Indian Village, where the round-domed shelters and other structures of the area's early inhabitants have been re-created. There is also an earthquake trail where you can see evidence of the San Andreas fault.

INVERNESS Most points of interest lie along Sir Francis Drake Boulevard, which rolls for miles and will carry you past this tiny town with country inns and ridgetop houses.

TOMALES BAY Like the Golden Gate, this finger-shaped inlet is a drowned river valley. Shacks and storefronts along Tomales Bay sell fresh local oysters, barbecued or on the half-shell. Most oysters in the Point Reyes area are Pacific oysters, imported from Japan in the 1930s to replace local oysters that had disappeared from San Francisco Bay because of pollution. Tomales Bay is one of the few areas where the smaller, sweeter Olympia oyster native to the Bay Area is still harvested. Gourmets consider Olympic oysters a special delicacy.

MOUNT VISION OVERLOOK Deeper in the park, a side road twists up to this overlook, where vista points sweep the peninsula.

DRAKES BAY OYSTER COMPANY ✉17171 Sir Francis Drake Boulevard, Inverness ✆415-669-1149 ✉415-669-1260 ✐www.drakesbayfamilyfarms.com Workers harvest the rich beds of an estuary here. The farm is a conglomeration of slapdash buildings, house trailers, and rusty machines. The shoreline is heaped over with oyster shells and the air is filled with pungent odors. Raw oysters are for sale. Even if you don't care for them, you might want to visit anyway. After all, when was the last time you saw an oyster farm?

The main road continues over folded hills that fall away to reveal sharp bluffs. Farm animals graze through fields smothered in wildflowers. There are ocean vistas stretching along miles of headland.

DRAKES BEACH On Drakes Beach you can picnic and beachcomb. Or gaze at the surrounding cliffs and wonder whether they truly resemble the White Cliffs of Dover. In that question resides a story told by one school of historians and vehemently denied by others. It seems that in 1579 the English explorer Sir Francis Drake anchored somewhere along the Northern California coast. But where? Some claim he cast anchor right here in Drakes Bay, others say Bolinas Lagoon, even San Francisco Bay. A brass plate, purportedly left by Drake, was discovered near San Francisco Bay in 1936; later it was believed that the plate had been first located near Drakes Bay and then moved; finally the plate was deemed a counterfeit. Find out more at the **Ken Patrick Visitor Center** (415-669-1250), which also features an aquarium and interactive computer displays. Saturday and Sunday only.

POINT REYES BEACH This windy ten-mile-long strip, also known as "North Beach" and "South Beach," is an ideal place for whale watchers. From there, it's not far to the end of Point Reyes' hammerhead peninsula. At one tip is **Chimney Rock**, a sea stack formed when the ocean eroded away the intervening land mass, leaving this islet just offshore. On the way to Chimney Rock you'll pass an **overlook** that's ideal for watching sea lions; then from Chimney Rock, if the day is clear, you'll see all the way to San Francisco.

POINT REYES LIGHTHOUSE 📞*415-669-1534* At the other tip of Point Reyes Beach is this lighthouse, an 1870s beacon located at the foggiest point on the entire Pacific coast. The treacherous waters offshore have witnessed numerous shipwrecks, the first occurring way back in 1595. The original lighthouse, constructed to prevent these calamities, incorporated over a thousand pieces of crystal in its intricate lens. A modern beacon eventually replaced this multifaceted instrument, although the antique is still on view. Walking the steps between the lighthouse and its observation platform is equivalent to ascending a 30-story building. The old lighthouse and an accompanying information center are still open to the public Thursday through Monday, weather permitting (lighthouse is inaccessible during winds exceeding 40 m.p.h.).

From Olema you can continue north on Route 1 or follow a looping 25-mile detour through the region's pastoral interior. On the latter, Sir Francis Drake Boulevard leads east past bald-domed hills and isolated farms. Livestock graze at the roadside while overhead hawks work the range. Grassland gives way to dense forest as you enter the realms of **Samuel P. Taylor State Park**. Then the road opens again to reveal a succession of tiny, woodframe towns.

WEST MARIN At San Geronimo, turn left on Nicasio Valley Road. This carries you farther into the pastoral region of west Marin, which varies so dramatically from the county's eastside suburban enclaves. Indeed, the inland valleys are reminiscent more of the Old West than the busy Bay Area. At the Nicasio Reservoir, turn left onto Point Reyes–Petaluma Road and follow it to Sir Francis Drake Boulevard, closing the circle of this rural tour.

From Olema, Route 1 continues north along Tomales Bay, the lovely fjord-shaped inlet. Salt marshes stretch along one side of the road; on the other are rumpled hills tufted with grass.

MARSHALL This waterfront village consists of fishing boats moored offshore and woodframe houses anchored firmly onshore.

TOMALES After Marshall the road turns inland to this falsefront town with a clapboard church and country homes. Then Route 1 continues past paint-peeled barns and open pastureland before turning seaward at Bodega Bay.

LODGING

MARIN HEADLANDS HOSTEL
$ 105 BEDS ✉*Fort Barry, Building 941* 📞*888-464-4872* 📠*415-331-3568*
🖳*www.norcalhostels.org*
Sometimes location is everything. That—plus a lively young clientele— is why I recommend this hostel. Also known as Golden Gate Hostel, the lodging is ideally located in the spectacular Marin Headlands section of

the Golden Gate National Recreation Area. Housed in two historic wood-frame buildings, this hostel's dormitory-style accommodations go for low prices. There are kitchen and laundry facilities available, a game room, a living room, and a few private rooms. Reservations are advised.

5 NORTH COAST MARIN COAST LODGING

GREEN GULCH FARM **h**idden

$$–$$$ 16 ROOMS   ✉ *1601 Shoreline Highway, Muir Beach*
📞 *415-383-3134* 📠 *415-383-3128* 🖥 *www.sfzc.org, ggfdirector@sfzc.org*

A Zen meditation center and organic farm located on a 115-acre spread in a lovely valley, Green Gulch is a restful and enchanting stop. Enroll in the Guest Practice Retreat Program, available between Sunday and Thursday with a three-night minimum. The schedule involves meditation, chanting, and bowing as well as morning chores and includes all meals (vegetarian, of course). Or you can simply rent a room by the night (at moderate to deluxe prices including meals) in their 12-room guest house, cottage, or guest center. With nearby hiking trails and beaches, it's a unique place. Closed in January.

THE PELICAN INN **h**idden

$$$–$$$$ 7 ROOMS   ✉ *10 Pacific Way, Muir Beach*   📞 *415-383-6000*
📠 *415-383-3424* 🖥 *www.pelicaninn.com, innkeeper@pelicaninn.com*

Most folks grumble when the fog sits heavy along the coast. At The Pelican Inn, guests consider fog part of the ambience. Damp air and chill winds add a final element to the Old English atmosphere at this bed and breakfast. Set in a Tudor-style building near Muir Beach, The Pelican Inn re-creates 16th-century England. There's a pub downstairs with a dart board on one wall and a fox-hunting scene facing on another. The dining room serves country fare like meat pies, prime rib, and fish and chips. To accompany the hearty English fare, the pub has a great selection of both local and international ales. Upstairs the period-print bedrooms contain time-honored antique furnishings, including canopied beds. Highly recommended; reserve well in advance.

SMILEY'S SCHOONER SALOON AND HOTEL

$–$$ 8 ROOMS   ✉ *41 Wharf Road, Bolinas* 📞 *415-868-1311* 📠 *415-868-0502*
🖥 *www.coastalpost.com/smileys, editor@coastalpost.com*

Located in the rustic town of Bolinas, Smiley's affords a three-minute walk to the beach. Accommodations are clean and nicely refurbished. The rooms are done in a rose color with antiques and have no radio, TV, phones, or other newfangled inventions. Six guest rooms are in the bungalows behind the saloon while two are above the bar. Light sleepers be forewarned: The bar downstairs is a favorite haunt of late-night revelers.

GRAND HOTEL

$ 2 ROOMS   ✉ *15 Brighton Avenue, Bolinas* 📞 *415-868-1757*

At this tiny business the two rooms share a bath and a kitchen. The proprietor also serves as a referral service for other places in town, so check with him about local accommodations.

HOSTELLING INTERNATIONAL—POINT REYES HOSTEL

$ 45 ROOMS   ✉ *P.O. Box 247, Point Reyes Station, CA 94956* 📞 *415-663-8811, 800-909-4776 ext. 168* 📠 *415-663-8811* 🖰 *www.norcalhostels.org*

Within Point Reyes National Seashore, this hostel provides low-rent lodging. In addition to 45 dorm-style accommodations, the hostel has a patio, kitchen, and a living room with a wood-burning stove. Perfect for explorers, it is situated two miles from the ocean near several hiking trails. The hostel is closed from 10 a.m. to 4:30 p.m. Reservations recommended.

BLACKTHORNE INN

$$$$ 5 UNITS   ✉ *266 Vallejo Avenue, Inverness Park* 📞 *415-663-8621*
📠 *415-663-8635* 🖰 *www.blackthorneinn.com, susan@blackthorneinn.com*

The Blackthorne is an architectural extravaganza set in a forest of oak, bay trees, and Douglas fir. The four-level house is expressive of the flamboyant "woodbutcher's art" building style popular in the 1970s. Using recycled materials (including windows from a Julia Morgan–designed building) and heavy doses of imagination, the builders created a maze of skylights, bay windows, and French doors, capped by an octagonal tower. A spiral staircase corkscrews up through this multi-tiered affair to the top deck, where an outdoor hot tub amid the trees. There are four bedrooms with private baths, and a hideaway suite with shared bath. Each room has been personalized; the most outstanding is the "Eagle's Nest," occupying the glass-encircled octagon at the very top of this Aquarian wedding cake. No children under 14 allowed.

MOTEL INVERNESS

$$–$$$ 7 UNITS   ✉ *12718 Sir Francis Drake Boulevard, Inverness* 📞 *415-236-1967, 866-453-3839* 🖰 *www.motelinverness.com, info@motelinverness.com*

Nearby in Inverness there's this motel, commanding a location along Tomales Bay that would be the envy of many well-heeled hostelries. Unfortunately, the architect who designed it faced the rooms toward the road, not the water. Only the newly added honeymoon suite overlooks Tomales Bay. Guests can, however, enjoy views of the bay in the motel's common room, which also features a billiards table. The entire motel is a nonsmoking establishment.

INVERNESS VALLEY INN

$$$ 25 ROOMS   ✉ *13275 Sir Francis Drake Boulevard, Inverness* 📞 *415-669-7250, 800-416-0405* 🖰 *www.invernessvalleyinn.com, info@invernessvalleyinn.com*

Situated on 15 quiet country acres, this inn offers an affordable retreat in the increasingly upscale Point Reyes area. Scattered over the well-groomed grounds are five contemporary A-frame buildings, each housing large, light, and airy rooms complete with kitchenettes, barbecues, and private patios. A saltwater pool, a hot tub, basketball hoops, and, of course, tennis courts round out the amenities. Perfect for families and active couples, the inn is a stone's throw away from secluded coves, spectacular hiking trails, excellent kayaking, and a private eight-acre wildlife preserve. And if you forgot your tennis rackets, the friendly owners will be glad to provide them. Pet-friendly.

TEN INVERNESS WAY

$$$ 5 ROOMS   ✉10 Inverness Way, Inverness   📞415-669-1648
📠415-669-7403   ✐www.teninvernessway.com, inn@teninvernessway.com

A favorite bed and breakfast lies along the flagstone path at Ten Inverness Way. The place is filled with pleasant surprises, like fruit trees and flowers in the yard, a library, and a warm living room with stone fireplace. The bedrooms are small but cozy, carpeted wall-to-wall, and imaginatively decorated with hand-fashioned quilts; all have private baths. If you want deluxe treatment, book the Meadow Suite, which includes exclusive use of the hot tub. It's a short stroll from the house to the shops and restaurants of Inverness. A full hot breakfast is provided in the morning. Another special treat: Tea and fresh-baked cookies are served in the afternoon, and wine and cheese in the evening.

POINT REYES LODGING   📞415-663-1872, 800-539-1872   ✐www.ptreyes.com

As country living goes, it's darn near impossible to find a place as pretty and restful as Point Reyes. People with wander in their hearts and wonder in their minds have been drawn here for years. Not surprisingly, country inns sprang up to cater to star-struck explorers and imaginative travelers. A good source for information on these local hostelries is this company, which offers 24-hour information on 16 inns and cottages in coastal Marin.

DINING

From the Marin Headlands region, the nearest restaurants are in the bayside town of Sausalito. Then, progressing north, you'll find dining spots scattered throughout the towns and villages along the coast.

SAND DOLLAR RESTAURANT

$$ AMERICAN   ✉3458 Route 1, Stinson Beach   📞415-868-0434   📠415-868-0159

Stinson Beach sports several restaurants; my favorite is the Sand Dollar, with facilities for dining indoors or on the patio. At lunch this informal eatery serves hamburgers and sandwiches. At dinner there are fresh fish dishes and pasta; they also serve vegetarian and meat dishes. With a fireplace and random artwork on the wall, it is a cozy local gathering point.

BOLINAS COAST CAFÉ

$$ CALIFORNIA CUISINE   ✉46 Wharf Road, Bolinas   📞415-868-2298
📠415-868-0660   ✐www.bolinascafe.com

Bring the kids and the dogs—this café is warm, welcoming, and casual. Specialties such as gardener's pie, tomato-fennel seafood stew, and linguine and clams use local organic produce, locally caught fish and shellfish, local dairy, and chemical-free meats. In the summer, the chefs barbecue oysters and salmon on the front patio. Breakfast on weekends. Closed Monday.

THE STATION HOUSE CAFÉ

$$ AMERICAN   ✉11180 Main Street, Point Reyes Station   ✆415-663-1515
✎www.stationhousecafe.com

Local residents highly recommend this place. Maybe it's the artwork along the walls or the garden patio. Regardless, it's really the food that draws folks from the surrounding countryside. The dinner menu includes fresh oysters, plus steak and fish dishes. Dinner may include entrées such as potato-crusted local fillet of sole with orange-basil beurre blanc and green beans or Niman Ranch osso bucco with vegetables and soft polenta. There's also a complete breakfast menu served all day, along with sandwiches and salads. Closed Wednesday.

PRISCILLA'S PIZZERIA & CAFE

$–$$ PIZZA   ✉12781 Sir Francis Drake Boulevard, Inverness   ✆415-669-1244

This woodframe café in the center of tiny Inverness serves delicious pizza and pasta as well as soups, sandwiches, and salads. The place has a touch of city style in a country setting; there are overhead fans and an espresso machine. Closed Tuesday.

NICK'S COVE

$$–$$$$ CALIFORNIA CUISINE   ✉23240 Highway 1, Marshall   ✆866-63-NICKS, 415-663-1033   ✆415-663-9751   ✎www.nickscove.com, relax@nickscove.com

Located on scenic Tomales Bay, Nick's was built in the 1930s and has been restored to its original glory. Situated directly on the water and elevated by pilings, the restaurant affords unmatched views from every table. Fresh seafood and steaks highlight the seasonal menu, which also boasts greens from the restaurant's very own garden. Try the oak-fired Arctic char or move straight to dessert for the toasted-almond cheesecake.

SHOPPING

Past Sausalito, the shopping scene along the North Coast is concentrated in a few towns. There are small shops scattered about in rural areas, but the best selection of arts and crafts is located around Point Reyes.

During the '60s and '70s, many talented people, caught up in the "back to the land" movement, migrated to the state's northern counties. Here they developed their skills and further refined their art. As a result, crafts like pottery, woodworking, weaving, stained-glass manufacturing, jewelry, and fashion designing have flourished.

CLAUDIA CHAPLINE GALLERY AND SCULPTURE GARDEN

✉3445 Shoreline Highway, Stinson Beach   ✆415-868-2308   ✎www.cchapline.com If the weather's nice, take a stroll through this gallery and sculpture garden. Featuring a variety of mixed media and three roomy skylight galleries, it's a great place to pick up an interesting work of art. Open Saturday and Sunday, or by appointment.

STINSON BEACH BOOKS   ✉3455 Shoreline Highway, Stinson Beach
✆415-868-0700 This shop may be located in a small town, but it offers a large variety of books. Compressed within the confines of the place is

an array of travel books, field guides, bestsellers, novels, children's books, etc. It's a great place to stop before that long, languorous day at the beach. Closed Tuesday from January through May.

GALLERY ROUTE ONE ✉*11101 Route 1, Point Reyes Station* ☎*415-663-1347* Route One spotlights sculptures, photographs, and paintings by contemporary regional artists. There's also mixed-media environmental art exhibits. Closed Tuesday.

SUSAN HAYES HANDWOVENS ✉*80 4th Street, Point Reyes Station* ☎*415-663-8057* 🖱*www.susanhayeshandwovens.com, susan@susanhayeshandwovens. com* The showroom here is a gorgeous tumble of the colored twill, rayon, wool, and handwoven textiles used to make coordinating separates. Custom orders are the specialty. There's also a wide selection of beautiful hats, gloves, handbags, and jewelry. Closed Monday and Tuesday.

SHAKER SHOPS WEST ✉*5 Inverness Way, Inverness* ☎*415-669-7256, 800-474-2537* 🖱*www.shakershops.com, shaker@shakershops.com* This is a marvelous store specializing in reproductions of Shaker crafts, particularly furniture. In addition to rag rugs, candlesticks, and woven baskets, there are beautifully handcrafted boxes. The Early American household items range from cross-stitch needlepoint to tinware. Touring the store is like visiting a mini-museum dedicated to this rare American community. Open Friday and Saturday, and by appointment.

NIGHTLIFE

SMILEY'S SCHOONER SALOON ✉*41 Wharf Road, Bolinas* ☎*415-868-1311* When the sun goes down in Bolinas, you are left with several options. Sleep, read, curl up with a loved one, fade into unrelieved boredom, or head for Smiley's. Since local folks often follow the latter course, you're liable to find them parka-to-parka along the bar. They come to shoot pool, listen to weekend live music, and admire the lavish wood-panel bar. Smiley's, after all, is the only show in town—and one of the longest continuously operating saloons in California (since 1851). Occasional cover.

OLD WESTERN SALOON ✉*11201 Route 1, Point Reyes Station* ☎*415-663-1661* Local folks in Point Reyes Station ease up to this wooden bar practically every night of the week. But on Friday, Saturday, and alternating Sundays, when the place features live rock, blues, country—you name it—and dancing 'til the wee hours, the biggest crowds of all arrive. Occasional cover.

BEACHES & PARKS

KIRBY COVE
✉*The beach is located in the Marin Headlands section of the Golden Gate National Recreation Area. Take the first exit, Alexander Avenue, after crossing the Golden Gate Bridge. Then take an immediate left, following the sign back toward San Francisco. Next, bear right at the sign for Marin Headlands. Follow Conzelman Road three-tenths of a mile to a turnout where a sign will mark the trailhead.* ☎*415-331-1540* 📠*415-331-6963* 🖱*www.nps.gov/goga*

🚶 🚲 🎣 This pocket beach, located at the end of a one-mile trail, nestles in the shadow of the Golden Gate Bridge. The views from beachside are unreal: Gaze up at the bridge's steel lacework or out across the gaping mouth of the Gate. When the fog's away, it's a sunbather's paradise; regardless of the weather, this cove is favored by those who like to fish. Facilities include a picnic area and toilets.

▲ There are four campsites for tents only; $25 per night. Reservations are required: 877-444-6777. Closed November through March.

UPPER FISHERMAN'S BEACH

✉ Located in the Marin Headlands section of the Golden Gate National Recreation Area. Follow the directions to Kirby Cove trailhead (see listing above). Continue on Conzelman Road for two and a third miles. Shortly after passing the steep downhill section of this road, you'll see a parking lot on the left with a trailhead. Follow the trail to the beach.

🚲 🐎 🛶 This is a long, narrow corridor of sand tucked under the Marin Headlands. With steep hills behind and a grand view of the Golden Gate in front, it's a perfect place for naturists and nature lovers alike. It is a popular beach for nudists, although not officially recognized as such. It cannot be found on maps or atlases, but local folks and savvy travelers know it well (some call it "Black Sands"). There are no facilities here.

RODEO BEACH

✉ Located in the Marin Headlands section of the Golden Gate National Recreation Area. After crossing Golden Gate Bridge on Route 101, take the first exit, Alexander Avenue. Bear right on Alexander Avenue, then go left on Bunker Road. Follow this road to Rodeo Beach. ☏ *415-331-1540* 📠 *415-331-6963* 🖥 *www.nps.gov/goga*

🚶 🚲 🐎 🛶 ⚓ A broad sandy beach, this place is magnificent not only for the surrounding hillsides and nearby cliffs, but also for the quiescent lagoon at its back. Given its proximity to San Francisco, Rodeo Beach is a favorite among the natives. The beach has restrooms, cold-water showers, and a picnic area. Pets on leashes are allowed. Beware of the strong undercurrents and rip tides.

▲ Though not permitted on the beach, camping is available at three campgrounds in the area. They are hike-in campgrounds, ranging from 100 yards to 3 miles. There are five sites at Haypress, three sites at Hawkcamp, and three sites at Bicentennial. No water, no fires, and no pets. These campgrounds are for tents only, all are free, but reservations and permits are required. Call the information number above for more details.

MUIR WOODS NATIONAL MONUMENT

✉ Off Route 1 on Panoramic Highway, about 12 miles north of the Golden Gate Bridge ☏ *415-388-2596* 📠 *415-389-6957* 🖥 *www.nps.gov/muwo*

🚶 If it weren't for the crowds, this redwood preserve would rank little short of majestic. Designated a national treasure by President Theodore Roosevelt in 1908, it features stately groves of tall trees. Salmon run the creeks from November to April; the best viewing times are a few days after a heavy storm. There are six miles of hiking trails, a snack bar, a gift shop, and restrooms. Day-use fee, $5.

MT. TAMALPAIS STATE PARK ___

✉ *Follow Route 1 north through Mill Valley; turn right on Panoramic Highway, which runs along the park border.* ☎ *415-388-2070* 📠 *415-388-2968*

🚶 🚴 🐎 Spectacularly situated between Mt. Tamalpais and the ocean, this 6300-acre park offers everything from mountaintop views to a rocky coastline. More than 50 miles of hiking trails wind past stands of cypress, Douglas fir, Monterey pine, and California laurel. Wildlife abounds. The countryside draws nature lovers and sightseers alike. The park's facilities include picnic areas, restrooms, a refreshment stand, and a visitors center (open weekends only). The park now offers wi-fi service. Every year since 1913 a mountain play has been staged in the amphitheater. Parking fee, $6.

▲ There are 15 tent sites at Pantoll Park Headquarters (415-388-2070); facilities in this well-shaded spot include picnic areas, restrooms, and running water; $15 per night. There's also camping at Frank Valley Horsecamp (800-444-7275), located near Muir Beach in the southwest end of the park. You'll find picnic tables, pit toilets, and running water. Reservations are required and can be obtained at park headquarters. For information on Steep Ravine Environmental Camp see the listing below.

MUIR BEACH

✉ *Route 1, about 16 miles north of San Francisco* ☎ *415-388-2596* 📠 *415-389-6957* 🌐 *www.nps.gov/muwo*

🚶 🚴 🐎 ⚓ 🏊 Because of its proximity to San Francisco, this spot is a favorite among local people. Located at the foot of a coastal valley, Muir Beach forms a semicircular cove. There's a sandy beach (with a rough surf) and ample opportunity for picnicking. Other than picnic tables the facilities are limited to toilets.

STEEP RAVINE ENVIRONMENTAL CAMP

✉ *Located along a paved road off Route 1, about one mile south of Stinson Beach. Turn at the sign.* ☎ *415-388-2070* 📠 *415-388-2968*

Set on a shelf above the ocean, this outstanding site is bounded on the other side by sharp slopes. Contained within Mt. Tamalpais State Park, it features a small beach and dramatic sea vista. This is a good place for nature study.

▲ There are seven tent sites ($15 per night) and ten rustic cabins ($75 per night). Reservations can be made up to seven months in advance for cabins; call 800-444-7275.

RED ROCK BEACH ___

✉ *Part of Mt. Tamalpais State Park, Red Rock is located off Route 1 about one mile south of Stinson Beach. Watch for a large (often crowded) parking area on the seaward side of the highway. Follow the steep trail down to the beach.*

🏊 ⚓ 🏖 One of the area's most popular nude beaches, this pocket beach is wall-to-wall with local folks on sunny weekends.

Well protected along its flank by steep hillsides, Red Rock is an ideal sunbathers' retreat. There are no facilities here.

STINSON BEACH PARK

✉ *Located along Route 1 in the town of Stinson Beach, 23 miles north of San Francisco*
✆ *415-868-1922*

One of Northern California's finest beaches, this broad, sandy corridor curves for three miles. Backdropped by rolling hills, Stinson also borders beautiful Bolinas Lagoon. Besides being a sunbather's haven, it's a great place for beachcombers and birdwatchers. To escape the crowds congregating here weekends, stroll up to the north end of the beach. You'll find a narrow sand spit looking out on Bolinas. You still won't have the beach entirely to yourself, but a place this beautiful is worth sharing. Because of currents from Bolinas Lagoon, the water at Stinson Beach Park is a little warmer than elsewhere along the Northern California Coast (but it's still brisk by Atlantic Coast standards). There are picnic areas with barbecues, outdoor showers and restrooms; in summer there are lifeguards and a snack bar. If you dare swim anywhere along the North Coast, it might as well be here, where the waters are a tiny bit warmer.

BOLINAS BEACH

✉ *Located at the end of Wharf Road in Bolinas*

Beginning near Bolinas Lagoon and curving around the town perimeter, this salt-and-pepper beach provides ample opportunity for walking. A steep bluff borders the beach. In the narrow mouth of the lagoon you can often see harbor seals and waterfowl. There are no facilities but the town of Bolinas is within walking distance.

AGATE BEACH AND DUXBURY REEF

✉ *From Olema–Bolinas Road in Bolinas, go up the hill on Mesa Road, left on Overlook Drive, and right on Elm Road. Follow Elm Road to the parking lot at the end; take the path down to the ocean.* ✆ *415-499-6387* ✆ *415-499-3795*

You could spend the whole day at Agate Beach gazing at the beautiful variety of stones under your feet. (Collecting is not permitted.) At low tide, Duxbury Reef to the south is also outstanding for tidepool gazing. Both are highly recommended for adventurers, daydreamers, and amateur biologists. There are portable restrooms.

HAGMAIER POND

✉ *On Route 1 go three and a half miles north of the Bolinas turnoff (at the foot of Bolinas Lagoon). You'll see a shallow parking lot on the right side of the highway. A dirt road leads uphill several hundred yards to the lake; take the first left fork.*

Favored by swimmers and nude sunbathers, this miniature lake offers a variation from nearby ocean beaches. It's fringed with grassland and bounded by forest, making it an idyllic spot within easy reach of the highway. There are no facilities.

SAMUEL P. TAYLOR STATE PARK _____

✉ *Located on Sir Francis Drake Boulevard, east of Route 1 and six miles from Olema* ☎ *415-488-9897* 📠 *415-488-4315*

🚶 🚴 🐎 ⛵ Located several miles inland, this redwood facility provides an opportunity to experience the coastal interior. The place is heavily wooded and offers close to 2900 acres to roam. In addition to the campgrounds, there are beautiful hiking trails through old-growth redwood groves, near a tranquil creek, and up to hilltops, offering sweeping views of the Olema Valley. Wildflowers adorn the park entrance and gentle trails. The park has picnic areas, restrooms, and showers. Wi-fi access is available. Parking fee, $6.

▲ There are 61 sites, 25 for tents only (no hookups); $11 to $25 per night. Reservations are recommended from Memorial Day through Labor Day; call 800-444-7275.

POINT REYES NATIONAL SEASHORE

✉ *Off Route 1, about 40 miles north of San Francisco* ☎ *415-464-5137* 📠 *415-663-8132* 🌐 *www.nps.gov/pore*

🚶 🚴 🐎 ⛵ 🎣 ⛵ 🚣 One of the great natural features of Northern California, this 77,000-acre park contains everything from wind-blown beaches to dense pine forests. No traveler should miss it. The park's facilities include three visitors centers, picnic areas, restrooms, and 140 miles of hiking trails.

▲ You may camp in any of four campgrounds, which are all accessible only by hiking trails or bikes. **Sky Camp**, with 12 primitive sites, sits on the side of Mt. Wittenberg, commanding stunning views of Drakes Bay. **Wildcat Camp** rests on a bluff above a pretty beach; there are 8 primitive sites. **Glen Camp** lies in a forested valley and has 12 primitive sites. **Coast Camp** nestles in a meadow near the beach; there are 14 primitive sites. Each camp is equipped with toilets, non-potable water, and picnic areas. Wood fires are not allowed; plan to bring alternate campfire materials. Permits are required; camping fee is $15 per night, but can raise to as much as $40 depending on the size of your group. You are limited to four nights in the park. Reservations are strongly recommended. For reservations call 415-663-8054 between 9 a.m. and 2 p.m. Monday through Friday, or download a camping form from the website and fax to 415-464-5149. Permits can be obtained Monday through Friday until 2 p.m. at Bear Valley Visitors Center.

LIMANTOUR BEACH

✉ *Once in Point Reyes National Seashore, follow Limantour Road to the end.*

⛵ This white-sand beach is actually a spit, a narrow peninsula pressed between Drakes Bay and an estuary. It's an exotic area of sand dunes and sea breezes. Ideal for exploring, the region shelters over 350 bird species. There's good (but cold) swimming and fishing seaside. The only facilities are toilets.

▲ None, but the Point Reyes Youth Hostel is located on the road to Limantour.

TOMALES BAY STATE PARK

✉ *From Route 1 in Olema take Sir Francis Drake Boulevard to Inverness. From Inverness it's another eight miles. When Sir Francis Drake forks, take the right fork, which becomes Pierce Point Road. Follow Pierce Point Road to the park.* ✆ *415-669-1140* 🖝 *415-669-1701*

🏃 ⛵ 🏖 ⛴ This delightful park, which abuts on Point Reyes National Seashore, provides a warm, sunny alternative to Point Reyes' frequent fog. The water, too, is warmer here in Tomales Bay, making it a great place for swimming, as well as fishing and boating. Or check out the self-guided nature trail for a description of the relationship between American Indians and local plants. The virgin grove of Bishop pine is a special treat. Rimming the park are several sandy coves; most accessible of these is Heart's Desire Beach, flanked by bluffs and featuring nearby picnic areas. From Heart's Desire a self-guided nature trail goes northwest to Indian Beach, a long stretch of white sand fringed by trees. Hiking trails around the park lead to other secluded beaches, excellent for picnics and day hikes. Dogs are restricted to the upper picnic area and must be kept on a leash. The park has picnic areas and restrooms. Day-use fee, $6.

SHELL BEACH

✉ *Once in Point Reyes National Seashore, take Sir Francis Drake Boulevard one mile past Inverness, then turn right at Camino del Mar. The trailhead is located at the end of this street; follow the trail three-tenths of a mile down to the beach.*

⛵ 🎣 🏖 ⛴ Actually part of Tomales Bay State Park, this pocket beach is several miles from the park entrance. As a result, it is often uncrowded. A patch of white sand bordered by steep hills, Shell Beach is ideal for swimming and picnicking. No dogs allowed. The only facilities are toilets.

MARSHALL BEACH

✉ *Once in Point Reyes National Seashore, take Pierce Point Road. Immediately after passing the entrance to Tomales Bay State Park, turn right onto the paved road. This road travels uphill, turns to gravel and goes two and six tenths miles to a gate. From the gate you hike one and a half miles down a steep trail to the beach.*

🏃 ⛵ 🎣 🚣 🚴 🏖 ⛴ This secluded beach on Tomales Bay is a wonderful place to swim and sunbathe, often in complete privacy. The beach is a lengthy strip of white sand fringed by cypress trees.

▲ Boat-in camping allowed on the beach with a permit; be sure to pack out everything you packed in. For information and permits, call 415-663-8054.

ABBOTTS LAGOON

✉ *Once in Point Reyes National Seashore, take Pierce Point Road. The trailhead is located along the roadside, two miles past the turnoff for Tomales Bay State Park; follow the trail one mile to the lagoon.*

🏃 Because of its rich waterfowl population and beautiful surrounding dunes, this is a favorite place among hikers and birdwatchers. From the lagoon it's an easy jaunt over the dunes to Point Reyes Beach. The only facilities are toilets.

KEHOE BEACH

✉ *Once in Point Reyes National Seashore, take Pierce Point Road. The trailhead is along the roadside four miles past the turnoff for Tomales Bay State Park; follow the trail a half-mile to the beach.*

🏃 🌊 Bounded by cliffs, this strand is actually the northern end of ten-mile-long Point Reyes Beach. It's a lovely place, covered with wildflowers in spring and boasting a seasonal lagoon. The isolation makes it a great spot for explorers. The only facilities are toilets (at the trailhead).

MCCLURES BEACH

✉ *Located in Point Reyes National Seashore at the end of Pierce Point Road. A steep trail leads a half-mile down to the beach.* 📞 *415-464-5100*

🏃 🌊 Of the many beautiful beaches in Point Reyes National Seashore, this beach is by far my favorite. It is a white-sand beach protected by granite cliffs that stand like bookends on either flank. Tidepool watching is a great sport here; if you arrive during low tide it's possible to skirt the cliffs along the south end and explore a pocket beach next door. But don't let a waxing tide catch you sleeping! Swimming is dangerous here; surf fishing, bird-watching, and driftwood gathering more than make up for it. Quite simply, places like this are the reason folks visit Northern California. The only facilities are toilets (at the trailhead).

POINT REYES BEACH

✉ *Located off Sir Francis Drake Boulevard, about 14 miles from park headquarters*

🌊 It will become wonderfully evident why this is nicknamed "Ten Mile Beach" when you cast eyes on this endless sand swath. A great place for whale watching and fishing, this is not the spot for swimming. Sharks, riptides, and unusual wave patterns make even wading inadvisable. Also the heavy winds along this coastline would chill any swimmer's plans. But that does not detract from the wild beauty of the place, or the fact you can jog for miles along this strand (also referred to as North Beach and South Beach). Restrooms are the park's only facilities.

DRAKES BEACH

✉ *Located off Sir Francis Drake Boulevard, 15 miles from park headquarters*

🏃 🚣 🌊 Edged by cliffs, this crescent beach looks out upon the tip of Point Reyes. Since it's well protected by Drakes Bay, this is a good swimming spot. It also provides interesting hikes along the base of the cliffs to the inlet at Drakes Estero. Facilities include picnic areas, restrooms, a visitors center, and a snack bar open weekends only during off-season.

OLEMA RV RESORT & CAMPGROUND

✉ *10155 Route 1, Olema* 📞 *415-663-8106, 800-655-2267* 📠 *415-663-8135*
🌐 *www.olemaranch.com*

This roadside camping park has facilities for trailers and tent campers. The price, however, ain't cheap—$30 to $35 for a tent and two people ($39 to $49 for RV sites). That will buy a plot of ground in a grassy area.

It's not exactly the great outdoors, but the place is strategically situated along Route 1 near the turnoff for Point Reyes National Seashore. There are picnic areas, restrooms, showers, a playground, a post office, wi-fi, and a laundromat.

▲ There are 230 tent/RV sites (full hookups available); $40 to $60 per night.

SONOMA AND MENDOCINO COAST

Just north of Marin County lie the coastlines of Sonoma and Mendocino, beautiful and still lightly developed areas. Placid rangeland extends inward while along the shoreline, surf boils against angular cliffs. Far below are pocket beaches and coves; offshore rise dozens of tiny rock islands, or sea stacks. The entire coast teems with fish—salmon and steelhead—as well as crabs, clams, and abalone. Rip currents, sneaker waves, and the coldest waters this side of the Arctic make swimming inadvisable. But the landscape is wide open for exploration, enchanting and exotic.

SIGHTS

BODEGA BAY   Jenner, Mendocino, and Fort Bragg are among the small towns along this endless coastline, but the first place you'll come to is a somewhat different type of community. In fact the fishing village of Bodega Bay might look vaguely familiar, for it was the setting of Alfred Hitchcock's eerie film *The Birds*. It's questionable whether any cast members remain among the population of snowy egrets, but the Bay still supports a variety of winged creatures. Conservation efforts have encouraged a comeback among the endangered brown pelicans and blue herons. Serious Hitchcock fans in search of familiar structures from the movie can take a short side trip inland along the Bay Highway to the town of **Bodega**. Here they'll find the old Potter schoolhouse and the church from the film.

LUCAS WHARF   ✉ *Route 1 and Smith Brothers Lane, Bodega Bay* Here, and elsewhere along this working waterfront, you can watch fishermen setting off into the fog every morning and hauling in their catch later in the day.

OCCIDENTAL   For a rustic detour, follow Coleman Valley Road when it departs from Route 1 north of Bodega Bay. It weaves through farmland and offers great views of ocean and mountains, and leads to the forest-rimmed village of Occidental.

JENNER   Just before Route 1 winds up to this woodframe town (population 170, elevation 13), is the newly named **Jenner Headlands**, a 5630-acre coastal ranch set to be officially acquired by the Sonoma Land Trust in 2009. (For current information, go to www.sonoma land trust.org.) The town itself is a quiet seaside whistle-stop with a handful of vacation inns located where the Russian River meets the ocean.

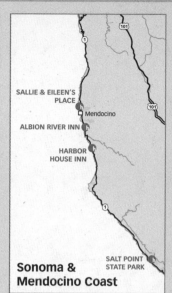

SALLIE & EILEEN'S PLACE
PAGE 336

Your own little private sanctuary in the woods—a nurturing, comfortable space for women only

ALBION RIVER INN
PAGE 338

Otherworldly cliffside views and mouthwatering California cuisine like grilled ginger-lime prawns

HARBOR HOUSE INN
PAGE 338

Charming, intimate dining room offering fresh, local foods with a roaring fire and sunsets over the ocean

SALT POINT STATE PARK
PAGE 343

6000 acres of coastline, forests, redwoods, and open range laced with hiking trails and rife with wildlife

FORT ROSS ☎707-847-3286, 707-847-3437 📠707-847-3601 ✉fria@mcn.org The Russians for whom the river is named were explorers and trappers sailing down the Pacific coast from Russian outposts in Alaska. They came in search of sea otters, growing food for their Alaskan settlements, and in hope of opening trade routes with the early Spanish settlers. In 1812 these bold outlanders went so far as to build this wooden fortress overlooking the ocean. The Fort Ross community included Native Alaskans, Russians, and local Koshaya Poms. The old Russian stronghold, 12 miles north of Jenner, is today a state historic park. Touring the reconstructed fort you'll encounter an old Russian Orthodox chapel, a stockade built of hand-tooled redwood, barracks and officers' houses, and two blockhouses (one seven-sided and another eight-sided). The Visitors Center includes a museum and exhibit auditorium. Admission.

ROUTE 1 From Jenner north through Fort Ross and beyond, this highway winds high above the coast. Every curve exposes another awesome view of adze-like cliffs slicing into the sea. Driving this corkscrew route can jangle the nerves, but the vistas are soothing to the soul. With the exception of scattered villages, the coastline remains undeveloped. You'll pass sunbleached wooden buildings in the old town of Stewarts Point. Then the road courses through Sea Ranch, a development bitterly opposed by environmentalists, which nevertheless displays imaginative contemporary-design houses set against a stark sea.

Inside the map:
- SALLIE & EILEEN'S PLACE
- Mendocino
- ALBION RIVER INN
- HARBOR HOUSE INN
- SALT POINT STATE PARK
- Sonoma & Mendocino Coast

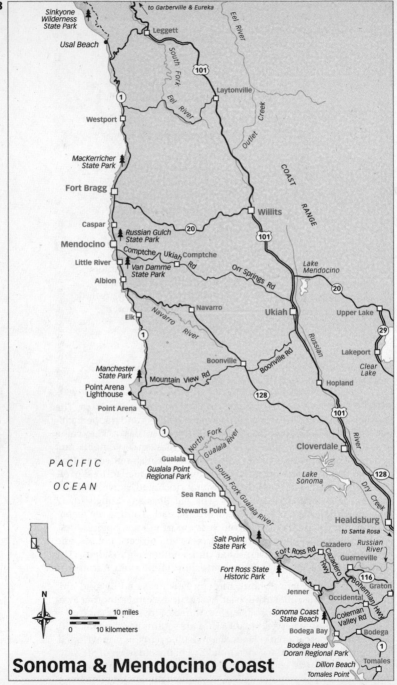

Sinkyone
Wilderness
State Park

to Garberville & Eureka

Leggett

Usal Beach

Eel River

South Fork
Eel
River

101

Laytonville

Westport

Outlet
Creek

MacKerricher
State Park

COAST

Fort Bragg

Willits

RANGE

Caspar

20

101

Russian Gulch
State Park

Mendocino

Comptche

Ukiah

Comptche

Lake
Mendocino

Little River

Comptche
Rd

Orr Springs Rd

20

Van Damme
State Park

Albion

Elk

Navarro

Navarro

River

Ukiah

Upper Lake

29

Lakeport

1

Russian

Clear
Lake

Boonville

Boonville Rd

Manchester
State Park

Mountain View Rd

Hopland

Point Arena
Lighthouse

128

101

Point Arena

1

North Fork
Gualala River

Cloverdale

River

128

Gualala

Gualala Point
Regional Park

South Fork Gualala River

Lake
Sonoma

Dry Creek

Sea Ranch

Stewarts Point

Healdsburg

to Santa Rosa

Salt Point
State Park

Fort Ross Rd

Cazadero

Russian
River

PACIFIC

OCEAN

Fort Ross State
Historic Park

Cazadero
Hwy

Guerneville

116

Graton

Jenner

Occidental

Bohemian Hwy

Sonoma Coast
State Beach

Coleman
Valley Rd

N

Bodega Bay

Bodega

0   10 miles

Bodega Head
Doran Regional Park

1

0   10 kilometers

Dillon Beach
Tomales Point

Tomales

Sonoma & Mendocino Coast

POINT ARENA LIGHTHOUSE ☎707-882-2777 ✉palight@mcn.org Just north of Point Arena, a side road from Route 1 leads out to this lighthouse. The original lighthouse, built in 1870, was destroyed in the 1906 San Francisco earthquake, which struck Point Arena even more fiercely than the bay city. The present beacon, rebuilt shortly afterwards, rises 115 feet from a narrow peninsula. The lighthouse is open for tours. The views, by definition, are outstanding. Open from 10 a.m. to 4:30 p.m. Admission.

SEASIDE VILLAGES In Mendocino County, the highway passes through tiny seaside villages. **Elk**, **Albion**, and **Little River** gaze down on the ocean from rocky heights. The coastline is an intaglio of river valleys, pocket beaches, and narrow coves. Forested ridges, soft and green in appearance, fall away into dizzying cliffs. The houses that stand amid this continental turmoil resemble Maine saltboxes and Cape Cod cottages.

MENDOCINO In this town, which sits on a headland above the sea, you'll discover New England incarnate. Settled in 1852, Mendocino was built largely by Yankees who decorated their village with wooden towers, Victorian homes, and a Gothic Revival Presbyterian church. The town, originally a vital lumber port, has become an artists' colony. With a shoreline honeycombed by beaches and a villagescape capped with a white church steeple, Mendocino is a mighty pretty corner of the continent.

MENDOCINO HEADLANDS STATE PARK ☎707-937-4700 Located atop a sea cliff, this park offers unmatched views of the town's tumultuous shoreline. From the bluffs you can gaze down at placid tidepools and wave-carved grottoes. The **Ford House** (735 Main Street, Mendocino; 707-937-5397), within the park, is an 1854 home with a small museum that also serves as a visitors center.

KELLEY HOUSE MUSEUM ✉45007 Albion Street, Mendocino ☎707-937-5791 ☏707-937-2156 ✉staff@mendocinohistory.org The best way to experience Mendocino is by stopping at this antique museum. Set in a vintage home dating from 1861, the museum serves as a historical research center (open Tuesday through Friday from 9 a.m. to 4 p.m.; appointments recommended). Closed Wednesday in summer.

Among Mendocino's intriguing locales are the **Chinese Temple**, a 19th-century religious shrine located on Albion Street (open by appointment only); the **Presbyterian Church**, a national historic landmark on Main Street; and the **MacCallum House**, a Gingerbread Victorian on Albion Street, which has been reborn as an inn and restaurant. Another building of note is the **Masonic Hall**, an 1866 structure adorned with a hand-carved redwood statue on the roof on Ukiah Street.

MENDOCINO ART CENTER ✉45200 Little Lake Street, Mendocino ☎707-937-5818, 800-653-3328 ☏707-937-1764 ✉www.mendocinoartcenter.org, mendoart@mcn.org After meandering the side streets, stop at this art center. Here exhibits by painters, potters, photographers, textile workers, and others will give an idea of the tremendous talent contained in tiny Mendocino. Nearly 300 one- to six-day workshops in ceramics, sculpture, computer arts, and textiles are offered annually. There's a pretty garden and a gift shop, and the complex also houses a local theater company.

JUG HANDLE STATE RESERVE ✉Along Route 1 about one mile north of Caspar ☎707-937-5804 ☏707-937-2953 North of town, on the way to Fort

Bragg, stop at this state reserve where you can climb an ecological stairway, which ascends a series of marine terraces. On the various levels you'll encounter the varied coast, dune, and ridge environments that form the area's diverse ecosystem.

MENDOCINO COAST BOTANICAL GARDENS ✉ *18220 North Route 1, Fort Bragg* ☎ *707-964-4352* 📠 *707-964-3114* 🖥 *www.gardenbythesea.org, info@ gardenbythesea.org* For a thoroughly delightful stroll to the sea, meander through these botanical gardens. This coastal preserve, with three miles of luxuriant pathways, is "a garden for all seasons" with something always in bloom. The unique Northern California coastal climate is conducive to heathers, perennials, fuchsias, and rhododendrons, which grow in colorful profusion here. Trails lead past gardens of camellias, ferns, and dwarf conifers to a coastal bluff with vistas up and down the rugged shoreline. Admission.

SKUNK TRAIN

✉ *Fort Bragg* ☎ *707-964-6371, 800-866-1690* 📠 *707-964-6754* 🖥 *www.skunk train.com, skunk45@adelphia.net* Maybe it's just the name, but I have to rank the ride on the Skunk train through the redwoods as one of my favorite scenic rail trips. You can board the train near the center of Fort Bragg for a 4-hour ride aboard a steam or diesel engine or a diesel-powered railcar. Dating from 1885, the Skunk was originally a logging train; today it also carries passengers along a 40-mile route through mountains and redwoods to the inland area of Northspur and back. For information, contact Sierra Railroad. Reservations recommended.

North of Fort Bragg, Route 1 runs past miles of sand dunes and traverses several small towns. Then, after having followed the coast all the way from Southern California, it abruptly turns inland. The reason is the mysterious Lost Coast of California. Due north, where no highway could possibly run, the King Range vaults out of the sea, rising over 4000 feet in less than three miles. It is a wilderness inhabited by black bears and bald eagles, with an abandoned lighthouse and a solitary beach piled with ancient Indian shellmounds.

LODGING

Though bed-and-breakfast prices are generally high, Northern California's inns are unparalleled in intimacy and personal care.

INN AT OCCIDENTAL

$$$$ 16 ROOMS ✉ *3657 Church Street, Occidental* ☎ *707-874-1047, 800-522-6324* 📠 *707-874-1078* 🖥 *www.innatoccidental.com, innkeeper@innatoccidental.com*

A few miles east of Bodega Bay, the Inn at Occidental is a charming Victorian homestead encircled by a wide porch bedecked with potted plants and white wicker rockers. The 16 guest rooms feature fireplaces, spa tubs, antiques, and original artwork. There is also a separate cottage with a full kitchen and two master suites. A full breakfast is included, as are afternoon wine and cheese.

JENNER INN AND COTTAGES

$$–$$$ 23 ROOMS ✉10400 Route 1, Jenner ☎707-865-2377, 800-732-2377 ☏707-865-0829 ⌕www.jennerinn.com, innkeeper@jennerinn.com

A prime Jenner resting spot is this bed and breakfast overlooking the river. Several buildings comprise the spread: You can rent a room, a suite, even a cottage. Many rooms have fireplaces and hot tubs, all have private decks. The rooms are lovingly decorated with antiques and comfy furnishings. Full breakfast included.

FORT ROSS LODGE

$$–$$$$ 22 ROOMS ✉20705 Route 1, Jenner ☎707-847-3333, 800-968-4537 ☏707-847-3330 ⌕www.fortrosslodge

A fair bargain can be found along the coast at Fort Ross Lodge, two miles north of the old Russian fort. Overlooking the ocean, this establishment consists of a cluster of woodframe buildings. The rooms have ocean views; the ceilings are knotty pine, and the varied decor includes everything from wicker to antique furniture. There are TVs, DVD players, refrigerators, patios equipped with grills, and private baths in all rooms, plus a community sauna and hot tub.

TIMBER COVE INN

$$$–$$$$ 50 ROOMS ✉21780 North Route 1, 15 miles north of Jenner ☎707-847-3231, 800-987-8319 ☏707-847-3704 ⌕www.timbercoveinn.com, info@timbercoveinn.com

Several lodges along the California coast reflect in their architecture the raw energy of the surrounding sea. Such a one is Timber Cove Inn. Set on 26 acres and elemental in style, it is a labyrinth of unfinished woods and bald rocks. The heavy timber lobby is dominated by a walk-in stone fireplace and sits astride a Japanese pond. The 50 guest rooms are finished in redwood with beams and columns exposed; they look a bit old and dated for my taste, but they do afford marvelous views of the mountains and open sea. Many have decks, fireplaces, and hot tubs. All have TVs and phones. Timber Cove, fittingly, rests on a cliff directly above the ocean. Raccoons are a common sight; if you have critter issues you might want to steel yourself before wandering the grounds at night.

STILLWATER COVE RANCH

$–$$ 7 UNITS ✉22555 Route 1, 16 miles north of Jenner ☎707-847-3227

Set on a beautiful 50-acre plateau above the ocean, Stillwater is set on lovely grounds and populated with peacocks, sheep, chicken, and cows. Formerly a boys' school, this complex of buildings has been transformed into a restful retreat. Accommodations are varied and include single rooms, large kitchenettes, and a cottage, all with fireplaces. Even the dairy barn can house guests: It's been converted to a bunkhouse with kitchen. Closed for ten days around Christmas.

SEA RANCH LODGE

$$$$ 20 ROOMS ✉60 Sea Walk Drive, Sea Ranch ☎707-785-2371, 800-732-7262 ☏707-785-2917 ⌕www.searanchlodge.com, reservations@searanchlodge.com

Sea Ranch is the ultimate Sonoma coast retreat. Miles of secluded beaches and hiking trails, fields of wildflowers, and beautiful bluffs make this resort a perennial favorite. The lodge, which wears its weathered wood siding with dignity, offers 20 rooms with ocean or ridge views. The decor emphasizes earth tones that blend in with the natural surroundings. There is a bar with a solarium, a store, and nearby hiking and biking trails.

MAR VISTA COTTAGES AT ANCHOR BAY

$$$ 12 UNITS ✉35101 South Route 1, Gualala ☎707-884-3522, 877-855-3522 📠707-884-4861 ✎www.marvistamendocino.com, renata@marvistamendocino.com

This is a community of 12 separate cottages scattered around nine acres of oceanview property. Each is an old woodframe affair with a sitting room and kitchen as well as a bedroom and bathroom. Several are equipped with decks, fireplaces, or wood stoves. A soaking tub and barbecue facility on the property are surrounded by trees; a short path leads across Route 1 to the beach. Guests can harvest their own organic greens and fruit from the garden and fetch fresh eggs from the hens. Completely nonsmoking. Pets welcome.

WHALE WATCH INN

$$$ 18 UNITS ✉35100 Route 1, Gualala ☎800-942-5342 ✎www.whalewatchinn.com, info@whalewatchinn.com

For ocean views and private beach access down a stairway right from the hotel, this is a real find. Five separate buildings have rooms ranging from standard bed-and-breakfast styles to spacious suites with elevated whirlpool tubs with sea views, fireplaces, and decks. Each accommodation is different and all are beautifully decorated with furniture that ranges from traditional mahogany to Southwestern-influenced pine. A perfect honeymoon retreat.

SEACLIFF INN

$$–$$$ 16 ROOMS ✉39140 South Route 1, Gualala ☎707-884-1213, 800-400-5053 📠707-884-1731 ✎www.seacliffmotel.com, information@seacliffmotel.com

Every one of the 16 rooms here stares straight at the Pacific Ocean, and some days you can see whales rubbing their bellies on the sandbar. Accommodations are a bit outdated but comfortable, with everything you need for an atmospheric retreat: fireplaces, private decks, two-person whirlpool tubs with ocean views, downy king-sized beds, coffee makers, and refrigerators stocked with complimentary champagne. The staff treats you like family.

Country inns of this genre are quite abundant farther north. Near the town of Mendocino there are numerous bed and breakfasts, some outstanding. The seaside towns of Elk, Albion, Little River, Mendocino, and Fort Bragg each house several.

HARBOR HOUSE INN

$$$$ 10 UNITS ✉5600 South Route 1, Elk ☎707-877-3203, 800-720-7474 📠707-877-3452 ✎www.theharborhouseinn.com, innkeeper@theharborhouseinn.com

Among the more renowned bed and breakfasts in the area is the Harbor House. Set on a rise overlooking the ocean, the house is built entirely of redwood. The living room alone, with its fireplace and exposed-beam ceiling, is an architectural feat. The house was modeled on a design exhibited at San Francisco's 1915 Panama–Pacific Exposition. Of the ten bedrooms and cottages, all are beautifully and individually decorated, many with ocean views, fireplaces, and antique appointments. The gardens are gorgeous, with paths leading down to the private beach. Rates include breakfast and dinner for two. The inn is closed the first two weeks in December.

ELK COVE INN & SPA

$$$–$$$$ 13 UNITS   ✉6300 South Route 1, Elk   ✆707-877-3321, 800-275-2967   📠707-877-1808   ✎www.elkcoveinn.com, innkeeper@elkcoveinn.com

A message in a guest room diary at Elk Cove Inn & Spa reads: "A view, with a room." The view is of knobby coast and simmering surf of ice blue and shaggy dunes falling away. The room is perfect for watching it all: a comfortable cabin with dramatic beamed ceiling, gas fireplace at the foot of your featherbed, carafe of port waiting on the nightstand. In the morning the proprietor lays out an elaborate buffet—coffee cakes, corned beef hash—in the main 1883 Victorian house, a short walk from the four bluff-top cabins. There are six guest rooms in the main house, some with dormer windows overlooking ocean, others with views of the riotous gardens. Four luxurious spa suites, three junior suites and an outdoor hot tub complete the picture.

HERITAGE HOUSE

$$$$ 40 ROOMS   ✉5200 North Route 1, Little River   ✆707-937-5885, 800-235-5885   📠707-937-0318   ✎www.heritagehouseinn.com, info@heritagehouseinn.com

This historic inn was constructed in 1877 and reflects the New England architecture popular then in Northern California. Baby Face Nelson is reputed to have hidden in the old farmhouse that today serves as the inn's reception and dining area. Most guests are housed in duplex cottages that overlook the rocky coastline. All of these 40 rooms have king-sized beds, ocean views, and private decks or patios.

GLENDEVEN

$$$–$$$$ 10 ROOMS   ✉8205 North Route 1, Little River   ✆707-937-0083, 800-822-4536   ✎www.glendeven.com, innkeeper@glendeven.com

The New England–style farmhouse that has transformed into Glendeven dates back to 1867. The theme is country living, with a meadow out back and dramatic views of the ocean and headlands nearby. The sitting room is an intimate affair with comfortable armchairs set before a brick fireplace. In the rooms you're apt to find a bed with wooden headboard, an antique wardrobe, and colorful orchids. Glendeven is as charming and intimate as a country inn can be. A full breakfast is delivered to your room.

LITTLE RIVER INN

$$–$$$$ 66 UNITS   ✉*7901 North Route 1, Little River*   ☎*707-937-3944*
www.littleriverinn.com, info@littleriverinn.com

A quaint 1850s-era house expanded into a mini-resort, this elegant inn still manages to be welcome-home cozy. With a day spa, a restaurant, a lounge, tennis courts, and a nine-hole golf course, the Little River offers guests a choice between running the gamut of on-site activities or relaxing in bed (the front desk will deliver any of their 400 movies). There's a variety of rooms, from simple to super luxurious, and almost all afford grand ocean views.

AUBERGE MENDOCINO

$$$ 11 UNITS   ✉*8200 North Route 1, two miles south of Mendocino*   ☎*707-937-0088, 800-347-9252*   📠*707-937-3620*
www.aubergemendocino.com, innkeeper@aubergemendocino.com

This scenic gem overlooks Van Damme State Park, with trails that deliver you instantly to rocky coast and the shiny bald heads of grey seals. Six rooms, three suites, a cottage, and a vacation rental home are extra spacious and decorated with pastel walls, folded linen draperies, antique dressers, and wood-burning hearths. Music streams through the living room. Breakfast, featuring savory items like fresh seasonal fruit, frittatas, and herbed cheese omelettes, is served by candlelight in the elegant dining room.

STANFORD INN BY THE SEA

$$$$ 41 UNITS   ✉*Route 1 and Comptche Ukiah Road, Mendocino*
☎*707-937-5616, 800-331-8884*   📠*707-937-0305*   *www.stanfordinn.com, info@stanfordinn.com*

Set where Big River meets the ocean, this bed and breakfast is both stately and whimsical. With bright red trim against dark wood paneling, the inn overlooks the Pacific headlands and its own meticulously well-kept organic garden. Families love it here, and visiting pets are pampered. Couples go for the intimate suites with Lexington furnishings, wood-burning fireplaces, DVD players (the inn stocks 1400 movies), and balconies. You'll also find an enchanting greenhouse pool with a balmy garden of palms and bougainvillea, and water that's bathtub-warm year-round. There's kayaking and redwood outrigger canoeing down Big River, and biking along Pacific cliff trails. Yoga classes are offered, as is massage. Not a detail has been overlooked.

MENDOCINO HOTEL

$$–$$$$ 51 ROOMS   ✉*45080 Main Street, Mendocino*   ☎*707-937-0511, 800-548-0513*   📠*707-937-0513*   *www.mendocinohotel.com, info@mendocinohotel.com*

Set in a falsefront building which dates to 1878, the Mendocino is a wonderful place, larger than other nearby country inns, with a wood-paneled lobby, two restaurants, and living quarters adorned with antiques. There are rooms in the hotel with both private and shared baths as well as quarters in the garden cottages out back. Some rooms are pet-friendly.

MACCALLUM HOUSE INN

$$–$$$$ 19 ROOMS   ✉*45020 Albion Street, Mendocino*   ☎*707-937-0289,*
800-609-0492   📠*707-937-2243*   💻*www.maccallumhouse.com,*
info@maccallumhouse.com

This is the queen of Mendocino, a Gingerbread Victorian built in 1882. The place is a treasure trove of antique furnishings, knick-knacks, and other memorabilia. Many of the rooms are individually decorated with rocking chairs, quilts, and wood stoves. Positively everything—the carriage house, barn, greenhouse, gazebo, even the water tower—has been converted into a guest room. Full breakfast included. Pet-friendly.

SWEETWATER SPA & INN

$$–$$$$ 20 UNITS   ✉*44840 Main Street, Mendocino*   ☎*800-300-4140*
💻*www.sweetwaterspa.com, lodging@sweetwaterspa.com*

From cozy watertower rooms and private suites to garden cottages and family lodgings, Sweetwater provides a variety of accommodations. Many of their units are pet-friendly and are right in the heart of Mendocino. They also operate a few lodging options in nearby Little River.

SEA GULL INN

$–$$$ 9 ROOMS   ✉*44960 Albion Street, Mendocino*   ☎*707-937-5204, 888-937-5204*
📠*707-937-3550*   💻*www.seagullbb.com, seagull1@mcn.org*

The Sea Gull has comfortable guest accommodations, some with ocean views. In a land of pricey hotels, this B&B establishment is a rarity. Choose to stay in the main house or in the cottage set in the garden.

JOSHUA GRINDLE INN

$$$–$$$$ 12 ROOMS   ✉*44800 Little Lake Road, Mendocino*   ☎*707-937-4143,*
800-474-6353   💻*www.joshgrin.com, stay@joshgrin.com*

Set on two landscaped acres overlooking Mendocino village and the coast, the Joshua Grindle is a 19th-century New England–style farmhouse with ten spacious rooms, all with sitting areas, and some with wood-burning fireplaces, whirlpool tubs, and ocean views. A separate two-bedroom home is also available. An inviting gathering spot during evening hours, the parlor offers a cheerful fire and an antique pump organ. Full breakfast included.

HILL HOUSE INN

$$$ 44 ROOMS   ✉*10701 Palette Drive, Mendocino*   ☎*707-937-0554, 800-422-0554*
💻*www.hillhouseinn.com*

If upon seeing this New England–style inn you're suddenly inspired to compile detective notes on a typewriter, don't be alarmed. This bed and breakfast set amid Victorian gardens was the site of the 1980s television series *Murder, She Wrote*. These days the elegant lodging boasts ocean view suites furnished with antiques and fireplaces; some with whirlpool tubs. In-room massage is available. Pet-friendly.

SALLIE & EILEEN'S PLACE

$$ 2 UNITS ✉Box 409, Mendocino, CA 95460 ☎707-937-2028
📠707-937-2918 🖱www.seplace.com, innkeeper@seplace.com

For women guests only, Sallie & Eileen's is a scenic, gay-friendly property owned and operated by a lesbian couple. It offers a studio A-frame cottage and a spacious cabin three miles from Mendocino, both with propane fireplaces. The studio has a kitchen area and a sunken tub, while the cabin, which can sleep up to six, has a loft bedroom, a woodstove, a deck, a full kitchen, and a private backyard. Pets allowed with a nominal extra fee.

BREWERY GULCH INN

$$$–$$$$ 10 ROOMS ✉9401 Coast Highway 1 North, Mendocino
☎800-578-4454 📠707-937-1279 🖱www.brewerygulchinn.com,
innkeeper@brewerygulchinn.com

Built with virgin redwood timbers salvaged from Big River, this is the ultimate bed and breakfast, oozing romance, luxury, and privacy. Perched on a bluff overlooking Smuggler's Cove, it's designed so each of its ten arts-and-crafts-style guest rooms (eight of which have private decks) has views of the crashing surf. Rooms are fitted with down comforters, fireplaces, and wi-fi access. The huge gourmet breakfast changes seasonally.

THE ATRIUM

$$–$$$ 10 ROOMS ✉700 North Main Street, Fort Bragg ☎707-964-9440,
800-287-8392 📠707-964-1770 🖱www.atriumbnb.com, info@atriumbnb.com

Right in the center of Fort Bragg and only blocks away from galleries and shops sits The Atrium. This lovely yellow Victorian inn offers ten charming rooms, each well-appointed and well-maintained. The indoor garden provides a serene resting spot, while those looking for outdoor scenery will be delighted by the proximity to the town's botanical gardens. An afternoon beverage service and a full breakfast are included.

WELLER HOUSE

$$–$$$ 9 ROOMS ✉524 Stewart Street, Fort Bragg ☎877-893-5537
🖱www.wellerhouse.com, innkeeper@wellerhouse.com

Originally built in 1886, this place is now on the National Registry of Historic Places. It now boasts a 900-square-foot redwood-paneled ballroom, six-person hot tub, and English gardens, and is home to the tallest land structure in Fort Bragg: a historic water tower. It's a great place for relaxing in one of nine antique-decorated guest rooms, and even better place for exploring the lavish surroundings.

LIVING LIGHT INN

$$$-$$$$ 10 ROOMS ✉533 East Fir Street, Fort Bragg ☎877-964-1384
✎707-964-1384 ✐www.livinglightinn.com, innkeeper@livinglightinn.com

For the eco-conscious traveler, this inn offers environmentally friendly amenities. Organic bedding, low-impact lighting, and organic beverages are just a few of the green touches. A Craftsman-style affair, each room here is individually decorated in earth tones and boasts its own New Age theme, such as Tranquility, Inspiration, or Harmony. The safari-chic Adventure Suite gives a nod to all things wild with its African-styled decor tamed by an intimate fireplace. Amenities include cable television and free wi-fi. A sandy beach is within minutes of the inn.

DINING

RIVER'S END RESTAURANT

$$-$$$ INTERNATIONAL ✉11048 Route 1, Jenner ☎707-865-2484 ext. 111
✎707-865-9621 ✐www.ilovesunsets.com, dine@rivers-end.com

For the best meal hereabouts (or for that matter, anywhere about), head for this restaurant. Situated at that momentous crossroad of the Russian River and Pacific Ocean (and commanding a view of both), this outstanding little place is a restaurant with imagination. How else do you explain a dinner menu that ranges from smoked filet mignon to racklettes of elk to almond-encrusted halibut? Not to mention good service and a selection of over 150 local wines. River's End is a great place for ocean lovers and culinary adventurers. Closed Monday through Thursday in winter. Closed January and first two weeks of February.

SALT POINT BAR AND GRILL

$$-$$$ SEAFOOD ✉23255 North Route 1, 17 miles north of Jenner ☎707-847-3234
✎707-847-3234 ✐www.saltpointlodgebarandgrill.com

This small restaurant serves three meals a day. The menu relies heavily on seafood—halibut, oysters, prawns—but also includes chicken, steak, and other dishes. At lunch, enjoy a variety of salads, sandwiches, or seafood selections. Breakfast offers an array of omelettes.

ST. ORRES

$$$$ CALIFORNIA CUISINE ✉36601 Route 1, Gualala ☎707-884-3303
✎707-884-1840 ✐www.saintorres.com, saintorres@yahoo.com

Okay, so St. Orres is yet another California cuisine restaurant. But it's the only one you'll see that looks as if it should be in Russia rather than along the California coast. With its dizzying spires, this elegant structure evokes images of Moscow and old St. Petersburg. The kitchen provides an everchanging menu of fresh game and fish dishes with an emphasis on organic, locally grown food. The fixed-price menu will include hot and chilled soups, poached salmon, rabbit, rack of lamb, stuffed wild boar, and several seasonal specialties. Even if you're not interested in dining, it might be worth a stop to view this architectural extravaganza. Dinner and occasional brunch. Closed Tuesday and Wednesday during winter.

BONES ROADHOUSE
$–$$ AMERICAN   ✉38920 South Route 1, Gualala   ☎707-884-1188

When you're ready for a great big burger after days of camping and you don't want to stop to clean up, Bones is the place—a traditional steakhouse that's good for the whole family. The pulled pork sandwich comes with a towering stack of succulent meat and crispy fries on the side. Add a cold beer or soda and settle back for some people-watching that's sure to include an eclectic crowd, from golden-age bikers to locals and professional types from the city.

ARENA COVE BAR & GRILL
$$–$$$ SEAFOOD   ✉790 Port Road, Point Arena   ☎707-882-2100   ☏707-882-2762

Arena Cove looks out on a pier as well as a series of ocean bluffs. With a hand-carved bar and woodplank dining room, it's a local seafood restaurant serving fresh salmon, sautéed prawns, and raw oysters. If oysters and homemade clam chowder don't interest you, there are steaks and chops at this good-ol'-style eating place.

HARBOR HOUSE INN
$$$$ CALIFORNIA CUISINE   ✉5600 South Route 1, Elk   ☎707-877-3203, 800-720-7474   ☏707-877-3452   🖰www.theharborhouseinn.com, innkeeper@theharborhouseinn.com

Although the dining room here Inn mainly serves guests at this bed and breakfast, there are three extra tables for two people each evening. A fire in the fireplace will keep you warm and cozy on a cold coastal night, and in the summer you can watch the sunset over the ocean out of the huge windows. The chef prepares a set menu, served at 7 p.m., with entrées such as salmon, pork tenderloin, or halibut. A vegetarian meal can also be prepared with advance notice. Reservations are required.

ALBION RIVER INN
$$–$$$$ CALIFORNIA CUISINE   ✉3790 North Route 1, Albion   ☎707-937-1919, 800-479-7944   ☏707-937-2604   🖰www.albionriverinn.com, innkeepers@albionriverinn.com

Set high on a cliff above the Albion Cove and the ocean is this plate-glass dining spot serving California cuisine, and specializing in otherworldly ocean views. Entrées include grilled ginger-lime prawns, roast breast of duck, and grilled filet mignon in pinot noir wine demi-glace, and can be perfectly paired with a selection from their award-winning wine list. Dinner only.

LITTLE RIVER INN

$$$–$$$$ CALIFORNIA CUISINE   ✉7901 North Route 1, Little River
☏707-937-3944 ⌘www.littleriverinn.com, lri@mcn.org

Casual elegance sets the tone at Little River Inn's garden-themed dining room. With fresh seafood such as Dungeness crab pot pie with leeks and a hint of sherry, and hickory-smoked prime rib with shallot au jus, the seasonal menu here is a mix of upscale California cuisine and traditional comfort fare. For dessert, don't miss the aptly named Chocolate Decadence.

RAVEN'S RESTAURANT

$$–$$$ VEGAN/VEGETARIAN   ✉Stanford Inn by the Sea, Route 1 and Comptche Road, Mendocino ☏707-937-5615, 800-331- ☏707-937-0305
⌘www.ravensrestaurant.com, info@stanfordinn.com

The sublime all-vegan cuisine here is as distinguished as it is delightful. With surprisingly hearty and uniquely flavored entrées prepared with organic vegetables (many straight from their on-site garden), the restaurant boasts a seasonal menu that will please even the most avid carnivore. Expect dishes such as grilled tangerine-sesame tofu, luscious portobello mousse with flaxbread, and baked falafel on grilled heirloom tomatoes with avocado tartare. Breakfast is vegetarian and includes more traditional dishes with a twist, like rose petal ricotta crêpes. Everything is served with fresh flowers—even the water.

BAY VIEW CAFÉ

$–$$ CONTINENTAL   ✉45040 Main Street, Mendocino ☏707-937-4197
☏707-937-2884

A morning ritual for locals and visitors alike is to climb the rough-hewn stairs to this loft-like café for coffee, French toast, or fluffy omelettes. On sunny afternoons, the deck overlooking Main Street and the coastal headlands makes an ideal lunch spot, especially for fish and chips or hot crêpe sandwiches. Dinner only on Friday and Saturday in winter.

MENDOCINO HOTEL

$$$–$$$$ CALIFORNIA CUISINE   ✉45080 Main Street, Mendocino
☏707-937-0511, 800-548-0513 ⌘www.mendocinohotel.com,
reservations@mendocinohotel.com

At this hotel you can enjoy California-style cuisine in the main dining room or out in the "garden room." The menu represents a mix of meat and seafood entrées such as prime rib, house-made ravioli, and roasted garlic scallop and jumbo shrimp embrochette. The ambience in this 19th-century building evokes Mendocino's early days.

MOOSSE CAFÉ

$$$ CALIFORNIA CUISINE   ✉390 Kasten Street, Mendocino ☏707-937-4323
☏707-937-3611 ⌘www.themoosse.com, manager@themoosse.com

Situated in a cozy little house, this café offers imaginative seasonal dishes and organically grown comfort food. Try their seafood dishes or pasta special. Finish with a homemade dessert. Closed most of January and Tuesday and Wednesday, except in summer.

955 UKIAH STREET

$$$ INTERNATIONAL   ✉*955 Ukiah Street, Mendocino* ☎*707-937-1955*
📠*707-937-5138* ⌨*www.955restaurant.com*

For French and California cuisine, 955 Ukiah Street is an address worth noting. Candles, fresh flowers, and impressionist prints set the tone here. Serving dinner only, it prepares brandied prawns, red snapper in phyllo pastry, roast duck, and calamari. For the diet-conscious, they also offer lighter dishes. Dinner only. Closed Monday through Wednesday.

CAFÉ BEAUJOLAIS

$$$ INTERNATIONAL   ✉*961 Ukiah Street, Mendocino* ☎*707-937-5614*
⌨*www.cafebeaujolais.com, cafebeau@mcn.org*

Mendocino's best-known dining room is well deserving of its renown. Situated in a small Victorian house on the edge of town, this restaurant serves designer dishes, which I try to sample on a regular basis. They offer an ever-changing global menu featuring local organic produce, wild and sustainably cultured seafoods, humanely raised meats, and more than 50 varieties of wine available by the glass. Excellent cuisine. No lunch Monday and Tuesday.

MACCALLUM HOUSE RESTAURANT

$$$–$$$$ CALIFORNIA CUISINE   ✉*45020 Albion Street, Mendocino*
☎*707-937-0289* ⌨*www.maccallumdining.com, info@maccallumhouse.com*

The dining rooms of the 1882 MacCallum House Restaurant are beautiful, the walls and ceilings covered with carved redwood and fir, the tables glittering with firelight and candlelight. Everything on the menu is excellent. Start with their house champagne cocktail and the smoked organic chicken flatbread with figs, bleu cheese, and caramelized onions. Then try the seared, black pepper–encrusted ahi with warm bacon-olive potato salad, or a grilled Niman Ranch steak with bourbon-glazed shallots and porcini butter. There's a lighter café menu served in the bar. Breakfast and dinner only.

MENDO BISTRO

$$–$$$ CALIFORNIA CUISINE   ✉*301 Main Street, Fort Bragg* ☎*707-964-4974*
📠*707-964-4949* ⌨*www.mendobistro.com, eat@mendobistro.com*

This bistro is Fort Bragg's best-kept secret. True to his stomping grounds, the chef/owner exclusively uses local produce, seafood, free-range meat, beer and wine. Fresh-made pastas, breads, and desserts also have a prominent place on his menu. A local favorite, Mendo Bistro offers diners a casual, elegant atmosphere with a picturesque view of Fort Bragg's historic downtown.

THE RESTAURANT

$$–$$$ CONTINENTAL   ✉*418 North Main Street, Fort Bragg* ☎*707-964-9800*
⌨*www.therestaurantfortbragg.com, info@therestaurantfortbragg.com*

Fort Bragg's favorite dining spot is easy to remember—The Restaurant. Despite the name, this is no generic eating place but a creative kitchen serving excellent dinners. It's decorated with dozens of paintings by local artist Olaf Palm, lending a sense of the avant-garde to this informal establishment. The menu offers seasonal entrées like sautéed prawns, rockfish, steaks, and vegetarian selections. Everything is house-made down to the stocks and dressings. Dinner only. Closed Tuesday and Wednesday. Closed first week of November and first two weeks of March.

SHOPPING

In the New England–style town of Mendocino you'll discover a shopper's paradise. Prices are quite steep, but the window browsing is unparalleled. Housed in the town's old Victorians and Cape Cod cottages is a plethora of shops. There are stores specializing in soap, seashells, candles, and T-shirts; not to mention bookstores, potters, jewelers, art galleries, and antique shops galore. Most shops are located along Mendocino's woodframe Main Street, but also search out the side streets and passageways in this vintage town.

WILLIAM ZIMMER GALLERY ✉10481 Lansing Street, Mendocino ✆707-937-5121 This noteworthy gallery houses an eclectic collection of contemporary and traditional arts and crafts.

HIGHLIGHT GALLERY ✉45052 Main Street, Mendocino ✆707-937-3132 Be sure to also check out this gallery, featuring, among other things, displays of handmade furniture, contemporary art, jewelry, ceramic, glass, and woodwork.

MENDOCINO ART CENTER ✉45200 Little Lake Street, Mendocino ✆707-937-5818 This cultural art center houses numerous crafts studios as well as art studios. Photography, sculpture, and ceramics are on display throughout the different galleries.

GALLERY BOOKSHOP AND BOOKWINKLE'S CHILDREN'S BOOKS ✉Main and Kasten streets, Mendocino ✆707-937-2665 Books are the order of the day here. It is a great resource for local literary events and a super shop for gifts and souvenirs.

NIGHTLIFE

CASPAR INN ✉14957 Caspar Road, Caspar ✆707-964-5565 ⌨www.caspar inn.com There's music four nights a week at this down-home bar. You'll find deejays, local bands as well as groups from outside the area. Hit it on the right night and the joint will be rocking. If you've overdone your partying by the end of the night, ask management about the rooms they have available. Cover for live music.

MENDOCINO HOTEL ✉45080 Main Street, Mendocino ✆707-937-0511 ⌨www.mendocinohotel.com For a quiet night on the town, enjoy a drink at this hotel. You can relax in a Victorian-style lounge or in an enclosed garden patio.

PATTÉRSON'S PUB ✉10485 Lansing Street, Mendocino ✆707-937-4782 For a pint of Guinness, a game of backgammon, local characters, and friendly chit-chat, slip into Patterson's. The pub is small, in keeping with its Irish persona, and furnished in dark wood and brass. There's occasional live entertainment.

BEACHES & PARKS

DILLON BEACH

✉*From Route 1 in Tomales take Dillon Beach Road west for four miles.*

🚶🚴🐎⛵🎣🛶🏊🚤🦪🌊 Located at the mouth of Tomales Bay, this beach is popular with boaters and clammers. The surrounding hills are covered with resort cottages, but there are open areas and dunes to explore. There are picnic areas and restrooms, groceries, boat rentals, and fishing charters. Day-use fee, $7.

⛺ Located nearby, Lawson's Landing (707-878-2443) has open-meadow tent/RV camping (no hookups); $23 to $26 per night. Take note: This campground hosts hundreds of trailers. Call in December and January for closures; they may lock the gates if it's too wet.

DORAN REGIONAL PARK

✉*201 Doran Beach Road; Off Route 1 in Bodega Bay* 📞*707-875-3540* 📠*707-875-2171* 🖥*www.sonoma-county.org*

🚶🚴🐎⛵🎣🛶🏊🚤🦪🌊 This peninsular park is situated on a two-mile stretch of sand between Bodega Harbor and Bodega Bay. With a broad sand beach and good facilities, it's an excellent spot for daytrippers and campers alike. Explore the tidal flats or fish up on the jetty. There are picnic areas, restrooms, and showers. Day-use fee, $6.

⛺ There are 134 tent/RV sites (no hookups); $19 per night.

BODEGA HEAD

✉*Off Route 1 in Bodega Bay along Bay Flat Road* 🖥*www.sonoma-county.org*

There are pocket beaches here dramatically backdropped by granite cliffs. A good place to picnic and explore, this is also a favored whale-watching site. There are restrooms and showers located in nearby Westside Park.

⛺ Westside Park (707-875-3540) has 47 tent/RV sites (no hookups); $16 per night for Sonoma County residents and $18 for nonresidents.

SONOMA COAST STATE BEACH

hidden

✉*Located along Route 1 between Bodega Bay and Jenner* 📞*707-875-3483* 📠*707-875-3876*

🚶🚴🐎🏊🎣🌊 This magnificent park extends for 19 miles between Bodega Head and the Vista Trail. It consists of a number of beaches separated by steep headlands; all are within easy hiking distance of Route 1. The beaches range from sweeping strands to pocket coves and abound with waterfowl and shorebirds, clams, and abalone. The park headquarters and information center is at Salmon Creek Beach, where endless sand dunes backdrop a broad beach. Schoolhouse Beach is a particularly pretty pocket cove bounded by rocky cliffs; Portuguese Beach boasts a wide swath of sand; Blind Beach is rather secluded with a sea arch offshore; and Goat Rock Beach faces the town of Jenner and is decorated with offshore rocks. Pick your poison—hiking, tidepooling, birdwatching, whale watching, camping, picnicking, fishing—and you'll find it waiting along this rugged and hauntingly beautiful coastline. Bodega Dunes, Salmon

Creek Beach, Schoolhouse Beach, Goat Rock, Portuguese Beach, and Wrights Beach have restrooms; Bodega Dunes and Wrights Beach also feature picnic areas. Day-use fee, $6.

▲ At Bodega Dunes, there are 98 tent/RV sites (no hookups); $25 per night. At Wrights Beach, there are 27 tent/RV sites (no hookups); $25–35 per night. Reservations are required; call 800-444-7275. At Pomo Canyon and Willow Creek you'll find 31 walk-in primitive sites; $15 per night; closed December through March.

FORT ROSS REEF CAMPGROUND

✉ *19005 Route 1, 12 miles north of Jenner; Watch for a cluster of white barns on the west side of the highway.* ✆ *707-847-3286* ✍ *707-847-3601*

🚶🚴 ⤚ ⚓ ⏚ Set in a canyon surrounded by bluffs, this facility is beautifully located near the ocean and features a redwood grove. It is a state park with spectacular surroundings and gorgeous views. There are picnic areas and restrooms. Day-use fee, $6.

▲ There are 21 tent/RV sites (no hookups); $15 per night. Closed November through March. Depending on the weather, fires may not be allowed.

STILLWATER COVE REGIONAL PARK

✉ *Route 1, about 16 miles north of Jenner* ✆ *707-847-3245* ✍ *707-847-3325*

🚶 ⤚ ⏚ Situated amid pine trees on a hillside above the ocean, this is a small park with access to a beach. The canyon trail leads up to the restored (but closed) Fort Ross Schoolhouse. There are picnic areas, restrooms, and showers. Day-use fee, $5.

▲ There are 22 tent/RV sites (no hookups); $20 per night. Reservations must be made at least ten days in advance; 707-565-2267.

OCEAN COVE STORE AND CAMPGROUND

✉ *Route 1, about 17 miles north of Jenner* ✆ *707-847-3422* ✍ *707-847-3624*
🖰 *www.oceancove.org*

🚶🚴 ⚓ ⤚ ⏚ This privately owned campground has sites on a bluff above a rocky shoreline. Anglers catch everything from salmon to rockfish. The scenery is mighty attractive, and the campsites are well removed from the road. There are hot showers and portable toilets. Day-use fee, $7.

▲ There are 150 tent/RV sites (no hookups); $19 per night; $2 extra for dogs. Closed December through March.

SALT POINT STATE PARK

✉ *Route 1, about 20 miles north of Jenner* ✆ *707-847-3221* ✍ *707-847-3843*
🚶🚴 ⤚ ⏚ Extending from the ocean to over 1000 feet elevation, this 6000-acre spread includes coastline, forests, and open range land. Along the shore are weird honeycomb formations called tafoni, caused by sea erosion on coastal sandstone. Up amid the stands of Douglas fir and Bishop pine there's a pygmy forest, where unfavorable soil conditions have caused fully mature redwoods to reach only about 20 feet in height. Blacktail deer, raccoons, mountain lions, and bobcats roam the area.

Miles of hiking trails lace the park, including one through a rhododendron reserve. After the fall rains, chanterelles and other favored mushrooms abound here. Pickers beware: Carefully identify anything you plan to eat, since some mushrooms can be fatal. There are picnic areas and restrooms. Day-use fee, $6.

▲ There are three campgrounds here with 108 tent/RV sites (no hookups); $25 per night. Reservations are required from March to October; call 800-444-7275.

GUALALA POINT REGIONAL PARK

 idden

✉ Located along Route 1 due south of Gualala   ☎ 707-785-2377
🖨 707-785-3741

🚶 🏊 ⛵ ⌛ Located where the Gualala River meets the ocean, this charming place has everything from a sandy beach to redwood groves. Across the river, there are kayak and canoe rentals. There are picnic areas, restrooms, and an information center. Day-use fee, $5.

▲ There are 23 tent/RV sites (no hookups), 1 hiker/biker site, 6 walk-in sites; $20 per night. Reservations: 707-565-2267; sonomacounty.org/parks.

MANCHESTER STATE PARK

✉ Located along Route 1, about eight miles north of Point Arena   ☎ 707-882-2463
🖨 707-937-2953

🚶 🎣 ⌛ This wild, windswept beach extends for miles along the Mendocino coast. Piled deep with driftwood, it's excellent for hiking. There are picnic areas, restrooms, and an information center.

▲ There are 18 tent/RV sites (no hookups) and 10 primitive, hike-in environmental sites; $15 per night; first-come, first-served. Reservations: 707-882-2463.

VAN DAMME STATE PARK

✉ Route 1, about 30 miles north of Point Arena, or three miles south of Mendocino
☎ 707-937-5804   🖨 707-937-2953

🚶 🚴 ⛵ ⌛ Extending from the beach to an interior forest, this 2069-acre park has several interesting features: a "pygmy forest" where poor soil results in fully mature pine trees reaching heights of only six inches to eight feet; a "fern canyon" smothered in different species of ferns; and a "cabbage patch" filled with that fetid critter with elephant ear leaves—skunk cabbage. This park is also laced with hiking trails and offers excellent beachcombing. Facilities include a visitors center, picnic areas, restrooms, and showers. Day-use fee, $6 for the fern canyon.

▲ There are 74 tent/RV sites (no hookups); $20 to $25 per night. The upper campground is closed in winter. Reservations are essential during the summer: 800-444-7275.

MENDOCINO HEADLANDS AND BIG RIVER BEACH STATE PARKS

✉ Located in the town of Mendocino

🚶 🎣 ⛵ ⌛ These adjoining parks form the seaside border of the town of Mendocino. And quite a border it is. The white-sand beaches are only part of the natural splendor. There are also wave tunnels, tide-pools, sea arches, lagoons, and 360-degree vistas that sweep from the surf-trimmed shore to the prim villagescape of Mendocino. The only facilities are restrooms; private canoe rental nearby.

RUSSIAN GULCH STATE PARK

✉Located along Route 1, two miles north of Mendocino ✆707-937-5804
✆707-937-2953

🚶🚴🐎 ⛴ Set in a narrow valley with a well-protected beach, this park has numerous features. There are marvelous views from the craggy headlands, a waterfall, and a blowhole that rarely blows. Rainbow and steelhead trout inhabit the creek while hawks and ravens circle the forest. There are picnic areas, restrooms, and showers. Day-use fee, $6.

⛺ There are 30 tent/RV sites (no hookups); $20 to $25 per night. Reservations: 800-444-7275.

MACKERRICHER STATE PARK

✉Along Route 1, about three miles north of Fort Bragg ✆707-937-5804
✆707-937-2953

🚶🚴🐎 🎣 ⛴ 🚣 Another of the region's outstanding parks, this facility features a crescent of sandy beach, dunes, headlands, a lake, a forest, and wetlands. Harbor seals inhabit the rocks offshore and over 90 bird species frequent the area. The park has picnic areas, rest-rooms, and showers.

⛺ There are 140 tent/RV sites (no hookups), ten walk-in and eight hike-and-bike sites ($3 per night, per person); $20 to $25 per night. Reservations: 800-444-7275.

REDWOOD COUNTRY

Near the nondescript town of Leggett, Route 1 joins Route 101. Logging trucks, those belching beasts that bear down upon you without mercy, become more frequent. You are entering Redwood Country.

This is the habitat of *Sequoia sempervirens*, the coastal redwood, a tree whose ancestors date to the age of dinosaurs and which happens to be the world's tallest living thing. These "ambassadors from another time," as John Steinbeck called them, inhabit a 30-mile-wide coastal fog belt stretching 450 miles from the Monterey area north to Oregon. Redwoods live five to eight centuries, though some have survived over two millennia, while reaching heights over 350 feet and diameters greater than 20 feet.

There is a sense of solitude here uncapturable anywhere else. The trees form a cathedral overhead, casting a deep shade across the forest floor. Solitary sun shafts, almost palpable, cut through the grove; along the roof of the forest, pieces of light jump across the treetops, poised to fall like rain. Ferns and a few small animals are all that survive here. The silence and stillness are either transcendent or terrifying. It's like being at sea in a small boat.

RICHARDSON GROVE STATE PARK

The Redwood Highway, Route 101, leads north to the tallest, densest stands of *Sequoia sempervirens*. At this state park the road barrels through the very center of a magnificent grove. A short nature trail leads through this virgin timber, though the proximity of the road makes communing with nature seem a bit ludicrous.

AVENUE OF THE GIANTS

North of Garberville, follow this 31-mile alternative route that parallels Route 101. The two-lane road winds along the Eel River south fork, tunneling through dense redwood groves.

HUMBOLDT REDWOODS STATE PARK

📞 707-946-2409 📠 707-946-2326 ⏚ *www.humboldtredwoods.org,* *hrsp@humboldtredwoods.org* Much of the Avenue of the Giants is encompassed by this 52,000-acre preserve with some of the finest forest land found anywhere—17,000 acres are virgin-growth redwood. Park headquarters contains a nice visitors center.

FOUNDER'S GROVE A nature trail loops through a redwood stand in this grove. The forest is dedicated to early Save-the-Redwoods League leaders who were instrumental in preserving thousands of redwood acres, particularly in this park.

ROCKEFELLER FOREST Near Founder's Grove is this forest, which has another short loop trail that winds through a redwood grove. Avenue of the Giants continues through towns that are little more than way stations and then rejoins Route 101, which leads north to Eureka.

LOST COAST

There are alternate routes to Eureka leading along the perimeter of California's Lost Coast region. One of the state's most remote wilderness areas, it is a tumbling region of extraordinary vistas. Here the King Range, with its sliding talus and impassable cliffs, shoots 4087 feet up from the ocean in less than three miles. No road could ever rest along its shoulder. The place has been left primitive, given over to mink, deer, river otter, and black bear; rare bald eagles and peregrine falcons work its slopes.

The range extends about 35 miles. Along the shore is a wilderness beach from which seals, sea lions, and porpoises, as well as gray

Redwood Country

Crescent City

TALL TREES GROVE

SAMURAI RESTAURANT

Eureka

SHAW HOUSE BED & BREAKFAST

THE LOST COAST

TALL TREES GROVE

PAGE 351

Small, old-growth redwood stand at the end of a three-mile hike past fern groves and mossy, twisted maple trees

SAMURAI RESTAURANT

PAGE 358

Classic and imaginative sushi, sukiyaki, and tempura in a simple dining room decorated with Japanese folk art

SHAW HOUSE BED & BREAKFAST

PAGE 355

Gothic 1854 home modeled after the *House of the Seven Gables* and furnished with precious period antiques

THE LOST COAST

PAGE 346

Primitive, tumbling region of unbelievable vistas and vibrant wilderness—home to river otter, black bear, and bald eagles

and killer whales, can be seen. There's also an abandoned lighthouse and the skeletons of ships wrecked on the rocks. Be aware that fires and winds have caused hundreds of trees to fall across trails in the area. To reach this remote area, from Route 101 near Redway take Briceland–Thorne Road, which turns into Shelter Cove Road as it winds through the King Range.

SHELTER COVE   This is a tiny bay neatly folded between sea cliffs and headlands. A point of embarkation for people exploring the Lost Coast, it has a few stores, restaurants, and hotels. Stock up here: The rest of this backcountry jaunt promises little more than a couple of stores.

Be Prepared

Keep in mind that the "Lost Coast" is a wilderness area and not a heavily monitored state park. Hikers and campers need to bring water or water purifiers, sturdy hiking boots, and insect repellent. If you want to hike the beach, use a tide table; hikers often get trapped for hours by the tides. Mountain bikers should stick to the area east of King Range. Black Sands Beach is closed to motorized vehicles.

Redwood Country

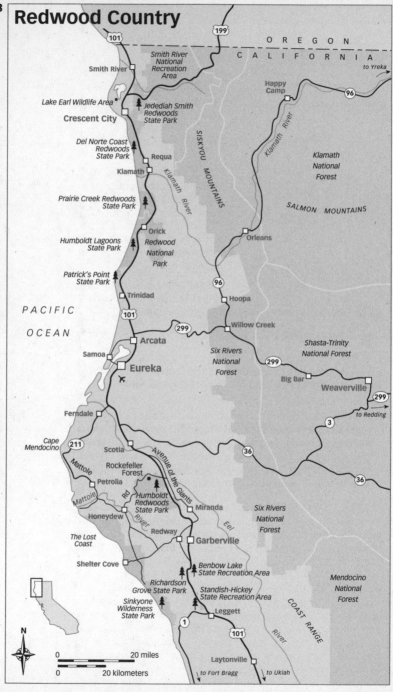

OREGON

CALIFORNIA

to Yreka

Smith River National Recreation Area

Smith River

Happy Camp

Lake Earl Wildlife Area

Jedediah Smith Redwoods State Park

Crescent City

Klamath National Forest

Del Norte Coast Redwoods State Park

Requa

Klamath

Prairie Creek Redwoods State Park

SALMON MOUNTAINS

Humboldt Lagoons State Park

Orick

Redwood National Park

Orleans

Patrick's Point State Park

Trinidad

Hoopa

PACIFIC OCEAN

Arcata

Willow Creek

Six Rivers National Forest

Shasta-Trinity National Forest

Samoa

Eureka

Big Bar

Weaverville

Ferndale

to Redding

Cape Mendocino

Scotia

Rockefeller Forest

Avenue of the Giants

Petrolia

Humboldt Redwoods State Park

Miranda

Six Rivers National Forest

Honeydew

Redway

The Lost Coast

Garberville

Shelter Cove

Benbow Lake State Recreation Area

Richardson Grove State Park

Standish-Hickey State Recreation Area

Mendocino National Forest

Sinkyone Wilderness State Park

Leggett

COAST RANGE

Laytonville

to Fort Bragg

to Ukiah

N

0   20 miles

0   20 kilometers

HONEYDEW Outside Shelter Cove you can pick up Kings Peak Road or Ettersburg–Honeydew Road, which connect with Wilder Ridge Road and lead to the general store town of Honeydew. This is a prime marijuana growing region and a colony of laidback locals is bound to be sitting on the stoop swapping tales.

PETROLIA Mattole Road heads northeast, meandering along the Mattole River, to this forest hamlet. Nestled in a river valley and marked by a white-steeple church, the town is a scene straight from a Norman Rockwell painting. Hawks glide overhead. Old men rock on their front porches.

MATTOLE ROAD This road ascends a succession of plateaus to a ranch land of unpainted barns and broad shade trees, then noses down to the coastline and parallels the waves for perhaps five miles. Here the setting is Scottish. Hillsides are grazed by herds of sheep and covered with tenacious grasses that shake in the sea wind. The gray sand beach is covered with driftwood. Along the horizon peaks rise in jagged motions, seemingly thrust upward by the lash of the surf.

CAPE MENDOCINO This is the westernmost point in the contiguous United States. Here you'll have broad views of the ocean, including the menacing shoals where countless ships have been slapped to timber. Next, the road curves up through forest and sheep-grazing lands before rolling down to the gentle pastureland near the unique town of Ferndale.

FERNDALE A Victorian-style hamlet set in the Eel River valley, this town is so perfectly refurbished it seems unreal. Main Street and nearby thoroughfares are lined with Gothic Revival, Queen Anne, Eastlake, and Italianate-style Victorians, brightly painted and blooming with pride. Tragedy struck this picturesque town in April 1992 when a 7.1-level earthquake and several powerful aftershocks rocked the entire area. Since then local residents have devotedly rebuilt the quaint Main Street district with its boutiques and gift shops and other affected neighborhoods.

FERNDALE MUSEUM ✉515 Shaw Avenue, Ferndale ✆707-786-4466 ☏707-786-4466 ⬧www.ferndale-museum.org, museum@ferndale-museum.org The best way to see the town is by stopping first at this museum. Here is an ever-changing collection of antiques and memorabilia from the region, plus an old blacksmith shop. There are sometimes maps available for self-guided walking tours of this historic community. It's an architectural wonder that shouldn't be missed. Closed Monday during summer and Monday and Tuesday during winter. Admission.

EUREKA Roughly 26,000 inhabitants make this the largest town on the Northern California coast. Founded in 1850, the town's first industry was mining; the name "Eureka" came from an old gold mining exclamation meaning "I found it!"

GREATER EUREKA CHAMBER OF COMMERCE ✉2112 Broadway, Eureka ✆707-442-3738, 800-356-6381 ☏707-442-0079 ⬧www.eurekachamber.com, chamber@eurekachamber.com Today fishing and lumbering have replaced more romantic occupations, but much of the region's history is captured in points of interest. Stop at the chamber of commerce on the way into town for maps, brochures, and information. Make certain to ask at the Chamber of Commerce for the **architectural tour** map. Closed on the weekends in winter.

CARSON MANSION ✉*2nd and M streets, Eureka* Eureka has over 100 glorious Victorian homes ranging from understated designs to this outlandish mansion, a multilayered confection that makes other Gothic architecture seem tame. It was built in the 1880s by William Carson, a wealthy lumber merchant with the same need for ostentation that afflicted the robber barons on San Francisco's Nob Hill. The Carson Mansion is a private club, but you can drive by and view its distinctive architecture.

COVERED BRIDGES
Of a more subdued nature are the covered bridges on the southern outskirts of town. To reach them from Route 101, take Elk River Road two miles to Berta Road or three miles to Zanes Road (there is a wooden span covering both). You'll enter a picture of red barns and green pasture framed by cool, lofty forest. The bridges, crossing a small river, evoke Vermont winters and New Hampshire sleigh rides.

FORT HUMBOLDT ✉*3431 Fort Avenue, Eureka* ☎*707-445-6567* ✆*707-441-5737* Built in the early 1850s to help resolve conflict between gold settlers and indigenous tribes of Yurok, Hoopa, Wiyot, and Mattole Indians, this fort has been partially restored. In addition to re-creating Army life (experienced here by a hard-drinking young officer named Ulysses S. Grant), the historic park displays early logging traditions. There's a drafty logger's cabin, a small lumber industry museum, a military museum displaying Army artifacts, a museum of American Indian artifacts, and a couple of remarkable old steam engines.

SEQUOIA PARK ✉*W Street between Glatt and Madrone streets, Eureka* This park provides a nifty retreat from urban life. Tucked into its 52-acre preserve is a petting zoo (closed Monday), a picnic area, a playground, and a thick stand of redwoods.

OLD TOWN Old Town is Eureka's answer to the nation's gentrification craze. This neighborhood was formerly the local bowery; the term "skid row" reputedly originated right here. It derived from the bums residing beside the nearby "skid roads," along which redwood logs were transported to the waterfront. Now the ghetto is gilded: old Victorians, woodframe warehouses, brick buildings, and clapboard houses have been rebuilt and painted striking colors. Stylish shops have sprung up and restaurants have opened.

CLARKE HISTORICAL MUSEUM ✉*240 E Street, Eureka* ☎*707-443-1947* ✆*707-443-0290* 🖱*www.clarkemuseum.org, clarkehistorical@att.net* Don't miss this museum with its outstanding collection of Northern California American Indian artifacts. Here are twined baskets, ceremonial regalia, and a dugout redwood canoe. It provides a unique insight into this splendid Humboldt Bay region before the age of gold pans and axe handles. There is also the museum's Victorian section, featuring items from the

Gold Rush and the timber and maritime industries. Closed Sunday and Monday.

MADAKET ✉*Eureka* ✆*707-445-1910* ✆*707-442-0514* This vintage motor vessel departs at the foot of F Street in Old Town, where the bowery meets the bay. For several well-invested dollars, you'll sail past an egret rookery, oyster beds, pelican roosts, ugly pulp mills, and the town's flashy marina. The cruises are weather-dependent; always call ahead. Closed October through April. Admission.

ARCATA Heading north from Eureka there are two towns worth noting. Arcata, home of Humboldt State University, is a student town with an outstanding collection of old Victorians. Be sure to circle the town square, which is movie-set picture perfect. For a self-guided architectural tour, obtain a map at the **Arcata Chamber of Commerce** (1635 Heindon Road, Arcata; 707-822-3619, fax 707-822-3515; www.arcatachamber.com, arcata@arcatachamber.com).

TRINIDAD One of the area's oldest towns, Trinidad perches above a small port. Sea stacks and sailboats lie anchored offshore, watched over by a miniature lighthouse. For a tour of the pocket beaches and rocky shores lining this beautiful waterfront, take a three-mile trip south from town along Scenic Drive.

REDWOOD NATIONAL PARK This national park is a fitting finale to the lengthy coastal journey. Park of parks, it's a necklace strung for over 33 miles along the coast. Among its gems are secluded beaches, elk herds, and some of the world's tallest trees. The first link in the chain is the **Redwood National and State Park Visitors Center** (119441 Route 101, Orick; 707-464-6101 ext. 1, fax 707-488-5335). In addition to information, the center issues permits for Tall Trees Grove.

TALL TREES GROVE _____ **h**idden

A three-mile round trip trail leads down a steep grade to this redwood stand boasting some of the loftiest of all California's redwoods. When you visit, notice the built-up sediment at the base of the trees. Look for the Libbey Tree, which at one point was the world's tallest tree. In the 1960s and 1970s, efforts to protect the surrounding Redwood Creek drainage from logging focused on the Tall Trees Grove, which was threatened by increasing sediment flow from upstream logging. With the creation of Redwood National Park in 1968 and added park lands in 1978, the Tall Trees Grove and lower Redwood Creek were given protection. Tall Trees Access Road requires a free permit, obtained at the visitors center in Orick. A maximum of 50 permits per day are given out on a first-come, first-served basis.

LADY BIRD JOHNSON GROVE _____ **h**idden

Located off Bald Hill Road on a one-mile trail, this grove represents another magnificent cluster of ancient trees. Named for the former first lady, who was instrumental in establishing the

352 Redwood National Park and advocated for many conservationist efforts, the old-growth stand winds to a ridge awash in bright greens from the footpath to the treetops.

GOLD BLUFFS BEACH Davison Road (day-use fee) leads along this remote beach eight miles to Fern Canyon. Here angular walls 50 feet high are covered with rioting vegetation.

ELK PRAIRIE Redwood National Park encompasses three state parks—**Prairie Creek Redwoods**, **Del Norte Coast Redwoods**, and **Jedediah Smith Redwoods**. Just after the main entrance to the first you'll pass this prairie, where herds of Roosevelt elk graze across open meadows. Immediately past the entrance, Cal Barrel Road, another short detour, courses through dense redwood forest.

COASTAL DRIVE Plan to turn off onto this gravel road paralleling Route 101. Its numerous turnouts expose extraordinary ocean vistas. The road snakes high above the coast before emptying onto the main highway near the mouth of the Klamath River.

MAIN PARK HEADQUARTERS ✉*1111 2nd Street, Crescent City* ☎*707-464-6101* 📠*707-464-1812* The Del Norte section of the park reveals more startling sea views en route to Crescent City, where the main park headquarters is located.

CRESCENT CITY–DEL NORTE COUNTY CHAMBER OF COMMERCE ✉*1001 Front Street, Crescent City* ☎*707-464-3174, 800-343-8300* 📠*707-464-9676* 🖳*www.northerncalifornia.net,* *cchamber@charterinter.com* There is travel information aplenty at the Main Park Headquarters and at this chamber of commerce building just across the street. Closed on weekends in winter.

BATTERY POINT LIGHTHOUSE ✉*Crescent City* ☎*707-464-3089* Perched on a rocky island off Route 101 in Crescent City is this lighthouse, an 1856 stone and masonry structure that is one of the best preserved original lighthouses on the Pacific Coast, and the fifth-oldest on the West Coast. At low tide from April through September visitors can walk across a spit of sand and rock to the lighthouse for tours of the house, the lantern room, and a small museum. Closed Monday and Tuesday, and weekdays from October through March. Admission.

LAKE EARL WILDLIFE AREA ✉*Old Mill Road, three miles north of Crescent City* ☎*707-464-2523* 📠*707-464-2871* 🖳*lakeearlwla@dfg.ca.gov* Woodlands, wetlands, grasslands—you'll find them all here. This preserve also offers secluded sand dunes and a sufficient number of bird species, over 300 at last count, to make it look like it was created by the Audubon Society. One of the finest birdwatching spots on the North Coast, this Pacific Flyway destination is the place to see hawks, falcons, bald eagles, Canada geese, and canvasback ducks. As many as 51,000 Aleutian Canadian geese stop here in the spring to fatten up before their 3000-mile non-stop flight back to the Aleutian Islands. Closed weekends.

Route 101 north to Route 199 leads to the park's Jedediah Smith section with its mountain vistas and thick redwood groves. The Smith River, rich in salmon and steelhead, threads through the region.

HIOUCHI INFORMATION CENTER ⊠*Route 199, four miles east of Route 101* ✆*707-464-6101* ⌕*707-464-1812* For further details on the remote Jedediah Smith area check with this information center. Closed mid-September to mid-June.

LODGING

BENBOW INN

$$$–$$$$ 54 ROOMS   ⊠*445 Lake Benbow Drive, Garberville* ✆*707-923-2124,* *800-355-3301* ⌕*707-923-2122* ⌕*www.benbowinn.com, benbow@benbowinn.com*
One of Northern California's finest old lodges is this imposing, Tudor-style inn. Located astride the Eel River, this regal retreat is bounded by lawns, gardens, and umbrella-tabled patios. The structure itself is a bold three-story manor in the English country tradition. The lobby, paneled in carved wood and adorned by ornamental molding, is a sumptuous sitting area with a grand fireplace. Jigsaw puzzles lie scattered on the clawfoot tables. The dining area and lounge are equally elegant. Guest quarters offer such flourishes as quilted beds with wooden headboards, hand-painted doors, period wallprints, marble-topped nightstands, and complimentary sherry. Visitors also enjoy tea and scones in the afternoon and evening hors d'oeuvres.

JOHNSTON MOTEL

$ 14 ROOMS   ⊠*839 Redwood Drive, Garberville* ✆*707-923-3327* ⌕*707-923-2108*
The cheapest lodging I've found in the southern redwoods area is this motel. Unlike the region's big-tag caravansaries, this 14-unit facility has rooms at budget prices. Don't expect a lot of shine. The plain rooms are small but comfortable.

Not that I have anything against Johnston's; it's just that Garberville is not my idea of paradise. For a few well-spent dollars more you can rent a room in any of several motels along redwood-lined Avenue of the Giants.

MIRANDA GARDENS RESORT

$$–$$$ 17 UNITS   ⊠*6766 Avenue of the Giants, Miranda* ✆*707-943-3011* ⌕*707-943-3584* ⌕*www.mirandagardens.com, info@mirandagardens.com*
This resort has everything from one- and two-person cottages to cabins with fully equipped kitchens. Some accommodations include whirlpools. All cabins boast a private patio or deck, some overlooking Redwood State Park. The place features a heated swimming pool, playground, and market. The facilities are tucked into a redwood grove with lush gardens, and the rooms are partially paneled in redwood. Continental breakfast during summer.

SHELTER COVE BEACHCOMBER INN

$–$$ 6 ROOMS ✉412 Machi Road, Shelter Cove ☎707-986-7551, 800-718-4789 ⬥www.sojourner2000.com/directory/beachcomber

Way out in Shelter Cove, at the southern end of California's remote Lost Coast, is this inn, which consists of three buildings with six units. Three rooms have kitchens and wood-burning stoves. All come with barbecue grills and patios, almost all with ocean views. Considering that the price tag on this luxury is reasonable and that Shelter Cove is one of the coast's most secluded hideaways, the Beachcomber Inn is well worth the effort.

MATTOLE RIVER ORGANIC FARMS COUNTRY CABINS

$$ 5 UNITS ✉42354 Mattole Road, Petrolia ☎707-629-3445, 800-845-4607 📠707-629-3445

Mattole River Organic Farms offers full-facility cottages (c. 1925) complete with kitchenettes. Each is plain but comfortably furnished ; most feature a sitting room and a bedroom. This rustic colony sits amid shade trees and is backdropped by forested hills.

SUNRISE INN AND SUITES

$$ 25 ROOMS ✉129 4th Street, Eureka ☎707-443-9751, 800-404-9751 📠707-443-9751

The cheapest lodging of all is in the neon motels along Route 101 on the outskirts of Eureka. Many advertise room rates on highway signs along the southern entrance to town. Sunrise Inn is perhaps the best of these. Because it is centrally located, guests can walk to Old Town and other points of interest. The rooms are simple but very clean, with carpeting and king or queen beds. Nearly half have jacuzzi tubs.

EAGLE HOUSE VICTORIAN INN

$$ 24 ROOMS ✉139 2nd Street, Eureka ☎707-444-3344 ⬥www.eaglehouseinn.com, eaglehouse@sbcglobal.net

This imposing Victorian inn has been operating as an inn since the 1880s, and many of the exquisitely detailed antiques date from the early days. Every room is different, but all boast the same high level of historic decor as the ornate lobby (which features a wood-burning stove), and all have modern amenities such as private baths, phones, and cable TV. The bay-view dining room on the second floor serves continental breakfast. The front street-level entrance leads directly into an Irish pub, a convivial spot for a drink and snack any day of the week.

CARTER HOUSE

$$–$$$$ 5 ROOMS ✉301 L Street, Eureka ☎707-445-1390, 800-404-1390 📠707-444-8067 ⬥www.carterhouse.com, reserve@carterhouse.com

Another of Eureka's spectacular bed and breakfasts is Carter House, one of the finest Victorians I've ever seen. This grand old four-story house is painted in light hues and decorated with contemporary artwork, lending an airy quality seldom found in vintage homes. The place is beautiful: Light streams through bay windows; oriental rugs are scattered across hardwood floors; there are sumptuous sitting rooms, and oak banisters that seemingly climb forever. In the seven rooms are antique nightstands and armoires, beds with bold wooden headboards, ceramic pieces, and original local artwork. Two private cottages with fireplaces, spa tubs, and full kitchens are also available. The price includes a full breakfast, complimentary wine, and cookies before bedtime.

HOTEL CARTER

$$$$ 23 ROOMS ⊠301 L Street, Eureka ✆707-444-8062, 800-404-1390
✉707-444-8067 ⌖www.carterhouse.com, reserve@carterhouse.com

Mark and Christi Carter added this hotel to their lodging empire a number of years ago. Its pale pine furniture and khaki-colored walls offer a refreshing counterpoint to the Carter House across the street. Accommodations are spacious; some have fireplaces and whirlpool baths. Complimentary breakfast is served in the ground-floor dining room, where colorful dhurrie rugs and silver candleholders add an elegant touch.

ABIGAIL'S ELEGANT VICTORIAN MANSION

$$$ 4 ROOMS ⊠1406 C Street, Eureka ✆707-444-3144
⌖www.eureka-california.com, info@eureka-california.com

Time-travel to the turn of the 20th century at Abigail's, an 1888 manse with a classic gingerbread exterior. This opulent inn offers four guest rooms with richly ornamental Victorian decor. You can wander into the Turkish Sitting Room and catch one of 700 period films, or check out the gramophones playing pre-1930 popular music. The stay here also comes with the option of participating in a variety of sporting and recreational opportunities, including tennis, croquet, and a five-hour backcountry wilderness safari ride on four-wheelers.

THE DALY INN

$$ 5 UNITS ⊠1125 H Street, Eureka ✆707-445-3638, 800-321-9656
✉707-444-3636 ⌖www.dalyinn.com, innkeeper@dalyinn.com

Built in 1905 by a local department store magnate, this inn is now an elegant bed and breakfast. Surrounded by colorful Victorian gardens, this picture-perfect inn has three comfortable rooms and two spacious suites, all furnished in early-20th-century antiques. A full breakfast and evening hors d'oeuvres are complimentary.

SHAW HOUSE
BED & BREAKFAST

$$–$$$$ 8 ROOMS ⊠703 Main Street, Ferndale; mailing address: P.O. Box 1369, Ferndale, CA 95536 ✆707-786-9958, 800-557-7429 ✉707-786-9758
⌖www.shawhouse.com, stay@shawhouse.com

For an extra dash of history in your nightly brew, there's the Shaw House in nearby Ferndale. It's only fitting to this bed and breakfast that Ferndale is an island in time where the Victorian era still remains. The Shaw House, built in 1854, is the oldest home in town and is on the National Historic Register. A Carpenter Gothic creation, it was modeled on Hawthorne's *House of the Seven Gables*. A library, two parlors, a dining room, and balconies are available to guests, and the home is furnished throughout with precious antiques. All rooms have private baths. Tea and cookies are served in the afternoon.

THE GINGERBREAD MANSION

$$$–$$$$ 11 UNITS ✉*400 Berding Street, Ferndale* ☎*707-786-4000,*
800-952-4136 📠*707-786-4381* 🖥*www.gingerbread-mansion.com,*
innkeeper@gingerbread-mansion.com

In a town chockablock with precious Victorians, one of the most precious of all is The Gingerbread Mansion. Turrets and gables, an intimate garden, interesting antiques, and a delicious home-made breakfast are among the features; but what you'll find particularly special about this bed and breakfast are the bathrooms. One has mirrored ceilings and walls; another, his-and-hers claw-foot tubs set near a tiled gas fireplace. The 11 distinct accommodations (4 are top-floor suites), are comfortably cozy. Afternoon tea and Godiva turn-down chocolates (port, too, for suite guests) are additional touches.

LADY ANNE

$$ 5 ROOMS ✉*902 14th Street, Arcata* ☎*707-822-2797*
🖥*www.humboldt1.com/ladyanne, ladyanne@humboldt1.com*

Set in a quiet residential neighborhood within walking distance of downtown, the Lady Anne has antique-appointed rooms in an 1888 Queen Anne–style home. You can sit on the porch or in a chair in the front yard and watch the world go by, or play the grand piano and guitars in one of the inn's two parlors. A full breakfast is served each morning.

TRINIDAD BAY
BED & BREAKFAST

$$$ 4 ROOMS ✉*Edwards and Trinity streets, Trinidad* ☎*707-677-0840*
🖥*www.trinidadbaybnb.com*

You will be hard pressed anywhere along the coast to find a view more alluring than the one here. This New England–style shingle house, set in a tiny coastal town, looks across Trinidad Bay, past fishing boats and sea rocks, seals and sandy beaches, to tree-covered headlands. Two of the country-style rooms are equipped with standard furnishings, private entrances, and come with a delivered breakfast. There is a fireplace and a living room for guests to share. Rates include breakfast.

TURTLE ROCKS OCEANFRONT INN

$$$$ 6 ROOMS ✉*3392 Patrick's Point Drive, Trinidad* ☎*707-677-3707*
🖥*www.turtlerocksinn.com, innkeeper@turtlerocksinn.com*

Turtle Rocks is located four and a half miles north of town on a rocky bluff overlooking seastacks that provide a refuge for barking seals.

Decorated with seashells, driftwood, turtle figurines, and fresh flowers, the contemporary bed and breakfast has six spacious guest rooms, each with a sitting area with facing divans, a king-sized bed, a private bath, and a private glass-paneled deck that's picture-perfect for whale-watching in spring or fall and enjoying sunsets any time of year. Free wi-fi access is also provided in all rooms. Trinidad State Beach and Trinidad Head Trail are close by, and Patrick's Point State Park, with its rock headlands and promontories, is less than a mile's walk. Rates include a full gourmet breakfast and beverages throughout the day.

HOSTELLING INTERNATIONAL— REDWOOD NATIONAL PARK

$ 32 BEDS ✉14480 Route 101 at Wilson Creek Road, Klamath ✆707-482-8265, 888-464-4872 ext. 552 📠707-482-4665 ✐www.redwoodhostel.org, info@redwoodhostel.org

Set in a 1908 settler's house, this hostel provides basic dormitory-style accommodations; there are two private rooms for couples and one family room. It's across the highway from a beach and features a laundry room, kitchen facilities, and a common room. Winter schedule varies, call ahead.

CRESCENT BEACH MOTEL

$$ 27 ROOMS ✉1455 Route 101 South, Crescent City ✆707-464-5436 📠707-464-9336 ✐www.crescentbeachmotel.com

Farther north in Crescent City, along the scimitar strand that gave the town its name, is Crescent Beach Motel. This motel has plate-glass views of the ocean. Rooms are small but decorated with oak furniture and a blue-green color scheme. They have TVs, and most rooms have those oh-so-priceless sea vistas.

DINING

BENBOW INN

$$$$ CALIFORNIA CUISINE/FRENCH ✉445 Lake Benbow Drive, Garberville ✆707-923-2124, 800-355-3301 📠707-923-2122 ✐www.benbowinn.com, benbow@benbowinn.com

Personally, my favorite dining place in these parts is at this inn. This Tudor lodge serves meals in a glorious dining room that will make you feel as though you're feasting at the estate of a British baron. The dinner menu relies on local produce and herbs grown in the inn's own garden. Though the menu changes seasonally, you are likely to find such items as lamb, salmon, scallops, and filet of beef. Breakfast and dinner served year-round; lunch served June to mid-September.

WOODROSE CAFÉ

$–$$ AMERICAN ✉911 Redwood Drive, Garberville ✆707-923-3191

In the southern redwoods region you'll be hard pressed to find a better restaurant than the Woodrose. It's not big on looks—just a counter, some tables and chairs, and a small patio out back. But the kitchen folk cook up some potent concoctions. That's why the place draws locals in droves. The breakfast menu offers buckwheat pancakes, lox and bagels, and spinach-and-feta-cheese omelettes. At lunch they make homemade soups, organic salads, sandwiches, and tofu burgers; no dinner served. The Woodrose Café is a good reason to visit otherwise drab Garberville. No lunch on Saturday and Sunday.

Proceeding north along the Avenue of the Giants, you'll encounter cafés in tiny towns like Miranda, Myers Flat, Weott, and Pepperwood. Most are tourist-oriented businesses, adequate as way stations, but undistinguished and slightly overpriced.

DJS BURGER BAR

$ AMERICAN   ✉*509 Wildwood Avenue, Rio Dell*   ☎*707-764-2924*

Non-chain eateries in Scotia are limited, so your best bet is to head half a mile over the Scotia Bridge to the popular DJs in Rio Dell. Locals gather here for chicken and beef tacos, BLTs, hot dogs, and the always popular bacon-cheeseburger-with-fries special. DJs has also been known to play host to regional festivities, such as Classic Car Night.

RESTAURANT 301

$$$–$$$$ CONTINENTAL   ✉*In the Hotel Carter, 301 L Street, Eureka*
☎*707-444-8062, 800-404-1390*   📠*707-444-8067*   🖥*www.carterhouse.com*

Eureka's historic Old Town section, a refurbished neighborhood of stately Victorians, supports several good restaurants. Located in the Hotel Carter, this spot offers fresh, inventive gourmet food, with imaginative entrées such as teriyaki-bourbon portobello mushroom and coffee-dusted venison medallions. The menu changes seasonally but usually features local fish, meat, and vegetarian dishes. Prix-fixe multicourse "Discovery" meals, complete with wine pairings for each course, are also available. Breakfast and dinner.

SEA GRILL

$$–$$$ SEAFOOD   ✉*316 E Street, Eureka*   ☎*707-443-7187*

A meal here is a chance to enjoy fine dining in a historic 1876 storefront. The place has an airy Victorian feel about it, with lots of peachy pastels, fabric drapes, and an antique mahogany bar. Oil paintings created by local artists add to the atmosphere. Chicken, steak, and seafood dishes are the specialties. No lunch Saturday through Monday. Closed Sunday.

SAMURAI RESTAURANT

$$ JAPANESE   ✉*621 5th Street, Eureka*   ☎*707-442-6802*

For Asian fare there's this simple dining room appointed with Japanese antiques and folk art. The menu includes seafood, standard sukiyaki, tempura, and teriyaki dishes. There's a large selection of imaginative sushi. You can also try the "Treasure Ship," a sampler of five different entrées. Dinner only. Closed Sunday and Monday.

SAMOA COOKHOUSE

$$ AMERICAN   ✉*Samoa Road, Samoa*   ☎*707-442-1659*   📠*707-442-1699*
🖥*www.samoacookhouse.net*

For a dining experience lumberjack-style, there's this neighborhood restaurant just outside Eureka. A local lumber company has opened its chow house to the public, serving three meals daily. Just join the crowd piling into this unassuming eatery, sit down at a school cafeteria–style table and dig in. You'll be served redwood-size portions of soup, salad, meat, potatoes, vegetables, and dessert—you can even ask for seconds. Ask for water and they'll plunk down a pitcher, order coffee and someone will bring a pot. It's noisy, crowded, hectic, and great fun. Reduced rates for children and seniors.

SEASCAPE RESTAURANT

$$–$$$ SEAFOOD ✉ *Trinidad Pier, Trinidad* ☏ *707-677-3762* ✆ *707-677-3987*
✐ *www.cheraeheightscasino.com*

There are only about three dozen tables and booths at this small and unassuming dining room. But the walls of plate glass gaze out upon a rocky headland and expansive bay. Situated at the foot of Trinidad Pier, the local eating spot overlooks the town's tiny fishing fleet. The dishes, many drawn from surrounding waters, include halibut, rock cod, salmon, crab, and shrimp. Landlubbers dine on beef fillet. Lunch and breakfast menus are equally inviting.

From Trinidad to the Oregon border the countryside is sparsely populated. Crescent City is the only town of real size, but you'll find nondescript cafés in such places as Orick, Klamath, and Smith River.

HARBOR VIEW GROTTO

$$ SEAFOOD ✉ *150 Starfish Way, Crescent City* ☏ *707-464-3815*

Crescent City—like the entire North Coast—is seafood country. Best place around is this family restaurant with an ocean view. This plate-glass eatery features a long inventory of ocean dishes—whole clams, fried prawns or oysters, scallops, red snapper, salmon, cod, halibut, and so on, not to mention the seafood salads and shrimp cocktails. There are also a few meat dishes (prime rib and steak), plus an assortment of sandwiches, chicken, and pasta dishes. Worth a stop.

SHOPPING

In Ferndale, a picturesque Victorian town south of Eureka, there's a covey of intriguing shops. The community has attracted a number of artisans, many of whom display their wares in the 19th- and early-20th-century stores lining Main Street. There are shops selling needlework, stained glass, and kinetic sculptures; others deal in ironwork, used books, and handknits. There are even stores specializing in "paper treasures," boots and saddles, dolls, and "nostalgic gifts." All are contained along a three-block section that more resembles a living museum than a downtown shopping district.

Eureka, too, has been gentrified. Most of the refurbishing has occurred in Old Town, where stately Victorians, falsefront stores, and tumbledown buildings have been transformed into sparkling shops and art galleries. Window browse down 2nd and 3rd streets from C Street to H Street and you're bound to find several inviting establishments. Of particular interest is the F Street corridor, which is becoming a nexus for the arts.

MORRIS GRAVES MUSEUM OF ART ✉*636 F Street, Eureka* ✆*707-442-0278* 📠*707-442-2040* ✐*www.humboldtarts.org* The crown jewel is the Humboldt Arts Council's museum, featuring seven galleries of local fine arts. Closed Monday through Tuesday.

NIGHTLIFE

Now don't misunderstand—California's northern coast and redwood region are wild and provocative places. It's just that the word "wild" up here is taken literally, as in wilderness and wildlife. Somehow the urban meaning of crazy nights and endless parties was never fully translated.

BENBOW INN ✉*445 Lake Benbow Drive, Garberville* ✆*707-923-2124* The Benbow features a fine old lounge with carved walls and an ornate fireplace. A pianist adds to the intimacy.

FERNDALE REPERTORY THEATER ✉*447 Main Street, Ferndale* ✆*707-786-5484* 📠*707-786-5480* ✐*www.ferndale-rep.org* Entertaining for almost three decades, the Ferndale Repertory Theater puts on a variety of plays and musicals year-round in an old movie theater.

BEACHES & PARKS

THE LOST COAST
hidden

✆*707-986-5400*

🚶🚴🏇🎣🚣🛥️⚓ California's coastal Route 1 is one of the greatest highways in America. Beginning in Southern California, it sweeps north through Big Sur, Carmel, San Francisco, and Mendocino, past ocean scenery indescribably beautiful. Then it disappears. At the foot of Redwood Country, Route 1 quits the coast and turns into Route 101.

The region it never reaches is California's fabled "Lost Coast." Most of the region is now protected as the King Range National Conservation Area. Four major trails traverse it: Cooskie Creek Trail is 12.8 miles of coastal prairie areas; King Crest Trail, which climbs the main coastal ridge for 11.5 miles, with views of the ocean and Eel River Valley; the nine-mile-long Chemise Mountain trail; and the 1.5-mile-long Lost Coast Trail–North along the wilderness beach. Before you go, it's good to get trail information from the King Range ranger station.

One of the wettest areas along the Pacific Coast, King Range gets about 100 inches of rain a year. The precipitation is particularly heavy from October to April. Summer carries cool coastal fog and some rain. Weather permitting, it's a fascinating region to explore—wild and virgin, with the shellmounds of American Indians who inhabited the area over a century ago still scattered on the beach.

Motels, restaurants, groceries, and boat rentals are available in Shelter Cove, at the south end of the Conservation Area. To get there from Garberville on Route 101, Redwood Drive leads to nearby Redway and then Briceland Road and then Shelter Cover Road lead southwest to Shelter Cove. About 15 miles down this road, Kings Peak Road forks northwest, paralleling the Conservation Area, to Ettersberg and Honeydew. Just before Kings Peak Road, Chemise Mountain Road turns off into Nadelos and Wailaki campgrounds.

▲ There are numerous tent/RV campgrounds (no hookups): Wailaki is for RVs and tents, Nadelos for tents only. Fees $8 per night. For information contact the Arcata Field Office (U.S. Bureau of Land Management, 1695 Heindon Road, Arcata, CA 95521; 707-986-5400, fax 707-825-2301; www.ca.blm.gov/arcata).

SINKYONE WILDERNESS STATE PARK

✉ *Located 30 miles west of Redway on Briceland Road or 50 miles north of Fort Bragg on County Road 431* 📞 *707-986-7711* 🖥 *707-986-7711*

🚶🏇⛵ This 7500-acre park below the southern tip of the King Range is known for the narrow and steep winding dirt roads leading to its interior. For this reason trailers and RVs are discouraged from entering the park—especially since there are no RV facilities. Featuring old-growth redwood groves and clear-cut prairies, the park hugs the southern section of the Lost Coast. The ranch house and visitors center are a mere 200 yards from awe-inspiring bluffs. Other facilities include picnic tables and pit toilets. Keep an eye out for the majestic Roosevelt elk who inhabit Sinkyone Wilderness State Park. Day-use fee, $6.

▲ There are 16 drive-in sites at Usal Beach and 17 hike-in sites at Needle Rock for tents only; fees up to $15 per night. All of the north end sites are hike-in only.

STANDISH-HICKEY STATE RECREATION AREA

✉ *Located along Route 101, two miles north of Leggett* 📞 *707-925-6482* 🖥 *707-925-6402*

🚶🛶🎣⛵ Near the southern edge of Redwood Country, this 1000-acre park primarily consists of second-growth trees. The single exception is a 1200-year-old giant named after the Mayflower pilgrim, Captain Miles Standish. The forest here also has Douglas fir, oak, and maple trees. The south fork of the Eel River courses through the area, providing swimming holes and fishing spots (catch-and-release only). There are picnic areas, restrooms, and showers. Day-use fee, $6.

▲ There are 99 tent/RV sites (no hookups) and 63 tent sites; $20 per night. Reservations recommended during summer; call 800-444-7275.

RICHARDSON GROVE STATE PARK

✉ *Route 101, about 18 miles north of Leggett* 📞 *707-247-3318* 🖥 *707-247-3308*

🚶🛶⛵ The first of the virgin redwood parks, this 2300-acre facility features a grove of goliaths. For some bizarre reason the highway builders chose to put the main road through the heart of the forest. This means you won't miss the redwoods, but to really appreciate them you'll have to disappear down one of the three hiking trails that loop through the grove. The south fork of the Eel River flows through the park, providing swimming and trout fishing opportunities. In the summer there are weekend campfires and kids' programs. The park has an information center, picnic areas, restrooms, and showers. Day-use fee, $6.

▲ There are 176 tent/RV sites (no hookups); $20 per night. Reservations: 800-444-7275.

BENBOW LAKE STATE RECREATION AREA
✉️ *Route 101, about 23 miles north of Leggett* 📞 *707-923-3238, 707-247-3318*
🖥️ *707-247-3300*

🚶🚴🏇⛵🚤🛶 One of the less desirable parks in the area, this facility fronts the Eel River near the dam that creates Benbow Lake. The lake is usually full and suitable for boating from July 1 to mid-September; it's a good idea to call first. Motorized boats are not allowed. Route 101 streams through the park's center, disrupting an otherwise idyllic scene. Nevertheless, there's good swimming and fishing in the river-lake. In summer there are weekend campfires and kids' programs here. There are picnic areas, restrooms, and showers. Note: At the time of this book's publication, the fate of Benbow Lake is uncertain due to state financial issues and environmental concerns relating to the damming of Eel River. Please call ahead to make sure the lake is accessible for any future reservations. Day-use fee, $6.

▲ There are 77 tent/RV sites (two have hookups) along the river; $20 per night. Closed in winter. Reservations: 800-444-7275.

HUMBOLDT REDWOODS STATE PARK

✉️ *Located along the Avenue of the Giants between Miranda and Pepperwood*
📞 *707-946-2409* 🖥️ *707-946-2618* 🌐 *www.humboldtredwoods.org*

🚶🚴🏇⛵🛶 One of the state's great parks, it is set within a 20-million-year-old forest. The park is a tribute to early conservationists who battled lumber interests in an effort to save the area's extraordinary trees. Today more than 100 miles of hiking trails lead through redwood groves and along the south fork of the Eel River. Within the park's 35-mile length there are also opportunities for swimming, biking, horseback riding (you must provide your own horse), fishing, or tree gazing. Facilities include an information center, picnic areas, restrooms, and showers. Day-use fee, $6.

▲ There are three different campgrounds (only one in the winter) with a total of 256 tent/RV sites (no hookups); $20 per night. (The best, most private sites are, appropriately enough, at Hidden Springs Campground.) There are also five hike-in camps. Reservations: 800-444-7275.

CLAM BEACH COUNTY PARK
✉️ *Located along Route 101, about 15 miles north of Eureka* 📞 *707-445-7652*
🖥️ *707-445-7409*

🚶🏇🎣🛶 There's a broad expanse of beach here with good views of surrounding headlands. As its name suggests, this place was once known for its clams; unfortunately for mollusk-lovers, clamming has diminished in the last few years. Still, it's a lovely local park. Horseback riders must provide their own horses. There's a picnic area and toilets.

▲ There are 27 open-ground tent/RV sites here (no hookups); $10 per night. No reservations accepted.

PATRICK'S POINT STATE PARK

✉*Off Route 101, about 25 miles north of Eureka* ✆*707-677-3570* 🖂*707-677-9357*

🏃 🚣 ⏚ This 650-acre park is particularly known for Agate Beach, a long crescent backdropped by wooded headlands. It's one-third of a mile from the main parking area. There are tidepools to explore, sea lions and seals offshore, and several miles of hiking trails. Leave Fido at home—dogs aren't allowed on the beach or trails. Drop by the reconstructed Yurok Indian village, where rangers will tell you about life on the coast before the Europeans showed up. The facilities here include picnic areas, restrooms, and showers. Day-use fee, $6.

▲ There are 124 tent/RV sites (no hookups); $20 to $23 per night. Reservations are recommended in the summer; call 800-444-7275.

HUMBOLDT LAGOONS STATE PARK

✉*15336 Highway 101, Trinidad; Off Route 101, about 40 miles north of Eureka*
✆*707-488-2169*

🏃 🚣 🎣 ⏚ ⏚ 🚤 ⏚ A 2000-acre facility, this beach park is full of surprises. The main entrance leads to a sandy beach tucked between rocky outcroppings and heaped with driftwood. Behind the beach an old lagoon has slowly transformed into a marsh of brackish water. Add the two areas together and you come up with a splendid park. Catch-and-release fishing at Stone Lagoon is good for cutthroat trout. Toilets and a visitors center are the only facilities.

▲ There are 12 environmental hike-in and boat-in sites; $12 per night.

REDWOOD NATIONAL AND STATE PARKS _____ idden

✉*Located along Route 101 between Orick and Crescent City; Jedediah Smith*
Redwoods State Park is along Route 199, nine miles east of Crescent City.
The park headquarters is at 1111 2nd Street, Crescent City. ✆*707-464-6101*
🖂*707-464-1812* 🌐*www.nps.gov/redw*

🏃 🚴 🏇 ⏚ ⏚ ⏚ Actually four parks in one, this 105,516-acre giant encompasses Prairie Creek Redwoods, Del Norte Coast Redwoods, Jedediah Smith Redwoods state parks and Redwood National Park. Together they stretch over 33 miles along the coast from Orick to the Crescent City region. Within that span, one of California's wettest areas (69 inches of rain yearly in Del Norte), are hidden beaches, ocean cliffs, deep redwood forests, and mile on mile of hiking trails.

Along the coast are wind-scoured bluffs and gently sloping hills. The beaches range from sandy to rocky; because of the rugged terrain in certain areas, some are inaccessible. In addition to beaches, many streams—including Prairie Creek, Redwood Creek, Klamath River, Mill Creek, and the Smith River—traverse this series of parks.

Hikers and redwood lovers will find that several spectacular groves lie adjacent to Routes 101 and 199. Others can be reached along uncrowded trails. Tan oak and madrone grow around the redwoods, while farther inland there are Jeffrey pine and Douglas fir.

Birdwatchers will encounter mallards, hawks, owl, shorebirds, quail, and great blue herons. The mammal population ranges from shrews and moles to rabbit and beaver to black-tail deer, Roosevelt elk, and an occasional bear. Along the coast live river otters and harbor seals. These and other features make the parks a natural for swimming, fishing, canoeing, and kayaking.

Facilities include information centers, picnic areas, restrooms, and showers. Day-use fee, $6 at campgrounds.

▲ In the national park, there are four hike-in campgrounds: Nickel Creek, with five sites; Flint Ridge and Demartin, each with ten sites; and Little Bald Hills has four sites and one group site. All are free and completely primitive. The incorporated state parks offer more campgrounds. **Prairie Creek Redwoods State Park** offers 67 tent/RV sites (no hookups); $20 per night. **Jedediah Smith Redwoods State Park** has 69 tent/RV sites (no hookups); $20 per night. And at **Del Norte Coast Redwoods State Park** you will find 131 tent/RV sites (no hookups); $20 per night. In winter, sites are on a first-come, first-served basis. For reservations contact Reserve America (800-444-7275; www.reserveamerica.com).

OUTDOOR ADVENTURES

SPORTFISHING

All along the coast, charter boats depart daily to fish for salmon, Pacific snapper, or whatever else is running. Most companies leave the dock at 6 a.m. and return by 3:30 p.m.

Marin Coast

CARUSO'S SPORTFISHING ✉Harbor Drive, Sausalito ✆415-332-1015 If you hanker to try your luck for salmon, contact Caruso's.

LOCH LOMOND LIVE BAIT HOUSE ✉Loch Lomond Marina, San Rafael ✆415-456-0321 This shop sells bait and tackle. They also cruise the bay for striper, halibut, and sturgeon.

Sonoma and Mendocino Coast

BODEGA BAY SPORTFISHING ✉1410 Bay Flat Road, Bodega Bay ✆707-875-3344 ✑www.usafishing.com Besides salmon charters, this company runs charters for halibut, rock cod, ling cod, albacore, and crab, as well as giant Humboldt squid. Whale-watching cruises run January through April, and in the summer there are sunset cruises.

ANCHOR CHARTER BOATS ✉*North Harbor Drive, Wharf Restaurant, Fort Bragg* ✆*707-964-4550* ✐*www.anchorcharterboats.com* Whatever your sportfishing tastes, Anchor Boats aims to please. Besides the usual rockfish, tuna, salmon, and whale-watching excursions, they'll also take you on extended trips.

Redwood Country

FULL THROTTLE SPORTFISHING ✉*Woodley Island Marina, 601 Startare Drive, Eureka* ✆*707-498-7473* ✐*www.fullthrottlesportfishing.com, gary@fullthrottle sportfishing.com* For deep-sea fishing trips in search of tuna, salmon, rockfish, or halibut, contact Full Throttle. Bait and all gear are provided.

RIVER RUNNING

With the Eel, Klamath, Smith, and Trinity rivers traversing many of the North Coast's parks, you're never far away from these mysterious fog-filled areas full of natural vegetation and wildlife.

ALL OUTDOORS ADVENTURE TRIPS ✉*1250 Pine Street, Suite 103, Walnut Creek* ✆*925-932-8993, 800-247-2387* ✐*www.aorafting.com* These experts offer professionally guided rafting excursions ranging from Class I to Class V. Trips are one-day to four-day affairs, with all food and lodging included.

BEYOND LIMITS ✉*P.O. Box 215, Riverbank, CA 95367* ✆*800-234-7238* ✐*www.rivertrip.com* In addition to running trips on the Stanislaus, American, and Yuba rivers (Class I to Class V), this group can arrange kayak and canoe trips.

REDWOODS & RIVERS ✉*P.O. Box 606, Big Bar, CA 96010* ✆*800-429-0090* ✐*www.redwoods-rivers.com, redriver@redwoods-rivers.com* This rafting company has half-day to five-day trips on the Trinity, South Fork Eel, Upper Eel, Lower Klamath, and Cal Salmon rivers for all levels, plus kayaking lessons and drift-boat fishing.

WHALE WATCHING

It is the world's longest mammal migration: 6000 miles along the Pacific coast from the Bering Sea to Baja California, then back again. The creatures making the journey measure 35 to 50 feet and weigh 40 tons. During the entire course of their incredible voyage they neither eat nor sleep.

Every year from mid-December to early February, the California gray whale cruises southward along the Northern California coast. Traveling in groups numbering three to five, these magnificent creatures hug the shoreline en route to their breeding grounds.

Since the whales use local coves and promontories to navigate, they are easy to spot from land. Just watch for the rolling hump, the slapping tail, or a lofty spout of spuming water. Sometimes these huge creatures will breach, leaping 30 feet above the surface, then crashing back with a thunderous splash.

Blue Skies, Gray Whales

California gray whales live to 40 or 50 years and have a world population numbering about 21,000. Their only enemies are killer whales and humans. They mate during the southern migration one year, then give birth at the end of the following year's migration. The calves, born in the warm, shallow waters of Baja, weigh a ton and measure about 16 feet. By the time they are weaned seven months later, the young are already 26 feet long.

Blue whales, humpback whales, dolphins, and porpoises also sometimes visit the coast. Gray whales can be seen again from March to mid-May, though farther from shore, during their return migration north. So keep an eye peeled: That rocky headland on which you are standing may be a crow's nest in disguise.

The best crow's nests from which to catch this aquatic parade are Muir Beach Overlook, Chimney Rock at Point Reyes National Seashore, Bodega Head State Park, Sonoma Coast State Beach, Salt Point State Park, Mendocino Headlands State Park, Shelter Cove or Trinidad Head in Humboldt County, and Point St. George up near Crescent City. Visitors to California's Central Coast also enjoy this annual event.

OCEANIC SOCIETY EXPEDITIONS ✉*Fort Mason Center, Quarters 35, San Francisco* ✆*415-474-3385* ✆*415-474-3395* ⌖*www.oceanic-society.org* Several outfits sponsor whale-watching cruises. During the winter and early spring, the Oceanic Society offers gray whale migration tours, which are led by qualified naturalists. June through November, full-day Farallon Islands trips to see humpback and blue whales are provided. Weekends only.

BOAT HOUSE ✉*1445 Route 1, Bodega Bay* ✆*707-875-3495* For a close look at our fellow mammals from January through April, contact this group (operated by Bodega Bay Sportfishing).

GOLF

From Marin to the Oregon border you'll find several clubs where it's relatively easy to get tee times.

Sonoma and Mendocino Coast
THE NEW LINKS AT BODEGA HARBOUR ✉*21301 Heron Drive, Bodega Bay* ✆*707-875-3538* This 18-hole course is hilly and scenic. Part of the course meanders around a freshwater marsh.

Redwood Country
EUREKA GOLF COURSE ✉*4750 Fairway Drive, Eureka* ✆*707-443-4808* ⌖*www.playeureka.com* In the home of that lofty tree, I recommend this 18-hole course nestled in redwoods. There's a pro shop, a driving range, a putting green, a restaurant, and carts.

DEL NORTE GOLF COURSE ✉*130 Club Drive, Crescent City* ✆*707-458-3214* ⌖*www.delnortegolf.com* In Crescent City, this challenging 18-hole golf course is set amidst redwoods.

The best bet for finding a tennis court without staying at the most expensive hotels is to call the local parks and recreation department.

Redwood Country

HIGHLAND PARK ✉*Highland and Glen streets, Eureka* Four courts.

HAMMOND PARK ✉*14th and E streets, Eureka* ✆*707-441-4226* Four courts.

CRESCENT CITY ✉*301 West Washington Boulevard, Crescent City* ✆*707-464-6141* Four lighted courts.

RIDING STABLES & PACK TRIPS

Riding along the hauntingly beautiful North Coast is not an experience easily forgotten.

FIVE BROOKS STABLES ✉*8001 Route 1, Olema* ✆*415-663-1570* ⌨*www.fivebrooks.com* There are few prettier places to ride than Point Reyes National Seashore, where you can canter through rolling ranch country and out along sharp sea cliffs. This company conducts mounted tours of this extraordinary area. Reservations required.

BIKING

Two-wheeling north of San Francisco is an invigorating sport. Not only is the scenery magnificent, but the accommodations aren't bad either. Many state and national parks sponsor campgrounds where cyclists and hikers can stay for a nominal fee.

Route 1 offers a chance to pedal past a spectacular shoreline of hidden coves, broad beaches, and sheer headlands. Unfortunately, the highway is narrow and winding—for experienced cyclists only.

Marin Coast

Point Reyes National Seashore features miles of bicycling, particularly along Bear Valley Trail.

Sonoma and Mendocino Coast

Other popular areas farther north include the towns of Mendocino and where level terrain and beautiful landscape combine to create a cyclist's haven.

Bike Rentals

CATCH A CANOE AND BICYCLES TOO! ✉*Coast Highway 1 at Comptche-Ukiah Road* ✆*707-937-0273* ⌨*canoe@mcn.org* In Mendocino, this shop rents and sells state-of-the-art equipment.

FORT BRAGG CYCLERY ✉*221-A North Main Street, Fort Bragg* ✆*707-964-3509* Located on the bicycle migration route between Canada and Mexico, this place rents bikes and does full-service repairs.

HIKING

To call California's North Coast a hiker's paradise is an understatement. After all, in San Francisco and north of the city is the Golden Gate National Recreation Area. Together with continuous county, state, and national parks it offers over 100,000 acres to be explored.

Within this ambit are trails ranging from trifling nature loops to tough mountain paths. The land varies from tidal areas and seacliffs to ranch country and scenic mountains. In the far north are the giant redwood forests, located within national parks and featuring networks of hiking trails.

All distances listed for hiking trails are one way unless otherwise noted.

Marin Coast

THE MARIN HEADLANDS   This is a region of bold bluffs and broad seascapes that contain many hiking paths in its unpredictable landscape.

The moderate **Kirby Cove Trail** (1 mile) leads from Conzelman Road down to a narrow beach. The views of San Francisco en route provide a lot of adventure for a short hike.

Beginning at Rodeo Beach, **Wolf Ridge Loop** (5 miles) follows the Coastal Trail and Wolf Ridge Trail, then returns along Miwok Trail. It ascends from a shoreline environment to heights with sweeping views of both San Francisco and Mt. Tamalpais.

The easy **Tennessee Valley Trail** (2 miles) winds along the valley floor en route to a small beach and cove. The trailhead sits off Route 1 at the end of Tennessee Valley Road.

MT. TAMALPAIS STATE PARK   ☎415-388-2070 ✎415-388-2968 About 45 miles of trails loop through this state park. These link to a 200-mile network of hiking paths through Muir Woods National Monument and Golden Gate National Recreation Area. Explorers are rewarded with a diverse terrain, startling views of the entire Bay Area, and a chance to hike within commuting distance of San Francisco. Most trails begin at Pan Toll Park Headquarters. Here you can pick up trail maps ($1) and descriptions from which to devise your own combination loop trails, or consult with the rangers in planning anything from an easy jaunt to a rugged trek.

Dipsea Trail (7.1 miles) is a favorite moderate path beginning in Mill Valley and heading along rolling hills, past sea vistas, then ending near Stinson Beach. The easiest way to pick up the trail is in Muir Woods, about a 3.5 miles from the Mill Valley trailhead.

Matt Davis Trail (3.8 miles) descends 1200 feet from Pan Toll Park Headquarters to Stinson Beach; you'll encounter deep woods, windswept knolls, and views of San Francisco and Point Reyes.

True to its name, **Steep Ravine Trail** (2.8 miles) angles sharply downward from Pan Toll Park Headquarters through a redwood-studded canyon, then joins the Dipsea Trail.

Redwood Creek Trail (2.5 miles) loops through several remarkable redwood stands. A favorite with tourists, this easy trail begins near Muir Woods park headquarters and is often crowded. So it's best hiked either early or late in the day.

There are numerous other trails that when combined form interesting loop hikes. For instance, from Bootjack picnic area in Mt. Tamalpais State Park, you can follow **Bootjack Trail** down a steep canyon of redwood and Douglas fir to Muir Woods, then take **Ben Johnson Trail** (4.2 miles) back up to Pan Toll Park Headquarters. From there it's a half-mile walk back to Bootjack. This moderate circle tour carries through relatively isolated sections of Muir Woods.

For a more challenging 9.4-mile circular trek to the top of Mt. Tamalpais, begin at Pan Toll Park Headquarters. Along Old Stage Road you'll encounter Mountain Home, an inn located along Panoramic Highway. Follow **Old Railroad Grade**. This will lead to West Point Inn, a cozy lodging place for hikers. From here you climb to the road that goes to East Peak, one of Mt. Tamalpais' three summits. If you choose to go on down the rocky **Fern Creek Trail**, you'll encounter Old Railroad Grade once more. En route are flowering meadows, madrone stands, chaparral-cloaked hillsides, and mountaintop views.

POINT REYES NATIONAL SEASHORE   Within its spectacular 72,000-acre domain, this park contains over 140 miles of hiking trails plus four hike-in campsites. The trails form a latticework across forests, ranch lands, and secluded beaches and along sea cliffs, brackish inlets, and freshwater lakes. Over 350 bird species inhabit the preserve. Black-tailed deer, Eurasian fallow deer, and spotted axis deer abound. You might also encounter raccoons, weasels, rabbits, badgers, bobcats, even a skunk or two.

Most trailheads begin near Bear Valley Visitors Center, Palomarin, Five Brooks, or Estero. For maps and information check with the rangers at the **Bear Valley Visitors Center** (415-464-5100, fax 415-464-5149; www.nps.gov/pore).

Hikers can learn about the nearby San Andreas Fault on the short **Earthquake Trail** (.6 mile) that begins from the Bear Valley Visitors Center and leads along the original rupture of the 1906 earthquake. The ground here shifted over 16 feet during that terrible upheaval.

 Woodpecker Trail (.7 mile) is an easy, self-guiding trail with markers explaining the natural environment. The annotated path leads to a horse "museum" set in a barn.

Also beginning near the visitors center, the **Bear Valley Trail** (4.1 miles) courses through range land and wooded valley to cliffs overlooking the Pacific Ocean. The park's most popular trail, it is level and may unfortunately be crowded with hikers and bicyclists.

Coast Trail (15.9 miles) runs between Palomarin (near Bolinas) and Limantour Beach. Hugging the shoreline en route, this moderate, splendid trail leads past four freshwater lakes and two camping areas, then turns inland to Hostelling International's lodge.

Olema Valley Trail (5.3 miles) parallels Route 1 as it tracks a course along the infamous San Andreas Fault. Originating from Five Brooks, it alternates between glades and forest while beating a level path to Dogtown. Moderate.

Estero Trail (8.6 miles) shadows the shoreline of Drakes Estero and provides opportunities to view local waterfowl as well as harbor seals, sea lions, and bat rays.

Redwood Country

HUMBOLDT REDWOODS STATE PARK   There are more than 100 miles of hiking and riding paths within Humboldt Redwoods State Park. Many lead through dense redwood stands, others meander along the Eel River, and some lead to the park's hike-in camps.

Founder's Grove Nature Trail (.5 mile) tunnels through a virgin redwood forest that once boasted the national champion coastal redwood. Though a storm significantly shortened the 362-foot giant, it left standing a cluster of equally impressive neighbors.

Rockefeller Loop Trail (.5 mile) ducks into a magnificent grove of old-growth redwoods. There are also longer trails leading deep into the forest and to the top of 3379-foot Grasshopper Peak.

Within McKinleyville's Clam Beach County Park is the **Hammond Coast Trail** (5 miles), which offers a spectacular trek to the Arcata Bottoms. Views of the ocean and the Trinidad Head can be seen from the northern peak of the trail, which then winds down to the Mad River Bridge.

REDWOOD NATIONAL AND STATE PARKS ✆*707-464-6101* ✆*707-464-1812* Comprising three distinct state parks and extending for miles along California's northwestern corner, Redwood National and State Parks' diverse enclave offers adventure aplenty to daytrippers and mountaineers alike. There are over 150 miles of trails threading the parks, leading through dense redwood groves, along open beaches, and atop wind-buffeted bluffs.

Berry patches and wildflowers dot the **Yurok Loop Trail** (1 mile) that begins near the terminus of Coastal Trail.

Enderts Beach Trail (.5 mile), south of Crescent City, features tidepools, seaside strolling, and primitive camping. It also offers access to the moderate **Coastal Trail** (8.2 miles), an old roadway that cuts through forests of redwood, alder, and spruce and features glorious ocean views.

PRAIRIE CREEK REDWOODS STATE PARK   There are numerous trails to enjoy within this state park.

Redwood Creek Trail (9 miles) leads from a trailhead two miles north of Orick to Tall Trees Grove, home of the world's tallest trees. There is backcountry camping en route; permits available at the trailhead.

Tall Trees Trail (1.6 miles) at Tall Trees provides a shorter route to the same destination as the Redwood Creek Trail: the world's tallest trees.

The **Lady Bird Johnson Grove Nature Loop Trail** (1 mile) winds through ancient redwood country.

A moderate trek, **Rhododendron Trail** (7.8 miles) begins at park headquarters and continues along the eastern ridge of the park, which is filled with rhododendrons.

James Irvine Trail (4.3 miles) goes from the Prairie Creek visitors center along a redwood ridge to Fern Canyon. For a longer loop (10.3 miles), head south on Gold Bluffs Beach, then pick up **Miner's Ridge Trail**. This last trail follows a corduroy mining road used early in the century.

Fern Canyon Trail (.8 mile) courses along a gulch dripping with vegetation.

An easy hike is the **Coastal Trail** (5 miles), which begins at Fern Canyon and parallels Gold Bluffs Beach.

The moderate **West Ridge Trail** (7.1 miles) traces a sharp ridgetop through lovely virgin forest, ending at the Butler Creek backpacking camp.

A marvelous innovation, the **Revelation Trail** (.3 mile) contains handrails and a tape-recorded description of the surroundings for the blind. For those of us gifted with sight, it provides a fuller understanding of the scents, sounds, and textures of a redwood forest.

The **Cathedral Trees Trail** (1.4 miles) heads along streams and meadows to elk country.

Reputedly one of the park's prettiest hikes, the **Brown Creek Trail** (1.2 miles) leads along streams and through old redwood stands.

DEL NORTE COAST REDWOODS STATE PARK   This state park offers several areas ideal for short hikes.

Coastal Trail (4 miles), located south of the state park, begins at Klamath River Overlook. In addition to ocean vistas, it offers a moderate walk through a spruce and alder forest, plus glimpses of sea lions, whales, and numerous birds.

The strenuous ancient Yurok Indian path, **Damnation Creek Trail** (2.1 miles), winds steeply down from Route 101 to a hidden cove and beach.

Hobbs Wall Trail (3.8 miles) leads through a former lumberjacking region.

Alder Basin Trail (1 mile) meanders along a stream through stands of willow, maple, and alder.

JEDEDIAH SMITH REDWOODS STATE PARK   Farther north from Alder Basin is this state park, which has a number of trails to hike.

Stout Grove Trail (.5 mile) highlights several spots along its short easy course: a 340-foot redwood tree, swimming and fishing holes, plus rhododendron regions.

Hiouchi Trail (2 miles), with its huckleberries, trilliums, and rhododendrons, is impressive. This nature trail goes right through a burned-out redwood; it also affords scenic vistas along the Smith River.

Hatton Trail (.3 mile) tours an ancient redwood grove.

Nickerson Ranch Trail (.8 mile) leads through a corridor of ferns and redwoods.

TRANSPORTATION

CAR

When traveling by car you can choose the ever-winding, spectacular coastal **Route 1**, which provides some of the prettiest scenery this side of Shangri-la. Or take **Route 101**, the faster, more direct freeway that follows an interior route.

AIR

ARCATA/EUREKA AIRPORT ⊠*133 V Street, Eureka* ☎*707-443-0826* ✎*www.hta.org* Arcata/Eureka Airport in McKinleyville is served by United Airlines and Horizon Air. On a bluff above the Pacific, this is one of the most beautiful small fields in California. **Humboldt Transit Authority** provides roughly hourly service (Monday through Friday) from Eureka and Arcata to the airport. There's limited service on Saturday.

BUS

GREYHOUND BUS LINES ☎*707-545-6495, 800-231-2222* ✎*www.grey hound.com* Greyhound travels the entire stretch of Route 101 between San Francisco and Oregon, including the main route through Redwood Country.

CAR RENTALS

It's advisable to rent an auto in San Francisco rather than along the North Coast. There are more rental agencies available and prices are lower. At the Arcata/Eureka Airport you can rent from **Avis Rent A Car** (800-331-1212), **Hertz Rent A Car** (800-654-3131), and **National Car Rental** (800-227-7368).

PUBLIC TRANSIT

GOLDEN GATE TRANSIT ☎*415-923-2000* ✎*www.goldengate.org* This transit system has bus service between San Francisco and Sausalito. It also covers Route 101 from San Francisco to Santa Rosa. Public transportation from San Francisco to Marin can become a sightseeing adventure when you book passage on a Golden Gate Transit **ferry boat** (415-455-2000).

MENDOCINO TRANSIT AUTHORITY ☎*800-696-4682* ✎*www.4mta. org* From Santa Rosa you can pick up coastal connections on MTA, which travels Route 1 from Bodega Bay to Point Arena. There's only one bus a day in either direction.

CENTRAL COAST

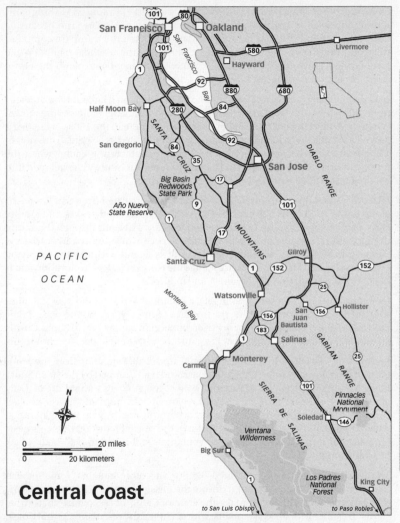

Central Coast

If the Central Coast were an oil painting, it would portray a surf-laced shoreline near the bottom of the frame. Pearly beaches and bold promontories would occupy the center, while forested peaks rose in the background. Actually, a mural would be more appropriate to the subject, since the coastline extends 150 miles from San Francisco to Big Sur. The artist would paint two mountain ranges parallel to the shore, then fill the area between with a patchwork of hills, headlands, and farmland.

Even after adding a swath of redwoods along the entire length of the mural, the painter's task would have only begun. The Central Coast will never be captured—on canvas, in print, or in the camera's eye. It is a region of unmatched beauty and extraordinary diversity.

Due south of San Francisco is Half Moon Bay, a timeless farming and fishing community founded by Italians and Portuguese during the 1860s. The oceanside farms are so bountiful that Half Moon Bay dubs itself the pumpkin capital of the world, and Castroville, farther south, claims to be the artichoke capital. While local farmers grow prize vegetables, commercial fishing boats comb the entire coast for salmon, herring, tuna, anchovies, and cod.

In the seaside town of Santa Cruz, on the other hand, you'll encounter a quiet retirement community that has been transformed into a dynamic campus town. When the University of California opened a school here in the 1960s, it created a new role for this ever-changing place. Originally founded as a Spanish mission in 1791, Santa Cruz became a lumber port and manufacturing center when the Americans moved in around 1849. Then in the late 19th century it developed into a tourist resort filled with elaborate Victorian houses.

Like every place on the Central Coast, Santa Cruz is reached from San Francisco along Route 1, the tortuous coast road that twists past sandy coves and granite cliffs. Paralleling it is Route 101, the inland freeway that leads through the warm, dry agricultural regions of the Salinas Valley. Between these two roadways rise the Santa Cruz Mountains, accessible along Routes 35 and 9. Unlike the low-lying coastal and inland farming areas, this range measures 3000 feet in elevation and is filled with redwood, Douglas fir, alder, and madrone.

Different still is the Monterey Peninsula, a fashionable residential area 125 miles south of San Francisco. Including the towns of Monterey, Pacific Grove, and Carmel, this wealthy enclave is a far cry from bohemian Santa Cruz. If Santa Cruz is an espresso coffeehouse, Monterey is a gourmet restaurant or designer boutique.

Farther south lies Big Sur, the most unusual area of all. Extending from the Monterey Peninsula for 90 miles along the coast, and backdropped by the steep Santa Lucia Mountains, it is one of America's most magnificent natural areas. Only about 1000 residents live in this rugged region of bald crags and flower-choked canyons. None but the most adventurous occupy the nearby Ventana Wilderness, which represents the southernmost realm of the coastal redwoods. Once a nesting place for rare California condors, Ventana is still home to wild boar, black bear, and mountain lion.

The Esselen Indians, who inhabited Big Sur and its mountains, took Spanish names to avoid being slaughtered during the missionary period. In recent years, they have been organizing to make the state of California recognize their tribal status. Together with the Costanoans, who occupied the rest of the Central Coast, the Esselen may have been here for 5000 years. By the time the Europeans happened upon California, about 10,000 American Indians lived near the coast between San Francisco and Big Sur. Elk and antelope ranged the region. The American Indians also hunted sea lions, gathered seaweed, and fed on oysters, abalone, clams, and mussels.

Westerners did not settle Big Sur until after 1850, and Route 1 did not open completely until 1937. During the 1950s, novelist Henry Miller became the focus of an artists' colony here. Jack Kerouac trekked through the area, writing about it in sev-

Over 300 years before settlers arrived in Big Sur, Monterey was already making history. As early as 1542, Juan Rodríguez Cabrillo, a Portuguese explorer in Spanish employ, set anchor off nearby Pacific Grove. Then in 1602 Sebastian Vizcaíno came upon the peninsula again and told a whale of a fish story, grandly exaggerating the size and amenities of Monterey Bay.

His account proved so distorted that Gaspar de Portolá, leading an overland expedition in 1769, failed to recognize the harbor. When Father Junípero Serra joined him in a second journey the next year, they realized that this gentle curve was Vizcaíno's deep port. Serra established California's second mission in Monterey, then moved it a few miles in 1771 to create the Carmel Mission. Neither Serra nor Portolá explored the Big Sur coast, but the Spanish were soon building yet another mission in Santa Cruz.

In fact, they found Santa Cruz much easier to control than Monterey. By the 1820s, Yankee merchant ships were plying Monterey waters, trading for hides and tallow. This early American presence, brilliantly described in Richard Henry Dana's classic Two Years Before the Mast, climaxed in 1846 during the Mexican War. Commodore John Sloat seized the town for the United States. By 1849, while Big Sur was still the hunting ground of American Indians, the adobe town of Monterey had become the site of California's constitutional convention.

An added incentive for these early adventurers, and modern-day visitors as well, was the climate along the Central Coast. The temperature still hovers around 67° in summer and 57° during winter; Santa Cruz continues to boast 300 sunny days a year. Explorers once complained of foggy summers and rainy winters, but like today's travelers, they were rewarded with beautiful spring and fall weather.

Perhaps that's why Monterey became a tourist mecca during the 1880s. Of course the old Spanish capital also developed into a major fishing and canning region during the early 20th century. It was then that John Steinbeck, the Salinas-bred writer, added to the already rich history of Monterey with his novels and stories. Much of the landscape that became known as "Steinbeck Country" has changed drastically since the novelist's day, and the entire Central Coast is different from the days of Serra and Sloat. But the most important elements of Monterey and the Central Coast—the foaming ocean, open sky, and wooded heights—are still here, waiting for the traveler with a bold eye and robust imagination.

SOUTH OF SAN FRANCISCO

An easy drive from the city, the coast south of San Francisco is full of surprises. You might see gray whales, watch the sea lions at Año Nuevo State Reserve, or visit one of the rural towns that dot this shoreline. The area along Route 1 between San Francisco and Santa Cruz also sports numerous beaches, bed-and-breakfast inns, and country roads that lead up into the Santa Cruz Mountains.

SIGHTS

DALY CITY   Preceding the beauty, however, is the beast. The road south from San Francisco leads through one of America's ugliest towns. In fact, Daly City is the perfect counterpoint to the bay city: it is as hideous as San Francisco is splendid. If Tony Bennett left his heart in San Francisco, he must have discarded a gallbladder in Daly City. This town was memorialized in Malvina Reynolds' song, "Little Boxes," which describes its "ticky tacky" houses and over-developed hillsides.

SAN ANDREAS FAULT   No matter, the suburban blight of Daly City soon gives way to Route 1, which cuts through Pacifica and curls into the hills. As the road rises above a swirling coastline you'll be entering a geologic hotspot. The San Andreas Fault, villain of the 1906 and 1989 earthquakes, heads back into shore near Pacifica. As the road cuts will reveal, the sedimentary rock along this area has been twisted and warped into bizarre shapes.

DEVIL'S SLIDE   Several miles south of Pacifica at this spot, unstable hillsides periodically collapse into the sea, prompting costly road closures. Construction of two multi-million dollar bypass tunnels is now underway, and is scheduled for completion by 2011. Route 1, which connects Pacifica to Montara and includes Devil's Slide, will remain open during construction. Updates are available through the California Department of Transportation District 4 (www.dot.ca.gov/dist4/dslide). When the new bypass is open, the Devil's Slide section of the highway will be closed and converted into a nature preserve. I should add that this is an area not to be missed. Drive carefully and you'll be safe to enjoy the outstanding ocean vistas revealed at every hairpin turn in this winding roadway. Rocky cliffs, pocket beaches, and erupting surf open to view. There are sea stacks offshore and, in winter, gray whales cruise the coast.

MONTARA   At this village, you will pass an old lighthouse whose utility buildings have been converted to a youth hostel. As the road descends toward Moss Beach, precipitous rock faces give way to gentle slopes and placid tidepools. Then in Half Moon Bay a four-mile-long white-sand beach is backdropped by new homes built on farmlands.

HALF MOON BAY   This area is the combination of the farm meeting the sea. It's a hybrid town, half landlubber and half old-salt. They are as likely to sell artichokes here as fresh fish. The town was named for its crescent beach, but thinks of itself as the pumpkin capital of the world. In October, this San Francisco suburb bedroom community hosts the **Art & Pumpkin Festival**, which draws over 300,000 people. At times the furrowed fields seem a geometric continuation of ocean waves, as if the sea lapped across the land and became frozen there. It is Half Moon Bay's peculiar schizophrenia, a double identity that lends an undeniable flair to the community.

From Half Moon Bay, a connecting road leads to Route 35 and Route 9, providing an alternate course to Santa Cruz; this will be covered below, in the "Santa Cruz Mountains" sightseeing section of this chapter. For now, let's stay on Route 1, which continues south, poised between the mountains and the sea.

HIGGINS–PURISIMA ROAD
On the southern outskirts of Half Moon Bay, watch for this country lane that curves for eight miles into the Santa Cruz Mountains, returning to Route 1. This scenic loop passes old farmhouses and sloping pastures, mountain meadows and redwood-forested hills.

JAMES JOHNSTON HOUSE   ☎650-726-0329 ⌂www.johnstonhouse.org, questions@johnstonhouse.org Immediately upon entering the bumpy Higgins–Purisima Road, you'll spy a stately old New England–style house set in a plowed field. That will be the James Johnston House, a saltbox structure with sloping roof and white clapboard facade. Dating back to 1853 and built by an original '49er, it is the oldest house along this section of coastline. The house is open to the public from January through September, the third Saturday of the month, or by appointment.

SAN GREGORIO   The farming plus fishing spirit of Half Moon Bay prevails as Route 1 continues south. A short distance from the highway, you'll encounter this weather-beaten little town. Once a resort area, today it reveals a quaint collection of sagging roofs and unpainted barns.

SAN GREGORIO GENERAL STORE   ✉Corner of Stage Road and Route 84, San Gregorio ☎650-726-0565 ⌂www.sangregoriostore.com Be sure to drop by this classic general store that's been around since the 1890s. You'll find live music here on weekend mornings.

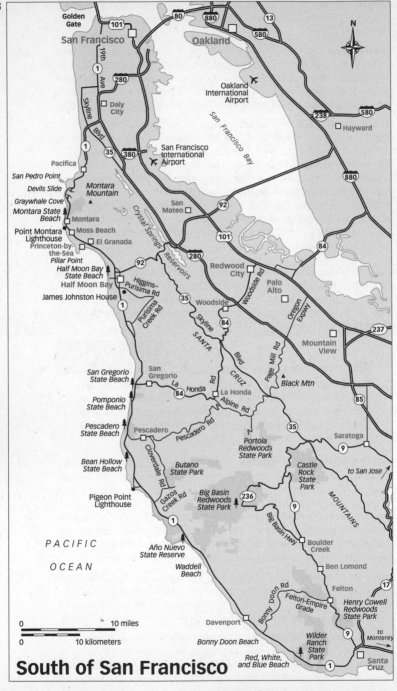

Golden
Gate
San Francisco
19th Ave
Skyline Blvd
Daly City
Pacifica
San Pedro Point
Devils Slide
Graywhale Cove
Montara State Beach
Montara
Point Montara Lighthouse
Moss Beach
El Granada
Princeton-by-the-Sea
Pillar Point
Half Moon Bay State Beach
Half Moon Bay
James Johnston House
Higgins–Purisima Rd
Purisima Creek Rd
San Gregorio State Beach
San Gregorio
La Honda Rd
Pomponio State Beach
Pescadero State Beach
Pescadero
Pescadero Rd
Alpine Rd
La Honda
Bean Hollow State Beach
Cloverdale Rd
Butano State Park
Portola Redwoods State Park
Pigeon Point Lighthouse
Gazos Creek Rd
Big Basin Redwoods State Park
Castle Rock State Park
Saratoga
to San Jose
Año Nuevo State Reserve
Big Basin Hwy
Boulder Creek
Ben Lomond
Felton
Waddell Beach
Bonny Doon Rd
Felton-Empire Grade
Henry Cowell Redwoods State Park
PACIFIC OCEAN
Davenport
Bonny Doon Beach
Red, White, and Blue Beach
Wilder Ranch State Park
to Monterey
Santa Cruz

Oakland
Oakland International Airport
Hayward
San Francisco Bay
San Francisco International Airport
Crystal Springs Reservoirs
San Mateo
Redwood City
Woodside Rd
Palo Alto
Oregon Expwy
Woodside
Mountain View
SANTA CRUZ
Page Mill Rd
Skyline Blvd
Black Mtn
MOUNTAINS

N

101
80
880
13
580
280
238
92
84
35
380
1
237
85
9
236
17

0 _____ 10 miles
0 _____ 10 kilometers

South of San Francisco

PESCADERO   Here is another timeworn town hidden a short way from Route 1. It's a woodframe hamlet of front-porch rocking chairs and white-steeple churches. The name translates as "fisherman," but the Portuguese and Italian residents are farmers, planting artichokes, Brussels sprouts, beans, and lettuce in the patchwork fields surrounding the town.

PHIPPS COUNTRY STORE & FARM ✉2700 Pescadero Creek Road, Pescadero ✆650-879-0787,   650-879-1032 📠650-879-1622 ✐www.phippscountry. com, phippscountry@earthlink.net A family-owned farm open to the public, Phipps offers a nursery, pottery studio, child-friendly barnyard, and a market selling dried beans, herbs, and other products grown on the premises. During the summer visitors can pick several varieties of berries. Admission.

PIGEON POINT LIGHTHOUSE ✆650-879-2120 The beacon several miles south of Pescadero is a 110-foot sentinel that's one of the nation's tallest lighthouses. The point gained a nasty reputation during the 19th century when one ship after another smashed on the rocks. In fact, Pigeon Point is named for the *Carrier Pigeon*, a Yankee clipper that wrecked on the rocks here in 1854. The lighthouse went up in 1872, and originally contained a 1000-piece lens. Doubling as a youth hostel, it now warns sailors while welcoming travelers. Although the lighthouse is closed to the public, the grounds remain open.

AÑO NUEVO STATE RESERVE ✆650-879-2025 📠650-879-2031 Miles of sand dunes border this enchanting park that contains an offshore island where two-ton elephant seals breed in winter. With its tidepools, exotic bird population, sea lions, and harbor seals, the reserve is a natural playground. The Ohlone Indians highly valued the region for its abundant fish and shellfish population. It was here they experienced their first contact with whites in 1769 when Juan Gaspar de Portolá trekked through en route to his discovery of San Francisco Bay. Today, visitors come to Año Nuevo to observe the elephant seals who return to breed each year from December through March. (For further information, see "Beaches & Parks" below.)

From here to Santa Cruz, the road streams past bold headlands and magnificent seascapes. There are excellent beaches to explore and marvelous vista points along the way. You'll also discover rolling farmlands where giant pumpkins grow at the edge of the sea.

WILDER RANCH STATE PARK idden

✆831-423-9703, 831-426-0505 About two miles north of Santa Cruz along Route 1 you'll discover Wilder Ranch. This 8000-acre spread has 30 acres that have been designated a "cultural preserve" because of the historic houses found on the property. Hiking trails allowing horses and bikes wind throughout. In addition to an 1839 adobe, the complex features an 1897 Queen Anne Victorian and a Greek Revival farmhouse dating to 1859, which recently re-opened as a hands-on living history museum. You can also tour the outlying barns and workshops portraying life on a turn-of-the-20th-century dairy farm, which this once was. Go on a weekend to see a living-history demonstration and the working Pelton waterwheel, used during the Gold Rush to operate mining equipment. Open Thursday through Sunday, and occasionally other weekdays; call for hours. Parking fee.

LODGING

HOSTELLING INTERNATIONAL— POINT MONTARA LIGHTHOUSE

$ 50 BEDS ✉Route 1 at 16th Street, Montara ☎650-728-7177, 888-464-4872
📠650-728-7058 ⌕www.norcalhostels.org, himontara@norcalhostels.org

If there were a hotel on the site of this hostel, it would easily charge $300 a night. Set on a bluff overlooking the ocean, on one of those dramatic points always reserved for lighthouses, the hostel charges down-to-earth prices. The daily fee buys you a bunk in a cozy dorm-style room. Couple and family rooms are also available. There is a kitchen, a common room, and laundry facilities in this old lightkeeper's house. This is a good spot for whale watching (November through April). Reservations are strongly recommended.

THE SEAL COVE INN

$$$–$$$$ 10 ROOMS ✉221 Cypress Avenue, Moss Beach ☎650-728-4114,
800-995-9987 📠650-728-4116 ⌕www.sealcoveinn.com, sealcoveinn@sealcoveinn.com

Located 30 minutes south of San Francisco and six miles north of Half Moon Bay, this inn is the perfect place to sojourn for one more night before heading farther afield. The decor has been freshly refurbished in a modern European style, but the setting is pure California, with seals, whales, long white beaches, and towering cypress trees sharing the surrounding acreage. A breakfast buffet, afternoon tea, and hors d'oeuvres come with each room.

PILLAR POINT INN

$$$ 11 ROOMS ✉380 Capistrano Road, Princeton-by-the-Sea
☎650-728-7377, 800-400-8281 📠650-728-8345 ⌕www.pillarpointinn.com,
reservations@pillarpointinn.com

The Cape Cod look has become very popular with establishments in the Half Moon Bay area. One of the foremost, Pillar Point is a fully modern bed and breakfast cloaked in 19th-century New England disguise. Overlooking the harbor, this inn combines VCRs, DVD players, televisions, and refrigerators with traditional amenities like featherbeds, window seats, and fireplaces. Every guest room has a private bath, and there's a deck overlooking the waterfront. Breakfast is a full-course affair.

MILL ROSE INN

$$$$ 6 ROOMS ✉615 Mill Street, Half Moon Bay ☎650-726-8750, 800-900-7673 📠650-726-3031 ⌕www.millroseinn.com, info@millroseinn.com

This is one of the finest country inns along the entire Central Coast. Built in 1902, the place is adorned with hand-painted wallpapers, European antiques, and colorful tiles throughout. The grounds resemble an English garden and include an enclosed gazebo with a jacuzzi and flagstone patio. Each of the six guest rooms is brilliantly appointed; even the least expensive displays an antique armoire, European featherbed, and marble-top dresser covered with old-style combs and brushes. The sitting room and spacious dining room are equally elegant.

BEACH HOUSE

$$$–$$$$ 54 ROOMS   ⊠4100 North Cabrillo Highway, P.O. Box 129, Half Moon Bay
☏650-712-0220, 800-315-9366   ☖650-712-0693   ⬠www.beach-house.com,
view@beach-house.com

Sitting right above the beach a few miles north of Half Moon Bay is this pleasant spot. This contemporary facility, designed in the style of a New England summer home, features "lofts" that include fireplaces and either a patio or private balcony. One of the most comfortable hotels along this stretch of coastline, it creates a sense of easy elegance. There's a lobby with fireplace, a heated pool and a jacuzzi, not to mention a succession of beautiful sunsets just beyond your patio door. Complimentary continental breakfast.

SAN BENITO HOUSE

$$–$$$ 12 ROOMS   ⊠356 Main Street, Half Moon Bay   ☏650-726-3425
⬠www.sanbenitohouse.com, inquiries@sanbenitohouse.com

Among lodgings on this stretch of coastline, San Benito is a personal favorite. Set in a 1905 building, it's a bed-and-breakfast inn with adjoining bar and restaurant. The less expensive rooms are small but quite nice. One room I saw featured a brass light fixture, hanging plants, quilted beds, framed drawings, and wood furniture. There are both shared and private baths. Add a sauna plus a country-inn ambience and you have a bargain.

ZABALLA HOUSE

$$–$$$ 14 ROOMS   ⊠324 Main Street, Half Moon Bay   ☏650-726-9123
⬠www.zaballahouse.net, zaballahouse@earthlink.net

The blue clapboard home of an early merchant in Half Moon Bay is now a bed and breakfast. Within the 1859 structure, the oldest in town, are 14 charming rooms, some with fireplaces and large whirlpool tubs. A friendly, unpretentious atmosphere prevails throughout, with guests encouraged to put their feet up in the parlor and relax with a good book. All guests enjoy a full breakfast buffet and afternoon wine and cheese.

HOSTELLING INTERNATIONAL—
PIGEON POINT LIGHTHOUSE

$ 58 BEDS   ⊠Route 1 at Pigeon Point Road, Pescadero   ☏650-879-0633,
888-464-4872   ☖916-443-4763   ⬠www.norcalhostels.org

Comparable to the low-cost lodging at the Point Montara Lighthouse, this hostel has a similarly dramatic windswept setting above the ocean. The rooms are in several shared cottages with kitchens, living rooms, and accommodations for couples. Rates, as in other American Youth Hostels, are budget. Guests have access to a private, clifftop hot tub for a small fee. Set beneath California's second tallest lighthouse on a beautiful shoreline, the hostel is a charming place to stay. Four private rooms are available for an additional charge. Reservations strongly advised; couples should call four to six months in advance.

ROADHOUSE RESTAURANT & INN

$$–$$$ 8 ROOMS ✉31 Davenport Avenue, Davenport ☎831-426-8801
☎831-426-8830 ⬧www.davenportroadhouse.com, info@davenportroadhouse.com

The refurbished Roadhouse boasts a sparse decor featuring bare white walls and clean, environmentally sound modern furniture in dark woods. The eight rooms have extra-thick mattresses and private baths. Oceanfront views, wine tastings, and massages give it a singular appeal.

DINING

NICK'S RESTAURANT

$$$ ITALIAN ✉100 Rockaway Beach, Pacifica ☎650-359-3903 ☎650-359-5624,
www.nicksrestaurant.net

Nick's has been operated by the same Greek-Italian-American family for more than eight decades and is still pulling in the Pacifica crowds. Wood sculptures of sea life decorate the walls, but the main attraction is the million-dollar view of Rockaway Beach. Nick's is known for its grilled crab sandwiches, sautéed prawns, and fettuccine angelina.

MOSS BEACH DISTILLERY

$$$$ SEAFOOD ✉140 Beach Way, Moss Beach ☎650-728-5595 ☎650-728-8135
⬧www.mossbeachdistillery.com

For dinner overlooking the ocean, there's nothing quite like Moss Beach. The place enjoys a colorful history, dating back to Prohibition days, when this area was notorious for supplying booze to thirsty San Francisco. Today it's a bustling plate-glass restaurant with adjoining bar and an indoor/outdoor patio with an incredible ocean view. The menu includes fresh seafood, gulf shrimp and Chicago steaks. The bootleggers are long gone, but those splendid sea views will be here forever. Brunch served on Sunday. Closed first three weeks of December.

BARBARA'S FISHTRAP

$$ SEAFOOD ✉281 Capistrano Road, Princeton-by-the-Sea ☎650-728-7049
☎650-728-2519

Speaking of seafood, Barbara's down on Half Moon Bay has some of the lowest prices around. Set in and around a small woodframe building smack on the bay, this unpretentious eatery features several fresh fish dishes daily. "The trap," as the locals call it, is liable to be serving fresh sea bass, local halibut, and salmon, as well as steak sandwiches and shellfish. Calamari rings are a specialty. Friendly, local, inexpensive— and highly recommended.

MEZZA LUNA

$$–$$$$ ITALIAN ✉459 Prospect Way, Princeton-by-the-Sea ☎650-728-8108
☎650-728-8201 ⬧www.mezzalunabythesea.com, dinner@mezzalunabythesea.com

Mezza offers an authentic taste of Southern Italy with contemporary dishes that include a variety of pastas with homemade sauces, fresh seafood, lamb, and veal. A favorite is the homemade, half-moon–shaped ravioli stuffed with fresh salmon and served in a tomato cream sauce. The ambience is wonderful as well: terracotta- and salmon-colored walls, arched windows, and tile floors resemble a true Italian trattoria.

DUARTE'S TAVERN

$$–$$$ AMERICAN ✉202 Stage Road, Pescadero ✆650-879-0464 ✆650-879-9460 ✍www.duartestavern.com

Once past Half Moon Bay, restaurants become mighty scarce. Practically anything will do along this lonesome stretch south; but rather than just anything, you can have Duarte's Tavern. Open since 1894, this restaurant and tavern has earned a reputation all down the coast for delicious food. There's a menu filled with meat and fish entrées, omelettes, and sandwiches. They also serve a variety of homemade desserts, and there's a full bar. Personally, I recommend trying the cream of artichoke soup and olallieberry pie. Breakfast, lunch, and dinner daily.

DAVENPORT ROADHOUSE
AT THE CASH STORE RESTAURANT

$$–$$$ CALIFORNIA CUISINE ✉1 Davenport Avenue, Davenport ✆831-426-8801 ✍www.davenportroadhouse.com, info@davenportroadhouse.com

I find the countrified atmosphere here a perfect match to the hearty, homestyle meals served here. It's decorated with colorful wall rugs, handwoven baskets, and fresh flowers. The cuisine at this eatery ranges from steak and eggs to grilled vegetable panini to gourmet pizzas made in a wood-burning oven. More ordinary fare—such as omelettes, hamburgers, and seafood—is also on the agenda. They also feature dinner specials such as salmon, lamb, and Cornish game hen. Breakfast, lunch, and dinner. Closed Monday.

NIGHTLIFE

BACH DANCING AND DYNAMITE SOCIETY ✉Miramar Beach, off Medio Road, Half Moon Bay ✆650-726-4143 ✍www.bachddsoc.org, info@bachddsoc.org

There's jazz, classical or world music most Sunday afternoons here. Situated beachfront off Route 1 about two miles north of the Route 92 intersection, it's renowned for quality sounds.

DAVENPORT ROADHOUSE AT THE CASH STORE BAR ✉1 Davenport Avenue, Davenport ✆831-426-8801 ✍www.davenportroadhouse.com

This place provides a mellow café-like setting. Live music is offered several nights a week. Check out their on-line calendar.

BEACHES & PARKS

GRAY WHALE COVE

✉Located along Route 1, three miles south of Pacifica. Watch for the parking lot on the east side of the highway. Cautiously cross the highway and proceed down the staircase to the beach ✆650-726-8819

This white-sand crescent is a clothing-optional beach. Tucked discreetly beneath steep cliffs, it is also a beautiful spot. The

undertow is strong, so swimming is not advised. The only facilities are toilets.

MONTARA STATE BEACH

✉ *The beach is located along Route 1, seven miles south of Pacifica. There is a trail leading to the beach from Route 1 and 2nd Street in Montara.*
📞 *650-726-8820, 800-444-7275* 📠 *650-726-8816*

🚶 🚴 🏇 🏊 🏄 ⛵ Though this half-mile beach may be a haven to nude sunbathers, police controls have been known to pass out tickets since it is prohibited. Volleyball players and frisbee throwers can be found everywhere. Backdropped by a rocky bluff, it's a very pretty place. Advanced surfers ride the swells. Visitors can go biking and horseback riding on McNee Ranch on the east side of the highway. The only facilities here are primitive toilets and parking is limited.

JAMES V. FITZGERALD MARINE RESERVE
✉ *Off Route 1 in Moss Beach about eight miles south of Pacifica* 📞 *650-728-3584*
🚶 Boasting the best facilities among the beaches in the area, this park also has a sandy beach and excellent tidepools. It's a great place to while away the hours watching crabs, sea urchins, and anemones. Since there are houses nearby, this is more of a family beach than the freewheeling areas to the immediate north and south. And since it is a reserve, there is no collecting of anything (even rocks). There are restrooms and a picnic area. Day-use fee, $5.

HALF MOON BAY STATE BEACH (OR FRANCIS BEACH)
✉ *All four park segments are located along Route 1 in Half Moon Bay.* 📞 *650-726-8820*
📠 *650-726-8816*

🚶 🚴 🏊 🏄 ⛵ Despite a four-mile-long sand beach, this park receives only a guarded recommendation. Half Moon Bay is a working harbor, so the beach lacks the seclusion and natural qualities of other strands along the coast. Of course, with civilization so near at hand, the facilities here are more complete than elsewhere. Also, Francis Beach is part of a chain of beaches that you can choose from, including Venice Beach, Roosevelt Beach, and Dunes Beach. Personally, I pick the last. Surfers head to the sandy beach break at Francis Beach and below Half Moon Bay jetty. Restrooms or toilets are available at all four beaches; picnic areas at Francis Beach. No dogs allowed. The beach parking lot closes at sunset. Day-use fee, $6.

⛺ There are 50 tent/RV sites (no hookups) and three additional tent sites at Francis Beach, available year round; $25 per night. Hiker/biker camp available at Francis; $3 per night. Reservations: 800-444-7275.

SAN GREGORIO STATE BEACH

✉ *Located along Route 1, about 15 miles south of Half Moon Bay. Entrance to the nude beach is several hundred yards north of the state beach entrance.*
📞 *650-879-2170* 📠 *650-879-2172*

🚶 🏊 🏄 ⛵ There is a white-sand beach here framed by sedimentary cliffs and cut by a small creek. Spanish explorer Gaspar de Portolá dropped anchor at San Gregorio in October 1769. Star of the show, though, is the nearby private nude beach (admission) north of the state beach, reputedly the first and one of the nicest beaches of its type in California. There are picnic areas and toilets at the state beach, no facilities at the nude beach. Day-use fee, $6.

POMPONIO STATE BEACH

✉Route 1, about 16 miles south of Half Moon Bay ☎650-879-2170 ℻650-879-2172

🚶 🏄 🍴 Less appealing than its neighbor to the north, this park has a white-sand beach that's traversed periodically by a creek. There are headlands on either side of the beach. Facilities include picnic areas and toilets. Day-use fee, $6.

PESCADERO STATE BEACH

✉Route 1, about 19 miles south of Half Moon Bay ☎650-879-2170
℻650-879-2172

🚶 🏄 🍴 Backed by sand dunes and saltwater marsh, this lovely park also features a wide beach. There are tidepools to the south and a wildlife preserve across the highway. Steelhead run annually in the streams here, while deer, blue herons, and egrets inhabit the nearby marshland. Rangers sometimes lead guided tours (call for availability). There are picnic areas and toilets.

BEAN HOLLOW
STATE BEACH

✉Located along Route 1, about 21 miles south of Half Moon Bay; Pebble Beach is about a mile north of Bean Hollow. ☎650-879-2170 ℻650-879-2172

🚶 🏄 🍴 The small sandy beach here is bounded by rocks, so sunbathers go elsewhere while tidepool watchers drop by. Particularly interesting is nearby Pebble Beach, a coarse-grain strand studded with jasper, serpentine, agates, and carnelians. The stones originate from a quartz reef offshore and attract rockhounds by the pack. But don't take rocks away—it's illegal. Also not to be missed is the blufftop trail between Bean Hollow and Pebble Beach, from which you can espy whales and seals in season. Facilities include a picnic area and toilets.

BUTANO STATE PARK ___ hidden

✉Located 22 miles south of Half Moon Bay. Coming from the north on Route 1, go 20 miles south of Half Moon Bay; turn left (east) on Pescadero Road, and then right on Cloverdale Road about four and a half miles to the park. Or, coming from the south, turn right (east) on Gazos Creek Road (two miles south of Pigeon Point Lighthouse) and then left on Cloverdale Road. ☎650-879-2040

🚶 🚴 🍴 This inland park, several miles from the coast, provides a welcome counterpoint to the beach parks. About 3600 acres, it features a deep redwood forest, including stands of virgin trees. Hiking trails traverse the territory. Not as well known as other nearby redwood parks, Butano suffers less human traffic. The park has picnic areas and restrooms. Day-use fee, $6.

▲ There are 21 drive-in sites and 18 walk-in sites; $25 per night. Camping by reservation only from Memorial Day to Labor Day: 800-444-7275.

AÑO NUEVO STATE RESERVE

✉Off Route 1, about 26 miles south of Half Moon Bay ☎650-879-2025, 650-879-0227 (recorded information) ☎650-879-2031 ⌕www.anonuevo.org

🤸 🚶 🚣 Awesome in its beauty, abundant in wildlife, this park is one of the most spectacular on the California coast. It consists of a peninsula heaped with sand dunes. A miniature island lies just offshore. There is a nature trail for exploring. Seals and sea lions inhabit the area; loons, hawks, pheasants, and albatrosses have been spied here. But most spectacular of all the denizens are the elephant seals, those lovably grotesque creatures who come here between December 15 and March 31 to breed. Back in 1800, elephant seals numbered in the hundreds of thousands; by the end of the century, they were practically extinct; it's only recently that they have achieved a comeback. When breeding, the bulls stage bloody battles and collect large harems, creating a spectacle that draws crowds every year. During breeding season, docents lead two-and-a-half-hour tours that must be booked eight weeks in advance by calling 800-444-4445. The tours cover seal-breeding areas, which otherwise are closed to the public throughout the breeding season; during the rest of the year the entire park and the seal rookery are open. Be forewarned that it's a three-mile roundtrip walk from the parking lot to the rookery. During the summer there are surf breaks off the end of beach, about ten minutes south of the rookery. Also be aware, the elephant seal population makes this beach attractive to sharks. The wildlife protection area is closed the first two weeks of December. The only facilities are toilets. Day-use fee, $6.

GREYHOUND ROCK _____

✉Located along Route 1, about 30 miles south of Half Moon Bay. From the parking lot at the roadside follow the path down to the beach.

🏖 One of the most secluded strands in the area, this beach is a beauty. There are startling cliffs in the background and a gigantic boulder—Greyhound Rock—in the foreground; the area is a favorite among those who love to fish. It is also, unfortunately, a favorite for thieves. Keep your valuables with you and lock your car. Although the beach has good conditions for swimming, it has been known to be "sharky." Restrooms and picnic areas are the only facilities.

WADDELL BEACH

✉Located along Route 1, seven miles north of Davenport ☎831-427-2288

🏄 🏖 🚣 A celebrated windsurfing and hang gliding destination, this beach is a great spot for water activities. It's part of the Big Basin Redwoods State Park and within the Theodore J. Hoover Natural Preserve, which adds to its ample birdwatching opportunities. Facilities include bathrooms; no dogs allowed.

BONNY DOON BEACH

✉ *Off Route 1, about eight miles north of Santa Cruz. Watch for the parking lot near the junction with Bonny Doon Road; follow the path across the railroad tracks and down to the beach.*

🏊 This spot ranks among the most popular nude beaches in California. Known up and down the coast, the compact beach is protected on either flank by rugged cliffs. There are dunes at the south end of the beach, caves to the north, plus bevies of barebottomed bathers in between. Currents are strong; be careful when swimming. Keep a close eye on your valuables. This beach has no security nor facilities.

RED, WHITE, AND BLUE BEACH

✉ *Off Route 1, five miles north of Santa Cruz. Watch for the red, white, and blue mailbox at Scaroni Road intersection; follow Scaroni Road a short distance west to the beach.*
📞 831-423-6332 📠 831-423-6332

🧍 🚶 🏖 🚤 🍴 There's a clothing-optional beach here surrounded by rocky headlands. There are also more RVs than at a Fourth of July picnic. The beach is monitored for safety and no cameras or dogs are allowed. Visitors have to pay upon entry. Of course, the beach does provide facilities and permit camping but somehow the management takes the nature out of bathing au natural. There are picnic areas, restrooms, and hot showers. Day-use fee, $12.

⛺ There are 35 sites; $18 per night, per person. Closed November through January.

SANTA CRUZ MOUNTAINS

For a hawk's-eye view of the Santa Cruz Mountains and redwood country, leave the coast at Half Moon Bay and catch Route 35 (Skyline Boulevard) south. This rustic highway climbs along a ridgetop, revealing vistas of both the ocean and San Francisco Bay. From the tangled undergrowth on either side of the road, scattered trees, pine and deciduous, stand against open sky.

SIGHTS

METHUSELAH   The forest gathers around you as Route 35 tunnels through dense, tall timber. You are entering a land of giants. A gate and small sign, three miles north of the Route 84 turnoff, mark Methuselah, a stately 1800-year-old redwood.

LA HONDA   For an interesting detour loop, take Route 84 (La Honda Road) south to this knotty-pine town decorated with a bar, a restaurant, and a post office. This forest retreat is novelist Ken Kesey's old stomping ground. During the halcyon days of the '60s, his band of Merry Pranksters, like rebels in the hills, swept down from La Honda through

HERITAGE GROVE

PAGE 388

Virgin redwood forest in San Mateo County Park with hiking trails meandering across 37 rolling acres

BIG BASIN REDWOODS STATE PARK

PAGE 388

California's oldest state park with 88 miles of hiking trails stretching from the ocean to the Santa Cruz Mountains

HENRY COWELL REDWOODS STATE PARK

PAGE 389

Stunning old-growth redwood forests, with 15 miles of majestic trails

Northern California and beyond. They were mind-guerrillas, set on overthrowing American consciousness with the "Trips Festival," a multimedia extravaganza of rock music, light shows, and street theater, raised to an electric pitch by massive doses of psychedelic drugs.

HERITAGE GROVE

Today La Honda has lapsed back into rural consciousness. Rather than tripping out or experiencing heavy life changes, you'll probably just pass through town and pick up Alpine Road, which returns to Route 35. En route you'll encounter Heritage Grove, a virgin redwood forest with a creek and hiking trails, and then emerge into rolling hill country marked by broad vistas.

BIG BASIN REDWOODS STATE PARK

Pick up Route 9 south, the redwood road that will eventually lead to Santa Cruz. Before this winding mountain road descends to the sea, it connects with an even narrower and more sinuous thoroughfare, Route 236, which goes to Big Basin Redwoods State Park. One of the area's prettiest parks, it offers nature trails galore, 2000-year-old redwood stands, and complete facilities for picnicking and camping.

Almost as fascinating as Big Basin Redwoods State Park's natural wonders is the history behind its founding. At the turn of the 20th century, most of these magnificent groves were marked for destruction by lumbermen. But Andrew P. Hill, a local photographer and conservationist, vowed to preserve the giants. Hill had been infuriated and inspired when an arrogant landowner refused him permission to photograph the redwoods because they were private property! Dedicated to "Save the Redwoods," Hill formed the Sempervirens Club, which lobbied for preservation of forests throughout the state. Today, you can hike to **Slippery Rock**, opposite a waterfall, where pioneer conservationists made a pact to protect the public's natural heritage.

Rejoining Route 9 in **Boulder Creek**, you'll find that this town, **Ben Lomond**, and **Felton** are central to the area's travel facilities. They house numerous antique stores and crafts shops. In addition to tourists, they also attract a lot of winter rain. In 1982 this became a disaster area: Almost two feet of rain fell in just 36 hours, hillsides collapsed, mudslides buried homes, and 21 people died in Santa Cruz County. Outside Ben Lomond, a dozen people are buried in mudslides so deep their bodies have never been recovered.

FELTON COVERED BRIDGE ✉*Covered Bridge Road* Now that you're convinced never to go near the region, let me tell you some of its marvelous features—like the Felton covered bridge (at the edge of town on Covered Bridge Road). A wood-plank span with sagging shingle roof, the structure dates from 1892 and has been named a state historical landmark. Appropriately, it's set in a secluded spot along the San Lorenzo River.

HENRY COWELL REDWOODS STATE PARK

✉*The park entrance is at 101 North Big Trees Park Road, Felton* ☎*831-438-2396* At this nearby state park there are 1750 acres of redwood forest to explore. Of the 15 miles of majestic trails, one leads to the dean of the forest, an ambassadorial, 285-foot tree that measures 16 feet wide. The oldest trees in the park date back some 1400 to 1800 years. When Gold Rush pioneer Henry Cowell bought the redwood-filled land in the 1800s he set up multiple lime kiln operations, but managed to spare the natural forests. His son Harry later donated a large portion of the family acreage to this state park as well as to local universities.

ROARING CAMP & BIG TREES NARROW GAUGE RAILROAD

✉*Graham Hill Road, Felton* ☎*831-335-4400* ⌂*www.roaringcamp.com* During the summer you can climb aboard the full-size Santa Cruz, Big Trees and Pacific Railway for a scenic eight-mile journey from the hillside town of Felton to the Santa Cruz boardwalk. In Felton you can catch the area's locomotive superstar, the Roaring Camp & Big Trees Narrow Gauge Railroad. This vintage steam engine whistles through redwood stands en route to Bear Mountain. Passengers are invited to picnic on the mountain, hike the area, then return on a later train.

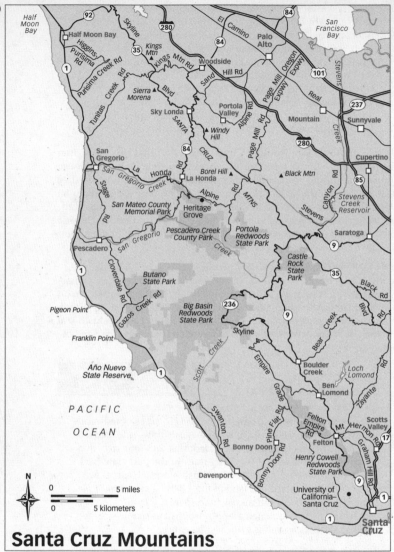

Santa Cruz Mountains

LODGING

Accommodations in the Santa Cruz Mountains cluster around the towns of Boulder Creek, Ben Lomond, and Felton. They are generally of two types: neon motels and piney lodges. The first is less expensive, the second more inviting.

MERRYBROOK LODGE

$$–$$$ 10 UNITS   ✉ 13420 Big Basin Highway, Boulder Creek   ☎ 831-338-6813
🖰 www.merrybrooklodge.net
This lodge, set in a redwood grove, has pretty cottages right on a creek.

They are one-bedroom structures, with a living room, kitchen, shower and porch. The floors are hardwood, the walls knotty pine, and as a final touch, there's a woodstove. For rustic living high in the mountains, you'll be hard pressed to find a more inviting place.

FELTON CREST INN BED AND BREAKFAST

$$$$ 4 ROOMS ✉780 El Solo Heights Drive, Felton ✆831-335-4011
🖱www.feltoncrest.com, hannapeters@comcast.net

Innkeeper Hanna Peters greets all her guests at this bed and breakfast with champagne and chocolate kisses. It's a pleasant arrival to an even more pleasing inn. All four rooms and suites are wonderfully furnished and most have either a jacuzzi or add-on whirlpool. Outside the house is a peaceful redwood glade, which keeps the surroundings green and lush year-round; it's close to Henry Cowell Redwoods State Park. Continental breakfast included.

DINING

TYROLEAN INN

$–$$$ GERMAN/BAVARIAN ✉9600 Route 9, Ben Lomond ✆831-336-5188
🖱www.tyroleaninn.com

This rustic little restaurant serves German and Bavarian dishes. During the dinner hour, they stoke the fires and prepare an array of German dishes. Sauerbraten, wienerschnitzel, and smoked pork chops with sauerkraut are among the offerings. Dinner only. Closed Monday.

SCOPAZZI'S INN

$$$–$$$$ AMERICAN/ITALIAN ✉13300 Big Basin Highway, Boulder Creek
✆831-338-6441 ✆831-338-6444 🖱www.scopazzisrestaurant.com

Around since 1912, Scopazzi's can still be trusted for a good meal. The place is perfectly fitted to its mountain environment, with wood-paneled walls, a lofty, exposed-beam ceiling and lots of windows for great views. Add a tile fireplace, a patio, and a lounge for a prize establishment in the heart of Santa Cruz redwood country. The menu is equal to all this: there are numerous dinners—chicken cacciatore, filet of sole, veal parmigiana—complete with soup, salad, relish plate, and dessert. At lunch they serve sandwiches, salads, pasta dishes, and several platters including veal cutlet and calamari. Closed Monday and Tuesday.

LA BRUSCHETTA

$$$ ITALIAN ✉5447 Route 9, Felton ✆831-335-3337

Hailing from Italy, Chef Luca Rubino brings his culinary expertise to this house *cum* restaurant in a residential neighborhood. This unpretentious place cooks up traditional Sicilian dishes with organic and homegrown ingredients, from *gamberoni in unido* (prawns, sautéed garlic, capers, tomatoes, and white wine) to *agnolotti alla ragusana* (round ravioli stuffed with wild mushrooms and ciocavello cheese, and draped in a butter and sage sauce). If the weather's nice, dine on their outdoor patio. No lunch Monday through Friday; weekend brunch.

PARKS

SAN MATEO COUNTY MEMORIAL PARK

✉ *9500 Pescadero Creek Road, about six miles from La Honda*
📞 *650-879-0212, 650-879-0238* 📠 *650-879-1034*

🚶 🚴 🛶 A 499-acre park, this redwood preserve is covered with hiking trails. There's a creekside swimming hole, a visitors center, and a redwood tree dating back 1500 years. In an area of extraordinary parks, this one's a sleeper, small but beautiful, and a good place to avoid the crowds found at more popular parks. It's known for its Mt. Ellen Nature Trail that takes visitors through a variety of habitats, from Pescadero Creek to the summit of Mt. Ellen. There's also the very special 37-acre Heritage Grove, an unusual stand of redwoods that are bigger and larger in diameter than others in the park. Facilities include picnic areas, restrooms, showers, a horse camp for those with horses, and a snack bar that also sells a few groceries. Day-use fee, $5.

⛺ There are 158 sites; $21 per night; hike-in sites are $10 per night.

PORTOLA REDWOODS STATE PARK

✉ *From Route 35, take Alpine Road west to Portola State Park Road.* 📞 *650-948-9098*

🚶 With dense stands of redwood, Douglas fir, and live oak, this natural facility is a great place for exploration. There are 18 miles of hiking trails, including one leading to Tiptoe Falls, a five-foot waterfall. Visitors can see pre-historic clam shells and other marine deposits from when the area was covered by the ocean. There are picnic areas, restrooms, and showers. Day-use fee, $6.

⛺ There are 53 sites ($25 per night) plus a backpack camp ($10 per night). Closed December through April.

CASTLE ROCK STATE PARK

✉ *The parking lot and trailhead are on Skyline Boulevard, two and a half miles south of the intersection with Route 9.* 📞 *408-867-2952*

🚶 🏇 A hiker's paradise, this semi-wilderness area of roughly 5000 acres has no entry roads. To experience the place you'll have to join the many hikers, backpackers, and rock climbers who number this among their favorite parks. The rewards are several: a network of trails, including one that descends 32 miles to the ocean; a waterfall; and Castle Rock, which crowns this retreat at 3214 feet. Hike-in campsites feature picnic areas, pit toilets, and running water. Parking fee, $6.

⛺ Permitted at 20 hike-in campsites; $10. For information, contact the park headquarters at 831-338-8861.

BIG BASIN REDWOODS STATE PARK

✉ *21600 Big Basin Way (Route 236), nine miles north of Boulder Creek; Route 9 connects with Route 236, leading to the park.* 📞 *831-338-8860*

🚶 🚴 🏇 California's oldest state park, this 18,000-acre expanse reaches from the ocean to a 2000-foot elevation. Within that domain are 2000-year-old redwoods, a sandy beach, 88 miles of hiking trails, 20 to 30 miles of mountain-biking trails, and a host of facilities. You'll also find Homo sapiens in tents, black-tailed deer, coyotes, bobcats, raccoons, and salamanders inhabiting the area, as well as over 250 bird species that either live here or drop by. It's highly recommended that you do also. There are picnic areas, a mini-museum, a snack bar, a grocery, a gift shop, restrooms, and showers. Day-use fee, $5.

▲ There are 183 designated sites plus several hike-in sites; also, four-person tent cabins are available. All sites are $25 per night; tent cabins are $65 per night. Reservations: 800-444-7275. (Two especially recommended campsites near park headquarters are the Blooms Creek and Huckleberry campgrounds.)

HENRY COWELL REDWOODS STATE PARK

hidden

✉ *Off Route 9, just south of Felton* 📞 *831-335-4598* 📠 *831-335-3156*

🚶 🚲 🏇 ⚓ ⛵ A 4140-acre park on the San Lorenzo River, it features a short nature trail (three-quarter-mile loop) through a redwood forest. One of the sequoias here measures 285 feet; there are also stands of Douglas fir and madrone. With 20 miles of hiking trails, picnic areas, a nature center, a bookstore, restrooms, and showers, it's a favorite among locals. Fishing is prohibited during summer, and alcohol is not allowed. Day-use fee, $6.

▲ There are 111 sites in a campground on Graham Hill Road three miles from the park center; $25 per night. Information: 831-438-2396. Closed December through March.

SANTA CRUZ

One of California's original missions, a University of California campus, a historic railroad, and some of the finest Victorian neighborhoods on the coast are just a few of the pluses in Santa Cruz. This town of more than 54,000 people is in many respects one big playground. It enjoys spectacular white sand beaches, entertaining nightlife, and an old-fashioned boardwalk amusement park. The city faces south, providing the best weather along the Central Coast. Arts and crafts flourish here, and vintage houses adorn the area.

SIGHTS

SANTA CRUZ COUNTY CONFERENCE AND VISITORS COUNCIL
✉ *1211 Ocean Street* 📞 *831-425-1234, 800-833-3494* 🖊 *www.santacruz.org, comments@ santacruz.org* This visitors center has information to help orient you with the area.

NATURAL BRIDGES STATE BEACH ✉ *End of West Cliff Drive* Route 1, California's magnificent coastal highway, veers slightly inland upon reaching Santa Cruz, which means it's time to find a different waterfront drive. Not to worry, the best way to begin exploring the place is at the north end of town around this state beach. A pretty spot for a picnic, this is the place to pick up West Cliff Drive, which sweeps the Santa Cruz waterfront.

EL PALOMAR

PAGE 401

Spacious cantina in a 1930s hotel serving Santa Cruz's best Mexican food and delicious specialty margaritas

VASILI'S GREEK RESTAURANT

PAGE 402

Lively taverna with authentic Greek favorites like kebabs and *saganaki*, a flaming cheese appetizer

CLIFF CREST BED & BREAKFAST INN

PAGE 399

1887 Victorian country inn with antique four-poster beds and a solarium illuminated with stained-glass windows

TWIN LAKES STATE BEACH

PAGE 404

Pretty mile-long beach and lagoon just outside of town where all of the locals relax

LIGHTHOUSE POINT   The shoreline is a honeycomb of tiny coves, sea arches, and pocket beaches. On a clear day you can see the entire 40-mile curve of Monterey Bay silhouette the skyline. Even in foggy weather, sea lions cavort on the rocks offshore, while surfers ride the challenging "Steamer Lane" breaks.

SANTA CRUZ SURFING MUSEUM ✉ 701 West Cliff Drive at Lighthouse Point ✆ 831-420-6289 ✐ www.santacruzsurfingmuseum.org, jlthompson@ci.santa-cruz. ca.us A testament to surfers is this tiny museum situated in the Mark Abbott Memorial Lighthouse at Lighthouse Point and overlooking "Steamers Lane." Here vintage photos and antique boards re-create the history of the Hawaiian sport that landed on the shores of Santa Cruz early in the 20th century. Closed Tuesday and Wednesday (only closed Tuesday in summer).

SANTA CRUZ MUNICIPAL PIER   Beach Street continues this coast-hugging route to this pier, a half-mile-long wharf lined with bait shops, restaurants, and fishing charters. Those early-morning folks with the sun-furrowed faces are either fishing or crabbing. They are here everyday with lawn chairs and tackle boxes. When reality overcomes optimism, they have been known to duck into nearby fresh fish stores for the day's catch. The pier is a perfect place to promenade, soak up sun, and seek out local color. It also provides a peaceful counterpoint to the next attraction.

SANTA CRUZ BEACH BOARDWALK ✉*400 Beach Street* ☎*831-423-5590* ☏*831-460-3336* ✐*www.beachboardwalk.com* The Boardwalk is Northern California's answer to Coney Island. Pride of the city, it dates back to 1907 and sports several old-fashioned rides. The penny arcade features vintage machines as well as modern video games. You'll find shooting galleries and candy stalls, coin-operated fortune tellers and do-it-yourself photo machines. Shops sell everything from baubles to bikinis. Then there are the ultimate entertainments: a slow-circling Ferris wheel with chairs suspended high above the beach; the antique 1911 Loof carousel (a National Historic Landmark), a whirl of mirrors and flashing color; a funicular whose brightly painted cars reflect the sun; rides with names that instantaneously evoke childhood memories—bumper cars, tilt-a-whirl, haunted castle; and that soaring symbol of amusement parks everywhere, the roller coaster. Closed most of December and most non-summer weekdays.

PACIFIC GARDEN MALL This playground for shoppers sits several blocks inland along Pacific Avenue. Pacific Garden Mall is a tree-lined promenade that stretches from Cathcart to Water streets. Beautifully executed, the entire mall is a study in urban landscaping and planning. On October 17, 1989, a 7.1 earthquake centered just a few miles from Santa Cruz sent most of the mall tumbling into the street, killing three people.

MUSEUM OF ART & HISTORY AT THE MCPHERSON CENTER ✉*705 Front Street* ☎*831-429-1964* ☏*831-429-1954* ✐*www.santacruzmah.org*, *vs@santacruzmah.org* Within walking distance of the mall are several places that merit short visits. This museum at the McPherson Center features changing exhibits that focus primarily on California art. Permanent exhibits relate to the social history of the Santa Cruz area, using photographs and artifacts. Closed Monday. Admission.

SANTA CRUZ MISSION ✉*High Street at Emmet Street in Mission Plaza* ☎*831-426-5686* ☏*831-423-1043* ✐*bpedrazzi@sbcglobal.net* A half-scale replica of the 1791 structure, this mission pales by comparison with the missions in Carmel and San Juan Bautista. Closed Monday.

SANTA CRUZ MISSION STATE HISTORIC PARK ✉*144 School Street near Mission Plaza* ☎*831-425-5849* ☏*831-429-2870* A remarkable piece of restoration, this historic park provides a fascinating timeline of California's past. This 1791 adobe home was built for and by the Ohlone and Yocut Indians who sold the property to Californios (children of Spanish settlers). Later part of it was bought by Irish immigrants. Various rooms document each of these periods with artifacts excavated on the site. Reflecting the difficulties of early-19th-century interior design, the Californio Room is decorated with mismatched wallpaper that was sent at different times from the East Coast. Touring is self-guided, but guided walks are available by appointment. Special events including cooking demonstrations, candlemaking, and brick-making take place occasionally, as does American Indian storytelling (call for dates). Closed Monday through Wednesday.

VICTORIAN HOUSES Santa Cruz's rich history has left a legacy of elegant Victorian houses. Although there are no guided tours, if you set

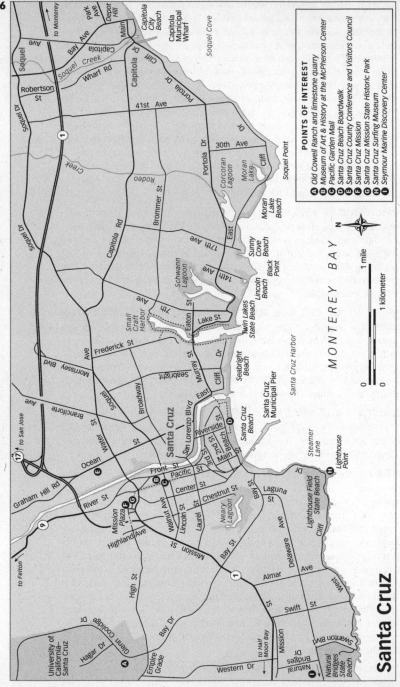

Santa Cruz

POINTS OF INTEREST

- Ⓐ Old Cowell Ranch and limestone quarry
- Ⓑ Museum of Art & History at the McPherson Center
- Ⓒ Pacific Garden Mall
- Ⓓ Santa Cruz Beach Boardwalk
- Ⓔ Santa Cruz County Conference and Visitors Council
- Ⓕ Santa Cruz Mission
- Ⓖ Santa Cruz Mission State Historic Park
- Ⓗ Santa Cruz Surfing Museum
- Ⓘ Seymour Marine Discovery Center

MONTEREY BAY

out on your own you won't be disappointed. In the Beach Hill area, not far from the Boardwalk, be sure to see the gem-like home at **1005 3rd Street**, counterpoint to the multilevel confection with Queen Anne turret at **311 Main Street**. Near Pacific Garden Mall is the Civil War–era **Calvary Episcopal Church** (532 Center Street), with its clapboard siding and shingle roof. The **200 block of Walnut Avenue** is practically wall-to-wall Victorians.

HOLY CROSS ROMAN CATHOLIC CHURCH ✉ *126 High Street* Located near the Santa Cruz Mission is this white-painted brick Catholic church. The steeple of this 1889 Gothic Revival beauty is a landmark for miles around.

FRANCISCO ALVIZA HOUSE ✉ *109 Sylvar Street* Nearby the Francisco Alviza House, vintage 1850s, is the oldest home in town.

Around the corner from the Francisco Alviza House, the **200 block of Mission Street** displays several homes built shortly afterwards. Nearby is **W. W. Reynolds House** (123 Green Street), which was an Episcopal Church in 1850.

UNIVERSITY OF CALIFORNIA–SANTA CRUZ ✉ *1156 High Street* ☎ *831-459-0111* ✐ *www.ucsc.edu* From this last Victorian cluster, High Street leads to the UC Santa Cruz campus. Turn right at Glenn Coolidge Drive and you'll find an information booth dispensing maps, brochures, and words of wisdom. Those stone ruins and sunbleached buildings nearby are the remains of the old Cowell ranch and limestone quarry from which 2000 of the campus acres were drawn.

No ivory tower ever enjoyed the view that UC Santa Cruz commands of Monterey Bay. Set on a hillside, with redwood forest and range land all around, the campus possesses incredible beauty. The university itself is divided into eight colleges, insular and self-defined, each marked by a different architectural style. The best way to see this campus is simply to wander: Walk the fields, trek its redwood groves, and explore the different colleges that make it one of the West's most progressive institutions. Of particular interest at UC Santa Cruz are the organic farm as well as the arboretum, with its Mediterranean garden and outstanding collection of Australian and South African plants.

SEYMOUR MARINE DISCOVERY CENTER ✉ *End of Delaware Avenue* ☎ *831-459-3800* ✐ *seymourcenter.ucsc.edu* Located at the Joseph M. Long Marine Laboratory, a University of California research facility, is this center. Part museum, part working lab, the center is dedicated to teaching the public about the role of research in ocean conservation and features hands-on displays, working aquarium exhibits, and a family-friendly touch tank. The 87-foot blue whale skeleton (the largest on display in the world) is a highlight. There are several tours daily. Closed Monday. Admission.

LODGING

When seeking overnight accommodations in Santa Cruz, the place to look is near the beach. That is where you'll want to be and, not surprisingly, where you'll find most hotels and motels. The problem during summer months is the cost. In winter you can have a room for a song, but come June the price tags climb.

SURFSIDE APARTMENTS

$$ 17 ROOMS ⊠ 311 Cliff Street ☎ 831-423-5302

This establishment, the best bargain in town, contains several cottages and houses clustered around a flower garden and courtyard. They truly are efficiency units: no telephone, parking facilities, or housekeeping services. But they are comfortably furnished, possess a friendly "beach cottage" feel, and they feature kitchens. Located two blocks from the Boardwalk, there are one- and two-bedroom apartments. They are only available from late June through Labor Day.

OCEAN ECHO MOTEL AND COTTAGES

$$-$$$$ 16 UNITS ⊠ 401 Johans Beach Drive ☎ 831-462-4192 ☎ 831-462-0658
⌖ www.oceanecho.com, beach@oceanecho.com

Ocean Echo is an excellent facility, located near a quiet neighborhood beach. This clapboard complex sits far from the madding Boardwalk crowd that's right on the beach. It represents a perfect choice for anyone seeking a studio or Cape Cod–style cottage. Some have kitchens and private patios, but all have microwaves and refrigerators. Continental breakfast included. Weekly rentals are sometimes available. On weekends there's a two-night minimum.

DREAM INN SANTA CRUZ

$$$-$$$$ 165 ROOMS ⊠ 175 West Cliff Drive ☎ 831-426-4330, 866-774-7735
☎ 831-427-2025 ⌖ www.dreaminnsantacruz..com

It's big and blocky with kitchy touches reminiscent of a Las Vegas resort, but the recently refurnished Dream Inn is also right on the beach. With pool, jacuzzi, oceanfront restaurants, and lounge, this multitiered establishment extends from a hilltop perch down to a sandy strand. The location can't be topped; the boardwalk and fishing pier are a short stroll away. Each of the guest rooms is sleek and modern with bright and contemporary furnishings; each sports a private balcony and ocean view. The question is whether you'll endure the sometimes noisy, semiplastic atmosphere for the sake of proximity to the Pacific. It's your call. (Being lazy myself, I'd book reservations in a minute.)

WEST CLIFF INN

$$$$ 9 ROOMS ⊠ 174 West Cliff Drive ☎ 831-457-2200, 800-979-0910
☎ 831-457-2221 ⌖ www.westcliffinn.com, westcliffinn@foursisters.com

A white Victorian mansion overlooking Monterey Bay, this romantic bed and breakfast boasts elegant guest rooms with fireplaces and king-sized beds; some include jetted tubs. Wraparound porches on both the first and second stories allow for quiet reading spots or comfortable areas to lounge and admire the view. In the morning, a large country-style breakfast is served. There's complimentary afternoon wine and hors d'oeuvres as well as fresh baked cookies in the evening. Champagne and signature teddy bears will await you upon arrival if requested (fee).

CLIFF CREST BED & BREAKFAST INN

$$$ 6 ROOMS ✉ *407 Cliff Street* ✆ *831-427-2609* 🖷 *831-427-2710*
🖰 *www.cliffcrestinn.com, info@cliffcrestinn.com*

Country inns are rare in Santa Cruz; this California custom is slowly catching on here. One exception is the Cliff Crest, a historic 1887 Victorian home with additional accommodations in an 1878 carriage house. Among the features of the house are a belvedere, a yard landscaped by the designer of San Francisco's Golden Gate Park, and a solarium illuminated through stained-glass windows. Rooms vary in cost from a small room with private bath to the spacious "Rose Room," which has a fireplace. In any case, the decor you're apt to find includes patterned wallpaper and four-poster beds in each room.

HOSTELLING INTERNATIONAL—SANTA CRUZ

$ 45 BEDS ✉ *321 Main Street* ✆ *831-423-8304, 888-464-4872*
🖰 *www.hi-santacruz.org, info@hi-santacruz.org*

There is also this hostel, located two blocks from the beach, wharf, and boardwalk. Set in restored Victorian cottages on well-located Beach Hill, it offers five dorm-style rooms and five private rooms. There are also hot showers, a kitchen, a dining area, internet access, and a common room; all linen provided free of charge. There is an 11 p.m. curfew. Non-members pay $3 more.

HARBOR INN

$–$$ 19 ROOMS ✉ *645 7th Avenue* ✆ *831-479-9731* 🖷 *831-479-1067*
🖰 *www.harborinnsantacruz.com*

Less distinguished, but considerably cheaper, is this inn across town. The place sits in a two-story stucco house in a semi-residential neighborhood a couple blocks from the beach. It supports 19 bedrooms, all with refrigerators and microwaves. Two rooms are two-story affairs suitable for families. There are both private and shared baths. All are spacious, attractive, and inexpensively furnished. The staff is helpful and friendly, making this place a fortuitous addition to the local housing scene.

Santa Cruz also has a string of neon motels within blocks of the Boardwalk. Count on them to provide small rooms with color television, wall-to-wall carpeting, nicked wooden tables, naugahyde chairs, stall showers, etc.; if they have any decorations at all, you'll wish they didn't. But if you're on a budget, for a night or two you can call them home. Their rates fluctuate wildly depending on the season and tourist flow. (Generally they charge budget prices in winter; summer prices escalate to the moderate range.)

BEACHVIEW INN

$ 22 ROOMS ✉ *50 Front Street* ✆ *831-426-3575, 800-946-0614*
🖰 *www.beach-viewinn.com, beachviewinn@yahoo.com*

The Beachview is a solid choice. Half a block from the Boardwalk and wharf, the motel has ocean views and a complimentary breakfast bar.

BIG 6 MOTEL

$$ 21 ROOMS   ✉335 Riverside Avenue   ☎831-423-1651

Located within walking distance of the beach, this motel sits in a two-story stucco building and contains rooms with private baths.

SUPER 8 MOTEL

$$ 24 ROOMS   ✉338 Riverside Avenue   ☎831-426-3707, 800-800-8000   🖳831-426-0547

Right next door to Big 6 is the Super 8, which has rooms decorated in a white and burgundy color scheme. Guests here enjoy lounging at the pool or soaking in the spa. Continental breakfast is included.

DINING

SANTA CRUZ BEACH BOARDWALK   Most Santa Cruz restaurants can be found near the Boardwalk or in the downtown area, with a few others scattered around town. Of course, along the Boardwalk the favorite dining style is to eat while you stroll. Stop at **Surf City Grill** for a corn dog, Italian sausage sandwich, or fried zucchini; sit down to a bowl of clam chowder or crab salad at the **Fisherman's Galley**; or pause at the **Barbary Coast** for cheeseburgers. For dessert there are caramel apples, ice cream, cotton candy, popcorn, and saltwater taffy. For inexpensive snacks, try the hot dog stand at the bottom of the steps in **Lovers Point Park** (Ocean View Boulevard at the foot of 16th Street). It's a local institution.

BEACH STREET CAFÉ

$$ AMERICAN   ✉399 Beach Street   ☎831-426-7621   🖳831-476-0654   ✐www.beachstreetcafe.com

If eating on the run proves a bit much, try one of the budget restaurants on Beach Street, across from the Boardwalk. Foremost is Beach Street Café, which houses the largest U.S. collection of Maxfield Parrish limited-edition prints. Breakfast begins with guacamole omelettes, bagels, croissants, or pancakes. Matter of fact, breakfast continues until late afternoon. Try the "Eggs Sardou" (artichoke bottoms with spinach, poached eggs, and hollandaise sauce). The "mile-high" burgers are worth trying to get your teeth around. No dinner.

EL PAISANO TAMALES

$ MEXICAN   ✉605 Beach Street   ☎831-426-2382

This spot has the standard selection of tacos, tostadas, enchiladas, and burritos. Closed Monday and Tuesday and from January to mid-February.

CASABLANCA RESTAURANT

$$$ NEW AMERICAN   ✉101 Main Street   ☎831-423-1570   🖳831-423-0235   ✐www.casablanca-santacruz.com, casabeach@aol.com

This cozy restaurant, with its overhead fans and Moroccan flair, is an excellent dinner choice. The place has a wraparound view of the ocean, not to mention a tony decor. The menu includes such gourmet selections as seared chicken with tarragon, sauteed prawns over capellini, and filet mignon with forest mushroom demi-glace. Casablanca boasts one of the largest selections of wines in Santa Cruz County. Dinner only.

IDEAL BAR AND GRILL

$$ SEAFOOD   ✉ *106 Beach Street*   ☎ *831-423-5271*   📠 *831-423-3827*
🖱 *www.idealbarandgrill.com, idealbar@aol.com*

This is a tourist trap with tradition. It's been one since 1917. It also has decent food (breakfast, lunch, and dinner), and a knockout view, especially from the outdoor deck right on the sand. The place is wedged in a corner between the beach and the pier, which means it looks out on everything, from boardwalk to bounding deep. The specialty is seafood—calamari, oysters, lobster, and salmon. Several pastas, plus a few meat and fowl dishes, round out the menu.

THE CATALYST

$ AMERICAN   ✉ *1011 Pacific Avenue*   ☎ *831-423-1338*   📠 *831-429-4135*
🖱 *www.catalystclub.com*

Among the many places in the Pacific Garden Mall area, my personal favorite is The Catalyst. I don't go there so much to eat as to watch. Not that the food is bad, it's just that The Catalyst is a scene. At night the place transmogrifies into a club with live music and unfathomable vibrations. By day, it's just itself, a cavernous structure with a glass roof and enough plants to make it an oversized greenhouse. Indeed, some of the clientele seem to have taken root. There are two bars if you're here to people watch.

EL PALOMAR

$$–$$$ MEXICAN   ✉ *1336 Pacific Avenue*   ☎ *831-425-7575*   📠 *831-423-3037*
🖱 *www.elpalomarcilantros.com, elpalomarrestaurant@msn.com*

I often join the locals here, their favorite Mexican restaurant, named the best Mexican restaurant by the readers of *Good Times*, a local entertainment newspaper, for several years running. This leafy establishment is housed in a beautiful 1930s hotel and sports soaring ceilings and large booths. El Palomar serves up such Mexican seafood dishes as prawn burritos and the José special—grilled skirt steak, snapper, and prawns. Homemade tortillas and specialty margaritas enhance the delicious fare. The taco bar, or cantina, offers more casual dining. Sunday brunch is also available.

BENTEN

$$–$$$ JAPANESE   ✉ *1541 Pacific Avenue, Suite B*   ☎ *831-425-7079*

For Japanese food there's this comfortable restaurant complete with a sushi bar. They serve an array of traditional dishes including sashimi, tempura, teriyaki, and a special plate called *kaki* fry (deep-fried breaded oysters). Understated and reliable. Closed Tuesday.

ALDO'S HARBOR RESTAURANT

$–$$ SEAFOOD/ITALIAN   ✉ *616 Atlantic Avenue*   ☎ *831-426-3736*   📠 *831-426-1362*
🖱 *www.aldos-cruz.com*

Aldo's, a café with patio deck overlooking Santa Cruz Harbor, whips up seafood dishes, pastas, soups, salads, and sandwiches. Conveniently located near Seabright Beach, this unassuming little place serves fresh seafood and home-baked breads. No dinner on Sunday.

EMILY'S GOOD THINGS TO EAT

$ AMERICAN ✉*1129 Mission Street* ✆*831-429-9866, 800-461-2976*
📠*831-429-6328* ✐*www.emilysbakery.com*

Emily Rielly, who's served two terms as town mayor, has been offering simple, delicious fresh-baked breads, tarts, cakes, crostatas, muffins, and sandwiches here since 1982. The friendly staff and the shop's motto—"Relax...you have plenty of time"—make this a pleasant stop in your travels. Pick up a daily special sandwich on crusty French bread, a hot cup of coffee, and linger on the deck overlooking Laurel Creek.

VASILI'S
GREEK RESTAURANT

$$ GREEK ✉*1501A Mission Street, Suite A* ✆*831-458-9808*

Opa! For Greek food and fun hit up Vasili's. It's a quirky place where the walls are chockablock with trinkets and the kebabs are great. Patrons like the flaming cheese appetizer *(saganaki)*, especially when the owner comes over and lights the dish up. Closed Monday.

SHOPPING

The central shopping district in Santa Cruz is along Pacific Garden Mall, a six-block strip of Pacific Avenue converted to a promenade. The section is neatly landscaped with flowering shrubs and potted trees and its sidewalks, widened for window browsers, overflow with people.

ARTISANS GALLERY ✉*1368 Pacific Avenue* ✆*831-423-8183* ✐*www.artisanssantacruz.com* You can stop by this gallery, which deals in fine handcrafts and gift items by local artists. They feature outstanding pottery, woodwork, glassware, and jewelry.

BOOKSHOP SANTA CRUZ ✉*1520 Pacific Avenue* ✆*831-423-0900* ✐*www.bookshopsantacruz.com* This is the finest among this college town's many wonderful bookstores.

PACIFIC AVENUE Strolling along this street, you will find galleries, gift stores, plus arts-and-crafts shops run by local artists.

NIGHTLIFE

THE CATALYST ✉*1011 Pacific Avenue* ✆*831-423-1336* 📠*831-423-7853* ✐*www.catalystclub.com* In Santa Cruz, this club is the common denominator. A popular restaurant and hangout by day, it becomes an entertainment spot at night. There's live music most weekday evenings in the Atrium, where local groups perform. But on weekends the heavyweights swing into town and The Catalyst lines up big rock performers. Some all-ages shows. Cover charge for live bands.

THE CROW'S NEST ✉*2218 East Cliff Drive* ✆*831-476-4560* ✐*www.crowsnest-santacruz.com* The Crow's Nest offers eclectic entertainment with an ocean view. On any given night they will be headlining jazz, reggae, salsa, rock, blues, or, on Sunday night, comedy. Cover.

KUUMBWA JAZZ CENTER ✉ *320 Cedar Street* ☎ *831-427-2227* 🖰 *www. kuumbwajazz.org* The unassuming Kuumbwa headlines top-name musicians most nights. All ages are welcome here. Cover.

BLUE LAGOON ✉ *923 Pacific Avenue* ☎ *831-423-7117* 🖰 *www.thebluelagoon. com* The crowd here dances to live hip-hop, house, and deejay music during the week, and watches live bands most Friday nights.

VINOCRUZ ———— (h)idden

✉ *725 Front Street, Suite 101; Off Cooper Street* ☎ *831-426-8466* 🖰 *www. vinocruz.com, info@vinocruz.com* The casual-yet sophisticated atmosphere and the Santa Cruz–based selection are draws here, but it's the knowledgable owners who bring people back time and again. This small shop boast stainless steel countertops and 150 varietals, all from Santa Cruz Mountain wineries. There are daily tastings, Saturday night movies in summer, and plenty of wine merchandise, from decanters to corkscrews to stemware. You'll be hardpressed to leave without taking home something for yourself.

MOE'S ALLEY ✉ *1535 Commercial Way* ☎ *831-479-1854* 🖰 *www.moesalley. com* The best reggae bands around make Moe's a regular stop, and it's a consistently good bet for all kinds of world music, blues, and jazz. The crowd is loud and appreciative, there's a full bar, and on weekends, spicy Indian food to nosh on with a cold beer. Cover charge most nights. Closed Monday.

BEACHES & PARKS

NATURAL BRIDGES STATE BEACH
✉ *Located at the end of West Cliff Drive near the western edge of Santa Cruz*
☎ *831-423-4609*

🏃 🛶 🎣 ⚓ 🏖 🚣 Northernmost of the Santa Cruz beaches, Natural Bridges is a small park with a half-moon-shaped beach and tidepools. All but one of the sea arches here have collapsed, leading local wags to dub the spot "Fallen Arches." This is a popular windsurfing spot in the summer. It's quite pretty, though a row of houses flanks one side. In the winter, surfers gather on the reef break. This is also an excellent spot to watch monarch butterflies during their annual winter migration (from October to late February). During these months there are weekend guided tours of the eucalyptus groves. Facilities include picnic areas, a visitors center, a bookstore, restrooms, and wi-fi access. No dogs are allowed on the beach. The visitor center is closed Monday and Tuesday in summer. Day-use fee, $6.

SANTA CRUZ BEACH
✉ *Located along Beach Street; access from the Municipal Wharf and along the Boardwalk*
🚴 🛶 🎣 ⚓ 🏖 🚣 ⛵ 🚣 Of the three major beaches extending along the Santa Cruz waterfront, this is the most popular, most crowded, and most famous. All for a very simple reason: the Santa Cruz Boardwalk, with its amusement park and restaurants, runs the length of the sand, and the Santa Cruz Municipal Pier anchors one end of the

beach. This, then, is the place to come for crowds and excitement. "Steamer Lane" is the Santa Cruz surfing hotspot. A series of reef breaks are located along West Cliff Drive, extending west to Lighthouse Point. Facilities include restrooms, showers, seasonal lifeguard, volleyball, restaurants, and groceries.

SEABRIGHT BEACH

✉ *Access to the beach is along East Cliff Drive at Mott Avenue, or at the end of 3rd Avenue.* 📞 *831-429-2850* 🖂 *831-475-8350*

Also known as Castle Beach, Seabright is second in Santa Cruz's string of beaches. This beauty extends from the San Lorenzo River mouth to the jetty at Santa Cruz Harbor. It's long, wide, and backdropped by bluffs. The views are as magnificent as from other nearby beaches, and the crowds will be lighter than along the Boardwalk. There are restrooms, fire rings, and a lifeguard in summer.

TWIN LAKES STATE BEACH

✉ *At East Cliff Drive and 7th Avenue, south of Santa Cruz Harbor* 📞 *831-429-2850* 🖂 *831-475-8350*

Just the other side of Santa Cruz Harbor is this odd-shaped beach. Smaller than the two beaches to the north, it is also less crowded. The park is 94 acres, with a lagoon behind the beach and a jetty flanking one side. A very pretty spot. Surfing is sometimes okay in winter or after a storm. There are restrooms and lifeguards during the summer.

LINCOLN BEACH, SUNNY COVE, MORAN LAKE BEACH

✉ *All three beaches are near East Cliff Drive. Blacks Beach (part of Twin Lakes State Beach) is at the end of 14th Avenue, Sunny Cove at the end of 17th Avenue, and Moran Lake Beach is near Lake Avenue.*

Located along the eastern end of Santa Cruz, these three sandy beaches are in residential areas. As a result, they draw local people, not tourists, and they're more difficult to get to. All are backdropped by bluffs. There are restrooms and picnic areas at Lincoln Beach and Moran Lake Beach; otherwise amenities are scarce. Parking is a problem throughout the area (though Moran Lake Beach has a parking lot where you can park all day for a fee during summer and weekends, otherwise free).

SANTA CRUZ TO MONTEREY

From Santa Cruz, coastal Route 1 heads south through Capitola, known for its sparkling beach and September Begonia Festival, and through Aptos, another bedroom community with equally pretty beaches.

THE FOREST OF NISENE MARKS STATE PARK ✆ *831-763-7063*
Aptos' most popular place these days is a foreboding forest located at latitude 37° 2' and longitude 121° 53'. That precise spot, at the end of a two-mile trail in the Forest of Nisene Marks State Park, is the **1989 earthquake epicenter.** A stake now marks ground zero of the 7.1 shaker that devastated Northern California. To reach the trailhead, follow Aptos Creek Road north from Aptos to the Nisene Marks parking lot. Admission.

RURAL SIDE TRIP   In nearby Rio del Mar, there's a rural side trip that carries you past miles of farmland before rejoining Route 1 near Watsonville. To take this side trip follow San Andreas Road, which tunnels through forest, then opens into rich agricultural acres. Intricately tilled fields roll down to the sea and edge up to the foot of the mountains. At the end of San Andreas Road, follow Beach Street to the ocean. The entire stretch of coastline is flanked by high sand dunes, a wild and exotic counterpoint to the furrowed fields nearby.

WATSONVILLE   Beach Street leads back into Watsonville. Central to the surrounding farm community, Watsonville is the world's strawberry-growing capital. It's also rich in **Victorian houses** and boasts a population of birds so diverse that the **Watsonville Chamber of Commerce** (449 Union Street; 831-724-3900, fax 831-728-5300; www.pajarovalley.com) hosts an annual Birding Festival, in addition to offering maps and guides year-round. Closed weekends.

MOSS LANDING   Back on Route 1, you'll pass Moss Landing, a weather-beaten fishing harbor. With its antique stores, an old bridge, bright-painted boats, and unpainted fish market, the town has a warm personality. There is one eyesore, however—a huge power plant with twin smokestacks that stand out like two sentinels of an occupying army. Otherwise the place is enchanting.

ELKHORN SLOUGH NATIONAL ESTUARINE RESEARCH RESERVE
✉ *1700 Elkhorn Road, Watsonville* ✆ *831-728-2822* ✐ *www.elkhornslough. org, info@elkhornslough.org* Nearby, Elkhorn Reserve is a 1400-acre world of salt marshes and tidal flats managed by a state and federal partnership between the California Department of Fish and Game and the National Oceanic and Atmospheric Administration. Within this delicate environment live some 400 species of invertebrates, 80 species of fish, and 300 species of birds (among them great blue heron, great egret, and acorn woodpeckers), as well as harbor seals. Guided tours on the weekend. To get to the visitors center from Route 1, follow Dolan Road for three miles, go left on Elkhorn Road, and then proceed two more miles. Closed Monday and Tuesday. Admission.

CASTROVILLE   Next in this parade of small towns is Castroville, "Artichoke Center of the World." Beyond it is a cluster of towns—

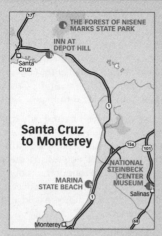

THE FOREST OF NISENE MARKS STATE PARK

PAGE 414

Hiking trails traversing redwood groves and fossil beds leading to the 1989 earthquake epicenter

INN AT DEPOT HILL

PAGE 409

Former train depot-turned-B&B with rooms representing international vacation spots like St. Tropez, Paris, and Portofino

NATIONAL STEINBECK CENTER MUSEUM

PAGE 409

Literary museum in historic downtown Salinas displaying manuscripts, photographs, and art exhibits

MARINA STATE BEACH

PAGE 415

Fluffy sand dunes offering great opportunities for hang gliding, fishing, or whale watching

Marina, Sand City, and Seaside—that probably represent the sand capitals of the world. The entire area rests on a sand dune that measures up to 300 feet in depth, and extends ten miles along the coast and as much as eight miles inland. From here you can trace a course into Monterey along wind-tilled rows of sand.

OLD MISSION SAN JUAN BAUTISTA ☎831-623-4528 ✎www.old missionsjb.org Time permitting, there's one overland excursion that must be added to your itinerary—a visit to this mission. While this graceful mission town, located 90 miles south of San Francisco, is easily reached from Route 101, the most inspiring route is via Route 156 from the Monterey Peninsula.

Anyone who has read Frank Norris' muckraking novel about the railroads, *The Octopus*, will recognize this placid village and its thick, cool adobe church. And anyone who remembers the climax to Hitchcock's *Vertigo* will instantly picture the mission, even though the bell tower that Jimmy Stewart struggled to climb was a Hollywood addition that you won't see at the real San Juan Bautista. Founded in 1797, the mission was completed in 1812. Today it numbers among California's most enchanting locales. With its colonnade and sagging crossbeams, the mission has the musty scent of history. The old monastery and church consist of a low-slung building roofed in Spanish tile and topped with a belfry.

MISSION CEMETERY ✉ *Old Mission San Juan Bautista* My favorite spot in this beloved town is this small plot bounded by a stone fence and overlooking valley and mountains. It's difficult to believe that over 4300 American Indians are buried here in unmarked graves. The few recognizable resting places are memorialized with wooden crosses and circling enclosures of stone. Shade trees cool the yard. Just below the cemetery, symbolic perhaps of change and mortality, are the old Spanish Road (*El Camino Real*) and the San Andreas Fault. The mission rests on a grassy square facing Plaza Hall.

PLAZA HALL ✉ *Old Mission San Juan Bautista* Originally a dormitory for unwed American Indian women, this structure was rebuilt in 1868 and used as a meeting place and private residence. Peek inside its shuttered windows or tour the building and encounter a child's room cluttered with old dolls, a sitting room dominated by a baby grand piano, and other rooms containing period furniture.

BLACKSMITH SHOP ✉ *Old Mission San Juan Bautista* Behind Plaza Hall sits this shop, now filled with wagon wheels, oxen yokes, and the "San Juan Eagle," a hook-and-ladder wagon drawn by a ten-man firefighting crew back in 1869.

PLAZA STABLE ✉ *Old Mission San Juan Bautista* Near the blacksmith shop is this stable, which houses an impressive collection of buggies and carriages.

PLAZA HOTEL ✉ *Old Mission San Juan Bautista* The Plaza lines another side of the square. Consisting of several adobe structures, the earliest built in 1814, the place once served as a stagecoach stop. Today its myriad rooms contain historic exhibits and 1860s-era furnishings.

CASTRO-BREEN ADOBE ✉ *Old Mission San Juan Bautista* Similar to the Plaza is this building decorated with Spanish-style pieces. Owned by a Mexican general and later by Donner Party survivors, it is a window into California frontier life.

SAN JUAN JAIL ✉ *Old Mission San Juan Bautista* An oversized outhouse constructed in 1870, and a **settler's cabin**, a rough log cabin built by East Coast pioneers in the 1830s or 1840s are also worthwhile sights.

STATE HISTORIC PARK ☎ *831-623-4526* ☎ *831-623-4612* All of the mission buildings are part of the state historic park that comprises San Juan Bautista. Like the plaza, 3rd Street is lined with 19th-century stores and houses. Here, amid porticoed haciendas and crumbling adobe, are antique stores, a bakery, restaurants, and other shops. Admission.

EL TEATRO CAMPESINO ✉ *705 4th Street, San Juan Bautista* ☎ *831-623-2444* ☎ *831-623-4127* ⌨ *www.elteatrocampesino.com, info@elteatrocampesino.com* This Latino company originated *Zoot Suit*, an important and provocative play that was eventually filmed as a movie. With a penetrating sense of Mexican-American history and an unsettling awareness of contemporary Latino social roles, it is a modern expression of the vigor and spirit of this old Spanish town.

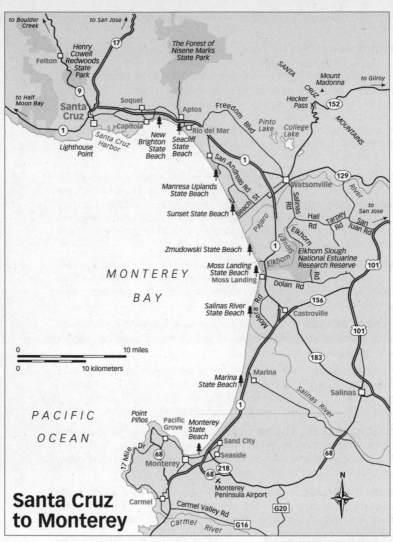

to Boulder Creek

to San Jose

Henry Cowell Redwoods State Park

The Forest of Nisene Marks State Park

Felton

17

SANTA

Mount Madonna

to Gilroy

Hecker Pass

152

9

to Half Moon Bay

Soquel

Aptos

Freedom Blvd

Pinto Lake

College Lake

CRUZ

Santa Cruz

1

Capitola

Rio del Mar

New Brighton State Beach

Seacliff State Beach

San Andreas Rd

1

MOUNTAINS

Lighthouse Point

Santa Cruz Harbor

Watsonville

129

River

to San Jose

Manresa Uplands State Beach

Beach St

Salinas Rd

Hall Rd

Tarpey Rd

San Juan Rd

Sunset State Beach

Pajaro

Elkhorn Rd

Zmudowski State Beach

1

Elkhorn Slough National Estuarine Research Reserve

101

MONTEREY

Moss Landing State Beach

Elkhorn

Moss Landing

Dolan Rd

BAY

Molera Rd

156

Salinas River State Beach

Castroville

101

0   10 miles

0   10 kilometers

183

Marina State Beach

Marina

Salinas River

PACIFIC

Salinas

Point Piños

1

OCEAN

Pacific Grove

Monterey State Beach

Sand City

17 Mile Dr

68

Seaside

68

Monterey

68

218

N

Monterey Peninsula Airport

G20

Santa Cruz to Monterey

Carmel

Carmel Valley Rd

G16

Carmel River

hidden

STEINBECK HOUSE

✉ *132 Central Avenue, Salinas* 📞 *831-424-2735* 📠 *831-757-5806* 🖘 *www. steinbeckhouse.com, steinbeckhouse@sbcglobal.net* In Salinas, south of San Juan Bautista via Route 101, the house in which author John Steinbeck grew up is located a few blocks from the National Steinbeck Center. It now serves as a gift shop and restaurant, open for lunch Tuesday through Saturday. Victorian tea service is offered the second Saturday of every month. Sunday tours during the summer. Reservations are recommended.

NATIONAL STEINBECK CENTER MUSEUM

✉ *1 Main Street, Salinas (eight miles southeast of Route 1 via Route 183)*
📞 *831-775-4721* 📠 *831-796-3828* ⌕ *www.steinbeck.org, info@steinbeck.org*

This museum, located in the heart of Oldtown Salinas (the historic downtown district), houses photographic, multimedia, and interactive exhibits about the life and work of Salinas-born author John Steinbeck, as well as a wing on the agricultural history of the region. It also contains a research archive of more than 45,000 manuscripts, first editions, newspaper and magazine articles, photographs, and other artifacts. The museum displays rotating art exhibits. There's also a store offering books, artwork, and apparel. Admission.

JOHN STEINBECK'S GRAVE

✉ *768 Abbot Street, Salinas* John Steinbeck's grave is in the Garden of Memories cemetery.

LODGING

CAPITOLA VENETIAN HOTEL

$$–$$$$ 19 ROOMS   ✉ *1500 Wharf Road, Capitola* 📞 *831-476-6471, 800-332-2780*
📠 *831-475-3897* ⌕ *www.capitolavenetian.com, information@capitolavenetian.com*

The Venetian is a mock Italian complex next to Capitola Beach. With its stucco and red tile veneer, ornamental molding, and carved wooden doors, it's a poor cousin to the grand villas of Venice. The guest rooms come equipped with kitchens. There are few wall decorations and the furnishings lack character, but the atmosphere is pleasant. Two-night minimum on weekend.

HARBOR LIGHTS MOTEL

$$–$$$$ 10 ROOMS   ✉ *5000 Cliff Drive, Capitola* 📞 *831-476-0505* 📠 *831-476-0235*
⌕ *www.harborlightsmotel.net, info@harborlightsmotel.net*

This motel is a few steps farther uphill from the beach from the Capitola Venetian Hotel and is similarly laid out but in a more modern fashion. This ten-unit stucco building has rooms with completely equipped kitchens and ocean views. The views of Monterey Bay are the real draw here.

INN AT DEPOT HILL

$$$$ 12 ROOMS   ✉ *250 Monterey Avenue, Capitola* 📞 *831-462-3376,*
800-572-2632 📠 *831-462-3697* ⌕ *www.innsbythesea.com,*
depothill@innsbythesea.com

Does a trip around the world interest you? If so, this inn might save you time and money without sacrificing the feel of the trip. This bed and breakfast, fashioned from a former train station, features internationally decorated rooms with names like "Paris,"

"Côte d'Azur," and "Portofino." There is a fireplace in each room and some come with a patio and hot tub. Full breakfast, hors d'oeuvres with wine, and dessert are included with a night's stay.

SEASCAPE BEACH RESORT

$$$$ 285 ROOMS ✉ *Seascape Resort Drive, Aptos* ☎ *800-929-7727*
🖥 *www.seascaperesort.com, info@seascaperesort.com*

Seascape is the place to go for a complete indulgence. It has 285 suites and villas with full kitchens or kitchenettes, fireplaces, wi-fi access, and HDTV. Amenities include in-room massage, a deluxe fitness center with 11 tennis courts, three swimming pools with outdoor hot tubs, a golf course, and 17 miles of beach.

PAJARO DUNES

$$$$ 140 UNITS ✉ *2661 Beach Road, Watsonville* ☎ *831-728-7400, 800-564-1771*
🖥 *www.pajarodunes.com, info@pajarodunes.com*

With two miles of beachfront, Pajaro Dunes is ideal for those who want to go down to the sea. Located midway between Santa Cruz and Monterey, this resort colony has condominiums, townhouses, and beachhomes that range from one to six bedrooms. While decorating schemes vary from beach contemporary to brass and glass, all units offer kitchens, fireplaces, decks, and barbecues. There are 19 on-site tennis courts. The big units are a good bet for large family groups. Two-night minimum stay is required for houses.

CAPTAIN'S INN

$$–$$$ 10 ROOMS ✉ *P.O. Box 570, Moss Landing Road, Moss Landing*
☎ *831-633-5550* 🖥 *www.captainsinn.com, res@captainsinn.com*

Built in 1906 for the Pacific Coast Steamship Company, Captain's has done a wonderful job of retaining its heritage. The ten guest rooms—divided between the main Steamship Company building and the accompanying waterfront boathouse—are decorated with nautical antiques and include private baths, high-speed internet, and king- or queen-sized beds, complete with feather pillows. An onsite mini-spa boasts warm stone massages, sea salt scrubs, and aromatherapy. Nature lovers will also be thrilled: the surrounding area is populated with seals, coastal birds, and the occasional surfacing whale.

POSADA DE SAN JUAN

$$ 33 ROOMS ✉ *310 4th Street, San Juan Bautista* ☎ *831-623-4030*
📠 *831-623-2378*

Accommodations are scarce in San Juan Bautista, but here they offer comfortable, unassuming rooms within walking distance of the mission and 3rd Street's shops and restaurants. The rooms are equipped with wetbars, oversized spa bathtubs, and gas fireplaces. Decorated in a hacienda style, this inn reflects the distinctly Mexican flavor of San Juan Bautista.

SAN JUAN INN

$$ 42 ROOMS ✉ *410 The Alameda, San Juan Bautista* ☎ *831-623-4380*

This reliable resting spot has an outdoor pool and hot tub, and each of its rooms comes with a coffeemaker, microwave, and cable TV. Or for $10 more, you can chose a slightly larger suite, which includes a subdivided livingroom. Note: The Inn is also the only place in town that allows pets.

SHADOWBROOK RESTAURANT

$$–$$$ SEAFOOD ✉1750 Wharf Road, Capitola ☏831-475-1511, 800-975-1511 📠831-475-7764 ✐www.shadowbrook-capitola.com, office@shadowbrook-capitola.com

The area's foremost dining room is actually outside Santa Cruz in a nearby suburb. True to its name, the multitiered Shadowbrook Restaurant, in operation since 1947, sits in a wooded spot through which a creek flows. Food is almost an afterthought at this elaborate affair; upon entering the grounds you descend either via a funicular or a sinuous, fern-draped path. Once inside, you'll encounter a labyrinth of dining levels and rooms, luxuriously decorated with potted plants, stone fireplaces, and candlelit tables. A mature tree grows through the floor and ceiling of one room here; in others, vines climb along the walls. When you finally chart the course to a table, you'll be offered a menu including prime rib, salmon, and other fresh seafood dishes. Definitely a dining experience. Live music some nights in the Rockroom Lounge. Sunday champagne brunch. No lunch.

Capitola Beach is wall-to-wall with seafood restaurants. They line the strand, each with a different decorative theme but all seeming to merge into a collection of pit stops for hungry beachgoers. If fresh fish is what you're after, any of them will do.

THE WHOLE ENCHILADA

$$ MEXICAN ✉Route 1 at Moss Landing Road, Moss Landing ☏831-633-3038 📠831-633-5391 ✐www.wenchilada.com, eat@wenchilada.com

Touted as the best Mexican restaurant in Monterey County, this eatery specializes in seafood dishes. The chef uses locally grown produce like Castroville artichokes and chiles, fresh fish, prawns, and oysters. Try the "whole enchilada" entrée—fillet of red snapper wrapped in corn tortillas topped with melted cheese and chile salsa. Save room for flan!

LIGHTHOUSE HARBOR AND GRILL

$ AMERICAN ✉7902 Route 1, Suite C, Moss Landing ☏831-633-3858

Next door to The Whole Enchilada is the Lighthouse, offering early breakfast (they open at 5:30 a.m. on weekdays) and lunch. Mexican dishes are available, but more standard fare such as omelettes dominate the menu. There are even whole wheat hotcakes. Dinner available Wednesday through Sunday.

LA CASA ROSA

$$ MEXICAN/CALIFORNIA CUISINE ✉107 3rd Street, San Juan Bautista ☏831-623-4563 📠831-623-1031

As for restaurants in San Juan Bautista, La Casa Rosa sits in an 1858 house. Open for lunch only, this family-run eatery features an "old California casserole," a "new California casserole," a chicken soufflé, and a seafood soufflé. The first entrée is made with cheese, meat sauce, and a corn base; the second dish features green chiles. La Casa Rosa is charming and intimate. Closed Tuesday.

JARDINES DE SAN JUAN

$–$$ MEXICAN   ✉*115 3rd Street, San Juan Bautista*
☏*831-623-4466* ☏*831-623-4340* ✐*www.jardinesrestaurant.com,*
info@jardinesrestaurant.com

This spot is recommended as much for its garden as its food. In addition to the usual tacos, burritos, and flautas, weekend specials get fancy: Veracruz-style red snapper served with *crema* on a bed of rice, or *pollos borrachos* cooked in sherry with ham and sausage. Friday and Saturday nights generally features a Paraguayan harpist.

SHOPPING

Located along Route 1 south of Santa Cruz, the coastal village of Moss Landing is a must for antique hounds. More than 20 shops offer a wide array of treasures from the good old days. Clustered around the intersection of Moss Landing Road and Sandholdt Road are several shops that warrant a close look.

WATERFRONT ANTIQUES ✉*7902 Sandholdt Road, Moss Landing* ☏*831-633-1112* ✐*www.waterfrontantiques.com* For furniture, nautical instruments, glass, and lamps, check out this shop.

THE LITTLE RED BARN ✉*8461 Moss Landing Road, Moss Landing* ☏*831-578-2198* To peruse a bit of everything, stop by this antique shop.

NIGHTLIFE

SHADOWBROOK RESTAURANT ✉*1750 Wharf Road, Capitola* ☏*831-475-1511* ✐*www.shadowbrook-capitola.com* For a relaxing evening, try Shadowbrook. Its soft lighting and luxurious surroundings create a sense of well-being, like brandy and a blazing fire. They present live music Saturday nights (and some weekday nights) in their Rockroom Lounge.

ZELDA'S ✉*203 Esplanade, Capitola* ☏*831-475-4900* Several of the restaurant lounges lining Capitola's waterfront have nightly entertainment. Over at Zelda's you can enjoy a quick drink on the patio, and live music on Thursday, Friday, and Saturday nights.

CAVA WINE BAR

✉*115 San Jose Avenue, Capitola* ☏*831-476-2282* ✐*www.cavacapitola.com,*
cavacapitola@gmail.com A hit with locals, this laid-back wine lounge comes with comfortable couches, a roaring fireplace, and often live music. The wine list includes sparkling whites along with full-bodied reds. In addition to wine, Cava offers a tapas menu that features salami and outstanding housemade cheeses. The

two owners—longtime friends Zach and Cliff—bring a lot of hospitality and plenty of wine knowledge.

FRANCO'S NORMA JEAN

✉10639 Merritt Street, Castroville ✆831-633-2090 A lively gay Latino crowd heats up this weekend-only club on Friday and Saturday nights. You'll find a small dancefloor and rotating deejays, along with a crew of regulars who come for the strong drinks and good company. It doesn't look like much from the outside—a plain stripmall exterior—but if you enjoy a slightly edgy gay nightlife scene, you'll feel right at home.

EL TEATRO CAMPESINO ✉705 4th Street, San Juan Bautista ✆831-623-2444 📠831-623-4127 ✎www.elteatrocampesino.com, info@elteatrocampesino.com From May to September summer productions are held in this theater; the Christmas show is staged in Mission San Juan Bautista.

BEACHES & PARKS

CAPITOLA CITY BEACH

✉Located in the center of Capitola ✆831-475-6522 📠831-475-6530

🏊 🎣 ⛵ 🚣 🏄 ⛱ 🎵 Sedimentary cliffs flank a corner of this sand carpet but the rest is heavily developed. Popular with visitors for decades, Capitola is a well-known resort community. Seafood restaurants line its shore and boutiques flourish within blocks of the beach. A great place for families because of the adjacent facilities, it trades seclusion for service. The ocean is well protected for water sports and in winter, surfers enjoy the breaks near the jetty, pier, and river mouth. Following a year of heavy storms, the beach often disappears under the high tide. There are restrooms, showers, bait and tackle shop, lifeguards, a fishing pier, and volleyball.

NEW BRIGHTON STATE BEACH

✉Off Route 1 in Capitola, four miles south of Santa Cruz ✆831-464-6330, 831-464-6329 📠831-685-6443

🏊 🎣 🎵 This sandy crescent adjoins Seacliff Beach and enjoys a wide vista of Monterey Bay. Headlands protect the beach for swimmers and beginning surfers. Clamming is also popular. Within its mere 94 acres, the park contains a forested bluff. A new Pacific Migrations Visitors Center (831-464-5620) within the beach houses exhibits about the roles of Chinese immigrants in local history. (Closed in winter.) There are picnic areas, fire pits, restrooms, and showers (for campers only). Day-use fee, $6.

⚲ There are 88 tent/RV sites (limited hookups) in a wooded area inland from the beach; $25 to $35 per night. Reservations are required (people book up to seven months in advance): 800-444-7275.

SEACLIFF STATE BEACH

✉ *Off Route 1 in Aptos, five miles south of Santa Cruz* ☎ *831-685-6442* 📠 *831-685-6443*

This two-mile strand is very popular. *Too* popular: During summer, RVs park along its entire length and crowds gather on the waterfront. That's because it provides the safest swimming along this section of coast. There are roving lifeguards on duty during the summer and a protective headland nearby. The visitors center offers guided walks year-round to look at fossils. Check for changing hours and tour schedules. The beach also sports a pier favored by anglers. It's a pretty place, but oh-so-busy. There are picnic areas, restrooms, and showers. Day-use fee, $6.

▲ There are 26 sites for RVs and self-contained vehicles (full hookups); $44 per night. Reservations are required: 800-444-7275.

THE FOREST OF NISENE MARKS STATE PARK ——

✉ *From Route 1 southbound take the Seacliff Beach exit in Aptos, five miles south of Santa Cruz. Take an immediate left on State Park Drive, pass over the highway, and then go right on Soquel Drive. Follow this for a half-mile; then head left on Aptos Creek Road. This paved road turns to gravel as it leads into the forest.* ☎ *831-763-7063* 📠 *831-763-7120*

This semi-wilderness expanse, several miles inland, encompasses over 10,000 acres. Within its domain are redwood groves, meandering streams, rolling countryside, and dense forest. About 30 miles of hiking trails wind through the preserve. Along them you can explore fossil beds, deserted logger cabins, old trestles, and railroad beds; you can also hike to the epicenter of the 1989 earthquake. The park is a welcome complement to the natural features along the coast. There are picnic tables and barbecues. Day-use fee, $6.

▲ There are six primitive sites; $5 per person per night. No water available. Reservations required: 831-763-7073.

MANRESA UPLANDS STATE BEACH ——

✉ *Located 13 miles south of Santa Cruz; from Route 1, take the Larkin Valley Road and San Andreas Road exit, turn right onto San Andreas Road and follow it several miles to the park turnoff.* ☎ *831-763-7064*

Here you'll find a strip of white sand bookended by blufftop homes. Popular with surfers, it provides a sweeping view of Monterey Bay. A bit more removed than other nearby beaches, Manresa nevertheless can be quite popular on summer afternoons. Facilities include restrooms, lifeguards (in summer), picnic tables, and, for campers, fire pits and showers. Campground closed October through March. Day-use fee, $6.

▲ There are 64 walk-in tent sites in Manresa Uplands Campground next to the beach; $25 per night. Reservations: 800-444-7275.

SUNSET STATE BEACH

✉ *Located 16 miles south of Santa Cruz; from Route 1, take the Larkin Valley and San Andreas Road exit, turn right onto San Andreas Road and follow it several miles to the park turnoff.* ☎ *831-763-7063* 📠 *831-763-7120*

Over three miles of beach and sand dunes create one of the area's prettiest parks. There are bluffs and meadows behind the beach as well as Monterey pines and cypress trees. This 324-acre park is a popular spot for fishing. Surfers also come here. But remember, there's more fog here and farther south than in the Santa Cruz area. There are picnic areas, restrooms, and showers. Day-use fee, $6.

▲ Permitted in 91 sites (no RV hookups), $25 per night; hiker/ biker camp available, $3 per person. One group site also available. Reservations: 800-444-7275.

ZMUDOWSKI, MOSS LANDING, AND SALINAS RIVER STATE BEACHES

✉ *All three are located off Route 1 within a few miles of Moss Landing* ☎ *831-649-2836*

These three state parks are part of a long stretch of sand dunes. They all contain broad beaches and vistas along Monterey Bay. Though relatively uncrowded, their proximity to Moss Landing's smoke-belching power plant is a severe drawback. Quite suitable anywhere else, they can't compete with their neighbors in this land of beautiful beaches. Surfing is good near the sandbar at Salinas River; great at Moss Landing, which draws locals from Santa Cruz. Each beach has portable toilets.

MARINA STATE BEACH

✉ *Located along Route 1, nine miles north of Monterey* ☎ *831-384-7695*

The tall, fluffy sand dunes at this 170-acre park are unreal. They're part of a giant dune covering 50 square miles throughout the area. A half-buried boardwalk takes you through the sand to the beach and gives you an up-close view of the unique vegetation. There are marvelous views of Monterey here, plus a chance to fish or sunbathe. It is also the perfect place to try out hang gliding. Swimming is allowed, though rip tides do occur. Regarding surfing, there's a great beach break in summer but it's dangerous in winter. There are restrooms and limited picnic areas.

MONTEREY

Over two million visitors visit the Monterey area every year. Little wonder. Its rocky coast fringed with cypress forests, its hills dotted with palatial homes—the area is unusually beautiful. The town of Monterey also serves as a gateway to the tumbling region of Big Sur.

For a tour of Monterey Peninsula, begin in Monterey itself. Here are historic homes, an old Spanish presidio, Fisherman's Wharf, and Cannery Row. Set in a natural amphitheater of forested hills, it is also home to one of the richest marine sanctuaries along the entire California coast. It's no surprise that this town, with a population that numbers 30,000 people, has served as an inspiration for Robert Louis Stevenson and John Steinbeck. With a downtown district that reflects small town America and a waterfront that once supported a rich fishing and canning industry, Monterey remains one of the most vital spots on the Central Coast.

SIGHTS

History in Monterey is a precious commodity that, in most cases, has been carefully preserved. Ancient adobe houses and Spanish-style buildings are so commonplace that some have been converted into shops and restaurants. Others are museums or points of interests that can be seen on a walking tour. For sightseeing tips and brochures, visit **Monterey County Convention and Visitors Bureau** (765 Wave Street; 831-657-6400, 800-555-6290). Closed Saturday and Sunday. If you need a little touring advice on the weekend, the **Monterey County Visitors Center** (401 Camino El Estero; 831-649-1770, 888-221-1010, fax 831-648-5373; www.montereyinfo.org) is open daily. You can download the official Monterey Guidebook on their website.

GUIDED TOURS—MONTEREY STATE HISTORIC PARKS

☎831-649-7118 ✉mshp@parks.ca.gov Tours of Monterey's historic buildings are available through the state park. The two-mile Path of History tour includes stops at museums, homes, gardens, and one of the nation's last remaining whalebone sidewalks. Beginning at the Pacific House Museum, these guided tours are a great way to see and learn about Monterey's history.

CUSTOM HOUSE

✉1 Custom House Plaza This 1827 structure is across from Fisherman's Wharf. In 1846, Commodore Sloat raised the American flag here, claiming California for the United States. Today the stone and adobe building houses displays from an 1830s-era cargo ship.

MARITIME MUSEUM OF MONTEREY

✉5 Custom House Plaza ☎831-375-2608 📠831-655-3054 ✉www.montereyhistory.org, info@montereyhistory.org You'll find model ships, a World War II exhibit, and a two-story-tall rotating lighthouse lens in this museum. Closed Monday. Admission.

PACIFIC HOUSE

✉10 Custom House Plaza Across the plaza rises this house (c. 1847), a two-story balconied adobe with a luxurious courtyard. The exhibits inside trace California's history from American Indian days to the advent of Spanish settlers and American pioneers.

CASA DEL ORO

✉210 Olivier Street at Scott Street ☎831-649-3364 Just behind Pacific House sits this tiny 1840s adobe that now houses the **Joseph Boston Store**, an old-fashioned mercantile shop selling Early American items. Closed Monday through Wednesday.

BRICK HOUSE

Diagonally across the intersection on Olivier Street behind an office complex stands the oldest brick house, purportedly

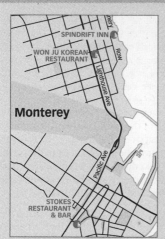

Monterey

SPINDRIFT INN

PAGE 423

Spacious, light-filled, waterfront inn with bay windows and woodburning fireplaces in elegant rooms

WON JU KOREAN RESTAURANT

PAGE 424

Traditional Korean eatery serving celebrated dishes like *bi bim bap* and *kalbi*

STOKES RESTAURANT & BAR

PAGE 423

California cuisine meets Mediterranean flavors—crispy polenta with Spanish chorizo and duck with pomegranate

the first such house in California. Adjacent to the brick house is the **Whaling Station**, an adobe with a balcony from which the early whalers spotted their migrating bounty.

CALIFORNIA'S FIRST THEATRE ✉*Scott and Pacific streets* ☎*831-646-6441* A block up the street from the Whaling Station is this theatre. It is still used to stage 19th-century melodramas that are performed by America's oldest continually operating theater troupe. The theater is closed indefinitely for renovations. Call for updates.

CASA SOBERANES ✉*6 Pacific Street* A left on Pacific Street leads to this Monterey-style house with red tile roof and second-story balcony. Completed in the 1840s, this impressive structure is also called "the house with the blue gate" for its entrance.

CASA SERRANO ✉*412 Pacific Street* ☎*831-372-2608* ⌨*www.montereyhistory.org* This 1843 home contains wrought-iron decorations over its narrow windows. Once home to a Spanish teacher who was Monterey's second *alcalde* (mayor), it is open for touring by appointment. For more information contact the Monterey History and Art Association.

FRIENDLY PLAZA This tree-shaded park serves as a focus for several important places. The **Monterey Museum of Art** (559 Pacific Street; 831-372-5477; www.montereyart.org) displays works and artifacts by early and contemporary California. Closed Monday and Tuesday. Admission. **La Mirada** (720 Via Mirada Avenue; 831-372-3689; www.montereyart.org) is housed in an old adobe with period furnishings. Closed Monday and Tuesday. Admission.

Author In Love

Robert Louis Stevenson, the vivacious but sickly Scottish writer, sailed the Atlantic and traveled overland across the continent to visit his wife-to-be Fanny Osbourne in Monterey. Writing for local newspapers, depending in part upon the kindness of strangers for sustenance, the fragile wanderer fell in love with Fanny and Monterey both. From the surrounding countryside he drew inspiration for some of his most famous books, including *Treasure Island*.

COLTON HALL ✉ *Pacific Street between Jefferson and Madison streets* Pierce Street, running along the upper edge of the plaza, contains a string of historic 19th-century homes. This is the site of California's 1849 constitutional convention, and the hall displays memorabilia from that critical event. The squat granite **Old Jail** next door, with wrought-iron bars across the windows, dates back to the same era. Across the street, **Casa Gutierrez** was built in 1846 by a cavalryman with 15 children.

LARKIN HOUSE ✉ *510 Calle Principal* ☎ *831-649-7118* After exploring the plaza, turn left into Madison Street from Pacific Street, then left again along Calle Principal to one of the town's most famous homes, the Larkin House. Designed in 1834 by Thomas Larkin, the antique home is now a house museum filled with period pieces. The only United States Consul to California lived here. Admission. Tours Wednesday, Friday, Saturday, and Sunday afternoons.

HISTORIC HOMES A right on Jefferson Street and another quick right on Polk takes you past a cluster of revered houses. Now a private club, **Casa Amesti** (516 Polk Street), built in 1824, was originally the home of a Spanish family named the Amestis. **Cooper-Molera Adobe** (525 Polk Street; 831-649-7118), across the road from Casa Amesti, includes a 19th-century museum and a "historic garden" of herbs and vegetables of the Mexican era. Grounds and store open daily, but for a guided tour call Monterey State Historic Parks for information. Admission. Facing each other on either side of Polk and Hartnell streets are the **Gabriel de la Torre Adobe** (c. 1836) and the **Stokes Adobe**, erected in the 1840s.

STEVENSON HOUSE ✉ *530 Houston Street* ☎ *831-649-7118* Backtrack along Polk Street one block to the five-way intersection, take a soft right onto Pearl Street, walk a few short blocks, then turn right on Houston Street to the Stevenson House, Robert Louis Stevenson's residence for several months in 1879. The house features personal belongings, original manuscripts, and first editions, all of which can be viewed on a guided tour. Admission. House open on weekends.

Two other places of historical note are located in Monterey, but a significant distance from the Path of History.

ROYAL PRESIDIO CHAPEL ✉ *550 Church Street* ☎ *831-373-4345* This chapel is a graceful expression of the 18th-century town. Decorative molding adorns the facade of the old adobe church while the towering belfry, rising along one side, makes the structure asymmetrical. Heavy wooden doors lead to a long, narrow chapel hung with dusty oil paint-

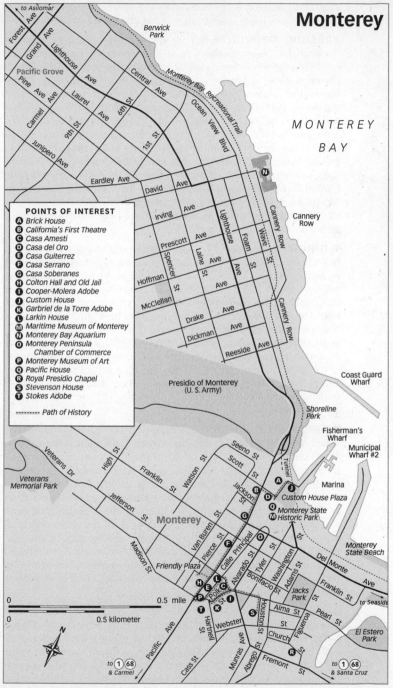

Monterey

to Asilomar

Forest Ave

Grand Ave

Lighthouse Ave

Pacific Grove

Pine Ave

Laurel Ave

Carmel Ave

Central Ave

6th St

Berwick Park

Monterey Bay Recreational Trail

Ocean View Blvd

9th St

1st St

Junipero Ave

Eardley Ave

David Ave

Irving Ave

Prescott Ave

Lighthouse Ave

Foam St

Wave St

Cannery Row

MONTEREY BAY

Cannery Row

N

Laine Ave

Spencer St

Hoffman Ave

McClellan Ave

Drake Ave

Dickman Ave

Reeside Ave

Cannery Row

Coast Guard Wharf

Presidio of Monterey (U. S. Army)

Shoreline Park

Fisherman's Wharf

Municipal Wharf #2

POINTS OF INTEREST
- **A** Brick House
- **B** California's First Theatre
- **C** Casa Amesti
- **D** Casa del Oro
- **E** Casa Guiterrez
- **F** Casa Serrano
- **G** Casa Soberanes
- **H** Colton Hall and Old Jail
- **I** Cooper-Molera Adobe
- **J** Custom House
- **K** Garbriel de la Torre Adobe
- **L** Larkin House
- **M** Maritime Museum of Monterey
- **N** Monterey Bay Aquarium
- **O** Monterey Peninsula
       Chamber of Commerce
- **P** Monterey Museum of Art
- **Q** Pacific House
- **R** Royal Presidio Chapel
- **S** Stevenson House
- **T** Stokes Adobe

-------- Path of History

Veterans Dr

High St

Franklin St

Watson St

Scott St

Seeno St

Jackson St

Tunnel

A

J

D

Marina

Custom House Plaza

Q Monterey State
M Historic Park

Veterans Memorial Park

Jefferson St

Monterey

Madison St

Van Buren St

Pierce St

G

F

O

Calle Principal

Alvarado St

Bonifacio St

Tyler St

Washington St

Adams St

Del Monte

Monterey State Beach

Friendly Plaza

H **L**
E **C**
P
Polk St
T **K** **I**

S

Houston St

Jacks Park

Franklin St

to Seaside

Alma St

Pearl St

Hartnell St

Webster St

Munras Ave

Abrego St

Church St

Figueroa St

R St

Fremont St

El Estero Park

Pacific Ave

Cass St

to ①⑥⑧ & Carmel

to ①⑥⑧ & Santa Cruz

Boardwalk

0   0.5 mile

0   0.5 kilometer

N

ings. This was the mission that Father Junípero Serra founded in 1770, just before moving his congregation a few miles south to Carmel.

PRESIDIO OF MONTEREY ✉*Pacific and Artillery streets* ☏*831-242-5555* ✆*831-242-5464* ✐*www.monterey.army.mil* The Presidio sits on a hill near the northwest corner of town. Established as a fort by the Spanish in 1770, it currently serves as a foreign language institute for the military. Argentine pirate Hipólito Bouchard sacked and burned the Monterey Presidio during his round-the-world rampage in 1818. There are cannons banked in a hillside, marking the site of Fort Mervine, built by the Americans in 1846. There's some evidence that the Presidio may also be the site of an ancient Costanoan Indian village and burial ground. And a granite monument at the corner of Pacific and Artillery streets marks the spot where in 1602 the Spanish celebrated the first Catholic mass in California. In addition to historic points, the Presidio grounds enjoy marvelous views of Monterey. You can look down upon the town, then scan along the bay's curving horizon. Due to heightened security, the Presidio is not open to the public.

MUNICIPAL WHARF #2 ✉*Located at the foot of Figueroa Street* Strangely, Monterey, which elsewhere demonstrates special care in preserving its heritage, has let its wharves and piers fall prey to tinsel-minded developers. Municipal Wharf #2 is a welcome exception. It's actually all that remains from the heyday of Monterey's fishing fleet. Here broad-hulled boats still beat at their moorings, while landlubbing anglers cast from pierside. Gulls perch along the handrails, sea lions bark from beneath the pilings, and pelicans work the waterfront. On one side is the dilapidated warehouse of a long-defunct freezer company. At the end of the dock, fish companies still operate. It's a primal place of cranes and pulleys, forklifts and conveyor belts. There are ice boxes and old packing crates scattered hither-thither, exuding the romance and stench of the industry.

FISHERMAN'S WHARF Then there is this parody of an actual wharf, much better known than the original. Fisherman's Wharf, like its San Francisco namesake, has been transmogrified into what the travel industry thinks tourists think a fishing pier should look like. Something was lost in the translation. Few fishing boats operate from the wharf these days; several charter companies sponsor glass-bottom boat tours and whale-watching expeditions. Otherwise the waterfront haven is just one more mall, a macadam corridor lined on either side with shops. There are ersatz art galleries, shops vending candy apples and personalized mugs, plus a school of seafood restaurants. A few outdoor fish markets still sell live crabs, lobsters, and squid, but the symbol of the place is the hurdy-gurdy man with performing monkey who greets you at the entrance.

Actually this is only the most recent in the wharf's long series of role changes. The dock was built in 1846 to serve cargo schooners dealing in hides. Within a decade the whaling industry took it over, followed finally by Italian fishermen catching salmon, cod, and mackerel. During the Cannery Row era of the '30s, the sardine industry played a vital part in the life of the wharf. Today all that has given way to a bizarre form of public nostalgia.

CANNERY ROW The same visionary who designed Monterey's Fisherman's Wharf appears responsible for the resurrection of Cannery Row. Made famous by John Steinbeck's feisty novels *Cannery Row* and *Sweet Thursday*, this oceanfront strip has been transformed into a neighborhood of wax museums and dainty antique shops. As Steinbeck remarked upon returning to the old sardine canning center, "They fish for tourists now."

Cannery Row of yore was an unappealing collection of corrugated warehouses, dilapidated stores, seedy hotels, and gaudy whorehouses. There were about 30 canneries, 100 fishing boats, and 4000 workers populating the place. The odor was horrible, but for several decades the sardine industry breathed life into the Monterey economy. The business died when the fish ran out just before *Cannery Row* was published in 1945.

Before the entire oceanfront strip was developed in the early 1980s, you could still capture a sense of the old Cannery Row. A few weather-beaten factories remained. Rust stained their ribbed sides, windows were punched, and roofs had settled to an inward curve. In places, the stone pilings of old loading docks still stood, haunted by sea gulls. Now only tourists and memories remain.

BUBBA GUMP SHRIMP CO. ⊠ *720 Cannery Row* ✆ *831-373-1884* ℘ *831-373-0354* ✑ *www.bubbagump.com, dtrombetta@bubbagump.com* One of the modern additions to the historic street is the first Bubba Gump Shrimp Co. in the country, located in the 1916 building that was once the reduction plant for the Monterey Canning Company.

In the middle you'll encounter the scene of the malling of Cannery Row. Old warehouses were renovated into shopping centers, new buildings rose up, and the entire area experienced a face lift.

MONTEREY BAY AQUARIUM ⊠ *Cannery Row and David Avenue* ✆ *831-648-4888, 800-756-3737* ℘ *831-648-4810* ✑ *www.montereybayaquarium.org* The most impressive feature is this aquarium, a state-of-the-art museum that re-creates the natural habitat of local sea life. Monterey Bay features one of the world's biggest submarine canyons, deeper than the Grand Canyon. At the aquarium you'll encounter nearly 200 exhibits and display tanks representing the wealth of underwater life that inhabits this mineral-rich valley. For instance, the Monterey Bay Habitats, a 90-foot-long acrylic enclosure, portrays the local submarine world complete with sharks, schooling fish, and wharf pilings. The Outer Bay Galleries contain, among other delights, a million-gallon tank filled with all kinds of ocean species, including black sea turtles, ocean sunfish, hammerhead sharks, barracuda, and the only tuna in an American aquarium; the Vanishing Wildlife exhibit allows a ground-floor view into the galleries. Another aquarium contains a living kelp forest crowded with fish. Don't forget the hands-on exhibits where you can pet bat rays and touch crabs, starfish, and sea cucumbers. And don't miss the deep-sea video images beamed several times a day live from research vessels in undersea Monterey Canyon, two miles beneath the surface of the bay. Definitely take the kids to the Splash Zone, where hands-on activities and animals like penguins, moray eels, and tropical sharks will keep them entertained for hours. Admission.

LODGING

The problem with lodging on the Monterey Peninsula is the same dilemma plaguing much of the world—money. It takes a lot of it to stay here, especially when visiting one of the area's vaunted bed and breakfasts. These country inns are concentrated in Pacific Grove and Carmel, towns neighboring on Monterey. The town of Monterey features a few such inns as well as a string of moderately priced motels. Budget travelers will do well to check into the latter and also to consult several of the Carmel listings in the book. Monterey's motel row lies along Munras Avenue, a buzzing thoroughfare that leads from downtown to Route 1. Motels are also found along Fremont Street in the adjacent town of Seaside. These are cheaper, drabber, and not as conveniently situated as the Munras hostelries.

RESORT 2 ME LODGING RESERVATIONS
☎831-642-6622, 800-757-5646 📠831-642-6641 ✎www.resort2me.com, info@resort2me.com Since overnight facilities fill rapidly around Monterey, particularly on weekends and during summer, it's wise to reserve in advance. Contact this free reservation agency for the Monterey Peninsula.

DAYS INN MONTEREY
$$–$$$ 35 ROOMS ✉1288 Munras Avenue ☎831-375-2168, 800-329-7466 📠831-375-0368
One standard located five blocks from downtown, the Days Inn features newly remodeled rooms with private baths. Tickets to the Monterey Bay Aquarium can be purchased at the front desk. Complimentary continental breakfast included.

OLD MONTEREY INN
$$$–$$$$ 10 ROOMS ✉500 Martin Street ☎831-375-8284, 800-350-2344 📠831-375-6730 ✎www.oldmontereyinn.com, omi@oldmontereyinn.com
For good cheer and elegance, this inn provides a final word. Glorious rhododendrons and camellias in a lavish garden surround this ten-room Tudor-style bed and breakfast. The house rests on a quiet street yet is located within a few blocks of downtown Monterey. The trimly appointed rooms feature feather beds, tile fireplaces, woodwork, and delicate wallhangings; five have whirlpool spa tubs. There are spacious dining and drawing rooms downstairs and the landscaped grounds are studded with oak and redwood. An elaborate breakfast is included; they'll even serve you in bed. You'll find this friendly little inn a perfect spot for an evening fire and glass of port. Spa services also available.

MERRITT HOUSE INN
$$$$ 25 ROOMS ✉386 Pacific Street ☎831-646-9686, 800-541-5599 📠831-646-5392 ✎www.merritthouseinn.com, merritthouseinn@usa.net
Located in the downtown district, Merritt House is not only an overnight resting place but also a stopping point along Monterey's "Path of History." Part of this lovely inn rests in a vintage 1830 adobe

home. Accommodations in the old house (three lavish suites) and the adjoining modern quarters (22 guest rooms) are furnished with hardwood period pieces and feature vaulted ceilings, fireplaces, and balconies. The garden abounds with magnolia, fig, pepper, and olive trees. Expanded continental breakfast is served.

SPINDRIFT INN

$$$$ 45 ROOMS   ✉*652 Cannery Row*   ☎*831-646-8900,*
800-841-1879 📠*831-646-5342* ✐*www.spindriftinn.com,*
reservations@innsofmonterey.com

Oceanfront on Cannery Row stands the Spindrift Inn, an elegant 45-room hotel. The lobby is fashionably laid out with skylight and sculptures and there is a rooftop solarium overlooking the waterfront. Guest rooms carry out the award-winning architectural motif with bay windows, hardwood floors, woodburning fireplaces, and built-in armoires. Continental breakfast delivered to your room; afternoon wine and cheese reception.

MONTEREY HOSTEL

$ 45 BEDS   ✉*778 Hawthorne Street*   ☎*831-649-0375*
📠*831-649-0375* ✐*www.montereyhostel.org, info@montereyhostel.org*

Three blocks from Cannery Row is this comfortable, family-friendly hostel with both traditional shared dorms and private rooms. There is free wi-fi throughout the building, and spacious common areas allow for community gatherings such as music and movie nights. Farmers' market tours, monthly potluck dinners, and weekend barbecues add to the hostel's charm and elevate it from a simple accommodation to an inviting home away from home. Every morning a do-it-yourself pancake breakfast is available.

MONTEREY FIRESIDE LODGE

$$–$$$ 27 ROOMS   ✉*1131 10th Street*   ☎*831-373-4172, 800-722-2624*
📠*831-655-5640* ✐*www.firesidemonterey.com, info@firesidemonterey.com*

Catering to a mixed gay and straight clientele is this cozy hostelry located just a short walk from downtown. Rooms are bright with country-style flair and feature gas fireplaces and free wi-fi. In addition to comfortable accommodations, they have a jacuzzi and patio. Continental breakfast included.

DINING

STOKES RESTAURANT & BAR

$$–$$$ CALIFORNIA CUISINE/MEDITERRANEAN   ✉*500 Hartnell Street*
☎*831-373-1110* 📠*831-373-1202* ✐*www.stokesrestaurant.com,*
stokes@stokesrestaurant.com

Few restaurants can compete with Stokes for ambience. Housed in an 1833 California adobe with stucco walls, artwork by local

424

artists, and European antiques, this restaurant serves California-Mediterranean cuisine including delicious pizzas and tapas. Featuring flavors from northern Italy, southern France, and Spain and an extensive wine list with French, Italian, Australian, and California vintages. No lunch. Closed the first week of January.

WON JU KOREAN RESTAURANT

$$–$$$ KOREAN   ⊠570 Lighthouse Avenue   ☏831-656-0672

Tasty *kalbi* and *bi bim bap* are among the traditional favorites at Won Ju. You'll find meat dishes as well as seafood and vegetarian options. Dinner comes with a Korean potato pancake, rice, and a wide variety of side dishes such as sesame-flavored spinach and spicy *kim chee* (pickled cabbage).

GIANNI'S PIZZA

$–$$ ITALIAN   ⊠725 Lighthouse Avenue   ☏831-649-1500

Eating at Gianni's is a guaranteed good time. You can feel it when you walk in the door of this casual restaurant. The tables sport red-and-white-checked tablecloths, there are bottles of wine and pictures of Italy on the walls, and on weekends banjo and accordion players serenade diners with lively tunes. You can order fresh pastas, hand-tossed, thick-crusted pizza, or oven-baked sandwiches from various stations, and they are prepared and delivered to your table. There's also a bar and wonderful gelato for dessert. No lunch Monday through Thursday.

ABALONETTI

$$–$$$ SEAFOOD   ⊠57 Fisherman's Wharf   ☏831-373-1851   ☏831-373-2058   ✎www.abalonettimonterey.com

One of Monterey Bay's most abundant seafood products is squid, the inky creature that often turns up on local restaurant menus as the more palatable-sounding calamari. Under any name, the best place to enjoy it is Abalonetti, a casual wharfside restaurant overlooking the bay. The menu presents calamari in an array of guises, including deep-fried, sautéed with wine and garlic, and baked with eggplant. Several more fresh fish specials round out the menu.

PLUMES COFFEE

$ COFFEE/SNACKS   ⊠400 Alvarado Street   ☏831-373-4526   ☏831-655-1621

Enjoy a cuppa java in a coffee shop quite unlike any you've ever visited before. At Plumes Coffee they grind the beans for each cup and brew it individually. So that your own special cup of coffee is not mistakenly served to someone else, you pick up your order under a picture of, say, a waterfall or sunset. Plumes also serves sweet treats from the best bakeries in the area. It's a free wi-fi hotspot, too.

FRESH CREAM

$$$$ CONTINENTAL   ⊠Heritage Harbor, 99 Pacific Street   ☏831-375-9798   ✎www.freshcream.com, dining@freshcream.com

Small and personalized with an understated elegance is the most fitting way to describe this highly recommended restaurant. Its grand-scale dining room features natural woods and atrium sky-lights. One wall is floor-to-ceiling windows that provide a great view of the bay. Service is excellent and the menu, printed daily, numbers among the finest on the Central Coast. On a given night you might choose from filet mignon in Madeira sauce, sautéed veal loin, pan-seared ahi tuna, duckling in black currant sauce, and rack of lamb. That's not even mentioning the appetizers, which are outstanding, or the desserts—such as a Grand Marnier soufflé—which should be outlawed. Food aside, Fresh Cream outdoes itself in wine selection alone. With a 3000-bottle wine cellar, they have won the coveted *Wine Spectator* Award of Excellence for 15 consecutive years. Four stars. Dinner only.

SHOPPING

In Monterey, there are stores throughout the downtown area and malls galore over on **Cannery Row**. Every year another shopping complex seems to rise along the Row. Already the area features cheese and wine stores, clothiers, a fudge factory, and a gourmet supply store. There's also a collector's comic book store, the inevitable T-shirt shop, knickknack stores, and galleries selling artworks that are like Muzak on canvas.

BOOK HAVEN ⊠*559 Tyler Street* ☎*831-333-0383* Stepping into this shop is like discovering a private library filled with antiquarian treasures. Bibliophiles and casual browsers will surely find what they are looking for in the store's collection of new, used, rare, paperback, hardcover, and antique books. Closed Sunday.

NIGHTLIFE

THE HIPPODROME ⊠*321 Alvarado Street* ☎*831-646-9244* ⊘*www.club octane.com* The hippest spot around is The Hippodrome. Entertainment changes nightly, with four different rooms featuring deejays spinning dance tunes plus an outdoor patio and go-go cages. "Upscale" dress code enforced on weekends. Closed Tuesday and Wednesday.

MONTEREY LIVE ⊠*414 Alvarado Street* ☎*831-646-1415* This is a performing arts venue featuring live music from every continent. You can get your groove on to West African harp, Australian folk, or Czech bluegrass.

PACIFIC GROVE

Projecting out from the northern tip of Monterey Peninsula is the diminutive town of Pacific Grove. Covering just 1700 acres, it is reached from Monterey along Lighthouse Avenue. Better yet, pick up Ocean View Boulevard near Cannery Row and follow as it winds along Pacific Grove's surf-washed shores. A quiet town with a lightly developed waterfront, Pacific Grove offers paths that lead for miles along a rock-crusted shore.

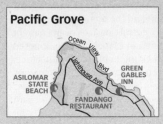

Pacific Grove

ASILOMAR STATE BEACH
PAGE 431

Mile-long sandy beach with snowy dunes located on a marine sanctuary teeming with wildlife

FANDANGO RESTAURANT
PAGE 430

Mediterranean favorites like lamb osso bucco and paella in a five different romantic dining rooms

GREEN GABLES INN
PAGE 429

Impressive Queen Anne bed and breakfast overlooking Monterey Bay with lavishly restored rooms

Costanoan Indians once dove for abalone in these waters. By the 19th century, Pacific Grove had become a religious retreat. Methodist Episcopal ministers pitched a tent city and decreed that "bathing suits shall be provided with double crotches or with skirts of ample size to cover the buttocks." The town was dry until 1969. Given the fish canneries in Monterey and teetotalers in this nearby town, local folks called the area "Carmel-by-the-Sea, Monterey-by-the-Smell, and Pacific Grove-by-God."

SIGHTS

Today Pacific Grove is a sleepy residential area decorated with Victorians, brown-shingle houses, and clapboard ocean cottages.

POINT PINOS LIGHTHOUSE ✉*North of Lighthouse Avenue* ☎*831-648-5716* ⌗*www.pgmuseum.org* The waterfront drive goes past rocky beaches to this lighthouse. When this beacon first flashed in 1855, it burned sperm whale oil. Little has changed except the introduction of electricity; this is the only early lighthouse along the entire California coast to be preserved in its original condition. The U.S. Coast Guard still uses it to guide ships; it is the oldest continually operating lighthouse on the West Coast. Two rooms have been restored to look as they did in Victorian times, and there's a short history of Emily Fish, the woman who ran the lighthouse in the 19th century. The lighthouse is open for self-guided tours. Open afternoons Monday through Thursday. Call for winter hours.

ASILOMAR STATE BEACH Sunset Drive continues along the sea to Asilomar State Beach. Here sand dunes mantled with ice plant front a wave-lashed shore. There are tidepools galore, plus beaches for picnics, and trails leading through the rolling dunes.

MONARCH BUTTERFLIES   Pacific Grove's major claim to fame lies in an area several blocks inland: around George Washington Park on Melrose Street and in a grove at 1073 Lighthouse Avenue. This otherwise unassuming municipality is known as "Butterfly Town, U.S.A." Every mid-October, brilliant orange-and-black monarch butterflies migrate here, remaining until mid-March. Some arrive from several hundred miles away to breed amid the cypress and oak trees. At night they cling to one another, curtaining the branches in clusters that sometimes number over a thousand. Then, at first light, they come to life, fluttering around the groves in a frenzy of wings and color.

PACIFIC GROVE MUSEUM OF NATURAL HISTORY   ⊠*Central and Forest avenues*   ✆*831-648-5716*   ✎*831-372-3256*   ✐*www.pgmuseum.org, pg museum@mbay.net*   This is an excellent small museum with exhibits on native animals and early peoples, and a touch gallery for kids. Closed Sunday and Monday.

JOHN STEINBECK COTTAGE   ⊠*147 11th Street*   This ivy-cloaked cottage is where John Steinbeck lived and wrote *In Dubious Battle* and *Of Mice and Men*. Unfortunately, it's not open to the public.

GOSBY HOUSE INN   ⊠*643 Lighthouse Avenue*   This century-old Victorian mansion, now an inn, is decorated in period antiques.

HART MANSION   ⊠*649 Lighthouse Avenue*   Next door to the Gosby House Inn is this mansion (now a full-service restaurant), another elaborate old Victorian house.

17 MILE DRIVE   From Pacific Grove, 17 Mile Drive leads to **Pebble Beach**, one of America's most lavish communities. This place is so exclusive that the rich charge a fee to anyone wishing to drive around admiring their homes. No wonder they're rich.

Galling as the gate fee might be, this is an extraordinary region that must not be missed. The road winds through pine groves down to a wind-combed beach. There are miles of rolling dunes tufted with sea vegetation. (The oceanfront can be as cool and damp as it is beautiful, so carry a sweater or jacket, or better yet, both.)

SPANISH BAY   Among the first spots you'll encounter is this bay where Juan Gaspar de Portolá camped during his 1769 expedition up the California coast. (The picnic area here is a choice place to spread a feast.) At **Point Joe**, converging ocean currents create a wild frothing sea that has drawn several ships to their doom.

SEAL ROCK AND BIRD ROCK   True to their nomenclature, these boulders are carpeted with sea lions, harbor and leopard seals, cormorants, brown pelicans, and gulls. Throughout this thriving 17 Mile Drive area are black-tail deer, sooty shearwaters, sea otters, and, during migration periods, California gray whales.

LONE CYPRESS   There are crescent beaches and granite headlands as well as vista points for scanning the coast. You'll also pass the Lone Cypress, the solitary tree on a rocky point that has become as symbolic of Northern California as perhaps the Golden Gate Bridge.

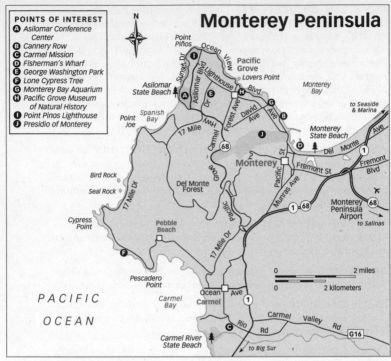

POINTS OF INTEREST
- Ⓐ *Asilomar Conference Center*
- Ⓑ *Cannery Row*
- Ⓒ *Carmel Mission*
- Ⓓ *Fisherman's Wharf*
- Ⓔ *George Washington Park*
- Ⓕ *Lone Cypress Tree*
- Ⓖ *Monterey Bay Aquarium*
- Ⓗ *Pacific Grove Museum of Natural History*
- Ⓘ *Point Pinos Lighthouse*
- Ⓙ *Presidio of Monterey*

Monterey Peninsula

PRIVATE HOMES The private homes en route are mansions, exquisite affairs fashioned from marble and fine hardwoods. Some appear like stone fortresses, others seem made solely of glass. They range from American Colonial to futuristic and were designed by noted architects like Bernard Maybeck, Julia Morgan, and Willis Polk.

GOLF COURSES This is also home to several of the world's most renowned golf courses—Pebble Beach, Spyglass Hill, and Poppy Hills—where the AT&T National Pro-Am Championship takes place each year. The ever-famous Cypress Point golf course is also nearby. More than the designer homes and their celebrity residents, these courses have made Pebble Beach a place fabled for wealth and beauty.

HUCKLEBERRY HILL The best part of the drive lies along the coast between the Pacific Grove and Carmel gates. Along the backside of 17 Mile Drive, where it loops up into Del Monte Forest, there are marvelous views of Monterey Bay and the San Gabilan Mountains. Here also is Huckleberry Hill, a forest of Monterey and Bishop pine freckled with bushes.

LODGING

ASILOMAR CONFERENCE CENTER

$$–$$$ 313 ROOMS   ✉ *800 Asilomar Boulevard*   ☎ *831-372-8016, 866-654-2878*
📠 *831-372-7227* 🖥 *www.visitasilomar.com, asilomarsales@dncinc.com*

Asilomar provides one of the area's best housing arrangements. Set in a state beach, it's surrounded by more than 100 acres of sand dunes and pine forests. The beach is a stroll away from any of the center's over three hundred rooms divided among 30 hotel lodges. There's a dining hall on the premises, as well as meeting rooms and recreational facilities (pool and volleyball court). Breakfast is included in the price. Catering primarily to groups, Asilomar does provide accommodations (depending on availability) for independent travelers. "Historic" rooms in the "rustic buildings" are small and spartan but adequate (*and* designed by Julia Morgan). They lack carpeting on the hardwood floors and include little decoration. The "standard" rooms are nicely appointed with wallhangings, study desks, and comfortable furnishings. Fireplaces are also available in some rooms, and every lodge includes a spacious lounge area with stone fireplace. In keeping with the restful atmosphere, the rooms have neither telephones nor televisions. No doubt about it, Asilomar is a splendid place at a relaxing price.

GOSBY HOUSE INN

$$$ 22 ROOMS   ✉643 Lighthouse Avenue   ✆831-375-1287, 800-527-8828
📠831-655-9621   🖰www.foursisters.com, gosbyhouseinn@foursisters.com

One of Monterey Peninsula's less expensive B&Bs, this century-old Victorian mansion offers over twenty refurbished rooms. Each is different, and all have been decorated with special attention to detail. In any one you are liable to discover an antique armoire, brass lighting fixtures, stained glass, or a Tiffany lamp. The two rooms in the carriage house have jacuzzi tubs. They are all small after the Victorian fashion, which sacrifices space for coziness. The full breakfast, afternoon wine and hors d'oeuvres, and nightly turn-down service add to the homey feeling.

GREEN GABLES INN

$$–$$$$ 11 ROOMS   ✉301 Ocean View Boulevard   ✆831-375-2095,
800-722-1774   📠831-375-5437   🖰www.foursisters.com,
greengablesinn@foursisters.com

This inn represents one of the region's most impressive bed and breakfasts. The house, a Queen Anne–style Victorian, dates from 1888. Adorned with step-gables, stained glass, and bay windows, it rests in a storybook setting overlooking Monterey Bay. Five bedrooms upstairs and a suite below have been fastidiously decorated with lavish antiques. Three of these share a bathroom, but offer the best ocean views. Set in a town filled with old Victorian homes, this oceanside residence is an ideal representation of Pacific Grove. There are also five separate units in a building adjacent to the main house. These are suites with private bath and fireplace. All rooms have king or queen beds; full breakfast, afternoon wine and cheese, yummy home-baked cookies, and access to the main house are included.

MARTINE INN

$$$–$$$$ 25 ROOMS   ✉ *255 Ocean View Boulevard* ☎ *831-373-3388,*
800-852-5588 📠 *831-373-3896* ⌕ *www.martineinn.com,*
don@martineinn.com

Commanding a front and center view of the spectacular waterfront is this pastel stucco Mediterranean-style villa with individually decorated rooms and one family suite, many with wood-burning fireplaces. Among the accommodations is the Edith Head Room, which has 1920s furnishings from the Hollywood costume designer's estate. A full sit-down breakfast and afternoon wine and hors d'oeuvres are included. There's a hot tub on-site, along with an antique game room and 1000-plus book library. There is a two-night minimum stay on high-season weekends.

DINING

FANDANGO RESTAURANT

$$$ MEDITERRANEAN/CONTINENTAL   ✉ *223 17th Street*
☎ *831-372-3456* 📠 *831-372-2673* ⌕ *www.fandangorestaurant.com*

Take a little stroll into town to Fandango and ask for the Cellar or Alcove rooms for the most romantic seating. Exquisitely prepared entrées such as abalone, paella, and rack of lamb, and an extensive wine list make this is a highly recommended dining destination. Reservations strongly suggested .

RED HOUSE CAFÉ

$$ CONTINENTAL   ✉ *662 Lighthouse Avenue* ☎ *831-643-1060*
⌕ *www.redhousecafe.com, info@redhousecafe.com*

The quaint, shingled Red House is a cozy place to join the locals for breakfast, lunch, or dinner. Morning brings Belgian waffles, frittatas, and croissant sandwiches, while the later meals feature oven-roasted chicken sandwiches and warm eggplant with fontina cheese. Breakfast on weekends only. Closed Monday.

PEPPERS MEXICALI CAFE

$–$$ MEXICAN/CENTRAL AMERICAN   ✉ *170 Forest Avenue* ☎ *831-373-6892*
📠 *831-373-5467* ⌕ *www.peppersmexicalicafe.com*

Peppers pays homage to the red chile and has attracted an incredible number of devotees, evident from the sometimes lengthy wait for a table. Chile posters and pepper prints by local artists decorate the walls, and the food focuses on Mexican and Central American seafood. Among the offerings are grilled prawns with fresh lime and cilantro dressing, grilled seafood tacos, MahiMahi Yucatan, and snapper Veracruz, as well as excellent versions of more mundane dishes such as tacos, burritos, and enchiladas. A full bar offers blue agave tequilas for some of the best margaritas in town. No lunch on Sunday. Closed Tuesday.

The main area for window browsing in town can be found along Lighthouse Avenue. Just above this busy thoroughfare, on 17th Street, artisans have renovated a row of small beach cottages. In each is a creatively named shop.

REINCARNATION VINTAGE CLOTHING ⊠214 17th Street ☎831-649-0689 This place sells vintage and vintage-inspired contemporary clothing, jewelry, and accessories. Closed Sunday.

MUM'S PLACE ⊠246 Forest Avenue ☎831-372-6250 ⏴www.mumsfurniture.com At Mum's, there's high-quality oak, maple, cherry, and pine furniture.

AMERICAN TIN CANNERY OUTLETS ⊠125 Ocean View Boulevard ☎831-372-1442 ☎831-372-5707 ⏴www.americantincannery.com From designer fashions to gourmet cookware, the shops here are a shopper's paradise. A good place to look for luggage, books, shoes, housewares, and linens, this renovated two-story complex has a variety of outlet stores. If you're looking for bargains in the Monterey area, don't miss this gem.

NIGHTLIFE

TERRACE LOUNGE ⊠1700 17-Mile Drive, Pebble Beach ☎831-647-7500, 831-625-8524 This lounge at Pebble Beach Resort is a thoroughly elegant, clubby place where pianists and small jazz groups play each night. The service is superb, and the view overlooking the 18th green of the Pebble Beach golf course is well worth the drive and the dressing up—be sure to wear a jacket.

BEACHES & PARKS

ASILOMAR STATE BEACH

⊠Located along Sunset Drive in Pacific Grove ☎831-646-6440 (ranger office) ☎831-372-3759 ⏴www.visitasilomar.com

🎣 🚶 🚴 ⛵ This oceanfront facility features over 100 acres of pine forest, snowy white sand dunes, tidepools, and beach. It's a perfect place for daytripping and exploring. The best surfing here is just off the main sandy beach. Since northern and southern currents run together here, the waters are teeming with marine life. Swimming is not recommended. The conference grounds feature historic buildings and enchanting grounds (overnight accommodations are described in "Lodging" above).

CARMEL

The first law of real estate should be this: The best land is always occupied by the military, bohemians, or the rich. Think about it. The principle holds for many of the world's prettiest spots. Generally the military arrives first, on an exploratory mission or as an occupying force. It takes strategic ground, which happens to be the beaches, headlands, and mountaintops. The bohemians select beautiful locales because they possess good taste. When the rich discover where the artists have settled, they start moving in, driving up the rents, and forcing the displaced bohemians to discover new homes, which will then be taken by another wave of the wealthy.

The Monterey Peninsula is no exception. In Carmel the military established an early beachhead when Spanish soldiers occupied a barracks in the old Catholic mission. Later the bohemians arrived in numbers. Poet George Sterling came in 1905, followed by Mary Austin, the novelist. Eventually such luminaries as Upton Sinclair, Lincoln Steffens, and Sinclair Lewis, writers all, settled for varying periods. Jack London and Ambrose Bierce visited. Later, photographers Ansel Adams and Edward Weston relocated here.

The figure most closely associated with this "seacoast of Bohemia" was Robinson Jeffers, a poet who came seeking solitude in 1914. Quarrying rock from the shoreline, he built the Tor House and Hawk Tower, where he lived and wrote haunting poems and epics about the coast.

Then, like death and tax collectors, the rich inevitably moved in. As John Steinbeck noted when he later returned to this artists' colony, "If Carmel's founders should return, they could not afford to live there. . . . They would instantly be picked up as suspicious characters and deported over the city line."

It's doubtful many would want to remain anyway. Today Carmel is so cute it cloys. The tiny town is cluttered with over four dozen inns, about six dozen restaurants, and more than 300 shops. Ocean Avenue, the main street, is wall-to-wall with merchants. Shopping malls have replaced artists' garrets, and there are traffic jams where there was once solitude.

SIGHTS

TUCK BOX   Typifying the town is the Tuck Box, a gingerbread-style building on Dolores Street between Ocean and 7th avenues (there are no street numbers in Carmel), or the fairy tale–like **Hansel-and-Gretel cottages** on Torres Street between 5th and 6th avenues.

Still, reasons remain to visit Carmel, which is reached from Monterey via Route 1 or from the Carmel gate along 17 Mile Drive. The window shopping is good and several galleries are outstanding. Some of the town's quaint characteristics have appeal. There are no traffic lights or parking meters, and at night few street lights. Drive around the side streets and you will encounter an architectural mixture of log cabins, adobe structures, board-and-batten cottages, and Spanish villas.

MISSION TRAILS PARK _____
A secret that local residents have long withheld from visitors is this park. No signs will direct you here, so watch for an entrance at the corner of Mountain View and Crespi avenues. Within this

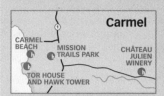

Carmel

CARMEL BEACH

MISSION TRAILS PARK

CHÂTEAU JULIEN WINERY

TOR HOUSE AND HAWK TOWER

CARMEL BEACH

PAGE 433

Sandy beach with views of the surrounding countryside and excellent birdwatching along the river

MISSION TRAILS PARK

PAGE 432

Quiet sanctuary with hiking trails through redwood and Monterey pine groves and wildflower meadows

TOR HOUSE AND HAWK TOWER

PAGE 433

American poet Robinson Jeffers' hand-crafted stone home—his 1920s writing haven

CHÂTEAU JULIEN WINERY

PAGE 435

Wine tastings at a French mansion with an 18-foot-long mahogany table

forest preserve are miles of hiking trails. They wind across footbridges, through redwood groves, and past meadows of wildflowers en route to Carmel Mission. There are ocean vistas, deer grazing the hillsides, and an arboretum seeded with native California plants.

CARMEL BEACH

Carmel's most alluring feature is the one that early drew the bohemians—the Pacific. At the foot of Ocean Avenue rests this beach, a snowy strand shadowed by cypress trees. From here, Scenic Road hugs the coast, winding above rocky outcroppings.

TOR HOUSE AND HAWK TOWER

✉26304 Ocean View Avenue; for information and reservations, call 831-624-1813 ✆831-624-3696 ✐www.torhouse.org, thf@torhouse.org Just before the intersection with Stewart Way, gaze uphill toward those two stone edifices. Poet Robinson Jeffers' Tor House and Hawk Tower seem drawn from another place and time, perhaps a Scottish headland in the 19th century. In fact, the poet modeled the house after an English-style barn and built the 40-foot-high garret with thick stone walls in the fashion of an Irish tower. Completed during the 1920s, the structures are granite and include porthole windows that Jeffers salvaged from a shipwreck. One-hour tours of the house and tower are conducted on Friday and Saturday by reservation. No children under 12 years allowed. Admission.

CARMEL RIVER STATE BEACH   Just beyond the Tor House and Hawk Tower stretches this state beach, a sandy corridor at the foot of Carmel Bay. For additional information, see the "Beaches & Parks" section below.

CARMEL MISSION BASILICA   ✉*Located on Rio Road just off Route 1* ☎*831-624-1271* Even for the non-religious, a visit to Carmel Mission Basilica becomes a pilgrimage. If the holiness holds no appeal, there's the aesthetic sense of the place. Dating back to 1770, its Old World beauty captivates and confounds. The courtyards are alive with flowers and birds. The adobe buildings have been dusted with time—their eaves are hunchbacked, the tile roofs coated in moss. Visitors can pick up brochures for self-guided tours. Docents do lead tours most days; check for availability. Admission.

Established by Father Junípero Serra, this mission is one of California's most remarkable. The basilica is a vaulted-ceiling affair adorned with old oil paintings and wooden statues of Christ; its walls are lime plaster made from burnt seashells. The exterior is topped with a Moorish tower and 11 bells.

Junípero Serra lies buried in the sanctuary, his grave marked with a stone plaque. There are also museum rooms demonstrating early California life—a kitchen with stone hearth and rudimentary tools, the state's first library (complete with waterstained bibles), and the cell where Father Serra died, its bed a slab of wood with a single blanket and no mattress. Close by, in the cemetery beside the basilica, several thousand American Indians are also buried.

POINT LOBOS STATE RESERVE

Just two miles south of Carmel lies this incomparable natural area of rocky headlands and placid coves. The park features hillside crow's nests from which to gaze out along Carmel Bay. Before Westerners arrived, the American Indians gathered mussels and abalone here. Later Point Lobos was a whaling station and an abalone cannery. Today it's a park intended primarily for nature hikers. You can explore pine forests and cypress groves, a jagged shoreline of granite promontories, and wave-lapped coves. Every tidepool is a miniature aquarium pulsing with color and sea life. The water is clear as sky. Offshore rise sea stacks, their rocky bases ringed with mussels, their domes crowned by sea birds. This region, also rich in wildlife and underwater life, should not be bypassed; for complete information, see the "Beaches & Parks" section below.

CARMEL VALLEY   As if its shoreline was not enough, Carmel also boasts an extraordinary interior. Carmel Valley Road leads from Route 1 into the distant hills, paralleling the Carmel River in its circuitous course. The lower end of the Carmel Valley promises fruit orchards and

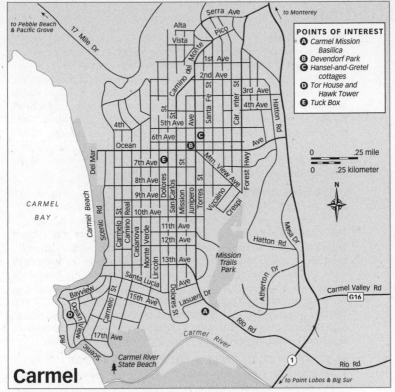

Carmel

fields of grazing horses before the road ascends into the wooded heights that separate Carmel from the farmlands of Salinas.

CHÂTEAU JULIEN WINERY

✉ *8940 Carmel Valley Road, five miles from Route 1* ☎ *831-624-2600* ✑ *www. chateaujulien.com* Set on 16 acres in the Carmel Valley, this grand estate produces ten high-quality varietals, including their crown jewel, merlot. Daily tastings are held within the winery's French-Swedish mansion at an 18-foot mahogany tasting table. Visitors may stroll the grounds, which include a garden terrace and picnic area. Fee.

GARLAND RANCH REGIONAL PARK

✉ *700 West Carmel Valley Road, nine miles from Route 1* ☎ *831-659-4488* ✑ *www.mprpd.org, info@mprpd.org* You may want to follow the trails that lead from the visitors center near the Carmel River through woodlands and meadows to **Snively's Ridge**, a 2000-foot peak in this 3700-acre regional park. Pick up a map at the visitors center for information about hiking and horseback riding.

LODGING

THE PINE INN

$$$–$$$$ 49 ROOMS   ✉Ocean Avenue between Lincoln and Monte Verde streets
📞831-624-3851, 800-228-3851   📠831-624-3030   🖱www.pineinn.com

This hotel, Carmel's oldest, dates back to 1889 and still possesses the charm that has drawn visitors for decades. The lobby is a fashionable affair with black lacquered furniture, dark, warm woods, and a brick fireplace. The less expensive accommodations are smaller but do have canopied beds, private baths, TVs, and phones common to all the rooms. Each room has touches of both Europe and the Far East. Rather than a country inn, this is a full-service hotel with restaurant and bar downstairs as well as room service for the guests.

L'AUBERGE CARMEL

$$$$ 20 ROOMS   ✉Monte Verde Street and 7th Avenue   📞831-624-8578
📠831-626-1018   🖱www.laubergecarmel.com, reservations@laubergecarmel.com

This classic French villa combines top-of-the-line luxury with elegant European style. Each guest room is richly appointed with burgundies, royal blues, and golds, from the floor-length drapes to the warmly lit table lamps. Contemporary amenities complement the old-world charm with flatscreen TVs and CD players; some rooms feature spacious soaking tubs and cozy floor heating. For an extra posh stay, you can take advantage of their in-room massage and spa services, including Shiatsu and essential oil rubs. This full-service hotel also boasts two signature restaurants and is just four easy blocks from the beach.

BEST WESTERN CARMEL'S TOWN HOUSE LODGE

$ 28 ROOMS   ✉5th and San Carlos streets   📞831-624-1261, 866-427-7482
📠831-625-6783   🖱www.bestwestern.com

It's a bare-bones motel, but convenient to the center of town, very clean, and certainly affordable. The rooms are large, with refrigerators, cable TV and free high-speed internet. An outdoor heated pool, sun deck with a fireplace, continental breakfast, and free parking make it a good choice for families on a budget, who may also want to book one of the two-bedroom accommodations.

COMFORT INN CARMEL BY THE SEA

$ 19 ROOMS   ✉Ocean Avenue and Torres Street   📞831-622-7090   📠831-622-7044
🖱www.comfortinn.com

A restored mansion that has a lovely garden setting a few blocks from downtown, this place offers rooms that are small but tastefully furnished and well-kept. Units have coffee makers, refrigerators, and cable TV. There's free wi-fi and a continental breakfast in the dining room, which features a large stone fireplace.

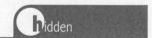

MISSION RANCH

$$–$$$$ 31 ROOMS   ✉26270 Dolores Street   📞831-624-6436,
800-538-8221   📠831-626-4163   🖱www.missionranchcarmel.com

Carmel's most closely kept secret is this hideaway resort set on 22 acres and overlooking the ocean at a distance. Scattered about the tree-shaded grounds at the Mission Ranch are triplex cottages and a quadraplex unit, 31 rooms in all, in addition to the older white clapboard farmhouse. There are tennis courts, trim lawns, and ancient cypress trees. With mountains in the background, the views extend across a broad lagoon and out along sandy beach-front. The ranch dining room is favored by local people, and the whole ranch was once owned by Clint Eastwood. A rare find indeed with continental breakfast included. On-site restaurant.

CARMEL RIVER INN

$$$–$$$$ 43 ROOMS   ✉ *Route 1 at Carmel River Bridge* ✆ *831-624-1575,*
800-882-8142 ✆ *831-624-0290* ✑ *www.carmelriverinn.com, info@carmelriverinn.com*
Located on the southern outskirts of town, this establishment has both a motel and woodframe cottages (the latter have greater appeal). The less expensive guest units are studio-size structures with wall-to-wall carpeting, televisions, refrigerators, and telephones; their interior designer was obviously a capable, if uninspired, individual. The pricier cottages vary in size and facilities, but all have DVD players, while some may contain extra rooms, a fireplace, or a kitchen. There's a heated pool and several patios.

HIGHLANDS INN, PARK HYATT CARMEL

$$$$ 48 ROOMS   ✉ *Route 1 about four miles south of Carmel* ✆ *831-620-1234,*
800-682-4811 ✆ *831-626-1574* ✑ *www.highlandsinn.hyatt.com*
Highlands Inn is one of those raw-wood-and-polished-stone places that evoke the muted elegance of the California coast. Ultramodern in execution, it features a stone lodge surrounded by wood-shingle buildings. The lodge houses two restaurants and an oceanview lounge while the neighboring structures contain the cozy guest rooms, each a warren of blond woods. Most have patios or balconies, and wood-burning fireplaces; several have double spa tubs. Parked on a hillside overlooking an awesome sweep of ocean, the inn is the ultimate in Carmel chic.

DINING

TUCK BOX

$–$$ AMERICAN   ✉ *Dolores Street between Ocean and 7th avenues*
✆ *831-624-6365* ✆ *831-626-3939* ✑ *www.tuckbox.com*
In Carmel, the thing to do is drop by the Tuck Box for afternoon tea. The establishment sits in a dollhouselike creation with a swirl roof and curved chimney. The prim and tiny dining room also serves breakfast and lunch. During the noon meal there are omelettes, sandwiches, shrimp salad, and Welsh rarebit. Tea includes scones, muffins, or home-made pie. Jams and scone mix are available for purchase. No dinner.

BAHAMA BILLY'S ISLAND STEAKHOUSE

$$–$$$ SEAFOOD/CARIBBEAN   ✉ *Barnyard Shopping Center, 3690 The Barnyard*
✆ *831-626-0430* ✑ *www.bahamabillys.com, manager@bahamabillys.com*
Crispy coconut prawns, crab mango bisque, and macadamia nut–crusted halibut are just a few of the reasons this upbeat local favorite recommends reservations. Though the menu concentrates on

Caribbean-style seafood, you'll also find a selection of prime steaks and several vegetarian options. The upscale tropical ambiance is complemented by a heated patio, full bar, and frequent live music in the bar.

TUTTO MONDO TRATTORIA

$$–$$$ ITALIAN   ✉*Dolores Street between Ocean and 7th avenues*   📞*831-624-8977*
📠*831-624-4102*   🖱*www.mondos.com, info@mondos.com*

Join the line in front of Tutto Mondo for good times and a great meal. As you step through the door you might think you're in Italy: Wine bottles, cooking utensils, and strings of garlic adorn the walls, and the staff is very friendly, often breaking into song for impromptu celebrations. If that isn't enough, the food is *molto delizioso*. You can't go wrong with a fresh pasta dish such as the San Remo (sun-dried tomatoes and goat cheese in cream sauce) or *la mafiosa* (calamari, prawns, and scallops in a spicy tomato sauce). Dinner specials include veal, seafood, fish, and chicken entrées, and at lunch sandwiches are added to the menu. Save room for the desserts, especially the tiramisu! You can also take home some of their housemade olive oil.

RIO GRILL

$$–$$$ SOUTHWESTERN   ✉*Crossroads Shopping Center, Route 1 and Rio Road*
📞*831-625-5436*   📠*831-625-2950*   🖱*www.riogrill.com, chris@riogrill.com*

Reasonably priced, casual, and contemporary. Who could ask for more than what they're offering at the critically acclaimed Rio Grill? The cuisine at this popular dining room is American grill with a Southwestern touch. Smoked chicken and artichokes and baby-back ribs with cayenne-sprinkled yam cakes are among the entrées. Sunday brunch available.

PATISSERIE BOISSIÈRE

$$ FRENCH   ✉*Mission Street between Ocean and 7th avenues*
📞*831-624-5008*   📠*831-626-9155*   🖱*www.patisserieboissiere.com*

This eatery belongs to that endangered species—the moderately priced French restaurant. The simple French country dining room adjoins a small bakery. In addition to outrageous pastries for breakfast, they offer brunch on the weekend. Entrées include coquilles St. Jacques, salmon in parchment paper, and braised lamb shank. Baked brie and French onion soup are also on the bill of fare. A bargain-hunter's delight in dear Carmel. No dinner on Monday and Tuesday.

THE RESTAURANT AT MISSION RANCH

$$–$$$$ AMERICAN   ✉*26270 Dolores Street*   📞*831-625-9040, 800-538-8221*
📠*831-625-5502*   🖱*www.missionranchcarmel.com*

Old-time Carmel residents will tell you about this restaurant, how it dates back over a century to the days when it was a creamery. Today it's just a warm, homey old building with a stone fireplace plus a view of a sheep pasture and the neighboring ocean (an outdoor patio is also available). The menu is a combo of fresh seafood and all-American fare: steak, prime rib, chicken, and pasta. Dinner served nightly along with entertainment from the Piano Bar, as well as Sunday jazz champagne brunch.

THE COVEY AT QUAIL LODGE

$$$–$$$$ CALIFORNIA CUISINE/MEDITERRANEAN   ⊠ *8205 Valley Greens Drive*   ☎ *831-620-8860, 888-828-8787*   ⊘ *www.quaillodge.com*

Of course, the ultimate dining place is The Covey at Quail Lodge in Carmel Valley. Set in one of the region's most prestigious hotels, The Covey is a contemporary European restaurant with a California influence, serving, for example, Alaskan king salmon with chanterelle and black truffle jus, and dungeness crab salad with blood orange and roasted hearts of palm. There's also an hour-long tapas serving and a changing, three-course *prix fixe* dinner menu available. Richly decorated, the restaurant overlooks the lodge's lake and grounds. Reservations, please. Breakfast and dinner. Closed Sunday and Monday.

SHOPPING

In Carmel, shopping seems to be the raison d'être. If ever an entire town was dressed to look like a boutique, this is the one. Its shops are stylish and expensive. The major shopping strip is located along Ocean Avenue between Mission and Monte Verde streets, but the best stores generally are situated on the side streets.

DOUD ARCADE   ⊠ *Ocean Avenue between San Carlos and Dolores streets*   This mall features artisan shops. You'll find leather merchants, potters, and jewelers.

Most of the artists who made Carmel famous have long since departed, but the city still maintains a wealth of art galleries. While many are not even worth browsing, others are outstanding.

CARMEL BAY COMPANY   ⊠ *Lincoln Street and Ocean Avenue*   ☎ *831-624-3868*   This company features unique home furnishings, as well as art and crafts by local artisans, potters, and woodworkers.

CARMEL ART ASSOCIATION GALLERY   ⊠ *Dolores Street between 5th and 6th avenues*   ☎ *831-624-6176*   ⊘ *www.carmelart.org*   This gallery is owned and operated by artists and offers paintings and sculpture by over 80 local figures.

CHAPMAN GALLERY   ⊠ *7th Avenue between Mission and San Carlos streets*   ☎ *831-626-1766*   ⊘ *www.chapmangallery.com*   The Chapman features works by local artists and doubles as a bookstore. They also offer professional framing services. Closed Sunday and Monday, except by appointment.

Carmel is recognized as an international center for photographers. Two of the nation's most famous—Ansel Adams and Edward Weston—lived here.

THE WESTON GALLERY   ⊠ *6th Avenue between Dolores and Lincoln streets*   ☎ *831-624-4453*   ⊘ *www.westongallery.com*   The Weston displays photos by both men, as well as works by other 19th- and 20th-century photographers.

PHOTOGRAPHY WEST GALLERY ✉*Dolores Street between Ocean and 7th avenues* ☎*831-625-1587* At Photography West, Weston and Adams are represented, as are Imogen Cunningham, Brett Weston, and Christopher Burkett. Closed Tuesday and Wednesday in January and sometimes in June.

THE PILGRIM'S WAY ✉*On Dolores Street between 5th and 6th streets* ☎*800-549-9922* ☎*831-624-4955* ⬦*www.pilgrimsway.com* Carmel, Big Sur, and the Central Coast are the home of a potpourri of metaphysical movements, so it's fitting that one of the coast's best bookstores, The Pilgrim's Way, is here. From animal health to Wicca, there are books and gifts for every category.

THE BARNYARD SHOPPING VILLAGE ✉*Route 1 and Carmel Valley Road* ☎*831-624-8886* ⬦*www.thebarnyard.com* This shopping village is an innovative mall housing about 50 shops and restaurants. Set amid flowering gardens is a series of raw wood structures reminiscent of old farm buildings. For the man with impeccable taste, visit **J. Lawrence Khaki's Men's Clothier** (831-625-8106, 800-664-8106). **Mountain and Sea Gallery** (831-626-7788) captures the area's rugged beauty in photographs.

NIGHTLIFE

THE FORGE IN THE FOREST ✉*Junipero Street and 5th Avenue* ☎*831-624-2233* The Forge is a restaurant-cum-bar with its copper walls, handcarved bar, and open fire. It's a classy spot for a cocktail.

THE RESTAURANT AT MISSION RANCH ✉*26270 Dolores Street* ☎*831-624-6436* ⬦*www.missonranchcarmel.com* The piano man at this piano bar plays standards until 11 nightly. It's one of the very few places in Carmel that stays open past 9, so it's a good bet for a relaxing after-dinner drink and romantic mood music. Views include an incredible, unobstructed look at Carmel River Lagoon and beach and occasional sightings of owner Clint Eastwood at the piano.

LOBOS LOUNGE ✉*Highlands Inn, Route 1, about four miles south of Carmel* ☎*831-620-1234* ☎*831-626-1574* ⬦*www.highlandsinn.hyatt.com* Possibly the prettiest place you'll ever indulge the spirits in is this lounge. An entire wall of this leather-armchair-and-marble-table establishment is plate glass. And the picture on the other side of those panes is classic Carmel—rocky shoreline fringed with cypress trees and lashed by passionate waves. If that's not entertainment enough, there's jazz on Friday and Saturday nights.

BEACHES & PARKS

CARMEL RIVER STATE BEACH
✉*Located at the end of Carmelo Road in Carmel (take Rio Road exit off Route 1)* ☎*831-624-2836* ☎*831-624-9265*

🚶 This beach would be more attractive were it not upstaged by Point Lobos, its remarkable neighbor to the south. Nevertheless, there's a sandy beach here as well as a view of the surrounding hills. The chief feature is the bird refuge along the river. The marshes offer willets, sandpipers, pelicans, hawks, and kingfishers, plus an occasional Canadian snow goose (and lots of gulls). The beach has restrooms.

POINT LOBOS STATE RESERVE

✉ Route 1, about three miles south of Carmel 📞 831-624-4909

🖥 www.pt-lobos.parks.state.ca.us, pointlobos@parks.ca.gov

🚶 🚲 🛶 ⚓ In a region packed with uncommonly beautiful scenery, this park stands out as something special. A 1225-acre reserve, only 456 acres of which are above water, it contains over 300 species of plants and more than 250 species of animals and birds. This is a perfect place to study sea otters, harbor seals, and sea lions. During migrating season in mid-winter and mid-spring, gray whales cruise the coast. Along with Pebble Beach, Point Lobos is the only spot in the world where Monterey cypresses, those ghostly, wind-gnarled coastal trees, still survive in the wild. There are 80-foot-high kelp forests offshore, popular with scuba divers who know the reserve as one of the most fascinating places on the coast. Reservations to dive are necessary and can be made up to two months in advance by phone or e-mail. There are picnic areas and restrooms. Dogs aren't allowed. Parking fee, $10.

PINNACLES
NATIONAL MONUMENT

hidden

✉ No road traverses the park. You must enter either on the east side by following Route 25 south from Hollister for 32 miles, then proceeding four miles west on Route 146; or on the west side along Route 146, about 13 miles east from Soledad (which is just off Route 101) 📞 831-389-4485 📠 831-389-4489

🖥 www.nps.gov/pinn, pinn_visitor_information@nps.gov

🚶 Set far inland amid the softly rolling Gabilan Mountains are the sharp, dramatic volcanic peaks that centerpiece this unusual park. Sheer spires and solitary minarets vault 1200 feet from the canyon floor. Comprising the weathered remains of a 23 million-year-old volcano, these towering peaks challenge day hikers and technical rock climbers alike. Rockclimbing is a major activity here in spring and fall (it's too hot in summer). There are caves to explore, and more than 30 miles of trails leading through the remnants of the volcano. Prairie falcons, coyote, gray fox, and bobcat roam the region, while golden eagles work the skies above. Since the cliffs are accessible only by trail, visitors should be prepared to hike. Bring water, durable shoes, loose clothing, and a flashlight for cave exploring. (Caves are subject to seasonal closures due to flooding and "bat protection.") The best time to visit is spring, when the wildflowers bloom, or autumn; summer brings stifling heat to the area and winter carries rain. The east side of the park has an information center, picnic areas, and restrooms. The west side offers a ranger station, picnic areas, and restrooms. There are limited concession services on the east side of the park. Day-use fee, $5. The lengthy drive to the east entrance makes for a long day trip. If you plan to hike, start early in the day.

⚑ Pinnacles Campground (www.pinncamp.com), a facility with more than 139 sites (some with partial RV hookups), sits inside the park's east side. Hot showers, a pool, and campground activities are perks. Fees range from $23 for tent sites, $36 for RV sites; group sites start at $75. A small grocery store with limited hours is also on-site.

BIG SUR

From Point Lobos, the highway hugs the coastline as it snakes south toward Big Sur. Like Route 1 north of San Francisco, this is one of America's great stretches of roadway. Situated between the Santa Lucia Mountains and the Pacific, Route 1 courses about 30 miles from Carmel to Big Sur, then spirals farther south along the coast toward San Luis Obispo and Los Angeles.

The Big Sur district is where the Santa Lucia Mountains encounter the Pacific. Backed by the challenging Ventana Wilderness, the region is marked by sharp coastal cliffs and unbelievable scenery. Though it's hard to conceive, Big Sur may be even more beautiful than the other sections of the Central Coast.

Along Route 1, each turnout provides another glimpse into a magic-lantern world. Here the glass pictures a beach crusted with rocks, there a wave-wracked cliff or pocket of tidepools. The canyons are narrow and precipitous, while the headlands are so close to the surf they seem like beached whales. Trees are broken and blasted before the wind. The houses, though millionaire affairs, appear inconsequential against the backdrop of ocean and stone. In summer 2008, a massive forest fire swept through Big Sur, destroying over 150,000 acres. A heroic effort by firefighters finally quelched the fire after it burned for nearly two weeks. However, much of the devastation remains and many state parks and backroads sustained substantial damage. Be sure to contact any listing before visiting.

SIGHTS

SOBERANES POINT

Eight miles south of Carmel, the hiking trails here lead out along the headlands. You can stand on a rock shelf directly above the ocean and gaze back at the encroaching hills.

PALO COLORADO ROAD

For an intriguing excursion into those hills, head about six miles up Palo Colorado Road, which intersects with Route 1 a couple of miles south of Garrapata Creek. Though paved, this country road is one lane. The corridor tunnels through an arcade of redwoods past log cabins and rustic homes. If you're feeling adventurous, follow the twisting eight-mile road to its terminus at Los Padres National Forest.

443

BIXBY CREEK BRIDGE   Back on Route 1 you'll traverse this bridge, which stretches from one cliff to another across an infernal chasm. Local legend cites it incorrectly as the world's longest concrete arch span. With fluted hills in the background and a fluffy beach below, it may, however, be the world's prettiest.

COAST ROAD ———————— hidden

For another incredible side trip, you can follow this road for about 11 miles up into the Santa Lucia Mountains. Climbing along narrow ledges, then corkscrewing deep into overgrown canyons, the road carries you past exquisite views of forests and mountain ridges. There are hawk's-eye vistas of the Pacific, the rolling Big Sur countryside, and Pico Blanco, a 3709-foot lime-rich peak. This is the old coast road, the principal thoroughfare before Route 1 was completed in the 1930s. Take heed: It is so curvy it makes Route 1 seem a desert straightaway; it is also entirely unpaved, narrow, rutted, and impassable in wet weather. But oh those views!

Coast Road begins at Bixby Bridge and rejoins Route 1 at Andrew Molera State Park. If instead of detouring you stay on Route 1, it will climb along **Hurricane Point**, a promontory blessed with sweeping views and cursed by lashing winds, and descend toward **Little Sur Beach**. This sandy crescent is bounded by a shallow lagoon. There are dunes and lofty hills all around, as well as shore birds. Another lengthy beach leads to **Point Sur Light Station** (831-625-4419), set on a volcanic headland. This solitary sentinel dates back to 1889. The only way to visit this lighthouse is by a three-hour guided tour. Tours run Saturday at 10 a.m. and 2 p.m., and Sunday at 10 a.m. There are additional tours added in summer, including a moonlight tour. Call for details. Admission.

BIG SUR   Then the road enters the six-mile-long Big Sur River Valley. Big Sur, a rural community of under 2000 people, stretches the length of the valley. Lacking a town center, it consists of houses and a few stores dotted along the Big Sur River. The place received its name from early Spanish settlers, who called the wilderness south of Carmel *El País Grande del Sur*, "the big country to the south."

Later it became a rural retreat and an artists' colony. Henry Miller lived here from 1947 until 1964, writing *Big Sur and the Oranges of Hieronymus Bosch*, *Plexus*, and *Nexus* during his residence. Today the artists are being displaced by soaring land values, while the region is gaining increased popularity among visitors. It's not difficult to understand why as you cruise along its knife-edge cliffs and timbered mountainsides. You can drive for miles past eye-boggling vistas, then turn back on Route 1 to the Monterey Peninsula, or continue on to a strange and exotic land called Southern California.

ANDREW MOLERA STATE PARK

PAGE 449

Hiker's paradise with 3 miles of beach and over 15 miles of rugged coastal trails

JULIA PFEIFFER BURNS STATE PARK

PAGE 450

Spectacular views on the coast, including the 80-foot-high McWay Waterfall cascading into the ocean

HENRY MILLER LIBRARY

PAGE 444

Live performances and great books in a woodframe library dedicated to the famous American writer

SIERRA MAR

PAGE 448

Polished California cuisine menu with fresh seafood and local produce served alongside dramatic views of the Pacific coast

HENRY MILLER LIBRARY

✉ *Route 1 about a mile south of Ventana Inn* ☎ *831-667-2574* ✐ *www.henry miller.org, magnus@henrymiller.org* There's not much to this library, but somehow the unassuming nature of the place befits its candid subject. Occupying a small woodframe house donated by Miller's friend Emil White, the museum contains volumes from the novelist's library as well as his evocative artworks. There's also local artwork and a great bookstore that hosts periodic concerts, readings, and workshops. Closed Tuesday.

Note: The massive Basin Complex wildfire in 2008, the largest in the last hundred years, scarred much of the surrounding forest, especially at Julia Pfeiffer Burns State Park. The fire was contained east of Highway 1, sparing the great majority of the coastal businesses that cater to the tourist industry.

LODGING

BIG SUR CAMPGROUND AND CABINS

$–$$$ 7 UNITS ✉ *Route 1* ☎ *831-667-2322* ✐ *www.bigsurcamp.com*
For a variety of accommodations, consider staying here. Set in a redwood grove along the Big Sur River, this 13-acre facility has campsites, RV sites, tent cabins, and A-frames and bills itself as a quiet retreat with

an enforced "quiet time" from 10 p.m. to 8 a.m. Camping out on the grounds includes access to hot showers, a laundry, a store, a basketball court, and a playground. The tent cabins consist of woodframe skeletons with canvas sides and transparent roofs. They come with beds, bedding, and towels, and share a bath house. The "cabins" along the river are neatly furnished but rather sterile. More intimate are the A-frame cabins with Franklin stoves, kitchens, and sleeping lofts. The newer modular units include pine floors with bedrooms as well as a kitchen and a private bath.

RIPPLEWOOD RESORT

$$–$$$ 18 UNITS   ✉ *Route 1* ☎ *831-667-2242, 800-575-1935* 📠 *831-667-2108*
🖥 *www.ripplewoodresort.com, info@ripplewoodresort.com*

Ripplewood has cabins and a café. The least expensive cabin is a small, basic duplex unit with redwood walls, a gas heater, and carpeting. It has a bath but lacks a kitchen. The more expensive units are larger, with kitchens, sitting rooms, spacious bedrooms, and decks, and are located above the river. My advice? Compromise with one of the riverfront cabins.

BIG SUR LODGE

$$$–$$$$ 61 UNITS   ✉ *47225 Route 1* ☎ *831-667-3100, 800-424-4787*
📠 *831-667-3110* 🖥 *www.bigsurlodge.com, info@bigsurlodge.com*

Located within Pfeiffer Big Sur State Park is this complex containing cottages with two to six units per cottage. The "lodge" represents a full-facility establishment complete with conference center, restaurant, gift shop, grocery, laundromat, and heated pool in the summer. It's very convenient, if undistinguished. The cottages are frame houses with wood-shingle roofs. They are simple in design, yet some have a kitchen and a fireplace. The interiors are pine and feature wall-to-wall carpeting and high beam ceilings; each cottage features a porch or a deck. Guests also receive complementary state park day passes.

DEETJEN'S BIG SUR INN

$$$–$$$$ 20 ROOMS   ✉ *48665 South Route 1* ☎ *831-667-2377* 📠 *831-667-0466*
🖥 *www.deetjens.com*

Big Sur has long been associated with bohemian values and an easy lifestyle. Today landed gentry and wealthy speculators have taken over many of the old haunts, but a few still remain. One such is Deetjen's, a slapdash affair where formality is an inconvenience. The place consists of a hodgepodge collection of buildings. The outer walls are unpainted and the doors have no locks, lending the residence a tumbledown charm. Rooms are roughhewn, poorly insulated, and rustic, but some have woodburning stoves. Throw rugs are scattered about, the furniture is traditional, and local art pieces along the wall serve as decoration. No in-room phones or TVs. If all this is beginning to discourage you, you're getting older than you think; after all, this offbeat hideaway does possess an enchanting quality.

VENTANA INN AND SPA

$$$$ 60 ROOMS   ✉ *Route 1* ☎ *831-667-2331, 800-628-6500* 📠 *831-667-0573*
🖥 *www.ventanainn.com, reservations@ventanainn.com*

When I'm ready to spend *beaucoup* bucks, I book lodging at the Ventana Inn. Set along 243 mountainside acres overlooking the Pacific Ocean, this fabled resort is the *ne plus ultra* of refined rusticity. Build-

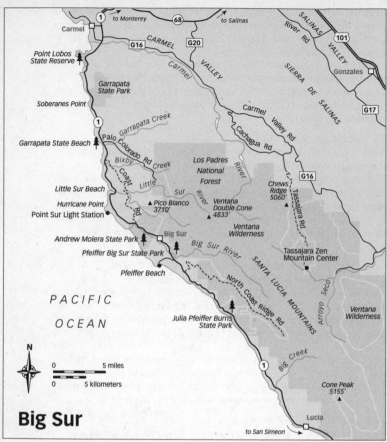

Big Sur

ings are fashioned from raw wood and most guest rooms and suites are equipped with tile fireplaces. There are cedar walls and quilt beds. With Japanese hot baths, saunas, two pools, a spa, a fitness room, a library, and a clothing-optional sun deck, the place exudes an air of languor. Guests enjoy a continental breakfast and afternoon wine and cheese, hike nearby trails, partake in activities like mushroom hunting and photography, and congratulate themselves for having discovered a secluded resort where doing nothing is a way of life. Leaving the kids at home is suggested.

POST RANCH INN

$$$$ 42 UNITS ✉ Route 1 ☎ 831-667-2200, 800-527-2200 🖷 831-667-2512
🖅 www.postranchinn.com, reservations@postranchinn.com

If, on the other hand, you spell Big Sur with a capital $, consider this cliff-edge hotel, located just across the highway from the Ventana Inn. Defying description, it is a testimony to rustic perfection. Consisting of over 40 separate units and designed to fit the surrounding landscape, some rooms are built into the hillside and covered by grass; others are perched on stilts high above the forest floor. Each room is decorated with wood and stone, has a king-size bed, and, best of all, offers an open view of the Pacific Ocean or tree-covered hillside. There are also two deluxe houses, complete with hot tubs and private terraces.

TASSAJARA ZEN MOUNTAIN CENTER

$$$ 15 UNITS   ✉39171 Tassajara Road   ☎415-865-1895; for reservations, call 415-865-1899   ⌨www.sfzc.org/tassajara, tassrez@sfzc.org

The ultimate resting place in this corner of the world is the Tassajara. Set deep in the Santa Lucia Mountains along a meandering country road, Tassajara has been a hot springs resort since the 1860s. Before that its salubrious waters were known to American Indians and the Spanish. When the Zen Center purchased the place in 1966, they converted it into a meditation center. There are only a few telephones and electrical outlets in the entire complex, making it ideal for people seeking serenity. Every year from May until September, the Zen Center welcomes day visitors and overnight guests to use the Japanese-style bath houses and natural steam showers. The hosts provide three vegetarian meals daily plus lodging in the private rooms and cabins dotted about the grounds. Day visitors are also welcome; shuttle service into the resort is available from Jamesburg, south of the Carmel Valley. In summer, Tassajara hosts a number of special workshops and retreats, including tea ceremonies and calligraphy writing. For day and overnight visits be sure to make your reservations far in advance, since this unique place is very popular. Closed September through April.

DINING

BIG SUR ROADHOUSE RESTAURANT

$$–$$$ CALIFORNIA CUISINE   ✉Route 1   ☎831-667-2264
📠831-667-2865   ⌨www.bigsurroadhouse.com

This restaurant has a prime location along Big Sur. The menu highlights fresh local seafoods and California fare with a Latin flair. The wine list features central California vintages. This small restaurant is a local favorite; reservations are recommended. Dinner only. Closed Tuesday.

FERNWOOD GRILL

$–$$ AMERICAN   ✉Route 1   ☎831-667-2422   📠831-667-2663
⌨www.fernwoodbigsur.com

This combination restaurant-bar-store with motel-like accommodations and RV hookups has a changing menu at the Fernwood Grill that usually includes hamburgers, salads, and the like. This local gathering spot is your best bet for an inexpensive lunch or dinner.

CIELO

$$$$ SEAFOOD ✉Route 1 ☏831-667-4242, 800-628-6500
🖱www.ventanainn.com, reservatons@ventanainn.com

Part of the extraordinary complex that includes the prestigious Ventana Inn, this is one of the region's most elegant dining places. Resting on a hillside overlooking the mountains and sea, it's a perfect spot for a special meal. At lunch you'll be served salad, steak sandwiches, or fresh pasta, either inside the wood-paneled dining room, or alfresco on a sweeping veranda. For dinner you can start with oysters on the half shell or roasted red and golden beet salad, then proceed to such entrées as glazed duck breast, sauteed venison, or fresh fish grilled over oak.

SIERRA MAR   **hidden**

$$$$ CALIFORNIA CUISINE ✉*Route 1* ☏*831-667-2800* 📠*831-667-2824*
🖱*www.postranchinn.com*

Whether or not you're staying at the Post Ranch Inn, you will hardly want to miss dinner at the resort's signature restaurant. The magnificent views of the ocean and surf 1100 feet below become tenfold more dramatic at dinner when the sun drops behind the Pacific. The menu features health-conscious California cuisine and changes daily. Among the prix-fixe menu selections are lean beef, seafood, poultry, and vegetarian dishes. The bar serves a light luncheon all afternoon. Reservations required.

NEPENTHE

$$-$$$$ AMERICAN ✉*Route 1* ☏*831-667-2345* 📠*831-667-2394*
🖱*www.nepenthebigsur.com, lpotter@nepenthebigsur.com*

Perched on a cliff 800 feet above the Pacific, this fabled dining spot has plenty of personality and offers another bird's-eye view. People come across the continent to line its curving bar or dine along the open-air patio. It's a gathering place for locals, tourists, and everyone in between. There are sandwiches, quiches, and salads for lunch. At dinner the menu includes fresh fish, broiled chicken, and steak. If you're not hungry, at least stop in for a drink—the scene is a must.

CAFÉ KEVAH

$-$$ AMERICAN ✉*Route 1* ☏*831-667-2344* 📠*831-667-2394*
🖱*www.nepenthebigsur.com*

For breakfast or lunch, try this outdoor restaurant downstairs at Nepenthe. Personally, I think it's a much better deal than its upstairs neighbor. They serve yummy breakfast fare, like eggs benedict and french toast, and lunch dishes with a Mediterranean focus. Their homemade pastries are the perfect companions for an afternoon gazing out at the ocean. Closed January to March and when it rains.

SHOPPING

COAST GALLERY
✉*49901 Route 1, 33 miles south of Carmel* ☏*831-667-2301*, *800-797-6869* 📠*831-667-2303* 🖱*www.coastgalleries.com* Set in a circular wooden structure resembling an oversized wine cask (and made from old water tanks) is one of Big Sur's best-known art centers. The Coast Gallery is justifiably famous for its displays of arts and crafts by local

artists. There are lithographs by novelist Henry Miller as well as paintings, sculptures, ceramics, woodwork, handmade candles, and blown glass by Northern California craftspeople. An adjoining shop features a wide selection of Miller's books.

NIGHTLIFE

BIG SUR RIVER INN ✉*Route 1* ☎*831-667-2700, 800-548-3610* ⬧*www.big surriverinn.com* Down in Big Sur the lights go out early. This is one place that has a wood-paneled bar overlooking the Big Sur River and keeps a candle burning. Live music on Sunday afternoon in the summer May through October.

BEACHES & PARKS

GARRAPATA STATE PARK

✉*It's along Route 1 about 7 miles south of Carmel. Watch for the curving beach from the highway; stop at the long turnout just north of the Garrapata Creek bridge. From here a path leads down to the beach.* ☎*831-649-2866*

This broad swath of white sand is particularly favored by local people, some of whom use it as a nude beach (which remains illegal). Easily accessible, it's nevertheless off the beaten tourist path, making an ideal hideaway for picnicking and skinny dipping. There are no facilities. A rough current and lack of lifeguards make swimming inadvisable.

ANDREW MOLERA STATE PARK

✉*Located along Route 1 about three miles north of Big Sur* ☎*831-667-2315* ✆*831-667-2886*

An adventurer's hideaway, this 4800-acre park rises from the sea to a 3455-foot elevation. It features three miles of beach and over 15 miles of hiking trails. The forests range from cottonwood to oak to redwood, while the wildlife includes mule deer, bobcat, harbor seals, and gray whales. Big Sur River rumbles through the landscape and surfers try the breaks on the beach. The only thing missing is a road: this is a hiker's oasis, its natural areas accessible only by heel and toe. The wilderness rewards are well worth the shoe leather. This is the only place in Big Sur where you can ride a horse; you can hire a horse from a concessionaire and check out Captain Cooper's Cabin, a late-19th-century pioneer log cabin. East Molera trail remains closed due to the Big Sur fire. Toilets are the only facilities. Day-use fee, $10.

There are 24 hike-in sites (tents only); $15 per night. Primitive facilities, but water and flush toilets are available.

PFEIFFER BIG SUR STATE PARK

✉*Located along Route 1 in Big Sur* ☎*831-667-2315* ✆*831-667-2886*

One of California's southernmost redwood parks, this 1000-acre facility is very popular, particularly in summer. With cottages, a restaurant, a grocery, a gift shop, picnic areas, restrooms, showers, and a laundromat on the premises, it's quite developed. However, nature still retains a toehold in these parts: the Big Sur River overflows with trout and salmon (fishing is prohibited, however), Pfeiffer Falls tumbles through a fern-banked canyon. With the Big Sur fire, most trails remain closed along with the Big Sur River Gorge. Call for updates. Day-use fee, $10.

▲ There are 204 sites for both tents and RVs (no hookups); $20 to $35 per night. Reservations: 800-444-7275.

PFEIFFER BEACH

✉ *Follow Route 1 for about a mile south past the entrance to Pfeiffer Big Sur State Park. Turn right onto Sycamore Canyon Road (unmarked), which leads downhill two miles to the beach.* ☎ *831-667-2315* 📠 *831-667-2886*

Of Big Sur's many wonders, this may be the most exotic. It's a sandy beach littered with boulders and bisected by a meandering stream. Behind the strand rise high bluffs that mark the terminus of a narrow gorge. Just offshore loom rock formations into which the sea has carved tunnels and arches. Little wonder poet Robinson Jeffers chose this haunting spot for his primal poem "Give Your Heart to the Hawks." The only facilities are toilets. Day-use fee, $5.

JULIA PFEIFFER BURNS STATE PARK

✉ *Route 1, about 11 miles south of Pfeiffer Big Sur State Park* ☎ *831-667-2315* 📠 *831-667-2886*

This 3700-acre extravaganza extends from the ocean to about 1500 feet elevation and is bisected by Route 1. The central park area sits in a redwood canyon with a stream that feeds through a steep defile into the ocean. Backdropped by sharp hills in a kind of natural amphitheater, it's an enchanting glade. A path leads beneath the highway to a spectacular vista point where 80-foot-high McWay Waterfall plunges into the ocean. Another path, one-and-eight-tenths miles north of the park entrance, descends from the highway to an isolated beach near Partington Cove that has been declared an underwater park (permit required). There are restrooms. Parking fee, $10. Note: The park sustained extensive fire damage from the 2008 Basin Complex wildfire. The redwoods are charred and not much else remains of the forest itself. All but one of the trails are closed. Check with the park for updated trail information.

▲ There are two hike-in environmental campsites for tents only; $15 to $20 per night with an eight-person maximum. Reservations are required; call 800-444-7275.

VENTANA WILDERNESS

✉ *From Route 1 in the Big Sur area, there are two entry points. The ranger station, where maps and fire permits can be acquired, is just south of Pfeiffer Big Sur State Park. For information and permits, contact the U.S. Forest Service (Monterey District, 406 South Mildred Avenue, King City, CA 93930).* ☎ *831-385-5434, 831-667-2315* 📠 *831-667-2886*

Part of Los Padres National Forest, this magnificent 216,500-acre preserve parallels Route 1 a few miles inland. It covers a broad swath of the Santa Lucia Mountains with elevations ranging from 600 feet to 5800 feet. Within its rugged confines are 237 miles of hiking trails. Wild boars and turkeys, mountain lions, and deer roam its slopes. Bald eagles soar the skies. The only facilities are ranger stations. However, much of the wilderness (areas north of Nacimiento-Fergusson Road) remain closed to public entry because of Big Sur fire damage. Parking fee, $4.

▲ There are hike-in sites only, which are free.

OUTDOOR ADVENTURES

SPORTFISHING

The Central Coast is renowned for its open-sea fishing. Charter boats comb the waters for rock cod, salmon, and albacore. Most trips leave the dock by 6 a.m. and return by 3 p.m.

South of San Francisco

HALF MOON BAY SPORTSFISHING ✉111 Johnson Pier, Princeton-by-the-Sea ☎650-726-2913 ⌨www.fishingboat.com If you want to test your skill, or luck, contact this company. They operate three boats, ranging from 55 to 65 feet. You can go deep-sea fishing for rock cod or ling cod any day of the week. April through November there's salmon fishing and December through March there's whale watching. Bait and tackle available.

Santa Cruz

LEO'S MARINE SUPPLY AND SPORTFISHING ✉2210 East Cliff Drive at the Santa Cruz Yacht Harbor ☎831-476-2648 ⌨www.mtmcharters.com To take a charter from Santa Cruz in search of tuna, salmon, or rock cod, call Leo's. Bait included, rods and tackle available. They run a 44-footer.

SANTA CRUZ BOAT RENTALS ✉Santa Cruz Municipal Pier ☎831-423-1739 ⌨www.santacruzboatrentals.net For do-it-yourself adventures, this company has 18 boats to rent and a 16-foot wood skiff that seats up to four adults. Motorized skiffs are available. Fishing gear is provided. There is also bait, tackle, and a gift shop.

Monterey

RANDY'S FISHING TRIPS ✉66 Old Fisherman's Wharf ☎831-372-7440 ⌨www.randysfishingtrips.com Spend the day on one of two boats with Randy's. Advance reservations recommended.

CHRIS'S FISHING FLEET ✉48 Old Fisherman's Wharf ☎831-372-0577 ⌨www.chrissfishing.com Chris's also offers charters and day-long fishing trips for albacore, salmon, and deep-sea catches.

WHALE WATCHING

To see the whales during their annual migration, head for whale-watching lookouts at Pillar Point in Half Moon Bay, the coast around Davenport, Point Pinos in Pacific Grove, or Cypress Point in Point

Lobos State Reserve. The summer whale-watching season typically runs from mid-June through September while the winter migration is viewable from mid-December to mid-March. (See the "Whale Watching" section in Chapter Five.)

South of San Francisco

HALF MOON BAY SPORTFISHING ✉ *21 Johnson Pier, Princeton-by-the-Sea* ☎ *650-726-2913* November through March, this company offers two whale-watching excursions daily. The party boat plies the coast in search of cetaceans, pinnipeds, and other marine life.

Monterey

RANDY'S FISHING TRIPS ✉ *66 Old Fisherman's Wharf* ☎ *831-372-7440* If you'd prefer a close look at these migrating mammals and other marine life—sea lions, seals, otters, sea birds—catch a cruise with Randy's. They can accommodate up to 48 people, and the two- or three-hour trip is fully narrated by a naturalist.

MONTEREY WHALEWATCHING ✉ *96 Old Fisherman's Wharf #1* ☎ *831-372-2203* ⊰ *www.montereywhalewatching.com* To catch glimpses of blue whales, humpbacks, and dolphins, hop on board a 75- or 100-foot vessel with Monterey Whalewatching. Trips last about three hours and feature a naturalist; sonar equipment is used to help locate whales.

CHRIS'S FISHING FLEET ✉ *48 Old Fisherman's Wharf* ☎ *831-372-0577* ⊰ *www.chrissfishing.com* Chris's offers cruises that last anywhere from two to six hours. Their three boats are fully equipped with fish finders and radar.

KAYAKING

Whether you are young or old, experienced or a novice, the Central Coast awaits discovery by sea kayak. Guided excursions of the bay or Elkhorn Slough afford an up-close and personal look at the region's greatest treasures.

Monterey

MONTEREY BAY KAYAKS ✉ *693 Del Monte Avenue* ☎ *831-373-5357, 800-649-5357* ⊰ *www.montereybaykayaks.com* Explore Monterey Bay and Elkhorn Slough, or paddle your way along the coastal waters with this outfitter. They also offer naturalist-led trips around the Monterey National Marine Sanctuary, where you'll see a wide variety of marine life. The tour to Elkhorn Slough goes through an inland saltwater marsh to view seals, otters, and birds. Reservations recommended.

ADVENTURES BY THE SEA ✉ *299 Cannery Row* ☎ *831-372-1807* ⊰ *www.adventuresbythesea.com, sales@adventuresbythesea.com* This company has double and single kayaks for rent. The twice-daily tours are led by a local docent who describes the history of Cannery Row, local geology, natural history, and native lore.

DIVING

The Central Coast offers premiere diving in Northern California. Although coastal waters are quite frigid, the unique kelp forests, wide array of fish, spotted harbor seals, and other fascinating marine life make for unforgettable diving.

Santa Cruz

ADVENTURE SPORTS ✉*303 Potrero Street #15* ☎*831-458-3648, 888-839-4286* ✐*www.asudoit.com, dennis@asudoit.com* This company offers everything from one- or two-week-long dive trips taking you to hotspots to brunch dives leaving from Monastery Beach. They rent and sell gear, and give classes ranging from beginning to assistant instructor. Closed Sunday.

Monterey

AQUARIUS DIVE SHOP ✉*2040 Del Monte Avenue* ☎*831-375-1933* ✐*www.aquariusdivers.com* This shop offers one- and two-tank beach dives as well as night dives. They rent and sell all the gear. Classes are offered for open water, advanced rescue, dive master, and nitrox. Reservations required.

MONTEREY BAY DIVE COMPANY ✉*225 Cannery Row* ☎*831-656-0454* ✐*www.montereyscubadiving.com* For morning or afternoon dives, contact this company. All equipment is available to rent.

Carmel

POINT LOBOS STATE RESERVE ✉*Route 1* ☎*831-624-8413* ✐*www.pt-lobos.parks.state.ca.us, pointlobos@parks.ca.gov* Point Lobos has some of the finest shore diving opportunities on the Pacific Coast. You'll spot sea otters, sea lions, and schools of fish. The numbers of divers per day is limited so reservations are a must (up to two months in advance to the day).

SURFING & WINDSURFING

Catching a wave when the surf's up near Lighthouse Point north of Santa Cruz is a surfer's dream. Known as "Steamer Lane," this stretch of coastline hosts many international surfing competitions. On the east side, Pleasure Point is a popular surf spot with several reef breaks. Mavericks Break, located north of Half Moon Bay, is world-renowned among surfers for its huge—sometimes deadly—waves. Even experienced wave riders need to be careful here. Avoid surfing too far north near Año Nuevo—the waters are popular with great white sharks.

FREELINE DESIGN ✉*821 41st Avenue, Santa Cruz* ☎*831-476-2950* ✐*www.freelinesurf.com* On the east side, long and short fiberglass boards, boogie-boards, and wet suits can be rented or purchased from Freeline Design.

O'NEILL'S SURF SHOP ✉*1115 41st Avenue, Capitola* ☎*831-475-4151* ✐*www.oneill.com* This one-stop surf mecca rents surfboards, boogie-boards, and wetsuits, and sells all the accessories.

CLUB ED ✉*Look for the trailer on Cowell Beach next to the Santa Cruz wharf* ☎*831-464-0177* ✐*www.club-ed.com* Catch the wind on a windsurfing board. Rentals and lessons are available at Club Ed, as are regular surfing lessons and equipment. Besides surfboards they also rent body boards and wetsuits.

RIDING STABLES

Exploring the coast and inland trails astride a galloping horse is one way to enjoy a visit to the Central Coast.

South of San Francisco

SEAHORSE AND FRIENDLY ACRES RANCH ✉ *2150 Route 1, Half Moon Bay* ☎ *650-726-9903* With its four-mile white-sand beach and surrounding farm country, Half Moon Bay is a choice region for riding. Seahorse and Friendly Acres Ranch, located on the coast, rents more than 150 horses. They also have pony rides for kids. No reservations are necessary.

Pacific Grove

PEBBLE BEACH EQUESTRIAN CENTER ✉ *Portola Road and Alva Lane, Pebble Beach* ☎ *831-624-2756* 🖰 *www.ridepebblebeach.com, info@ridepebblebeach.com* There are escorted tours at the Equestrian Center. A one-and-a-half-hour ride takes you through the forest and down to the beach. Call ahead to reserve a horse.

GOLF

For golfers, visiting the Monterey Peninsula is tantamount to arriving in heaven. Pebble Beach is home to the annual AT&T National Pro-Am Golf Championship. Several courses rank among the top in the nation.

PEBBLE BEACH GOLF COURSE ✉ *17 Mile Drive, Pebble Beach* ☎ *831-625-8518, 800-654-9300* With stunning views of the rugged coastline, Pebble Beach is the most noted. Four U.S. Open Tournaments have been held here. The 7th, 8th, 17th, and 18th holes are world-renowned as highly difficult ocean holes. Reservations are required a day in advance for non-hotel guests.

SPYGLASS HILL GOLF COURSE ✉ *Stevenson Drive, Pebble Beach* ☎ *831-625-8563, 800-654-9300* Spyglass Hill, known as one of the toughest courses in the nation, has six of the holes with ocean views while the rest are set in the forest. Reservations are required.

DEL MONTE GOLF COURSE ✉ *1300 Sylvan Road, Monterey* ☎ *831-373-2700* Set on a century-old property, Del Monte is a relatively flat course studded with ancient trees.

PACIFIC GROVE GOLF COURSE ✉ *77 Asilomar Avenue, Pacific Grove* ☎ *831-648-5777* Pacific Grove overlooks Monterey Bay and the Pacific Ocean. It has a pro shop and driving range.

BIKING

The **Pacific Coast Route** follows Route 1 through the entire Central Coast area to Big Sur and beyond. There are camping sites along the way. The ocean views and rolling pastures make this an ideal course to peddle, if you are experienced and careful.

Both Santa Cruz and Monterey have bike paths for beginners and skilled riders alike. Especially good for touring are **17 Mile Drive**, the bike trail along the bayshore from **Seaside to Marina**, the trail from **Seaside to Lover's Point** (via Cannery Row), and the roads in **Point Lobos State Reserve**.

Bike Rentals
BAY BIKE RENTALS ✉*585 Cannery Row, Monterey* ✆*831-655-2453* 🖱*www. baybikes.com* Bay Bike Rentals carries hybrids, mountain bikes, tandems, and surreys (four-wheeled, pedal-powered vehicles).

HIKING

To fully capture the beauty and serenity of the region's woodlands, chaparral country, and beaches, explore its hiking trails. The Santa Cruz and Santa Lucia mountains offer several hundred miles of trails through fir, madrone, and redwood forests. Getting lost, so to speak, among these stands of ancient trees is a splendid way to vacation. Or hike the inland hills with their caves and rock spires. Down at the sea's edge you'll discover more caves, as well as tidepools, sand dunes, and a world of marine life.

All distances listed for hiking trails are one way unless otherwise noted.

South of San Francisco
AÑO NUEVO STATE RESERVE   If you've an urge to see elephant seals breeding, take the three-mile guided walk led by docents at Año Nuevo State Reserve. To protect these mammoth mammals, the preserve is open during breeding season only to those on the guided tours. Tours are scheduled from December through March. The tours are popular and space is limited so make reservations well in advance; call 800-444-4445. To explore this area after mating season, you can hike on your own past sand dunes, tidepools, and sea caves. Follow **Año Nuevo Trail** (2.5 miles), beginning at the west end of the parking lot, to Año Nuevo Point.

Santa Cruz Mountains
SKYLINE-TO-THE-SEA TRAIL ✆*831-338-8860, 831-338-8861* 🖱*www.big basin.org, info@bigbasin.org* For a backpacking trip over the Santa Cruz Mountains, take this magnificent 28.4-mile (roundtrip) trail. The route begins at Saratoga Gap (Skyline Boulevard and Route 9) or Castle Rock State Park (adding three miles to the trek) and climaxes on the Pacific shore. Campgrounds at Waterman Gap, Big Basin, and along Waddell Creek provide resting places for hikers traveling this heavily forested path. Be sure to make reservations for campsites.

CASTLE ROCK STATE PARK   For hikers and beginning rock climbers, Castle Rock State Park offers a chance to try out skills and enjoy magnificent views. **Castle Rock Trail** (3 miles) is a moderate hike through oak and madrone woodlands. The trail starts at the south side of the Skyline Boulevard parking lot. Castle Rock is about a half-mile from the trailhead. Continue along the Castle Rock Trail, then pick up the **Saratoga Gap Trail** (2.8 miles), which leads to Castle Rock Trail Camp.

BIG BASIN REDWOODS STATE PARK There are hikes for everyone along the 60 miles of trails in Big Basin Redwoods State Park, the oldest of California's state parks. Covering 18,000 acres, Big Basin has spectacular trails leading to waterfalls and redwood groves. **Redwood Trail** (.6 mile) is a self-guiding nature trail easy enough for the entire family. Take the trail that begins west of the parking lot and stroll past a grove of giants.

Berry Creek–Sunset Loop Trail (11 miles) is an arduous trek through the most beautiful scenery in the park. Follow Redwood Trail, then pick up Skyline-to-the-Sea Trail, which will run into Berry Creek Trail. The trek climaxes at Lower and Upper Berry Creek Falls, which tumble more than 50 feet over sandstone cliffs. A return on the Sunset Trail completes the journey; allow about six hours.

The **Howard King Trail** (3.5 miles) begins at the Middle Range Fire Road and ascends gradually to Mt. McAbee overlook. En route you'll encounter meadows, old-growth redwoods, and views of the Pacific.

Monterey Area
POINT LOBOS STATE RESERVE One of California's most beautiful spots is the six-mile shoreline at Point Lobos State Reserve. The park is laced with trails leading to tidepools, sandy coves, and whale-watching vistas.

Cypress Grove Trail (.8 mile) is one of the most popular (and populated) in the park, leads through a stand of Monterey cypress trees and offers cliff-top views of the ocean.

Bird Island Trail (.8 mile) takes you through coastal shrubbery to two exquisite white-sand beaches—China Cove and Gibson Beach. The path also overlooks Bird Island, a refuge for cormorants and brown pelicans.

Beginning near Piney Woods, **Pine Ridge Trail** (.7 mile) goes inland through forests of Monterey pines and Coast live oak. Deer, squirrel, and such birds as pygmy nuthatches and chestnut-backed chickadees make this a tranquil nature hike.

South Shore Trail (1 miles), an oceanside walk between Sea Lion Point and the Bird Rock parking area, allows close looks at tidepool life and shore birds. You can also play amateur geologist, examining multicolored patterns in sedimentary rocks.

PINNACLES NATIONAL MONUMENT For rock climbers and hikers alike, Pinnacles offers great sport. Because of the summer heat and winter weather, it's recommended that you come in spring or fall to explore the park's rock spires, talus caves, and covered canyons. At any time of year, bring plenty of water and a flashlight.

Hiking along the narrow ledges of **High Peaks Trail** (5.4 miles), you'll find splendid views of the entire park. The steep trail begins across from the Chalone Creek picnic area, travels up through the High Peaks and ends up at the Moses Spring parking lot. Allow at least three to four hours.

Old Pinnacles Trail (2.3 miles) begins at Chalone Creek picnic area and goes along relatively level terrain near the west fork of the creek to Balconies Caves.

Juniper Canyon Trail (1.8 miles) starts near the west end of the park at the Chaparral ranger station and climbs 760 feet to connect with the park's east side High Peaks Trail. It's the steepest trail in the monument.

Big Sur

VENTANA WILDERNESS   Over 240,000 acres of rugged mountain terrain comprise the Ventana Wilderness of Los Padres National Forest. About 200 miles of hiking trails make it easy to explore the Santa Lucia Mountains while escaping the trappings of civilization. Several roads off Route 1 will take you onto the preserve. Big Sur Station is the only staffed coastal entrance. However, after the Big Sur fire of 2008 much of Ventana's trails are closed. Check www.ventanawild.org/trails for the latest information on hiking trail closures and openings.

Bottchers Gap–Devils Peak Trail (4 miles) is a steep hike through coniferous forests to spectacular vistas overlooking the northern section of the Ventana Wilderness.

Kirk Creek–Vicente Flat Trail (5.1 miles) winds along ridgelines that afford mountain views.

Pine Ridge Trail (27 miles) begins at Big Sur Station and carries two miles to the park boundary before heading into the Ventana Wilderness. First stop is Ventana Camp, near the Big Sur River. Then the trail leads past several campgrounds and ends at China Camp.

TRANSPORTATION

CAR

From San Francisco, coastal highway **Route 1** is the most scenic way to explore the Central Coast. In the Santa Cruz Mountains, **Routes 35** and **9** lead through redwood forests and rural towns. **Route 101**, which runs inland parallel to the coast is the fastest route. Numerous side roads lead from this highway to points along the Central Coast. Be careful when driving along the coast in the summer—thick fogs occasionally creep in, making for dangerous driving conditions.

AIR

MONTEREY PENINSULA AIRPORT ✉Route 68 and Olmstead Road ☏831-648-7000 ⬦www.montereyairport.com Several airlines fly regular schedules to this airport. American Eagle Airlines, Allegiant Air, ExpressJet, United, United Express, and US Airways, service this area from San Francisco and other departure points.

BUS

GREYHOUND BUS LINES ✉425 Front Street ☏831-423-1800, 800-231-2222 ⬦www.greyhound.com Greyhound has continual service to Santa Cruz from San Francisco and Los Angeles.

TRAIN

AMTRAK ✆ *800-872-7245* For railroad buffs, Amtrak offers daily service on the "Coast Starlight." The train runs from Seattle to Los Angeles with stops in Oakland, San Jose, and Salinas (11 Station Place). Once in Salinas, passengers can transfer to a Greyhound or Monterey–Salinas Transit bus.

CAR RENTALS

If flying directly into Monterey, you can rent a car at the airport from **Alamo** (800-327-9633), **Avis Rent A Car** (800-331-1212), **Budget Rent A Car** (800-527-0700), **Enterprise** (800-736-8222), **Hertz Rent A Car** (800-654-3131), or **National Car Rental** (800-227-7368). Additional rental agencies are located in town; try **American International Rent A Car** (800-392-8724).

PUBLIC TRANSIT

SAN MATEO COUNTY TRANSIT (SAMTRANS) ✆ *800-660-4287* ✐ *www.samtrans.com* This agency, which departs from the Daly City and Colma BART stations, has local bus service to Pacifica, Moss Beach, and Half Moon Bay. Bus service is also available between Año Nuevo and San Mateo and Half Moon Bay during seal season (January through March). Reservations are required (through SamTrans).

SANTA CRUZ METROPOLITAN TRANSIT DISTRICT ✆ *831-425-8600* From Waddell Creek in northern Santa Cruz County, the Santa Cruz Metropolitan Transit District covers Route 1 as far south as Watsonville.

MONTEREY–SALINAS TRANSIT COMPANY ✆ *831-899-2555* ✐ *www.mst.org* From Watsonville, connections can be made to Monterey and Big Sur via this transit company. These buses carry passengers to many points of interest including Cannery Row, Point Lobos, and Andrew Molera and Pfeiffer Big Sur State Parks (seasonal). Buses from Monterey to Big Sur run twice daily from Memorial Day to Labor Day, and on weekends year-round.

GOLD COUNTRY & HIGH SIERRA

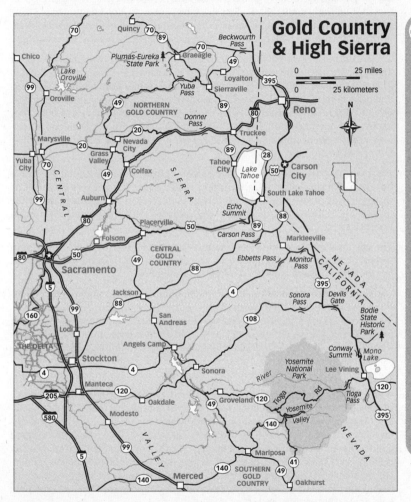

Gold Country & High Sierra

Setting out from a flat, warm, agricultural region several hundred feet above sea level, this chapter ends far past timberline, amid snow-domed peaks 13,000 feet high. The rivers that irrigate the farmland begin high in the Sierra Nevada. These whitewater currents slice through the mountains, carving canyons and dumping rich minerals along the riverbanks. Among the precious metals is one that altered the course of California history. It also gave its name to the foothill region that lies between the heights and the lowlands—the Gold Country.

Sacramento rests at the heart of California's Central Valley, the richest farming area in the world. Sacramento's other business is politics; this city of 454,000 is the state capital. Originally, however, its business was gold. No yellow metal was ever found along Sacramento streets. Sacramento made its fortune supplying the gold fields, providing men and materials for the nearby strikes.

The man who founded the town was also directly responsible for the original discovery of gold. John Sutter created Sacramento in 1839 when he built a fort to protect the huge land grant that the Spanish government bestowed upon him. Using American Indians as serfs, he set out to create an inland empire, New Helvetia. With Sacramento as headquarters, his domain spread to the nearby Sierra foothills.

Then occurred an event of historic import, which should have secured his power and fortune. Instead, it destroyed him. Gold was discovered on John Sutter's land. That was January 1848. By the next year, machinists and farm hands, scoundrels and preachers, filled with hope and a hunger for gold, began descending in mobs. Over 40,000 miners arrived in 1849; three years later there were 100,000. They came to John Sutter's land. His workers quit to join the miners, farmland fell fallow, projects went unfinished, buildings were stripped for firewood. By 1852, Sutter was bankrupt.

His town, however, boomed. In 1854, Sacramento became the capital. By 1856 it boasted California's first railroad, and in 1860 the city was a center for the Pony Express. The transcontinental railroad was conceived in Sacramento, and by the turn of the century, this river town was adorned with the beautiful Victorian homes it still displays.

The precious metal that built Sacramento was found throughout the Gold Country east of the capital. There a rich vein of quartz and gold, the Mother Lode, parallels the Sierra Nevada range for several hundred miles.

The Gold Country became a land of dreams, but its gold fields were often a nightmare. Eventually $2 billion worth of yellow metal was mined, yet for many argonauts, prospecting meant coming up empty-handed and then facing inflated prices for provisions. Little wonder that most of the towns that mushroomed in the wilderness have long since vanished. The towns remaining go by names such as Mariposa, Sonora, Coloma, and Nevada City. Still maintaining antique buildings and old mining scars, they are located along a 300-mile stretch of Route 49.

If time and territory can possibly be compared, perhaps the historic importance of the Gold Rush is equal to the grandeur of the mountains that forged the gold. The Sierra Nevada is the largest single mountain range in the country. It's a solitary block of earth, tilted and uplifted, 430 miles long and 80 miles wide. A mere child in the long count of geologic history, it rose from the earth's surface a few million years back and did not reach its present form until 750,000 years ago. During the Pleistocene epoch, glaciers spread across the land, grinding and cutting at the mountains. They carved river valleys and deep canyons, and sculpted bald domes, fluted cliffs, and stone towers.

The glaciers left a landscape dominated by ragged peaks where lakes number in the hundreds and canyons plunge 5000 feet. There are cliffs sheer as glass that compete with the sky for dominance. It is, as an early pioneer described it, a "land of fire and ice."

To the pioneers, however, the beauty of the place was of little consequence compared to its magnitude. The Sierra Nevada was a hellish gateway to the promised land, the final obstacle before entering California. The first to cross it was Jedediah Smith, a mountain man who followed the Stanislaus River in 1827. Then, in 1841, the Bidwell-Bartleson party became the first emigrant wagon train to trek the Sierra. By 1845, the mountain migration route was opening as 250 settlers crossed; twice that number traveled the "California Trail" the next year. Present-day hikers can explore a network of old emigrant trails throughout the mountains. Trees still living near timberline bear blazes left by pioneers back in the 1850s.

Before the settlers, Maidu and Miwok peoples hunted the western slopes, while Washoes and Paiutes stalked the eastern heights of Nevada. Today much of the land is preserved in a series of state parks and national forests. There's Calaveras Big Trees with its solitary trails through dense sequoia stands; Mono Lake, a prehistoric sea adorned with rock statues; and the High Sierra wilderness, domain of backpackers and golden eagles.

The hot spot of the Sierras is Lake Tahoe, an alpine resort that goes year-round. Tahoe enjoys 300 sunny days annually, but also manages to receive 18 feet of snow. Skiers and snowboarders challenge its slopes at Squaw Valley, Alpine Meadows, Sugar Bowl, and a dozen other runs. Spring and fall carry crisp weather to Tahoe; since summers are warm, anglers, boaters, and waterskiers replace snow lovers.

In the Gold Country, winter usually brings rain, spring covers the hillsides with wildflowers, and summers are hot. Not so hot, however, as Sacramento. There the weather can be torrid, though spring and fall are cool and winter is foggy and overcast.

That means Yosemite enjoys the finest weather of all: summers are mild, and in winter Yosemite Valley itself receives little snow while the high country is wide open to skiers. Climate is only one of the elements that makes Yosemite a special place. The park is our national heritage etched in stone; a land where glaciers, sequoias, and alpine meadows are ringed by stately mountains. If Sacramento is the state capital, then Yosemite is the capital of the Sierra, representing in its angled cliffs and tumbling rivers a unique land of gold and granite. Since businesses in the area may be seasonal, travelers should call ahead.

SACRAMENTO

Remember those quizzes in grammar school?

What's the capital of Illinois?

—*Chicago.*

No, Springfield. How about New York?

—*Brooklyn.*

Wrong, dodo, it's Albany. And Florida?

—*Orlando.*

No, not Miami either, but Tallahassee.

The state capital is never where it should be. It's rarely obvious, and almost never the state's big, famous city. They always put the capital in

THE FIREHOUSE

PAGE 469

Historic restaurant with award-winning wine list and California cuisine featuring dijon-roasted lamb and steak Delmonico

FACES

PAGE 472

Lively nightclub catering to gay men with three dancefloors and drink specials at 16 different bars

ERNESTO'S MEXICAN FOOD

PAGE 470

Upscale Mexican dining in a festive atmosphere with eclectic south-of-the-border menu and mouth-watering margaritas

INN AND SPA AT PARKSIDE

PAGE 467

Chic Tuscan-style bed and breakfast with individually decorated rooms and a luxurious spa—ultimate relaxation

some backwater no one ever heard of, hoping that because it's the capital the place will become great. It never does. It only means kids have to spend four times as long doing their homework.

California is no different. The seat of government should be San Francisco or Los Angeles. But instead it's Sacramento, which is north of both those cities. Sacramento is actually closer to a town called Vacaville, which translates as "cow town."

Sacramento is not my favorite city. (Neither is Harrisburg, Pennsylvania, nor Jefferson City, Missouri.) Not that it's a bad place. In fact, Sacramento is more than the capital city: It's also a gateway to the Gold Country and the center of the richest agricultural area in the world. If you decide to tour the town, you'll discover it has several faces. Who knows? Sacramento might even become your favorite capital.

SIGHTS

AMTRAK 📞 *800-872-7245* One entertaining way to reach Sacramento is by train. Daily rail service from the San Francisco Bay Area is very convenient. The ride is especially fun for children. Best of all, the train stops just a couple of blocks from the most interesting part of town.

OLD SACRAMENTO ✉ *Between the Sacramento River and Route 5* A National Historic Landmark, this neighborhood provides a perfect introduction to the Gold Country. Lined with wooden sidewalks and heavy masonry storefronts, its streets date to Sacramento's gilded era. Once considered the city's skid row section, Old Sacramento today is a 28-acre historic park comprising more than 100 restored and re-created buildings. The neighborhood can easily be seen in the course of a short walking tour.

CALIFORNIA STATE RAILROAD MUSEUM ✉*2nd and I streets* ☎*916-323-9280, 916-445-6645* 📠*916-327-5655* ✐*www.californiastaterailroadmuseum. org, rrmuseuminfo@parks.ca.gov* The high point of any visit to Old Sacramento is this railroad museum. The sights, sounds, and smells of the railroads are evocatively displayed here. Trains hoot, station yard dogs bark, and steam engines hiss as you wander past antique locomotives and narrow-gauge passenger trains. Docents are always on hand to explain the history of railroading. There's a full-scale diorama showing the construction of the transcontinental railroad in the High Sierra during the 1860s. If the re-creation is not enough for you, take a six-mile train ride on a historic locomotive from the nearby Central Pacific Freight Depot (every weekend from April through September). Admission.

B. F. HASTINGS BUILDING ✉*2nd and J streets* Behind the iron doors of this 1852 structure is a museum commemorating the western headquarters of the Pony Express.

EAGLE THEATRE ✉*925 Front Street* ☎*916-323-6343* A walking tour will carry you past this 1849 playhouse where Gold Rush–era plays and dramas are occasionally presented. Free guided tours are available, complete with a slideshow about Old Sacramento.

GLOBE ✉*Foot of K Street* Stop to check out this replica of an 1833 brig that sailed around Cape Horn in 1849. On board are exhibits and interactive displays about Sacramento River history.

OLD SACRAMENTO SCHOOLHOUSE ✉*Front and L streets* With its bolted desks and wood stoves, this schoolhouse evokes the days of stern taskmasters and heavy discipline. Past the balconied buildings and brick warehouses is a sense of nostalgia that remains throughout this antique enclave.

STATE CAPITOL BUILDING From Old Sacramento, walk south to Capitol Mall, a tree-lined boulevard, and follow it to the State Capitol Building. Set in a gracefully landscaped park, adorned with statuary and lofty pillars, it's an impressive sight. Looking like capitols everywhere, the Roman Corinthian structure is capped with a golden dome and dominated by a grand rotunda. What makes this building different from others is that many rooms have been restored and are open to the public. The old governor's office has been furnished with period pieces, equipped with a coal-burning pot-bellied stove, and returned to its 1906 glory. The state treasurer's office has been converted to a historical condominium—half re-creating 1906 and the other half portraying the Depression era.

ASSEMBLY AND SENATE GALLERIES ✉*10th Street between L and N streets* ☎*916-324-0333* 📠*916-445-3628* ✐*www.capitolmuseum.ca.gov* Wander up to the third floor of the Capitol Building when the legislature is in session and you can sit in the gallery watching the solons battle it out.

Sacramento

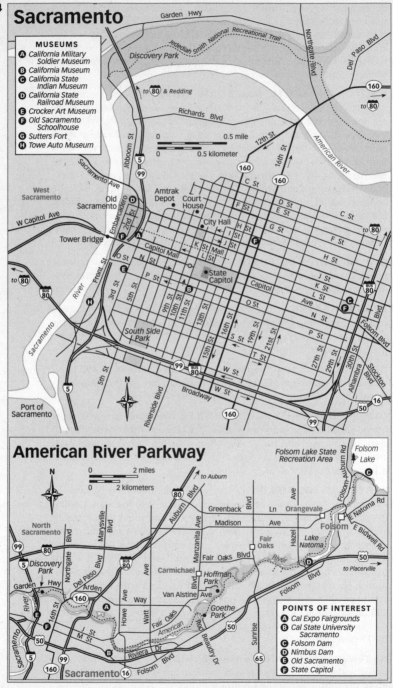

MUSEUMS
- Ⓐ California Military Soldier Museum
- Ⓑ California Museum
- Ⓒ California State Indian Museum
- Ⓓ California State Railroad Museum
- Ⓔ Crocker Art Museum
- Ⓕ Old Sacramento Schoolhouse
- Ⓖ Sutters Fort
- Ⓗ Towe Auto Museum

Garden Hwy
Jedediah Smith National Recreational Trail
Discovery Park
Northgate Blvd
Del Paso Blvd
to 80 & Redding
Richards Blvd
American River
12th St
16th St
160
160
0   0.5 mile
0   0.5 kilometer
Sacramento Ave
Jibboom St
99
5
West Sacramento
Old Sacramento
C St
D St
C St
to 80
Amtrak Depot
Court House
F St
E St
City Hall
H St
G St
F St
W Capitol Ave
Embarcadero
2nd St
3rd St
Tower Bridge
Capitol Mall
K St / J St
L St Mall
K St
L St
H St
to 80
O St
N St
State Capitol
Capitol
J St
K St
L St
Ave
to 80
BUS 80
Front St
River
3rd St
5th St
9th St
10th St
11th St
13th St
P St
O St
N St
Sacramento
South Side Park
15th St
16th St
19th St
21st St
S St
P St
27th St
29th St
30th St
Folsom Blvd
BUS 80
99
BUS 80
W St
T St
Broadway
W St
Stockton Blvd
Alhambra Blvd
5
Port of Sacramento
5th St
Riverside Blvd
N
160
99
50
16

American River Parkway

Folsom Lake State Recreation Area
Folsom Lake
N
0   2 miles
0   2 kilometers
to Auburn
80
Auburn Blvd
Folsom-Auburn Rd
Ⓒ
North Sacramento
Greenback Blvd
Ln
Orangevale
E Natoma Rd
99
80
Marysville Blvd
Madison
Ave
Hazel
Folsom
E Bidwell Rd
5
Discovery Park
Del Paso Blvd
Northgate Blvd
BUS 80
Manzanita Ave
Fair Oaks
Lake Natoma
River
Folsom Blvd
to Placerville
Garden Hwy
Arden
Way
Ave
Carmichael
Fair Oaks Blvd
Hoffman Park
Ⓓ
160
Ⓐ
Van Alstine Ave
Howe
Watt
Fair Oaks
American
Goethe Park
Folsom Blvd
Ⓔ
16th St
Beaudry Dr
50
Sunrise
Ⓕ
J St
50
M St
Ⓑ
Riviera Dr
65
5
99
160
Sacramento 16
Folsom Blvd

POINTS OF INTEREST
- Ⓐ Cal Expo Fairgrounds
- Ⓑ Cal State University Sacramento
- Ⓒ Folsom Dam
- Ⓓ Nimbus Dam
- Ⓔ Old Sacramento
- Ⓕ State Capitol

Both the Assembly and Senate galleries are sometimes open to visitors, even when the Legislature is not in session. Like the rooms downstairs, they feature antique furnishings and traditional decor, but the chambers also incorporate such newfangled devices as automatic vote counters and electronic sound systems. A museum offers exhibits about California history and government; a film and free guided tours are available. The Capitol is wheelchair accessible.

CAPITOL PARK   Having listened to the legislators ramble on, you'll be ready to adjourn to Capitol Park. Surrounding the Capitol Building, this urban oasis includes a trout pond, cactus and rose gardens, and a grove of trees transplanted from Southern battlefields to memorialize the Civil War dead. There's also a Vietnam memorial to Californians lost in that war.

THE CALIFORNIA MUSEUM ✉*1020 O Street* ☎*916-653-7524* 🖷*916-653-0314* ✐*www.californiamuseum.org, info@californiamuseum.org* This facility, initially established to showcase the contents of the state archives, now also features ever-changing exhibits that focus on the history, culture, and people of the Golden State. One of the big draws is the annual California Hall of Fame exhibit, honoring outstanding Californians such as Dave Brubeck, Jane Fonda, Sally Rice, Theodor Geisel ("Dr. Seuss"), Quincy Jones, Jack Nicholson, Tiger Woods, and Alice Waters. Also look for the California's Remarkable Women exhibit, which honors the state's female powerhouses. Admission. Closed Monday.

SUTTER'S FORT ✉*2701 L Street* ☎*916-445-4422* ✐*www.parks.ca.gov* From the east end of Capitol Park, Capitol Avenue leads to Sutter's Fort. It was back in 1839 when John Sutter founded Sacramento, building an adobe fort near the American River. Having received a 76-square-mile land grant from the Spanish, he named the domain "New Helvetia" after his native Switzerland. The fort became a cultural and strategic center for all Northern California. Donner Party survivors sought refuge here, Captain John Fremont and Kit Carson visited, and in 1846, during the Mexican War, a key Spanish leader was imprisoned and the American flag raised over the fort.

The original fortress has long since dissolved to dust and a re-created version raised in its stead. Lacking the feel of authenticity, it nevertheless possesses some interesting displays. There are weaving rooms with large but primitive looms, plus living quarters complete with rusty utensils and the most uncomfortable beds imaginable. You'll see a cooper shop where buckets and barrels were fashioned, museum cases portraying early California life, and a room hung with traps and animal skins. Admission.

CALIFORNIA STATE INDIAN MUSEUM ✉*2618 K Street* ☎*916-324-0971* Here you will gather an idea of California before the advent of Sutter and his Mexican benefactors. On permanent display are tools, baskets, dance regalia, and other items from California's first peoples. Admission.

SACRAMENTO CONVENTION & VISITORS BUREAU ✉*1608 I Street* ☎*916-808-7777, 800-292-2334* 🖷*916-808-7788* ✐*www.discovergold.org, scvb@cityofsacramento.org* The capital city features several points of interest. Contact the visitor bureau for information. Closed weekends.

CROCKER ART MUSEUM ✉*216 O Street* ✆*916-808-7000* ☏*916-264-7372* ✐*www.crockerartmuseum.org, cam@cityofsacramento.org* This museum provides a grand example of Californian art and sculpture as well as decorative arts from Europe and Asia. But the entire collection is dominated by the building it is housed in. With its parquet floors and repoussé ceilings, the E. B. Crocker mansion represents the ultimate artwork. Browsing the museum means wandering through a grand ballroom, along sweeping staircases, and past walls carved by hand. If you can overcome the impact of the interior, there are many interesting artworks to study, including special exhibits that rotate. Or you can adjourn to the glass-walled gallery, which houses part of the museum's contemporary California art collection. Children will enjoy the museum's student artwork and craft activities. In 2007, the museum began an expansion project that will triple the size of the current facility and quadruple the temporary exhibition space, allowing "blockbuster" exhibitions to come to Sacramento. The new digs will include a 7000-square-foot courtyard and indoor/outdoor café, twice as much parking, a 300-seat auditorium, and an education center. The $100 million project is scheduled to be complete in 2010. In the meantime, the "old Crocker" remains open for business. Closed Monday. Admission.

GOVERNOR'S MANSION ✉*1526 H Street* ✆*916-323-3047* ☏*916-322-4775* The Governor's Mansion houses no governors. Not any longer, that is. It did serve as home to 13 state leaders from 1903, when it was built, until 1966, when Ronald Reagan and wife Nancy refused to live there. The rest of the story is typical of California's wacky history. Reagan decided to build a new mansion, which wasn't ready until he left the governorship and went on to other things. The place was completed in time for Jerry Brown to occupy it. But it looked more like an architectural testimonial to Reagan than a house. Brown refused to take up residence, preferring to slap a mattress on an apartment house floor and call it home. Which he did—for eight years. The next governor finally decided he'd like to move in, but the legislature, controlled by the opposition party, refused to let him have the place.

Anyway, that's the tale of the "new" governor's mansion. The 30-room old mansion became a museum open to tours. It's a decorative Victorian structure that looks like a woodframe wedding cake. Within many rooms are antiques and artifacts from the early 20th century. Admission.

TOWE AUTO MUSEUM ✉*2200 Front Street* ✆*916-442-6802* ☏*916-442-2646* ✐*www.toweautomuseum.org, info@toweautomuseum.org* You can relive the development of the automobile and discover the visionary who brought us the modern convenience here. Approximately 170 cars are on display at any one time, featured in rotating exhibits with themes such as the Dream of Mobility, the Dream of Luxury, and the Dream of Cool. In addition to unusual cars—a 1906 Model K, a 1966 Cobra—the museum also houses automotive costumes, tools, and equipment. Admission.

CALIFORNIA MILITARY MUSEUM ✉*1119 2nd Street* ✆*916-442-2883* ☏*916-442-7532* ✐*www.militarymuseum.org, camilitarymuseum@sbcglobal.net* A tribute to the men and women of California who have served in the U.S. Armed Forces since the Spanish-Mission period, this museum exhibits nonactivated weapons, uniforms, and artifacts. In addition to profiling the California National Guard's role in the country's major wars, the museum looks at peacetime relief work such as the rescue efforts following the 1906 earthquake. Closed Monday. Admission.

FARMS

For a taste of country life right here in the city, you can pick your own fruits and vegetables at one of Sacramento's farms. Many of the region's farmers allow visitors to wander the fields, plucking produce right from the tree. The seasons are summer and autumn, but it's best to call ahead to find out what's ripe; costs for picking are minimal. For a list of farms in the Sacramento area and elsewhere, contact **Small Farm Center at University of California–Davis** (530-752-8136; www.calagtour.org).

LODGING

Every city has its motel row, a single street illuminated in neon and offering dozens of overnight possibilities. In Sacramento it's West Capitol Avenue, a busy highway extending out from the city's freeway nexus. As you buzz along this boulevard, the motels fly past in furious fashion, becoming a blur along the periphery of vision. B&B inns, many of which are in the fine old mansions that were built in Sacramento during the early part of the 20th century, now provide a welcome alternative to motels and faceless business hotels.

INN AND SPA AT PARKSIDE

$$$$ 11 ROOMS ✉2116 6th Street ☎916-658-1818, 800-995-7275
☎916-658-1809 ⌖www.innatparkside.com, info@innatparkside.com
Once a stately mansion built in 1936, the Parkside now serves as an extravagant boutique hotel. Decorated in Old World elegance with an Asian twist, some of the 11 rooms feature jacuzzi tubs. Evening wine-and-cheese service, in-room breakfast, and heavenly spa facilities make this one of Sacramento's most romantic places to stay.

SACRAMENTO HOSTEL

$ 9 ROOMS ✉925 H Street ☎916-443-1691
Considered one of the finest examples of 19th-century Italianate Stick–style architecture in California, this mansion sits on a tree-lined street in the heart of downtown. It boasts a grand entry, vaulted ceilings, wood paneling, chandeliers, fireplaces with original hand-painted tiles, a wraparound veranda, and a full kitchen, plus lots of public areas to spread out and marvel that it all comes at such a low price. There are six dorm rooms and three private rooms, one of which also has a private bath. Other useful amenities include on-site laundry facilities, ample parking, DSL and free wi-fi, secure lockers, and bag and bike storage.

CITIZEN HOTEL

$$$–$$$$ 198 ROOMS   ✉926 J Street, Sacramento   ☎916-447-2700,
800-738-7477   📠916-447-2701   🖥www.citizenhotelsacramento.com

Warm yellow- or olive green-striped walls, brass furnishings, and hatbox-inspired lights create a stately yet whimsical ambiance at Sacramento's haute boutique hotel, the Citizen. This 14-floor brick and terra cotta affair is designed to pay homage to politicians of the past and also play host to contemporary figures coming to the state capitol. A 3000-foot tented roof deck provides sweeping views of the city, and an upscale on-site restaurant offers California cuisine. For a posh stay with all the amenities, head here.

STERLING HOTEL

$$$$ 17 ROOMS   ✉1300 H Street   ☎916-448-1300, 800-365-7660   📠916-448-8066
🖥www.sterlinghotel.com

The Sterling doesn't have to be as pretty as it is to succeed. A typical guest room has a four-poster bed, armoire, Henredon furniture, fine art, an elegant chandelier, and a jacuzzi in the marble-tiled bathroom. When this 1894 mansion was remodeled, 17 accommodations were arranged on the three upper floors and the cellar was converted into a restaurant.

AMBER HOUSE

$$$$ 10 ROOMS   ✉1315 22nd Street   ☎916-444-8085, 800-755-6526
📠916-552-6529   🖥www.amberhouse.com, info@amberhouse.com

The 1905 Craftsman-style main house and century-old Colonial Revival home that comprise the Amber House are radiant. Each of the guest rooms is named for a poet or composer; all have private baths. Among the amenities are marble bathrooms with jacuzzis, canopy beds, and antique washstands. A lovely patio/garden area can serve as the setting for the full breakfast.

LE RIVAGE HOTEL

$$$–$$$$ 101 ROOMS   ✉4350 Riverside Boulevard, Sacramento
☎800-323-7500   📠916-706-3384   🖥www.lerivagehotel.com,
rivage.info@lerivagehotel.com

Set on the banks of the Sacramento River and just two miles from downtown, this European-inspired beauty comes with super-attentive service and a ton of amenities. The large rooms have high-end bedding, big flat screen TVs, free wi-fi, safes, refrigerators, coffeemakers, and a clawfoot soaking tub in the marble bath. Down by the river just out the door there's a private 25-slip marina, bocce ball court, huge firepits, and spectacular views. A full-service spa and excellent seafood restaurant round out the menu of pleasures.

THE FIREHOUSE

$$$–$$$$ CALIFORNIA CUISINE   ✉1112 2nd Street   ✆916-442-4772
📠916-442-6617   🖱www.firehouseoldsac.com,
comments@firehouseoldsac.com

Sacramento's capital restaurant is this plush Victorian-style dining room set in an 1850s-era fire station. The specialty here is California cuisine, as in cinnamon-scented pork tenderloin and Moroccan-spiced lamb. During summer you can dine outdoors in a brick courtyard. No lunch on Saturday. Closed Sunday.

DELTA KING

$$–$$$ SEAFOOD   ✉Foot of K Street   ✆916-441-4440, 800-825-5464
🖱www.deltaking.com, dking@deltaking.com

Climb aboard the *Delta King*, a five-decked riverboat that serves as a floating restaurant, hotel, and cultural curiosity. Seafood, of course, is the specialty, but you'll also find steaks and other meats on the menu.

MULVANEY'S B&L

$$–$$$ AMERICAN   ✉1215 19th Street, #100   ✆916-441-1771

Chef Patrick Mulvaney gets many of his ingredients from small area farmers, using first-rate products. The menu is short and changes constantly. One staple is the delectable New York steak Mulvaney, adorned with foie gras butter and served with sautéed arugula and baked potato wedges. There's also a wonderfully moist, mesquite-smoked pork chop. Ravioli is a specialty, stuffed with a changing array of fresh greens. Locals love this tiny red brick spot, once the home of the town's fire department—call early for reservations.

RICK'S DESSERT DINER

$ BAKERY   ✉2322 K Street   ✆916-444-0969   🖱www.rickdessertdiner.com

A favorite neighborhood haunt for locals with a discerning sweet tooth, Rick's is a tiny little retro-style joint that turns out a parade of decadent goodies. The on-site bakery has a repertoire of some 200 cakes and pies—Key lime pie and carrot, German chocolate, midnight torte, and poppy seed cakes are just a fraction of the 30 or so daily offerings.

BIBA

$$$–$$$$ ITALIAN   ✉2801 Capitol Avenue   ✆916-455-2422
🖱www.biba-restaurant.com, biba@biba-restaurant.com

Italian specialties here include lasagna, osso buco *alla Milanese*, homemade stuffed pasta, and braised rabbit with prosciutto. Among the featured pasta dishes you might find a fresh seafood linguine and angelhair pasta with sun-dried and fresh tomatoes. The mirrored, off-white dining room features modern art. No lunch on Saturday. Closed Sunday.

ERNESTO'S MEXICAN FOOD

$$ MEXICAN ✉1901 16th Street ☎916-441-5850
🖋www.ernestosmexicanfood.com

There's a reason that, come Friday or Saturday night, you'll probably have to wait up to an hour for a table at Ernesto's. Actually, there's a menu full of reasons. Stand-outs include the *carnitas*, the *chile colorado*, and the *chile verde*. Whatever you choose, chances are it'll be made with the freshest available ingredients. This lively midtown eatery also has outside patio dining, a full bar (try the margaritas or the mojitos), and occasional live music on the weekends.

CASA GARDEN RESTAURANT

$–$$ CALIFORNIA CUISINE ✉2760 Sutterville Road ☎916-452-2809
🖋www.casagardenrestaurant.org

I'm all for enjoying gourmet California cuisine in a garden setting and contributing to a good cause at the same time. Casa Garden serves up such specialties as Chinese dumpling and roasted vegetable salad, chicken with artichoke crowns, turkey enchiladas, and salad nicoise. The menu changes weekly. The staff are all volunteers, and all proceeds go to the Sacramento Children's Home. The restaurant only serves lunch from Monday through Friday. Reservations recommended.

CO DO

$–$$ VIETNAMESE ✉6665 Stockton Boulevard ☎916-427-8305

Little Saigon, in the midst of the scruffy South Sac area, is where locals in the know go for outstanding Asian food. A standout in the crowd of Vietnamese eateries, Co Do (the nickname for Hue, the old Vietnam capital city) specializes in charbroiled meats, the signature of central Vietnamese cuisine. Order the rice plate with lightly blackened and caramelized chopped pork and sweet and juicy shrimp, a wonderful way to expand your Asian horizons beyond *pho*, the beef noodle soup that is a staple of most Vietnamese restaurants.

SHOPPING

There are four prime sections for shoppers in the capital city: Old Sacramento, K Street, the Arden Fair Mall, and the 57th Street Antique Mall.

OLD SACRAMENTO First among the shopping choices, and lowest on the scale of price and variety, is Old Sacramento, a warren of 19th-century buildings that have been renovated and converted into shops and malls. Within the course of a few short blocks are knickknack stores, antique shops, and clothiers.

CALIFORNIA STATE RAILROAD MUSEUM STORE ✉111 I Street
☎916-324-4950, 800-417-7245 🖰www.csrmf.org Kids will love this Old Sacramento museum store, which has books, hats, T-shirts, and toys.

K STREET Another shopping district lies along K Street, a 14-block pedestrian walkway. Extending from Old Sacramento past the Capitol Building to 14th Street, this street-cum-shopping mall is lined with stores. There are major department stores, small shops, and fashionable restaurants along the strip. Also, the mall has been attractively landscaped with fountains and flowering trees, lending a natural feel to this consumer park.

EVANGELINE'S ✉113 K Street ☎916-443-2181 🖰www.evangelines.com For a trip into the fantastic, bizarre, frightening, or down-right hilarious, stop by Evangeline's. The store carries a huge selection of costumes, toys, gag gifts, novelty items, wigs, cards, and collectors' TV and film memorabilia. Great for keeping the kids (not to mention yourself) entertained, as well as for gifts for most occasions.

MIDTOWN This area, or "the grid" as locals call it, is newest addition to Sacramento shopping. Home to small boutiques, trendy salons, excellent restaurants, and the city's "Lavender Hill" gay entertainment district, Midtown has grown up in the midst of a charming neighborhood of wooden Victorian homes and tree-lined sidewalks. The second Saturday of each month, more than 40 galleries stay open late and offer entertainment and snacks to shoppers wandering the streets.

GINGER ELIZABETH CHOCOLATES ✉1801 L Street ☎916-706-1738 🖰www.gingerelizabeth.com This sweet little bon-bon of a shop in Midtown would be right at home on the Left Bank. Stop in after dinner to sip one of four kinds of hot chocolate, topped with fresh whipped cream or homemade vanilla bean marshmallows. Then pick up a box of exquisite, hand-dipped chocolates to send home. Closed Monday.

NEWSBEAT ✉1050 20th Street ☎916-448-2874 For magazines and newspapers from all over the world, cards, small gifts, snacks, and soft drinks, this Midtown newsstand is open every day from 7 a.m. to 10 p.m.

ARDEN FAIR MALL ✉1689 Arden Way ☎916-920-1167 🖰www.ardenfair.com This mall just north of downtown is a newer, shinier version of the downtown K Street mall, and is anchored by Nordstrom, Macys, Sears, and JC Penney, with more than 160 national chains and small boutiques scattered among the giants.

57TH STREET ANTIQUE MALL ✉875 57th Street ☎916-451-3110 Four miles west of downtown is this 10,000-square-foot antique mall. Take a trip down memory lane with close to 100 vendors who hawk varied antiquarian wares.

NIGHTLIFE

After sundown in the state capital, there are two places to look for entertainment. Old Sacramento, the city's historic sector, has several saloons and dancehalls. Better yet, head for the downtown area, where you'll find an array of nightclubs and watering holes.

FANNY ANN'S SALOON ✉*1023 2nd Street* ✆*916-441-0505* 🖷*916-441-7189* 🖳*www.fannyannsaloon.com* Without doubt the weirdest spot in Old Sacramento is Fanny Ann's, a multitiered bar and restaurant. The staircase rises past an endless series of rooms, each decorated in high tack fashion with old boots, wagon wheels, dangling bicycles, and striped barber poles. The main action occurs along the ground-floor bar where drinkers line up elbow to elbow or hit the dancefloor Thursday, Friday, and Sunday nights.

FOX & GOOSE ✉*1001 R Street* ✆*916-443-8825* 🖳*www.foxandgoose.com* For a laid back atmosphere, this place delivers. There's 15 beers on tap, darts, and live music on the weekend. Occasional cover.

THE TORCH CLUB ✉*904 15th Street* ✆*916-443-2797* 🖳*www.torchclub.net* This Sacramento blues club started life as a bar in 1934, the year Prohibition ended. From a watering hole for politicians, it evolved into a beloved local institution, pouring generous drinks and showcasing the hottest local, regional, and national blues performers. There's a large dancefloor and the place is open every night.

FACES ───────────────────────── **h**idden

✉*2000 K Street* ✆*916-448-7798* 🖷*916-448-2000* 🖳*www.faces.net* With room for 556 guests, Faces is Sacramento's largest gay nightclub. There's dancing to a mix of house, R&B, Latin, country, and disco music and a chance to relax on three floors or one of three patios. Sixteen bars offer ample opportunity to quench that thirst. Occasional cover.

PARKS

AMERICAN RIVER PARKWAY

✉*To reach River Bend Park, follow Route 50 east from Sacramento for several miles to the Bradshaw Avenue exit. Turn left on Bradshaw Avenue and then right on Folsom Boulevard. From Folsom Boulevard, Rod Beaudry Road leads to River Bend Park. To reach Ancil Hoffman Park from Route 50 east take the Watt Avenue exit. Turn right on Fair Oaks Boulevard, then right on Van Alstine Avenue. Turn left on California Avenue, then right on Tarshes Drive. This will take you through the main gate of the park.* ✆*916-875-6672* 🖷*916-875-6632* 🖳*www.sacparks.net, parkinfo@saccounty.net*

This chain of parks stretches for 23 miles along the American River, providing access for anglers, bikers, hikers, and picnickers. The parkway leads from Discovery Park in Sacramento to Nimbus Dam near Lake Folsom. Unfortunately, access roads do not follow the river too closely, so to reach the water you must use a series of side roads. The parkway provides opportunities to explore the riverbanks and engage in the area's numerous watersports. There are also miles of equestrian and bike trails. Within the park are picnic areas and restrooms. Day-use fee, $5. Three major parks lie along this strip—Discovery Park, River Bend Park, and Ancil Hoffman Park.

SOUTHERN GOLD COUNTRY

Extending from Mariposa to the restored Gold Rush town of Columbia, the southern Mother Lode consists of gentle, rolling foothill country laced by rivers that pour down from the Sierra Nevada. Sparsely populated, it is dotted with small towns, covered bridges, a steam railroad, and numerous monuments to the region's 19th-century heyday. Sonora is the region's hub, a good base for excursions into the Gold Country's emerald forests.

SIGHTS

MARIPOSA   A likely place to start is this historic town. The mine here was discovered in 1849 by the famous scout Kit Carson and became part of the 45,000-acre tract owned by his colleague, Colonel John C. Fremont.

MARIPOSA MUSEUM ✉5119 Jessie Street, Mariposa ☎209-966-2924 📠209-966-2924 ⌨www.mariposamuseum.com, mmhc@sti.net This museum displays a collection of artifacts from the Gold Rush era ranging from children's boots to Indian baskets to mining tools. Closed weekdays in January. Admission.

BULLION STREET   Along Bullion Street, on a hill overlooking town, the **old jail** and **St. Joseph's Catholic Church** still stand. A study in contrast, the jail is a squat granite building with formidable iron door, while the church is tall and slender with a lofty steeple. Most impressive of these period structures is the **Mariposa County Courthouse**. The state's oldest court of law, it was built back in 1854 with wooden pegs and square-cut nails. Still in use, the courtroom contains a wood stove, kerosene lanterns, and original wooden benches.

CALIFORNIA STATE MINING AND MINERAL MUSEUM ✉Mariposa County Fairgrounds, south of Mariposa on Route 49 ☎209-742-7625 📠209-966-3597 ⌨mineralmuseum@sti.net Gold—the mineral that shaped this area's history—is the focus here. Also on display are California diamonds and benitoite (the state gem), as well as gems and minerals from around the world. Among the historic mining artifacts is a scale model of a quartz mill. Closed Tuesday in winter. Admission.

HORNITOS _____

North of Mariposa, this ghost town offers a memorable side trip. Just pick up Old Toll Road in Mt. Bullion, then catch Hornitos Road; on the way back take Bear Valley Road. All are paved country roads leading through tree-studded hills on the 25-mile roundtrip detour. A Mexican-style village centered around a plaza, Hornitos was a hideout for the notorious bandito Joaquin

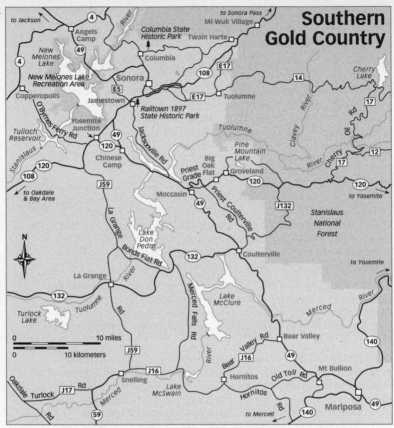

Murieta. According to legend, this Robin Hood figure, a semi-mythical hero to the Spanish miners, used a secret tunnel in the fandango hall to escape the law.

The Anglos in this rowdy mining town also claimed a famous citizen. Domingo Ghirardelli, the San Francisco chocolate manufacturer, built one of his earliest stores here in 1859. Several walls still remain, as do many of the town's old buildings. There's also an old jail, measuring little more than the size of a cell but possessing granite walls two feet thick.

The community contains something more than ruins of brick and stone. Because of its removal in time and space, Hornitos reflects the old days more fully than surrounding towns. There are windmills and range fences, grazing cows and crowing roosters. The tiny population goes about its business with an intensity not unlike that of the 15,000 who once lived here. And up on a hill, at a point closer to heaven than the rest of town, the old stone-and-wood church gazes down on the scene.

The region between Mariposa and Jamestown represents the least developed section of the Gold Country. It's a perfect place to capture a pure sense of the past. Particularly picturesque is the stretch from Mariposa to Coulterville, where Route 49 weaves wildly through the Merced River valley. The sharp slopes and hairpin turns provide grand vistas of the surrounding mountains.

COULTERVILLE   Nestling beneath forested slopes, Coulterville is an architectural hodgepodge that includes several historic buildings. Walk down Main Street to see an old Western saloon and Chinese boutique, both of which have been in operation since 1851. It's also worth stopping downtown to check out **Whistling Billy**, an eight-ton steam engine that dates back to the Gold Rush era.

NORTHERN MARIPOSA COUNTY HISTORY CENTER ✉Coulterville ✆209-878-3015 📠209-878-0744 ⌀www.home.inreach.com/nmchc, nmchc@inreach.com   This history center sits astride a sturdy stone-and-iron structure, the former home of McCarthy Pharmacy and Coulterville Hotel. Closed Monday and Tuesday (though tours can be arranged by appointment); closed January.

CHINESE CAMP   In this falsefront town with a gilded past, are ruins of the Wells Fargo building, a 19th-century store, plus an old church and cemetery. Once home to 5000 Chinese miners, this placid area was the scene of a violent tong war. About 2000 members of the Yan Wo and Sam Yap fraternities settled a mining dispute in 1856 with pikes, tridents, and axes.

KNIGHT'S FERRY ✉Route 120   From Chinese Camp, another detour (35 miles roundtrip) leads west on Route 120 to Knight's Ferry. This gold town on the Stanislaus River features a rare California sight—a covered bridge. Built on a stone foundation, the wood-plank span adds an air of New England to the old mining center. The local general store has been operating over a century. Among the many Gold Rush–era buildings still standing is the unmarked **Dent House**, owned by relatives of former President Ulysses S. Grant, and visited by Grant himself in 1854.

JAMESTOWN ✉Route 49, north of Chinese Camp   More commercially developed than mining centers to the south, this town has been ambitiously gentrified. Its restored hotels, attractive restaurants, and antique shops are a prelude to the new, improved Gold Country awaiting you. *High Noon* and *Butch Cassidy and the Sundance Kid* were filmed here.

RAILTOWN 1897 STATE HISTORIC PARK ✉5th Avenue and Reservoir Road, Jamestown ✆209-984-3953 📠209-984-4936 ⌀www.railtown1897.org, railtowninfo@parks.ca.gov   This park hosts a roundhouse museum with a blacksmith shop, a turntable, and historic locomotives. On weekends in April through October, you can also ride several miles through Mother Lode country aboard a steam-powered train.

SONORA   This town marks the center of the southern Gold Rush region. The seat of Tuolumne County and one of the largest towns in the Mother Lode, it has been preeminent almost since its founding in 1848.

Settled by Mexicans, Sonora gained an early reputation both for its law-lessness and commercial potential. When rich strikes were discovered here, racist Americans pushed the Mexicans out of the action. They levied a $20-a-month residence tax on "foreigners," which they soon repealed when local merchants complained that the emigration of Mexican miners was hurting business!

Much of Sonora's history is written in its architecture. The best way to explore it is with a walking-tour brochure available from the **Tuolumne County Museum and Historical Society** (158 West Bradford Avenue, Sonora; 209-532-1317; www.tchistory.org). With about 20 points of in-terest, the tour will carry you through the historic and geographic heart of the old "Queen of the Southern Mines."

COLUMBIA STATE HISTORIC PARK ⊠ *Route 49, Columbia* ✆ *209-588-9128* 📠 *209-532-5064* Of the countless gold towns strung along Route 49, Columbia is not to be missed. Much of the old mining center has been preserved as Columbia State Historic Park and offers visitors a look at the old days, including a chance to pan for gold. Here is a window on 19th-century life in the Sierra foothills. The refurbished buildings and rare artifacts create a picture that will help make sense of the random ruins found elsewhere in the Mother Lode.

You can wander the several streets that comprise this time-capsule town or take a stagecoach ride complete with a faux hold-up by masked ban-dits. You'll pass the old newspaper office, livery stable, and schoolhouse. There are hook-and-ladders so ancient they resemble Roman chariots, and a dentist's office containing fiendish-looking tools. Former Chinese residents are represented by a temple and herb shop, while the nearby apothecary remains stocked with Western-style potions and nostrums.

The old justice court serves the legal system no longer. It does, however, serve the public as it is open for touring. Over at the blacksmith shop are tools that bear an unsettling resemblance to those in the dentist's office. Like the four dozen buildings in this outdoor museum, it pres-ents a perfect reconstruction of an imperfect era.

LODGING

ROYAL CARRIAGE INN
$$$–$$$$ 16 UNITS   ⊠ *18239 Main Street, Jamestown* ✆ *209-984-5271* 📠 *209-984-1675* 🖢 *www.royalcarriageinn.com*

Jamestown features several historic hotels that have been refurbished. One example is the Royal Carriage, a hostelry with a small lobby. Ac-commodations are small and simply decorated. You'll find wall-to-wall carpeting, patterned wallpaper, and furnishings that range from pock-marked dressers to brass beds. Ask for a room facing north, since the other side abuts another building, or rent one of the cottages out back.

JAMESTOWN HOTEL
$$–$$$ 8 ROOMS   ⊠ *18153 Main Street, Jamestown* ✆ *209-984-3902, 800-205-4901* 📠 *209-984-4149* 🖢 *www.jamestownhotelcom, info@jamestownhotel.com*

This is one of the best-restored hostelries in the Gold Country. An at-tractive two-story brick building with a balconied falsefront, it blends modern comforts such as whirlpool tubs with old-fashioned Victorian decor, including floral wallpaper, brass beds, patchwork quilts, and wicker settees. A full breakfast is served.

SONORA DAYS INN

$$ 65 ROOMS ✉160 South Washington Street, Sonora ☎209-532-2400, 800-580-4667 📠209-532-4542 🖊www.sonoradaysinn.com, info@sonoradaysinn.com

Set in a sprawling Spanish-style structure, this full-service hotel features a restaurant and seasonal, rooftop swimming pool. The inn is made up of two buildings—a motel near the parking lot and the historic hotel. You'll encounter simulated-wood desks and naugahyde chairs, as well as telephones, televisions, and wi-fi access. The rooms are tidy and equipped with lovely tile showers.

CITY HOTEL

$$$ 10 ROOMS ✉Main Street, Columbia ☎209-532-1479, 800-532-1479 📠209-532-7027 🖊www.cityhotel.com, info@cityhotel.com

Staying at the City Hotel, situated in Columbia State Historic Park, is almost a civic responsibility. The ten-room hotel, dating from 1856, has been nicely restored and furnished with period pieces. There's a dining room and saloon downstairs. The guest rooms feature rugs across refinished pine floors, patterned wallpaper, and wall sconces. All include half-baths, with shared showers down the hall. "Balcony rooms" include patios overlooking the town's quiet Main Street.

HARLAN HOUSE

$$–$$$ 5 ROOMS ✉22890 School House Street, Columbia ☎209-533-4862 📠209-533-9080 🖊www.harlan-house.com

One of Columbia's finest homes at the turn of the 20th century sits on a hill across from the old schoolhouse. You'll sleep among Victorian and other American antiques, lounge in front of your own fireplace, and relax on a shady front porch.

DINING

CAFÉ SMOKE

hidden

$$ MEXICAN ✉Main Street, Jamestown ☎209-984-3733 📠209-984-4306

When Mexican food sounds appealing, consider this lively café. It's a friendly, upbeat place decorated with local artwork, Mexican tile floors, and potted cacti. The menu features the full gamut of Mexican-style dishes and the adjoining saloon cooks up some mean margaritas.

THE CITY HOTEL

$$–$$$$ AMERICAN/CONTINENTAL ✉Main Street, Columbia ☎209-532-1479, 800-532-1479 🖊www.cityhotel.com, info@cityhotel.com

For gourmet dining in a Gold Rush–era atmosphere, eat here. Built in 1856, the hotel is part of Columbia State Historic Park. The dining room is appointed in period with brass chandeliers, high-back chairs, and gold-framed oil paintings. Dinner is an extravaganza featuring roasted rack of lamb, pan-seared salmon, and roast breast of pheasant. The food is delicious and highly recommended. Closed Monday and the first two weeks in January.

BANNY'S CAFÉ

$$ CALIFORNIA CUISINE ✉ *83 South Stewart Street, Suite 1, Sonora* 📞 *209-533-4709* 📠 *209-533-0747* ✎ *www.bannyscafe.com, linlog@mlode.com*

This being Gold Country, you might expect to find mostly meat and potatoes, but Banny's offers a more sophisticated menu. At lunch, opt for a grilled chicken sandwich with spinach, red onion, and sundried tomato aioli on focaccia. For dinner, try chorizo and clam paella with roasted red pepper and tomato *rouïlle*, or pan-roasted duckling with dried cherry mango Madeira chutney. Daily quiches and a salad menu are also available. No lunch on Sunday.

PEPPERY GAR & BRILL

$$ AMERICAN ✉ *13494 Mono Way, Sonora* 📞 *209-533-9033*

This lively restaurant draws chilled skiers in with the promise of a hot, juicy burger after a day in the snow. Locals frequent the place too for the 14 on-tap brews, big-screen TVs, and the custom beer mugs that line the bar. In addition to burgers, the menu features a variety of sandwiches, pastas, pizzas, and salads—but it's the signature clam chowder that sets the Peppery apart from other mom-and-pop eateries. If you want to savor traditional flavors in an all-American atmosphere, grab a table here.

PIE IN THE SKY PIZZERIA

$$$ ITALIAN ✉ *2493 State Highway 108, Mi Wuk Village; About 14 miles west of Sonora* 📞 *209-586-4251*

With a sign claiming to serve the "Best Pizza in the World," this place gives itself a lot to live up to. But by offering generous toppings slathered over deep-dish crusts—a welcome treat at a snowy 4400 feet—it pulls off the claim without a hitch. The neighborhood feel and old-time style of the tiny eatery keep the locals coming back—and in a town of under 2000 people, that's a very good thing.

SEVEN SISTERS

$$$$ STEAK/SEAFOOD ✉ *Black Oak Casino, 19400 Tuolumne Road North, Tuolumne* 📞 *209-928-9363, 877-747-8777* ✎ *www.blackoakcasino.com*

Arugably the nicest restaurant in the area—and without a doubt the most expensive—this slick hotel-style dining room comes complete with mountaintop views of the Sierras. The menu ranges from fresh greens and pastas to sophisticated seafood dishes such as potato-crusted halibut served with passionfruit beurre blanc. You'll also find quality meat selections like pan-seared filet mignon with sweet crab and blackened pork chop with red onion marmalade. Sunday brunch available. Closed Monday and Tuesday.

SHOPPING

JAMESTOWN There are almost as many antique stores here as saloons. Dotted along falsefront Main Street are shops selling pieces that date back almost as far as the stores themselves. Matter of fact, other than an occasional pharmacy, hardware store, and knickknack shop, that's pretty much all you'll find here.

SONORA   Up in Sonora, you'll encounter a full-blown shopping scene. This is the commercial center for Southern Gold Country. Washington Street is lined with stores along its entire length. Since the shops cater to local residents, many are service outlets of little interest to travelers. But you will find clothiers, camera stores, jewelers, art galleries, bookshops, and antique stores.

COLUMBIA CANDY KITCHEN ⊠*22726 Main Street, Columbia* ✆*209-532-7886* Columbia has its own collection of shops—mostly antique, some touristy. Satisfy your sweet tooth at the Candy Kitchen, where much of the appetizing assortment of hard candy, taffy, fudge, and chocolate is dipped, pulled, and made on-site.

NIGHTLIFE

Jamestown is one place that remembers its past. Main Street in this 19th-century community is still decorated with a string of drinking spots.

NATIONAL HOTEL ⊠*18183 Main Street, Jamestown* ✆*209-984-3446, 800-894-3446* ✎*www.national-hotel.com, info@national-hotel.com* For casual drinking in an easy setting, this hotel bar is perfect. The atmosphere is rich with deep colors and Gold Rush history.

THE RAWHIDE SALOON ⊠*18260 Route 108, Jamestown* This get-down country bar is complete with pool tables, jukebox, dancefloor, and wide-screen TV. On Friday and Saturday night, country-and-western and rock bands crank up and wail into the wee hours. Cover for live music.

SIERRA REPERTORY THEATRE ⊠*11175 Washington Street, Columbia State Historic Park* ✆*209-532-3120* ✎*www.sierrarep.org, srt@mlode.com* In Columbia, the Sierra players perform dramas, musicals, and comedies year-round at the Fallon House Theatre.

SONORA HIGH SCHOOL ⊠*430 North Washington Street, Sonora* ✆*209-532-5511* ✎*www.sonorahs.k12.ca.us* For a true small-town experience, head to one of the Sonora High School games that bring out the locals. In the fall, football rules the field. In the winter, boys' and girls' basketball draws plenty of crowds and affords a great opportunity to people-watch.

BLACK OAK CASINO ⊠*19400 Tuolumne Road North, Tuolumne* ✆*877-747-8777* ✎*www.blackoakcasino.com* Much of the area's nightlife centers around this major American Indian enterprise about nine miles east of Sonora. Owned by the Mi Wuk tribe, the casino features slots, card tables, and theme buffets 24 hours a day. **Willow Creek Lounge** offers classic drinks, a dancefloor, and live entertainment until 2 a.m. If you're looking for family fun, the casino also boasts a bowling alley and an underground arcade open until about 10 p.m.

PARKS

COLUMBIA STATE HISTORIC PARK
⊠*Located off Route 49 about three miles north of Sonora* ✆*209-588-9128*
🚶 🐎 A fully reconstructed Gold Rush town, this park represents an ex-

traordinary outdoor museum. It stretches across many acres and provides a graphic representation of life in mid-19th-century California. Facilities include restrooms, picnic areas, restaurants, groceries, hotels, a museum, and much more.

▲ There is no camping in the park, but two private campgrounds for tents and RVs are close to the park. **'49er RV Ranch** (www.49rv.com) charges $33.90 double nightly for tent camping; full hookups and cable available. **Marble Quarry RV Park** (209-532-9539; www.marblequarry. com, info@marblequarry.com) collects $25 for partial hookups, $35 for full hookups and cable. Both feature picnic areas, hot showers, and other facilities. My vote goes to Marble Quarry RV Resort, where the folks are particularly friendly.

NEW MELONES LAKE TUTTLETOWN RECREATION AREA

✉ 7200 Reynolds Ferry Road, Sonora 📞 209-536-9094

🚶 🚴 🐎 ⛵ ⚓ 🛶 🚤 One of two scenic recreation areas around New Melones Lake, Tuttletown offers a great spot for outdoor activities, including water sports. Birdwatching is also a popular pasttime here, as both American bald eagles and great horned owls make their homes in the varied habitat, especially in the winter. You may also catch a glimpse of mule deer, gray foxes, California quail, red-tail hawks, and osprey.

▲ Tuttletown Campground features 161 sites with a few spaces big enough for larger RVs; there are also 65 sites at Acorn; $14 to $18 per night. Reservations recommended.

NEW MELONES LAKE GLORYHOLE RECREATION AREA

✉ Gloryhole is about 16 miles north of Sonora. 📞 877-444-6777

🚶 🚴 ⚓ 🎣 🚣 🛶 🚤 Set on the shores of spacious New Melones Lake, this area is popular with boaters and anglers. The entire lake is surrounded by oak trees and rolling hills, making it a pretty place to picnic. It was even more beautiful, conservationists claim, before the reservoir was created by the controversial Melones Dam, which flooded the historic Stanislaus River Valley. The **Visitor Center/ Museum** (209-536-9543; fax 209-536-9652; www.usbr.gov, pguida@ mp.usbr.gov) addresses this controversy, and also features exhibits on Miwok culture, local ecology, and Gold Rush and mining history. Both recreation areas have toilets and showers.

▲ There are 140 sites (including hike-ins) at Gloryhole Campground; $14 to $18 per night; two-week limit. Reservations recommended.

STANISLAUS NATIONAL FOREST

✉ From Route 49 you can take Route 120, Route 108, or Route 4 east through the forest. 📞 209-532-3671 📠 209-533-1890 💻 www.fs.fed.us/r5/stanislaus

🚶 🚴 🐎 🎿 ⛷ ⚓ 🎣 ⛵ 🛶 🚤 Rising along the western slope of the Sierra Nevada, this rugged region extends from the Gold Country to Yosemite National Park. Elevations range from 1100 to over 11,000 feet, and there are hiking trails through much of the forest's 1700 square miles. Since it parallels Route 49 and represents the nearest high country to San Francisco, Stanislaus is quite popular. Among its attractions are the Merced, Tuolumne, Clavey, Stanislaus, and Mokelumne rivers, which have cut deep canyons through the forest. Within the park is Pinecrest Recreation Area, which includes a 300-acre lake at 5500 feet. This is *the* summertime spot for families and groups who want to spend a day on the water. Throughout the park there are also ponderosa pine, incense cedar, cottonwood, and willows. Grouse, quail, black bear, and blacktail deer inhabit the mountains and wildflowers grow in brilliant profusion throughout the spring. Within the forest are picnic areas and restrooms; ranger stations are dotted around the area.

⚐ There are 49 campgrounds, including Pinecrest Campground, which has 200 sites; $19 per night; and Fraser Flat Campground, which has 38 sites; $15 per night. Some campgrounds are on a first-come, first-served basis; others by reservation only.

CENTRAL GOLD COUNTRY

Mark Twain and Bret Harte helped immortalize it. Birthplace of the California Gold Rush and a good place to visit American Indian landmarks, the central Mother Lode is also home to giant sequoias and wineries, a famous frog jumping contest, white-water rafting, and some favorite hiking trails. Spread out along Route 49 between Angels Camp and Placerville, this area is a great escape.

SIGHTS

MARK TWAIN CABIN

✉*Jackass Hill Road* About nine miles north of Sonora, a side road leads from Route 49 to the reconstructed Mark Twain Cabin, where the fledgling writer lived for five months during the 1860s. It was Twain's Gold Country story, "The Celebrated Jumping Frog of Calaveras County," that first propelled him to fame.

ANGELS CAMP

An annual jumping-frog contest takes place every May up in this old mining town, which Twain visited during his California sojourn. The community boasts several antique buildings and a museum, but its chief notoriety is literary; it hosted not only the creator of Huckleberry Finn, but also Bret Harte, who probably used the mining center as a model in his story, "The Luck of Roaring Camp."

GOLD CLIFF MINE ADVENTURE ✐*caverns@caverntours.com* Descend underground and tour mineral-rich caverns for a look at how the original forty-niners mined—and found—millions in gold. These guided group trips explore two different mines and include rafting over

HIDDEN LISTINGS

HISTORIC CARY HOUSE HOTEL

PAGE 489

Restored 1857 hotel decorated with dark wood trim and antiques—known as the "Jewel of Placerville"

SHENANDOAH VALLEY

PAGE 486

Prosperous wine-growing region in the Sierra foothills dotted with small vineyards specializing in zinfandel and syrah

CALAVERAS BIG TREES STATE PARK

PAGE 492

Cavernous state park with 18 miles of hiking trails traversing two groves of giant sequoias

ANGELS CAMP

PAGE 481

Charming mountain town—once a booming Gold Rush community that inspired Mark Twain's first successful novel

a 100-foot-deep flooded shaft. Hardhats and gloves are required for this family-friendly adventure.

From Angels Camp, Route 4 leaves Route 49 and heads east toward the High Sierra. On the way it passes several points of interest, including wineries, limestone caverns, the town of Murphys, and Calaveras Big Trees State Park.

IRISH VINEYARDS

✉2849 Route 4, Vallecito 📞209-736-1299 🖂www.irishvineyard.com, irish@goldrush.com Just before Murphys you'll come to Vallecito. Turn right at Parrotts Ferry Road, left on Batten Road, and soon you'll bump into Irish Vineyards, a family-owned and -operated winery fermenting a handful of red and white wines. Their tasting room is open Friday through Tuesday, and by appointment.

IRONSTONE VINEYARDS ✉1894 Six Mile Road, Murphys 📞209-728-1251
📠209-728-1275 🖂www.ironstonevineyards.com, service@ironstonevineyards.com
Whereas Irish Vineyards measures a wee 8.3 acres, Ironstone weighs in at 1150 acres. In addition to daily wine tastings, there's a gourmet deli,

a museum, a jewelry shop, a culinary exhibition center, and an outdoor amphitheater.

MURPHYS This attractive little town was established by two Irish brothers in 1848. Originally home to eager gold miners, today Murphys is comprised of about 2000 residents, and it boasts a pleasant downtown that still maintains its historic charm. The area also showcases just over a dozen family-owned wineries, many of which provide tasting rooms along the town's quaint Main Street. Contact the **Murphys Business Association** (www.visitmurphys.com, info@visitmurphys.com) for more information.

MURPHYS HISTORIC HOTEL ⊠*457 Main Street, Murphys* ☎*209-728-3444, 800-532-7684* ✎*www.murphyshotel.com, reservations@murphyshotel.com* Among the historic buildings fronting Murphys' treelined streets is this hotel. Built in 1856, it has housed an impressive assemblage of guests, among them Bret Harte, Jacob Astor, Jr., Count Von Rothschild, and Ulysses S. Grant.

CALAVERAS BIG TREES STATE PARK ⊠*Located along Route 4 about 25 miles east of Angels Camp* ☎*209-795-2334* ✆*209-795-7306* Many of the 19th-century luminaries signing the Murphys Hotel guest book were en route to the "Big Trees," which had been recently discovered and were fast becoming a world-famous tourist destination. Today Calaveras Big Trees State Park preserves these "Monarchs of the Forest." The park rests at 4000 to 5000 feet elevation. Within it are two groves of giant sequoias, the largest living things on earth. Closely related to coastal redwoods, these trees trace their ancestry back to the age of dinosaurs. One tree in the park stands 320 feet high, another measures 27 feet in diameter. Like their coastal cousins, they create a hushed sense of awe that cannot be described, but must be experienced as you stand amidst these mountain goliaths. Admission.

SAN ANDREAS The spirit of '49 remains alive and well on Route 49 as it continues north from Angels Camp. There are buildings of note in this old Gold Rush town.

MOKELUMNE HILL The argonaut community of Mokelumne Hill contains a Main Street lined with old-time buildings, including an **IOOF hall** that represents the Gold Country's first three-story structure.

COUNTRY TOURS _____ **h**idden

Two country tours in this region will carry you past ancient mining claims tucked in the mountains. Little evidence remains of the '49ers, but the routes lead through pretty places away from civilization. First is an alternative 25-mile route from Angels Camp to San Andreas via Dogtown, Calvaritas, and Mountain Ranch roads. These country lanes wind past rolling ranchlands and mountain streams. Second is a westward course 11 miles each way to Campo Seco. From Mokelumne Hill take Route 26 to Paloma Road to Campo Seco Road. Settled by Mexicans in 1849, **Campo Seco** reveals its gilded past in a series of stone ruins lining the road.

Central Gold Country

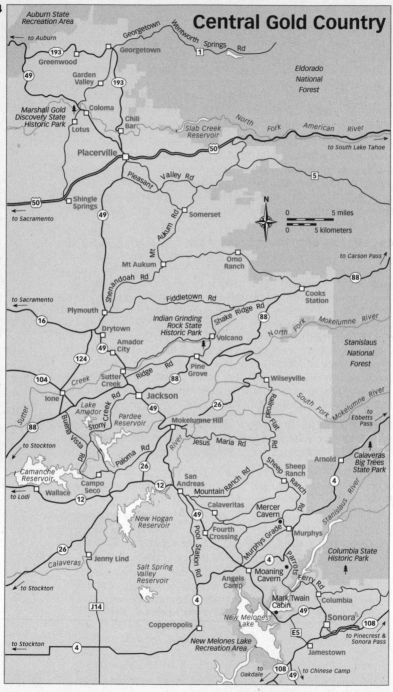

JACKSON   During the surge and flutter of the gold rush in 1849, French tradesman Louis Tellier set up a post in this town located at the fork of a creek. By 1853, Jackson had its own post office and stagecoach service. Today the historic town features some of its original structures, most impressively, the two-story brick **Masonic Building**, which has been standing since 1854. To fully appreciate the history, take the walking tour starting at the Amador Museum and visit the 19th-century cemetery, old jail house and myriad Western-style architecture throughout town. Maps for this self-guided tour are available at the **Amador County Chamber of Commerce** (9125 Peek Street, Suite B, Jackson; 209-223-0350; www.amadorcountychamber.com, info@ amadorcountychamber.com), which is closed on weekends.

AMADOR   COUNTY   MUSEUM ✉225 Church Street, Jackson ✆209-223-6386 In addition to a balconied Main Street, Jackson features this museum. One of the region's best, it honors the Chinese with displays of abacuses, Chinese drums, and coolie hats. Also here are a Kennedy Mine Model (open on weekends; fee), geologic showcases, and a photograph collection featuring the dourest-looking people imaginable. Closed Monday, Tuesday, and December.

SUTTER CREEK   The next town along Route 49 is named for the man on whose land gold was first discovered, John Sutter. Sutter Creek warrants a walking tour, too. Within a few blocks along Main and Spanish streets are dozens of buildings and homes rich with history.

VOLCANO   This well-preserved mining center, located on Sutter Creek Road about 12 miles east of the town of Sutter Creek, was a booming town of 5000 back in the days of the argonauts. In addition to a Masonic hall, express office, and three-story hotel, the community sports another relic—"Old Abe." According to local folks, this cannon was used during the Civil War to warn off Confederate sympathizers who sought to divert the town's gold to the Rebel cause. There are other motives for visiting this mountainside retreat.

MOANING CAVERN AND MERCER CAVERNS ✉Moaning Cavern ✆209-736-2708, 866-762-2837 ✆209-736-0330 ✐www.caverntours.com, caverns@ caverntours.com ✆209-728-2101 ✆209-728-2101 ✐www.mercercaverns.com These extraordinary limestone formations descend hundreds of feet underground; guided tours lead into the subterranean cathedrals where rock formations are twisted into bizarre figures. Entering them is like descending into an ice palace filled with sparkling creations. Above ground, you can mine for gemstones in a flume system or walk the interpretive nature trail. If you prefer a fullbore spelunking tour at Moaning Cavern or in another nearby cavern, you can schedule that as well. For an extra thrill, strap in to the twin zip lines that race 1500 feet above scenic trails near the caverns. No experience is necessary to launch from one tower and hit speeds of over 40 mph. Admission at both.

INDIAN GRINDING ROCK STATE HISTORIC PARK ✉Pine Grove–Volcano Road ✆209-296-7488 ✆209-296-7528 On the same road two miles from Volcano is this state historic park, an authentic roundhouse still used by local Miwok. Here along a limestone outcropping the

Miwok Indians gathered to collect acorns and grind seeds, berries, and nuts. Using the limestone bedrock as a natural mortar, they eventually ground over a thousand cavities in the rock. These unusual mortar holes, together with several hundred petroglyphs, can be toured along a self-guided trail. You'll also pass facsimile displays of bark houses, granaries, and a Miwok playing field. An on-site museum covers Sierra American Indian tribes. Admission.

AMADOR CITY   North from Sutter Creek, Route 49 bisects Amador City. The focus of a quartz mining operation, this pretty community still contains many of its original brick and woodframe buildings.

DRYTOWN   It was the creek, not the miners, that was dry in neighboring Drytown. Matter of fact, the place contained about 25 saloons during its golden youth.

SHENANDOAH VALLEY WINE-GROWING REGION

From Plymouth, just north of Drytown, take a side trip up Shenandoah Road (County Road E16) to the Shenandoah Valley wine-growing region. Vineyards have prospered here since Gold Rush days and at present almost two dozen wineries dot the area. Many are clustered along a ten-mile stretch of Shenandoah Road.

SOBON ESTATE

✉*14430 Shenandoah Road, Plymouth* ✆*209-245-6554* ▨*209-245-5156* ✑*www.sobonwine.com, info@sobonwine.com* Foremost in Shenandoah Valley wine region is Sobon, which dates from 1856. Enjoy the tasting room or take a self-guided tour through the original cellar. This rock-walled enclosure still contains the old handmade oak casks and hewn wooden beams. Specializing in zinfandel, Sobon also produces French syrah and viognier. While this winery is open daily, others have limited schedules and often require reservations.

APPLE HILL   Located on a mountain ridge east of Placerville, this area is crowded with orchards where for a modest fee you can pick your own apples. Many of the orchards lie just off Route 50 on Carson Road. If visiting between September and December during the apple harvest, ask at the **El Dorado County Chamber of Commerce** (542 Main Street, Placerville; 530-621-5885; www.visit-eldorado.com) for information about Apple Hill.

PLACERVILLE   One of the largest towns in the Mother Lode, Placerville has been heavily developed and lacks the charm of neighboring villages. There are a few historic places remaining, however.

GOLD BUG MINE   ✉*2635 Gold Bug Lane, off Bedford Avenue, one mile from downtown Placerville* ✆*530-642-5207* ▨*530-642-5238* Step between the timbers and explore a narrow stone tunnel that leads deep into the earth here. One of the few mines open to the public, Gold Bug also features a weatherbeaten stamp press mill used to grind gold from bedrock. Closed weekdays from November through February.

ROUTE 193 Placerville also served as a supply center for other mining towns, including several that can be visited via a side trip along Route 193. Just north of town you can pick up this mountain road and follow it in a 28-mile semicircle, rejoining Route 49 a few miles south of Auburn. In the course of its arc, the road curls along the sides of the mountains as it curves up from the American River Valley. There are open views of pine-fringed peaks and dark green canyons. Among the old mining communities are **Chili Bar**, perched astride the American River, **Georgetown** with its antique buildings lining a boulevard-wide Main Street, and the one-street town of **Greenwood**.

MARSHALL GOLD DISCOVERY STATE HISTORIC PARK ✉*Route 49, Coloma* ☎*530-622-3470* 📠*530-622-3472* This country detour is recommended only if you plan to cover the Placerville to Auburn span along Route 49 as well. Otherwise you'll miss Marshall Gold Discovery State Historic Park. Like Columbia, this park features the remains of the Gold Rush town of Coloma. It also happens to be the place where it all began. Here on January 24, 1848, James Marshall found shining metal in a sawmill owned by himself and John Sutter. "Boys," Marshall exclaimed, "I believe I have found a gold mine." The history of California and the West was changed forever. Within the park, a self-guiding trail leads past a reconstruction of Sutter's mill and to the discovery site on the banks of the American River. With the skeletal-looking mill on one hand and a foaming river on the other, it's an eerie sensation standing on the spot that once lured tens of thousands across a continent. There's also a museum with display cases portraying the days of '49 and a miner's cabin complete with long johns and animal pelts hanging from the rafters. In all, this 574-acre park features two dozen points of interest and is second only to Columbia in its ability to evoke California's glittery past. Admission.

LODGING

QUERENCIA
$$$$ 4 ROOMS ✉*4383 Sheep Ranch Road, Murphys* ☎*209-728-9520* 🖰*www.querencia.ws, info@querencia.ws*
Set on 80 acres above Murphys is this sumptuous 6500-square-foot architectural delight that's home to an indoor waterfall. Four spacious guest rooms offer king- or queen-size beds, gas fireplaces, tile showers, and private patios or balconies. You'll also find a wine cellar and a reading room. The grounds at this secluded enclave are interlaced with paths ripe for exploration; guests can also stroll through the flower, herb, and vegetable gardens.

MURPHYS HISTORIC HOTEL
$$–$$$$ 9 ROOMS ✉*457 Main Street, Murphys* ☎*209-728-3444, 800-532-7684* 📠*209-728-1590* 🖰*www.murphyshotel.com, reservations@murphyshotel.com*
I get a kick out of spending the night in the same room where Mark Twain once slept at Murphys Historic Hotel. I wonder if I'd feel richer or just less funny if I stayed in William Randolph Hearst's room there, but

so far I haven't tried. The place dates to 1856 and also numbers among its previous guests Ulysses S. Grant and Black Bart. The nine rooms are still maintained much as they were back when, with oak wardrobes, antique dressers, and patterned wallpaper. Each room has the name of a famous guest painted on the door; all share baths. For a historic splurge, book the presidential suite, containing the same bed on which Grant slept. (There's also an adjoining motel, but staying there contradicts the reason for coming to Murphys.)

IONE HOTEL

$$ 14 ROOMS ✉ *25 West Main Street, Ione* 📞 *209-274-6082* 📠 *209-274-0750*

Step back into the days of yore at this restored inn dating from the 1850s. Today, the guest rooms, each located on the second floor with easy balcony access, are all decorated with antiques. Three units have clawfoot tubs, while all are fully carpeted and air-conditioned. For an added thrill, request the more rustic Room 13. It's supposedly haunted by a ghost named George.

NATIONAL HOTEL

$$ 22 ROOMS ✉ *2 Water Street, Jackson* 📞 *209-223-0500* 📠 *209-223-4845*

One of the better bargains in all the Gold Country is found here. This hulking hotel claims every California governor since 1862 (until 1960) as a guest, not to mention Presidents Garfield and Hoover. Standard rooms are small, furnished with antiques, and some have TVs. There's a Western-style saloon downstairs.

SUTTER CREEK INN _____

$$–$$$ 17 ROOMS ✉ *75 Main Street, Sutter Creek* 📞 *209-267-5606*
📠 *209-267-9287* ✎ *www.suttercreekinn.com, info@suttercreekinn.com*

This inn provides the most commodious lodging in town. Innkeeper Jane Way has been running this facility since 1966 and doing so with special flair. Among her trademarks are four rooms with swinging beds, a complete country-style breakfast, and a spacious lawn with secret gardens, shade trees, and hammocks for lounging guests. Some of the guest rooms are located in the main house, a New England–style home built of redwood in 1859; others are located in the cottages that dot the grounds. Each room is individual in size, decor, and furnishings, but all feature private baths and many have fireplaces and private patios. There's also a library where guests can cozy up with a good book.

IMPERIAL HOTEL _____

$$ 9 ROOMS ✉ *14202 Highway 49, Amador City* 📞 *209-267-9172*
✎ *www.imperialamador.com, info@imperialamador.com*

This whimsical, restored Victorian hotel houses six rooms on the second floor of the original 1879 building and three larger ones in a 1930s garden cottage. Hotel accommodations have high ceilings and original brick walls. Cottage rooms have private entrances, whirlpool jacuzzi tubs for two, fireplaces, and refrigerators. All are decorated in the style of the Gold Rush days, with period furniture and layers of ornamentation. There are no phones or TVs in the rooms, encouraging guests to mingle over cocktails in the bar or choose a book from the well-stocked library.

RANCHO CICADA RETREAT

$$–$$$ 26 UNITS ✉10001 Bell Road, Plymouth ☎209-245-4841, 877-553-9481 ☏209-245-3357 ⌫www.ranchocicadaretreat.com, ranchocicada@gmail.com

This gay resort located along the Cosumnes River offers rustic accommodations in two comfortably furnished cabins (year-round) and 24 cabins/tents set on platforms and equipped with mattresses (May through October, weather permitting). Although it caters primarily to private groups, the resort also welcomes individuals. The grounds include rock gardens, lawns, hiking trails, a large hot tub, and places for sunbathing, volleyball, croquet, and swimming. Reservations required.

HISTORIC CARY HOUSE HOTEL

$$$ 38 ROOMS ✉300 Main Street, Placerville ☎530-622-4271 ☏530-622-0696 ⌫www.caryhouse.com, manager@caryhouse.com

When it was built in 1857, the three-story Historic Cary Hotel was reputed to be the finest hotel in the Gold Country. Its name was changed twice, and in 1915 it was demolished and rebuilt using the same bricks. In 1997, after a complete renovation, the original name was restored. The lobby is richly appointed with floral carpeting and dark wood trim. The guest accommodations are Victorian in style. All have private baths and air conditioning, and most have kitchenettes and king- or queen-size beds.

ALBERT SHAFSKY HOUSE BED & BREAKFAST

$$ 3 ROOMS ✉2942 Columa Street, Placerville ☎530-642-2776, 866-385-6466 ⌫www.shafsky.com, stay@shafsky.com

In the heart of the historic district, this Queen Anne Victorian offers rooms with private baths and fireplaces. Taffeta curtains, damask and velvet chairs, and period-style mahogany furniture provide the romantic atmosphere. Free wi-fi, refrigerators, satellite TV, and the daily paper bring it up to date.

SIERRA NEVADA HOUSE

$$ 6 ROOMS ✉835 Lotus Road, Coloma ☎530-626-8096 ☏530-626-8565 ⌫www.sierranevadahouse.com, info@sierranevadahouse.com

A town fixture since the 1850s, this B&B has been a hotel for miners and a silent movie house. Rebuilt after a 1925 fire, it houses Buford's Bar and a café downstairs and renovated rooms upstairs. Decorated with antiques in a subdued style, all have private baths and open to an outdoor veranda with superb views of the valley.

DINING

MURPHYS HISTORIC HOTEL

$$ AMERICAN ✉ *457 Main Street, Murphys* ☎ *209-728-3444, 800-532-7684*
📠 *209-728-1590* 🖂 *www.murphyshotel.com, reservations@murphyshotel.com*

A 19th-century hostelry, Murphys features an informal dining room. Though there are antiques dotted about, the restaurant lacks the charm of the hotel. The Continental menu features a full breakfast, lunch, and an array of dinnertime spreads.

VILLA BUSCAGLIA'S

$$–$$$ ITALIAN ✉ *1218 Jackson Road, Jackson* ☎ *209-223-9992*
🖂 *www.buscaglias.com*

First opened as a miners' tavern in 1905, this property was eventually bought by the Buscaglia family, who in 1919 added a restaurant. Today, both tavern and restaurant are going strong. The restaurant serves regional Italian cuisine such as fettuccine with pancetta and cream sauce, or seafood cannelloni in lobster cream sauce, but you can also find steaks, lamb, veal, and osso buco. The romantic decor resembles Old World Italy, with stucco, brick walls, and fireside seating. Closed Monday and Tuesday.

GOLDEN STAR RESTAURANT & SALOON

$$$ AMERICAN ✉ *25 West Main Street, Ione Hotel, Ione* ☎ *209-274-6082*
🖂 *www.ionehotel.com, info@ionehotel.com*

A restored 19th-century bar stands as the centerpiece of the Golden Star. Fashioned into a Chicago-style pub, this restaurant features chandeliers, shiny wooden floors, and the feel of the Old West. Dine on pasta, steaks, or other hearty cowboy fare. Local wines complement any meal. Breakfast and lunch served daily; dinner served Tuesday through Sunday.

ZACHARY JACQUE

$$$–$$$$ FRENCH ✉ *1821 Pleasant Valley Road, Placerville* ☎ *530-626-8045*
🖂 *www.zacharyjacques.com*

This provincial French restaurant is trimly appointed with paintings and decorative china plates. Wood paneling and a cozy fireplace add to its warm appeal. Though the menu is seasonal, you can always choose from staples like rack of lamb, duck with walnuts and apples, and wild salmon with béarnaise sauce. Closed Monday and Tuesday.

SHOPPING

There are several arts and crafts shops in Angels Camp, Murphys, Jackson, and Volcano. Then, proceeding north, you'll encounter a pair of towns with antique buildings that have been remodeled into charming shops.

SUTTER CREEK Within a couple of blocks are no fewer than a dozen antique shops. Of course in this historic town, the stores as well as their contents are antiques: Even the local plumbing company is situated in an 1869 building.

OLD HOTEL ANTIQUES ✉*68 Main Street, Sutter Creek* ✆*209-267-5901*
Along the 19th-century Main Street are shops like this one. It boasts
Depression glass, old Coca-Cola advertisements, and antique jewelry.

AMADOR CITY   This city has been renovated in like fashion. Route
49 barrels through the center of this aged town, past handicrafts shops,
art galleries, and those places that seem more plentiful than restaurants—antique stores.

PLACERVILLE   This community serves as a regional shopping area
for the Central Gold Country, with stores of all sizes.

GOLD HILL OLIVE OIL COMPANY ✉*5601 Gold Hill Road, Placerville*
✆*530-621-7073* ✐*www.goldhilloliveoilco.com* Check out this olive oil company for a fine selection of quality, locally manufactured olive oils—not
to mention vinegars, health and beauty products, and even actual olive
trees! Closed Monday through Thursday.

NIGHTLIFE

There are nondescript bars in Angels Camp, San Andreas, and Mokelumne Hill.

MURPHYS HISTORIC HOTEL ✉*457 Main Street, Murphys* ✆*209-728-
3444, 800-532-7684* ✐*www.murphyshotel.com* Up at the old Murphys there's
an old-time miners' saloon. The crowd here is drawn not only by the
nightlife, but also because of the fame of this hostelry. There's occasional live music.

NATIONAL HOTEL ✉*2 Water Street, Jackson* ✆*209-223-0500* There's a
Western-style saloon in the historic old National Hotel. The place is
complete with bright red wallpaper, gilded mirrors, and glittery chandeliers. On weekends DJs and live bands are offered.

PJ'S ROADHOUSE ✉*5641 Mother Lode Drive, Placerville* ✆*530-626-0336*
✐*www.pjsroadhouse.net* Just outside Placerville, PJ's hosts bands every
Friday and Saturday night. Other evenings you can play shuffleboard,
shoot pool, or watch sports on big-screen televisions.

COLOMA CLUB ✉*7171 Route 49, Coloma* ✆*530-626-6390* ✐*www.coloma
club.com* There are rock-and-roll or country bands every weekend here.
It's a down-home bar complete with pool table and dancefloor as well
as karaoke nights.

Theater
High culture is also part of the Gold Country tradition. If visiting during
a weekend in summer, you might take in a show by one of the region's
many repertory groups. Several feature traditional drama, though most
present light melodramas.

VOLCANO THEATRE COMPANY ✉*Volcano* ✆*209-223-9076* ✐*www.
volcanotheater.org* Out in Volcano, the theatre company headlines at the
Cobblestone Theatre. Their season runs April through October.

COLOMA CRESCENT PLAYERS ✉*380 Monument Road, Coloma* ☏*530-626-5282* ✐*www.oldecolmatheatre.com* These local players are featured at the Coloma Theatre.

PARKS

CALAVERAS BIG TREES
STATE PARK _____

✉*Highway 4; four miles northeast of Arnold* ☏*209-795-2334*

🚶 🚵 🎿 ⚓ Straddling the north fork of the Stanislaus River, this magnificent park covers almost 6300 acres of mountainous terrain. Its 18 miles of hiking trails lead along deep canyons and riverside beaches. The chief attractions, however, are the two groves of giant sequoias. Of particular interest is the South Grove, explored along a five-mile trail, which still possesses a sense of the primeval. Facilities in the park include an information center, museum, picnic areas, and restrooms. Day-use fee, $6.

⚑ There are 74 sites at Northgrove Campground and 55 sites at Oak Hollow Campground; both campgrounds have showers; $20 per night.

INDIAN GRINDING ROCK
STATE HISTORIC PARK _____

✉*14881 Pine Grove–Volcano Road, Pine Grove off Route 88; About 12 miles east of Jackson* ☏*209-296-7488* 🖷*209-296-7528*

🚶 Set at about 2400-feet elevation, this facility features interesting American Indian displays in the Regional Indian Museum. There are bedrock mortars, petroglyphs, and a reconstructed Miwok village complete with dwellings. The forest is filled with manzanita and ponderosa pine, as well as black oak trees from which the Miwok gathered acorns. Facilities include picnic areas, restrooms, and showers. Day-use fee, $6.

⚑ There are 23 sites; $20 per night. Also on these grounds are seven "bark houses," primitive campsites that are representative of the Miwok way of life. Each of these houses can accommodate up to six people; $20 per night.

MARSHALL GOLD DISCOVERY STATE HISTORIC PARK

✉*310 Back Street, Coloma* ☏*530-622-3470* ✐*marshallgold@parks.ca.gov*

🚶 🚲 ⛵ 🚣 ⚓ This re-created Gold Rush town off of Route 49 was the site of the original strike. The primary interest is historic and the park is fully described in the "Central Gold County" section above. Canoeing and kayaking are at North Beach only. Facilities include an information center and museum, historical buildings and displays, picnic areas, and restrooms. Day-use fee, $5.

⚑ Camping is not permitted within the park, but there are campgrounds located nearby. The closest is **Coloma Resort** (6921 Mount Murphy Road, Coloma, off Route 49; 530-621-2267, fax 530-621-4960; www.colomaresort.com). It has over 100 campsites; fees are $45 per night (showers and general store are available).

AMERICAN RIVER RESORT ✉*6019 New River Road, Coloma* ☎*530-622-6700* 🖱*www.americanriverresort.com* Near Marshall Gold Discovery State Historic Park is this resort, with riverside sites for $30 to $35 per night (showers, restaurant, grocery, and swimming pool on the premises; open seasonally).

CAMP LOTUS ✉*5461 Bassi Road, Lotus* ☎*530-622-8672* 🖷*530-622-0103* 🖱*www.camplotus.com* A few miles from Coloma this camp has riverbank camping and is very popular with river rafters ($30 per night on Friday and Saturday. $21 per night the rest of the week; fees are based on three people). There's a deli here with sandwiches and espresso drinks, and a store selling camping and rafting supplies. Closed November through January.

NORTHERN GOLD COUNTRY

This forested region features colorful pinnacles, covered bridges, mining museums, and some of the state's more notable Victorians. The fastest growing part of the Gold Country, it also offers cross-country skiing, inviting river swimming holes, ghost towns, and 19th-century hotels that are a journey back in time. Extending from Auburn to Sierra City, the northern section of the Mother Lode is traversed by the historic transcontinental railroad.

SIGHTS

AUBURN Auburn, like Placerville, has grown too large to enjoy the rural charm of other Mother Lode communities. The only section of note is "Old Town," built near the American River in the 19th century. There's an interesting walking tour through this brick-and-woodframe neighborhood, which you should take after obtaining an Old Town map from the **Auburn Chamber of Commerce** (601 Lincoln Way, Auburn; 530-885-5616, fax 530-885-5854; www.auburnchamber.net, info@auburnchamber.net). Closed weekends. Among the sights are a trim three-story firehouse capped with a bell tower, an old town antique shopping center, and a maze of falsefront streets.

NORTH STAR MINING AND PELTON WATERWHEEL MUSEUM ✉*End of Mill Street on Allison Ranch Road, Grass Valley* ☎*530-273-4255* 🖱*www.nevada countyhistory.org* The mines to the north along Route 49 were a far cry from the simple mining claims that started the Gold Rush. Prominent during the latter half of the 19th century, these big buck operations were heavily industrialized. Grass Valley, for instance, has 367 miles of tunnels running beneath its streets. The town's North Star Mining and Pelton Waterwheel Museum displays the sophisticated machinery that replaced the gold pan and rocker. Closed mid-October through April.

EMPIRE MINE STATE HISTORIC PARK ✉*10791 East Empire Street, Grass Valley* ☎*530-273-8522* 🖷*530-274-1960* At this historic park you can view the engineering office and machine shops of the richest hardrock

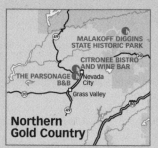

HIDDEN LISTINGS

Northern
Gold Country

MALAKOFF DIGGINS STATE HISTORIC PARK
PAGE 500

3000 remote acres with a well-preserved Gold Rush town and miles of trails sloping from river beds to alpine heights

CITRONEE WINE BAR
PAGE 498

Charming spot pairing fresh, seasonal, organic foods with an impressive array of wines from Italy, Spain, and Australia

THE PARSONAGE BED & BREAKFAST
PAGE 497

Historic bed and breakfast decorated with authentic Victorian pieces honoring Gold Country pioneer spirit

gold mine in California. Walk about 50 feet into the black entranceway of a shaft that leads nearly a mile down and wander through the many buildings comprising this multimillion dollar venture. With its eroded hillsides, the surrounding area presents a graphic illustration of how mining destroyed the landscape. It's ironic that the rich mine owners, whose opulent homes you can view here, chose to build their estates in neighborhoods they were turning to rubble heaps. Admission.

GRASS VALLEY Despite the scars, Grass Valley still reveals several pretty sections. Along Mill and Main streets, the gas lamps, awnings, balconies, and brick facades remain from the gold era.

Grass Valley's most famous resident was Lola Montez, a dancer notorious for her love affairs with European notables such as Alexander Dumas, Czar Nicolas I of Russia, and "Mad" King Ludwig of Bavaria. After a performance tour of Gold Country opera houses, Montez retired to a house in Grass Valley, but scandal pursued her. Though prostitutes worked the streets of this mining town openly, the aging mistress of a foreign king aroused moral indignation. Montez was ultimately forced to flee California after horsewhipping a local newspaper editor who had attacked her in print. Her seven-year-old protégée, Lotta Crabtree, eventually became a nationally renowned theatrical entertainer.

A replica of the Lola Montez House contains the **Grass Valley Chamber of Commerce** (248 Mill Street, Grass Valley; 530-273-4667, fax 530-272-5440; www.grassvalleychamber.com, info@ grassvalleychamber.com), where you can obtain brochures and walking maps. Closed Sunday.

NEVADA CITY This was once the third largest city in California. Still grand by local standards, it nevertheless has a country village charm. There are gaslights, turreted houses, and balconied stores along Broad Street. Much of the Victorian elegance remains amid the widow's walks, church steeples, and gingerbread facades, and the downtown is listed on the National Register of Historic Places.

NEVADA CITY CHAMBER OF COMMERCE ⊠ *132 Main Street, Nevada City* ✆ *530-265-2692* 🖨 *530-265-3892* ✐ *www.nevadacitychamber.com, info@ nevadacitychamber.com* A walking map of Nevada City is available from the chamber of commerce. It will guide you through the historic heart of town. Closed Sunday.

MALAKOFF DIGGINS STATE HISTORIC PARK ⊠ *23579 North Bloomfield–Graniteville Road* ✆ *530-265-2740* For an adventurous side trip from town, head to Malakoff Diggins. While it is a fully developed park, this area is so remote it represents a good example of "hidden California." Huge cliffs show the destructive force gold mining had on this region. Also here is a 7800 bedrock tunnel that once served as a drain from the mountain to the farmland downstream.The journey to this park will carry you over the Yuba River, where the scenery is startling and the seclusion splendid.

The park includes the rustic town of **North Bloomfield**, built during the 1850s as one of the nation's largest hydraulic gold-mining centers. There's a livery stable filled with wagons, plus a whitewashed church, a saloon, an 1890s furnished home, and an old general store, all neatly preserved. The immediate area has been heavily eroded by hydraulic mining, which involves washing away hillsides with hoses, then sifting gold from the mud. Bald cliffs and a miniature lake remain as evidence of these destructive techniques. But the rest of the region is wild and untouched, wide open for exploration. Tours are available daily during the summer and on weekends in winter. Admission.

BRIDGEPORT COVERED BRIDGE

To delve deeper into the mountains, continue north from Nevada City on Route 49. Towns are few and far in this region of tall pines and deep river valleys. About 13 miles from town you can take a 14-mile (roundtrip) detour along Pleasant Valley Road to this covered bridge in South Yuba River State Park. Stretching 230 feet, it is reputedly the West's longest single-span covered bridge.

DOWNIEVILLE Route 49 follows a serpentine course along the Yuba River as it climbs to this enchanting town cradled in a canyon. The crooked streets and tin-roof houses of this 1849 settlement are completely encircled by mountains. The town gallows and many picturesque buildings still stand in this natural amphitheater.

SIERRA CITY Higher still is Sierra City, built in the shadow of the Sierra Buttes. The highway streams past fruit orchards and alpine meadows en route to this avalanche-plagued town, then climbs 6700-foot Yuba Pass and heads for the High Sierra.

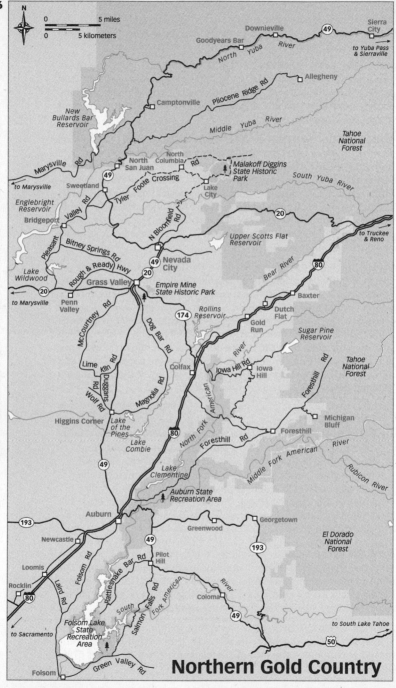

Northern Gold Country

TRAVELODGE

$$ 76 UNITS ✉13490 Lincoln Way, Auburn ✆530-885-7025, 877-885-7025
✆530-885-9503

The Travelodge is a 1970s time warp, with comfortable units spread across three buildings. Rooms offer king- and queen-sized beds, vanities, and small tables convenient for workaholics and families that like to dine in. There's a seasonal swimming pool and whirlpool on the premises.

GRASS VALLEY COURTYARD SUITES

$$-$$$ 36 ROOMS ✉210 North Auburn Street, Grass Valley ✆530-272-7696
✆530-272-1203 ✑www.gvcourtyardsuites.com, info@gvcourtyardsuites.com

Rooms range from a basic but spacious king to a super-size queen with two beds, full kitchen, and separate living room. This hotel/B&B combo is nestled in a quiet neighborhood just one block from Main Street. Amenities include a spa and seasonally heated pool, fitness center and sauna, and guest laundry facilities. Rooms are stocked with coffeemakers, microwaves, refrigerators, DVD players, and DSL connections.

NATIONAL HOTEL

$$-$$$ 9 ROOMS ✉211 Broad Street, Nevada City ✆530-265-4551
✆530-265-2445 ✑www.thenationalhotel.com

Anchoring the center of Nevada City, the National claims to be the oldest continuously operating hotel west of the Rockies. With its bar, dining room, and Victorian decor, the place has served travelers since the 1850s. Accommodations vary from rooms that are plain but comfortable to suites that feature love-seats, canopy beds, and 19th-century frills.

THE PARSONAGE
BED & BREAKFAST

$$-$$$ 6 ROOMS ✉427 Broad Street, Nevada City ✆530-265-9478,
877-265-9499 ✆530-265-8147 ✑www.theparsonage.net

For a true living-history experience, delve into the secret treasures of The Parsonage. Each of the six bedrooms honors a Dane family pioneer who settled in the Gold Country in the 1850s. The house is decorated with authentic period pieces and attention to detail is a way of life. The full breakfast includes fresh baked muffins and croissants, and homemade jams and fresh fruit, all served on Haviland china. Closed first two weeks of January.

EMMA NEVADA HOUSE

$$-$$$ 6 ROOMS ✉528 East Broad Street, Nevada City ✆530-265-4415,
800-916-3662 ✆530-25-4416 ✑www.emmanevadahouse.com

This lovely Victorian was the childhood home of 19th-century opera star Emma Nevada and has been restored to a shine. In a quiet location steps from the historic district, it offers sunny decks, a wraparound porch, understated decor, and breakfast served in the hexagonal Sun Room. Guest rooms all have private baths and queen- or king-sized beds. The top choice for honeymooners is the Empress's Chamber, with its wall of windows, ivory and burgundy tones, and a jacuzzi tub for two.

DINING

LATITUDES RESTAURANT, GALLERY AND BAR-CAFÉ

$$–$$$ INTERNATIONAL   ✉130 Maple Street, Auburn   ☎530-885-9535
🖰www.latitudesrestaurant.com

Latitudes serves up a colorful selection of worldly dishes in an 1870 Victorian home. Try the savory curried tofu with papaya chutney or the filet mignon with rosemary potatoes. Deck seating wraps around a huge, 200-year-old oak tree, and beneath the restaurant are a bar and art gallery. The lunch menu includes lighter fare such as falafel and salads. Sunday brunch. Closed Monday and Tuesday.

CITRONEE BISTRO AND WINE BAR

$$ FRENCH   ✉320 Broad Street, Nevada City   ☎530-265-5697
🖰www.citroneebistro.com.

Fresh, local, seasonal, organic, and sustainable are the bywords for this charming French-decor bistro. There's an impressive stock of wines from Italy, Spain, and Australia. Buy a bottle from the attached wine shop and enjoy it with a daily special, which might include such exotic fare as braised rabbit with cognac, orange, and dried prunes or a tender grilled filet mignon with puréed potatoes and roasted shallots drizzled with veal reduction and black truffle oil. Dinner only. Closed Tuesday.

FRIAR TUCK'S

$$$–$$$$ CONTINENTAL   ✉111 North Pine Street, Nevada City   ☎530-265-9093
🖰www.friartucks.com

Here you can dine in the Sherwood Forest room (dominated by a faux oak tree), high-backed booths in the main room, or in the Pine Street Room overlooking the historic district. With its brick walls and dark interior, the restaurant is reminiscent of an old gold mine. But fresh flowers and a guitarist performing through dinner add warmth to one of the region's most popular restaurants. Fondue is the specialty, with steak, chicken, meatball, shrimp, and cheese versions available; you can also order teriyaki steak, ribs, roast duck, or fresh fish. Dinner only.

THE COUNTRY ROSE CAFE

$$–$$$$ SEAFOOD   ✉300 Commercial Street, Nevada City   ☎530-265-6248

This café is the latest incarnation of an 1861 brick building originally built as a grocery store. Huge trees shade the patio; inside, copper pots and pans and bouquets of dried flowers decorate the walls. Seafood is the specialty here: Salmon with spinach and brie and halibut with almond crust number among the favorites. Steak, pasta, and lamb are also served. The menu changes weekly. Lunches tend toward soups, sandwiches, and an array of specials. Closed Monday.

AUBURN This town contains expansive shopping sections and serves as a regional center for folks throughout the central Mother Lode. Window browsing Auburn's "Old Town" section is tantamount to a historic adventure. Most of the 19th-century buildings have been converted to shops. The Empire Livery Stable is now a minimall, the old Hop Sing Laundry and Chinese Joss Houses are antique stores. Located along Sacramento, Washington, and Commercial streets are other new shops in old clothing.

NEVADA CITY Grass Valley and Nevada City are the chief shopping destinations in the northern Mother Lode area. The better of the two is Nevada City, where early stores have received a face-lift. And if you're looking for books about Gold Country history, you've definitely come to the right place; independent bookstores seem to thrive here. Within a few blocks of the historic district, you'll find **Harmony Books** (231 Broad Street, Nevada City; 530-265-9564), **Brigadoon Books** (108 North Pine, Nevada City; 530-265-3450), and **Wisdom Café and Gallery** (426 Broad Street, Nevada City; 530-265-4204). You'll also find a jewelry shop beside the family barber, a T-shirt store near an old saloon, and an oriental rug shop next door to a historic hotel. The best places to browse are along Broad, Commercial, and North Pine streets. Happy hunting!

NIGHTLIFE

MCGEE'S ANNEX ✉ *315 Broad Street, Nevada City* ✆ *530-265-3205* Nevada City has two varied nightspots within a few doors of one another. McGee's Annex is a posh, brick-walled drinking emporium with overhead fans and stained glass decoration that's good for a quiet cocktail. There are deejays on weekends. Cover.

CIRINO'S ✉ *309 Broad Street, Nevada City* ✆ *530-265-2246* This dark wood saloon exudes historic Gold Rush–era charm and offers a great spot for an evening drink or late-night Italian dish. Friday and Saturday nights are especially popular with locals.

PARKS

AUBURN STATE RECREATION AREA

✉ *The ranger station is located along Route 49 about one mile south of Auburn.*
✆ *530-885-4527* ✉ *asra@cyber.com*

🚶🚴🏇⚓⚓⚓⚓⚓⚓ This sprawling facility covers over 30,000 acres and includes Lake Clementine, a small reservoir. Long and narrow in its configuration, the park follows the American River basin for about 30 miles. There are opportunities to swim and fish in this former placer mining region. It's also a great hiking destination with 58 miles of trails, some near the water, some climbing to lookout points. Portable toilets are the only facilities.

▲ Permitted in 35 primitive sites; $15 to $24 per night.

FOLSOM LAKE STATE RECREATION AREA

✉️*Located along Folsom–Auburn Road between Auburn and Folsom* 📞*916-988-0205*
📧*folsom@sna.com*

🚶🚴🏇⛵️🎣🛶🚤🏊‍♂️ One of California's most popular parks, this mammoth facility completely encircles Folsom Lake's 75-mile shoreline. Visitors come to boat, waterski, ride horseback, picnic, swim, and camp. Anglers try for trout, bass, perch, and sturgeon. There are also 65 miles of hiking trails around the lake. Quite crowded in summer, the park is best visited during the week. Facilities include a water education center at Folsom Dam, an information center, a marina, picnic areas, restrooms, and showers. Day-use fee, $7.

▲ There are 150 sites in two campgrounds; $20 per night.

MALAKOFF DIGGINS
STATE HISTORIC PARK _____

✉️*From Nevada City, take Highway 49 north for 11 miles and make a right onto Tyler Foote Road. Follow the paved road 17 miles to Derbec Road, which leads to the park.* 📞*530-265-2740*

🚶🚴🎣🛶 Remote and beautiful, this 3000-acre facility includes a well preserved Gold Rush town. The park rests near the Yuba River, where anglers catch rainbow and brook trout; there are also black bass and bluegill in nearby Blair Reservoir. The park's slopes, climbing from 2200 to 4200 feet, are open to hikers. Swimming is good in the reservoir. The park has an information center and museum, picnic areas, and restrooms. Day-use fee, $6.

▲ Permitted in 30 sites, $15 per night. There are also three rustic cabins for rent; $35 per night.

PLUMAS-EUREKA STATE PARK

✉️*From Route 49 north of Sierra City take Gold Lake Road to Graegle, then go five miles west on County Road A14, which begins near the intersections of Routes 89 and 70.*
📞*530-836-2380*

🚶🚴🎿 Set deep in the Sierra, this 5500-acre spread contains waterfalls, creeks, and two small lakes. The park rises from 4600 feet to 7447-foot Eureka Peak and is home to the pileated woodpecker, the largest woodpecker in North America, and the calliope hummingbird, the smallest of its kind on the continent. The park is also home to golden eagles, great blue herons, deer, and beaver. This area is also a pioneer ski region, which hosts winter sports events. Displays in the museum focus on the hard-rock mining of the area. During the summer, gold panning is offered. Get some basic instructions and tips, then try your hand at the sport. Call ahead to sign up. Other facilities include an information center, picnic areas, restrooms, and showers.

▲ There are 67 sites (including 14 walk-in). Reservations are required from May 15 to August 15, the rest of the year is first-come, first-serve; $20 per night. Reservations: 800-444-7275.

LAKE TAHOE AREA

There aren't many places in America where you can waterski from one state to another. Nor can I think of many spots perfect for wilderness hiking during the day and shooting craps at night. And how many lakes can you name that are so clear you can see objects 75 feet below the surface? One of the West's most unique areas, the Lake Tahoe region is a remarkable blend of nature and kitsch.

In addition to its raw beauty and Nevada gambling, Lake Tahoe is also very popular simply because it is so easily accessible. From Route 49 in the Gold Country, numerous highways lead east into the Sierra and on toward Tahoe. The main road from San Francisco is Route 80, a fast, efficient freeway that bisects Sacramento and traverses the Sierra about 12 miles north of Lake Tahoe.

SIGHTS

EMIGRANT TRAIL MUSEUM AT DONNER MEMORIAL STATE PARK ⊠*Donner Pass Road, Truckee* ☏*530-582-7892* ☏*530-550-2347* During the terrible winter of 1846–47, a party of stalwart pioneers, unable to cross the Sierra because of drifting snow, camped for the winter. Many perished from exposure and hunger, others went insane, and some resorted to cannibalism. Today the Emigrant Trail Museum commemorates their passing. There is also a monument on the grounds. Its base stands 22 feet high—the depth of the snow that winter. Today Route 80, the transcontinental interstate, passes within yards of the Donner Party's tragic resting place. Admission.

TRUCKEE   For a more hospitable sense of the Old West, truck on over to Truckee, two miles east on Route 80. This 19th-century town sits astride a mountain pass high in the Sierra. Framed by forested slopes, Truckee is a woodframe town overlooking an old railroad yard and depot. The main street, Commercial Row, is lined with falsefront buildings. Clapboard warehouses and meeting halls with second-story balconies remain from the town's old lumbering and railroad days. Then as now, Truckee was a gateway. Today it leads to the gambling palaces and ski resorts of Tahoe.

SQUAW VALLEY   To tour one of the most famous of the ski resorts, head south from Truckee toward Lake Tahoe on Route 89, and follow the signs. The 1960 Winter Olympics put this vale on the map, and ski bums have been making the pilgrimage ever since. Ringed by 8200-foot-high mountains, and sprinkled with lodges and condos, it's a favored jet-set landing ground.

LAKE TAHOE   As soon as the highway from Squaw Valley rises to meet Lake Tahoe, it becomes evident why the region's rivers run fast and pure. This lake, situated 6225 feet above sea level, contains water so clear that objects 75 feet below the surface are sometimes visible. With depths reaching an incredible 1645 feet, it is the biggest alpine lake of

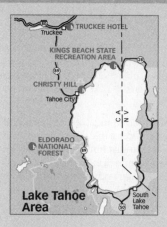

Lake Tahoe Area

TRUCKEE HOTEL

PAGE 505

Sprawling 1873 falsefront building with rooms chock-full of Old West charm and crowded with character

KINGS BEACH STATE RECREATION AREA

PAGE 513

Sandy strip by the water—perfect spot for swimming, windsurfing, and family-friendly fun

CHRISTY HILL

PAGE 510

Fresh California cuisine like Hawaiian *ono* in mango, ginger, and lime sauce in a wraparound glass dining room

ELDORADO NATIONAL FOREST

PAGE 516

Massive wilderness rising 10,000 feet from the Gold Country to the High Sierra—a hiker's paradise

such purity in all North America. Tahoe is 22 miles long and measures 72 miles around. The entire lake is framed by 10,000-foot mountain peaks, a translucent gem set in a granite ring.

Unlike nearby lakes of glacial origin, Tahoe was formed by faulting. About 150 million years ago the basin was created when the Carson Range rose to the east while the Sierra Nevada grew to the west, leaving a giant trough between. When volcanoes dammed the end of the basin, rain and snow filled the natural bowl to brimming. Washoe Indians eventually inhabited the lakeshore regions, and enjoyed uninterrupted predominance until 1844 when Captain John Fremont and Kit Carson, searching a mountain pass into California, "discovered" the lake. By the 1870s, with the advent of the railroad, Tahoe emerged as a popular resort area. The Washoe have some remaining presence, though. Lake Tahoe is named for a Washoe word meaning "lake" or "water in high place."

Today the tourist scene along this alpine jewel centers around the "North Shore" and the "South Shore." The former includes a series of small towns, each featuring resort facilities, restaurants, and various attractions. The latter highlights South Lake Tahoe, the region's most populous town.

On either shore, crossing the border between California and Nevada is like passing from one country to another. The reason is simple—gambling. It's legal in Nevada, but not in California. Within a few steps of the border rise the casinos of Incline Village and Stateline, with their brilliant lights and promise of quick and easy wealth.

Mark Twain visited the lake over a century ago, long before the gaming palaces, and was overwhelmed. "As it lay there with the shadows of the mountains brilliantly photographed upon its still surface," he remarked in *Roughing It*, "I thought it must surely be the fairest picture the whole earth affords."

Tahoe. The word still carries power. But in recent decades it has become a riddle, an oxymoron. To some it conjures images of dark casinos and fateful gaming tables. To others it evokes thoughts of pristine trackless wilderness and oceanic depths. Never the twain shall meet: Tahoe is an environmental battleground. Developers, wedded to tomorrow's dollar, struggle against environmentalists committed to yesterday's beauty. Every fight the conservationists lose results in more structures along the lake, greater erosion, and another cloud across that glassy water. The resource they seek to protect is a magical place.

To see Lake Tahoe fully, you should circle the entire lake, a loop of about 70 miles. The loop cuts through dense conifer forests, then passes dramatic outcroppings of granite. Intermittently the highway opens onto broad lake vistas, swept by westerly winds and adorned with the sails of careening sloops. Along the way are private residences worthy of a prince, magnificent stone edifices with lawns rolling down to the lip of the lake, leaded-glass mansions that appear drawn from *The Great Gatsby*.

TAHOE MARITIME MUSEUM ✉*5205 West Lake Boulevard, Homewood* ☎*530-525-9253* 📠*530-525-9283* 🖥*www.tahoemaritimemuseum.org* Starting from Tahoe City, head south along Route 89, past Homewood Mountain Resort. Nearby you can take a look at Tahoe's seafaring history at this non-profit museum brimming with photographs and collectibles from the early 1900s. The museum also boasts over 25 historic vessels, many of which still shuttle guests during summer months. A fishing exhibit rounds out the displays with antique equipment and a vintage wooden boat.

VIKINGSHOLM ☎*530-525-7232* As you approach the south end of the lake, you'll come to the best known of all the great Lake Tahoe estates, Vikingsholm, a 38-room castle. Open for tours in the summer, this unusual structure was designed along the lines of a 9th-century Norse fortress. It's built of granite and hand-hewn timbers and marked by a series of towers. Admission. Anchored offshore, near Vikingsholm, is tiny **Fanette Island**, where a stone teahouse built to similar specifications still sits.

EMERALD BAY As if all this extraordinary stonework were not enough, the Vikingsholm castle rests beside two-mile-long Emerald Bay. From the vista point located along Route 89, this spectacular cove, guarded by lofty conifers, presents the most picturesque site along the entire lake.

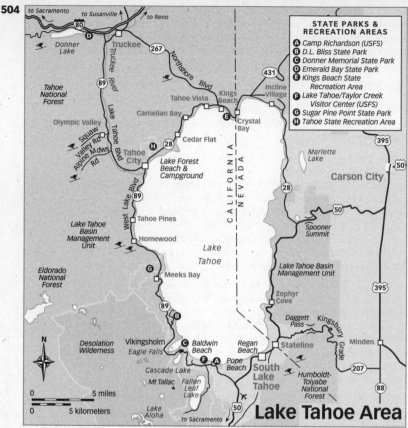

to Sacramento to Susanville to Reno

STATE PARKS & RECREATION AREAS
Ⓐ Camp Richardson (USFS)
Ⓑ D.L. Bliss State Park
Ⓒ Donner Memorial State Park
Ⓓ Emerald Bay State Park
Ⓔ Kings Beach State Recreation Area
Ⓕ Lake Tahoe/Taylor Creek Visitor Center (USFS)
Ⓖ Sugar Pine Point State Park
Ⓗ Tahoe State Recreation Area

Lake Tahoe Area

EAGLE FALLS At the far end of Emerald Bay, poised between two peninsulas, is a slender opening into the lake; at the near edge, cascading along granite steps, is Eagle Falls. A short path leads from the vista point to a wooden footbridge below the falls, or you can hike one mile down from the vista point to Vikingsholm.

BALDWIN BEACH AND POPE BEACH Continuing around the south end of the lake, you'll pass the **Lake Tahoe Visitors Center** (775-588-4591, 775-588-4598) and the turnoffs to two of the best beaches on the lake—Baldwin Beach and Pope Beach.

TALLAC HISTORIC SITE ESTATES Along the western outskirts of South Lake Tahoe, between the two beaches, are the Tallac Historic Site Estates, representing more of Tahoe's fabulous old mansions. Here you can stroll through the woods on a path strewn with pine needles. You'll pass a cluster of old brown-shingle buildings, a log cabin, and the fabled estates. These include the Pope House, built in 1884; Valhalla, a brown-shingle beauty; and the McGonagle estate, a prestigious house designed ironically in the fashion of a log cabin. Closed in winter. The Estate Trail lies between the Lake Tahoe Visitors Center and Camp Richardson Resort.

SOUTH LAKE TAHOE   Turning east onto Route 50, continue to the town of South Lake Tahoe. Originally an 1860s mining town, this lakeside area was quickly transformed into a resort haven as early as the 1880s. Since then, its popularity has grown due to its proximity to the huge alpine lake and numerous activities, including water and snow recreation. Today, with nearly 35,000 residents, including the surrounding Stateline area, it remains a booming center for tourists and visitors alike, boasting numerous restaurants, inns, and shops. The **Lake Tahoe South Shore Chamber of Commerce** (775-588-1728, fax 775-588-1941) can provide additional information.

NEVADA SIDE   East of South Lake Tahoe, at the gambling village of **Stateline**, you'll cross into the state of Nevada. Continue north along the east side of the lake. Soon after passing through the village of Glenbrook, turn north (left) onto Route 28, which passes pretty **Spooner Lake**, curves around the lake's northern perimeter, crosses back into California at **Crystal Bay**, and eventually brings you back to the point where you began.

LODGING

ROYAL GORGE RAINBOW LODGE

$$$ 30 ROOMS   ✉9411 Hillside Drive, Soda Springs; 16 miles east of Truckee off Route 80   ☏530-426-3871, 800-500-3871   📠530-426-9221   ✍www.royalgorge.com, reservations@royalgorge.com

If you prefer a base of operations from which to experience the wild, this wilderness lodge sits amid the largest network of cross-country trails in the nation. It's an 80-year-old building formerly used by hunters. The private rooms share baths and offer modern conveniences like heat, electricity, a sauna, and an outdoor hot tub. The lodge's chef specializes in French country cuisine. Nearby are secluded warming huts where you can enjoy afternoon tea.

TRUCKEE HOTEL

$$–$$$ 37 ROOMS   ✉Corner of Bridge Street and Commercial Row, Truckee   ☏530-587-4444, 800-659-6921   📠530-587-1599   ✍www.thetruckeehotel.com, thetruckeehotel@sierra.net

In a chic and flashy area like Lake Tahoe, where everything was constructed tomorrow, it's a pleasure to discover a place such as the Truckee Hotel. Built in 1873, and nicely renovated, this four-story falsefront building sprawls across an entire block. The guest rooms, with either shared or private bath, possess an Old West charm. They are full of antiques and crowded with character. Even if you don't plan on staying there, the hotel is well worth a visit.

SUN AND SAND LODGE

$$–$$$ 26 UNITS   ✉8308 North Lake Boulevard, Kings Beach   ☏530-546-2515, 800-547-2515   📠530-546-0112   ✍www.sunandsandlodge.com, laketahoe@aol.com

For lakefront lodgings on the North Shore, try this knotty-pine motel with units near the water. There's a sandy beach along one edge of the property and a sunny smile at the front desk.

RUSTIC COTTAGES

$$–$$$ 20 ROOMS   ✉7449 North Lake Boulevard, Tahoe Vista   📞530-546-3523,
888-778-7842   📠530-546-0146   ✍www.rusticcottages.com, rustic@rusticcottages.com

How can anyone go wrong at a place named Rustic Cottages? With cottages clustered across the street from the lake, this charming complex offers a clapboard alternative to the chic lodges hereabouts. The houses are neatly furnished and feature knotty-pine interiors; all are tucked under an awning of pine trees. Some units have kitchens, some have fireplaces, many have both. It's a cute and cozy place. Many of the units are pet-friendly.

TAHOE VISTA INN & MARINA

$$$$ 6 UNITS   ✉7220 North Lake Boulevard, Tahoe Vista   📞530-546-8222,
800-521-6656   📠530-546-0667   ✍www.sierravacations.com, info@sierravacations.com

You could get lost in the enormous suites at this beachfront inn. Five of the six accommodations in this multilevel, wood-shingled inn offer sweeping lake views. They each have bedrooms, as well as a living room, stone fireplace, full kitchen, and private porch. A few of the suites have jacuzzis. Sun pours through windows into rooms lightened even more by soft grays and off-white modern decor. Worth the price.

SUNNYSIDE RESTAURANT AND LODGE

$$$–$$$$ 23 ROOMS   1850 West Lake Boulevard, Tahoe City   📞530-583-7200,
800-822-2754   📠530-583-2551   ✍www.sunnysideresort.com

Mountain lodge meets high-class resort at the redwood, multi-gabled Sunnyside. Nestled in pine woods and sitting before its own marina, the lodge features a cozy country lobby with river rock fireplace adorned with hunting trophies. Ducks and decoys are everywhere in the 23 lakefront or lakeview accommodations, simply furnished in wicker and wood and featuring individual touches like an old sea chest or armoire. Many have fireplaces and wet bars. There is free wi-fi throughout the lodge.

RESORT AT SQUAW CREEK

$$$$ 405 ROOMS   ✉400 Squaw Creek Road, Olympic Valley   📞530-583-6300,
800-327-3353   📠530-581-6632   ✍www.squawcreek.com, info@squawcreek.com

This resort lures guests with extravagant accommodations that are showcased by a stream and waterfall which plunge 250 feet through the property. Situated a half-mile from Squaw Valley's vaunted ski slopes, the resort is a summer destination as well as winter hideaway. For warm-weather enthusiasts there are two tennis courts, an 18-hole golf course, bike paths, miles of equestrian and hiking trails in the surrounding mountains, and an aquatic center with three pools and a water slide, and a full-service spa. In winter it provides ice skating facilities, dog sled tours, and easy access to the ski slopes with an on-site property.

ROCKWOOD LODGE BED & BREAKFAST

$$–$$$ 5 ROOMS   ✉5295 West Lake Boulevard, Homewood   📞530-525-5273,
800-538-2463   📠530-525-5949   ✍www.home.inreach.com/rockwood

Established in 1939 as Tahoe's first B&B, this west shore treasure has a huge stone fireplace in the parlor, hand-hewn beams, and pine paneling throughout. European and American antiques are accented with Laura Ashley fabrics and all rooms have feather beds, down comforters, sitting areas, and either private showers or private baths. Evening desserts, early continental breakfast, and later full breakfast are all included.

HISTORIC CAMP RICHARDSON RESORT & MARINA

$$$–$$$$ 50 UNITS   ✉1900 Jameson Beach Road, South Lake Tahoe
☎530-541-1801, 800-544-1801   🖷530-541-1802   ⬧www.camprichardson.com,
info@camprichardson.com

A multifaceted facility, Richardson Resort sits along a pretty beach on the western outskirts of South Lake Tahoe. In addition to a spacious lodge with traditional guest rooms, this historic establishment has cabins for rent as well as a multitude of campsites. The lodge is a classic mountain retreat. It offers a cozy lobby with knotty-pine walls, log beams, and a stone fireplace. The rooms are neatly if unimaginatively decorated. The cabins are rustic in appearance, but furnished in comfortable fashion. Woodframe in construction, they are set around the resort's wooded acres not far from the lake, with some located right on the water's edge. The cabins include complete kitchen facilities. A gazebo with a hot tub is on the grounds for hotel guests, too. In summer the resort only rents cabins by the week. No pets allowed.

SKY LAKE LODGE

$$ 23 ROOMS   ✉2644 Lake Tahoe Boulevard, South Lake Tahoe   ☎530-544-0770

This motel is located on the South Shore's main drag. The guest rooms here are nicely furnished and decorated with flair; all have phones, carpets, color televisions, and stall showers. Ask for a room away from the highway.

INN BY THE LAKE

$$$–$$$$ 100 UNITS   ✉3300 Lake Tahoe Boulevard, South Lake Tahoe
☎530-542-0330, 800-877-1466   🖷530-541-6596   ⬧www.innbythelake.com,
info@innbythelake.com

Tahoe travelers who just have to be where the action is will find refined charm amid the chaos along Route 50 at this stone-and-shingle inn. The accommodations, set back from the highway on landscaped grounds, feature blond woods and lush pastel bedspreads and wallhangings. Many view the lake across the street; suites have full kitchens. There's also a pool, sauna, and bi-level hot tub.

LAKELAND VILLAGE BEACH & MOUNTAIN RESORT

$$$ 209 UNITS   ✉3535 Lake Tahoe Boulevard, South Lake Tahoe   ☎530-544-1685,
800-822-5969   ⬧www.lakeland-village.com, stay@lakeland-village.com

A family-friendly option is Lakeland Village, located on 19 acres of woodland on Lake Tahoe's southern shore. The condo units come with fireplaces, fully equipped kitchens, and balconies—some with outstanding views. The resort also provides outdoor heated pools, hot tubs, and tennis courts.

SAIL IN MOTEL APARTMENTS

$$ 3 ROOMS   ✉861 Lakeview Avenue, South Lake Tahoe   ☎530-544-8615,
800-303-8246   🖷530-544-3098   ⬧www.sailinmotel.com, sailinmotel@aol.com

Positively the best lodging bargain in hectic South Lake Tahoe is the Sail In Motel. Not only is the place away from the busy section of town, it's also located right on a beach. The rooms are few, which might be why the owners have taken such care in furnishing them. The interior decoration shows imagination. And the exterior? Step outside and you'll find a knockout view of Lake Tahoe.

HANSEN'S RESORT

$$–$$$ 9 UNITS   ✉1360 Ski Run Boulevard, South Lake Tahoe
☎530-544-3361   📠530-541-3824   🖱www.hansensresort.com,
info@hansensresort.com

Another recommended spot is Hansen's, on the road to Heavenly Valley ski area. A collection of cabins tucked beneath arching pines, this facility is splendidly situated. It's a short stroll to the center of South Lake Tahoe or to the ski region. For a quiet but convenient retreat, the place is ideal. There are nine individual cabins (most with a bedroom, a living room, and a kitchen). All facilities are pine-paneled, very well-furnished, and immaculately clean. Cool and spiffy.

HOLLY'S PLACE

$$$–$$$$ 8 UNITS   ✉P.O. Box 13197, South Lake Tahoe, CA 96151   ☎530-544-7040,
800-745-7041   📠530-541-6543   🖱www.hollysplace.com, reservations@hollysplace.com

Holly's provides a serene getaway in the pines just two blocks from the lake. Each of its eight cabins are architecturally different. One is a converted barn and another a former greenhouse. They all have natural knotty-pine walls, carpeting, a couch, and a kitchen. There's a recreation room with movies and a ping-pong table. Gay-friendly.

At the very edge of South Lake Tahoe, near the gambling casinos and Nevada border, are countless motels. These are all within walking distance of the gaming tables and cater mainly to gamblers. Because of competitive rates, they can also be attractive to travelers. Unfortunately, they're often crowded and their rates fluctuate wildly. Count on paying more during the summer and on weekends. Even the rates quoted below constitute little more than an estimate. I'll list two of the area's motels; it's advisable to shop among others nearby for the best deal.

7 SEAS INN AT TAHOE

$–$$ 17 ROOMS   ✉4145 Manzanita Avenue, South Lake Tahoe   ☎530-544-7031,
800-800-7327   📠530-544-1208   🖱www.sevenseastahoe.com,
info@sevenseastahoe.com

Just two blocks from the beach, the 7 Seas has eclectically furnished rooms (some with Navajo prints, some with dark silky decor), but they're all comfortable. This pet-friendly accomodation includes king- or queen-sized beds, and some rooms boast gas fireplaces and whirlpool tubs. A continental breakfast is served.

BLUE JAY LODGE

$–$$ 50 ROOMS   ✉4133 Cedar Avenue, South Lake Tahoe   ☎530-544-5232,
800-258-3529   📠530-544-0453   🖱www.bluejaylodge.com, info@bluejaylodge.com

Basic, but comfortable with pale hues and floral prints, the Blue Jay offers cozy, clean rooms near winter activities centers. Rooms feature cable TV, VCRs, and coffeemakers, and there is an outdoor seasonal pool for guest use. Some rooms include fireplaces, kitchenettes, or jacuzzi tubs.

OLD POST OFFICE CAFÉ

$ DINER ✉ *5245 North Lake Boulevard, Carnelian Bay* ✆ *530-546-3205*

The folks here only serve breakfast and lunch, but they do it with country flair. Popular with locals, the restaurant offers pancakes, waffles, and omelettes from the early hours. By lunchtime, the griddle is blazing with a variety of chicken breast sandwiches and the cook is ladling out homemade soup and chili. No dinner.

RIVER RANCH RESTAURANT AND LODGE

$$–$$$ AMERICAN ✉ *2285 River Road, Tahoe City* ✆ *530-583-4264, 866-991-9912*
✍ *www.riverranchlodge.com*

During the summer, dine on this restaurant's sprawling outdoor patio and watch river rafters roll down the Truckee River. When winter comes around, head indoors and cozy up near a roaring fire. Both casual and formal, River Ranch's menu is as varied as its seating options. Try hamburgers and hot dogs on the deck, or portobello mushroom Napoleon and roasted elk loin in the lavish dining room. The food is as enjoyable as the view.

BACCHI'S INN

$$–$$$$ ITALIAN ✉ *2905 Lake Forest Road, Tahoe City* ✆ *530-583-3324*
✆ *530-583-4924*

Famed for its minestrone soup, this Italian eatery serves family-style meals, which is appropriate as it has been owned and operated by the same family for three generations. The dining room, open for dinner only, is decorated with traditional red-checkered tablecloths and lantern candles.

TAHOE HOUSE

$ DELI ✉ *625 West Lake Boulevard, Route 89, Tahoe City* ✆ *530-583-1377,*
877-367-8246 ✆ *530-583-4909* ✍ *www.tahoe-house.com, tahoehouse@ltol.com*

This stop is owned by a Swiss family. Mainly a bakery, gourmet shop, and deli, their delicious sandwiches can be ordered to go, or enjoyed at a comfy little nook in front of the fireplace. Definitely give their fresh bread a try, and don't get me started on their pastries, cookies, and fruit tarts.

ROSIE'S CAFÉ

$$–$$$ AMERICAN ✉ *571 North Lake Boulevard, Tahoe City* ✆ *530-583-8504*
✍ *www.rosiescafe.com, rosiescafe@aol.com*

Rosie's is one of those laid-back eating spots California is famous for harboring. Just across the street from the lake, the place is bizarrely decorated with old sleds, bicycles, skis, and wall mirrors. It's open all day and into the night, featuring imaginative cuisine. At breakfast there are lots of egg specialties. Lunch consists of salads, sandwiches, tostadas, and more. Come dinner, the menu expands to include pasta, vegetarian and stir-fry dishes, roast duckling, steak, and seafood. Tasty and popular.

WOLFDALE'S

$$–$$$ INTERNATIONAL ✉ *640 North Lake Boulevard, Tahoe City* ✆ *530-583-5700*
✆ *530-583-1583* ✍ *www.wolfdales.com*

Living in the Bay Area, I guess I'm spoiled when it comes to great dining experiences. That's why, when visiting Lake Tahoe, dinner at Wolfdale's is one of the few I'll settle for. Located on Tahoe's north shore, the eatery touts itself as a "cuisine unique restaurant." It's well known, critically acclaimed, and has had the same owner/chef since 1978. The menu changes frequently but always offers fresh seafood, quality meats, and unusual game. Dinner only. Closed Tuesday, except in July and August.

CHRISTY HILL

$$$–$$$$ CALIFORNIA CUISINE   ✉*115 Grove Street, Tahoe City*
📞*530-583-8551*   ✍*www.christyhill.com*

With a wraparound glass dining room and outdoor seating, this chalet-style restaurant commands great lake views that complement its modern, minimalist decor. This eating spot is highly regarded by guests and locals. Fresh food in light sauces are Christy Hill's hallmark, with entrées such as Hawaiian *ono* in mango, ginger, and lime sauce. Closed Monday.

EVAN'S AMERICAN GOURMET CAFÉ

$$$–$$$$ INTERNATIONAL   ✉*536 Emerald Bay Road, South Lake Tahoe*
📞*530-542-1990*   ✍*www.evanstahoe.com, tahoewino@aol.com*

A lovely little Tahoe cottage houses Evan's, where the menu ranges from Continental to Asian to American regional. Soft lighting and cream-and-burgundy tones with gold accents set off an appealing room of only 11 tables. The far-ranging menu might include entrées such as grilled garlic tenderloin of beef with gorgonzola cheese. Killer homemade desserts. Dinner only.

THE BURGER LOUNGE

$ AMERICAN   ✉*717 Emerald Bay Road, South Lake Tahoe*   📞 *530-542-4060*

When you crave a hamburger in Tahoe, this is where you go. Try a Jiffy Burger with peanut butter, cheese, and bacon or head straight for the classic juicy burger cooked on the charcoal grill, topped with a fresh bun, and served with an order of pesto, garlic, or regular fries that will satisfy four people. There's no beer, it's cash only, and there's always a line for what some call a "plate of heaven."

RED HUT CAFE

$ AMERICAN   ✉*2749 Lake Tahoe Boulevard, South Lake Tahoe*   📞*530-541-9024*
✍*www.redhutcafe.com*

Traditional diner fare is at its best when served up at the Red Hut. Only offering breakfast (starting at 6 a.m.!) and lunch, it's a great way to start your day. Choose from egg dishes or pancakes and waffles (even coconut ones), or all-American classics like grilled cheese and hamburgers for lunch. Prepare for some tasty grub in a homey and relaxed joint.

SPROUTS CAFÉ

$ CAFE   ✉*3123 Harrison Avenue, South Lake Tahoe*   📞*530-541-6969*

Looking for something fresh, healthy, and organic? Check out Sprouts, which specializes in fresh-squeezed juices, smoothies, sandwiches, and wraps made with ingredients like tofu, hummus, brown rice, and fresh veggies. This café's not *strictly* vegetarian, but boy is it veggie-friendly. Order your food to go, or relax at one of the many tables. The counter staff is super-friendly and super-spunky.

THE NAKED FISH
$$–$$$ JAPANESE   ✉ *3940 Lake Tahoe Boulevard, South Lake Tahoe*
📞 *530-541-3474*   ✐ *www.thenakedfish.com, info@thenakedfish.com*

This superb sushi bar also has a full kitchen with cooked entrées such as tempura teriyaki, grilled salmon, and mac and cheese for the kids. The specialty rolls are innovative combinations of sweet and sour, spicy and cool that are hands-down menu favorites. The Sierra Powder Roll combines white fish, albacore, and asparagus topped with wasabi to-biko and wasabi cream sauce. Order a few along with a cold Japanese beer and or one of several fine *sakes*.

Among the cheapest places to eat on the South Shore are the casino hotels just across the border in Stateline, Nevada. All of them feature "gambler's specials" of one sort or another: breakfast for a buck or perhaps a full-course meal in a good restaurant at budget prices.

TOWN SQUARE BUFFET
$$ INTERNATIONAL   ✉ *50 Route 50, Stateline, Nevada*   📞 *775-588-6211*
📞 *775-588-3110, 800-648-3322*   ✐ *www.horizoncasino.com*

At the Horizon Casino Resort, this buffet provides an incredible spread that on a typical night will include Mexican and Chinese selections, as well as American favorites such as prime rib. A salad and gourmet dessert bar caps off the feast.

HARVEY'S LAKE TAHOE
$$$$ SEAFOOD   ✉ *Route 50, Stateline, Nevada*   📞 *775-588-2411, 800-427-8397*
✐ *www.harveys.com, info@harveys.com*

Over at Harvey's, there's a huge, 12-station seafood buffet. Dinner only. Closed Monday through Wednesday.

HARRAH'S LAKE TAHOE RESORT
$$$ AMERICAN   ✉ *Route 50, Stateline, Nevada*   📞 *775-588-6611*   📞 *775-586-6607*
✐ *www.harrahstahoe.com*

Harrah's has a Forest Buffet up on the 18th floor where you can enjoy an array of dishes as well as a panoramic view. Typical specialties include pizza, a pasta and Asian bar, and baked turkey. The catch, of course, is that you must escape from the casino before gambling away the money you just saved on breakfast, lunch, or dinner.

SHOPPING

THE WHITE BUFFALO   ✉ *10116 Donner Pass Road, Truckee*   📞 *530-587-4446*
✐ *www.whitebuffalotruckee.com* In downtown Truckee, this shop show-cases American Indian crafts such as pottery, kachinas, dreamcatchers, jewelry, and rugs.

VILLAGE AT NORTHSTAR   ✉ *3001 Northstar Drive, Truckee*   📞 *800-217-7554*
✐ *www.villageatnorthstar.com* This is the retail heart of the massive Northstar Resort on Tahoe's north shore. Lots of trendy shops, restaurants (from fine dining to fast food), and the flagship North Face store surround an ice rink. In the winter, shoppers can roast s'mores at one of

the fire pits. In the summer, take a "Star Tour" at the resort and enjoy live music on the weekends. A ski-in, ski-out Ritz-Carlton hotel and condo complex is slated to open here in late 2009, which will certainly attract more upscale shops and dining.

TAHOE/TRUCKEE FACTORY STORES ✉ *12047 Donner Pass Road, Truckee* ✐ *www.tahoetruckeefactorystores.com* Here you'll find outlets for familiar national brands such as Izod, Bass, Van Heusen, and Dansk.

FACTORY STORES AT THE Y ✉ *Routes 50 and 89, South Lake Tahoe* Outlet stores for popular name brands can be found at the Y.

GALLERY KEOKI ✉ *The Village at Squaw Valley, 1850 South Village Road, Suite 42, Olympic Valley* ✆ *530-583-1404, 800-995-3654* ✐ *www.gallerykeoki.com* If you're staying at Squaw Valley, stop in at this gallery, which features Lake Tahoe photographs captured by local resident Keoki Flagg, as well as works by Picasso, Miró, and Dalí.

NIGHTLIFE

For a get-down, stomping good time, the place to head is Truckee. This Old West town, 12 miles north of Lake Tahoe, has as many saloons as any self-respectin' frontier outpost. These saloons wail through the weekend with live music, all of them are hat brim to hat brim with ten-gallon locals. This is a Wild West town that knows how to party.

BAR OF AMERICA ✉ *10042 Donner Pass Road at Bridge Street, Truckee* ✆ *530-587-3110* ✐ *www.barofamerica.net* At this bar there's live jazz, blues, or rock-and-roll music every Friday and Saturday. Cover on summer weekends.

BLUE COYOTE BAR & GRILL ✉ *10015 Palisades Drive, Truckee* ✆ *530-587-7777* This lively bar is where you'll find the locals after a day of skiing or water sports, watching sports on the 16 TVs and filling up on huge orders of pub fare. The full bar also has 12 beers on tap. There are frequent theme parties and dance nights.

There are waterfront lounges and other nightspots around Lake Tahoe, particularly along the North Shore and in South Lake Tahoe. The real action, though, lies across the line in Nevada. Here legalized gambling has resulted in miles of neon casinos.

These garish, enticing establishments offer slot machines, roulette wheels, keno, and sports betting as well as gaming tables for poker, blackjack, and other pastimes. The clubs also have plush lounges featuring top-name entertainers. As a result, the shows are extravaganzas complete with dance troupes and orchestras.

On the North Shore, the scene centers around Incline Village. Down along the South Shore everyone gravitates over to Stateline, Nevada. Here a string of casinos lines a Vegas-like strip.

ASPEN LOUNGE ✉ *Route 50, Stateline, Nevada* ✆ *775-588-6211* ✐ *www.horizoncasino.com* One top club is the Aspen, which offers live music and dancing on weekends.

HARVEY'S RESORT HOTEL ⊠*Route 50, Stateline, Nevada* ☎*775-588-2411*
Be sure to check out the live music almost nightly at Harvey's.

MONTBLEU RESORT CASINO & SPA ⊠*55 Highway 50, Stateline,
Nevada* ☎*775-588-3515, 888-829-7630* ⊘*www.montbleuresort.com, questions@mont
bleuresort.com* The MontBleu Theatre showroom features theatrical
lighting, terraced seating, and a production-sized stage—a perfect platform for comedians such as Dana Carvey and Paul Rodriguez. The
venue also hosts classic acts such as Earth Wind & Fire, Boz Scaggs,
Smokey Robinson, and the Neville Brothers.

PARKS

DONNER MEMORIAL STATE PARK
⊠*Located just off Route 80, two miles west of Truckee* ☎*530-582-7892*
☎*530-550-2347*

Set in a pine-and-fir forest astride three-
mile-long Donner Lake, this facility lies north of Lake Tahoe. It was here
in the winter of 1846–47 that the ill-fated Donner party, trapped in
heavy snow, was confronted with cannibalism or death. Today the accommodations are more commodious. There are campgrounds, a museum, and a resident population of porcupines, beaver, raccoons, and
bears (plus perhaps the ghosts of several hungry pioneers). In addition
to an information center and museum (open year-round), the park features picnic areas, restrooms, and showers. Closed August to Memorial
Day. Day-use fee, $6.
▲ Permitted during the summer in 150 sites; $25 per night.

TAHOE NATIONAL FOREST
⊠*Located northwest of Lake Tahoe, the region is traversed by Routes 20, 49, 80, 89, and
267. The Tahoe National Forest Headquarters is located at 631 Coyote Street, Nevada City.*
☎*530-265-4531* ☎*530-478-6109* ⊘*www.fs.fed.us/r5/tahoe*

Rising from the Gold Country to the
Sierra crest, this mammoth forest covers over 800,000 acres. Its scenic
beauty and recreation facilities make it very popular year-round.
Swimming and horseback riding opportunities are available during
warm months, with skiers taking over in winter. Hunters, anglers, and
gold panners also frequent the area. Within the forest are picnic areas
and restrooms.
▲ There are 68 campgrounds throughout the forest; $10 to $42 per
night. Located at Sugar Pine Reservoir, Giant Gap Campground has 30
sites; $14 to $42 per night. At Jackson Meadow Reservoir, you'll find
Pass Creek Campground, which has 30 sites; $12 per night. Reserva-
tions required (877-444-6777).

KINGS BEACH
STATE RECREATION AREA
⊠*Located in Kings Beach along Route 28, about 12 miles east of Tahoe City*
☎*530-546-4212* ⊘*www.ntpud.org, ntpud@ntpud.org*

A tiny eight-acre plot, this facility is important because it's one of the few public beaches near Nevada on

the North Shore. Anticipate a sandy beach plus a picnic area, playground, parasail and jet ski rentals, and restrooms.

LAKE FOREST BEACH AND CAMPGROUND
✉ Off Route 28 along Lake Forest Road about two miles east of Tahoe City
☎ 530-583-3796 ext. 29 📠 530-583-8452 ✍ lvannoy@tcpud.org

🚴 ⛵ 🏊 🎣 🚤 🛶 🌅 These are two discrete units situated within walking distance of one another (about a mile apart). The beach consists of a stretch of sand bordered by aspen trees. There are picnic areas and toilets. The campground, which is inland from the lake, features sites near a grove of trees. It's equipped with picnic areas and a playground. Parking fee for boat launch only, $10.

🏕 There are 20 sites, first-come, first-served; $15 per night. Campground closed November to mid-April.

TAHOE STATE RECREATION AREA
✉ Route 28 just east of Tahoe City ☎ 530-525-7232 or 530-583-3074 📠 530-525-3380
✍ sierrahq@jps.net

🚶 🚴 ⛵ 🌅 Little more than a pocket park, this 62-acre facility possesses a small patch of lakefront property. The beach is unattractive, but the area behind it is studded with shady conifer trees. Facilities here include picnic area and restrooms. Closed Labor Day to Memorial Day.

🏕 There are 20 sites; $25 per night.

SUGAR PINE POINT STATE PARK
✉ Route 89 about ten miles south of Tahoe City ☎ 530-525-7232 📠 530-525-4114
✍ sierrahq@jps.net

🚶 🚴 ⛵ 🌅 One of the Tahoe region's most precious jewels, this magnificent park extends along almost two miles of lakefront. Inland it runs nearly four miles. Within that expanse is a forest of Jeffrey and sugar pines. The lakefront is dotted with sandy beaches, and the park possesses several historic structures, among them a pioneer log cabin and an old mansion that's been converted to a museum. There are also hiking trails, a tennis court, picnic areas, restrooms, and showers. Day-use fee, $6.

🏕 There are 175 forested sites; $25 per night.

D. L. BLISS AND EMERALD BAY STATE PARKS
✉ Both parks are along Route 89; D. L. Bliss is 17 miles south of Tahoe City, Emerald Bay is 22 miles south. ☎ 530-525-7232 📠 916-654-6374

🚶 🚴 ⛵ 🚤 🌅 These contiguous beauties curve along six miles of lakefront. Within their borders lie some of the area's most picturesque sites. Emerald Bay, a narrow cove bounded all around by dense forest, is a shimmering body of water. A spectacular waterfall feeds the cove. The forest that dominates both parks includes Jeffrey and ponderosa pines, incense cedar, quaking aspen, mountain dogwood, and willows. Wildflowers and berries flourish throughout the area. Tours of **Vikingsholm Mansion** (530-525-7277) are held daily. There are picnic areas, restrooms, and showers in both parks. Day-use fee, $6.

🏕 There are 149 sites at D. L. Bliss and 100 sites plus 20 boat-in sites at Emerald Bay; $25 per night. Camping is allowed from late spring to early fall, depending on weather conditions.

✉ *Located a few miles southwest of Lake Tahoe; accessible from Route 89 or Route 50*

🚶🏇 ⛺ 🚣 ⚓ This preserve, extending across 63,475 acres of alpine terrain, is a favorite among outdoor adventurers. With elevations ranging from 6500 to 10,000 feet, the domain encompasses about 130 lakes. Juniper, fir, and pine grow along the streams that tumble through the mountains, but large stretches, stripped by glacial action, are devoid of trees and appear like a moonscape. Because of heavy snowfall, the best time to explore is summer. Other than miles of hiking trails, there are no facilities here. A wilderness permit is necessary to enter. Contact the Taylor Creek Wilderness (530-543-2736) for more information.

⛺ ☎ *530-647-5415* Camping is hike-in only (not even strollers or bikes are allowed). Because of heavy summer use, there's a reservation fee and quota system. Some wilderness permits can be reserved up to 90 days in advance; others are available on a first-come, first-served basis.

LAKE TAHOE BASIN MANAGEMENT UNIT

✉ *Located along Route 50 around the lake's south shore. For more information contact the Taylor Creek Visitors Center on Route 89 along the western outskirts of South Lake Tahoe, near Fallen Leaf Lake.* ☎ *530-543-2400*

🚶🚴🏇 🚣 ⛺ 🚤 This extremely beautiful region is concentrated around the south shore of Lake Tahoe. Its 148,800 acres include some of Tahoe's prettiest beaches (see listing below), several campgrounds, picnic areas, plus ski and horseback riding opportunities; restrooms throughout. Day-use fee at several locations.

⛺ ☎ *530-587-3558* 📠 *530-587-6914* There are several campgrounds surrounding Lake Tahoe. My favorite is Meeks Bay, located on a pretty white-sand beach; there are 40 sites; $14 per night. There are also campsites in another part of Tahoe National Forest north of Lake Tahoe; these are located along Route 89 between Truckee and Tahoe City.

SOUTH SHORE BEACHES

✉ *Located along Route 89 west of South Lake Tahoe* ☎ *530-543-2400*

🚴🏇 🚣 ⛺ 🚤 Located within a few miles of South Lake Tahoe are several of the region's loveliest beaches. Matter of fact, the stretch from Baldwin Beach, near Emerald Bay, to the edge of South Lake Tahoe, is a golden swath of sandy beach dotted by a few businesses and private homes. Edged by trees and vegetation, backdropped by mountains, it's an idyllic site overlooking the entire lake. The sandy skein includes Baldwin Beach and Pope Beach. There are picnic areas, restrooms, and information centers at the Tallac Historic Site and Taylor Creek Center (admission).

HISTORIC CAMP RICHARDSON RESORT & MARINA

✉ *Located on Route 89 near the western outskirts of South Lake Tahoe* ☎ *530-541-1801, 800-544-1801* 🖱 *www.camprichardson.com, info@camprichardson.com*

🚶🚴🏇 🚣 ⛺ 🚤 This lakefront facility includes a campground among its many features. Situated in piney woods within strolling distance of the beach, this private campground is part of a full-facility complex that includes access to a marina, lawn sports, riding stable, and bike rentals. There are also picnic areas, restrooms, and showers. Closed from November to mid-March. No pets allowed.

🔺 There are more than 250 sites, some with RV hookups. Fees are $23 for tent sites; $28 for water and electric hookups; $31 for water, electric, and sewage hookups.

REGAN BEACH

✉️ *Located five blocks from Route 50 on Lakeview Avenue at Sacramento Street, South Lake Tahoe*

Not really a beach, this is an open picnic area along the waterfront. Nevertheless, it's nicely landscaped with a lawn and shade trees. Central to South Lake Tahoe, the park is still off the main thoroughfare. Facilities include picnic tables, barbecue grills, sand volleyball courts, and restrooms.

ELDORADO BEACH

✉️ *Along Route 50 near the intersection with Lakeview Avenue, South Lake Tahoe*

This pocket park, with its patch of sand, commands a sweeping view of the lake. Unfortunately, it's located right on a busy highway. Things can become rather schizophrenic with pristine nature extending out before you and civilization rumbling along behind. But its location in the center of South Lake Tahoe makes it popular nonetheless. The only facilities are picnic tables.

ELDORADO NATIONAL FOREST

✉️ *Routes 50 and 88 traverse the region.* 📞 *530-644-6048*

Rising from 1620 to 10,380 feet, this 668,000-acre national forest extends from the Gold Country to the High Sierra southwest of Lake Tahoe. Within its domain are numerous lakes, plus over 600 miles of fishing streams. Anglers try for brown, rainbow, and eastern brook trout; birdwatchers search out golden and bald eagles, quail, and several owl species; hunters stalk deer and bear. There are also 350 miles of hiking trails in the foothills and high Sierra. There are picnic areas and restrooms within the forest.

🔺 There are 60 campgrounds, including the beautiful Silver Lake and Caples Lake campgrounds, along Route 88; $8 to $18 per night.

LAKE TAHOE TO YOSEMITE

There are few better ways to experience High Sierra country than by following the mountain roads leading from Lake Tahoe to Yosemite. Route 89 South heads from South Lake Tahoe and intersects with Route 395, which in turn links with Route 120, the back road into Yosemite.

Along the way are views of bald-domed mountains, lofty and elegant, backdropped by even taller ranges. The road courses just below the ridge of the world, where jagged peaks dominate the sky, with valleys spread below, flat and broad. There are alpine meadows wild with flowers and aspen trees palsied in the wind.

MONITOR PASS The route from Lake Tahoe to Yosemite cuts through this pass, an 8300-foot plateau across which early pioneers and gold seekers once trekked. Today it is unchanged, tufted with grass, like an elevated prairie. Then the highway dives into boulder-strewn defiles, along rumbling rivers with white water like lace. There are tiny towns along the way—Topaz, Coleville, and Bridgeport—plus an occasional rest area.

MONO LAKE ✉ *Route 395* ✆ *760-647-6595* ✎ *760-647-6377* ✐ *www.monolake.org, info@monolake.org* In the mountains high above Yosemite, Route 395 arrives at Mono Lake, one of California's strangest and most controversial spots. The lake was inhabited for five thousand years by the Kuzedika, a Northern Paiute Indian tribe, who thrived on a high-protein diet of fly pupae and brine shrimp mixed with ground piñon nuts. The name "Mono," which comes from the language of the neighboring Yokut Indians, means "fly eaters." Located along the western edge of the Great Basin, it's a saline-alkaline body of water, the remnant of a prehistoric inland sea. At first glance it seems eerie and forbidding, an alien place with weird stalagmite-like formations that resemble a moonscape.

Actually, those spire-shaped figures are "tufa" towers, composed of calcite and formed by the confluence of freshwater springs and salt water. Many have taken the form of delicate statuary, rising like minarets and rock candy mountains from the surface. They create a provocative landscape of bone-white rock against turquoise water.

The reason these underwater fossils are presently above the lake surface is the key to a bitter environmental controversy. For over five decades, the distant city of Los Angeles drained water from streams feeding the lake. Together with natural evaporation, that action dropped the lake level about 40 feet and doubled salinity.

Since Mono Lake breeds brine shrimp and brine flies, favored food for gulls, it is home to the world's second-largest California gull population. Eared grebes and red-necked phalaropes also gather in great numbers. Their habitat has been threatened because water diversions drastically lowered the lake. In 1994, the State Water Board intervened, declaring that water diversion must decrease. Now the lake is at half its ordered level. Thirsty Los Angeles will continue to divert a small amount of water, but Mono Lake has been mandated to reach a stabilization level in 10 to 15 years. However, the future of this surreal and beautiful lake still hangs in the balance due to increasing development pressure, Los Angeles' constant demand for water, and climate change.

INYO NATIONAL FOREST Just beyond Mono Lake, Route 395 meets Route 120, along the backside of Yosemite. Before entering the park, the road cuts through Inyo National Forest, where jagged peaks angle upwards so sharply they seem like fortress walls. Below the road, other cliffs dive into gorges of granite and swirling water. The waterfalls cutting into these rockfaces have worked at the granite for thousands of years, barely chiseling a bed.

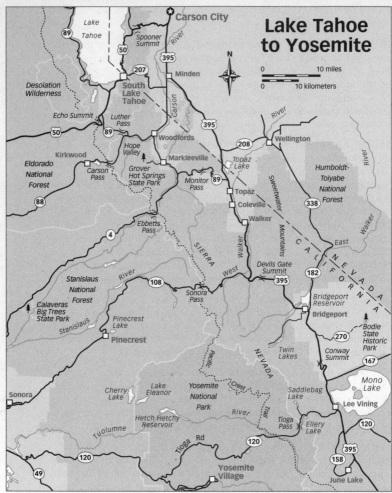

The road spirals up through **Tioga Pass** (9941 feet) and streams past **Ellery Lake**, an alpine crystal set at 9523 feet. Then it begins a steady descent into one of the country's prettiest parks—Yosemite.

LODGING

SORENSEN'S RESORT

$$–$$$$ 30 UNITS   ✉ 14255 Route 88, Hope Valley   ☎ 530-694-2203, 800-423-9949
🖰 www.sorensensresort.com, info@sorensensresort.com

Set high in the Sierras, just off a highway, there is a perfect mountain facility called Sorensen's. The 30 cabins (including ten log cabins) are scattered among a grove of aspen trees and look out upon rugged granite heights. The newer log cabins include efficiency kitchens, where other cabins have complete kitchen facilities and everything you need for a few secluded days in the hills. Nicely remodeled and decorated with wallhangings, they have a rustic charm. Some cabins feature gas fireplaces, many have free-standing wood stoves, and two have hot tubs. Sorensen's also operates the **Hope Valley Resort** down the road, which offers fly-fishing instruction, walking tours, and llama treks. Cross-country skiing is excellent here.

CAPLES LAKE RESORT

$$–$$$$ 14 UNITS   ✉*1111 Route 88, Kirkwood*   ☎*209-258-8888*   ✆*209-258-8898*
⌨*www.capleslakeresort.com, caples@volcano.net*

Caples is an alpine jewel. Set on a sparkling lake at 7800 feet, it features a lodge and eight individual cabins. There are fishing and boating facilities available, and the resort is also favored by skiers. The six B&B rooms in the lodge have private baths. And views of lake and mountains are extraordinary. The cabins have complete kitchen units (plus those oh-so-outrageous views). There's a marina with fishing boat and kayak rentals and a convenience store. Closed November to mid-December, April, and May.

BRIDGEPORT INN

$$ 25 UNITS   ✉*205 Main Street, Bridgeport*   ☎*760-932-7380*   ✆*760-932-1160*
⌨*www.thebridgeportinn.com, reservation@thebridgeportinn.com*

Deep in the mountains hardly seems the place to find a historic hotel. But here it is, contained in an 1877 white-shingle building. Add a valley setting surrounded by snowy peaks and it becomes an even more remarkable establishment. Downstairs there is a white-linen dining room and an Irish bar, as well as a parlor with chandelier and granddaddy wood stove. The restored Victorian rooms are appointed with Monterey furniture. The decor is period, simple and elegant. Be sure to ask for a room in the inn proper. Open March 1 to the day before Thanksgiving.

TIOGA PASS RESORT

$$–$$$ 14 UNITS   ✉*Route 120, Lee Vining*   ☎*254-241-6259*
⌨*www.tiogapassresort.com, reservations@tiogapassresort.com*

Situated at 9600 feet, directly above Yosemite National Park, is Tioga Pass. With log cabins, motel rooms, a restaurant, and other facilities, this is a perfect jumping-off place for the adventure-minded. The resort is surrounded by Inyo National Forest, providing ample opportunity for trout fishing, hiking, and boating during the summer, and cross-country skiing during the winter. The cabins come complete with kitchens and can be rented on a nightly or weekly basis. There are also motel units that are rented nightly. This resort's proximity to Yosemite makes it extremely popular, so book your reservations early. Summer season runs from mid-May to mid-October; winter season runs from the week before Christmas through April.

DINING

OFF THE WALL BAR & GRILL

$$$–$$$$ AMERICAN   ✉*1501 Kirkwood Meadows Drive, Kirkwood*   ☎*209-258-7365*

For an outstanding overall dining experience, try this Kirkwood Lodge restaurant. The atmosphere is designed for comfort, with oversized chairs and a fireplace, and the location affords great views of the surrounding mountains. Specials include lobster ceviche, osso buco, and the local favorite, shaved prime rib sandwich with horseradish. Open daily for lunch and appetizers, Friday and Saturday for dinner (reservations required).

MEADOWCLIFF

$–$$ DINER   ✉ *Route 395, Coleville*   📞*530-495-2180*   🖊*www.meadowcliff.com, stay@meadowcliff.com*

Restaurants are rare and far between along Route 395, but this is a homey café en route. The folks hereabouts serve standard breakfasts, and hamburgers and chili at lunch. Grab a table out back for spectacular views of the bordering cliffs. No dinner.

BRIDGEPORT INN

$$–$$$ AMERICAN   ✉*205 Main Street, Bridgeport*   📞*760-932-7380*
🖊*www.thebridgeportinn.com, reservation@thebridgeportinn.com*

The 1877 Bridgeport Inn contains a very attractive dining room. With its ceiling fans and antique wall fixtures, the place radiates a congenial atmosphere. The dinner menu, offering prime rib, veal chops, lobster, and catch-of-the-day, is deluxe in price, but breakfasts and lunches here are fairly inexpensive. Open March 1 to the day before Thanksgiving. No lunch on Wednesday.

TIOGA PASS RESORT

$$ DINER   ✉*Route 120, Lee Vining*   📞*254-241-6259*   🖊*www.tiogapassresort.com, reservations@tiogapassresort.com*

Way up behind Yosemite, more than 5000 feet above the valley, there's a friendly restaurant at Tioga Pass. Serving three meals daily, this mountain retreat features a menu ranging from sandwiches to homemade chili to hearty full-course dinners with delicious homemade desserts. It's particularly welcome for travelers heading from the High Sierra down to Yosemite.

NIGHTLIFE

WOLFCREEK RESTAURANT AND CUTTHROAT SALOON

✉*14830 Route 89, Markleeville*   📞*530-694-2150* For after-dinner drinks in an old-time bar, head over to Wolfcreek. Once the Alpine Hotel back in the boom days when the town of nearly 3000 was the gateway to the mines of Silver Mountains, it's now a low-key watering hole. Occasionally closed in winter.

PARKS

HUMBOLDT-TOIYABE NATIONAL FOREST

✉*The easiest access is along Routes 89 and 395, south of Lake Tahoe. For information, contact the Bridgeport Ranger District at Route 395, Bridgeport.*   📞*760-932-7070*
🖊*www.fs.fed.us/r4/htnf*

This is the biggest national forest in the lower 48 states. Its 6 million High Sierra acres reach from Lake Tahoe to Mono Lake and extend across the California border into Nevada. Routes 89 and 395, the main High Sierra roads between Lake Tahoe and Yosemite, traverse the heart of Toiyabe. In addition to alpine meadows and rugged mountain peaks, it contains coniferous forests inhabited by deer, black bear, porcupine, and mountain lion. There are numerous hiking trails and trout streams. Skiing, canoeing, and rafting are also popular here. Permits are required for wilderness backpacking. Facilities include picnic areas and restrooms.

▲ There are 38 campgrounds; $11 to $20 per night. Reservations: 877-444-6777.

GROVER HOT SPRINGS STATE PARK

✉Off Route 89, about four miles from Markleeville 📞530-694-2248
📠530-694-2502 ✏grover@gbif.com

🚶🚴🚣⛱ Set in a mountain meadow and backdropped by 8000-foot peaks, this 650-acre park is a lovely sight. The Toiyabe National Forest and Mokelumne Wilderness Area completely surround it; hiking trails lead from the park to lakes and other points throughout the forest. There is fishing for rainbow and cutthroat trout. The central attractions, however, are the springs. Water from underground springs bubbles up at 148° and is cooled to an inviting 102° to 104° for the park's hot bath (fee). This, together with a swimming pool, is situated in the meadow and open to the public. If you long for an outdoor hot pool in an alpine setting, this is the ticket. Other facilities include picnic areas, restrooms, and showers. Closed for two weeks in September. Day-use fee, $6.

▲ There are 76 sites (20 winter sites) in two campgrounds within walking distance of the pools. Campgrounds require reservations from about May 15 to Labor Day; during the rest of the year sites are on a first-come, first-served basis; $25 per night. Reservations: 800-444-7275.

INYO NATIONAL FOREST

📞760-873-2500 ✏inyovis/r5_inyo@fs.fed.us

🚶🚴🏇🎿🏂🏔⛱🚣🏊🚤⛴ Part of this sprawling facility lies along both Route 395, near Mono Lake, and Route 120, directly above Yosemite. Within this section of Inyo are several excellent campgrounds that have picnic areas access is along Routes 395 and 120. For information, contact the Lee Vining Ranger District at Route 120, Lee Vining.

▲ There are 90 campgrounds. Particularly recommended are Tioga Lake Campground and Ellery Lake Campground, both located along Route 120 directly above Yosemite. They're situated on lovely alpine lakes; $17 per night.

YOSEMITE NATIONAL PARK

It is a national institution, one of America's foremost playgrounds, a spectacular park climbing across the Sierra Nevada from 2000 feet elevation to a dizzying 13,000 feet—Yosemite. Within its domain is a valley whose sheer granite cliffs have been carved by the cold blade of a glacier. It's a region of bald domes, sunshot waterfalls, and stately sequoias. At the lower elevations are broad mountain meadows browsed by deer. During summer the place riots with wildflowers; in winter it's cloaked in snow. For general information on the goings-on in Yosemite, contact 209-372-0200; www.nps.gov/yose.

SIGHTS

YOSEMITE VALLEY Formed about two million years ago, this Sierra canyon has a flat meadow floor surrounded by vertical precipices. It seems that glacial action tore away softer sections of granite, leaving the more durable rocks like El Capitan and Half Dome.

For thousands of years, the Ahwahneechee and other Indians inhabited the valley. After its "discovery" by whites in the 19th century, the region became a curiosity point for tourists. To protect the place, President Lincoln in 1864 declared Yosemite Valley and the Mariposa Grove to be public parks. Several years later, John Muir, a Scottish naturalist, moved to Yosemite and began a campaign to further protect the natural environment by having it declared a national park. In 1890 his efforts succeeded.

The valley which Muir saved must be experienced; it cannot adequately be described. It was once a massive lake fed by the glaciers that created the surrounding cliffs. Erosion and stream sediment eventually filled it, creating fields rich in vegetation.

CLOUDS REST Above the valley bed, vertical cliffs extend on either side to the limit of sight. In the far distance rises Clouds Rest, at 9926 feet the highest mountain visible from the valley.

HALF DOME In front of Clouds Rest stands this monstrous rock, which appears to have been cleft in two by the hand of God, leaving a sheer wall 2000 feet straight up.

MIRROR LAKE This mountain jewel is named for the peaks reflected in its gleaming waters.

ROYAL ARCHES At this sight granite shells have been formed into great arcs by uplift and tilt.

SENTINEL ROCK This is the last remnant of a mammoth block of granite, the rest of which has been cracked and dumped into the valley. It's named for its resemblance to a watchtower.

LEANING TOWER Yosemite's sweeping tower, which gains its name from the rock's disconcerting tilt, offers a classic climb.

CATHEDRAL SPIRES At the summit of these granite shafts, rising about 2000 feet above the floor, is a stunning view of El Capitan and Yosemite Valley.

THREE BROTHERS These imposing forms take their name from a legend about three of the sons of Chief Tenaya.

YOSEMITE FALLS Yosemite Falls, among the world's tallest waterfalls, tumble 2425 feet in three dramatic cascades.

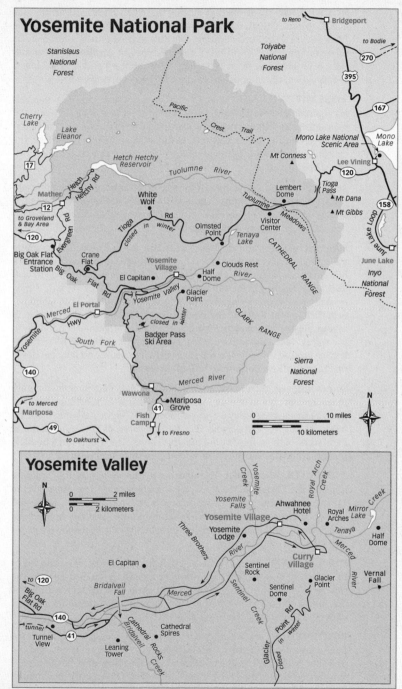

Yosemite National Park

Stanislaus
National
Forest

Toiyabe
National
Forest

to Reno

Bridgeport

to Bodie

270

395

167

Cherry
Lake

Lake
Eleanor

Mono Lake National
Scenic Area

Mono
Lake

17

Hetch Hetchy
Reservoir

Mt Conness

Lee Vining

Tioga Pass

120

158

Mather

Tuolumne River

White
Wolf

Rd

Lembert
Dome

▲ Mt Dana

June Lake Loop

12

Tioga

closed in winter

Olmsted
Point

Tuolumne

Meadows

Visitor
Center

▲ Mt Gibbs

to Groveland
& Bay Area

120

Big Oak Flat
Entrance
Station

Evergreen Rd

Crane
Flat

Tenaya
Lake

CATHEDRAL RANGE

June Lake

Inyo
National
Forest

El Capitan

Yosemite
Village

Clouds Rest

Half
Dome

River

Big Oak Flat Rd

Yosemite Valley

Glacier
Point

CLARK RANGE

El Portal

Merced Hwy

closed in winter

Badger Pass
Ski Area

Yosemite

South Fork

Sierra
National
Forest

Merced River

140

Wawona

to Merced

Mariposa

41

Mariposa
Grove

N

Fish
Camp

to Fresno

0   10 miles

49

to Oakhurst

0   10 kilometers

Yosemite Valley

N

0   2 miles

0   2 kilometers

Yosemite
Creek

Royal Arch Creek

Creek

Yosemite
Falls

Ahwahnee
Hotel

Mirror
Lake

Yosemite Village

Royal
Arches

Tenaya

Three Brothers

Yosemite
Lodge

Half
Dome

El Capitan

River

Curry
Village

Sentinel
Rock

Merced

to 120

Bridalveil
Fall

Merced

Sentinel
Dome

Glacier
Point

Vernal
Fall

Big Oak
Flat Rd

Sentinel Creek

River

140

tunnel

Cathedral
Bridalveil

Cathedral
Spires

Glacier Point Rd

closed in winter

Tunnel
View

41

Leaning
Tower

Rocks

Creek

EL CAPITAN King of kings among these grand geologic formations is El Capitan. This hard granite giant measures twice the size of the Rock of Gibraltar. Rock climbers, ant-like in proportion, inch along its unyielding walls. Composed of several types of granite, its sheer cliff rises over 3000 feet from the valley floor. Solitary and unshakable, it seems to peer down upon the human antics occurring far below.

YOSEMITE VILLAGE ☎209-372-0200 ✐*www.yosemite.org* Yosemite Valley is generally a beehive of activity. The busiest spot of all is this cluster of buildings and shops along the northern wall of the valley. The visitor center keystones the complex. In addition to an information desk, the center hosts a photographic display of the valley and a regionally oriented bookstore.

Also within Yosemite Village is a shop selling prints by the great photographer Ansel Adams, whose shots of the valley are renowned for their beauty and mystery. There's an art center nearby, as well as a post office, gift shop, grocery, and restaurants.

Summer, holidays, and weekends are particularly crowded in Yosemite Valley. In recent years the place has sometimes assumed the quality of a human zoo, with traffic jams and long lines. If possible, it's best to visit during the week or in the off-season, and to arrive before 10 a.m. A particularly nice time to visit is in May (before Memorial Day), when the waterfalls are at their peak due to snow melt and the dogwood is in bloom. Best of all, the summer crowds have not yet descended upon the valley. Also consider walking, bicycling, or using the free shuttle service around the valley; it will save you a headache and help cut down on the traffic flow. Parking is difficult in season.

Something else to remember: Yosemite Valley covers seven square miles, and everyone seems intent on crowding into its confines. For good reason—the valley is an extraordinary sight and must not be missed. But there are almost 1200 square miles of Yosemite National Park, some of them hardly touched by visitors. These outer reaches also possess singular beauty and should be part of your itinerary.

YOSEMITE MUSEUM Next door to the village is the building housing the Yosemite Museum. Exhibits illustrate the cultures of the Miwok and Paiute peoples who once inhabited the area, while the gallery has rotating exhibits on Yosemite Valley. Directly behind the museum spreads a village complete with bark dwellings called *umachas* and earth-covered houses.

HIGH SIERRA Plan to visit the High Sierra country above the valley by following Route 120, Tioga Road, in its eastward climb toward the top of the mountain range. This road is closed during snowy months, but in periods of warm weather it leads past splendid alpine regions with meadows, lakes, and stark peaks.

WHITE WOLF At about 7000 feet, Route 120 passes a virgin stand of red fir, then continues up to this tranquil meadowy area. The lodge here provides cabins, a campground, and a restaurant. Past White Wolf a spectacular view of the **Clark Range** is revealed. The scenic area is named for Galen Clark, who both explored and worked to protect Yosemite.

OLMSTED POINT From here, a short trail leads to a granite dome that looks down toward the north side of Half Dome and up to Tenaya Lake.

TENAYA LAKE This long, slender body of water, set at 8149 feet, is shadowed on either side by bald rockfaces. Beyond Tenaya Lake is **Mt. Conness**, which is 12,590 feet in elevation.

TUOLUMNE MEADOWS The highlight of the journey is sweeping Tuolumne Meadows, with its information center, campground, lodge, store, and restaurant. Statistically speaking, this wonderland constitutes the Sierra's largest subalpine meadow. Located at 8600 feet, its sunglinted fields are populated with smooth granite boulders and cut by a meandering stream. Conifers border the meadow and are in turn backdropped by bald domes and sharp faces. In summer, mountain wildflowers carpet the hillsides with brilliant shades of red, blue, and yellow, counterpointing the hard gray rocks with gentle forms and soft colors.

LEMBERT DOME A lopsided peak carved by glaciers, this dome has glittering patches of glacial polish that can still be seen along its surface.

MOUNTAIN PEAKS At 13,053 feet, **Mount Dana**'s sprawling ridge is the second-highest peak in Yosemite. Near Tioga Pass, **Mount Gibbs** offers a beautiful view from its 12,764-foot-high peak.

TIOGA PASS Constructed at 9941 feet, this roadway marks the highest automobile pass in California. It is also the gateway to Mono Lake, and to other mountain roads. On these you can travel north to Oregon, south toward Death Valley, or turn around and return to that extraordinary valley now over 5000 feet below.

BRIDALVEIL FALL An interesting trip from Yosemite Valley carries you along Route 41 to the park's southwestern boundary. Shortly after leaving the valley, the road passes this beautiful waterfall, where a short path leads to a 620-foot cascade. Tumbling along a sharp rockface, buffeted by breezes, the waterfall twists into intaglio designs. The edges of the cascade are blown to mist and fall like soft rain on the people below.

TUNNEL VIEW Soon after Bridalveil Fall, just before burrowing into the mountain, the highway arrives at Tunnel View. From here, Yosemite Valley looks like God's playpen, bounded by sharp walls and domed in azure sky. On the right, you'll see the hanging valley from which Bridalveil Falls descends. Behind it are Cathedral Rocks, appearing like hunchbacks bent to meet the valley. Sentinel Rock is a stone rapier, and Half Dome, from this unique angle, takes the form of a dolphin's bottlenose. To the left, a single figure predominates, its vertical profile at once alluring and frightening—El Capitan.

GLACIER POINT For an even finer view, follow the long side road that corkscrews up to 7214-foot-high Glacier Point. The vital fact here is that you are *above* Yosemite Valley, looking into the chasm and outward along its granite profile. You're also on the brink of a 3200-foot precipice (there but for the grace of a handrail go we all). Gaze out and you'll see that Half Dome now has transformed into a bird's head. Across the valley a three-tiered cascade, Yosemite Falls, tumbles thousands of feet. This is the most spectacular of all Yosemite viewpoints, with the High Sierra stretching along a limitless series of snowcapped peaks. Below, the Merced River meanders past camps and hotels deep in Yosemite Valley. Glacier Point is open only during the summer.

PIONEER YOSEMITE HISTORY CENTER ✉*Wawona* The main road continues through miles of tall, cool forest to Wawona, a small settlement in the park's southwest corner. Here, just past an old covered bridge, is this historic center. There are log cabins and houses dating back well into the 19th century, plus a blacksmith shop and Yosemite transportation company office. This intriguing outdoor museum also features a collection of wagons and buckboards.

MARIPOSA GROVE Beyond, near the park's south entrance, rises Mariposa Grove. Most impressive of Yosemite's three giant sequoia groves, it can be reached by tram in summer or along a two-and-a-half-mile trail. Within the grove stands Grizzly Giant, a 1500-year-old forest denizen. Giant sequoias, the world's largest living things, can weigh more than two million pounds. Within this grove are about 200 trees measuring over ten feet in diameter. Unlike redwoods, which hug the cool, moist coastal areas, sequoias flourish between 5000 and 8000 feet in sunny climates. Here in the cathedral silence of the grove, these forest giants number not only among the earth's biggest life forms, but its most regal as well.

LODGING

Accommodations in Yosemite are varied, plentiful, and, paradoxically, difficult to reserve. Four million people a year pour through the park's granite arches, many in search of a place to rest their wonder-struck heads. As a result, the park provides several locations with facilities ranging from canvas tents to cabins to cottages to hotel rooms to deluxe suites.

Most facilities are located right in the valley—at the Yosemite Lodge, Curry Village, and The Ahwahnee Hotel. Others—White Wolf, Tuolumne Meadows, and Wawona—are situated in distant parts of the park and offer retreats from the crowds in the valley. Prices quoted below are summer rates; during the week in winter, rates are sometimes significantly lower.

YOSEMITE RESERVATIONS, DNC PARKS & RESORTS AT YOSEMITE, INC. ✉*6771 North Palm Avenue, Fresno, CA 93704* ☎*801-559-5000* 📠*559-456-0542* ✐*www.yosemitepark.com* Particularly during the summer months, facilities are booked far in advance. Matter of fact, it's not a bad idea to make reservations the year before your arrival. During the colder months the situation eases; even then, however, weekends, holidays, or good skiing snow can draw summer-size crowds back to the park. To make your reservations, contact Yosemite Reservations, DNC Parks & Resorts at Yosemite, Inc.

YOSEMITE LODGE AT THE FALLS
$$$ 250 UNITS ☎*209-372-1274* ✐*www.yosemitepark.com*
This lodge hosts several styles of accommodations. Foremost are the lodge rooms; these are motel-type affairs in a series of low-slung buildings near the central lodge facility. One I stayed in was nicely furnished in oak, modern in design, spacious, and quite comfortable. It had a tele-

phone and television, and enjoyed a private patio looking out upon a pine grove. Deer browsed 20 feet from the window.

CURRY VILLAGE

$$ 418 UNITS ☏209-372-8333, 559-252-4848 (reservations) 📠209-372-4816 ✐www.yosemitepark.com

Over at Curry Village, in a nearby section of the valley, cabins are available at the same prices. Hotel rooms here have natural wood furnishings and stall showers. The wall decorations are tastefully selected and some rooms have lofts providing extra sleeping areas. The village also contains around 400 "canvas tent cabins," which provide an excellent means to visit Yosemite at an inexpensive price. They're wall tents on raised wooden platforms, with mosquito screens, windows, and canvas flaps for privacy. Furnishings include beds with complete bedding, food storage lockers, plus time-battered shelves; basic but sufficient. Most of the tents are not heated, so prepare accordingly for winter stays. People staying in any Curry facility have access to the sitting room, swimming pool (seasonal), shops, and restaurants on the premises. Due to rockslides, parts of the village will be closed until mid-2009. Closed weekdays from January through March.

THE AHWAHNEE

$$$$ 123 ROOMS ☏559-252-4848 📠559-456-0542 ✐www.yosemitepark.com

Yosemite provides the opportunity to bivouac in a flowering meadow, sleep in a pine forest, or rest yards away from the world's greatest geologic wonders. Nowhere, though, are the accommodations as grand and dramatic as they are here. Built in 1927, the place is an architectural marvel, a multitiered building of wood and stone backdropped by rainfluted cliffs. Its manicured lawns and natural arbors place it among world-class hotels. The high-ceilinged interior is decorated after American Indian designs with intricate rugs and patterned glass. There are grand fireplaces large enough to stand inside and chandeliers that belong in a castle. Befitting the rest of the hotel, the bedrooms are spacious affairs decorated in the same motif. Even if you decide not to stay here at least plan to tour the hotel. It's a singular feature in an extraordinary park.

TUOLUMNE MEADOWS LODGE

$ 70 UNITS ☏209-372-8413 ✐www.yosemitepark.com

Nestled along Route 120 at 8775 feet, Tuolumne Meadows has tent cabins available. These are similar to the facilities in the valley, consisting of a bed, complete bedding, sparse furnishings, and, to warm those chilly mountain nights, a wood stove. There is no electricity; candles are provided. The experience here is somewhere between hotel living and camping; bathrooms and showers are shared. The lodge contains a dining room and lobby available to tent sleepers. The entire complex sits near a beautiful meadow bounded by thick forest. Idyllic and easy. Open early June to mid-September.

WHITE WOLF LODGE

$$ 28 UNITS ☏209-372-8416 ✐www.yosemitepark.com

White Wolf, located midway between Yosemite Valley and Tuolumne Meadows at 7892 feet, has tent cabins as well as four wood cabins with private baths. With its nearby hiking trails, it makes a great escape hatch. Closed in winter and early spring.

THE REDWOODS IN YOSEMITE

$$$$ 125 UNITS ✉Box 2085, Wawona Station, CA 95389 📞866-628-0424
💻www.redwoodsinyosemite.com

This is a privately owned facility within the park. Here, cabins are set in the woods just off a side road. Accommodations range from one- to six-bedroom vacation homes, which all include decks and barbecues.

TENAYA LODGE AT YOSEMITE

$$$$ 244 ROOMS ✉1122 Route 41, Fish Camp 📞559-683-6555, 800-635-5807
📠559-683-6147 💻www.tenayalodge.com, tenayareservations@dncinc.com

One of the great frustrations of visiting Yosemite National Park is trying to land a reservation at the often sold-out Ahwahnee Hotel. Now this equally stunning lodge offers rooms near the park's southern entrance. The hotel has a spacious lobby decorated with American Indian art, nicely landscaped grounds, indoor and outdoor pools with jacuzzis, and a variety of recreational programs centered around the park. The resort-style lodge also offers a bar and lounge and an exercise room. The only drawback is the 45-minute trip down to the Yosemite Valley floor.

DINING

YOSEMITE VILLAGE

$–$$ DELI/AMERICAN 💻www.yosemitepark.com

At the northern edge of the valley, this village provides three dining possibilities. In addition to the budget-priced **Degnan's Delicatessen** (209-372-8454), there's an informal dining room called **Degnan's Loft** (209-372-8381). Dominated by a mammoth fireplace, this restaurant boasts a daily assortment of appetizers and decent pizza. The **Village Grill** (209-372-1207) serves basic dinner fare, with a menu featuring hamburgers, chicken strips, and ice cream. Lunch only. Closed in winter.

FOOD COURT

$ INTERNATIONAL 📞209-372-1265

Over at Yosemite Lodge at the Falls there is an affordable food court. It doesn't take much imagination to picture this area, serving steam-tray food at low, low prices. Though the meals sometimes sit too long above the steam, and the dining hall is cavernous and impersonal, this is a place for anyone who believes that a full stomach shouldn't mean an empty wallet.

MOUNTAIN ROOM RESTAURANT

$$$ STEAK/SEAFOOD 📞209-372-1281 💻www.yosemitepark.com

This restaurant provides an upscale step to a large but comfortable dining room. An exposed-beam ceiling adds a touch of class to the surroundings, where dinner is served. The interior is dominated by expansive windows and photographs of local sights, all of which is enough to make you forget the menu. To refresh your memory, they serve steak, steak, and steak—as in sirloin, prime rib, filet mignon, and New York cut. They also have tasty seafood and pasta dishes—broiled salmon, rainbow trout almandine, pepper-vodka penne or breast of chicken. Dinner only.

CURRY VILLAGE

$ INTERNATIONAL 📞209-372-8307 🖳www.yosemitepark.com

Curry Village features five dining locations with offerings such as burgers, pizza, Mexican fast food, meat and potatoes, and all-you-can-eat buffets. Call for winter hours.

AHWAHNEE DINING ROOM

$$$$ CONTINENTAL 📞209-372-1489 🖨209-372-1463 🖳www.yosemitepark.com

For special occasions, or just a personal indulgence, there's the Ahwahnee. An entire wing of this grand old hotel is dedicated to the fine art of dining. Part of the experience simply involves sitting in the dining room, a high-ceilinged affair with exposed-log beams. The interior is fashioned of stone and glass, with wood-paneled sections painted in American Indian designs. Service is impeccable. The breakfast menu is standard; lunch includes salads and sandwiches. Dinner is the hotel's premier meal. Appetizers range from oyster mushroom artichoke ravioli to Dungeness crab cake and cornbread quesadillas. Entrées include pan-seared organically farmed salmon and butter-braised rabbit. Dining here is an experience unto itself. Reservations required; dress code.

TUOLUMNE MEADOWS LODGE

$$ AMERICAN 📞209-372-8413 🖳www.yosemitepark.com

Farther up the highway, you'll encounter Tuolumne Meadows, a mountain hideaway with surprisingly sophisticated cuisine. The dining tent beside the Tuolumne River features a variety of beef, fish, chicken, and vegetarian offerings, as well as soups, salads, and desserts. They also serve hearty breakfasts, but no lunch. Reservations required for dinner. Open early June to mid-September.

WAWONA HOTEL

$$–$$$ INTERNATIONAL 📞209-375-1425 🖨209-375-6601
🖳www.yosemitepark.com

Over at Wawona, located in the park's southwest corner, is this splendid hotel. An old establishment in the style of the Deep South, it contains a white-linen dining room that overlooks manicured lawns. Decorated with antique photos of Yosemite and illuminated by hand-painted lamps, it's a regal affair. In addition to a breakfast buffet, they feature a hearty lunch. Dinner presents angus beef, trout, and vegetarian lasagna. Such good food and elegant surroundings are hard to match out here deep in the forest. A special barbecue dinner is available on Saturday during the summer, and Sunday brunch is served from Easter through Thanksgiving and during the Christmas holidays. Closed the first two weeks of December; open Friday through Sunday only from mid-January to mid-March.

NIGHTLIFE

MOUNTAIN ROOM BAR 📞559-252-4848 In Yosemite National Park, this spacious, oak-paneled lounge is complete with fireplace. The perfect spot for a late-night brandy, the room is walled-in glass and looks out toward Yosemite Falls. If you need a taste of the "real world," there's a large-screened TV that shows major sporting events.

AHWAHNEE BAR ✆ *209-372-1489* Over at the beautiful Ahwahnee, you'll encounter this intimate bar, a plushly appointed drinking place. Live music most weekends.

PARKS

YOSEMITE NATIONAL PARK
✉ *Located along Routes 120, 140, and 41 about 200 miles southeast of San Francisco*
✆ *209-372-0200* ✑ *www.nps.gov/yose*

🏃 🚵 🐎 🏕 ⛵ 🚣 🎣 One of the country's most extraordinary and renowned parks, this 761,000-acre giant offers every activity from sightseeing a spectacular glacial valley to skiing alpine meadows. About 95 percent of the park has been targeted for wilderness status. Its domain spreads from 2900 to 13,000 feet, climbing from the foothills to the roof of the Sierra. Since its features are so extensive, Yosemite is discussed at length in most other sections of this chapter, so consult them for details. Among the many facilities here are hotels, restaurants, stores, museums, shuttle service, organized nature programs, information centers, picnic areas, restrooms, showers, a ski area, almost 800 miles of hiking trails, stables, and more than 600 miles of riding trails. Day-use fee, $20 (good for one week). For information on weather, road conditions, and campground status, call 209-372-0200.

⛺ Camping is permitted in campgrounds in Yosemite Valley and throughout the park ($15 fee in Yosemite Valley). There is a seven-day limit in the valley during the summer, fourteen days in other areas. Since the park's 1500 sites are in great demand, arrive early; some campsites are on a first-come, first-served basis. Call the reservation center at 877-444-6777 to secure a site. Wilderness permits are required for backcountry camping; these are available at the Yosemite Valley visitors center, and in Big Oak Flat, Yosemite Valley Wilderness Center, Tuolumne Meadows, and Wawona (209-372-0740; www.yosemitepark. com).

There are also five High Sierra camps with dormitory tents and dining facilities. Spaced about seven miles apart and open during the summer, these are ideal for hikers exploring the high country. Contact High Sierra Reservations, Yosemite Concession Services (6771 North Palm Avenue, Fresno, CA 93704; 801-559-5000; fax 559-456-0542; www. yosemitepark.com).

OUTDOOR ADVENTURES

FISHING

Pick almost any lake or river in the Gold Country and High Sierra, bait a hook, and you're bound to come up with trout for dinner.

Sacramento
SACRAMENTO SPORT FISHING GUIDES ✉ *1531 Wyant Way, Sacramento* ✆ *916-487-3392, 800-344-4871* ✑ *www.fishingtrips.com, captjack@fishingtrips. com* These fishing guides can arrange trips on the Sacramento River for

striped bass and sturgeon from March through May. Stripehead bass trips are available in September and October.

Southern Gold Country
MOCCASIN POINT MARINA ✉11405 Jacksonville Road, Jamestown ☎209-989-2206 This place rents fishing boats on Lake Don Pedro, where anglers try for bass, crappie, trout, and salmon.

Lake Tahoe Area
TAHOE SPORT FISHING ✉Tahoe Keys Marina, 900 Ski Run Boulevard, South Lake Tahoe ☎530-541-5448, 800-696-7797 ⌨www.tahoesportfishing.com This is one of the area's best bets. A morning or afternoon charter includes drinks, bait and tackle, and fish cleaning. Common catches are mackinaw, rainbow, and brown trout and kokanee salmon.

DON SHEETZ GUIDE SERVICE ☎530-541-5566, 877-270-0742 ⌨www.tahoefishingguides.com Don Sheetz offers trips for mackinaw trout from the Tahoe Keys Marina.

MILE HIGH FISHING CHARTERS ☎530-541-5312, 866-752-3474 ⌨www.fishtahoe.com Mile High Charters offers Tahoe Keys Marina trips for mackinaw trout.

WATER SPORTS

From rafting and waterskiing on the American and Sacramento rivers to sailing and windsurfing on Lake Tahoe, the Gold Country and High Sierra are prime places for water sports.

Sacramento
AMERICAN RIVER RAFTING ✉11257 South Bridge Street, Rancho Cordova ☎916-635-6400 ⌨www.raftrentals.com This company will shuttle you back to your car after a three-and-a-half-hour lazy kayak or raft ride. Open May through August.

Lake Tahoe Area
CAMP RICHARDSON RESORT MARINA ✉1900 Jameson Beach Road, Camp Richardson ☎530-542-6570 ⌨www.camprichardson.com The place for recreational boating—including sailing, canoeing, ski boating, and board sailing—is Lake Tahoe. And Camp Richardson rents 18-foot Bow Riders and personal water crafts. Open May through September.

RIVER RUNNING

Whitewater rafting in the Gold Country and High Sierra combines spectacular scenery with high adventure.

Sacramento
AMERICAN RIVER RECREATION ✉P.O. Box 465, Lotus, CA 95651 ☎800-333-7238 ⌨www.arrafting.com Talk to this company for runs on the American, Klamath, and Merced rivers. Trips range from Class III to V, and last up to five days. Closed October through March.

Southern Gold Country

BEYOND LIMITS ADVENTURE TOURS ✉ P.O. Box 215, Riverbank, CA 95367 ✆ 209-869-6060, 800-234-7238 ⌨ www.rivertrip.com Beyond Limits provides trips on various rivers. They also rent rafts, and any camping gear you might need.

ZEPHYR WHITEWATER EXPEDITIONS ✉ P.O. Box 510, Columbia, CA 95310 ✆ 209-532-6249 ⌨ www.zrafting.com From April through September, Zephyr Expeditions leads tours of the Tuolumne, Kings, Merced, and American rivers. Trips are on a six-person raft and last from a half day to five days.

Central Gold Country

CHILI BAR OUTDOOR CENTER ✉ P.O. Box 554, Coloma, CA 95613 ✆ 530-621-1236 ⌨ www.cbocwhitewater.com This company runs Class III and IV rapids on the American River.

GOLD RUSH WHITEWATER RAFTING ✉ 6260 Route 49, Lotus, CA ✆ 530-295-8235, 800-900-7238 📠 530-626-7631 ⌨ www.goldrushriver.com This company has half-day, full-day, and overnight excursions on the American River. They also offer a heart-pounding trip on the Kaweah River with Class III to Class IV-plus runs.

Northern Gold Country

TRIBUTARY WHITEWATER TOURS ✉ 20480 Woodbury Drive, Grass Valley ✆ 530-346-6812, 800-672-3846 ⌨ www.whitewatertours.com, rafting@whitewatertours.com In business for more than two decades, this tour company leads expeditions on the American, Yuba, and Truckee rivers; difficulty ranges from Class II to Class V. Closed in winter.

Lake Tahoe Area

MOUNTAIN AIR SPORTS ✉ 55 West Lake Boulevard, Tahoe City ✆ 530-583-5606 ⌨ www.truckeeriverrafting.com Call this outfitter for a family ride on the gentle Class I Truckee River. Open in summer only. Don't forget your sunscreen!

ROCK CLIMBING

YOSEMITE MOUNTAINEERING SCHOOL AND GUIDE SERVICE ✉ Badger Pass, Yosemite National Park ✆ 209-372-8444 ⌨ www.yosemitemountaineering.com Ready to scale a sheer granite cliff? Then Yosemite National Park is your playground. Lessons and guides are available at this school and guide service.

BALLOON RIDES

A hot-air balloon may not get you there sooner, but it will carry you higher while offering spectacular views of Sacramento's rich farm country.

MOUNTAIN HIGH BALLOONS ✉ Truckee ✆ 530-587-6922, 888-462-2683 For a flight above the Sierras, call Mountain High from May through mid-October. There are several special surprises in store for you, and kids under ten fly free with an adult.

If sifting dirt along cold mountain streams sounds like fun, try your luck panning for gold. You may not strike it rich, but then again, who knows?

Southern Gold Country
GOLD PROSPECTING ADVENTURES ⊠18170 Main Street, Jamestown ☎209-984-4653, 800-596-0009 ⊲www.goldprospecting.com, info@goldprospecting. com These adventure guides will take you to their own private 1849 gold-mining camp. You'll find Mark Twain's cabin as well as original pistols, lanterns, and flumes used during that serendipitous era.

CALIFORNIA GOLD ⊠P.O. Box 1132, Jamestown, CA 95327 ☎209-984-4914 ⊲www.goldfun.com California Gold offers a five-hour mining trip where you'll dig and pan for gold just like the '49ers did.

Central Gold Country
ROARING CAMP MINING CO. ⊠P.O. Box 278, Pine Grove, CA 95665 ☎209-296-4100 This is the place to contact for daily guided tours along the Mokelumne River. They also have cabins and tent camping where you can vacation while seeking out your fortune. Closed October through April.

SKIING

The center of California snow sporting lies in the Sierra, where large resorts surround Lake Tahoe and extend south toward Yosemite National Park and beyond. Squaw Valley played host to the 1960 Winter Olympics and numerous other resorts have won plaudits from world-class skiers. With temperatures hovering between 20 and 40 degrees and snowfall measuring 200 to 400 inches, the region is ideal for winter sports.

The season begins in late fall and sometimes lasts until May. During those frosty months dozens of ski areas offer both downhill and cross-country skiing.

Contact the **California Ski Industry Association** (One Market Street, Steuart Tower, Suite 2660, San Francisco, CA 94105; 415-543-7036, fax 415-543-0112; www.californiasnow.com, info@californiasnow.com) for full information on skiing in California.

SUGAR BOWL ⊠Norden ☎530-426-9000 📠530-426-3723 ⊲www.sugarbowl. com, info@sugarbowl.com Sugar Bowl has 1500 acres of skiable terrain accessed by 13 chairlifts. Seventeen percent of the 83 runs are beginner slopes, 45 percent are for intermediate, and 38 percent are for experts. There are two terrain runs for snowboarders designed by Noah Salasnek, plus a 19-foot super pipe. They rent downhill skis and snowboards.

NORTHSTAR RESORT ⊠Six miles east of Truckee on Route 267 ☎530-562-1010 ⊲www.northstarattahoe.com, northstar@boothcreek.com With 17 lifts and more than 80 runs, there is plenty to keep you busy here. The summit reaches 8610 feet and the vertical drop is 1722 feet. There are several terrain parks for freestyle skiers and riders. There are also extensive cross-country and snowshoe trails, and a snowtube run. The rental shop has downhill, telemark, and Nordic skis, snowshoes, and snowboards.

SQUAW VALLEY ✉2007 *Olympic Valley* ✆530-583-6985, 800-545-4350 ✍*www.squaw.com, squaw@squaw.com* Nestled in the High Sierra amidst 8000 acres of wilderness preserve with 4000 skiable acres, Squaw Valley boasts 33 lifts, six mountain peaks, and a 2850-foot vertical drop. Twenty-five percent of the runs are beginner slopes, 45 percent are intermediate, and 30 percent are expert. The snowboard park includes one super pipe and three terrain parks; it is one of several runs open until 9 p.m. Lessons for skiing, telemarking, and snowboarding are available, and they rent all necessary equipment. Squaw Valley also has ice skating, snow tubing, and an indoor climbing wall. There are instructors for every level of skier or snowboarder, snow school for children, and enough diversions to keep even a non-skier content.

Snow Motion

As a travel destination, California offers everything. Even during winter, when rain spatters the coast and fog invades the valleys, the Golden State has one more treat in its bottomless bag—snow. No sooner has the white powder settled than skiers and snowboarders from around the world make a beeline for the region's high-altitude resort areas. They come to schuss through fir forests in the Cascades, challenge the runs above Lake Tahoe, and breathe the beauty of Yosemite at Christmas.

Many resorts focus on downhill and alpine-style skiing and boarding and provide complete facilities for their athletic guests. Some, like Squaw Valley, are self-contained villages offering every facility imaginable. Such "G-rated" resorts often feature boutiques, pools, tennis courts, groceries, restaurants, and après-ski spots.

The more demanding Nordic style of cross-country skiing is the adventurer's way to explore the slopes—fill a daypack, strap on skis or a snowboard, and take off across the mountains. In the pack are extra clothes, food, water, flashlight, knife, map, compass, blanket, matches, equipment repair tools, and a first-aid kit.

Unrestricted by ski lifts and marked runs, cross-country skiers venture everywhere that geography and gravity permit. Their sport is tantamount to hiking on skis, with the entire expanse of the Sierra Nevada their domain. Some skiers disappear into the wilderness for days on end, emerging only when supplies run low. Particularly favored by these explorers is Desolation Wilderness, a stark, glaciated region just west of Lake Tahoe.

Nordic lodges offer moonlight tours through alpine meadows, overnight trips to backwoods cabins, cross-country races, and guided tours of the High Sierra. There are workshops in snow survival and winter photography. Or maybe you're ready for the Tahoe-version triathlon—six miles cross-country skiing, followed by twelve miles bicycling, six miles running, and finished off with a mere five miles kayaking along the Truckee River. What better time than winter to work up a sweat.

ALPINE MEADOWS ✉*2600 Alpine Meadows Road, Tahoe City* ☎*530-583-4232, 800-441-4423* 🖱*www.skialpine.com, info@skialpine.com* This is a skier's paradise with 12 chairlifts and more than 100 runs (25 percent beginner, 40 percent intermediate, and 35 percent expert). A terrain park for snowboarders has a half pipe and natural jumps. The base elevation is 6835 feet, and the steepest vertical drop is 60°. Lessons are available, and they rent downhill and telemark skis, big feet, and snowboards.

HOMEWOOD MOUNTAIN RESORT ✉*5145 West Lake Boulevard, Homewood* ☎*530-525-2992, 877-525-7669 (winter)* 🖱*www.skihomewood.com, smile@skihomewood.com* Located six miles south of Tahoe City, Homewood Resort features a base elevation of 6230 feet and a 1650-foot vertical drop. Seven chairlifts cover the 60 runs (15 percent beginner, 50 percent intermediate, and 35 percent advanced). Shredwood Forest is a run made for boarders and skiers who like quarter and half pipes. Ski and snowboard lessons and rentals are available.

HEAVENLY SKI RESORT ✉*Wildwood and Saddle roads, South Lake Tahoe* ☎*775-586-7000* 🖱*www.skiheavenly.com, info@skiheavenly.com* For 4800 acres of pure white powder, head over to Heavenly. Catering to downhill skiers and snowboarders, the resort has a base elevation of 6540 feet. There are 30 lifts and 95 runs (20 percent beginner, 45 percent intermediate, and 35 percent expert). Six snowboard parks have jumps, rails, tables, funboxes, and a half-pipe. Lessons are available for skiing and snowboarding. Hotels, restaurants, infant and child day care, and day lodges round out the amenities.

KIRKWOOD SKI RESORT ✉*1501 Kirkwood Meadows Drive, Kirkwood* ☎*209-258-6000* 🖱*www.kirkwood.com, info@kirkwood.com* Located in a lovely alpine valley, Kirkwood sports 2300 acres of skiable terrain along with a 2000-foot vertical drop. The base elevation is at 7800 feet. There are 14 lifts and more than 65 runs (15 percent beginner, 50 percent intermediate, and 35 percent expert). Three terrain parks have jumps, spines, and a half pipe. There are also 80 kilometers of groomed cross-country trails. They offer lessons for downhill and cross-country skiing, and snowboarding. All equipment is available to rent.

ROYAL GORGE SKI RESORT ✉*9411 Hillside Drive, Soda Springs* ☎*530-426-3871* 🖱*www.royalgorge.com, info@royalgorge.com* Cross-country skiers can contact this resort, which encompasses 9172 acres of skiable terrain. You can rent Nordic skis and travel over 330 kilometers of groomed trails.

Yosemite National Park

BADGER PASS SKI AREA ✉*Glacier Point Road, Yosemite National Park* ☎*209-372-8430* 🖱*www.yosemitepark.com* Located 29 miles from Yosemite Valley, Badger Pass features five chairlifts, ten runs, and an 800-foot vertical drop.

YOSEMITE MOUNTAINEERING SCHOOL AND GUIDE SERVICE ✉*Badger Pass, Yosemite National Park* ☎*209-372-8344* 🖱*www.yosemitemountaineering.com* Forty-five kilometers of trails are groomed at this school and guide service. Countless miles of ungroomed trails are also open for exploration. Cross-country ski, telemark, and snowshoe rentals are available at the Badger Pass Ski Area.

Ski Rentals
PORTER'S SKI & SPORT ✉️*501 North Lake Boulevard, Tahoe City* 📞*530-583-2314* 🖱️*www.porterstahoe.com* Porter's in Tahoe City rents snowboards and skis.

SLEIGH RIDES

CAMP RICHARDSON CORRAL ✉️*Camp Richardson* 📞*530-541-3113, 877-541-3113* You'll feel like you're in a Currier & Ives print when you climb aboard a sleigh for a romantic winter ride. Camp Richardson offers rides on winter weekends, weather permitting. Reservations are recommended. Sleigh rides offered December through February.

RIDING STABLES

Cantering through the parks of Sacramento or packing in to the Sierra wilderness . . . nothing brings you closer to the Old West than horseback riding.

Sacramento
SHADOW GLEN RIDING STABLES ✉️*4854 Main Avenue, Fair Oaks* 📞*916-989-1826* 🖱️*www.shadowglenstables.com* For one- and two-hour trail rides through an oak-filled meadow near the American River, contact Shadow Glen. Lessons are given year-round; trails are open April through November.

Lake Tahoe Area
CAMP RICHARDSON CORRAL ✉️*Emerald Bay Road, Camp Richardson* 📞*530-541-3113, 877-541-3113* Around Lake Tahoe, call Camp Richardson. Their guided one- and two-hour trips pass aspen, pine, and fir trees en route to Fallen Leaf Lake. You must make reservations a day or two in advance.

ALPINE MEADOWS STABLE ✉️*355 Alpine Meadows Road, Tahoe City* 📞*530-583-3905* In the spring, Alpine Meadows will take you on a ride through wildflower-filled meadows and forests. It is not uncommon to see deer or black bears. Open Memorial Day to October.

HIGHLAND LLAMA TREKKERS ✉️*14223 Highland Drive, Grass Valley* 📞*530-273-8105* 📠*530-273-8105* 🖱️*llamahi@nccn.net* For expeditions of another kind, call this group, which offers multiday trips through Tahoe National Forest (July through October), Trinity Alps Wilderness Area (July and August) and Mokelumne Wilderness (August). Year-round daytrips traverse privately owned wilderness areas in Auburn and Grass Valley.

Yosemite National Park
YOSEMITE NATIONAL PARK 📞*209-372-1000* 🖱️*www.yosemitepark.com* There are stables in the Valley, at Wawona, and at Tuolumne Meadows. Most of the Yosemite stables are closed in winter.

Exploring the Gold Country and High Sierra by bicycle can be an exhilarating experience. It's an area best toured by physically fit folks on mountain bikes. Almost all roads are open for bikes, but heavy traffic, steep grades, and the high altitude make for an arduous journey. To enjoy touring this area, cyclists should plan their trips carefully, if possible scouting out the routes in advance.

Sacramento
JEDEDIAH SMITH MEMORIAL BICYCLE TRAIL   This memorial trail runs along the American River Parkway for 30 miles and is ideal for a family outing.

Northern Gold Country
AUBURN STATE RECREATION AREA   More than 100 miles of mountain bike trails are offered here. The two-mile **Stagecoach Trail** (2 miles) runs from Russell Road in Auburn to the old Foresthill Bridge on the north fork of the American River. **Old Lake Clementine Road** meanders for nine miles along the American River. To ride past a creek through oak-and-pine-filled meadows, try the nine-mile **Olmsted Loop Trail**.

DOWNIEVILLE   Roads came slowly to the northern Gold Country. Decades after the Gold Rush, many people lived in areas that could only be reached by single-track mountain trails impassable in wagons. Many such trails still exist around Downieville, making the little town a mountain bike mecca.

Lake Tahoe Area
Tahoe National Forest   When it comes to mountain biking, few places can beat the Sierra Nevada. Some of the best off-road trails are found in Tahoe National Forest. At the **Tahoe National Forest Office** (631 Coyote Street, Nevada City; 530-265-4531; www.fs.fed.us/r5/tahoe, psexton@fs.fed.us) you can pick up information on mountain biking trails throughout the region. Other trails in the area that are not in the national forest include **Flume Trail** just off Spooner Summit at the junction of Routes 50 and 28. It offers challenging rides of 10 to 30 miles. **Angora Lakes Trail** (12 miles roundtrip) in the Fallen Leaf Lake area is another possibility.

KIRKWOOD SKI AREA ⊠*Route 88, Kirkwood* ☎*209-258-6000, 800-967-7500* ✎*www.kirkwood.com, info@skikirkwood.com*   Thirty miles south of Lake Tahoe is this resort offering a mountain biking program in the summer months. There are 50 miles of trails within the Kirkwood property. Spring wildflower and fall foliage trips are highly recommended. In addition, the resort provides easy access to hundreds of miles of trails in the **Eldorado National Forest**. The easy **Kirkwood Meadow Loop** (6 miles) is a good way to get acclimated. If you're in great shape and feeling ambitious, take the grueling **Mr. Toad's Wild Ride** off Luther Pass. The 35-mile trip runs from Hope Valley to the Tahoe basin. One of the most famous mountain bike trails in the Lake Tahoe region, this thrill-a-minute downhill ride is for skilled mountain bikers only. Following Saxon Creek down a deep, steep valley, it plunges 2200 feet in just three miles. Wear a helmet and protective gear! Start by taking Route 89 south of South Lake Tahoe for about five miles to the Big Meadow parking area, a trailhead for the Tahoe Rim Trail. Ride two and a half miles northeast along the rim trail, a strenuous uphill climb that leaves you poised at the start of Mr. Toad's ride. Take a left and hang on. The ride ends at Oneidas Street near the Lake Tahoe Airport. Turn left to return to Route 89 or right to continue into town on the much easier three-mile **Powerline Ride**. Alternatively, ride from Kirkwood to Hope Valley up **Old Luther Pass Road** to the Grass Lake area (40 miles). **Schneider Camp** (7 miles) is another enjoyable ride offering great views of Caples Lake. Remember, it takes a few days to adjust to the high altitude; also plan on drinking plenty of fluids.

Yosemite National Park

LOOP TRAIL   This is a paved eight-mile trail, which circles the valley floor and takes you as far as Mirror Lake-Meadow.

Bike Rentals

AMERICAN RIVER BICYCLE SHOP ⊠ *9203 Folsom Boulevard, Sacramento* ✆ *916-363-6271* For bike rentals and information in Sacramento, contact this bicycle shop. They rent hybrids and sell accessories.

YUBA EXPEDITIONS ⊠ *Route 49, Downieville* ✆ *530-289-3010* ⊘ *www.yubaexpeditions.com* For bike rentals, trailhead shuttles, and guided tours, contact Yuba Expeditions.

DOWNIEVILLE OUTFITTERS ⊠ *208 Main Street, Downieville* ✆ *530-289-3505* ⊘ *www.downievilleoutfitters.com* This local enterprise offers rentals, shuttles, and organized group trips.

CYCLE PATH MOUNTAIN BIKES ⊠ *1785 West Lake Boulevard, Tahoe City* ✆ *530-581-1171* Mountain bikes are the speciality here. If you are interested in a tour ask about the custom-designed trips of the area.

OLYMPIC BIKE SHOP ⊠ *620 North Lake Boulevard, Tahoe City* ✆ *530-581-2500* ⊘ *www.olympicbikeshop.com* One of the area's oldest and most popular bike spots, Olympic always has a large selection of street and mountain bikes for sale and rent, along with clothing, guidebooks, maps, and expert repair service.

CURRY VILLAGE ✆ *209-372-8319* ⊘ *www.yosemitepark.com* At Yosemite National Park you can rent single-speed cruisers and Schwinns with trailers at Curry Village. Open March to October, weather permitting.

YOSEMITE LODGE BIKE STAND ✆ *209-372-1208* There are single-speed bike rentals available at the Yosemite Lodge Bike Stand.

HIKING

The Gold Country and High Sierra represent two of nature's most magnificent contributions to Northern California. In the old mining territory you'll find groves of giant sequoias to explore. Then in the High Sierra, Lake Tahoe and Yosemite National Park offer networks of trails and Desolation Wilderness provides the closest wilderness area to San Francisco. All distances listed are one way unless otherwise noted.

Central Gold Country

CALAVERAS BIG TREES STATE PARK   Three trails wind through this state park's ancient forest of giant sequoias. **North Grove Trail** (1 mile) is a gentle loop through a stand of sequoia, ponderosa, and sugar pine. Included along the way is **Three Senses Trail** (600 feet) where you can touch, smell, and hear the forest around you. **South Grove Trail** (5 miles), more remote and primitive, winds up Big Trees Creek past nearly 1000 giant sequoias.

Northern Gold Country

MALAKOFF DIGGINS STATE HISTORIC PARK   Though formerly the site of one of the world's largest hydraulic mining operations, Malakoff Diggins State Historic Park has been partially healed by nature. About 15 miles of trails lead past mining-era ruins, colorful pinnacles, minarets, and lakes created by the miners. **Blair Trail** (1.5 miles) is an easy hike on a tree-shaded path that ends at an old-time swimming hole. Beginning at Shoot Hill Campground, **Rim Trail** (3 miles) leads to a vista point above the pond at the site of the diggings.

Lake Tahoe Area

DONNER LAKE RIM TRAIL   Though this 23-mile trail is scheduled for completion in 2010, a serviceable portion is already finished. In total, the trail, which will encircle Donner Lake, will provide excellent views of Mt. Rose, Castle Peak, and the Pacific Crest, and will include an alternative route for bicycles. For more information contact the Truckee Donner Land Trust (530-582-4711; john@tdland trust.org).

DONNER SUMMIT   The summit offers **Summit Lake Trail** (2 miles), located off Route 80 near the Donner Summit rest stop. It is an easy hike to Summit Lake through a conifer forest and flowering meadows.

Sandridge Lake Trail (6 miles) begins on the Pacific Crest Trail near Donner Summit and carries through pine and fir forests. It passes two alpine meadows en route to a small lake.

DESOLATION WILDERNESS   Because of its easy accessibility, this area is extremely popular with daytrippers and campers alike. The number of backpackers is therefore held to a quota from June 15 to Labor Day, and a wilderness permit is required year-round of all who enter (for further information, consult Chapter One).

Mt. Tallac via Gilmore Lake Trail (6.1 miles) starts near Glen Alpine Creek and ends at Mt. Tallac Summit. From the summit, you'll have one of the region's most dramatic views of Lake Tahoe.

Pacific Crest Trail to Lake Aloha (3.5 miles) begins with a ride in a water taxi operated by Echo Lake Resort (530-659-7207). Closed Labor Day to Memorial Day. The trail, one of the most heavily traveled in Desolation

Wilderness, leads to sparkling mountain lakes. (It's another two-and-a-half miles to the lake if you opt to bypass the water taxi.)

Meeks Bay Trail (8 miles) starts near Meeks Bay Resort and follows the northern part of lengthy Tahoe–Yosemite Trail to glimmering Rubicon Lake.

Bay View Trail to Mid-Velma Lake (4.8 miles) offers some stunning views of Lake Tahoe.

Glen Alpine to Lake Aloha Trail (5.8 miles) starts near Glen Alpine Spring and winds up at Lake Aloha.

Eagle Falls–Eagle Lake Trail (1 mile) begins at the Eagle Falls picnic area and traverses the cascade along a wooden footbridge. Then it crosses a blocky talus slope that offers beautiful views of the Tahoe Basin, and finally arrives at Eagle Lake.

Lake Tahoe has numerous hiking adventures. One of the most popular—and most trafficked—hikes is **Five Lakes Trail** (3 miles), which begins on Alpine Meadows Road off Route 89. This fairly steep trail goes past beautiful alpine scenery to a group of small, cold mountain lakes.

Shirley Lake Trail (2.5 miles) traverses spectacular Squaw Valley and passes stunning waterfalls. If you're so inclined, take the tram up and then hike down.

Rubicon–Emerald Point Trail (4.7 miles) passes Lake Tahoe's only lighthouse and offers wonderful views of Emerald Bay.

Loon Lake Trail (4.5 miles), beginning at Loon Lake Campground, is an easy 4.5-mile hike through a wild area. The trail crosses seasonal creeks as well as fir and pine groves en route to Spider Lake.

Yosemite National Park

Called the "Incomparable Valley," Yosemite is the place for hikers to seek the solitude, excitement, and grandeur of the wilderness. More than 100 hiking trails, both within and outside Yosemite Valley, lace the park. Remember, multiday hikes require a wilderness permit. Trails can be closed due to storm, fire damage, or the seasons, so call ahead before planning your hike. All distances listed are one way unless otherwise noted.

Mist Trail (3.5 miles) trek starts at Happy Isles trailhead about a mile away from Vernal Fall. It is a moderate to strenuous hike that continues up to Nevada Fall.

Half Dome Hike (8.2 miles) is a strenuous path that parallels the Mist Trail, then meets it above Nevada Fall and continues up to Half Dome.

Valley Floor–West Loop Trail (6.9 miles) carries past Bridalveil Fall, Cathedral Rocks, and El Capitan.

Valley Floor–Mirror Lake–Meadow Loop Trail (3 miles) wends past Mirror Lake Meadow and Half Dome along a tree-shaded route and takes a two-mile trek to reach. The lake is naturally evolving into a meadow and dries by the end of summer. The trail also features views of treacherous Tenaya Canyon.

Yosemite Falls Loop Trail (7.2 miles roundtrip), an eight- to ten-hour hike, climbs to the top of Upper Yosemite Fall.

Sentinel Dome Trail (1.2 miles) leaves from Glacier Point Road and carries across bedrock to the summit of Sentinel Dome. At the top are views of El Capitan, Yosemite Falls and Half Dome.

Little Yosemite Valley Trail (7.9 miles) is a semi-loop trek that is best hiked in two days. The trail is a major starting point for backpackers heading deep into Yosemite. Watch out for bears!

Half Dome Trail (8.6 miles) is a well-known arduous mountain climb that ends at the most spectacular summit in the park. The last 400 feet are on cables on this seasonal trail. Not a hike for acrophobes.

Lembert Dome–Dog Lake Loop Trail (4.2 miles) begins in the Tuolumne Meadows parking lot and leads to the top of Lembert Dome. It continues to Dog Lake with views of Mt. Dana, Mt. Gibbs, and Mt. Lewis.

One of the most popular trails in Tuolumne Meadows, **Elizabeth Lake Trail** (4.5 miles) offers impressive views of the usually snowcapped Cathedral Range on its way from Tuolumne Meadows to a beautiful alpine lake.

Harden Lake Trail (2.5 miles) is an easy hike from White Wolf Campground to one of the area's warmest lakes.

Alder Creek Trail to Bishop Creek (3.5 miles) is a moderate half-day trek in the Wawona area. Hard to find but very beautiful, this trail is best hiked in springtime when the creeks flow and the temperature is moderate. One of the most outstanding features is the flowering plant life, including mountain misery, a lightly scented shrub.

Panorama Trail from Glacier Point to Nevada Falls (8.5 miles) is one of the more scenic routes into the valley. It begins at the Glacier Point parking lot and gives startling views of Tenaya Canyon, Half Dome, Illilouette Fall, Clouds Rest, Nevada, and Vernal falls—to name just a few! (Transportation is available back to Glacier Point.)

Pohono Trail (13 miles) also starts from Glacier Point. Following the south rim of Yosemite Valley, it offers spectacular views as it descends 1800 feet to the Wawona Tunnel. This trail is known for its abundance of wildflowers in spring and early summer.

May Lake Trail (1.1 miles) makes its way through cool forest and across granite slabs to reach May Lake High Sierra Camp. Although it's hard to get reservations for the camp, fishing for rainbow and brook trout is permitted in the lake.

Mono Pass Trail (4.2 miles) is level but due to altitude, is one of the park's most ambitious hikes and takes all day. The scenery and the 10,600-foot altitude will leave you breathless.

TRANSPORTATION

CAR

The large section of the state covered in this chapter is serviced by numerous highways. From San Francisco, **Route 80** travels northeast directly to Sacramento, then bisects the Gold Country, and continues into the High Sierra, passing within ten miles of Lake Tahoe's North Shore. The quickest way to the South Shore is via **Route 50** from Sacramento. To reach Yosemite, follow the freeways leading east from San Francisco, then pick up either **Route 120** or **Route 140** into the park. The Gold Country can be toured along **Route 49**.

AIR

SACRAMENTO INTERNATIONAL AIRPORT *www.sacairports.org*
Several major airlines fly here. These include Alaska Airlines, America West, American Airlines, Continental, Delta Air Lines, Horizon Air, Northwest Airlines, Southwest Airlines, and United Airlines.

RENO–TAHOE INTERNATIONAL AIRPORT *www.renoairport.com*
Airlines with flights into this airport include Alaska Airlines, America West Airlines, American Airlines, Continental Airlines, Delta Air Lines, Frontier Airlines, Horizon Air, Southwest Airlines, and United Airlines.

BUS

GREYHOUND BUS LINES *800-231-2222* *www.greyhound.com* Greyhound provides service to Sacramento and Lake Tahoe.

TRAIN

AMTRAK *800-872-7245* *www.amtrak.com* Train aficionados can climb aboard Amtrak for an excursion to Sacramento, South Lake Tahoe, or Yosemite. From Oakland, the "Coast Starlight" provides service to Sacramento, while the "Zephyr" carries passengers to Truckee in the Tahoe area.

YOSEMITE AREA REGIONAL TRANSPORTATION SYSTEM (YARTS) *877-989-2787* *www.yarts.com* Those traveling to Yosemite from Oakland or Los Angeles can take Amtrak's "San Joaquin" to Merced, where YARTS provides connecting bus service into Yosemite Valley.

CAR RENTALS

The following agencies are at Sacramento International Airport: **Alamo Rent A Car** (800-462-5266), **Avis Rent A Car** (800-331-1212), **Budget Rent A Car** (800-763-2999), **Dollar Rent A Car** (800-800-4000), **Hertz Rent A Car** (800-654-3131), and **National Rent A Car** (800-227-7368). Other agencies offer airport pick-up service. Check the Yellow Pages for agencies in town.

SACRAMENTO REGIONAL TRANSIT ✆916-321-2877 ⌗www.sacrt. com Sacramento is serviced by this transit organization.

TAHOE AREA REGIONAL TRANSIT (TART) ✆530-550-1212 ⌗www. laketahoetransit.com TART services North Lake Tahoe and offers a shuttle service between Tahoe City and Truckee.

BLUE GO ✆530-541-7149 In South Lake Tahoe, Blue Go provides transportation around the South Shore.

YOSEMITE SHUTTLE ✆209-372-1240 ✆209-372-8443 ⌗www.yosemitepark. com In Yosemite Valley, a free shuttle bus ferries folks between various points of interest.

TOURS

LAKE TAHOE CRUISES ✆800-238-2463 To travel between the south and north shores of Lake Tahoe in winter, try Lake Tahoe Cruises.

NORTH TAHOE CRUISES ✉850 North Lake Boulevard, Tahoe City ✆800-218-2464 ⌗www.tahoegal.com North Tahoe Cruises explores the west shore of the lake and Emerald Bay from mid-May through October.

FAR NORTH

California's best-kept secret is a sprawling, thinly populated area full of history and incredible natural beauty. Much of the sector's lush terrain is virtually untouched. Reaching from Redding to Oregon and from the Coast Range to Nevada, the Far North encompasses a huge swath of California. Siskiyou, Modoc, Shasta, and Lassen counties are part of this tumbling block of territory.

A wilderness of alpine lakes and granite heights, its mountains include the Klamath, Marble, Salmon, Trinity, and Warner ranges. Foremost is the Cascade Range, extending south from Washington and Oregon. Mt. Shasta, rising over 14,000 feet, is lord of the land, a white-domed figure brooding above a forested realm. Lassen Peak, its infernal cousin, is an active volcano that last erupted in 1921.

Sprinkled along the region's panoramic byways are tiny hamlets where traffic lights are nonexistent. Virtually every town with more than a gas station has a museum showcasing its early history, but the most revealing glimpses are in the countryside, where small farms keep in step with an ancient drummer.

The Far North represents "hidden California" in its truly pristine state. Thousands of lakes and rivers make it a paradise for whitewater rafting. Chinook run 50 pounds and the fishing is excellent for trout and bass as well. Most of the region is preserved in a series of national forests, making it a retreat for hikers and campers.

The wilderness here has given birth to all sorts of things—rare species, trophy fish, and big game animals. But the most prized find of all may not even exist. For over a century, people have been sighting an elusive creature, kin perhaps to the abominable snowman, named Bigfoot. Said to range in height up to 14 feet, he weighs as much as 800 pounds. His skin is dark and tough as leather; hair covers his entire body. Bigfoot has a flat nose, short ears, human-like features, and walks with a ten-foot stride. He inhabits deep river valleys and thick forests, leaving huge footprints in the untrammeled wilderness.

In addition to a rich mythology, the countryside boasts a history that dates back millions of years, when volcanic activity created the Cascade Range and other geologic forces formed neighboring mountains. Modoc, Paiute, Pit River, and Shoshone peoples originally inhabited the Far North, fishing its endless waterways and hunting the surrounding forests. The region was not opened to Europeans until 1817 when Captain Luis Arguello, a Spanish adventurer, probed the wilderness. By the 1840s, American wagon trains were rolling through the territory. When gold was discovered around the end of the decade, prospectors began panning the rivers.

The original inhabitants, pushed from their lands by settlers and gold-seekers, struck back in the "Modoc War." During the tragic climax in 1873, the U.S. Army fought a pitched battle in the Lava Beds area against a group of Modocs led by Chief Kientpoos, also known as Captain Jack. "Nobody will ever want these rocks," the American Indian leader pleaded. "Give me a home here."

Except for a handful of descendants, the American Indians have disappeared, but cowboys continue to ride the range, thanks in part to a thriving cattle business. With ranches everywhere, particularly around Alturas, the Far North ranks as the largest beef-producing region in the state. Since practically any place that's not a granite mountain or alpine lake is covered with forest, the lumber industry is also an important factor in the economy.

Tourism reigns as the biggest source of local revenue. Despite a major chemical spill along the Sacramento River in 1991, the Far North remains a year-round vacation zone. The spill, which resulted from a train derailment north of Dunsmuir, was contained, though fishing is limited to catch and release between Lake Siskiyou and Scarlett Way and between Sweetbriar Bridge and Shasta Lake.

Everywhere else in the Far North aquatic enthusiasts arrive in ever-increasing numbers during the warm summer months and skiers pile in during the winter. Many facilities shut down during the cold season, and many roads are closed, so sightseers are advised to visit between late spring and early fall. Mid-summer brings large crowds, so if touring then, plan ahead, make reservations well in advance.

Regardless of the season, the Far North rarely disappoints the adventurous traveler. A land of giant dams and endless waterways, it is a wonderland for outdoor sports and a place of exquisite beauty.

REDDING

Route 5 runs like a spine through this rural region, moving north and south from Sacramento to Oregon. Redding, capital of the "Inland Empire," is the closest facsimile around to a buzzing metropolis. This town of 90,000 folks is also the major jumping-off point for sightseers.

From here, it's less than an hour along Route 299 to Whiskeytown, Shasta, and Trinity lakes, as well as the history-book towns of Shasta and French Gulch. Farther north on Route 5 are the ski slopes of Mt. Shasta and the antique town of Yreka. Route 44 leads from Redding to Lassen Volcanic National Park, and Route 395 winds into the far northeast corner of California.

SIGHTS

SHASTA-CASCADE WONDERLAND ASSOCIATION ⊠1699 Route 273, Anderson &530-365-7500, 800-474-2782 ⚲530-365-1258 ⊘www.shasta cascade.org No matter where you plan to visit, you should contact this association, which also serves as a California Welcome Center. The friendly staff is knowledgeable and can provide you with a comprehensive visitors guide. Furthermore, the association offers a free 64-page guide to a series of scenic byways that surrounds Redding. Most range from one to four hours in length, making for pretty and interesting side trips.

TURTLE BAY EXPLORATION PARK ⊠840 Auditorium Drive &530-221-8200, 800-887-8532 ⊘www.turtlebay.org, info@turtlebay.org All of Redding's major sightseeing attractions are clustered together at this expansive complex, which is an ongoing $47 million project set on both banks of the Sacramento River. It's linked by the **Sundial Bridge**, a steel, glass, and granite footbridge. The $23 million architectural marvel, designed by renowned Spanish architect Santiago Calatrava, features a graceful 217-foot pylon in the form of a working sundial. (The sundial's shadow is cast on the Spanish-tile plaza at the north end, where time markers are situated.) The bridge is open daily from 6 a.m. to midnight. A general admission fee gives you access to all the sites on the grounds.

TURTLE BAY MUSEUM At the heart of the complex is this museum, which features a multitude of interactive exhibits including computers, microscopes, and puzzles. Its art gallery has fascinating rotating historical displays re-creating local pioneer and American Indian life as well as selected contemporary items. The museum also houses a natural science display. At various times daily animals are brought out from their indoor cages for a show-and-tell session. Also check out the river aquarium with underwater fish viewing and the large, ever-changing Exploration Hall.

MCCONNELL ARBORETUM This beautiful and educational arboretum is just a short jaunt north of the main complex. Located along the Sacramento River, it provides 20 acres of gardens, including medicinal plants, wildflowers, and grass. Visitors can walk or bike the nature

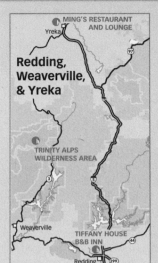

Redding, Weaverville, & Yreka

MING'S RESTAURANT AND LOUNGE

PAGE 556

Classic Chinese fare like kung pao chicken and roast duck at one of Yreka's favorite night spots

TRINITY ALPS WILDERNESS AREA

PAGE 557

Stunning landscape where 9000-foot peaks plummet into glacial canyons, pristine streams, and alpine lakes

TIFFANY HOUSE BED & BREAKFAST INN

PAGE 548

Cozy, impeccably decorated rooms filled with antiques in a picturesque Victorian home

trails where turtle ponds allow you to see the indigenous western pond turtles up close. The seasonal wetlands, streams, and oak woodland landscape this 200-acre preserve. During summer months, a **Butterfly House** features about 1000 live butterflies inside a greenhouse filled with flowering plants.

PAUL BUNYAN'S FOREST CAMP   Located just outside the Turtle Bay Museum is this woodsy, pseudo-rustic play area for kids along the bank of the Sacramento River. There is also a life-size replica of a logging camp. Exhibits show how to identify trees and make forest crafts. A nature trail presents a cross-section of Northern California forests.

LODGING

LA QUINTA INN

$$ 141 ROOMS   ✉ 2180 Hilltop Drive   ✆ 530-221-8200, 800-531-5900   ✐ www.lq.com

For a last, luxurious taste of civilization before heading into the hills, try La Quinta. This stylish establishment features positively huge rooms with plush wall-to-wall carpeting. The furnishings have a cherrywood finish with pastel upholstery and the decor is quite inviting. Despite the proximity to Route 5, this is an extremely quiet inn.

HAMPTON INN & SUITES

$$ 80 ROOMS   ✉ 2160 Larkspur Lane   ✆ 530-224-1001   ✆ 530-224-1101
✐ www.hamptoninn.com

The newest hotel in Redding offers sparkling clean rooms, super-soft beds, free wi-fi, an exercise room, swimming pool, and a full American breakfast, making it one of the best deals in town. Guest rooms feature coffeemakers, hair dryers, irons, and cable TVs. A guest laundry and on-site convenience store make this a good place to unwind and regroup in the middle of a long road trip.

TIFFANY HOUSE
BED & BREAKFAST INN

$$–$$$ 5 ROOMS   ✉*1510 Barbara Road*   ☏*530-244-3225*
🖥*www.tiffanyhousebb.com, tiffanyhse@aol.com*

In a town where the lodging scene is dominated by chain motels and motor inns, this bed and breakfast is a delightful exception. A late Victorian home in a residential area with a great view of distant Lassen Peak, it has three upstairs guest rooms, each with private bath, queen-sized bed, and sitting area plus special touches like hand-crocheted bedspreads and embroidered pillowcases. There is also a separate cottage with a seven-foot spa tub and an antique laurel wreath iron bed. The parlor is furnished in Victorian-era antiques. There is also a music room with an upright piano and old-time sheet music; afterwards, you can plunge into the backyard pool. A full gourmet breakfast is served in the dining room or outdoors in the gazebo.

ECONOMY INN

$ 28 ROOMS   ✉*525 North Market Street*   ☏*530-246-9803*   ☏*530-244-5011*

This is a great economical choice. The inn features standard amenities, as well as in-room refrigerators and microwaves.

RODEWAY INN

$$ 62 ROOMS   ✉*532 North Market Street*   ☏*530-243-5291, 800-243-1106*
☏*530-243-8328*   🖥*www.rodeway.com*

The comfortable Rodeway is located in the heart of Redding's neon motel strip. The biggest and best of the bunch, it boasts 62 clean but sterile rooms. Amenities include cable television in your room, free wi-fi access, and a swimming pool and spa on the grounds.

TRAVELODGE

$$ 41 ROOMS   ✉*540 North Market Street*   ☏*530-243-5291, 800-525-9055*

Bargain hunters take note: You'll find many inexpensive motels along this strip, each proudly displaying its nightly rates as part of a local price war. The Redding Travelodge features rooms with kitchenettes, free wi-fi, and cable television. There is also an indoor spa.

BRIDGEHOUSE BED
& BREAKFAST

$$–$$$ 4 ROOMS   ✉*1455 Riverside Drive*   ☏*530-247-7177*
🖥*www.reddingbridgehouse.com*

This cottage-style B&B overlooks the Sacramento River and is a short stroll away from the Sacramento River Trail, the historic downtown areas, and the Sundial Bridge. There are four bridge-themed rooms; the Sundial Bridge room echoes the look and feel of the nearby span with opaque glass doors, tiles, and amazing views. All rooms are large and elegantly decorated in a clean-lined early 20th-century style and include private baths, flat-screen TVs, and free wi-fi. There's also a weight room and extensive continental breakfast.

DINING

CASA RAMOS

$–$$$ MEXICAN   ✉️*995 Hilltop Drive* 📞*530-224-7223*

It's tough to bust your budget while dining in Redding. In fact, with the prices as low as the surroundings are pleasant (as they are at this bright eatery), there's no reason to even stretch your dollar. This Mexican eatery is decorated with sunflowers, imported tiles, and archways. And then there's the food—an extensive menu includes everything from a *chile relleno*, taco, and enchilada combination to *huevos rancheros*.

C. R. GIBBS AMERICAN GRILLE

$$–$$$ AMERICAN   ✉️*2300 Hilltop Drive* 📞*530-221-2335* 📠*530-221-2867* ✍️*www.crgibbs.com, info@crgibbs.com*

A special Redding restaurant is this welcoming bar and grill. Its bright, modern, wood-trimmed blue-and-white interior features an open exhibition kitchen that lets you watch as your meal is prepared and a central bar that offers a carefully selected assortment of California wines and microbrews as well as "the biggest selection of martinis around." The seasonal menu includes full dinner entrées such as almond-crusted halibut and grilled ribeye steak, along with salads, sandwiches, pasta dishes, and a creative array of brick oven–baked pizzas. Sunday brunch.

BUZ'S CRAB

$–$$ SEAFOOD   ✉️*2159 East Street* 📞*530-243-2120* 📠*530-243-4310* ✍️*www.buzscrab.com, fish@buzscrab.com*

This funky fish joint has been a local favorite since it opened in 1968, serving up spicy crab cakes, mesquite-grilled seafood, huge baskets of hot fish and chips, Cajun halibut, and salmon burgers. Seasonal specials include a hearty crab cioppino. Clam chowder is always on the menu, and fresh sourdough bread is baked twice a day. The wharf-style atmosphere, seafaring decor, moderate prices, and heart-healthy menus items make this a must-visit for seafood lovers.

MARKET STREET STEAKHOUSE

$$ AMERICAN   ✉️*1777 Market Street* 📞*530-241-1777*

A tidy little brick restaurant next to the historic Cascade Theatre, this spot has built up a solid reputation for absolutely top-of-the-line steaks of every cut. The grilled steak salad is a simple, supremely tasty affair of cold, just-picked greens, strips of hot grilled New York steak, and bleu cheese crumbles. This eatery is popular and doesn't take reservations, so plan on waiting in the bar, which is loud, friendly and always busy. For romance and great people watching, ask for the outside patio.

LIM'S CAFE

$ CHINESE/AMERICAN ✉*592 North Market Street* ☎*530-241-9747*

It looks like a typical roadside restaurant, complete with flashing neon sign and naugahyde booths, but Lim's offers a large selection of Chinese and American dishes. The Asian dinners include a combo plate that consists of chicken noodle soup, pork chow mein, sweet and sour pork, and fried shrimp. For those with an American palate, there are chicken dishes, sandwiches, and steaks.

SHOPPING

TURTLE BAY MUSEUM STORE ✉*840 Auditorium Drive* ☎*530-243-8850*

www.turtlebay.org, info@turtlebay.org If you're in the market for locally produced arts and crafts, this museum shop has jewelry, handcrafted pottery, baskets, and wood crafts. Postcards and booklets describing the area's history are also available.

SHASTA OUTLETS ✉*1699 Route 273, Anderson* ☎*530-378-1000* Just south

of Redding in Anderson lies Shasta Outlets, with close to 40 stores offering a smorgasbord of clothing, accessories, housing items, and shoes. Retailers include Mikasa, Van Heusen, and The Gap.

NIGHTLIFE

CASCADE THEATRE ✉*1731 Market Street* ☎*530-243-8886, 530-243-8877*

(box office) *www.cascadetheatre.org* Originally built in 1935, this Art Deco theater has been transformed into a state-of-the-art, multi-use performance center. The Cascade, home to the Redding City Ballet and the Northstate Symphony, features a variety of music (Count Basie Orchestra, Indigo Girls), theater, and dance productions.

RIVERFRONT PLAYHOUSE ✉*1620 East Cypress Avenue* ☎*530-221-1028,*

530-241-4278 (box office) *www.riverfrontplayhouse.net* For a peek into Redding's community theater, check out the Riverfront Playhouse, which has been producing musicals, dramas, and comedies since 1982.

REDDING TO WEAVERVILLE

Rising up from the Central Valley, the road from Redding to Weaverville leads west toward the gateway to one of Northern California's premier recreational destinations. While best known for water sports, this area is also the place to find old mining towns, historic commercial districts, and American Indian landmarks.

SIGHTS

SHASTA From Redding, Route 299 leads west for a few miles to the late, great gold mining outpost of Shasta. This brickfront ghost town was the region's "Queen City" back in the 1850s, producing over $100,000 in gold dust every week. A trail leads along a row of old ruins.

SHASTA STATE HISTORIC PARK ✉Route 299W, Shasta ✆530-243-8194
✆530-225-2038 Here you'll find a restored county courthouse, American
Indian artifacts, antique photos, Wanted posters, and paintings by early
California artists. The old jail features holograms, and an 1880s mercantile store stands nearby. Closed Monday and Tuesday. Admission.

WHISKEYTOWN LAKE ✉Route 299 Five miles farther west from
Shasta State Historic Park lies this lake, one of California's best boating,
fishing, camping, and swimming spots. With 36 miles of shoreline,
green rolling hills, tiny wooded islands, and dense stands of ponderosa
pine, it's a paradise for backcountry explorers.

FRENCH GULCH _____ **h**idden

✉Trinity Mountain Road This historic mining town, settled in 1849,
is situated off Route 299. Once an important way station on the
Old Oregon Pacific Trail, it's a place where time has refused to
budge for the last 100 years. The townsfolk still take family walks
down Main Street, paint their picket fences white, and rarely lock
their bikes.

WEAVERVILLE From French Gulch, Route 299 winds past beautiful
mountain vistas en route to this country-style Victorian town shaded
by honey locusts. In addition to its small-town charm, Weaverville has
a colorful past worth exploring.

JAKE JACKSON MEMORIAL MUSEUM ✉708 Main Street, Weaverville
✆530-623-5211 At this museum, displays re-create the tragedy and romance of the Gold Rush days. There's a complete blacksmith's shop, as
well as early mining tools (including a stamp mill used for obtaining
gold from ore), archaic medical supplies, and a fascinating display of
Chinese weapons, gowns, and money. From January through March,
they are only open on Tuesday and Saturday afternoon.

WEAVERVILLE JOSS HOUSE STATE HISTORIC PARK ✉Main
and Oregon streets, Weaverville ✆530-623-5284 ✆530-623-5284 This historic park,
known as the "Temple Amongst the Forest Beneath the Clouds," has always appealed to me as one of the region's most unique places since it
is here that Chinese Taoists have worshipped since 1874. Nestled in a
grove of trees near a wooden footbridge, this temple is a tribute to the
Chinese miners whose hard labor brought them neither riches nor acceptance in the Old West. Closed Monday and Tuesday. Admission.

Three Great Lakes

Established by Congress in 1965, **Whiskeytown-Shasta-Trinity National
Recreation Area** is spread over 400 miles and consists of three large lakes
north of Redding: Whiskeytown Lake, Shasta Lake, and Trinity Lake. With
environments that vary from coniferous forest to mountain lake, hiking,
horseback riding, swimming, and boating are just a few of the sports available
here. Bear, mountain lion, raccoon, and deer are plentiful throughout the area
and bald eagles and osprey are often spotted soaring in the sky. The recreation area is jointly administered by the National Park Service and the
National Forest Service.

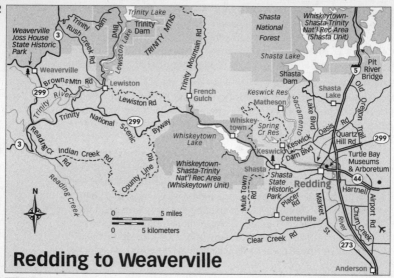

Redding to Weaverville

LODGING

WEAVERVILLE VICTORIAN INN

$$ 65 ROOMS ✉2051 Main Street 299 West, Weaverville ☎530-623-4432
📠530-623-4264

To complete the sense of old-time California, stay at this inn. The guest rooms are huge; 17 of them have hot tubs. There's a pool on the premises and you'll be within walking distance of the town's outdoor activities and sights, including an interesting old drugstore to poke around in and an active Taoist temple.

RED HILL MOTEL

$–$$ 14 UNITS ✉Red Hill Road, Weaverville ☎530-623-4331 📠530-623-4341
🖰www.redhillresorts.com, redhill@snowcrest.net

Tucked away in a woodsy corner, the Red Hill delivers comfortable rooms and cabins. Most of the quaint accommodations feature knotty-pine walls and cable television, but the best deals are the individual cabins. Some of these include full kitchenettes, afford ample privacy, and cost a few dollars more. They also offer knockout views of the Trinity Alps through the pines.

DINING

THE GARDEN CAFÉ

$ AMERICAN ✉Corner of Routes 299 and 3, Weaverville ☎530-623-2058
🖰whitmoreinn@hotmail.com

Sitting on the upper part of a two-story flat, this café provides an excellent vantage point for studying the town's street life. Mornings, sample homefries, the breakfast burrito, or the French toast. At lunch, you'll find vegetarian and classic sandwiches, quiche, fresh fish, and gourmet salads. On warm days, you can eat outdoors on the deck. Dinner served Friday, Saturday, and Sunday only. Closed Tuesday.

LA GRANGE CAFÉ

$$–$$$ BISTRO/CALIFORNIA CUISINE   ✉ *520 Main Street, Weaverville*
📞 *530-623-5325*

A restaurant here offering a dozen microbrews and 135-plus wines? Sure enough—La Grange, situated in a renovated brick building on Main Street, is Weaverville's take on fine dining. Specials include their national prize–winning buffalo ragoût, as well as veal piccata, venison bratwurst, and braised rabbit.

SHOPPING

HIGHLAND ART CENTER ✉*503 Main Street, Weaverville* 📞*530-623-5111* On Saturday evenings, locals head here for a monthly reception. The center, a non-profit established in the 1960s, sells locally made works of all types. Closed Sunday from January through April.

STEVE HUBBLE STUDIO ✉*410 Center Street, Weaverville* 📞*530-623-3900* Behind the Highland Art Center is this studio, a working art gallery where you can see the artist in action, painting mainly landscapes and dogs. His hours fit his fancy, so call ahead.

BUDMAN'S BOOK MINE ✉*106 Main Street, Weaverville* 📞*530-623-6251* A nice little shop, Budman's has a section devoted to local authors. They also have occasional book signings.

NIGHTLIFE

NEW YORK SALOON ✉*225 Main Street, Weaverville* 📞*530-623-3492* Weaverville nightlife is scarce at best, but there's some entertainment to be enjoyed at the New York Saloon. You don't visit this 1859 bar for dancing or karaoke—you go just to enjoy the sense of a time gone by (and to play a little ping-pong or pool).

TRINITY PLAYERS ✉*101 Arbuckle Road, Weaverville* 📞*530-623-8695* The town's local theater troupe, the Trinity Players, performs out of their own theater. The season tends towards the comedic and musical, although their Independence Day production is usually a melodrama from the gold-digging era.

BEACHES & PARKS

WHISKEYTOWN-SHASTA-TRINITY NATIONAL RECREATION AREA—WHISKEYTOWN UNIT

✉*Along Route 299 around eight miles west of Redding* 📞*530-246-1225*
📞*530-246-5154* ✎*www.nps.gov/whis*

The main event here is Whiskeytown Lake, a 3220-acre body of water that's ideal for swimming, canoeing, and sailing. There are beaches at Brandy Creek and Oak Bottom; the fishing for bass, kokanee salmon, and brown and rainbow trout is good. There are picnic areas, restrooms, a summer hamburger stand at both beaches, an information center, and canoe rentals at Oak Bottom. Rangers often lead free educational programs; call for information.

▲ For campers, there are 37 RV sites (no hookups) at Brandy Creek; $7 to $14 per night. Reservations are available at Oak Bottom (800-365-2267), which offers 42 RV sites and 100 tent sites; $14 to $18 per night. You'll also find seven primitive campgrounds (permit required). Day-use fee, $5.

WEAVERVILLE TO YREKA

The best path between Weaverville and Yreka is Route 3—a sinuous track plagued with fast-moving lumberjacks on wheels. It does, however, offer extraordinary mountain vistas. The old California-Oregon Wagon Road, it parallels Trinity Lake and the Trinity Alps on its 105-mile journey back to civilization at Yreka.

If you're feeling even more adventurous, you can travel west from Weaverville on Route 299 into Humboldt County, connect with Route 96, and head north into Salmon River country. This winding roadway passes Six Rivers National Forest and approaches whitewater stretches of the mighty Klamath River. Slow but scenic, it's the long way home to Yreka, doubling the distance to 213 miles, and leading along poorly maintained roads.

SIGHTS

TRINITY LAKE   If you opt for Route 3, watch for the Buckeye Creek Road turnoff about seven miles from Weaverville. Turn right and you'll discover some striking panoramas of Trinity Lake, a 16,500-acre expanse that's part of the Whiskeytown-Shasta-Trinity National Recreation Area.

SCOTT MUSEUM OF TRINITY CENTER ⊠*Airport Road, Trinity Center* ☎*530-266-3378* At the Scott Museum, you'll see displays representing the pioneer days, everything from Indian baskets to snowshoes for horses. It also boasts one of the country's largest collections of barbed wire—nearly 500 different samples. Open Tuesday through Saturday, June through August.

TRINITY ALPS WILDERNESS AREA   To explore this wilderness area, or for a closer look at the mountains, go eight miles past Trinity Center and turn left on Coffee Creek Road. It carries past waterfalls and rushing rivers, through deep forest and dark canyons. Just past the North Fork Coffee Creek Bridge lies this wilderness area, with its granite peaks and glacial lakes.

CALLAHAN   Back on Route 3, continue north into the placid Scott Valley region. Callahan, once an important trade center, still sports boardwalks and 19th-century buildings along its one-block commercial strip. Other small towns along the way—Etna, Greenview, and Fort Jones—also feature antique buildings.

YREKA   In Yreka, you'll find a reconstructed mining town, as well as hiking trails and a fishing lake in **Greenhorn Park**, located on Greenhorn Road.

Wandering around Yreka can feel a little like taking part in a treasure hunt—the treasures, in this case, being the town's assortment of **historical statues** and **murals**. In particular, keep your eyes open for local artist Ralph Starritt's metal sculptures, which include a gold-panning miner at the Route 5 offramp (Exit 775) and, just south of town on Route 5, an enormous metallic cow. Yreka has also commissioned several historical murals, including those located at the intersections of South Broadway and Lane Street, South Broadway and Butte Street, and West Miner and 3rd Street.

SISKIYOU COUNTY MUSEUM   ✉ *910 South Main Street, Yreka* ☎ *530-842-3836* 📠 *530-842-3166* 🌐 *www.co.siskiyou.ca.us/museum,*   *hismus@att.net* At Siskiyou's county museum are displays of American Indian artifacts, as well as exhibits on mining, the military, and Chinese pioneers. There are also vintage photographs, hand-colored panoramic images of Yreka and vicinity in the 1920s, and pioneer, logging, and Chinese exhibits. The Davis Cabin, part of this excellent facility, was built in 1856. Closed Sunday and Monday. Admission.

MINER STREET   Be sure to visit this timeworn commercial row, where most of the buildings have been standing since the late 19th century, and explore the town's **Victorian home district** (bounded by 3rd, Oregon, Gold, and Lane streets).

SISKIYOU COUNTY COURT HOUSE   ✉ *311 4th Street, Yreka* Some of the wealth that built these grand homes is displayed at the local court house. Here, behind a glass case, rests a king's ransom in gold nuggets from neighboring mines.

LODGING

KOA TRINITY LAKE
$$ 20 UNITS   ✉ *Route 3, Trinity Center* ☎ *530-266-3337, 800-715-3337* 📠 *530-266-3820* 🌐 *www.trinitylakekoa.com, trinitylake@koa.net*

"A complete 90-acre vacation village on Trinity Lake" is the way this place bills itself. The multifaceted enclave consists of fully equipped cottages, a trailer park, 80 campsites, a marina with rental boats, supermarket, gas station, and more. Although the cabins don't have TV or phones, they have fully equipped kitchens and provide a good location for exploring the nearby Trinity Alps. Some cottages house up to six people; there are two- and three-day minimums on weekends and holidays, respectively.

HISTORIC CARRVILLE INN
$$$ 5 ROOMS   ✉ *Carrville Loop Road, Trinity Center* ☎ *530-266-3511* 📠 *530-266-3778* 🌐 *www.carrvilleinn.com, info@carrvilleinn.com*

The Carrville is a gracious abode imbued with the glory of pure laziness: the swinging hammock beckons, the pool invites contemplative laps, and the veranda evokes images of napping with that book you've always meant to read. You can also wander out to the barn to visit the pot-belly pig, llamas, and peacocks. Enjoy appetizers in the evening, then retire to the saloon to pound away on the dancehall piano or play a quiet game of checkers. The rooms are decorated in Victorian flare, with ceiling fans and fresh flowers.

ECONOLODGE INN & SUITES

$ 44 ROOMS ✉️*526 South Main Street, Yreka* 📞*530-842-4404* 📠*530-841-0439*

You won't find much in the way of exotic rentals up in Siskiyou County, but the EconoLodge does have a few extras to make it stand out from the rest—like exceptionally spotless rooms, kitchenettes, color televisions, and a pool. The accommodations at this neon motel are comfortably but unimaginatively furnished.

BEST WESTERN MINER'S INN

$$ 134 UNITS ✉️*122 East Miner Street, Yreka* 📞*530-842-4355* 📠*530-842-4480*

If the EconoLodge is already booked, try this Best Western. With over one hundred accommodations (some are two-bedroom apartments with kitchenettes), it has two swimming pools and a free continental breakfast; a coffee shop is nearby.

DINING

MING'S RESTAURANT AND LOUNGE _____

$–$$ CHINESE ✉️*210 West Miner Street, Yreka* 📞*530-842-3888*
📠*530-842-3889*

Chinese dishes, teriyaki steak, and seafood are the main attractions here. The menu offers crab legs, roast duck, and several different combination plates. Locals fill the place at lunch for the full buffet that includes traditional favorites beef and broccoli, kung pao chicken, egg flower soup, and chicken chow mein. Don't miss the sesame chicken for dinner.

NATURE'S KITCHEN

$ VEGETARIAN ✉️*412 South Main Street, Yreka* 📞*530-842-1136*

This diner will be a welcome sight for vegetarians. Breakfast means an assortment of baked goods and coffee. Lunch brings a menu of salads, cold and hot sandwiches, and a delicious veggie chili burger. Desserts are made with local honey and organic wheat flour. No dinner. Closed Sunday.

CASA RAMOS

$–$$ MEXICAN ✉️*145 Montague Road, Yreka* 📞*530-842-7172*

For traditional Mexican fare, stop in here. You'll find a selection of tamales and enchiladas, as well as favorites like the *carne asada* dinner and steak or chicken fajitas.

SHOPPING

JAMES PLACE ✉️*216 3rd Street, Yreka* 📞*530-842-5454* ✉️*jamesplace@nctv. com* Antique stores are one of Yreka's strongest attractions. James Place is reputedly the largest single-owner shop of its type in the Pacific

Northwest, and has been doing business since 1971. Here you'll find vintage clothing, quilts, miniatures, and folk art. There's also a large variety of antique toys, including dolls, stuffed bears, and carousel animals. Closed Sunday.

PARKS

SHASTA-TRINITY NATIONAL FOREST

✉ *The forest is northeast, south, and west of Redding. Principal access is from Routes 3, 5, 89, and 299; Forest headquarters is located at 3644 Avtech Parkway, Redding.*
☎ *530-226-2500*   *530-226-2470*   *www.fs.fed.us/r5/shastatrinity*

These are just two of the 131 lakes found in this seemingly unending paradise. It's visited by more than five million people each year, but there's still plenty of room to spare within the forest's 2,121,546 acres. About 3100 miles of hiking trails, including part of the Pacific Crest Trail, wind through the forest. Towering Mt. Shasta, the region's most prominent peak, overlooks nearly 2000 miles of tributaries and streams. Wildlife includes bald eagles, ospreys, great blue herons, black bears, mule deer, striped skunks, gray fox, and golden-mantled squirrels. There are numerous visitors centers, restrooms, and picnic areas throughout the forest. For Whiskeytown, Shasta, and Trinity Lakes, and for Trinity Alps Wilderness Area and Mt. Shasta, see listings below.

There are more than 100 campgrounds; $6 to $14 per night. Some free campsites (without facilities) are scattered throughout the forest, and with a wilderness permit and a campfire permit you can camp anywhere in the forest, though it's best to check before you go for periodic area closures.

WHISKEYTOWN-SHASTA-TRINITY NATIONAL RECREATION AREA—TRINITY UNIT

✉ *Parallel to Route 3, just a few miles north of Weaverville*   ☎ *530-623-2121*
530-623-6010

This unit's centerpiece is Trinity Lake, which boasts 145 miles of shoreline and sits in the shadow of the Trinity Alps. Popular for swimming, waterskiing, and houseboating, it's also recommended for trout and smallmouth bass fishing. There are picnic areas and restrooms; restaurants, groceries, and boat rentals.

Some of the ten forest service campgrounds are located on a sandy beach at Clark Springs; $6 to $16 per night depending on the site. There are also cabin rentals near the lake.

TRINITY ALPS WILDERNESS AREA

✉ *Located 48 miles west of Redding, the area is accessible from Routes 299 and 3.*   ☎ *530-623-2121, 530-623-6106*   *530-623-6010*

A high, sharp mountain range, the Trinity Alps vault from glacial canyons to 9000-foot heights. In addition to startling granite peaks, the region contains alpine lakes, pristine streams, and giant talus boulders. There are no facilities here. A wilderness permit is required (for overnight use), as is a free campfire permit.

▲ Permitted for backpacking campers; no fee. Motorized vehicles are not allowed within the wilderness area.

SIX RIVERS NATIONAL FOREST

✉*Extending 140 miles along the western perimeter of the Far North, this facility is accessible from Route 101 (via Routes 36, 96, 299, and 199).* ☎*707-442-1721* 📠*707-442-9242* ✍*www.fs.fed.us/r5/sixrivers*

🚶 🚵 🐎 ⛵ 🛶 🚤 🎣 Stretching from the Oregon border almost into Mendocino County, this million-acre playground is the home of six major waterways—the Smith, Klamath, Trinity, Mad, Van Duzen, and Eel rivers. Although there are 400 miles of hiking trails, fishing is the most popular sport, followed by river rafting. There are picnic areas and restrooms.

▲ Permitted in 18 specified campgrounds and in other areas throughout the forest; $8 to $15 per night; group sites are extra. A cabin is available from June to October at Smith River; $75 for up to eight people. Fire permits are required for fires outside of developed areas. For more information call any of the national forest's ranger districts: Smith River National Recreation Area (Gasquet 707-457-3131), Orleans Ranger District (Orleans 530-627-3291), Lower Trinity Ranger District (Willow Creek 530-629-2118), or Mad River Ranger District (Mad River 707-574-6233). Reservations are available at Smith River, and for several campgrounds in the Orleans and Willow Creek areas; all other campgrounds are first-come, first-served. Closed Labor Day to Memorial Day.

REDDING TO MT. SHASTA

A cross between Valhalla and Shangri-la, Mt. Shasta is the quintessential Cascade mountain backdrop. Driving north from Redding toward the volcanic peak, you'll pass manmade and natural attractions alike before ascending this magic mountain.

SIGHTS

SHASTA LAKE   Due north along Route 5, you'll encounter this extremely popular recreation area, a paradise for naturalists and statisticians alike. Why the strange combination of interests? Because Shasta Lake, with its 370-mile shoreline and 30,000-acre expanse, is the largest manmade lake in the state. Its four arms stretch into the Sacramento, McCloud, and Pit rivers, as well as Squaw Creek. It boasts 17 types of game fish, a colony of houseboats, hiking trails, and every other possible outdoor diversion imaginable.

SHASTA DAM   Then there's Shasta Dam, located along Shasta Dam Boulevard five miles west of Route 5. Three times taller than Niagara Falls, it measures 602 feet, making it the second highest dam in the United States. Nearly seven years of labor and six and a half million cubic yards of concrete went into its completion. If those superlatives are insufficient, continue north on Route 5 a few miles and you'll cross **Pit River Bridge**, the world's highest double-deck bridge.

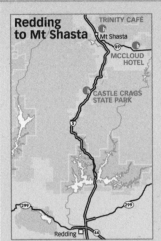

Redding to Mt Shasta

TRINITY CAFÉ

MCCLOUD HOTEL

CASTLE CRAGS STATE PARK

Redding

TRINITY CAFÉ
PAGE 563

Fresh, seasonal California-Mediterranean fare like cabernet-braised lamb with mint pesto in a romantic urban bistro

MCCLOUD HOTEL
PAGE 562

Old-fashioned, lovingly restored 1916 house with four-poster beds, overstuffed chairs, and antique vanities

CASTLE CRAGS STATE PARK
PAGE 565

Breathtaking, 6000-foot-high, glacier-polished granite spires towering over winding trails beside the Sacramento River

LAKE SHASTA CAVERNS ✉20359 Shasta Caverns Road, Lakehead ☎530-238-2341, 800-795-2283 📠530-238-2386 ✐www.lakeshastacaverns.com, shastacav@aol.com From the nearby town of **O'Brien** (population: two), you can visit these caverns. Guides will take you on a 15-minute ride across the lake by boat, then along a picturesque road by bus, to this mazework of limestone caves. Within are strangely shaped stalactites and awesome stalagmites, dating back perhaps 250 million years. This natural statuary comes in the form of spires and minarets, stone curtains and Disneyesque figures. Inside these tunnels, the temperature is always 58° with 95 percent humidity. Admission. Call for seasonal hours.

CASTLE CRAGS STATE PARK ✉Off of Castle Creek Road, Castella ☎530-235-2684 Castle Crags, northward along Route 5 in Castella, is a land of granite domes and startling landscapes. From vista points, you can gaze out upon the Cascade Range.

MOUNT SHASTA Foremost among these majestic peaks is awesome Mount Shasta, a 14,162-foot giant that carries five glaciers along its flanks. Dominating the skyline, it consists of two volcanic cones and features alpine lakes, flower-filled meadows, and deep forests. For a closer look at this sacred mountain, follow Route A10 through Mt. Shasta Recreation Area. The road winds to an elevation of 6800 feet and offers a different view at every hairpin turn.

MCCLOUD ✉P.O. Box 372, McCloud, CA 96057 ☎530-964-3113 ✐www.mccloudchamber.com, contact@mccloudchamber.com In the shadow of Mount Shasta along Route 89 sits McCloud, one of California's most picturesque villages. A lumber center established in 1897, McCloud was a company town until the mid-1960s. It still maintains much of its original architecture as well as its economic base of logging and tour-

Redding to Mt. Shasta

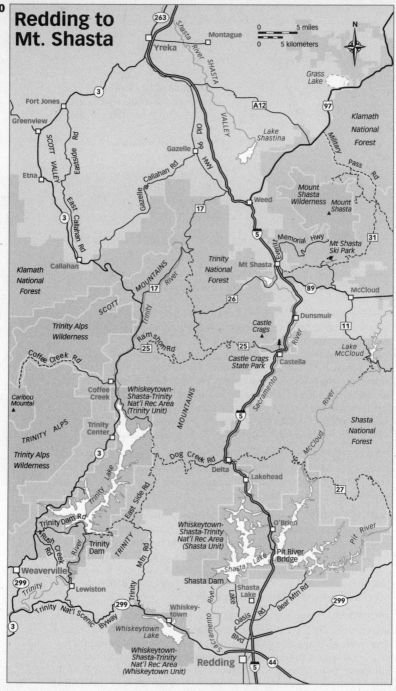

ism. In the winter, it's a mecca for skiers. The **McCloud Chamber of Commerce** doesn't have an office, but you can write to them and request information.

LODGING

TSASDI RESORT

$$ 20 UNITS ✉19990 Lakeshore Drive, Lakehead ✆530-238-2575, 800-995-0291 📠530-238-8660 ✐www.tsasdiresort.com, tsasdi@snowcrest.net

Idyllically situated in the Sacramento Arm of Shasta Lake, this resort is the perfect place to get away from it all without leaving all the conveniences behind. It offers cabins that come complete with kitchens, patio decks, picnic tables, and barbecues. Fairly plush by rustic standards, they have knotty-pine interiors and sit in a black oak forest overlooking Shasta Lake. The facilities also include a heated swimming pool, private dock, recreation room, and small convenience store. During the summer, cabins rent by the week only.

ANTLERS RESORT & MARINA

$$$–$$$$ 20 UNITS ✉20679 Antlers Road at Shasta Lake, Lakehead ✆530-238-2553, 800-238-3924 📠530-238-2340 ✐www.shastalakevacations.com, antlers@shastalakevacations.com

Antlers rents both houseboats and cabins. Many folks claim the only way to experience Shasta Lake is by houseboat, but the thrill doesn't come cheap. Prices for the smallest seagoing accommodations start in the ultra-deluxe range, with a three-day minimum. You can make the costs quite reasonable, however, by bringing along a few friends. The comforts of home include a complete kitchen, bathroom, and TV with VCR or DVD. Landlubbers may find the housekeeping cabins more to their liking, with rates starting lower than the houseboats. Rustic but well appointed, half have wood stoves and all include open porches. These are among the most comfortable cabins on the lake (seven-night minimum during the summer).

PACKERS BAY MARINA

$$$$ 5 UNITS ✉Packers Bay Marina at Shasta Lake ✆530-275-5570, 800-331-3137 📠530-275-5570 ✐www.packersbay.com, info@packersbay.com

South of Antlers Resort is this houseboat haven. The houseboats are well maintained and come complete with kitchen, barbecue, and stereo system. All you need to add is food, linens, pillows, and gasoline. Each of the five available houseboats sleeps 10 to 16 people. There's a four-day minimum off-season and a one-week minimum from early June until early September. Closed October through April.

BAVARIA LODGE

$ 8 UNITS ✉4601 Dunsmuir Avenue, Dunsmuir ✆530-235-4707 📠530-235-4707 ✐moreinfo@bavarialodge.net

Town living is combined with a touch of rusticity here. Eight log cabins sit along the edge of town. Nothing fancy, mind you; each is decorated with a few paintings along raw-wood walls and all but two are equipped with a fully stocked kitchenette. The entire complex is nestled in the trees.

RAILROAD PARK CABOOSE MOTEL

$$ 25 UNITS ✉100 Railroad Park Road, Dunsmuir 📞530-235-4440, 800-974-7245 🖰www.rrpark.com

I've slept in all kinds of places, from tents to palaces, but I've rarely spent the night in accommodations as unique as the converted cabooses here. Part of the Railroad Park Resort, this historic hostelry features cabooses transformed into sleeping units. The facility also offers four cabins, two with kitchens. The adjacent restaurant is housed in old railroad cars. Amenities at the resort include a swimming pool and jacuzzi.

ALPENROSE COTTAGE GUEST HOUSE

$-$$ 2 ROOMS ✉204 East Hinckley Street, Mount Shasta 📞530-926-6724 🖰www.snowcrest.net/alpenrose, alpenrose2946@sbcglobal.net

The two-story Bavarian-style Alpenrose is an ideal retreat. Panoramic views of Mount Shasta, walking distance to town, and proximity to skiing, hiking, rafting, and cycling make this a great vacation base. A lovely deck makes for great lounging. There's a complete kitchen, a charming garden, free wi-fi, and a TV room. Reservations are recommended—there are only two rooms offered. Free laundry facilities. No credit cards.

WOODSMAN HOTEL

$$ 42 ROOMS ✉1121 Mt.Shasta Boulevard, Mount Shasta 📞530-926-3411 📠530-926-3426 🖰www.woodsmanhotel.com, mtshastahotels@gmail.com

Nestled among 100-foot evergreens right at the Town Center, this lodge-style hotel has spacious, sparely furnished rooms paneled in knotty pine, with down comforters on the comfortable beds, spa toiletries, and plasma TVs. Suites include full kitchens, a boon for families.The hotel also is within easy walking distance to several good restaurants.

MCCLOUD HOTEL

$$-$$$$ 16 ROOMS ✉408 Main Street, McCloud 📞530-964-2822, 800-964-2823 📠530-964-2844 🖰www.mccloudhotel.com, mchotel@snowcrest.net

A registered National Historic Landmark dating to 1916, the McCloud was, in its former incarnation, a 93-room boarding house for single lodgers and the town's teachers. Condemned in 1982, it emerged in 1995 as a B&B, after a total renovation. Each room is unique and individually designed; some have four-poster beds. In many rooms, the upholstery of the couches and chairs matches the wallpaper and curtains. Breakfast is served in the lobby sitting room or, if you're staying in a suite, is brought directly to you.

DINING

RAILROAD PARK DINNER HOUSE AND LOUNGE

$$-$$$$ AMERICAN ✉100 Railroad Park Road, Dunsmuir 📞530-235-4611, 800-974-7245 🖰www.rrpark.com

For an incredible view of 4000-foot granite spires and a nostalgic trip back to the time when the railroad was king, climb aboard the Railroad Park Dinner House and Lounge. You'll discover two restored dining cars—decorated with antique hand tools, steam gauges, and plush pile carpeting—which brilliantly re-create the romance of the rails. Specialties include chicken dishes, seafood entrées, or prime rib dinners; children's plates include chicken nuggets and home-made mac and cheese. Dinner only. Closed in winter, depending on weather. Open Friday and Saturday (for other nights, call ahead).

CAFÉ MADDALENA

$$–$$$ CONTINENTAL ✉*5801 Sacramento Avenue, Dunsmuir* ✆*530-235-2725*
✍*www.cafemaddalena.com*

This café's enticing blend of continental cuisines—Spanish, French, Italian, and North African—has won it the loyal following of locals and food critics alike. Located in Dunsmuir's historic Railroad District, the café features a handsome wood-paneled dining room, an open kitchen, and, during the summer, outside garden seating. The bistro serves only seasonally fresh dishes such as herb-roasted rack of lamb with ratatouille or Spanish seafood stew with tomatoes, peppers, saffron, and rice. Closed Monday through Wednesday, and December through March. Reservations recommended.

MICHAEL'S

$$$ AMERICAN ✉*313 North Mount Shasta Boulevard, Mount Shasta*
✆*530-926-5288* ✍*530-926-5288* ✍*michaelsinc@snowcrest.net*

"Welcome back to homemade food—eat and enjoy" is the rule at Michael's. This downtown restaurant offers seafood, pasta, sandwiches, and a long list of wine and beer. At lunchtime, try the Rancho-burger, while pasta alfredo, linguine with white clam sauce, Russian ravioli, and prime rib top the dinner listings. A large window provides a breathtaking view of Mt. Shasta from the dining room. Closed Sunday, Monday, and Tuesday.

TRINITY CAFÉ

$$$ CALIFORNIA CUISINE/MEDITERRANEAN ✉*622 North Mount Shasta Boulevard, Mount Shasta* ✆*530-926-6200* ✍*www.trinitycafe.net*

Here, fine Californian and Mediterranean dishes are prepared with the freshest seasonal ingredients and served in a romantic, urban bistro environment. Entrées include cabernet-braised lamb with mint pesto, duck prosciutto over watercress and goat cheese salad, and butternut squash gnocchi with oyster mushrooms and candied hazelnuts. The café also offers an extensive (mostly Californian) wine list. Reservations recommended. Dinner only. Closed Monday.

SAY CHEESE PIZZA & SPORTS BAR

$–$$ PIZZA ✉*304 Maple Street, Mount Shasta* ✆*530-926-2821*

You can shoot some pool or try your hand at pinball while waiting for your order at Say Cheese. At this sports-themed pizza parlor, pictures of sports stars decorate the walls. Pizza and sandwiches dominate the menu, and there's a great salad bar.

BLACK BEAR DINER

$–$$ AMERICAN   ✉401 West Lake Street, Mount Shasta   ☎530-926-4669
✐www.blackbeardiner.com

The Black Bear has taken the diner one step further with a themed restaurant specializing in bears. Pictures of black bears and old-time shots of Mt. Shasta decorate the walls, and you can chow down on sandwiches and burgers with names like the Papa Bear—a half-pound of ground beef on a grilled French roll with Swiss cheese, bacon, tomato, and lettuce, with a mountain of fries on the side.

LILY'S RESTAURANT

$$–$$$ AMERICAN   ✉1013 South Mount Shasta Boulevard, Mount Shasta
☎530-926-3372   ✐www.lilysrestaurant.com, lilys@snowcrest.net

Past the picket fence, flower trellis, and leaded-glass doors of Lily's, you'll discover a huge, filling breakfast (try the salmon omelette). For lunch and dinner, they have lots of vegetarian options, from an eggplant hoagie to veggie burgers. They also serve charbroiled hamburgers and a delicious shrimp and crab sandwich. Thai dishes, Mexican staples, and even Italian influences are represented here.

THE MOUNT SHASTA RESORT RESTAURANT

$$–$$$$ STEAK/SEAFOOD   ✉1000 Siskiyou Lake Boulevard, Mount Shasta
☎530-926-3030, 800-958-3363   ✐www.mountshastaresort.com,
generalinfo@mountshastaresort.com

Part of a 50-chalet exclusive resort, this restaurant offers stunning vistas of Mt. Shasta past the resort's own golf course amidst a wine-influenced atmosphere of teal green carpets and burgundy tabletops. The chef creates an array of pasta, chicken, beef, pork, lamb, seafood, and vegetarian entrées that include shrimp and scallop sauté pasta, chicken marsala, shrimp scampi, and prime rib.

SHASTA SUNSET DINNER TRAIN

$$$$ AMERICAN   ✉328 Main Street, McCloud   ☎530-964-2142, 800-733-2141
✐www.shastasunset.com, info@shastasunset.com

For a different sort of dining experience, hop aboard the Shasta Sunset, which operates three-hour-long dinner runs. The mahogany-paneled dining cars with their antique brass lamps and luxurious upholstery harken back to the glory days of travel. The four-course dinner is pricey, but it's an experience you'll never forget. During the summer months, theme nights from wine tasting to murder mysteries are featured. If you can't afford it, there are open-air excursions through September that cover the same route. Trains run Friday and Saturday in June and October through December. They also operate Thursday, July through September.

SHOPPING

RUDDLE COTTAGE   ✉5815 Sacramento Avenue, Dunsmuir   ☎530-235-2022
✐www.ruddlecottage.net, jayne@ruddlecottage.net   Artist Jayne Bruck-Fryer makes jewelry from fused glass salvaged from a Burning Man installation and bits of glass found on the site of this shop, a former pool hall and bar which burned down in 1965. Other goodies include Java Jacket jewelry, recycled coffee cup sleeves cut into whimsical shapes and

adorned with beads and wire. Usually open from 11 a.m. until 3 p.m., but call ahead to confirm.

VILLAGE BOOKS ✉*320 North Mount Shasta Boulevard, Mount Shasta* ✆*530-926-1678* ✐*www.villagebooks-mtshasta.com* This shop specializes in books on the Mount Shasta region and works by local authors.

THE FIFTH SEASON ✉*300 North Mount Shasta Boulevard, Mount Shasta* ✆*530-926-3606* ✆*530-926-1337* ✐*www.thefifthseason.com* Even if you're not planning to take a run down the nearby slopes, The Fifth Season warrants a walk-through. This sports trading post provides ski equipment, mountaineering and bicycling gear, and a complete line of all-weather clothing.

GOLDEN BOUGH BOOKSTORE
✉*219 North Mount Shasta Boulevard, Mount Shasta* ✆*530-926-3228, 877-674-7282* ✐*www.goldenboughbooks.com* The Golden Bough caters to the many spiritual seekers who look to nearby Mt. Shasta for magical power. For books about local folklore, or for a dash of friendly conversation, drop by.

THE GALLERY ✉*201 North Mount Shasta Boulevard, Mount Shasta* ✆*530-926-2334* ✐*www.thegalleryinmtshasta.com* This is a large gallery space full of prints and paintings, jewelry, and wall hangings by local artists and American Indians.

NIGHTLIFE

MCCLOUD RIVER LODGE
✉*140 Squaw Valley Road, McCloud* ✆*530-964-2700* ✐*www.mccloudlodge.com, mccloudlodge@aol.com* Evenings tend to be quiet in the Mount Shasta region, but there is nightlife if you look for it, at least on some nights. Here the atmosphere is rustic; trophies and carved wooden plaques decorate the walls. Old-fashioned tools hang from the ceiling beams and cattle brands are burned into the posts. In the winter, customers are warmed by a century-old wood-burning stove in the center, and in the summer there's a grassy lawn with picnic tables in the back. There's live music—bluegrass, blues, rock and country—on Saturday evenings and line dancing on Wednesday. If that's not to your liking, play a game of pool or darts instead.

PARKS

CASTLE CRAGS STATE PARK
✉*Six miles south of Dunsmuir, just west of Route 5 in Castella* ✆*530-235-2684*
🚶 🏊 ⚓ They might look like the work of an avant-garde sculp-

tor, but the granite spires highlighting this 4000-acre facility were created more than 200 million years ago. In addition to the hiking on these 6000-foot statues, the park features rafting along the Sacramento River. The park has picnic areas, restrooms, and showers. Day-use fee, $6 per vehicle.

▲ There are 76 tent sites, three RV sites, and six trailer sites (no hookups); $20 per night.

WHISKEYTOWN-SHASTA-TRINITY NATIONAL RECREATION AREA—SHASTA UNIT

The lake is off Route 5 about ten miles north of Redding. 530-275-1587, 530-275-1589 (visitor center) 530-275-1512

California's largest artificial lake, Shasta Lake boasts 370 miles of shoreline in Whiskeytown's Shasta Unit. The lake's water temperature in the summer months averages 76°, making it ideal for houseboating, swimming, windsurfing (although winds are usually tame), and waterskiing. Fishing is excellent year-round, with bass, trout, bluegill, and sturgeon among the most frequent catches. There are restrooms, picnic areas, and boat ramps; restaurants, groceries, boat rentals, and hotel facilities are located near the lake.

▲ Camping is permitted in several forest service campgrounds, including some reached only by boat; free to $30 per night, depending on the campsite.

MT. SHASTA RECREATIONAL AREA

About 55 miles north of Redding off Route 5; Turn east on Everitt Memorial Highway (Route A10). 530-926-4511 530-926-5120 *www.fs.fed.us/r5/shastatrinity*

Dominated by 14,162-foot Mt. Shasta, this facility is favored by sightseers and climbers alike. Here you can explore living glaciers, whitewater canyons, and pristine lakes. A county road rises to 7800-feet elevation and hiking trails crisscross the mountain. Facilities include picnic areas and restrooms.

▲ There are six campgrounds, including two on the south side of the mountain; $10 to $12 per night.

KLAMATH NATIONAL FOREST

Accessible along Routes 96 and 97 530-842-6131 530-841-4571 *www.r5.fs.fed.us/klamath*

Fishing and river rafting are popular sports in this remote park. Covering parts of five different mountain ranges, it extends from Oregon across most of Siskiyou County. The Klamath, Scott, and Salmon rivers are explored here by many commercial outfitters, while fishing lodges have sprouted up near Happy Camp. Motorized boats are prohibited. Also within the forest is **Marble Mountain Wilderness Area**, a 213,363-acre preserve crowded with wildlife and sport fish. There are picnic areas and restrooms at some of the trailheads.

▲ There are 34 campgrounds with 377 sites; free to $15 per night. For more information contact any of the four ranger districts: Happy Camp (Happy Camp; 530-493-2243), Scott River (Fort Jones; 530-468-5351), Salmon River (Fort Jones; 530-468-5351), or Goosenest (Macdoel; 530-398-4391).

NORTHEAST LOOP

The best way to explore California's hidden northeastern corner is along a 400-plus mile odyssey from Redding. Heading east to Lassen Peak and beyond, it will carry you past mountain lakes and one-street towns. Then turning north, you'll skirt the Warner Mountains, detour to Lava Beds National Monument, and return to Redding via lonely Route 299.

SIGHTS

LASSEN VOLCANIC NATIONAL PARK ✉About 50 miles from Redding off Route 44 ☎530-595-4444 ⌖530-595-3262 ✑www.nps.gov/lavo, lavo_information@ nps.gov This is the first stop on your wilderness expedition. Lassen Peak, a 10,457-foot volcano, is the highlight and high point of this extraordinary region. It is part of the same mountain chain that brought you the Mt. St. Helens catastrophe. Lassen's last eruptions were between 1914 and 1921. Spewing fumes and ash 20,000 feet in the air, one explosion tore away an entire side of the mountain and flicked 20-ton boulders down the hillside. Today it's still a semi-active volcano, and the surrounding area is filled with steam vents, mud pots, and moonscape features.

The Lassen Volcanic National Park Road curves along three sides of the volcano, reaching an elevation of 8512 feet. Along this magnificent roadway are startling views of Lassen Peak, which still reveals scars from its furious eruptions. Also be sure to see **Bumpass Hell**, near the southern park boundary; it's a roaring region of boiling springs, mud pots, and pools colored gold and turquoise. (Although this 106,000-acre park is open year-round, the Lassen Volcanic National Park Road may be closed from the end of October until mid-June. If you're traveling during the ski season, consider taking Route 36 east from Red Bluff to the park's southwest entrance.)

KOHM YAH-MAH-MAH-NEE VISITOR CENTER ✉Lassen Volcanic National Park, PO Box 100, Mineral, CA 96063 ☎530-595-4480 ⌖530-595-3262 Interactive exhibits, a small auditorium, and a reception desk complete with guest permits and myriad park information are all available at this recently constructed visitor center. In addition, a gift shop and concession-style restaurant are part of the new structure, which sees about 400,000 visitors a year.

LAKE ALMANOR From Lassen, Route 36 heads east to Lake Almanor, a crystal blue expanse which mirrors the surrounding mountains. Measuring 52 square miles and bounded by evergreen forests, it's a prime place for swimming, boating, and waterskiing. Among the sport fish here are brown and rainbow trout as well as bass. Over 50 other lakes dot this pristine region and 500 miles of streams tumble through the area.

There are restaurants and lodgings in Chester, Susanville, and other small towns along the way. The **Lassen County Chamber of Commerce**

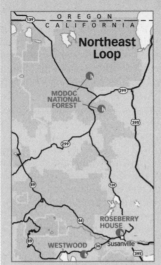

MODOC NATIONAL FOREST

PAGE 574

Remote acres of obsidian cliffs, lava tubes, open rangeland, and sweeping vistas, all with very few visitors

ROSEBERRY HOUSE

PAGE 571

Four charming, understated, sun-filled rooms with 19th-century antique furniture—cozy spot for quality R&R

WESTWOOD

PAGE 568

Tiny, quaint logging town where Paul Bunyan and Babe the Blue Ox were made heroes of American folklore

(601 Richmond Road, Susanville; 530-257-4323, fax 530-251-2561; www.lassencountychamber.org, director@lassencountychamber.org) can help you get your bearings in this sparsely populated region. Closed Saturday and Sunday.

EAGLE LAKE   Outside Susanville, a 28-mile (roundtrip) detour on County Road A1 leads to one of the state's biggest natural lakes. The high alkaline content of the 22,000-acre body of water has created an environment that supports an incredible variety of animal life. In addition to the native Eagle Lake trout, there are antelope, porcupine, deer, white pelicans, and a rare species of osprey along its shores.

Leading into the state's vast, empty northeastern corner, Route 395 proceeds north through high desert country. Sage brush hills and whistling winds are your sole companions. You'll pass **Standish** (population 388), **Litchfield** (population 376), **Termo** (population 61), and **Madeline** (population 26) en route to the grand metropolis of **Alturas** (population 2800).

WESTWOOD

If you're interested in American folklore, be sure to take a detour to this tiny historic logging town, where Paul Bunyan became a folk hero. Although the legend of Paul Bunyan had been told for generations in the lumber camps of the northeastern U.S., he was unknown outside the logging community. In 1913, the Walker family moved their mill from Minnesota to the northern Sierras, where they created the town of Westwood.

The Walkers hired W. B. Laughead to promote the new town and their company's Paul Bunyan Pine products by writing a series of small books on the exploits of Paul Bunyan and his blue ox Babe between the years of 1914 to 1944. Today, the mill is gone, but Paul Bunyan lives on in the annals of American folklore, and a giant statue of Paul and Babe stands guard at the edge of town.

MODOC COUNTY MUSEUM ✉*600 South Main Street, Alturas* 📞*530-233-2944* This museum has an extensive collection of Paiute and Pit artifacts and the counter from a turn-of-the-20th-century general store with its inventory of corsets, high button shoes, and other period pieces. There's also an entire wall of weaponry, a rock and gem collection, and an intriguing exhibit on the region's bird life. Another display tells the story of Fort Bidwell, the pioneer military headquarters for this region. Here you'll learn about California's last Indian battle. Closed Sunday and Monday, and from November through May. Admission.

ALTURAS CHAMBER OF COMMERCE ✉*522 South Main Street, Alturas* 📞*530-233-4434* 📠*530-233-4434* 🖰*www.alturaschamber.org* The local chamber of commerce can provide information and direct you to local attractions. Closed weekends.

LAVA BEDS NATIONAL MONUMENT ✉*Along Route 161* 📞*530-667-8100* 📠*530-667-2737* 🖰*www.nps.gov/labe* One recommended stop is this monument. It's a land of cinder cones, craters, and 30,000-year-old lava flows. It also features one of the world's finest series of lava tube caves, many open to exploration (the total number is over 700 caves). Once occupied by the Modoc people, this volcanic area contains numerous petroglyphs and pictographs.

KLAMATH BASIN NATIONAL WILDLIFE REFUGE ✉*Tulelake, off Route 139; Head five miles west on East-West Road, then a half-mile south on Hill Road.* 📞*530-667-2231* 📠*530-667-8337* Nearby Klamath Basin National Wildlife Refuge is a migration point for one of the greatest concentrations of waterfowl on the continent. Together with neighboring areas, it draws two million birds during the spring and fall, including mallards, pintails, and snow geese. Vehicle fee for certain areas, $3.

MCARTHUR–BURNEY FALLS MEMORIAL STATE PARK ✉*530-335-2777* 📠*530-335-5483* From this remote preserve you can return to civilization, following Route 139 and then Route 299 as it cuts an alpine path back to Redding. Before leaving the wilderness entirely, stop at McArthur–Burney Falls Park. Located midway between Mount Shasta and Lassen Park, it features a spectacular waterfall, fed by springs, which cascades over a 129-foot cliff. Ornamented with rainbows and an emerald pool, this fall was reputedly deemed the eighth wonder of the world by President Theodore Roosevelt. It's a fitting climax to this long, lonely loop into California's most secluded realm. Admission.

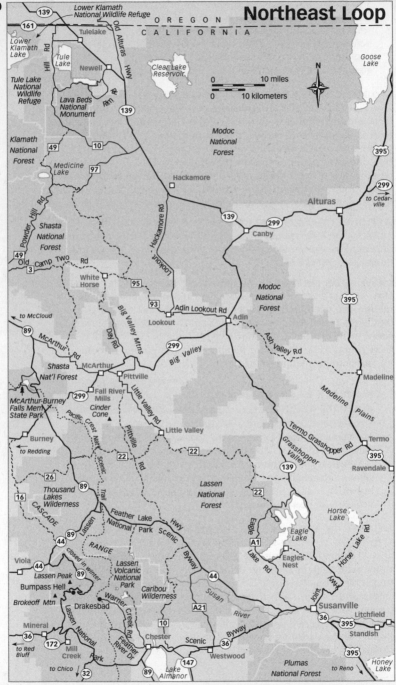

Northeast Loop

LASSEN MINERAL LODGE

$$–$$$ 20 ROOMS   ⊠*Route 36 East, Mineral*   ☎*530-595-4422*   📠*530-595-4452*
✐*www.minerallodge.com*

Modern amenities can be found at this lodge, although it was established in 1896. Here the rooms are conventionally styled with wall-to-wall carpeting, some with wood paneling. Rooms with kitchenettes are available, as are RV and tent sites. A restaurant, general store, and ski shop are also on the grounds.

CEDAR LODGE

$ 12 ROOMS   ⊠*Junction of Routes 36 and 89, Chester*   ☎*530-258-2904*
📠*530-258-2016*   ✐*www.cedarlodgefun.com, cedarlodge@cedarlodgefun.com*

Tucked between Mount Lassen and Lake Almanor you'll find this lodge. More of a motel than rural lodge, its cedar walls surround rather bland furnishings—such as second-hand store bedroom sets—but in such Technicolor territory, your eyes probably need a rest. The rooms that come equipped with kitchenettes offer a lot of space.

TIMBER HOUSE LODGE

$ 8 ROOMS   ⊠*501 Main Street, Chester*   ☎*530-258-2989*

Farther east from Cedar Lodge, set among towering pines, is the Timber House. The rooms here are plain but comfortable, with large beds, shower-tub combinations, televisions, and wood furnishings. There's also a restaurant.

DRAKESBAD GUEST RANCH

$$$–$$$$ 19 ROOMS   ⊠*End of Warner Valley Road, Chester*   ☎*530-529-1512*
ext. 120   📠*530-529-4511*   ✐*www.drakesbad.com*

Drakesbad Ranch looks like it hasn't changed for generations. This resort, with its rustic wood-paneled rooms and hardwood floors adorned by braided rugs, sits at the end of a gravel road within Lassen National Park. The cabins are lit by kerosene lanterns and the pool warmed by thermal hot springs. Guests enjoy simple pleasures like horseback rides, horseshoes, hiking, fishing, volleyball, and badminton. The place is so popular, reservations often must be made a year in advance for the June to mid-October season. Three meals are included in the room rate.

ROSEBERRY HOUSE

$$ 4 ROOMS   ⊠*609 North Street, Susanville*   ☎*530-257-5675*
✐*www.roseberryhouse.com, roseberryhouse@frontiernet.net*

For comfort, privacy, and quiet, try one of the four rooms at Susanville's sole bed and breakfast. Aside from quality 19th-century antique furniture and decorations, there's not much in the way of baubles or gimmicks here—just what you want after a long day. A freshly made, full breakfast awaits you in the dining room each morning.

MILL CREEK LODGE

$-$$ 2 ROOMS   ✉*Nine miles east of Likely, check website for directions*
📞*530-233-4934* ✐*www.millcreeklodge.com, mcgarvas@gotsky.com*

Staying in this cozy country lodge located about 20 miles south of Alturas is a nice break from busy city motels and hotels. The two spacious rooms share a large bath on the second floor loft and the innkeepers will cook a full breakfast to order every morning. You can bring your own alcohol and call ahead to arrange for dinner. It's quiet, warm, and just the spot to enjoy a peaceful evening in the country after a day of exploring.

SUPER 8 MOTEL

$-$$ 48 ROOMS   ✉*511 North Main Street, Alturas* 📞*530-233-3545*
📠*530-233-3305*

Located within half a mile of the Modoc County Museum, the Super 8 has 48 rooms. It's a typical, generic motel with the usual dresser-desk combination and dime-store paintings; the staff is friendly, though, and it also happens to be the nicest place in town.

COCKRELL'S HIGH DESERT LODGING

$-$$ 2 UNITS   ✉*Star Route 11-A, County Road 31, Cedarville* 📞*888-279-2209*
✐*www.highdesertlodging.com*

For breathtaking views of snow-capped mountains and lush fields, spend the night (or week) at Cockrell's. There are two three-bedroom houses with fully equipped kitchens and a backyard jacuzzi. Located on a working ranch, it's a great getaway and affords a truly Western experience.

DINING

KOPPER KETTLE CAFE

$$ DINER   ✉*Route 36 and Myrtle Street, Chester* 📞*530-258-2698*
📠*530-258-3182*

This café has the formica-counter-and-metal-chair appearance of a typical coffee shop, but the food is great. Just ask any of the local residents who crowd into this gathering spot. For a hearty breakfast, try the pork chops and eggs, which come with hash browns, toast, and applesauce. For lunch, there are giant hamburgers and fries, while dinner provides a selection of excellent fried chicken, liver and onions, and roast beef. If you're on a budget, it's a good place to chow down.

THE ST. BERNARD LODGE

$$ AMERICAN   ✉*44801 Route 36 East, ten miles west of Chester* 📞*530-258-3382*
✐*www.stbernardlodge.com*

The St. Bernard is one of those rare roadside inns that serves gourmet quality food. With its wood-paneled walls, lace tablecloths, and snowshoes on the wall, you might think you were in the Alps. Specialties include hamburgers, steaks, scampi, seafood, and fried chicken. Breakfast is also served Thursday through Monday (summer) and weekends (winter).

NIPA'S CALIFORNIA CUISINE

573

$-$$ THAI   ✉1001 North Main Street, Alturas   ☎530-233-2520

Nipa's serves up quality, no-frills Thai food. Popular dishes include the cashew chicken and the pad thai. The restaurant also offers a variety of beers and wines.

BRASS RAIL RESTAURANT

$$ AMERICAN   ✉395 Lakeview Highway, Alturas   ☎530-233-2906

The Brass Rail, located just outside of the Alturas city limits, dishes up hefty portions of traditional Basque cuisine. It's a family-style restaurant, so when you and your compadres sit down, be prepared for lots of food, fun, and conversation. A prix-fixe menu gets you wine, homemade bread, salad, soup, an entrée, and coffee (doggy bags are often served with the food). Favorites include top sirloin, lamb steak, and scallops. No lunch on Saturday. Closed Monday.

8 FAR NORTH   NORTHEAST LOOP PARKS

SHOPPING

COUNTRY VICTORIAN CHARM ✉718 Main Street, Susanville ☎530-257-8392 You'll find some unusual gifts at this elegant boutique, such as handmade Victorian dolls, handcrafted furniture, pewter picture frames, Victorian angels, and everlasting floral arrangements.

THE HEALTH NUT ✉2204 Main Street, Susanville ☎530-257-5800 Stop in here to load up on delicious and nutritious snacks to help energize you through the day. This store carries a full spectrum of health foods, from fresh smoothies and juices to aromatherapy and sports nutrition products to breads and dried fruits and nuts.

NIGHTLIFE

You will find restaurant bars and local saloons in small towns throughout the Far North. Many are short on entertainment, but provide a glimpse into this roughhewn, backwoods region.

BRASS RAIL RESTAURANT ✉395 Lakeview Highway, Alturas ☎530-233-2906 This is a great place to stop for a drink. The lounge is a low-light affair with a late-night bar and occasional musical entertainment.

PARKS

LASSEN NATIONAL FOREST

✉Accessible from Routes 44, 32, 36, and 89   ☎530-257-2151   📠530-252-6428
🌐www.fs.fed.us/r5/lassen

🚶🚴🏇🎣🏕🚣⛴🚢🛶 Sprawling across 1,100,000 acres, this giant facility fronts numerous lakes, including the popular Lake Almanor and Eagle Lake. It also contains **Thousand Lake Wilderness**, with its glacier-carved valley and 9000-foot peaks; **Caribou Wilderness**, a pine-forested plateau area featuring numerous lakes; and **Ishi Wilderness**, a 41,000-acre oak brushland with pine-covered plateaus. Facilities include picnic areas and restrooms.

▲ There are sites in 39 campgrounds; $10 to $15 per night for standard sites. Reservations: 872-444-6777.

LASSEN VOLCANIC NATIONAL PARK

✉ *The Lassen Volcanic National Park Road (closed during the snow season) bisects the park, which is located about 50 miles east of Redding.* ☎ *530-595-4444* ☎ *530-595-3262* ⌨ *www.nps.gov/lavo, lavo_information@nps.gov*

🚶 🏇 🚴 ⛵ ⛴ 🛶 Lassen Peak, a 10,457-foot plug dome volcano, tops the horizon in this 106,000-acre coniferous forest. Manzanita Lake provides limited catch-and-release fishing. This area is popular with sightseers, cross-country skiers, and hikers (there are 150 miles of hiking trails). Motorized boats are prohibited. The park has picnic areas, restrooms, and a snack bar (open in summer).

▲ There are sites in eight campgrounds; $10 to $16 per night. The Manzanita Lake and Summit Lake campgrounds are the most popular, right off the Lassen Volcanic National Park Road.

MCARTHUR–BURNEY FALLS MEMORIAL STATE PARK

✉ *Off Route 89 about 11 miles northeast of Burney* ☎ *530-335-2777* ☎ *530-335-5483*

🚶 🚴 🚵 🎣 ⛴ 🛶 🚤 The chief attraction at this 910-acre facility is its 129-foot waterfall, but the park also features a ponderosa pine forest, lake and stream fishing, and a bird population that includes bald eagles, black swifts, owls, and ospreys. The beach and swim area of the lake prove popular. Picnic areas and restrooms are within the park. Day-use fee, $6.

▲ There are 121 campsites; $20 per night. There are also 12 one-room cabins for $65 per night and 12 two-room cabins for $85 per night. Reservations are required Memorial Day through Labor Day: 800-444-7275.

LAVA BEDS NATIONAL MONUMENT

✉ *Off Route 139; 26 miles northwest of Canby* ☎ *530-667-8100* ☎ *530-667-2737* ⌨ *www.nps.gov/labe*

🚶 🚴 Known primarily for its extensive network of lava tube caves (over 700 of them), this amazing place features an active volcano, high desert plateaus, and large wilderness area. There are 25 miles of hiking trails. The visitors center provides free flashlights, which are essential for exploring, and sells headgear ($3.25), which is highly recommended for entering the caves. A bicycle helmet is also acceptable as headgear. A visitor center and restrooms are the only facilities. Day-use fee, $10.

▲ There are 43 designated campsites; $10 per night.

MODOC NATIONAL FOREST

✉ *Located both east and west of Alturas, this noncontiguous facility is accessible from Route 395 or Route 299.* ☎ *530-233-5811* ⌨ *www.fs.fed.us/ r5/modoc, mailroom/r5_modoc@modoc.fs.fed.us*

🚶 🚴 🏇 ⛷ 🏕 🚴 ⛴ 🚤 🛶 Nestled in the remote northeastern corner of California, this 1,654,392-acre facility is infrequently visited. Nevertheless, its features include obsidian cliffs, lava tubes, volcanic craters, open rangeland, basalt-domed plateaus, and mountain meadows. There are 118 miles of trails, plus numerous lakes and streams with fishing for trout and bass.

The Warner Mountains and South Warner Wilderness are part of the forest. Toilets are the only facilities.

▲ There are 20 campgrounds; $6 to $7 per night for sites with tested water and garbage facilities; free for campsites without these amenities.

OUTDOOR ADVENTURES

FISHING

Some of the best year-round fishing in the American West is found right here in the Far North. Steelhead, salmon, trout, and sturgeon run the region's countless rivers, while trout and bass inhabit the mountain lakes. For an unforgettable adventure, check with one of the many outfitters offering fishing expeditions.

Redding Area

THE FLY SHOP ✉*4140 Churn Creek Road, Redding* ☏*530-222-3555, 800-669-3474* ⌨*www.theflyshop.com* Professional guides here will tailor a trip to suit your abilities and interests year-round.

Weaverville to Yreka Area

KLAMATH RIVER OUTFITTERS ✉*3 Sandy Bar Road, Somes Bar* ☏*530-469-3349, 800-748-3735* ⌨*www.klamathriveroutfitters.com* This outfitter can lead you to the region's great fishing holes in fall and spring. They also provide summer rafting trips.

TRINITY FLY SHOP ✉*Bottom of Ohio Hill, on Old Lewiston Road, Lewiston* ☏*530-623-6757* ⌨*trinityflyshop.com* This shop arranges flyfishing trips on the Sacramento and Trinity rivers. They offer both half- and full-day trips on rafts and furnish flies and all gear.

Redding to Mt. Shasta Area

TED FAY FLY SHOP ✉*5732 Dunsmuir Avenue, Dunsmuir* ☏*530-235-2969* ⌨*www.tedfay.com* Just off the interstate and right next to the Sacramento River, this fly shop and guide service has been around for more than 50 years, offering every conceivable flyfishing gadget as well as knowledgeable guides.

JACK TROUT INTERNATIONAL FLY FISHING AND GUIDE SERVICE ✉*P.O. Box 94, Mount Shasta, CA 96067* ☏*530-926-4540* ⌨*www.jacktrout.com* Jack Trout International will take you on hiking excursions to local rivers or their own private ranch for a fruitful day of fishing. They rent all the equipment you may need.

RIVER RAFTING

If your favorite carnival ride is the roller coaster, you're ready for the adrenaline-pumping, spine-chilling thrill of whitewater river rafting. At one time it was strictly a sport for daredevils, but more and more vacationing adventurers are taking to the rapids. As a result, over 60 professional guide services in Northern California now combine expertise and equipment in a variety of tour packages.

Whether you're looking for a true test of nerve or prefer excitement in smaller doses, these knowledgeable river pilots can provide an enjoyable whitewater experience. You're liable to wind up in the drink at least once, especially if you choose one of the more challenging runs. But getting wet is part of the intoxicating rush created by a fast-moving stretch of river. There's also the serenity of paddling past untracked forests and bald mountains. In spite of river rafting's increasing popularity, the Far North's endless river system makes it a solitary wilderness activity.

Tours vary in length from one to seven days, and generally include food and all the equipment necessary except sleeping bags. Camping is usually the rule, but lodge trips are also available.

River rafting is primarily a summertime sport, centered in the Klamath, Shasta, Trinity, and Six Rivers National Forests. The most frequently explored routes include Hell's Corner Gorge in the Upper Klamath River, the Salmon River, and Upper Sacramento River. For whitewater pioneers, Burnt Ranch Gorge in the south fork of the Trinity River, the Scott River, and Lower McCloud River Canyon offer unmatched challenges.

WHITEWATER VOYAGES ✉5225 San Pablo Dam Road, El Sobrante, CA 94803 ✆510-222-5994 ✐www.whitewatervoyages.com In spring and summer, Whitewater offers half- to three-day river trips.

WILDERNESS ADVENTURES ✉108 Ski Village Drive, Mount Shasta, CA 96067 ✆530-926-6282, 800-323-7238 ✐www.wildrivertrips.com To experience the thrill of a river run, contact this company. Besides that, they'll point out plenty of wildlife—eagles, deer, hawks, beavers, and otters.

BOATING

Whether you prefer gliding across a crystal-blue lake in a rowboat, on waterskis, or paddling a canoe, the Far North resorts will cater to every desire.

Redding Area
BRIDGE BAY RESORT ✉10300 Bridge Bay Road, Redding ✆530-275-3021, 800-752-9669 ✐www.sevencrown.com To spend your days idling away on the water, contact this resort. They rent houseboats, ski boats, patio boats, Sea Doos, and fishing boats for use on Shasta Lake.

Redding to Weaverville Area
OAK BOTTOM MARINA ✉Oak Bottom Marina Northwest, Whiskeytown ✆530-359-2269 ✆530-359-2027 Nestled in a valley surrounded by trees and water, Oak Bottom rents waterskis, innertubes, and several kinds of recreational boats for use on Whiskeytown Lake. For those who like to sail, there are small sailboats. Closed October through March.

Redding to Mt. Shasta Area

Shasta Lake provides ample opportunities for fishing, waterskiing, and houseboating.

ANTLERS RESORT & MARINA ✉*20679 Antlers Road, Lakehead* ☎*530-238-2553, 800-238-3924* ⌨*www.shastalakevacations.com, antlers@shastalakevacations.com* Antlers rents houseboats, patio boats, and Sea Doos.

SHASTA MARINA RESORT ✉*18390 O'Brien Inlet Road, Lakehead* ☎*530-238-2284, 800-959-3359* ⌨*www.shastalake.net* Located on the Sacramento arm of Shasta Lake, Shasta Marina offers houseboats. They also rent wakeboards and skis.

Weaverville to Yreka Area

CEDAR STOCK MARINA ✉*Trinity Lake, 45810 Route 3, Trinity Center* ☎*530-286-2225, 800-255-5561* ⌨*www.cedarstock.com, info@cedarstock.com* Situated in the lovely Trinity Alps, Cedar Stock is the perfect spot to rent a houseboat. They also rent speed boats, patio boats, and fishing boats. Water-ski equipment and innertubes are available here.

BALLOON RIDES & GLIDING

SHASTA VALLEY BALLOONS ✉*Mount Shasta* ☎*530-926-3612* 📠*530-926-3612* ⌨*www.hot-airballoons.com* There are few more peaceful ways to explore the Shasta area than in a hot-air balloon. This company operates daily one-hour flights, which include brunch and a champagne toast. It also offers meditation flights.

SKIING

Ski enthusiasts can explore the Far North's winter wonderland on both downhill runs and cross-country treks. The skiing is particularly popular around 14,162-foot Mt. Shasta. **Shasta Cascade Wonderland Association** (www.shastacascade.com) provides information on downhill skiing as well as miles of trackless wilderness.

Redding to Mt. Shasta Area

MT. SHASTA BOARD & SKI PARK ✉*Ski Park Highway and Route 89, Mount Shasta* ☎*530-926-8686, 800-754-7427* ⌨*www.skipark.com, info@skipark.com* Located at the foot of beautiful Mt. Shasta, this park features three chairlifts that accommodate both skiers and snowboarders, and a 1390-foot vertical drop. You can also cross-country ski on the 30 kilometers of groomed Nordic trails. Most of the runs are beginning or intermediate level.

Northeast Loop

LASSEN VOLCANIC NATIONAL PARK ✉*Mineral* ☎*530-595-4444* ⌨*www.nps.gov/lavo* Lassen's most popular Nordic trails begin at the southwest entrance (near Mineral) and lead to such enticing spots as the Sulphur Works—an active geothermal area with running hot springs and steaming sulphur. On the north side of Lassen, there's a nice beginner trail around Manzanita Lake (1.6 miles) and a popular medium-difficulty trail up the drainage of Manzanita Creek (10 miles). No rentals are available in the park.

GOLD PANNING

THE NEW 49'ERS ✉*Happy Camp* ☎*530-493-2012* 🖨*530-493-2095* 🌐*www. goldgold.com* Seek your fortune in gold in the Klamath River and its tributary creeks. For a very minimal fee, you can spend a weekend or even a week mining with this private club, which has 60 river miles of placer claims on National Forest Service land near Happy Camp. The club operates hands-on training in high banking every summer. Bring your tent or an RV. You may strike it rich, or just have a good time picking up some new skills.

RIDING STABLES & PACK TRIPS

For the ultimate Western-style vacation, consider a horseback expedition through the Far North's mountainous wilderness. Experienced guides offer pack trips deep into this region of lost mountains and alpine rivers.

Weaverville to Yreka Area

TRINITY TRAILS RIDE BY COFFEE CREEK RANCH ✉*Trinity Center* ☎*530-266-3343,* *800-624-4480* 🖨*530-266-3597* 🌐*www.coffeecreekranch.com, ccranch@tds.net* This upscale dude ranch also offers specials to non-guests, including packing on horses into the Trinity Alps Wilderness Area for vacations, fishing, and deer and bear hunting. Closed November through May.

Northeast Loop

South of Lake Almanor you can explore the Plumas National Forest by horseback. Ride through the Lakes Basin (Gold Lake Highway) or Bucks Lake (off Route 70, north of Quincy) recreation areas.

REID HORSE & CATTLE COMPANY, INC. ✉*1540 Chandler Road, Quincy* ☎*530-836-0940* 🌐*www.reidhorse.com* This company operates guided trail rides out of Bucks Lake Stables, ranging from one hour expeditions to day-long trips. They also operate Gold Lake Stables, which offers overnight trips.

BIKING

Biking in the Far North is a challenge rewarded with spectacular mountain scenery. It's a region for cyclists with experience: The climbs are often steep and the narrow-shouldered roadways are traveled by lumber trucks and RVs. But there are several highways well worth exploring. Beginner to moderate trails can be found.

Weaverville to Yreka Area

Route 3 passes Trinity Lake and the historic town of Callahan on a

Redding to Weaverville Area

For a ride through Shasta State Historic Park and along Whiskeytown
Lake, try Route 299 outside Redding. Be careful; it's a popular road with
heavy traffic.

Northeast Loop

Route 89 from Mt. Shasta to McArthur–Burney Falls State Park rolls
from 2000 to 4500 feet elevation while passing pristine countryside and
tiny towns. Route 44 between Lassen Volcanic National Park and Susanville traverses unspoiled timber country.

Bike Rentals

BIKES ETCETERA ✉️ *2400 Athens Avenue, Redding* 📞 *530-244-1954* Here
they rent and repair bikes, and also offer literature on area trails.

HIKING

More than any other part of the state, the Far North earns the description "Hidden California." Inhabited by black bears, coyotes, black-
tailed deer, and an occasional bald eagle, the land offers hikers a
glimpse of nature in its unspoiled state. The Trinity Alps feature more
than 500 miles of trails for exploring glacial lakes, cool forests, and
silent meadows. Mt. Shasta's snow-domed summit rewards mountaineers with otherworldly views, and Lassen Peak reveals the explosive
side of this highly volcanic countryside.

Redding to Weaverville Area

For a scenic, moderate, two-hour hike, turn off to the right from Route
299 on Crystal Creek Road, about a mile west of the French Gulch turnoff. After a couple of miles the road deteriorates into a washed-out former logging road that is no longer maintained. Follow this road on foot
for about two miles to reach Crystal Creek Falls, a string of cascades that
fall a total of 200 feet, set in a pocket of primeval forest.

Weaverville to Yreka Area

Trinity Alps Wilderness Area is an extraordinary haven for backpackers.
Less crowded than other California wilderness areas, it possesses knife-
edge peaks, deep pine forests, and lakes crowded with trout. You can
camp anywhere in the forest with a wilderness permit (and a campfire
permit, if you plan to build a fire). **Tangle Blue Lake Trail** (4 miles) begins off Route 3 and leads through a flowering meadow to a lake
rimmed by jagged peaks. It is an easy-to-moderate trail.

The Trinity Alps section of the **Pacific Crest Trail** (17 miles) starts at
Scott Mountain Campground. It's one of the most scenic trails in the
wilderness area, carrying past alpine lakes, meadows, and forests.

There's a choice to make when hiking the **Caribou Basin and Sawtooth
Ridge Trail** (9.6 miles). You can follow an age-old trail across Caribou
Mountain, or take a newer trail that's easier to trek, more crowded, and

is two miles longer. Both hikes lead past mountain lakes and afford singular views from Sawtooth Ridge.

Stuart Fork to Emerald, Sapphire, and Mirror Lakes Trail (14.5 miles) is one of the most popular hikes in the Trinity Alps. It's one of Northern California's most picturesque hikes, resembling the Alps. It traverses an area teeming with wildlife en route to three subalpine lakes and is easy to moderate.

Beginning at Coffee Creek Road, the **Adams Lake Trail** (2.5 miles) leads to a tiny lake shadowed by a 7500-foot granite mountain and can be difficult to hike because of the steep path.

For a journey to three excellent fishing lakes, take **Big Bear Lake Trail** (4.7 miles), located off Route 3. This steep path climbs through fir and cedar forests and past thickets of willow and alder. An added treat is the 200-foot Bear Creek waterfall. En route, beware of rattlesnakes basking in the sun.

Mavis Lake–Fox Creek Lake Trail (4.7 miles) leads to another group of lakes. Beginning seven miles from Callahan, it climbs through heavy timber country to four trout lakes.

A lake covered with lilypads and a desolate canyon populated by coyotes, deer, and black bears are the destinations along **Boulder Lake to Poison Canyon and Lilypad Lake Trail** (4 miles). A steep ridge makes this a hike for the hearty.

Redding to Mt. Shasta Area

MT. SHASTA RECREATION AREA   Unparalleled adventure awaits skilled mountaineers at this recreation area. The 14,162-foot Mt. Shasta is accessed via three routes: **Horse Camp to Avalanche Gulch Trail**, **Mt. Shasta Ski Bowl Lodge Trail**, and **Horse Camp to Shastina Trail**; however, only expert climbers can accomplish this feat.

At Bunny Flat, hikers will find the trail to Horse Camp and the beginning of the Avalanche Gulch climbing route. Hikers entering the Mt. Shasta Wilderness can self-issue a wilderness permit at the trail head. Climbers going above 10,000 feet need to self-issue an additional summit pass (fee, $15).

Northeast Loop

LASSEN VOLCANIC NATIONAL PARK   This park offers 150 miles of hiking trails leading past lava flows, volcanic craters, and boiling mud pots. Most of these trails are moderate to strenuous. For trail information call 530-595-4444.

Starting from the park's southwest entrance station, **Brokeoff Mountain Trail** (3.7 miles) carries past open meadows and thick forest. Offering scenic views of Mt. Shasta, it's also an excellent route for flower-gazing and birdwatching.

For a hike to a 75-foot waterfall, follow **Mill Creek Falls Trail** (2.3 miles) along its scenic course.

Ridge Lakes Trail (1.1 miles) cuts through fir and pine forests and arrives at two jewel-like lakes (which become a single lake when the water level rises). This strenuous hike has a 1000-foot elevation change.

The largest hydrothermal area in Lassen lies along **Bumpass Hell Trail** (1.5 miles). One of the region's most dramatic hikes, the trail passes hot springs, steam vents, and mud pots.

Still, the finest hike in the park is **Lassen Peak Trail** (2.5 miles). Leading to the summit, it provides 360° degree views of the surrounding countryside and reveals evidence of recent volcanic activity. Hikers should be in good physical condition, bring water, jackets, sunscreen, and hats and turn back in case of thunderstorms.

Devastated Area Trail (.3 mile) offers an easy way to see a variety of rock formations and park panoramas. Highlights of this walk are volcanic formations from the May 1915 eruption and lava flow. Wheelchair accessible.

Even if I can't bring home a bouquet of blooms, I enjoy trekking **Paradise Meadows Trail** (1.5 miles), which is the best spot for summer wildflowers. Beginning at the Hat Lake parking area, the moderate trail climbs for a mile before reaching the meadows. Bring a lunch—this is a lovely place to picnic.

Beginning near the Loomis Museum parking lot is **Chaos Crags and Crags Lake Trail** (1.8 miles). Along this relatively easy walk are half a dozen immense crags, as well as wildflowers and a variety of geologic formations. During wet years a small lake forms in a "recently" (300-year-old) collapsed dome at the top of the trail.

Terrace, Shadow, and Cliff Lakes Trail (1.5 miles) begins at a high elevation and follows a flower-banked path to three lakes.

Crystal Lake Trail (.4 mile) begins on the east side of Juniper Lake and goes through forests and meadows to one of the park's most beautiful lakes.

For views of Lassen and other nearby peaks, climb **Inspiration Point Trail** (.8 mile). It tracks through western white pine and red fir forests and offers unforgettable vistas.

Cinder Cone Trail (2 miles) travels up one of the nation's most perfectly formed cinder cones. The trail begins at Butte Lake Campground. High-top boots are recommended due to difficult footing.

Beginning at Badger Flat, the Lassen Park section of the **Pacific Crest Trail** (17 miles) carries past Soap Lake, Fairfield Peak, Lower Twin Lake, Swan Lake, Pilot Mountain, Boiling Springs Lake, and Red Mountain to Little Willow Lake. In this area, the trail (which in its entirety extends from Canada to Mexico) is fairly level and can be hiked in two days at a comfortable pace.

TRANSPORTATION

CAR

From San Francisco, **Route 80** connects with **Route 5**, which leads through the heart of the Far North. It passes through Redding, Dunsmuir, Mount Shasta, and Yreka en route to Oregon.

AIR

REDDING MUNICIPAL AIRPORT ✉ *6751 Woodrum Circle* ✆ *530-224-4321* Horizon Air, Skywest Airlines, and United Express fly into Redding Municipal Airport.

BUS

GREYHOUND BUS LINES ✆ *800-231-2222* ✐ *www.greyhound.com* Greyhound travels Route 5, stopping in Redding.

TRAIN

AMTRAK ✆ *800-872-7245* ✐ *www.amtrak.com* Amtrak provides daily service on their "Coast Starlight" to Redding and Dunsmuir.

CAR RENTALS

Avis Rent A Car (800-331-1212) and **Hertz Rent A Car** (800-654-3131) have facilities at Redding Municipal Airport.

INDEX

LODGING INDEX

LODGING SERVICES

DINING INDEX

h

DINING INDEX

HIDDEN GUIDES

Adventure travel or a relaxing vacation?—"Hidden" guidebooks are the only travel books in the business to provide detailed information on both. Aimed at environmentally aware travelers, our motto is "Where Vacations Meet Adventures." These books combine details on unique hotels, restaurants and sightseeing with information on camping, sports and hiking for the outdoor enthusiast.

PARADISE FAMILY GUIDES

Ideal for families traveling with kids of any age—toddlers to teenagers—Paradise Family Guides offer a blend of travel information unlike any other guides to the Hawaiian islands. With vacation ideas and tropical adventures that are sure to satisfy both action-hungry youngsters and relaxation-seeking parents, these guides meet the specific needs of each and every family member.

Ulysses Press books are available at bookstores everywhere. If any of the following titles are unavailable at your local bookstore, ask the bookseller to order them.

You can also order books directly from Ulysses Press
P.O. Box 3440, Berkeley, CA 94703
800-377-2542 or 510-601-8301
fax: 510-601-8307
www.ulyssespress.com
e-mail: ulysses@ulyssespress.com

HIDDEN GUIDEBOOKS

____ Hidden Arizona, $16.95
____ Hidden Baja, $14.95
____ Hidden Belize, $15.95
____ Hidden Big Island of Hawaii, $14.95
____ Hidden Boston & Cape Cod, $14.95
____ Hidden British Columbia, $18.95
____ Hidden Cancún & the Yucatán, $16.95
____ Hidden Carolinas, $17.95
____ Hidden Coast of California, $19.95
____ Hidden Colorado, $15.95
____ Hidden Disneyland, $13.95
____ Hidden Florida, $19.95
____ Hidden Florida Keys & Everglades, $15.95
____ Hidden Georgia, $16.95
____ Hidden Hawaii, $19.95
____ Hidden Idaho, $14.95
____ Hidden Kauai, $14.95
____ Hidden Los Angeles, $14.95
____ Hidden Maine, $15.95
____ Hidden Maui, $15.95
____ Hidden Miami, $14.95

____ Hidden Montana, $15.95
____ Hidden New England, $19.95
____ Hidden New Mexico, $15.95
____ Hidden Oahu, $14.95
____ Hidden Oregon, $15.95
____ Hidden Pacific Northwest, $19.95
____ Hidden Philadelphia, $14.95
____ Hidden Puerto Vallarta, $14.95
____ Hidden Salt Lake City, $14.95
____ Hidden San Diego, $14.95
____ Hidden San Francisco & Northern California, $19.95
____ Hidden Seattle, $14.95
____ Hidden Southern California, $19.95
____ Hidden Southwest, $19.95
____ Hidden Tahiti, $19.95
____ Hidden Tennessee, $16.95
____ Hidden Utah, $16.95
____ Hidden Walt Disney World, $13.95
____ Hidden Washington, $15.95
____ Hidden Wine Country, $14.95
____ Hidden Wyoming, $15.95

PARADISE FAMILY GUIDES

____ Paradise Family Guides: Kauaʻi, $17.95
____ Paradise Family Guides: Maui, $17.95

____ Paradise Family Guides: Big Island of Hawaiʻi, $17.95

Mark the book(s) you're ordering and enter the total cost here ⇨ ☐

California residents add 8.75% sales tax here ⇨ ☐

Shipping, check box for your preferred method and enter cost here ⇨ ☐

☐ BOOK RATE   FREE! FREE! FREE!
☐ PRIORITY MAIL/UPS GROUND   cost of postage
☐ UPS OVERNIGHT OR 2-DAY AIR   cost of postage

Billing, enter total amount due here and check method of payment ⇨ ☐

☐ CHECK   ☐ MONEY ORDER
☐ VISA/MASTERCARD _____ EXP. DATE_____

NAME_____PHONE _____
ADDRESS_____
CITY_____ STATE_____ ZIP _____

MONEY-BACK GUARANTEE ON DIRECT ORDERS PLACED THROUGH ULYSSES PRESS.

ABOUT THE CONTRIBUTORS

Ray Riegert is the author of eight travel books, including *Hidden Coast of California*. His most popular work, *Hidden Hawaii*, won the coveted Lowell Thomas Travel Journalism Award for Best Guidebook as well a similar award from the Hawaii Visitors Bureau. In addition to his role as publisher of Ulysses Press, he has written for the *Chicago Tribune*, *Saturday Evening Post*, *San Francisco Chronicle* and *Travel & Leisure*. A member of the Society of American Travel Writers, he lives in the San Francisco Bay area with his wife, co-publisher Leslie Henriques.

Carolyn Patten, the update author for this edition, is the author of *The Insider's Guide to Palm Springs*. She has worked as a tourism public relations professional and freelance writer, specializing in the off-the-beaten path delights of California and Oregon. She lives in Portland, Oregon.